Integrated Korean

Advanced Intermediate 1

Integrated Korean

Advanced Intermediate 1

Ho-min Sohn & Eun-Joo Lee

KLEAR Textbooks in Korean Language

This textbook series has been developed by the Korean Language Education and
Research Center (KLEAR) with the support of the Korea Foundation.

Library of Congress Cataloging-in-Publication Data

Integrated Korean : advanced intermediate 1 / Ho-min Sohn and Eun-Joo Lee.
    p. cm. — (KLEAR textbooks in Korean language)
  ISBN 978–0–8248–2568–3 (pbk. : alk. paper)
    1. Korean language—Textbooks for foreign speakers—English. I. Ho-min Sohn and
  Eun-Joo Lee.
  II. Series.

PL913.I5812 2003
495.7'82421—dc21   00–033782

Camera-ready copy has been provided by the authors.

University of Hawai'i Press books are printed on acid-free paper
and meet the guidelines for permanence and durability of the Council
on Library Resources.

FLIP

CONTENTS

Preface

Unlike cognate languages of English such as Spanish, French, and German, Korean is one of the most difficult languages for English speakers to learn because of its profoundly distinct cultural features, entirely different sound patterns and vocabulary, unique writing system, predicate-final sentence structure, word structure with extensive agglutination of suffixes, intricate hierarchical system of honorifics, and so on. To optimize and maximize English speakers' learning of this truly foreign language, therefore, textbooks must be based on the soundest pedagogical principles and approaches, on the one hand, and must deal adequately with the huge linguistic, sociolinguistic, and cultural differences between Korean and English, on the other. The *Integrated Korean* series was designed and developed to meet diverse student needs with these requirements in mind.

Integrated Korean consists of five levels: Beginning (textbooks 1 and 2 and workbooks 1 and 2), Intermediate (textbooks 1 and 2 and workbooks 1 and 2), Advanced Intermediate (textbooks 1 and 2), Advanced (textbooks 1 and 2), and High Advanced (textbooks 1 and 2). Each level can be covered in two semesters or three quarters, assuming five class hours per week for the Beginning and Intermediate levels and three class hours per week for the Advanced Intermediate, Advanced, and High Advanced levels.

The lessons in *Integrated Korean* are sequenced in terms of the proficiency students are expected to achieve. For each lesson, special efforts have been made to integrate all five language skills (listening, speaking, reading, writing, and culture) properly to provide authentic situations and materials as much as possible, to explain detailed grammatical patterns, vocabulary items, and cultural aspects from a contrastive perspective, to give students relevant examples and exercises for each grammatical point, and to include extensive student-centered communicative and task/function activities.

The Beginning and Intermediate levels should allow students to master the basics of the language and to communicate in spoken and written forms in most essential daily situations. Following a schematic overview of the language and the Han'gŭl writing system, each lesson begins with a page of lesson objectives, followed by model conversations, related narration, new words and expressions, culture, grammatical points, and tasks/functions, in that order. For students' easy reference, extensive appendices, including predicate conjugation, useful semantic classes, a grammatical index, and glossaries (Korean-English and English-Korean) are provided. Students' factual knowledge and the basic language skills learned in the textbooks are further reinforced through extensive drills and skill-building activities in the workbooks and on the CDs.

In the Advanced Intermediate, Advanced, and High Advanced levels, a wide variety of interesting authentic reading materials is introduced to help students achieve high levels of proficiency not only in interpersonal but also in interpretive and presentational communication. Each lesson consists of pre-reading activities, a main reading text, model dialogues (Advanced Intermediate only), comprehension questions, new words, useful expressions, exercises, discussion and composition, and further reading. English translations of the main reading text and the model dialogues are also provided.

On behalf of the Korean Language Education and Research Center (KLEAR), I extend my heartfelt thanks to the following individuals who, functioning as main authors of different volumes of *Integrated Korean,* worked devotedly and tirelessly over a long period until the final versions were produced:

> Sungdai Cho, State University of New York at Binghamton
> Young-mee Cho, Rutgers University
> Jiha Hwang, Harvard University
> Eun-Joo Lee, Stanford University
> Hyo Sang Lee, Indiana University
> Young-Geun Lee, University of Hawai'i at Manoa
> Duk Soo Park, University of Sydney
> Carol Schulz, Columbia University
> Ho-min Sohn, University of Hawai'i at Manoa
> Sung-Ock Sohn, University of California, Los Angeles
> Hye-sook Wang, Brown University
> Jaehoon Yeon, University of London

The Korean-language specialists named below graciously cooperated on the project by providing sample dialogues, reading materials, or sample lessons, and by reviewing draft versions:

> Andrew Byon, State University of New York at Albany
> Sunny Jung, University of Southern California
> Gwee-Sook Kim, Princeton University
> Hae-Young Kim, Duke University
> Youngkyu Kim, University of Hawai'i at Manoa
> Sek Yen Kim-Cho, State University of New York at Buffalo
> Young-Key Kim-Renaud, George Washington University
> Haejin Koh, Korea University
> Dong Jae Lee, University of Hawai'i at Manoa

Jeyseon Lee, University of California, San Diego
Miseon Lee, Northwestern University
Sunae Lee, University of California, Santa Barbara
Sangsuk Oh, Harvard University
Kyu J. Pak-Covell, Defense Language Institute
Yong-Yae Park, Seoul National University
Joe J. Ree, Florida State University
Yoo Sang Rhee, Defense Language Institute
Heisoon Yang, Ewha Womans University
Seok-Hoon You, Korea University
Soo-ah Yuen, University of Hawai'i, Kapiolani Community College

I am also grateful to the many research assistants who helped the main authors. Special thanks go to Jeannie Kim, Haejin Koh, and Gabiel Sylvian, who provided English translations, and to Julie Sohn, who did some two thousand line drawings. Eun-Joo Lee and Seungbong Baek deserve special recognition for their dedicated service as managing assistants during the project period.

The *Integrated Korean* series and all its sister volumes (*Composition, Chinese Character Studies, Selected Readings, Modern Literature Reader, Modern Short Stories, Language in Culture and Society,* and *Grammar and Usage Dictionary*) are the outcome of eight years of intensive collaborative work by many Korean-language experts under KLEAR's Korean Language Textbook Development Project. This monumental project was initiated and financially supported by the Korea Foundation. KLEAR owes a great deal to past and present presidents of the Korea Foundation and their staffs. I would also like to express my sincere thanks to the members of the Korea Foundation's textbook review committee for their valuable comments at the initial stage of the project, and to the KLEAR board members for their continued support. Finally, I would like to extend my sincere appreciation to the National Foreign Language Center in Washington, D.C., for granting Andrew Mellon fellowships to four KLEAR members for the preparation of the original project guidelines in 1994; to the Center for Korean Studies and the Department of East Asian Languages and Literatures of the University of Hawai'i for providing office space and moral support; and to the University of Hawai'i Press (notably Patricia Crosby, Ann Ludeman, and Nancy Woodington) for editing and publishing the KLEAR textbooks.

Ho-min Sohn, KLEAR President

제1과 대인 관계

(Lesson 1: Interpersonal relations)

PRE-READING QUESTIONS

1. 부드러운 인간 관계를 맺기 위해서는 어떤 것들이 중요하다고 생각합니까?

2. 여러분은 "첫인상"에 대해서 어떻게 생각합니까? 첫인상이 중요합니까? 아니면, 중요하지 않다고 생각합니까? 그렇게 생각하는 이유는 무엇입니까?

3. 자기의 분야에서 성공하는 비결이 무엇이라고 생각합니까?

GAINING FAMILIARITY

1. 대학생활
   신입생 환영회, 교환 학생, 학사, 석사, 박사, 동아리, 선배, 후배

2. Phatic expressions
   처음 뵙겠습니다; 인사하세요. 여기는. . . ; 실례지만 혹시. . .

현대인의 성공 비결

현대는 인간 관계의 시대입니다. 현대 사회만큼 인간 관계가 중요한 시대는 없었던 것 같습니다.

인간 관계가 얼마나 중요한가를 조사한 기관들이 있습니다. 미국의 카네기재단에서는 사회적으로 성공한 사람들 1만 명을 대상으로[1.1] "성공의 비결"을 알아보았습니다.

"어떻게 돈 많이 벌었습니까?"

"어떻게 승진이 빨랐습니까?"

"어떻게 그 힘든 일을 해냈지요?"

"어떻게 유명해졌습니까?"

이런 질문들에 대하여 놀랍게도 머리, 기술, 노력으로 성공한 사람이 불과 15%이고, 나머지 85%가 인간 관계를 잘 해서 성공했다는 겁니다.[1.2]

또 하버드대학에서도 비슷한 조사를 했습니다. 하버드대학에서는 졸업생 중에서 실직자를 대상으로, "왜 직장을 그만두셨습니까?"하는 실직의 이유를 물어 보았습니다. 그 결과 일을 잘 못해서 쫓겨난 사람보다 인간 관계가 나빠서 그만두게 된 사람이 자그마치 두 배나 되었다고 합니다.

이 두 조사의 공통점은 무엇입니까? 한마디로 인간 관계의 중요성이죠. 다시 말해서[1.3] 인간 관계가 좋은 사람은 성공하고 인간 관계가 나쁜 사람은 실패하기 쉽다는 결론입니다.

대화

1

(1.5세 교포 사라 정은 3학년 때 한국의 한국대학에 1년간 교환 학생으로 갔다. 신입생 환영회에서 한국대학의 박영규 교수를 만난다.)

사라: 저, 실례지만 혹시 박영규 교수님 아니세요?

박 교수: 네. 맞는데요. 누구신가요?[1.4]

사라: 전 하와이대학에서 교환 학생으로 온 정사라라고 하는데요.

박 교수: 아 그래요? 반가워요. 그런데 날 어떻게 알지요?

사라: 저, 작년 봄 하와이대학 한국학 연구소에서 교수님 강연을 들었거든요.[1.5] 그렇지 않아도[1.6] 연구실로 한번 찾아뵈려고 했었는데요.

박 교수: 아 그래요?

사라: 교수님, 말씀 낮추세요.[1.7]

박 교수: 그래 여기서 무슨 공부를 하려고 유학 왔지?

사라: 한국 문학을 공부하려고요.

박 교수: 아 그래. 한국말이 굉장히 유창한데 어디서 배웠지?

사라: 전 다섯살 때 부모님을 따라 하와이로 이민 갔거든요. 부모님하고 한국말을 썼다가 영어를 썼다가 그랬어요.[1.8] 그리고 대학에서 한국 문학을 전공하고 있어요.

박 교수: 그래 대학원에서도 한국 문학을 전공할 건가?

사라: 네. 한국 문학으로 박사 과정까지 공부해 보려고 해요.

박 교수: 한국에 있는 동안 많이 배우기 바래.

사라: 네. 열심히 해 보겠습니다.

박 교수: 그럼 난 볼일이 있어서 이만 가 봐야겠는데 시간 날 때 한번 사무실로 찾아와.

사라: 네. 교수님 감사합니다. 안녕히 가세요.

2

(맑은 가을날 사라는 캠퍼스 벤치에 앉아서 교환 학생으로 온 마이클 존스를
기다리고 있다. 사라가 잘 아는 영문과 2학년 이소영이 지나간다.)

사라: 소영아 어디가니?

소영: 어머 언니. 도서관에요. 언니는 여기서 뭘 하세요?

사라: 응 마이클 존스라고 뉴욕에서 교환 학생으로 온 친구를
기다리고 있어. 아 저기 오는군.

마이클: 미안해요, 사라 씨. 오는 길에 아는 과 선배를 만나서 이
야기 좀 하느라고 늦어졌어요.

사라: 괜찮아요. 마이클 씨, 인사하세요. 여기는[1.9] 이소영이에요.

마이클: 처음 뵙겠습니다. 마이클 존스라고 합니다. 뉴욕 콜롬비아
대학에서 금년 봄에 유학 왔어요. 경제학과 3학년이에요.

소영: 안녕하세요? 영문과 이소영이에요. 사라 언니한테서 말씀
많이 들었어요. 마이클 씨는 한국말을 아주 잘 하시네요.

마이클: 천만에요. 아직 한국 예절을 몰라서 실수하기 일쑤예요.[1.10]
존대법을 제대로 못 써서 큰 일이에요.

소영: 아직도 한국은 생활 방식이나 언어 사용에 유교적인 데가
많기 때문에 서양 사람들에게는 낯설 거예요. 그런데 마이
클 씨, 경제학과 4학년 김영호 선배 아세요?

마이클: 그럼요. 잘 알지요. 조금 전에 길에서 만난 선배가 바로
그 분이에요. 그런데 그 선배를 어떻게 아세요?

소영: 그 오빠하고 같은 동아리에 있어요. 지금 도서관에서 그
오빠를 만나기로 했거든요.

마이클: 그렇지 않아도 영문과 후배를 만나러 간다던데 바로 소영
씨였군요. 세상 정말 좁네요.

사라: 말씀 도중 실례지만[1.11] 소영아, 영호 오빠 기다리시겠다.

소영: 참 내 정신 좀 봐.[1.12] 전 이만 가봐야겠네요.

Comprehension Questions

1. **Reading Comprehension.** "현대인의 성공 비결"을 읽고 맞고(Ⓣ) 틀린(Ⓕ) 것을 지적하거나 질문에 대답해 보세요.

   (1) 현대 사회에서는 인간 관계보다는 개인적인 능력이
   더 중요하다.   Ⓣ Ⓕ

   (2) 카네기재단 조사에 의하면 대부분의 사람들이 머리, 기술,
   노력으로 성공했다.   Ⓣ Ⓕ

   (3) 하버드대학의 조사에 의하면 일을 잘 못해서 직장을
   잃은 사람이 인간 관계가 나빠서 직장을 잃은 사람의
   두 배가 된다.   Ⓣ Ⓕ

   (4) 카네기재단은 성공한 사람들에게 어떤 질문을 했습니까?

   (5) 지은이는 현대인의 성공 비결이 무엇이라고 생각합니까?

   (6) 카네기재단의 조사에 의하면 "성공의 비결"은 무엇입니까?

   (7) 인간 관계에 관해 조사한 기관으로는 어떤 기관이 있습니까?

   (8) 카네기재단과 하버드대학 조사의 공통점은 무엇입니까?

   (9) 하버드대학 조사에 의하면 실직하게 되는 중요한 이유는
   무엇입니까?

   (10) 하버드대학에서는 어떤 사람들을 대상으로 하여 조사를
   했습니까?

2. **Listening Comprehension.** 대화를 듣고 맞고(Ⓣ) 틀린(Ⓕ) 것을 지적하거나 질문에 대답해 보세요.

   대화 1
   (1) 사라는 한국에서 1년 동안 지낼 것이다.   Ⓣ Ⓕ
   (2) 사라는 박 교수님을 연구실에서 뵈었다.   Ⓣ Ⓕ
   (3) 사라는 한국 역사를 공부하려고 한국에 왔다.   Ⓣ Ⓕ

(4) 사라는 언제 미국으로 이민을 갔습니까?

(5) 사라는 대학원에서 무엇을 전공할 계획입니까?

(6) 사라는 전에 어디에서 박영규 교수님을 만났습니까?

대화 2

(1) 소영과 영호 선배는 같은 동아리 회원이다. T F

(2) 마이클은 자신이 한국 존대법은 잘 알지만 한국 예절은 잘 모른다고 생각한다. T F

(3) 마이클은 사라와의 약속에 왜 늦었습니까?

(4) 마이클은 언제 한국으로 유학을 왔습니까?

(5) 마이클이 왜 "세상이 정말 좁네요"라고 했습니까?

New Words

1.5세 교포 1.5-generation Korean resident in a foreign country (a Korean who was born in Korea, emigrated in childhood, and became a citizen of the country of residence)

가을날 *n.* an autumn day

강연 *n.* lecture, address. 강연하다 to lecture on, talk about ¶강연회 lecture meeting ¶공개 강연 public lecture

결과 *n.* result ¶그 결과 as a result (of that)

결론 *n.* conclusion

경제학과 *n.* department of economics. 경제 economy; 경제학 economics

곱다 *adj.* to be refined, beautiful, lovely, nice, good-looking ¶고운 꽃 a pretty flower ¶고운 여자 a pretty woman ¶고운 말 refined language ¶고운 목소리로 in a sweet voice

공통점 *n.* point of sameness, common feature. 공통(성) commonness ¶공통 분모 common denominator

굉장히 *adv.* splendidly; exceedingly. 굉장하다 to be grand, imposing, splendid, magnificent

과정 *n.* course of study, curriculum, program, course ¶박사 과정 Ph.D. program

교환 학생 *n.* exchange student

그래 *adv.* well, by the way, so

그러자 *adv.* thereupon, thereon, and (just) then

그러지요 contr. of 그렇게 하지요 I will do so

그만두다 *v.* to quit, end, discontinue, give up ¶공부를 그만두다 to give up one's studies ¶일을 그만두다 to lay aside one's work ¶회사를 그만두다 to resign from a company

그야 contr. of 그거야, 그것이야 as for that, talking about that, so far as that is concerned

금년 *n.* this year

기관 *n.* institution; organ; organization

기술 *n.* skill, technique, ability, talent

나누다 *v.* to share, divide, exchange ¶말씀 나누다 to converse

나머지 *n.* rest, remainder

낯설다 *adj.* to be unfamiliar, not acquainted with ¶낯선 사람 a stranger ¶낯선 곳 unfamiliar place

놀랍게도 *adv.* to one's surprise, amazement, shock; surprisingly enough

대상 *n.* the object; the subject

대인 관계 *n.* interpersonal relations. 대인 personnel, interpersonal; 관계 relation

대학원 *n.* graduate school

도중 *n.* middle of the way; in the middle of; on the way ¶집에 가는 도중 on the way (back) home

동아리 *n.* school organization; social club; group

머리 *n.* intelligence, intellect, brain; the head

맺다 *v.* to form (a connection, relationship); to tie or knot; to conclude

박사 *n.* Ph.D. (degree)

배 *n.* double; twofold (= 2배); times; -fold ¶배로 하다 to double ¶3배가 되다 to be tripled

부드럽다 *adj.* to be soft, tender, smooth ¶부드러운 목소리 a gentle voice

불과 *adv.* only, merely, no more than ¶불과 이십 명 only twenty people

사회적으로 *adv.* socially

상대방 *n.* other (opposite) party; other side (= 상대편). 상대 facing each other; opposition; relativity; ~방 direction; side

서양 *n.* the West; *adj.* Western ¶서양 문명 Western civilization

석사 *n.* M.A. (degree)

선배 *n.* an elder, senior, superior. *ant.* 후배 a junior, inferior, subordinate

성공(의) 비결 secret of success. 성공 success, achievement; 비결 a secret ¶건강(의) 비결 secret of health ¶성공의 비결은 근면과 정직이다. The secret of success is hard work and honesty.

세상 *n.* the world; society; life ¶세상이 싫어지다 to become weary of life

승진 *n.* promotion. 승진하다 to get promoted

시대 *n.* period, age, era; times

신입생 환영회 party (reception) to welcome new students

실수하다 *v.* to make a mistake. 실수 mistake, blunder, slip ¶말을 실수하다 to make a slip of the tongue

실직자 *n.* jobless person, the unemployed. 실직 unemployment, job loss; 실직하다 to lose one's employment, be out of work

실패하다 *v.* to fail, go wrong

알아보다 *v.* to recognize, notice; to inquire, investigate, examine, search ¶못 알아보다 to be unable to recognize

어른 *n.* adult; elder ¶마을의 어른 elders of the village

어이 *interj.* hey! (used to an inferior)

언어 사용 language usage

여기 *n., adv.* here, this place; this person (when introducing someone)

영문과 *n.* department of English (language and literature)

예절 *n.* etiquette, protocol, good manners (= 예의) ¶예절을 지키다 to follow (abide by, observe) requirements of etiquette (good manners)

원만하다 *adj.* to be smooth, harmonious, satisfactory, perfect. 원만 perfection, integrity, soundness ¶원만한 가정 a happy home

유교적이다 *adj.* to be Confucian

유창하다 *adj.* to be fluent

유학 오다 *v.* to come to study. *ant.* 유학 가다 to go abroad to study

이민(을) 가다 *v.* to emigrate to ¶그들은 작년에 미국으로 이민을 갔다. They emigrated to the United States last year.

익히다 *v.* to acquaint oneself with, learn, gain skill in ¶자동차 운전을 익히다 to learn to drive a car

인간 관계 *n.* human relations

일쑤 *n.* habitual practice, habit

자그마치 *adv.* as much (many, long) as; a little; a few ¶그 기차 사고에서 자그마치 열 명이 죽었다. As many as ten passengers were killed in that train wreck. ¶술을 자그마치 마셔. Don't drink too much.

적응 *n.* adaptation. 적응하다 to adapt oneself (to), adjust oneself (to) ¶새 환경에 적응하다 to adapt oneself to new circumstances

제대로 *adv.* as it is; properly, well, without a hitch, in orderly fashion ¶나는 숙제를 제대로 했다. I did the homework in a proper way.

조사하다 *v.* to investigate, research, examine (into). 조사 investigation, research, examination

존대법 *n.* rules of honorifics

중요성 *n.* importance. 중요하다 to be important ¶중요성이 있다 to be of importance

쫓겨나다 *v.* to be driven (out of), evicted (from), dismissed (from) ¶학교에서 쫓겨나다 to be expelled from school ¶직장에서 쫓겨나다 to be dismissed from one's post

참 *interj.* oh! indeed!

찾아뵙다 *v.* to visit (a superior). 찾아보다 to visit; 찾다 to look for; to find; 뵙다 to see (a superior)

첫인상 *n.* first impression. ¶첫인상이 좋다 to give a good first impression

카네기재단 *n.* Carnegie Foundation

학사 *n.* B.A. (degree)

한국 문학 *n.* Korean literature

한국학 연구소 center for Korean studies

한마디로 *adv.* in a word, in short, briefly

현대인 *n.* modern person; the moderns. 현대 the present age (time); modern (times); a contemporary

혹시 *adv.* by any chance, possibly ¶혹시 김민수 씨를 아세요? Do you happen to know Mr. Kim, Min-su?

환영 *n.* welcome. 환영하다 to give a warm welcome (to)

Useful Expressions

1.1 ~을/를 대상으로 taking (something/someone) as a (research) subject

A contraction of ~을/를 대상으로 하여. 대상 means 'the subject' and 하여 means 'making, taking.'

일만 명을 **대상으로** "성공의 비결"을 조사했다.
They investigated "the secret of success," taking 10,000 people as subjects.
실직자를 **대상으로** 실직의 이유를 물어 보았다.
Taking jobless people as subjects, they asked the reasons for unemployment.

1.2 ~다는 겁니다 it is/was said/reported/found that

~다는 겁니다 and ~다는 거예요 are contractions of ~다고 하는 것입니다 and
~다고 하는 것이에요, respectively. 겁니다 means 'it is that,' 'the fact is' (see
4.5). ~다는 or ~다고 하는 is an indirect quotation marker. Together, the phrases
mean 'it is/was said (reported, found) that.'

1.3 다시 말해서 in other words

This pattern literally means 'by saying (it) again.' Similar expressions with the
same meaning are 다시 말하면 (*lit.,* 'if (I) say it again') and 다시 말하자면 (*lit.,*
'if we are to speak about it again').

1.4 ~는가요?/(으)ㄴ가요? (polite question form)

Compared to questions with ~요, questions with ~는가요/(으)ㄴ가요 are more
indirect and sound more polite. 누구세요? 'Who are you?' is direct and sounds
somewhat blunt, but 누구신가요? 'May I ask who you are?' is much softer and
more polite because ~는가/(으)ㄴ가 connotes the speaker's 'wondering whether'
the questioned event or state is true or not. ~는가요 occurs after a verb and
~(으)ㄴ가요 after an adjective (은 after a consonant and ㄴ after a vowel).

사라는 **자는가요**?   Is Sara sleeping? (I wonder.)
밖이 **밝은가요**?   Is it bright outside? (I wonder.)
대인 관계가 **중요한가요**?   Are interpersonal relations so important? (I wonder.)

1.5 ~거든요 because, since, as, indeed

This sentence ending politely indicates the speaker's reason or justification for an
event, an action, a state, or his/her or somebody else's earlier speech. Sometimes
it simply means 'surely, certainly, indeed.'

민지 씨 왜 우세요?　　　　　　Minji, why are you crying?

어머니 생각이 **나거든요**.　　　Because I miss my mother.

밖에 또 비가 와요.　　　　　　It's raining outside again.

장마철**이거든요**.　　　　　　　(That's) because it's a long rainy season.

사람들이 민지 씨가 되게 부자라대요.

People say that you are very rich, Minji.

그런 말 들을 때마다 기분이 **좋거든요**.

I certainly feel good whenever I hear such words.

1.6　그렇지 않아도 (= 그러잖아도) as a matter of fact

The literal meaning of 그렇지 않아도 is 'even if it were not so.' Its derived meanings include 'even without a person's doing (saying) something' and 'as a matter of fact.'

그렇지 않아도 곧 한번 뵙고 싶었어요.

(Independently of this meeting,) I had intended to see you one of these days.

그렇지 않아도 피곤한데 일을 더 하라고 해요.

I am already tired, and still he asks me to work more.

그렇지 않아도 소영 씨를 만나러 간다고 했어요.

As a matter of fact, he said he would go to see you, So-yŏng.

1.7　말씀 낮추세요 Please lower your speech (level).

This idiomatic expression is often used by younger to older when the older person keeps using polite or deferential speech. This is particularly the case if the older person is the younger one's in-group or an acquaintance.

1.8　~다(가) ~다(가) 하다 (alternation of actions or states)

When two ~다(가) 'while doing/being' constructions are followed by 하다 'do' or 그러하다 'do so,' the meaning is one of alternation.

많은 사람들이 들어왔**다(가)** 나갔**다(가)** **했**다.

A lot of people kept coming in and going out.

이가 아프다(가) 괜찮다(가) 그래요.
I have a tooth that bothers me on and off.

비가 오다(가) 말다(가) 그랬다.
It rained on and off.

1.9 여기, 저기, 거기 this person, that person (over there), that person (near you)

The place expressions 여기, 저기, and 거기 are used to indicate an adult when one is performing introductions.

여기는 이소영이고 거기는 사라예요.
This is So-yŏng Lee, and that (near you) is Sarah.

1.10 ~기(가) 일쑤이다 always to be doing (something unpleasant)

일쑤이다 'to be a habitual practice' follows a verb with the nominalizing suffix ~기 to express habitual action. The nominalized verb functions as the subject of 일쑤이다. This construction is used only when the action has a negative or unpleasant connotation, as in:

그 남자는 거짓말하기(가) 일쑤예요.
The man tells a lie every time he turns around.

이 애는 울기(가) 일쑤야.
This child is a constant crybaby.

우리 누나는 남 흉보기(가) 일쑤예요.
My older sister always finds fault with others.

1.11 말씀 도중 실례지만 excuse me for interrupting, but

This polite formula expression is used when interrupting a conversation between adults. The person using this formula may or may not be one of the participants in the conversation. The expression consists of 말씀 'talk; word' (polite form), 도중 '(in) the midst,' 실례 'discourtesy, impoliteness, rudeness,' and (이)지만 'to be. . . , but.'

1.12 내 정신 좀 봐 I completely forgot about it.

내 정신 좀 봐 is addressed to oneself and is used upon suddenly realizing that one has completely forgotten about something important because of involvement in something else (verbal or nonverbal). Literally, it means 'Oh, look at my mind!'

Exercises

1. 관련된 단어들끼리 연결하여 문장을 만들어 보세요.

    (1) 승진   •   • 알아보다   _____

    (2) 비결   •   • ~(이)나 되다   _____

    (3) 자그마치 •   • 빠르다   _____

    (4) 이민   •   • 가다   _____

    (5) 말씀   •   • 낮추다   _____

2. 아래의 설명과 맞는 단어나 표현을 본문에서 찾아 쓰세요.

    (1) 알려져 있지 않은 좋은 방법: _____

    (2) 직업을 잃어버린 사람: _____

    (3) 직위가 오름: _____

    (4) 이름이 알려져 있음: _____

    (5) 일을 하는 곳, 일자리: _____

    (6) 말을 아주 잘하다: _____

3. 보기에서 적당한 말을 골라 빈칸을 채우세요.

> 보기: 한마디로, 시대, 자그마치, 대상, 전공

    (1) 현대만큼 인간 관계가 중요한 _____는 없었던 것 같습니다. 현대는 인간 관계의 _____입니다.

(2) 사회적으로 성공한 사람들을 _____으로 성공의 비결을 알아보았습니다.

(3) 인간 관계가 나빠서 직장을 그만둔 사람이 _____ 두 배나 되었다.

(4) 이 두 조사의 공통점은 _____ 인간 관계의 중요성이다.

(5) 대학에서 한국어를 _____했다.

4. 밑줄 친 말과 비슷한 단어를 보기에서 고르세요.

(1) 성공한 사람들을 대상으로 성공의 비결을 <u>알아보았습니다</u>.

　　a. 조사하여 보았습니다　　　　b. 통지하였습니다
　　c. 알려 보았습니다　　　　　　d. 해냈습니다

(2) 하버드대학에서도 <u>비슷한</u> 조사를 했습니다.

　　a. 똑같은　　　　　　　　　　b. 거의 같은
　　c. 아주 다른　　　　　　　　　d. 거의 다른

(3) <u>다시 말해서</u> 인간 관계가 좋은 사람은 성공하고 인간 관계가 나쁜 사람은 실패하기 쉽다는 결론입니다.

　　a. 즉　　　　　　　　　　　　b. 그래서
　　c. 또　　　　　　　　　　　　d. 그러나

5. "~는/(으)ㄴ가요"를 사용해서 대화를 완성하세요.

(1) A: 김 선생님 _____
　　B: 지금은 좀 괜찮으세요.

(2) A: 밖에 _____
　　B: 비가 멈춘 것 같군요.

(3) A: 한국 축구팀이 네덜란드에 _____
　　B: 아니오. 3:0으로 지고 말았어요.

6. "~거든요"를 사용해서 다음 대화를 완성하세요.

(1) 마크: 날씨가 꽤 추워졌지요?
　　민지: _____

(2) 마크: 민지 씨는 요즘 뭐가 그렇게 좋아서 항상 싱글벙글하세요?

민지: _____

(3) 마크: 왜 교통이 전혀 막히지 않지요?

민지: _____

7. "그렇지 않아도"를 사용하여 대화를 완성하세요.

> 보기: A: 안녕하세요? (만나고 싶다)
>
> B: 안녕하세요? 그렇지 않아도 만나고 싶었어요.

(1) A: 선생님 늦어서 죄송합니다. (전화하다)

B: _____

(2) A: 이 선생님이 일을 또 시키셨어요? (피곤하다)

B: 네, _____ 또 시키셨어요.

(3) A: 영호 씨가 소영 씨 만나고 싶어하던데요. (만나러 가는 중이다)

B: _____

8. "~다(가) ~다(가) 하다"를 사용하여 대화를 완성하세요.

> 보기: A: 이가 아프다면서요?
>
> B: 네. 그런데 계속해서 아픈게 아니고 (아프다, 괜찮다) 아프다(가) 괜찮다(가) 그래요.

(1) A: 내일 영문학하고 경제학하고 시험이 두 개나 있다며?

B: 응. 그래서 (영문학 공부를 하다, 경제학 공부를 하다)

_____

(2) A: 오늘 아침 드셨어요?

B: 네. 아침에 출근길에 (운전을 하다, 빵을 먹다) _____

_____

    (3) A: 오늘 날씨가 참 이상하지요?

         B: 네, 하루 종일 _____

9. "~기(가) 일쑤이다"를 사용하여 다음 대화를 완성하세요.

    (1) A: 마이클이 아침잠이 많다며?

         B: 응. 그래서 (지각하다) _____

    (2) A: 이번 학기에 여섯 과목을 듣는다고?

         B: 응. 숙제가 너무 많아서 (밤을 새우다) _____

    (3) A: 저는 건망증(forgetfulness)이 심해요.

         B: 저도 그래요. 그래서 (버스에 우산을 두고 내리다) _____

        _____

10. "~을 대상으로"를 이용하여 문장을 만드세요.

> 보기: 초등학생을 대상으로 하루에 몇 시간 공부하는지
> 물어 보았다.

    (1) _____

    (2) _____

11. "다시 말해서"를 써서 문장을 만드세요.

    _____

    _____

12. Partner와 모범 대화 1과 2를 자연스럽게 따라해 보세요. 대화하면서 "~거든요," "말씀 낮추세요"와 "말씀 도중 실례지만"을 적절하게 써 보세요.

Discussion and Composition

1. 자기 소개를 하세요. 자기 소개를 할 때는 성명, 고향, 출신 고등학교, 현재 듣는 수업, 전공, 원하는 직업, 취미를 꼭 말하세요. 반 친구들이 자기 소개를 할 때 잘 듣고 빈칸을 채우세요.

성명			
고향 (국가, 도시)			
출신 고등학교			
현재 듣는 수업			
전공			
원하는 직업			
취미			

성명			
고향 (국가, 도시)			
출신 고등학교			
현재 듣는 수업			
전공			
원하는 직업			
취미			

성명			
고향 (국가, 도시)			
출신 고등학교			
현재 듣는 수업			

전공			
원하는 직업			
취미			

성명			
고향 (국가, 도시)			
출신 고등학교			
현재 듣는 수업			
전공			
원하는 직업			
취미			

성명			
고향 (국가, 도시)			
출신 고등학교			
현재 듣는 수업			
전공			
원하는 직업			
취미			

2. 원만한 대인 관계를 가지려면 어떤 말과 행동을 하여야 하는지 아래에 적고 교실에서 이야기해 보세요. 예를 들면 남의 장점(merit, good point)을 칭찬 (praise)하는 것은 대인 관계에 크게 도움이 됩니다. 사람은 누구나 칭찬을 받고 싶어하기 때문입니다.

(1) _____

(2) _____

(3) _____

(4) _____

(5) _____

3. 1.5세란 무슨 뜻인가요? 1.5세는 1세 또는 2세와 어떻게 다르다고 생각하세요?

4. "유교적인 사고방식"이라는 말을 많이 하는데 유교가 무엇인지요? 유교적인
사고방식이 서양의 기독교적인 사고방식과 어떻게 다른지 조사하여 글을 써
보세요.

5. 유교적인 사고방식과 기독교적인 사고방식의 장점과 단점(merits and demerits)
은 무엇이라고 생각하는지를 교실에서 토론(debate)하세요.

Further Reading

고운 말씨

사회 계급 제도가 있던 조선시대에 백정 노인이 고깃간을 하고 있었는데 어느 날 양반 두 사람이 고기를 사러 왔다.

"어이, 백정. 고기 한 근 주게."

"그러지요."

박 씨는 솜씨 좋게 칼로 고기를 베어 주었다. 함께 온 양반은 고깃간 주인이 비록 백정의 신분이긴 하지만 나이 많은 사람에게 말을 함부로 하기가 거북했다.

"박 서방, 여기 고기 한 근 주시게."

"예, 고맙습니다."

기분 좋게 대답한 박 씨는 그 양반에게 고기를 잘라 주었다. 먼저 고기를 산 양반이 보니 자기가 받은 것보다 갑절은 되어 보였다. 그 양반은 화가 나서 소리를 질렀다.

"이놈아, 같은 한 근인데 어째서 이 사람 것은 크고 내 것은 작으냐?"

그러자 박 씨가 대답했다.

"네, 손님 고기는 백정이 자른 것이고, 이 어른 고기는 박 서방이 잘랐으니까요."

갑절 double, two times (as much), twofold (= 배; 두 배); 거북하다 to feel uncomfortable; 고깃간 butcher shop; 근 a *kun,* a catty (a unit of weight equivalent to 601.04 gm); 말씨 way (manner) of speaking, use of words, mode of expression, speech, accent; 박 서방 "Old Pak" (서방 is a familiar title now used to a son-in-law, but formerly to adult servants); 백정 butcher (Chosŏn dynasty), member of the lowest class (once engaged chiefly in execution, grave digging, butchery, leatherwork, and wickerwork); 사회 계급 제도 class system; 손님 고기 your (*lit.,* esteemed guest's) meat; 솜씨 좋게 skillfully; 신분 social position, standing; 양반 aristocrat, nobleman, gentleman (the two upper classes [civil and military] of old Korea); 이 어른 고기 this gentleman's meat; 이놈아 you damn guy (*cf.* 이놈 this damn guy; 아 plain vocative particle); 조선시대 Chosŏn dynasty (1392-1910); 지르다 to shout, cry aloud; 함부로 rudely, roughly, at random; indiscriminately

1. 백정 노인에게 고기를 산 두 양반 중 어떤 사람이 고기를 더 많이 받았습니까?

2. 두 양반 중 한 양반이 백정 노인에게 말을 함부로 하지 않은 이유는 무엇입니까?

3. "어이, 백정. 고기 한 근 주게." 보다 "박 서방, 여기 고기 한 근 주시게."가 어느 점(points)에서 더 고운 말씨입니까?

4. Translate the selection "고운 말씨."

LESSON 1. INTERPERSONAL RELATIONS

Modern People's Secret to Success

The present age is the age of interpersonal relations. Although [interpersonal relations are important in] any age and any society, in no other time have they been as important as in the present age.

There are organizations that have investigated the magnitude of the importance of interpersonal relations. The United States' Carnegie Foundation has looked into the secrets of success of ten thousand successful people:

How did you make a lot of money?
How did you get promoted quickly?
How did you accomplish such a difficult task?
How did you become famous?

It was found through asking these questions that surprisingly, only 15 percent [of people] said that they succeeded by their intelligence, talent/skill, or effort. The remaining 85 percent said that they succeeded because they managed interpersonal relations well.

Harvard University also conducted a similar study. Harvard based its study on graduates who became unemployed, asking such questions as "Why did you quit your job?" to elicit reasons for unemployment. The study's findings indicated that bad interpersonal relations caused twice as much job loss as did incompetence.

What do the results of these two investigations have in common? In a word, the importance of interpersonal relations. Those with good interpersonal relations succeed, while those with bad ones are likely to fail.

CONVERSATION

1

(Sarah Jŏng is a 1.5-generation Korean-American student. In her third year of college, she went to Han'guk University in Korea as an exchange student for a year. While attending the freshman welcoming party, she met Professor Yŏng-Kyu Pak of Han'guk University.)

Sarah: Excuse me, but aren't you, by any chance, Professor Yŏng-Kyu Pak?

Prof. Pak: Yes, I am. May I ask who you are (lit., who you might be)?

Sarah: I'm Sarah Jŏng, an exchange student for a year from the University of Hawaii.

Prof. Pak: Oh, is that right? I'm pleased to meet you. But how do you know me?

Sarah: Last spring I attended your (lit., the professor's) lecture at the Center for Korean Studies at the University of Hawaii. As a matter of fact, I was going to go to your office to greet you.

Prof. Pak: Oh, is that right?

Sarah: By the way, Professor, please lower your speech [level] to me.

Prof. Pak: Well, what did you come to Korea to study?

Sarah: I came to study Korean literature.

Prof. Pak: Oh, I see. Your Korean is very fluent. Where did you learn it?

Sarah: I immigrated to Hawaii with my parents when I was five. I continued to speak Korean and English (lit., at times) at home with my parents. When I entered college, I ended up majoring in Korean literature.

Prof. Pak: So, will you be studying Korean literature in graduate school, too?

Sarah: Yes. I would like to attain a Ph.D. in Korean literature.

Prof. Pak: I hope you'll learn a lot during your year in Korea.

Sarah: I'll try my best.

Prof. Pak:	Well, I have some things to do, so I must leave (first). But when you have time, call and come to my office.
Sarah:	Yes. Thank you, Professor. Good-bye.

2

(On a clear autumn day, Sarah is seated on a bench on campus waiting for Michael Jones, who has come [to Korea] as an exchange student. So-yŏng Lee, a second-year English-language student whom Sarah knows well, passes by.)

Sarah:	So-yŏng, where are you going?
So-yŏng:	Oh, Sarah (*lit.,* older sister). (I'm on my way) to the library. What are you doing here (older sister)?
Sarah:	I'm waiting for Michael Jones, an exchange student from New York (*lit.,* a student who came as an exchange student from New York). Oh, there he comes.
Michael:	I'm sorry, Sarah. On the way here I ran into a senior of mine in economics and talked with him, so I'm late.
Sarah:	That's okay. By the way, Michael, say hello. This (*lit.,* here) is So-yŏng Lee.
Michael:	Glad to meet you. I'm Michael Jones. I came to study in Korea from Columbia University in New York in the spring of this year. I'm a junior in economics.
So-yŏng:	Pleased to meet you. I'm So-yŏng Lee, a sophomore in the English language and literature department. I've heard about you from (*lit.,* older sister) Sarah. You speak Korean very well, Michael.
Michael:	Not at all. I still don't know Korean etiquette, so I'm constantly making mistakes. I don't use honorifics properly, and it's a big problem.
So-yŏng:	Korea has a very Confucian approach to lifestyles and use of language, and this must be unfamiliar to Western people. By the way, Michael, do you know (senior) Yŏng-ho Kim in fourth-year economics?
Michael:	Of course. I know him well. The person I just met was (senior) Yŏng-ho Kim. How do you know him?
So-yŏng:	I am in the same club with him (*lit.,* that older brother). I'm supposed to meet him at the library now.
Michael:	In fact, he said he was going to meet a junior of his in the

	English language and literature department, so that was you. It's really a small world.
Sarah:	Sorry to interrupt, but, So-yŏng, don't you think (*lit.*, older brother) Yŏng-ho is waiting?
So-yŏng:	My goodness, where are my senses? I'll see you again.

제2과   노래방

(Lesson 2: *Noraebang*)

PRE-READING QUESTIONS

1. 노래방에 가 보았습니까? 주로 어떤 때에 누구와 노래방에 갑니까?

2. 가요, 클래식, 팝송 중 어떤 음악을 좋아합니까? 그 이유는 무엇입니까? 이 세 가지 장르의 차이는 무엇이라고 생각합니까?

3. 여러분은 주로 어떻게 음악을 듣습니까? CD, MP3, 미니디스크, 카세트 테이프 중 어떤 것을 주로 사용합니까?

GAINING FAMILIARITY

1. 노래, 곡, 노래방, 가라오케, 합창, 18번

2. 음악, 대중 음악, 전통 음악, 교회 음악, 실내 음악, 음악가, 음악회, 음악당, 음악 영화, 국악

3. 가요, 민요, 대중 가요 (= 유행가), 가곡, 가수

4. 음악의 장르
   클래식, 가스펠, 록, 팝(송), 뉴에이지, 랩, 힙합, 메탈, 블루스, 소울, 재즈, 펑크, 포크, 프로그레시브 록

한국인과 노래

음악과 인간은 깊은 관계가 있다는 것을 우리는 잘 알고 있다. 문명 사회이건 원시 사회이건[2.1] 사람이 살고 있는 데에는 음악이 있고 노래가 있다. 한국 사람들은 유난히 음악을 즐기는 민족이다.

여러 기록과 연구에 따르면,[2.2] 오랜 옛날부터 한국 사람들은 풍부한 음악 문화의 전통을 이어 왔다. 이러한 한국 전통 음악을 국악이라고 하는데, 국악에는 중국 음악의 영향을 받아 발달된 것과 한국에서 창조된 것이 있다. 한국에서 창조된 것은 향악, 향가, 민요, 가곡, 농악, 판소리 등을 들 수 있다. 그리고 전통 음악이 아닌 장르도 대단히 많다. 대중 가요는 그중 하나인데 가요 또는 유행가라고도 한다.

서양 음악도 한국 음악에서 중요한 위치를 차지하고 있다. 1885년부터 미국 선교사들이 한국 사람들에게 찬송가를 가르치기 시작했는데, 그 이후 클래식, 팝송, 록 등 온갖 장르의 서양 음악이 들어왔고 지금도 계속 들어오고 있다.

일반 한국 사람들은 한국에서 살건 외국에서 살건 간에 대중 가요를 가장 많이 부른다. 여러 비공식 모임에서 한 사람씩 또는 합창으로 노래 부르기를 좋아한다. 그러므로 외국인이 한국 사람들과 깊이 친해지려면 한국 노래나 외국 노래를 한 곡쯤 부를 준비를 항상 하고 있는 것이 바람직하다. 서양 사람들에게는 이것이 힘들지 모른다. 그러나 한국 사람들의 모임에서 서슴없이 노래 한 곡을 부를 때 한국 사람들의 감정과 기분과 정신의 문이 활짝 열릴 것이다.

요즘 노래방이라는 건전한 새 문화가 한국인 사회에 널리 퍼지고 있다. 수많은 노래방이 한국은 물론이고[2.3] 한국 사람이 살고 있는 세계의 많은 나라에서 손님을 기다리고 있다. 노래방은 복잡한 생활에서 오는 스트레스를 노래로 마음껏 푸는 장소일 뿐 아니라 따뜻한 인간 관계를 맺는 장소이기도 하다.

대화

1

(현주, 사라, 마이클이 원식이의 생일 파티 계획을 세우고 있다.)

현주: 이번 금요일이 원식이 생일인데 계획 좀 세워 봤니?

사라: 아직 특별한 계획은 못 세웠는데. 그냥 저녁 먹고 같이 노래방이나 가는 게 어때? 원식이 노래방 가는 거 좋아하잖아.

마이클: 노래방 가자고?[2.4] 노래방 가면 재밌긴 한데,[2.5] 원식이는 노래 너무 좋아해서 마이크 한번 잡으면 안 놓잖아.

(현주와 사라 웃는다.)

사라: 하긴 그래.[2.6] 전에도 원식이랑 노래방에 한번 같이 갔는데 혼자 연속 다섯 곡을 부르더라.

마이클: 완전히 원식이 독무대가 되겠군.

현주: 야. 그래도 생일인데 봐 주자.

마이클: 그러지 뭐.

현주: 그럼 어느 노래방으로 갈까?

마이클: 나랑 사라는 최신 가요 잘 모르니까 팝송이 좀 많은 데로 가자.

현주: 그러자. 참, 저녁은 어떻게 할까?

사라: 그냥 그날 강남역에서 만나서 원식이더러[2.7] 정하라고 하는 게 어떠니?

현주: 그게 좋겠다. 강남역 근처에 식당도 많고 노래방도 많으니까. 또 이동할 필요 없이 거기서 저녁 먹고 노래방에 가면 되겠구나.

마이클: 그럼 금요일날 강남역 뉴욕제과 앞 6시 괜찮니?

현주, 사라: 응. 괜찮아.

현주: 원식이한테는 내가 연락할게.

2

(현주, 원식, 사라, 마이클이 강남역 앞 무지개 노래방에 와 있다.)

종업원: 몇 분이세요?

마이클: 네 명이요.

종업원: 이쪽으로 오세요.

(현주, 원식, 사라, 마이클이 종업원이 안내해 준 방으로 들어간다.)

종업원: 몇 시간 하실 거예요?

현주: 글쎄요. 우선 1시간만 하고요, 더하고 싶으면 말씀드릴게요.

종업원: 네. 그러면 재미있게 노세요.

현주: 야, 시간이 돈이다. 빨리 정해.

사라: 오늘이 원식이 생일이니까 우리 생일 축하 노래로 시작할까?

마이클: 그러자. 근데 생일 축하 노래 몇 번이냐?

사라: 잠깐만, 찾아보고. 아, 여기 있다. 1122번.

원식: 리모콘 어디 있냐?

현주: 저기 텔레비전 위에 있다.

(마이클, 사라, 현주가 생일 축하 노래를 불렀다.)

마이클, 사라, 현주: 축하해 원식아.

원식: 고맙다. 이번엔 내가 답례로 한 곡 뽑을게.

현주: 그래, 네 18번 불러라.

사라: 원식이 18번이 뭔데?

현주: 들어 보면 알아. 전통 가온데 원식이가 진짜 가수보다 더 잘 불러.

마이클: 기대되는데.

토요일 밤

Calypso

조성욱 작사 조성욱 작곡 김세환 노래

긴 — 머 리 짧 은 치 마 아 름 다 운 그 녀 를 보 면
세 상 에 서 제 일 가 는 2.8 믿 음 직 한 그 이 를 보 면
아 름 다 운 노 래 소 리 멀 리 멀 리 퍼 져 — 갈때

무 슨 말 을 하 여 야 할 까
무 슨 말 을 하 여 야 할 까 오 토 요 일 밤
회 망 에 찬 내 일 을 위 해

에 — 토 요 일 밤 토 요 일 밤

에 나 그 대 — 를 만 나 리 —

토 요 일 밤 토 요 일 밤 에 나 그 대 — 를

만 나 리 라 D. S.

토 요 일 밤 토 요 일 밤 나 그 대 — 를 만 나

리 — 그 대 — 를 만 나 리 라 —

「어머니 노래부르기」(1991). 현대 음악 출판사

남행 열차

내용		영용		대지	
	1215		1127		911

정혜경 작사
정혜경 작곡
김수희 노래

비내리는호남 선
비내리는호남 선

남 행 열 차에——
마 지 막 열차——

혼 들 리— 는
기 적 소— 리

차 창 너 머로——
슬 피 우 는데——

빗물이흐르 고
눈물이흐르 고

내—눈물도흐르 고—
내—눈물도흐르 고—

잃 어 버—린 첫
잃 어 버—린 첫

— 사 랑 도—흐르네——
— 사 랑 도—흐르네——

깜 빡깜— 빡—이

「노래방대백과」 (1995). 세광 음악 출판사 pp. 142-143

Comprehension Questions

1. **Reading Comprehension.** "한국인과 노래"를 읽고 맞고(Ⓣ) 틀린(Ⓕ) 것을 지적하거나 질문에 대답해 보세요.

    (1) 대중 가요는 한국 전통 음악의 장르이다.   Ⓣ   Ⓕ

    (2) 지은이는 한국 사람들은 특별히 음악을 즐기는 민족이라고 생각한다.   Ⓣ   Ⓕ

    (3) 지은이는 한국이나 외국에 사는 한국 사람 모두 대중 가요를 가장 많이 부른다고 주장한다.   Ⓣ   Ⓕ

    (4) 지은이는 노래방은 복잡한 생활에서 오는 스트레스를 푸는 장소이지만 인간 관계를 맺기에 적당한 장소는 아니라고 생각한다.   Ⓣ   Ⓕ

    (5) 한국의 전통 음악을 무엇이라고 합니까?

    (6) 한국에서 창조된 전통 음악에는 어떤 것들이 있습니까?

    (7) 서양 음악은 언제부터 한국에 들어오기 시작했습니까?

    (8) 지은이는 외국인이 한국인들과 깊이 친해지려면 어떻게 해야 한다고 생각합니까?

    (9) 한국인이 오랜 옛날부터 풍부한 음악 전통을 이어왔다는 것을 어떻게 알 수 있습니까?

2. **Listening Comprehension.** 대화를 듣고 맞고(Ⓣ) 틀린(Ⓕ) 것을 지적하거나 질문에 대답해 보세요.

대화 1

    (1) 현주가 원식이에게 연락하기로 했다.   Ⓣ   Ⓕ

    (2) 마이클은 처음 사라가 노래방에 가자고 했을 때 아주 좋은 생각이라고 했다.   Ⓣ   Ⓕ

    (3) 현주, 사라, 마이클, 원식이는 다음 금요일날 강남역 근처에서 저녁을 먹고 노래방에도 갈 것이다.   Ⓣ   Ⓕ

(4) 원식이 생일날 어느 식당에서 저녁을 먹을지는 원식이가
정할 것이다. Ⓣ Ⓕ

(5) 마이클은 어떤 노래방에 가고 싶어합니까?

(6) 원식이 생일날 저녁은 어디에서 먹기로 했습니까?

(7) 현주, 사라, 마이클은 원식이 생일에 무엇을 하기로 했습니까?

대화 2

(1) 원식이는 노래방에서 자신의 18번인 생일 축하 노래를 불렀다. Ⓣ Ⓕ

(2) 원식이 생일날 노래방에서 제일 먼저 어떤 노래를
불렀습니까?

New Words

18번 *n.* (one's) favorite song

가곡 *n.* a song in the classical style

가수 *n.* singer, vocalist ¶오페라 가수 opera singer ¶유행가 가수 singer of popular songs

가요 *n.* song, ballad ¶대중 가요 popular song

감정 *n.* feeling, emotion, sentiment

강남역 *n.* Kangnam subway station

건전하다 *adj.* to be healthy, sound. 건전 health; soundness

계속 *n., adv.* continuation; continuously, uninterruptedly (= 계속해서; 계속적으로)

계획 *n.* plan ¶계획하다 to plan, make a plan ¶계획을 세우다 to plan

곡 *n.* tune, piece, melody; song

국악 *n.* traditional Korean music

그게 *contr.* of 그것이

그대 *pr.* you (archaic; used in songs, novels, etc.) (= 당신)

그러지 뭐 *contr.* of 그렇게 하지 뭐 Let's do so. 뭐 (from 무엇) just; what else

근처 *n.* neighborhood, vicinity; nearby

기대 *n.* expectation, anticipation. 기대하다 to expect, look forward to, anticipate, count on; 기대되다 to be expected; I can't wait ¶큰 기대를 걸다 to hope much (from a person) ¶너무 기대를 크게 가져서는 안돼. You must not set your expectations too high.

기록 *n.* record

기분 *n.* mood, frame of mind, feeling

기억 *n.* memory, recollection, remembrance. 기억하다 to remember; 기억력 the power of memory ¶기억(속)에 남다 to remain in one's memory

기적 *n.* steamwhistle ¶기적을 울리다 to give a whistle

깜빡(깜박)이다 *v.* to flicker, twinkle, wink (= 깜빡(깜박)거리다) ¶멀리 불빛이 깜빡(깜박)인다/거린다. A light is flickering in the distance.

끊임없이 *adv.* constantly, continually; successively. 끊임없다 to be continuous

남행 열차 *n.* southbound train. 남행 going south, southbound; 열차 train ¶상행 열차 up train (bound to Seoul) ¶하행 열차 down train (departing from Seoul)

너머로 *adv.* opposite from; over; beyond; through. 너머 opposite side; 로 toward; through ¶창 너머로 보다 to look through a window ¶할머니는 안경 너머로 나를 보았어요. Grandma looked at me from over her glasses.

노래방 *n. noraebang* (a room similar to a Japanese *karaoke* room)

농악 *n.* instrumental music of peasants

눈물 *n.* tears (weeping)

뉴욕제과 *n.* the New York Bakery

답례 *n.* return courtesy; return salute. 답례하다 to return a salute ¶그의 선물에 대한 답례로 무엇을 할까? What shall I give him in return for his present?

대중 가요 *n.* popular song

대중 음악 *n.* popular music

더러 *ptcl.* to (indirect object marker)

독무대 *n.* sole master of the stage. 독~ sole; 무대 stage ¶미아의 독무대다. Mia has the stage all to herself.

되겠다 it will be good (fine, O.K.) ¶빨리 가면 되겠어요. It will be O.K. if you go there quickly.

들다 *v.* to raise, hold up, hold; to mention; to enumerate ¶예를 들면 for example

등 *n.* and the like, etc.

리모콘 *n.* remote control

마음껏 *adv.* to one's heart's content, as one wishes, with one's whole heart 마음 heart, mind; ~껏 to the full extent of, to the utmost of ¶마음껏 먹다 to eat all one can ¶마음껏 울다 to cry one's heart out ¶마음껏 사랑하다 to love with one's whole heart

만나리(라) will meet (him/her) (archaic; = 만나겠다)

만날 순 없어도 *contr.* of 만날 수는 없어도 although unable to meet

맺다 *v.* to form; to tie; to conclude ¶인간 관계를 맺다 to form a relationship ¶끝을 맺다 to wind up

멀리 *adv.* far, far off, far away; (from) afar

무지개 *n.* rainbow

문명 사회 *n.* civilized society

뭐니뭐니해도 *adv.* after all; all things considered

민요 *n.* folk song, ballad

믿음직하다 *adj.* to be reliable, dependable, trustworthy; to be authentic ¶믿음직한 사람 promising man, person of promise, reliable person ¶매우 믿음직하게 생각하다 to repose great trust in (a person)

바람직하다 *adj.* to be desirable; to be advisable ¶바람직하지 않은 사람 undesirable person

발달되다 *v.* to be developed. 발달하다 to develop; 발달 development, growth

봐주다 *v.* to give special treatment, go easy on. 보다 to see, look after; 주다 (to do) for

비공식 *n.* informality; unofficial nature ¶비공식 회의 informal meeting

빗물 *n.* rainwater. 비 rain, 물 water

뽑다 *v.* to pull out, take out, draw; to sing (used colloquially among close friends; a more general form is 부르다 'to sing')

생일 축하 노래 *n.* "Happy Birthday" song

서슴없이 *adv.* without hesitation; unreservedly

선교사 *n.* missionary

슬피 *adv.* sadly, sorrowfully. 슬프다 to be sad

안내하다 *v.* to guide, lead the way; to usher (a person) in ¶안내서 a guide book ¶그 소녀는 나를 내 좌석으로 안내했다. The girl ushered me to my seat.

연구 *n.* study, research, investigation. 연구하다 to study, do research

연락하다 *v.* to contact; to communicate (with); to inform. 연락 contact, communication

연속 *n., adv.* continuing, continuation, succession; continuously, successively

영향 *n.* influence, effect

온갖 *pre-n.* all kinds of; every kind of; various

완전히 *adv.* completely; perfectly

우선 *adv.* first of all

원시 사회 *n.* primitive society

위치 *n.* situation; location; position, place

유난히 *adv.* unusually; particularly; uncommonly

유행가 *n.* popular song ¶유행가 가수 a pop(ular) singer

이동하다 *v.* to move (from one place to another) (= 옮기다). 이동 movement, transfer

이어 오다 *v.* to inherit; to uphold; to cherish. 잇다 to connect, tie, link

이후 *n., adv.* after; henceforth, hereafter ¶그 이후 since then, thereafter

인간 *n.* a human being; mankind, humanity

일반 *n.* (being) general, common, popular ¶일반 사람들 the general public

자꾸만 *adv.* repeatedly; frequently (emphatic form of 자꾸) ¶자꾸(만) 때리다 to strike repeatedly ¶비가 자꾸(만) 온다. It keeps on raining.

작곡 *n.* (musical) composition ¶A씨 작곡 composed by Mr./Ms. A ¶작곡가 composer

작사 *n.* song writing ¶이 노래는 그가 작사 작곡했다. He wrote both the words and music for this song.

장소 *n.* place; position; site

재밌긴 하다 contr. of 재미있기는 하다. It's true that it is fun.

전통 *n.* tradition; convention

전통 가요 *n.* old-style Korean pop song

전통 음악 *n.* traditional music

정신 *n.* mind, spirit, soul

정하다 *v.* to decide; to fix ¶값을 정하다 to fix the price

주로 *adv.* mainly, chiefly, primarily

진짜 *n.* the genuine article, the real stuff ¶진짜와 가짜를 가리다 to tell the real [originals] from the false [imitations] ¶이 종이꽃은 꼭 진짜 같아요. These artificial flowers are so lifelike.

차다 *v.* to be full (of) ¶그의 앞날이 희망에 차 있다. His future is full of hope. ¶스케줄이 꽉 차 있다 to have a full schedule

차지하다 *v.* to occupy, hold; to take; to have

차창 *n.* car window; train window

찬송가 *n.* hymn; psalm ¶찬송가를 부르다 to sing a hymn

참 *adv.* by the way; nearly; very; well

찾아보다 *v.* to look for (it) ¶모르는 단어의 뜻을 사전에서 찾아보았다. I looked up a word whose meaning I did not know.

최신 가요 *n.* current popular song, brand-new song

출판사 *n.* publishing company

판소리 *n.* *p'ansori* (a long Korean epic song)

팝송 *n.* popular song

퍼지다 *v.* to spread out, widen, broaden ¶그 소식은 빠르게 퍼졌다. The news spread like wildfire. ¶이 노래는 학생들 간에 널리 퍼져 있다. This song is very popular with the students. ¶퍼져 가다 to be spreading (퍼지다 to spread; 가다 to go, continue)

풀다 *v.* to untie, loosen, solve; to let out; to dispel; to remove ¶머리를 풀다 to loosen one's hair ¶문제를 풀다 to solve a problem ¶수수께끼를 풀다 to work out a puzzle ¶스트레스를 풀다 to let out stress

풍부하다 *adj.* to be rich, abundant, plentiful

합창 *n.* choral singing; ensemble. 합창하다 to sing together, sing in chorus

향가 *n.* old Korean folk songs (ballads); Korea's native songs

향악 *n.* indigenous Korean music

호남선 *n.* Honam (Seoul-Cholla province) line. 호남 the southwestern section of Korea (*lit,.* south of the lake)

혼자 *n., adv.* one person; alone; by oneself

활짝 *adv.* widely, extensively ¶활짝 갠 하늘 a cloudless sky ¶창문을 활짝 열다 to throw open the window ¶꽃이 활짝 피다 to be in full bloom

희망 *n.* hope, wish. 희망하다 to hope (for) ¶희망에 찬 젊은이 young hopefuls ¶희망에 찬 말 hopeful words ¶인생에 새로운 희망을 가지고 with a new hope in life

희미하다 *adj.* to be faint, dim, vague. 희미하게 faintly, dimly, vaguely; 희미해지다 to become faint, dim, vague

Useful Expressions

2.1 ~건/거나 . . . ~건/거나 whether . . . or; either . . . or; and; regardless of

This pattern is used to enumerate two or more alternative events, actions, or states. It may be translated either as 'and' (usually in positive sentences) or 'or' (usually in negative sentences).

그 사람은 마시거나 먹거나 하여 돈을 다 써 버렸다.
He spent his last penny on food and drink.

비가 오거나 눈이 내리거나 하면 오지 마세요.
Please don't come if it rains or snows.

2.2 ~에 따르면 according to

~에 따르면 consists of the particle 에 'at, to,' the verb stem 따르 'follow, go with' and the suffix ~면 'if.' It is similar in meaning and usage to ~에 의하면 'according to' (where 의하다 means 'to be due to, depend on') and can replace that phrase, as in 학생들 말에 따르면/의하면 'according to what students say.' 의하면 sounds slightly more formal than 따르면.

신문 보도에 따르면, 이번 비행기 사고로 120명이 사망했어요.
According to a newspaper report, 120 people were killed in the plane accident in question.

일기 예보에 따르면 내일 전국에 눈이 내린대요.
According to the weather forecast, we will have snow all over the country.

2.3 ~은/는 물론이다 there is no doubt that, it goes without saying that, it is a matter of course that

물론 (lit., 'don't discuss') is a Sino-Korean adverb variously meaning '(as a matter) of course, beyond dispute, surely, without doubt, without question, needless to say.' When 물론!, 물론이야, and 물론이에요 are used independently, they mean 'of course!' (emphatic).

A: 너 안 가지?   You won't go, will you?
B: 물론이지!   Of course not!

우리 형은 영어는 물론 독일어도 잘 한다.
My older brother knows German very well, not to mention (not to speak of, let alone) English.

2.4   ~자고? are you suggesting (asking) that we do ~?

The ending ~자 (proposal) and the quotative particle 고, followed by rising intonation, make up this pattern. Although there is no verb of suggesting or asking, the question intonation provides the meaning. A similar pattern is the command quotation ~라고? 'Are you asking that I/(s)he~?' as in 내가 가라고? 'Are you asking that I go?'

A: 모두 노래 좋아하잖아?   We all like to sing, don't we?
B: 그러니까 노래방 가자고?   So are you suggesting that we go to a *noraebang*?

A: 지금 시간 없어.   We don't have time.
B: 밥 빨리 먹자고?   Are you suggesting that we eat right away?

2.5   ~기는 (or 긴) 하다 it is true that ~ (but)

~기는 하다 consists of the nominalizing suffix ~기 + the particle 는 'as for' + the verb 하다 'to do, to be.' It is used when the speaker admits the truth of an action or state, but with some reservation. Compare 그 집이 좋다 'That house is good' with 그 집이 좋긴 하다 'It's true that that house is good [but I cannot afford it, and so on].' Instead of 하다, the verb or adjective before ~기는 can be repeated without any change in meaning: 좋기는 하다 = 좋기는 좋다.

노래방에 가면 재미있긴 **하겠는데** 지금 시간이 없네요.
It's true that going to a *noraebang* would be fun, but I don't have time now.
이 책을 읽어보기는 **했지만** 너무 어려워서 잘 이해하지 못했어요.
I did read this book, but it was too difficult [for me] to understand.

2.6   하기는 그래(요) that is certainly true

This idiomatic expression is a contraction of 그러하기는 그래(요) (*lit.,* 'as for doing/being so, that is so').

원식이는 마이크 한번 잡으면 안 놓잖아.
Wŏn-sik hardly lets others use the microphone once he grabs it.

하긴 그래.
That's very true.

저 가수가 노래는 잘 하는데 나이가 너무 많아요.
That singer sings very well, but he is too old.

하긴 그래요. 그래서 젊은 사람들한테 인기가 별로 없어요.
That's very true. That's why he is not very popular among young people.

2.7   ~더러 (specialized indirect object marker)

The particle 더러 is similar to 에게 and 한테 in meaning. Unlike those two, however, which have no restrictions, 더러 is usually used only in indirect quotations. 이것을 마이클더러 주세요 'Please give this to Michael' would not be acceptable.

원식이더러/에게/한테 정하라고 하는게 어떠니?
How about asking Wŏn-sik to decide about it?

박 선생님더러/에게/한테 지금 가시자고 하세요.
Please tell Professor Park that we should leave now.

2.8   제일가다/일등가다/첫째가다 to be best, to be first rate

The verb 가다 'to go' idiomatically combines with a noun meaning 'best' to mean 'to be the best, to be first rate.'

우리 형은 자기 반에서 공부가 **첫째가요**.
My older brother is the best student (*lit.,* in study) in his class.

세상에서 **제일가는** 믿음직한 그이
my (reliable) beloved, who is the best in the world

세계에서 **일등가는** 단거리 선수
a sprinter who is (*lit.,* ranks) the best in the world

2.9   ~(으)리(라) I/(s)he/it will

This sentence ending is obsolete in contemporary spoken Korean, but it occurs in songs and novels. The contemporary counterpart is ~겠다 'I intend to do; I presume that ~.'

그대를 **만나리(라)**. (= 당신을 만나겠어요) I will meet you.

2.10 Modifying clauses

As observed in 비내리는 호남선 남행 열차 'the southbound Honam line train on which it is raining,' a modifying clause (technically a relative clause) can modify a noun, a pronoun, or a noun phrase. A modifying clause consists of clause + modifier suffix (such as ~는 [non-past after a verb], ~은/ㄴ [non-past after an adjective; past after a verb], or ~을/ㄹ [prospective after a verb or adjective]: 먹는, 가는; 좋은, 큰; 먹은, 잔; 먹을, 갈, 좋을, 클. English relative clauses require a relative pronoun and a preposition, as in 'the train on which it is raining'; Korean relative clauses lack these elements. 비내리는 남행 열차 is literally 'the raining south bound train.' Similarly:

말이 많은 여자	a woman who is talkative
비가 많이 내리는 도시	the city where it rains a lot
선생님이 졸업하신 대학교	the university from which our professor graduated
젊어지는 샘물	the spring water by which people become younger

Exercises

1. 관련된 단어들끼리 연결하여 문장을 만들어 보세요.

(1) 대중 가요 •   • 세우다 _____

(2) 전통   •   • 잇다   _____

(3) 스트레스   •   • 풀다   _____

(4) 인간 관계 •   • 맺다   _____

(5) 계획   •   • 부르다 _____

2. 아래의 설명과 맞는 단어나 표현을 본문에서 찾아 쓰세요.

(1) 보통과 아주 다르게: _____

(2) 처음으로 만들어지다: _____

(3) 여러 사람이 소리를 맞추어 노래함: _____

(4) 말이나 행동이 거칠 것 없이: _____

(5) 건실하고 완전한: _____

(6) 가장 새로움: _____

(7) 끊이지 않고 죽 이음: _____

(8) 옮기어 다님: _____

3. 보기에서 적당한 말을 골라 빈칸을 채우세요.

> 보기: 그러므로, 그러나, 그리고, 특히

(1) 한국 사람들은 비공식 모임에서 노래 부르기를 좋아한다. _____ 외국인이 한국 사람들과 친해지려면 노래 한 곡쯤 부를 준비를 하고 있는 것이 바람직하다.

(2) 한국에서 창조된 한국의 전통 음악으로는, 향악, 향가, 민요, 가곡, 농악, 판소리 등을 들 수 있다. _____ 전통 음악이 아닌 장르도 대단히 많다.

(3) 한국 사람들은 유난히 음악을 즐기는 민족이다. _____ 노래 부르기를 좋아한다.

(4) 서양 사람들에게는 이것이 힘들지 모른다. _____ 한국 사람들의 모임에서 서슴없이 노래 한 곡을 부를 때 한국 사람들의 감정과 기분과 정신의 문이 활짝 열릴 것이다.

4. 밑줄 친 말과 반대되거나 대조(contrast)되는 말을 써서 새 문장을 만드세요.

(1) <u>전통 음악</u>으로는 향악, 향가, 민요, 가곡, 농악, 판소리 등을 들 수 있다.

_____

(2) <u>서양</u> 음악도 한국 음악에서 중요한 위치를 차지하고 있다.

_____

(3) 요즘 노래방이라는 <u>건전한</u> 문화가 한국인 사회에 널리 퍼지고 있다.

_____

(4) 많은 한국인들은 노래방에서 <u>스트레스를 푼다.</u>

_____

5. 보기와 같이 주어진 말이 들어가는 단어를 3개 이상 써 보세요.

> 보기: 친 (親, friendly, parents): 친지, 양친, 친척, 친구, 친절

　(1) 국 (國, country, nation): _____

　(2) 인 (人, man): _____

　(3) 비 (非, no, not, wrong): _____

　(4) 방 (room): _____

6. "~자고"나 "~라고"를 사용해서 대화를 완성하세요.

> 보기: A: 아이고 피곤해서 죽겠어. (자자)
>   B: 우리 벌써 자자고?

　(1) A: 영화 타이테닉이 볼만하대요. (보러 가자)

　　　B: _____

　(2) A: "남행열차" 잘 부르시지 않아요? (불러 보라)

　　　B: _____

　(3) A: 이번 주말에 무슨 계획 있으세요? (소풍 가자)

　　　B: _____

7. 다음 보도들(reports)을 출처(source)를 밝히는 문장으로 바꾸세요.

> 올해 물가는 안정될 것이다. (믿을만한 소식통 reliable source)
> 된장이 암 예방에 좋다.
> 　(뉴잉글랜드 저널 오브 메디슨 New England Journal of Medicine)
> 여성 흡연 인구가 증가하고 있다.
> 　(1998년도 보건복지부 Ministry of Public Health and Welfare)
> 90년도에 비해 97년도에 교통 통신비 지출이 크게 늘어났다.
> 　(통계청 Bureau of Statistics)

> 보기: 믿을만한 소식통에 따르면 올해 물가는 안정될 거래요.

(1) _____

(2) _____

(3) _____

8. "~기는 하다"를 사용하여 보기처럼 대화를 완성하세요.

> 보기: A: 마이클이 노래를 잘 불러요.
> B: 마이클이 노래를 잘 부르기는 하지만 소리가 너무
> 커서 귀가 아파요.

(1) A: 그 배우는 얼굴이 예뻐요.

B: _____

(2) A: 그 부부는 행복하게 살고 있어요.

B: _____

(3) A: 우리 선생님은 아시는 것이 아주 많아요.

B: _____

9. "하기는 그래(요)"를 사용하여 보기처럼 대화를 완성하세요.

> 보기: A: 요즘은 돈이 없으면 사람 노릇도 못 하겠어. (노릇
> function, role)
> B: 하긴 그래. 돈 없으면 집에 들어 앉아서 노래나 불러야지.

(1) A: 남한과 북한이 사이 좋게 지내야지 서로에게 좋지 않겠어?

B: _____

(2) A: 행복한 가정에 복이 온대. 싸우지 말고 잘 살아. (복 blessing)

B: _____

(3) A: 또 미역국 먹고 싶지 않으면 그만 놀고 열심히 공부해야 해.

(미역국 먹다 to fail an exam)

B: _____

10. "더러"를 사용하여 보기처럼 대화를 완성하세요.

> 보기: A: 저녁은 어디서 할까?
>
> B: 원식이더러 정하라고 하면 어때?
>
> (How about asking Wŏn-sik to decide?)

(1) A: 호텔 예약은 누가 하지요?

B: (Ask your younger brother to do that) _____ 하라고 해.

(2) A: 이번 일은 네가 잘못했다며?

B: (Who said that I did wrong?) _____ 누가 그래?

(3) A: 너 나 좀 도와 줘.

B: (Father told me to go on an errand.) _____ 심부름을 가라고 하셨어.

11. 다음 영문을 한국말로 옮기세요.

(1) the house from which I just came (out)

_____

(2) the river where there is no water

_____

(3) the sound of children fighting (the sound that children are fighting)

_____

12. "제일가다/일등가다/첫째가다"를 사용하여 문장을 만들어 보세요.

(1) _____

(2) _____

(3) _____

Discussion and Composition

1. 여러분이 대화 1에 나오는 현주라고 생각하고 원식이한테 이메일을 보내 보세요. 원식이 생일에 어디서, 누구와, 무엇을 하고 싶어하는 지를 물어 보세요. 그리고 원식이한테 저녁 식사 장소를 정하라고 부탁하세요.

```
받는 이:
함께 받는 이:
제목:
본문:




```

2. (Group work) 파티 계획을 세워 보세요. 언제, 어디서, 어떤 주제로 파티를 할지, 누구 누구를 초대할지, 파티에서 무엇을 할 것인지를 계획해 보세요. 여러 명이 의견을 나눌 때는 다음 표현을 사용해 보세요.

```
• ~는게 어때/어떠니?      • ~기는 한데 . . .
• ~자고?                  • 하긴 그래.
• 그게 좋겠다.
```

3. 다음은 음악에 관한 의견들입니다. 아래의 의견 중 여러분이 동의하는 의견 두 개와 동의하지 않는 의견 두 개를 골라 보고 그 이유를 말해 보세요.

```
• 음악을 듣고 있으면 집중이 안 돼서 공부를 할 수 없다.
• 전통 음악이나 고전 음악은 지루하다.
• 음악은 역시 클래식이 최고이다.
```

> • 대학생들은 전통 가요(or country music)를 좋아하지 않는다.
> • 영화 음악은 주로 주부들이 좋아한다.
> • 연세가 드신 분들은 힙합을 좋아하지 않는다.
> • 운동할 때 워크맨을 듣는 것은 좋지 않다.
> • 뮤직 비디오는 청소년에게 해롭다.

4. 학교 신문에 음악 특집 기사를 써 보세요. (특집 기사 feature article)

(1) 다음의 주제 중에서 하나를 정하세요.

> • 영화나 드라마에서 음악이 중요한가?
> • 인기 가요 (survey)
> • ~을/를 좋아하세요? (survey)
> • 최근에 어떤 콘서트를 가 보았어요?
> • 월드컵송/올림픽송을 누가 부르면 좋을까요? (survey)
> • 자신이 좋아하는 노래나 가수에 대한 기사
> • 기타 (etc.)

(2) 선택한 주제에 관계된 정보(information, data)를 모으고 기사를 쓰세요.

Further Reading

1. 다음 노래의 가사를 읽고 영어로 옮기세요. 그리고 가능하면 이 노래를 배워서 불러 보세요.

마법의 성

노래: 더 클래식
작사, 작곡: 김광진

믿을 수 있나요. 나의 꿈속에서 너는 마법에 빠진 공주란 걸. 언제나 너를 향한 몸짓엔 수많은 어려움뿐이지만. 그러나 언제나 굳은 다짐뿐이죠. 다시 너를 구하고 말 거라고. 두 손을 모아 기도했죠. 끝없는 용기와 지혜를 달라고.

(후렴 [refrain])

마법의 성을 지나 늪을 건너, 어둠의 동굴 속 멀리 그대가 보여. 이제 나의 손을 잡아 보아요. 우리의 몸이 떠오르는 것을 느끼죠. 자유롭게 저 하늘을 날아가도 놀라지 말아요. 우리 앞에 펼쳐질 세상이 너무나 소중해 함께라면.

_____

_____

_____

_____

_____

_____

_____

2. 다음 신문 기사를 읽고 질문에 답하세요.

"아드린느를 위한 발라드" 리처드 클레이더만 내한 공연

"아드린느를 위한 발라드"로 유명한 프랑스 출신의 팝피아니스트 리처드 클레이더만이 오는 12월에 서울과 부산에서 공연 무대를 갖는다. 리처드 클레이더만의 내한 공연은 이번이 다섯 번째다.

그는 오는 12월 17일 오후 7시 30분 부산 롯데호텔 대공연장, 12월 20일 오후 7시 30분 서울 잠실 올림픽공원내 펜싱 경기장에서 각각 공연한다.

연주곡으로는 "아드린느를 위한 발라드"(Ballade pour Adeline)를 비롯해 "러브 이즈 인 디 에어" (Love Is in the Air), "브라질리아" (Brasilia), "웨스트 사이드 스토리 메들리" (*West Side Story* Medley), "비틀스 메들리" (Beatles Medley) 등 17곡이 예정돼 있다. 051-244-4452.

(서울 = 연합) 정천기 기자 (중앙일보 2000년 10월 6일)

각각 each, respectively, separately; 경기장 arena, stadium; 공연 public performance; 내한 공연 a performance or concert in Korea by foreign artists; 내공연장 large performance hall; 무대 the stage; 비롯하다 to begin, start, originate in; 연주곡 musical program, repertoire; 예정되다 to be prearranged, scheduled; 오는 coming, next, forthcoming (오는 토요일 'next Saturday'); 출신 origin, birth, from

---

1. 리처드 클레이더만은 누구입니까?

2. 리처드 클레이더만은 어디에서 공연을 합니까?

3. 리처드 클레이더만은 내한 공연을 몇 번 했습니까?

4. 리처드 클레이더만은 어떤 곡을 연주할 예정입니까?

LESSON 2. *NORAEBANG*

Koreans and Song

We are all aware of the deep relationship between humanity and music. All human societies, whether civilized or primitive, have music and songs. Koreans have a particular love for music and especially love singing.

Many historical records and studies attest to the rich and continuous tradition of Korean musical culture. Korea's traditional music is called *kugak*. Korean *kugak* was influenced partially by Chinese music and partially by native developments. Examples of native developments include native music (*hyangak*), native songs (*hyangga*), folk songs (*minyo*), tunes (*kagok*), farmers' music (*nongak*), *p'ansori*, and so on. There are also many nontraditional genres of music. Popular music (*taejung kayo*) is one example (and is also called *yuhaengga*).

Western music is also an important part of Korean music. American missionaries began teaching hymns to Koreans in 1885. Later on, all sorts of Western music entered the country, including classical, pop, rock music, and the rest. These are still entering Korea today.

In general, Koreans—whether living in Korea or abroad—sing popular music (*taejung kayo*) more often than any other form. They enjoy taking turns singing these songs, or singing as a group, at various informal gatherings. If a foreigner wishes to become closer to Korean friends, it's a good idea to prepare at least one song to sing. It may be difficult for Westerners to sing before a group. But when one sings a song without reserve at a Korean gathering, the door to Koreans' emotion, mood, and spirit swings wide open.

Nowadays in Korean society, singing rooms (*noraebang*) are becoming widespread as a healthy new form of culture. Many singing rooms await guests not only in Korea, but also in many other countries, wherever Koreans reside. Singing rooms not only offer a place for people to unwind from the complex world outside, but also a place to strike up acquaintances.

CONVERSATION

1

(Hyǒn-ju, Sarah, and Michael are planning Wǒn-sik's birthday party.)

Hyǒn-ju: This Friday is Wǒn-sik's birthday. Have you made (*lit.*, tried to make) plans?

Sarah: I haven't made any particular plans yet. How about just having dinner and going to *noraebang* together? You know that Wŏn-sik likes going to noraebang.

Michael: Go to noraebang? It's true that it's fun to go to noraebang, but you know that Wŏn-sik really likes to sing. Once he gets a hold of the microphone, he doesn't let go.

(Hyŏn-ju and Sarah laugh.)

Sarah: That's true (*lit.,* indeed). The last time I went to noraebang with Wŏn-sik, he sang five songs in a row all by himself.

Michael: It's going to turn (completely) into Wŏn-sik's one-man stage.

Hyŏn-ju: You guys, it's his birthday. Let's cut him some slack.

Michael: Well, all right.

Hyŏn-ju: Then which noraebang shall we go to?

Michael: Because Sarah and I don't know the latest popular songs, let's go to one that has a lot of English songs (*lit.,* pop songs).

Hyŏn-ju: Let's do that. By the way, what shall we do about dinner?

Sarah: How about if we meet at Kangnam station that day and ask Wŏn-sik to decide?

Hyŏn-ju: That sounds good. Because there are many restaurants and noraebang in the vicinity of Kangnam station, we can eat and go to noraebang there without having to go from one place to another.

Michael: Then, is Friday at six in front of the New York Bakery at Kangnam station O.K.?

Hyŏn-ju, Sarah: Yes, fine.

Hyŏn-ju: I'll contact Wŏn-sik.

2

(Hyŏn-ju, Wŏn-sik, Sarah, and Michael are at the "Rainbow" *noraebang* in front of Kangnam station.)

Employee: How many people?

Michael: Four (people).

Employee: Come this way, please.

(Hyŏn-ju, Wŏn-sik, Sarah, and Michael enter the room the employee has ushered them to.)

Employee: How many hours would you use (*lit.,* do) the room?

Hyǒn-ju:	Well, we will begin with one hour only. We will let you know if we need more hours.
Employee:	Well, then, enjoy (*lit.,* have fun playing).
Hyǒn-ju:	Hey, time is money. Choose quickly.
Sarah:	Because today is Wǒn-sik's birthday, shall we start with "Happy Birthday"?
Michael:	O.K. But what's the number for "Happy Birthday"?
Sarah:	Wait a moment. Let me look it up. Oh, here it is. Number 1122.
Wǒn-sik:	Where is the remote control?
Hyǒn-ju:	It's on top of the television over there.
(Michael, Sarah, and Hyǒn-ju sing "Happy Birthday" song.)	
Michael, Sarah, Hyǒn-ju:	Congratulations, Wǒn-sik.
Wǒn-sik:	Thanks. As a return courtesy, I'll choose one this time.
Hyǒn-ju:	Yes, sing your favorite song (*lit.,* #18).
Sarah:	What's his favorite song?
Hyǒn-ju:	You'll know when you hear it. It's an old-style Korean pop song, and Wǒn-sik sings it better than a real singer does.
Michael:	I can't wait (*lit.,* it is expected).

Saturday Night

1. What shall I say when I see her, lovely with her long hair and short skirt?
2. What shall I say when I see him, the world's best and most trustworthy?
3. The sound of beautiful song spreads far, far toward a hopeful tomorrow.

Refrain: Oh, on Saturday night. I shall meet her/him on Saturday night. I will be meeting her/him on Saturday night.

Southbound Train

1. On the southbound train of the Honam line the rain is falling; over the shaking window the rainwater is streaming. My tears too are falling, and lost first love is flowing.

2. On the last train of the Honam line the rain is falling; a whistle cries sadly.

Tears are falling, my tears too are falling, and lost first love is flowing.

Refrain: The one I met then, the one without words, is hazy, flickering in my memory. We're going farther apart still, but though we cannot meet, do not forget: I have loved you.

제3과　한가위

(Lesson 3: Ch'usŏk [Harvest moon day])

PRE-READING QUESTIONS

1. 추석(한가위)에 대해 무엇을 알고 계세요?

2. 추석은 한국의 제일 큰 명절입니다. 여러분의 나라에도 추석과 비슷한 명절이 있으면 무엇인지 말해 보세요.

3. 추석의 대표적인 음식은 송편입니다. 여러분은 송편을 먹어 본 적이 있습니까? 송편에 대해 아는 대로 말해 보세요.

GAINING FAMILIARITY

1. 한국의 명절
   설, 정월 대보름, 단오, 추석

2. 한가위
   차례, 성묘, 송편, 보름달, 강강술래, 오곡, 햇곡식, 햇과일

한국인의 큰 명절 추석:
송편, 성묘 그리고 강강술래

옛날부터 전해 내려오는 말 중에 "더도 덜도 말고[3.1] 8월 한가위만 같아라"라는 말이 있다. 8월 한가위에는 오곡이 풍성하고 과일이 무르익고 서늘한 가을 바람이 불기 시작하기 때문에 이 때가 4계절 중 가장 좋다는 뜻이다.

음력으로 8월 15일이 한가위 또는 추석이다. 추석은 설, 정월 대보름, 단오 등과 함께 한국 민족의 큰 명절이다. 한 해의 힘든 농사를 마치고 조상님께 감사를 드리며 다음 해의 풍년을 기원하는 날이다. 추석은 옛 신라 시대부터 시작된 명절이다. 추석의 큰 행사로 차례를 꼽을 수 있다. 조상님께 감사하며 햇곡식, 햇과일로 차례 상을 차린다. 이른 아침 차례를 지내고 나면[3.2] 조상의 산소를 찾아 성묘를 한다.

추석에는 어느 명절 때보다도 음식이 풍부하다. 그중 대표적인 음식이 송편이다. 송편은 멥쌀을 가루로 빻아 반죽해서 빚는다. 팥, 깨, 콩, 대추, 잣 등을 넣고 손끝으로 빚는다. 송편은 마치 반달과 같은 모습이다. 송편은 음력을 사용하던 조상들이 달에 대한 고마움으로 만들던 떡이라고 한다.

1년 중 가장 넉넉하고 풍성한 추석에는 여러 가지 놀이도 있다. 설날의 윷놀이, 단오의 그네뛰기 등 전통 놀이가 있듯이 추석 하면[3.3] 강강수월래를 꼽는다. 추석이 되면[3.4] 둥근 보름달 아래서 큰 원을 만들어 돌며 흥겹게 춤을 추는 것이 강강수월래이다.

요즘도 추석이 되면 전통 음식과 함께 곳곳에서 민속 놀이를 즐기는 모습을 보게 된다. 또 추석이 되면 고향을 찾는 행렬이 줄을 잇는다. 가족, 친지들이 한자리에 모여 조상에게 감사하는 추석은 한국 민족의 큰 명절이다.

「한국화보」 (1997년 9월), 김민아, HEK홍보기획공사

대화

1

(오늘은 한가위날. 사라는 하와이에 계신 김수진 선생님께 전화를 건다.)

사라: 선생님, 저 사라예요.

김 선생님: 어머, 사라구나. 오늘이 한국 추석일 텐데,[3.5] 그렇지 않아도 전화하려고 했었어. 그래 송편은 먹었니?

사라: 조금 이따가 김영호 교수님댁에 가서 송편도 먹고 맛있는 거 많이 먹을 거예요.

김 선생님: 잘 됐구나. 난 또 명절을 혼자 보내는 건 아닌지 걱정했거든. 여기 마침 이 선생님이 계시는데, 선생님께서 너하고 통화하고 싶으시댄다.[3.6] 잠깐만 기다려. (잠시 후)

이 선생님: 사라니?

사라: 선생님, 안녕하셨어요? 전화 자주 드리지 못해서 죄송합니다.

이 선생님: 아니야. 한국에서 여러 가지로 바쁘지? 선생님이 이따가 전화는 드리겠지만, 김영호 교수님하고 사모님께 안부 전해 드리고.[3.7] 참 교수님 댁에 갈 때 빈손으로 가지 말고, 근처 상가에서 꽃이나 과일 같은 걸 좀 사 가지고 가면 좋겠다.

사라: 네, 선생님. 그렇지 않아도 벌써 다 사 놨어요.[3.8]

이 선생님: 그래, 그래야지.[3.9] 그리고 시간이 되면, 박경진 교수님도 찾아뵙고.

사라: 네, 저도 그랬으면 좋겠는데, 교수님께서 몇 달 전에 순천으로 이사 가셨대요.

이 선생님: 그래? 그러면, 너무 멀어서 못 가 뵙겠구나. 어쨌든 거기서도 추석 잘 보내거라.

사라: 네, 이 선생님도요. 안녕히 계세요.

2

(사라는 김영호 교수님 댁에서 집으로 돌아오는 길에 교대역 앞에서 제임스를 만났다.)

사라: 어, 제임스 오빠.

제임스: 어, 사라야. 여기 웬일이니?

사라: 저희 과 김영호 교수님 댁에 다녀오는 길이에요. 선생님께서 추석에 혼자 있는 교환 학생들을 초대하셨거든요.

제임스: 그래? 그런데, 오늘 왜 이렇게 서울 시내가 한산하니?

사라: 추석이잖아요. 모두들 고향으로 내려가서 그럴 거예요. 오늘 아침 뉴스에서 보니까, 어젯밤 고속 도로가 너무 막혀서 광주까지 가는 데 열두 시간이 넘게[3.10] 걸렸다던대요.

제임스: 그래?

사라: 오빠는 여기서 뭐 하고 계세요?

제임스: 어, 나는 저녁 먹으러 잠깐 나왔는데, 식당이 다 문을 닫았네. 난 추석날 이렇게 식당이 문을 다 닫는지 몰랐어.

사라: 오빠 그럼 마침 잘 됐네요.[3.11] 저희 집에 가서 저녁 같이 먹어요. 선생님 사모님께서 갈비찜하고 송편을 좀 싸 주셨거든요.

제임스: 그래? 그럼 그럴까? 학교 근처에 살지?

사라: 네.

(제임스와 사라는 지하철을 타기 위해 지하도로 내려간다.)

제임스: 학교 근처면 1구역이니 2구역이니?

사라: 1구역이요.

(제임스, 지하철 표 사는 곳에서 표를 산다.)

제임스: (매표원에게) 1구역 2장이요. (사라에게 표를 주며) 그럼 갈까?

사라: 오빠 그쪽은 3호선이에요. 저희는 2호선 타야 되니까 이쪽으로 가야겠네요.

제임스: 맞어. 난 아직도 지하철 타는 게 헷갈린단 말이야.[3.12]

Comprehension Questions

1. **Reading Comprehension.** "한국인의 큰 명절 추석: 송편, 성묘 그리고 강강술래"를 읽고 맞고(Ⓣ) 틀린(Ⓕ) 것을 지적하거나 질문에 대답해 보세요.

   (1) 추석은 조선 시대부터 시작되었다.　　　　　　　Ⓣ　Ⓕ

   (2) 추석이 되면 가족과 친지들이 한자리에 모인다.　Ⓣ　Ⓕ

   (3) 요즘은 한가위가 되도 민속 놀이를 즐기는 모습을 볼
   수가 없다.　　　　　　　　　　　　　　　　　Ⓣ　Ⓕ

   (4) 송편은 어떻게 만듭니까?

   (5) 추석은 무엇을 하는 날입니까?

   (6) 한국 민족의 큰 명절로는 무엇이 있습니까?

   (7) 한가위의 대표적인 전통 놀이는 무엇입니까?

   (8) "더도 덜도 말고 8월 한가위만 같아라"는 무슨 뜻입니까?

2. **Listening Comprehension.** 대화를 듣고 맞고(Ⓣ) 틀린(Ⓕ) 것을 지적하거나 질문에 대답해 보세요.

   대화 1

   (1) 사라는 김영호 교수님 댁에 선물을 가지고 갈 것이다.　Ⓣ　Ⓕ

   (2) 사라는 서울에 혼자 있기 때문에 추석날 송편을 먹지 못했다.　Ⓣ　Ⓕ

   (3) 사라는 추석날 김영호 교수님과 박경진 교수님께 전화를
   드릴 것이다.　　　　　　　　　　　　　　　　　Ⓣ　Ⓕ

   (4) 사라는 왜 김영호 교수님 댁에 갔습니까?

   (5) 사라는 왜 박경진 교수님 댁에 갈 수 없습니까?

   대화 2

   (1) 사라의 집에 가려면 지하철 3호선을 타면 된다.　Ⓣ　Ⓕ

   (2) 제임스는 추석날 식당이 다 문을 닫는지 몰랐다.　Ⓣ　Ⓕ

(3) 제임스와 사라는 저녁에 갈비찜과 송편을 먹을 것이다.   ⊤   �ⓕ

(4) 왜 서울 시내가 한산합니까?

(5) 제임스는 어디에서 저녁을 먹을 겁니까?

New Words

가루 *n.* powder; flour ¶쌀을 가루로 갈다 to grind rice into flour

갈비찜 *n.* steamed short ribs

강강수월래 *n. kanggang suwŏllae* (a Korean circle dance, usually danced by girls under the full moon; song accompanying the dance, *lit.,* 'Strong enemies are coming from across the sea'). Contracted to 강강술래

계절 *n.* season, time of year

건 contr. of 것은 ¶이건 (= 이것은) this ¶용호가 아픈 건 아니니? Isn't it that Yongho is sick?

걸 contr. of 것을 ¶과일 같은 걸 많이 먹어라. Have much fruit or something.

교대역 *n.* Kyodae subway station. 역 station; 교대 (= 교육대학교) teachers' college

그네뛰기 *n.* swinging (on a swing). 그네 a swing; 뛰다 to run, swing (on a swing)

기원하다 *v.* to pray, supplicate, wish for ¶빨리 병이 나으시기를 기원합니다. I pray for your early recovery from illness.

깨 *n.* sesame

꼽다 *v.* to count (on one's fingers); to take (something as an example) ¶나는 날짜를 꼽았다. I counted the days on my fingers. ¶그는 마을에서 첫째 가는 부자로 꼽힌다. He is taken to be the richest man in the village.

넉넉하다 *adj.* to be enough, to be plenty ¶식사가 넉넉하게 준비되었다. Sufficient food was prepared.

농사 *n.* farming, agriculture ¶농사를 짓다 to engage in agriculture (farming), to farm

다지다 *v.* to harden, strengthen, solidify, consolidate ¶그는 나와의 관계를 다지고자 했다. He wanted to strengthen his relationship with me. ¶그는 사회적 지위를 다지기 위해 무척 애썼다. He struggled to consolidate his position in society.

단오 *n.* Tano festival (fifth day of the fifth month of the lunar calendar)

닮다 *v.* to be (look) like, resemble, take after, be similar to

대추 *n.* Chinese date; jujube

대표적이다 *adj.* to be representative (of). 대표 representation; a representative. 대표하다 to represent ¶대표적 학생 model (typical) student

만 *ptcl.* only, just; as much as, so far as

멥쌀 *n.* non-glutinous rice

명절 *n.* major holidays; national holidays; festival days

모습 *n.* features, looks, appearance, shape, figure

무르익다 *v.* to become ripe, mature, mellow ¶무르익은 감 ripe (and soft) persimmons ¶무르익은 술 well-aged wine

민속 놀이 *n.* folk game. 민속 folk (ethnic) customs, folkways; 놀이 game

반죽하다 *v.* to knead. 반죽 kneading ¶밀가루를 반죽하다 to knead flour

보름달 *n.* full moon (occurs on the fifteenth night of a lunar month). 보름 fifteen days, fifteenth day (of a lunar month)

빈손 *n.* empty hand ¶빈손으로 empty-handed; not taking a present

빚다 *v.* to brew (rice wine); to make dough (만두, 송편); to make; to form

빻다 *v.* to grind; to powder

산소 *n.* grave, tomb, ancestral burial ground

설 *n.* New Year's Day, first day of the year (= 설날)

성묘 *n.* visit to one's ancestral tomb ¶성묘 가다 to visit one's ancestral tomb

송편 *n. songp'yŏn.* rice cake steamed on a layer of pine needles

안부 *n.* safety; regard ¶안부를 묻다 to inquire after someone's health

옛 *pre-n.* old, olden, archaic, ancient ¶옛 친구 an old friend ¶옛말 archaic word ¶옛글 ancient writings

옛날 *n.* old times; antiquity. 옛 old, ancient ¶먼 옛날 the distant past

오곡 *n.* the five grains; all kinds of grain ¶오곡밥 rice (cooked) with four other staple grains

원 *n.* circle ¶달은 원 모양을 하고 있다. The moon is round.

윷놀이 *n.* playing *yut* (the four-stick game)

음력 *n.* lunar calendar. *ant.* 양력 solar calendar ¶음력 8월 15일 August 15 of the lunar calendar

잇다 *v.* to join (one thing to another), connect, link. *ant.* 끊다 to cut (off), sever ¶줄을 잇다 to line up ¶줄을 이어 in a line

잣 *n.* pine nuts

전하다 *v.* to convey, transmit, pass, impart ¶전해 내려오다 to have been passed down

정월 대보름 *n.* January Full Moon Day (January 15 by the lunar calendar). 정월 January (in lunar calendar); 보름 full moon; day 15 by the lunar calendar

조상 *n.* ancestor, forefather, forebear; ancestry ¶인류의 조상 the progenitor of the human race ¶조상신 ancestral god ¶단군은 한국 민족의 조상이다. Tan'gun is the forefather of the Korean people.

차례 *n.* rite honoring one's ancestors ¶차례(를) 지내다 to hold a service honoring one's ancestors

찾아뵙다 *v.* to visit (a senior person)

추석 *n.* Ch'usŏk, the Korean Thanksgiving; Harvest Moon Day

추수감사절 *n.* Thanksgiving Day

친지 *n.* acquaintance, friend

콩 *n.* bean; pea; soybean ¶땅콩 peanut, ground nut

팥 *n.* red bean

풍년 *n.* year of abundance; good harvest ¶금년은 풍년이 들 것 같다. We shall probably have a good harvest this year.

풍부하다 *adj.* to be abundant, plentiful, ample, rich. 풍부 abundance, plenty, wealth ¶풍부한 음식 abundance of food ¶풍부한 지식 a great store of knowledge

풍성하다 *adj.* to be abundant; to be affluent ¶풍성한 수확 an abundant crop of rice

한가위 *n.* Korean Thanksgiving (August 15 by the lunar calendar) (= 추석)

한산하다 *adj.* to be at leisure, be off work; to be inactive; to be dull ¶시장이 한산하다. The market is dull. ¶거리가 이 시간에는 한산해요. The traffic is light about this time.

한자리 *n.* same table. 자리 seat

함께 *adv.* together ¶~과(와) 함께 together with, along with

햇곡식 *n.* new crop, the year's new grain. 햇~ new; 곡식 grain

햇과일 *n.* newly harvested fruit, fresh fruit

행렬 *n.* parade (of people)

행사 *n.* event, function ¶연중 행사 annual function ¶경축 행사 (event of) celebration

헷갈리다 *v.* to be confused, be thrown off, be distracted, have scattered thoughts ¶아이들이 떠들어서 내 정신이 헷갈린다. The children are too noisy for me to concentrate.

흥겹게 *adv.* delightfully, merrily, joyously. 흥겹다 to be delightful, joyous, cheerful. ¶그들은 파티에서 흥겹게 놀았다. They had a lot of fun at the party.

Useful Expressions

3.1 ~도 (말고) ~도 말고 neither. . . nor. . ., but

In this idiomatic pattern, 도 is an emphatic particle. 말고 'not being, not . . . but' consists of the verb 말다 'to stop, to cease; don't' and the suffix ~고 'and.'

더도 **(말고)** 덜도 **말고** 8월 한가위만 같아라.
Be just like the 15th of August, neither more nor less.
밥도 **(말고)** 술도 **말고** 잠만 자고 싶어요.
I need neither food nor drink. I just want to sleep.

3.2 ~고 나다 to have just finished (doing)

~고 나다 literally means 'to do something and come out.' It usually occurs with a subjunctive suffix, for example, ~(으)니(까), ~어서/아서, ~더니, or ~(으)면. ~고 나면, literally 'if (when) one does something and comes out,' means 'after having finished (doing),' and ~고 나니 means 'now that one has finished (doing).'

차례를 지내고 **나면** 조상의 산소를 찾는다.
After holding their ancestor-memorial services, they visit their ancestral tombs.
하고 싶은 말을 하고 **나니** 속이 시원하다.
Now that I have had my say, I feel the easier for it.

3.3 N하면 if (when) one does (says, thinks) about N; speaking of N

A contraction of N(이)라고 (말)하면 'when we say (talk about) N.'

추석**하면** 강강술래를 꼽는다.

When we say Ch'usŏk, we take *kanggang suwŏllae* (as the most important event).

사과**하면** 후지사과가 제일 맛있다.

Speaking of apples, fuji apples taste the best.

3.4 [Time word]~이/가 되다 to come; to be

When the verb 되다 'to become, get, grow' occurs after a time word subject, it means 'to come' or 'it is (was, will be).'

추석**이 되면** 고향을 찾는 행렬이 줄을 잇는다.

When Ch'usŏk comes, a parade of people lines up to return to their birthplaces.

벌써 2시**가 되었군**.

It is already two o'clock!

아침**이 되니까** 새가 울기 시작한다.

As morning comes, the birds begin to chirp.

3.5 ~(으)ㄹ 텐데 be supposed to do/be, and/but/so

This expression is a contraction of ~(으)ㄹ 터인데, which is a combination of ~(으)ㄹ 터이다 'to be supposed to; ought to; be going to, intend to; must, should, would' and the background information provider ~ㄴ데 'in the circumstance that; and; but; so.'

비가 올 **텐데** 가지 마세요.

It is supposed to rain, so please don't go.

오늘이 **추석일 텐데** 송편 먹었니?

Today must be Ch'usŏk, (and) did you eat *songp'yŏn*?

3.6 ~댄다 (they/he/she) say(s) that

~댄다 is a more colloquial variant of the indirect quotation ending ~단다, which is itself a contraction of ~다고 한다. Thus, 통화하고 싶으시댄다, 통화하고 싶으시단다, and 통화하고 싶으시다고 하신다 all mean the same thing. Notice that the honorific suffix ~(으)시 occurs only for the subject before ~댄다 and ~단다. In the full form, the honorific must also occur with the 하다 verb, as in 하신다.

3.7   ～고 and also, please (why don't you)

When the coordinating suffix ～고 'and (also)' occurs at the end of a sentence, it may connote a mild command—'please; why don't you'—in addition to the meaning 'and (also)～.' Examples:

큰어머니께 안부전해 드리고. (= 그리고 큰어머니께 안부 전해 드려라.)
And also, please give our regards to your aunt.
시간이 되면 큰아버지하고 성묘도 가고. (= 그리고 시간이 되면 큰아버지하고 성묘도 가라.)
And also, if you have time, why don't you visit our ancestral graves with your uncle?

3.8   ～어/아 놓다 to do something for later; ～어/아 두다 to do something and keep it that way (or for future use)

Both patterns above occur after a verb stem and have similar meanings. They are frequently interchangeable but have slight differences in connotation because of the basic meanings of 놓다 'to put (down), place' and 두다 'to keep, place.' 놓아 두다 'to put down something and keep it that way' is an acceptable construction, but *두어 놓다 is meaningless.

오늘 밤에 준비 다 **해 놔야** 해.	I'll have to prepare all of them tonight.
그 책을 거기에 그대로 **놓아 두세요**.	Leave the book there as it is.
마늘은 미리 **사 뒀잖**아.	As for garlic, remember we already bought it.
우리는 제주도로 여행갈 계획을 **세워 놓았어**.	We have made a plan to take a trip to Cheju Island.

3.9   ～어야지(요)/아야지(요) I suppose/suggest one must

～어야지(요)/아야지(요) formed from ～어야/아야 하지(요), which literally means 'I suppose/suggest that it will do only if one does/is.' It is similar in meaning to ～어야/아야 해(요) 'must, have to.' But while ～어야/아야 해(요) denotes straightforward obligation, ～어야지(요)/아야지(요) includes the speaker's supposition or strong suggestion.

배추가 얼기 전에 김장을 **해야지**.

I've got to (I suppose I should) do *kimjang* before the cabbages freeze.

할머니께 텔레비전을 하나 사 **드려야지요**.

I suppose you must buy a TV set for your grandmother.

3.10 넘게 more than

넘게 is the adverbial form of 넘다 'to exceed.' When it occurs after a number expression, for example, 열 시간 'ten hours,' 나이 사십 'forty years of age,' or 사람 이백 명 'two hundred people,' it indicates that the intended numbers are greater than the number given. Note that the particle used after the number must be the subject particle 가/이.

광주까지 가는 데 열두 시간이 **넘게** 걸렸다.

It took more than twelve hours to get to Kwangju.

그 회의에 백 명이 **넘게** 참석했다.

More than one hundred people participated in that conference.

3.11 마침 잘 됐다 perfect timing!

Composed of 마침 'just in time,' 잘 'well,' and 됐다 'turned out,' this idiomatic expression is used when everything works out.

마침 잘 됐다. 우리 함께 구경가자.	Perfect! Let's go sightseeing together.
제 때 와 주서서 **잘 됐어요**.	I am glad that you came just in time.

3.12 말이다 I mean; you know

말이다, which is composed of 말 'words, language' and the copula 이다 'to be' means 'I mean; I am saying; you know.' Its question form means 'are you saying . . . ? (what, who, where. . .) do you mean? do you mean. . . ?' It can be inserted after nominal, verbal, or adjectival phrases for casual or emphatic purposes.

머리도 잘 손질하고 **말이야**.	And be sure that your hair is in place, you know.
어느 책 **말이에요**?	Which book do you mean?

말이다 is also used to emphasize a quoted clause as in ~단 말이다, ~(느)냔 말이다, ~잔 말이다, ~란 말이다, and so on. These are contractions of ~다고 하는 말이다, ~(느)냐고 하는 말이다, ~자고 하는 말이다, and ~라고 하는 말이다, respectively.

빨리 가란 말이야.
I am requesting that you go right away.

우리 언제 떠나야 하느냔 말이에요?
I am asking when we must leave.

시간이 없는데 걸어가잔 말이에요?
Are you asking that we walk, even though we don't have time?

쇠고기가 질기단 말이에요.
The beef's tough, you know.

Exercises

1. 관련된 단어들끼리 연결하여 문장을 만들어 보세요.

   (1) 풍년   •   • 지내다   _____

   (2) 성묘   •   • 기원하다   _____

   (3) N하면   •   • 하다   _____

   (4) 마침   •   • 을/를 꼽는다 _____

   (5) 차례   •   • 잘 되다   _____

   (6) 마치   •   • 같다   _____

2. 아래의 설명과 맞는 단어나 표현을 본문에서 찾아 쓰세요.

   (1) 넉넉하고 많다: _____

   (2) 자기 세대(generation) 이전의 모든 세대분들: _____

   (3) 무덤, 무덤이 있는 곳: _____

   (4) 새해의 첫날: _____

   (5) 전화로 말을 주고 받다: _____

   (6) 태어나서 자란 곳: _____

3. 보기에서 적당한 말을 골라 빈칸을 채우세요.

> 보기: 명절, 빚는다, 차린다, 흥겹게, 잇는다, 안부, 서늘한

(1) 추석은 설, 정월 대보름, 단오 등과 함께 한국 민족의 큰 _____이다.

(2) 조상님께 감사하며 햇곡식, 햇과일로 차례 상을 _____.

(3) 송편은 멥쌀을 가루로 빻아 반죽하여 _____.

(4) 둥근 보름달 아래서 큰 원을 만들어 돌며 _____ 춤을 추는 것이 강강술래이다.

(5) 추석이 되면 고향을 찾는 행렬이 줄을 _____.

(6) 선생님께 _____를/을 전해 드린다.

(7) 오곡이 풍성하고 과일이 무르익고 _____ 가을 바람이 불기 시작하기 때문에 이때가 4계절 중 가장 좋다는 뜻이다.

4. 밑줄 친 말과 가장 비슷한 단어나 표현을 보기에서 고르세요.

(1) "더도 덜도 말고 8월 한가위만 같아라"라는 말이 있다.

    a. 말하고   b. 아니고

    c. 해내고   d. 좋고

(2) 오늘 왜 이렇게 서울 시내가 한산하니?

    a. 북적거리니   b. 한가하지만 산만하니

    c. 복잡하니   d. 한가하고 조용하니

(3) 어젯밤 도로가 너무 막혀서 광주까지 가는 데 열두 시간이 넘게 걸렸다던데요.

    a. 교통 체증이 심해서   b. 도로 공사를 해서

    c. 교통 사고가 나서   d. 도로가 좁아서

(4) 나는 저녁 먹으러 잠깐 나왔는데, 식당이 다 문을 닫았네.

    a. 영업을 안 하네   b. 없어졌네

    c. 영업 중이네   d. 사라졌네

5. 보기와 같이 주어진 말이 들어가는 단어를 3개 이상 써 보세요.

> 보기: 친 (親, friendly, parents): 친지, 양친, 친척, 친구, 친절

(1) 해 (year): _____

(2) 조 (祖, ancestor): _____

(3) 년 (年, year, age): _____

(4) 중 (中, middle, among): _____

(5) 화 (話, talk, conversation, story): _____

6. "～고"를 사용한 문장으로 바꾸세요.

(1) 큰아버지 찾아뵙고 꼭 안부 전해 드려라.

    → 큰아버지 찾아뵙고 꼭 _____

(2) 건강이 제일이니까 밥은 꼭 제때 제때 먹어라.

    → 건강이 제일이니까 _____

(3) 기숙사 생활 힘드니까 어려운 일 있으면 연락해라.

    → 기숙사 생활 힘드니까 _____

7. "넘게"를 넣어 대화를 완성하세요.

> 보기: A: 추석 전날 고속 도로가 많이 막혔다면서요?
>   B: 네. (광주까지 12시간이 걸리다) 광주까지
>   가는 데 12시간도 넘게 걸렸어요.

(1) A: 어제 성희 씨 결혼식에 사람들이 많이 왔어요?

    B: 네. (200명이 오다) _____

(2) A: 어제 푹 쉬었어요?

    B: 네. (10시간 자다) _____

(3) A: 뉴욕에서 한국까지 가려면 오래 걸려요?

    B: 네. (14시간 걸리다) _____

8. "마침 잘 됐다"를 사용하여 다음 대화를 완성시키세요.

> 보기: A: 어디 가니?
>   B: 도서관에 가.
>   A: (책 찾으러 도서관에 가다) 마침 잘 됐네. 나도 책 찾으러 도서관에 가는 길이야.

(1) A: 오늘 남대문 시장에 갈까 하는데, 같이 갈래요?
   B: (청바지를 하나 사다) _____

(2) A: 오늘 수업 끝나고 뭐하니?
   B: 오랜만에 영화나 볼까 생각 중이야.
   A: (영화 본 지 오래되다) _____

(3) A: 이번 학기 한국어 수업 듣니?
   B: 응.
   A: _____

9. "~도 (말고) ~도 말고"를 사용하여 다음 대화를 완성하세요.

(1) A: 너 어제 또 밤새웠구나?
   B: 요 며칠 잠을 못 잤더니 _____

(2) A: 오늘이 추석이니까 저기 저 달을 보면서 소원(wishes)을 말해 봐.
   B: _____

(3) A: 생일 선물로 뭐 해 줄까?
   B: _____

10. "~고 나다"를 사용해서 다음 문장을 완성하세요.

(1) _____, 후련해요. (after finishing the exam)

(2) _____, 갑자기 졸려요. (after eating until full)

(3) _____, 목도 마르고 피곤해요. (after working out too much)

11. "~어/아 놓다/두다"를 사용하여 대화를 완성하세요.

> 보기: A: 언제 이렇게 저녁을 준비하셨어요?
>
> B: 오늘은 저녁을 할 시간이 없을 것 같아서 (반찬을 미리 만들다) 반찬을 미리 만들어 놨어요.

(1) A: 오늘은 너무 바빠서 점심도 못 먹을 것 같아.

　　 B: 내가 그럴 줄 알고, (아침을 든든히 먹다) _____

(2) A: 어 여기 책꽂이에 꽂혀 있던 책 어디로 갔지?

　　 B: (책상에 놓다) _____

(3) A: 이번 추석에는 기차 여행을 한번 해 볼까 해요.

　　 B: 추석 연휴에는 기차 표를 사기가 힘들대요. (미리 표를 사다) _____

(4) A: 사라야, 보고서 다 썼니? (어제 벌써 쓰다)

　　 B: 어제 벌써 _____

12. 다음은 당신의 일주일 계획표입니다. "~어야지(요)/아야지(요)"를 넣어 질문에 답하세요.

	월	화	수	목	금	토	일
오전	도서관	영화	연극	②	**보기**	공항	청소
오후	①	미팅	소개팅		한국어	③	독서

> 보기: A: 금요일 오전에 뭐 하세요?
>
> B: 오후에 한국어 수업이 있으니까 밀린 숙제 해야지요.

(1) A: 월요일 오후에는 뭐 하세요?

　　 B: 오전에는 도서관에서 공부를 할 거니까 _____

(2) A: 목요일에는 뭐하세요?

　　B: 화요일 수요일 연속으로 놀 거니까 _____

　　　_____

(3) A: 토요일 오후에 뭐 하세요?

　　B: 오전에 친구가 한국에서 오니까 오후에는 _____

　　　_____

13. "N하면"을 사용하여 다음 대화를 완성시키세요.

> 보기: A: 어떤 사과가 맛있어요?
>
> 　　　B: (대구 사과) 사과하면 대구 사과가 제일 맛있어요.

(1) A: 누가 노래를 잘 해요?

　　B: (성희) _____

(2) A: 누가 야구를 잘 해요?

　　B: _____

(3) A: 컴퓨터를 사려고 하는데 어떤 컴퓨터가 좋을까요?

　　B: _____

14. "말이다"를 넣어서 대화를 끝내세요.

> 보기: A: 그 교통 사고가 언제 났다고요?
>
> 　　　B: 지난 화요일에 났단 말이에요.

(1) A: 어제 저녁 누구를 만나셨다고요?

　　B: _____

(2) A: 동생이 게으르다고요?

　　B: 네, 걔가 무척 게으르_____

(3) A: 일하기 싫으면 먹지도 마!

　　B: 뭐라고요? 일하기 싫으면 죽으_____

(4) A: 뭐라 하셨어요?

　　B: 너 오늘 왜 학교에 안 가_____

Discussion and Composition

1. '추석'과 '추수감사절'에 대해 이야기해 보세요. 두 명절의 역사, 음식, 명절
   에 주로 하는 일 등을 비교해 보세요.

2. 이야기한 내용을 정리하여 두 명절을 비교하는 글을 써 보세요.

> 글을 쓸 때 다음과 같은 단어를 사용하세요.
> 반면에, 그러나, 이와는 반대로, 다른 점은, 그렇지만,
> 마찬가지로, 비슷한 점은

Further Reading

다음 신문 기사를 읽고 질문에 답하세요.

내년 추석 항공 예약 10분 만에 매진

대한항공과 아시아나항공은 21일 오후 3시부터 내년 추석 연휴 기간 (10월 3일~6일) 국내선 항공권 예약을 시작했는데, 대부분의 노선이 약 10분 만에 예약이 끝났다. 대한항공은 이날 직원을 평소보다 70명 늘린 1백70명을 동원하여, 예약을 (1) _____ 추석 연휴 기간 중 국내선 항공기의 좌석이 불과 30분 만에 동이 났다. 대한항공은 서울~광주, 서울~대구, 서울~포항, 서울~예천, 서울~군산 등 대부분의 노선이 약 10분 만에 항공권 예약이 모두 끝났다. 그러나 항공편이 비교적 많은 서울~부산 노선은 30분 만에 예약이 끝났다고 대한항공은 밝혔다.

　아시아나항공의 경우도 대한항공과 거의 같은 시간에 예약이 끝났다. 특히 아시아나항공의 경우 예약 신청이 쏟아지는 바람에 예약 단말기의 기능이 잠시 마비되었었다. 이는 전국의 2천 개 여행사 예약과 PC를 통한 일반인들의 예약이 한꺼번에 몰렸기 때문이라고 했다.

국내선 domestic lines; 기능 function; 노선 route, line; 늘리다 to increase; 단말기 (computer) terminal; 대부분 greater part (of), majority; 동원하다 to mobilize; 동이 나다 to be sold out (= 동나다); 마비되다 to be paralyzed, stopped; 만에 in less than; only (in a certain amount of time); 매진 selling out; 몰리다 to come together, cluster; 바람에 in conjunction with, as a consequence of; 밝히다 to make (a matter) public, make (a matter) clear; 불과 only, merely; 쏟아지다 to pour (in, out, down); 연휴 consecutive holidays, holidays in a row; 예약 booking, reservation; 일반인 ordinary people; 직원 staff, personnel; 평소 ordinary times; 한꺼번에 at once, all together; 항공 airline, aviation; 항공권 plane ticket; 항공편 flight

---

1. 밑줄 친 곳 (1)에 알맞은 말은 무엇입니까?

　　a. 받았으나　　　b. 받았고　　　c. 받았으므로　　　d. 받아서

2. 대한항공은 평소에 몇 명의 직원이 예약을 받습니까?

   a. 70명   b. 170명   c. 240명   d. 100명

3. 대한항공의 경우 서울~부산 노선의 예약이 좀 늦게 끝난 이유는 무엇입니까?

4. 아시아나항공의 예약 단말기 기능이 마비된 이유는 무엇입니까?

LESSON 3. CH'USŎK (HARVEST MOON DAY)

Ch'usŏk, Korea's Great National Holiday:
Songp'yŏn, Visitations to the Ancestral Graves, and the Korean Circle Dance

Among the sayings passed down from ancient times, there is one that goes "Be no more and no less but just like August 15." The meaning is that this time is the best of the four seasons. Grain is plentiful, fruit has ripened, and the ovenlike heat [of summer] has given way to cool autumn breezes.

Ch'usŏk falls on August 15 of the lunar calendar. For Koreans Ch'usŏk is a major national holiday like New Year's Day, January Full Moon Day, and Tano festival day. At Ch'usŏk one gives thanks to the ancestors and prays for the next year's bounty after (completing) a year of arduous farming. Ch'usŏk's origins go as far back as the (ancient) age of Silla. A proper ancestor-memorial service is a big event of Ch'usŏk. As we give thanks to our ancestors, we prepare an ancestor-memorial table with newly harvested crops and fruits. The morning after the service, people visit the ancestral graves and cut the weeds around them.

Food is more plentiful at Ch'usŏk than at any other national holiday. The characteristic Ch'usŏk food is *songp'yŏn,* made with non-glutinous rice that has been powdered and mixed. Filled with red beans, sesame seeds, beans, Chinese dates, or pine nuts, and shaped with the fingertips, this rice cake has the form of a half-moon. It is said to have been made in thanks to the moon by our ancestors, who followed the lunar calendar.

A variety of games also takes place at Ch'usŏk, the most bountiful time of year. There are *yut-nori* on New Year's Day and swings on Tano day, but at Ch'usŏk one thinks of the Korean circle dance. When Ch'usŏk comes, people sing contentedly while going around in a large circle under the full moon. This is the circle dance.

Even nowadays one can sometimes see the traditional food and (the playing of traditional) games of Ch'usŏk. At Ch'usŏk people line up to return to their birthplace. At Ch'usŏk, families and friends (scattered all over the nation) gather in one place to thank their ancestors. Ch'usŏk is the Korean people's great holiday.

From Min-ah Kim, *The Monthly Pictorial of Korea* (September 1997)

CONVERSATION

1

(Today is the fifteenth of August. Sarah phones Kim Sŏnsaengnim in Hawaii early in the morning.)

Sarah:	Sŏnsaengnim, it's me, Sarah.
Kim Sŏnsaengnim:	Oh, it's you, Sarah. (As it is,) I was going to call you since today must be Ch'usŏk. Have you eaten *songp'yŏn*?
Sarah:	I'll be going to Professor Yŏng-ho Kim's house in a little while, so I'll have *songp'yŏn* and a lot of delicious food.
Kim Sŏnsaengnim:	All right. I worried that you might be alone on the holiday. By the way, Yi Sŏnsaengnim is here. He wants to talk to you. Hold on a moment.
Yi Sŏnsaengnim:	(a little later) Is it Sarah?
Sarah:	How are you? I'm sorry I haven't kept in touch (lit., called very often).
Yi Sŏnsaengnim:	Oh, no. You certainly are busy in Korea. Although I'll be calling them later, give our regards to Professor Yŏng-ho Kim and his wife. By the way, when you go to Professor Kim's house, don't go empty-handed. Stop by a store nearby and buy (and take) fruits or something.
Sarah:	Yes, Sŏnsaengnim. As it is, I've already bought them (lit., all).
Yi Sŏnsaengnim:	Good, that's good. And if you have time, visit Professor Kyŏngjin Park.
Sarah:	Yes, that would be nice, but it says that he moved to Sunch'ŏn two or three months ago.
Yi Sŏnsaengnim:	Then you probably won't be able to go, because it is too far. Anyway, have a good Ch'usŏk holiday.
Sarah:	Yes, you too (lit., Yi Sŏnsaengnim). Good-bye.

2

(On the way home from Professor Yŏng-ho Kim's house, Sarah meets James in front of the Kyodae subway station.)

Sarah: Oh, (older brother) James.

James: Oh, Sarah. What brings you here?

Sarah: I'm on my way from Professor Yŏng-ho Kim's house, because he invited exchange students who are alone on Ch'usŏk.

James: Oh, I see. By the way, why is Seoul (city) so quiet today?

Sarah: As you know, it's Ch'usŏk. Everyone has gone down to their hometown, that's why. I heard on this morning's news that it took more than twelve hours to get to Kwangju last night because there was so much congestion on the highways.

James: Really?

Sarah: What are you doing here, older brother?

James: Oh, I came out for a little while to have dinner, but all the restaurants are closed. I didn't know that all restaurants closed their doors (*lit.,* to this extent) on Ch'usŏk.

Sarah: Then you're in luck. Come have dinner with me at my house. Professor Kim's wife gave (*lit.,* wrapped) me some steamed short ribs and *songp'yon.*

James: Really? Shall I do that, then? You live near school, don't you?

Sarah: Yes.

(James and Sarah go down to take the subway.)

James: If it's near school, then, is it one section or two sections?

Sarah: One section.

(James buys tickets at the subway ticket booth.)

James: (To the ticket agent) Two for one section. (Giving Sarah a ticket) Okay, let's go.

Sarah: That way is the #3 line, older brother. Since we have to take the #2 line, we have to go this way.

James: You're right. I still get confused (when it comes to) taking the subway, you know.

제4과 유머 인생

(Lesson 4: A life of humor)

PRE-READING QUESTIONS

1. 여러분이 최근에 들은 재미있는 이야기는 어떤 것이 있습니까? 네 명이 한 그룹이 되어 이야기를 해 보세요.

2. 한국의 인터넷 사이트에서 재미있는 유머를 찾아 보고, 수업 시간에 발표하세요.

3. 여러분이 알고 있는 유명한 사람들 중에 가장 유머 있는 사람은 누구입니까? 그룹을 만들어 서로 이야기 한 다음, 가장 유머가 있다고 생각하는 사람을 한 명 뽑아 보세요.

GAINING FAMILIARITY

1. 풍자, 해학, 우스갯소리, 재치, 농담, 익살, 패러디, 개그, 코미디, 위트

2. "웃음이 있는 곳에 만복이 온다."

3. "웃음은 보약보다 낫다."

유머 인생

유머(우스갯소리)는 우습고 재미있고 소화까지 돋구며 보약 구실
까지 한다고 합니다. 그래서 유머는 동서고금을 통하여[4.1] 어느 사
회에나 있습니다. 여기에서는 서울 한국경제신문이 출판한 「유머
인생」 (1994)이란[4.2] 책에 실린 서양 유머와 한국일보 일요신문에
나오는 한국 유머 중 몇몇을 골라서 소개합니다.

횡재

선생님: 자니야, 너 어째서 지각했지?
자니: 어떤 사람이 1달러짜리 지폐를 잃어 버렸습니다.
선생님: 그래서 그걸 찾아 주느라고?
자니: 아닙니다. 제가 그걸 꼭 밟고 있었습니다.

서스펜스

환자의 방으로 안내를 받은 의사는 몇 분 후 스크류드라이버를 달
라고 했다.[4.3] 그리고 나서[4.4] 얼마 후에는 끌과 망치를 찾았다. 환자
의 부인은 아찔했다.

부인: 그 양반 어디가 탈난 거예요,[4.5] 선생님?
의사: 아직 알 수 없어요. 가방이 열리지 않네요.

부사장

새로 부사장이 된 사람이 어찌나[4.6] 자랑을 하는지 아내가 듣다 못
해[4.7] 쏴 붙였다.

아내: 흔해 빠진 게[4.8] 부사장인데 뭘 그래요. 아니, 슈퍼마켓에는
         자두 담당 부사장까지도 있습디다.[4.9]

화가 난 남편은 부인의 말을 반증할 생각으로 슈퍼마켓에 전화를
걸어 자두 담당 부사장을 찾았다.

슈퍼 직원: 포장된 걸 담당하는 부사장하고 포장되지 않은 걸
           담당하는 부사장하고 계신데, 어느 분을 바꿔 드릴
           까요?

뿌리

미국에서 온 사람이 영국인 친구와 함께 런던 거리를 드라이브하
고 있었는데 영국 사람은 자동차의 윈드스크린을 청소해야겠다는
이야기를 했다. 그러자 미국 사람은 윈드스크린이 아니라 윈드실
드라고 해야 한다며[4.10] 바로잡아 주었다.

영국인: 하지만 여기선 윈드스크린으로 통해.
미국인: 그럼 안 되지. 따지고 보면 자동차야 우리 미국 사람들
        이 만들어 낸 것이고, 그 때 우리가 윈드실드라고 이름
        을 붙인 거야.
영국인: 그건 그래. 하지만 미국 사람들이 사용하는 말은 누가
        만들어 냈는데?

딸과 며느리

부인1: 댁의 딸은 어떤 남자한테 시집갔어요?
부인2: 아주 좋은 신랑을 만났어요. 아침 늦게까지 잠을 자게

하고, 매일같이 미장원에 가게 한대요. 그리고 부엌일은
아예 하지 못하게 하면서 매일 밤 외식을 한대요.

부인1: 거 참 좋겠네요. 그러면 아드님은 어떤 여자하고
　　　결혼했고요?

부인2: 그 쪽은 문제가 많아요. 게을러 빠져 가지고[4.11] 매일 아침
　　　늦잠을 자고 나서는 노상 미장원에서 시간을 보낸대요.
　　　부엌일은 거들떠보려고도 하지 않으면서 남편을 졸라
　　　가지고 외식만 하려 한대요.

너 혼자 틀렸어!

쪽지시험을 본 다음날, 선생님이 학생들에게 정답을 불러 주며 답을 맞춰 보고 있었다. 그러다 어젯밤 늦게까지 시험지를 채점하느라 너무 피곤했던 선생님이 셋째 문제 답이 2번인데 1번이라고 잘못 말했다.

　까짝 놀란 반 학생들 대부분이 "어! 선생니이임~" 하면서 어리둥절해 하고 있는데 맨 뒤에서 들리는 최불암 학생의 목소리.

　"와! 하나 맞았다!"

정신없는 할아버지

한 노인이 아들의 집에 가기 위해 차를 타고 고속 도로를 달리던 중 아들에게서 전화가 왔다.

　"아버지, 지금 고속 도로에 계시죠?"

　"그래, 왜?"

　"지금 어떤 차 한 대가 고속 도로에서 거꾸로 달리고 있다고 뉴스에 나왔거든요. 조심하시라구요!"

그러자 노인이 대답했다.

"정말 정신없는 놈이구만.[4.12] 그런데 한 대가 아니다 얘. 수백 대가 전부 거꾸로 달리고 있어!"

나처럼 해 볼래?

길 가던 한 여자가 베란다 의자에 앉아 있는 할아버지를 보고 다가갔다. 그녀는 웃으며 말을 붙였다.

"그렇게 행복하게 장수하시는 비결이 뭐지요?"

"하루에 담배는 세 갑씩 피우고, 술은 여섯 병, 기름 많은 음식을 많이 먹고, 운동은 전혀 하지 않는 거지요."

"정말 믿을 수가 없네요. 올해 연세가 몇이신데요?"

"응. 스물 여섯."

같이 가 처녀

어떤 할머니가 있었다. 어느 날 밤에 동네 길을 걸어오는데 뒤에서 웬 남자가 "같이 가 처녀"라고 말하는 것이었다. 할머니는 못 들은 척 그냥 집으로 왔지만 마음 속으로 자신이 아직도 처녀같이 보인다는 기쁨에 잠을 이룰 수 없었다.

그 다음 날도 같은 곳을 지나가는데 남자의 목소리가 또 들려왔다. "같이 가 처녀 . . ." 할머니는 그날 밤 역시 설렘에 잠을 설쳤다. 다음날 "이번엔 한번 받아 줄까"하고 생각한 할머니는 단단히 마음을 먹고 지나갔다.

그때 뒤에서 들려오는 남자의 목소리. 그러나 자세히 들어 보니 그 소리는 다음과 같았다.

"갈치가 천원~!"

Comprehension Questions

1. **Reading Comprehension.** 본문의 유머를 읽고 맞고(T) 틀린(F) 것을 지적하거나 질문에 대답해 보세요.

횡재

    (1) 자니는 어떤 사람이 잃어버린 돈을 찾아 주었다.   T   F

    (2) 자니가 지각한 이유는 무엇입니까?

서스펜스

    (3) 의사는 혼자 환자의 방으로 들어갔다.   T   F

    (4) 환자의 부인이 아찔했던 이유는 무엇입니까?

뿌리

    (5) 영국인은 자동차의 윈드실드를 청소해야겠다고 말했다.   T   F

    (6) 미국인은 왜 미국 영어가 맞다고 주장했습니까?

딸과 며느리

    (7) 부인2는 같은 처지의 며느리(daughter-in-law)와 딸을
        다른 관점으로 평가하고 있다.   T   F

    (8) 부인2의 며느리는 어떤 여자인가요?

부사장

    (9) 부사장이 된 남편이 전화를 한 슈퍼마켓에는 자두 담당
        부사장이 한 명 있었다.   T   F

    (10) 남편은 왜 슈퍼마켓에 전화를 했습니까?

2. **Listening Comprehension.** 본문의 유머를 듣고 맞고(T) 틀린(F) 것을 지적하거나 질문에 대답해 보세요.

너 혼자 틀렸어!

(1) 세 번째 문제는 최불암 학생만 맞았다.   T   F

같이 가 처녀

(2) 할머니는 연세가 많지만 젊어 보여서 어떤 남자가 따라왔다.   T   F

(3) 할머니는 무슨 소리를 잘못 들었습니까?

나처럼 해 볼래?

(4) 할아버지는 하루에 담배도 많이 피우고 술도 많이 마시지만
아주 건강하다.   T   F

(5) 할아버지는 실제 연세가 어떻게 됩니까?

정신없는 할아버지

(6) 할아버지가 수백 대의 자동차가 거꾸로 달리는 것을 본
이유는 무엇입니까?

New Words

갈치 *n.* hair-tail; scabbard fish

갑 *n.* case, box, packet ¶담배 한 갑 one pack of cigarettes

거꾸로 *adv.* backward; inversely; inside out; upside down

거들떠보다 *v.* to pay attention (to), take notice (of) ¶미아는 나를 거들떠
보지도 않았다. Mia showed me little attention.

거 참 *adv.* contr. of 그것 참 that really

게을러 빠지다 *adj.* to be intolerably lazy [derogatory]. 게으르다 to be lazy;
빠지다 (to be) extreme

고르다 *v.* to choose, select, single out ¶가장 좋은 것을 골랐다. I selected
the best one.

고속 도로 *n.* freeway, highway

구실 *n.* role, function; duty ¶미아는 동생들에게 어머니 구실을 하고 있어요.
Mia is taking on a mother's role for her younger siblings. ¶그는
안내자로서 제 구실을 다했다. He did his whole duty as a guide.

그러다(가) *adv.* in that manner, (in) that way, like that; while doing that

그럼 *adv.* contr. of 그러면 (derived from 그렇게 하면 if you do so, then. . .)

¶그럼 안 되지. You shouldn't do so.

그리고 나서 *adv.* contr. of 그리하고 나서 after that, and then; after doing that

꼭 *adv.* tightly, firmly ¶그 창문을 꼭 닫으세요. Please shut the window tight. ¶선생님은 내 손을 꼭 쥐었어요. The teacher gripped my hand tightly.

끌 *n.* chisel

노상 *adv.* always, all the time; habitually (= 항상, 늘) ¶노상 좋은 일만 있는 것이 아니다. Good things do not always occur.

놈 *n.* fellow; guy [derogatory] ¶정신없는 놈 absent-minded guy

농담 *n.* joke; pun

늦잠을 자고 나서는 after sleeping late in the morning

다가가다 *v.* to step (go) near, approach

단단히 *adv.* firmly, strongly, solidly ¶단단히 마음을 먹다 to be firmly determined, make a firm resolution

달라고 하다 *v.* to ask (someone) to give (something) to him/her

담당하다 *v.* to take charge of, be responsible for. 담당 charge ¶저 형사가 그 사건을 담당하고 있어요. That police detective is in charge of the case.

대부분 *n., adv.* most (of); a great (large, major) portion (of); mostly; for the most part ¶손님은 대부분이 여자였다. The customers were mostly women.

댁 *n.* you [honorific]; one's house, residence [honorific] ¶댁의 양반 your husband ¶댁은 누구세요? Who are you? ¶김 선생님은 댁에 계실까요? Do you think Mr. Kim is at home?

도움이 되다 *v.* to be helpful ¶크게 도움이 되다 to be of much help ¶그것은 이 문제를 이해하는 데 도움이 될 것이다. That may be helpful in understanding this issue.

돋구다 *v.* to raise; to stimulate; to make (a degree or standard) higher (= 돋우다). 돋다 to rise, come up; ~구/우 (causative suffix) ¶입맛을 돋구다 to stimulate the appetite

동네 *n.* village; neighborhood

동서고금 *n.* all places and times. 동서 east and west; Orient and Occident; 고금 ancient and modern ages ¶동서고금을 통하여 가장 훌륭한 학자 the greatest scholar of all places and times

듣다못해 *adv.* (being) unable to continue to listen to

따지고 보면 *adv.* after all. 따지다 to calculate; to inquire into; 보면 if we look at (it)

딴 *pre-n.* other; another; else; different ¶딴 일 other matters ¶딴 곳 another place ¶딴 모자는 없어요? Don't you have any other hat?

마음(을) 먹다 *v.* to intend to, mean to, think of ¶그는 위대한 과학자가 되려고 마음먹고 있다. He is firmly determined to become a great scientist.

만복 *n.* great happiness; all kinds of good luck

말을 붙이다 *v.* to speak to, address (= 말을 건네다)

망치 *n.* hammer

맞다 *adj.* to be right, correct

맞추다 *v.* to check, adjust; to match, compare; to assemble; to guess correct ¶답을 맞추다 to check answers

맡다 *v.* to take charge of; to take up; to obtain; to undertake ¶내가 맡은 일 the business in my charge ¶이 사건은 김 변호사가 맡았다. Attorney Kim was entrusted with this case.

매일같이 *adv.* (almost) every day (*lit.,* like every day) ¶매일같이 네 생각만 하고 있어. Not a day passes without my thinking of you.

맨 *pre-n.* the very; the extreme. 맨 끝 the very end; 맨 처음 (at) the very first; 맨 뒤 the very last (end)

몇몇 *n., pre-n.* some; several; a few. 몇 how many; several; a few ¶몇몇 사람 several persons ¶몇몇은 죽고 몇몇은 다쳤다. Some people were killed, others wounded.

미장원 *n.* beauty salon

바꿔 드리다 *v.* [honorific of 바꿔 주다] to exchange, barter; to replace, change; (in telephone calls) to put (someone) on the phone ¶(in a telephone conversation) A: 누구를 바꿔 드릴까요? To whom would you like to talk? B: 김 교수님을 좀 바꿔 주세요. May I talk to Professor Kim?

바로잡다 *v.* to straighten, correct; to care for, remedy ¶그분은 자기 아들의 나쁜 버릇을 바로잡아 주었다. He remedied his son's bad habits.

반증하다 *v.* to prove the contrary. 반증 disproof, contrary evidence

받아 주다 *v.* to accept, respond favorably, to listen to, comply with

발표하다 *v.* to report, announce, express

베란다 *n.* veranda, porch

보약 *n.* restorative, tonic. 보~ strengthening; 약 medicine ¶인삼은 보약으로 쓰인다. Ginseng is used as a tonic.

부사장 *n.* vice president. 부~ vice, deputy, associate ¶부교수 associate professor ¶부시장 deputy mayor

불러 주다 *v.* to call out

비결 *n.* secret; key; mysteries (of) ¶성공의 비결 the key to success

뿌리 *n.* root

사회 *n.* society, community. 사회적 social ¶사회적 지위 one's social position ¶사회 문제가 되다 to become a social issue ¶어느 사회에나 in any society

서스펜스 *n.* suspense

서양 *n.* Western countries, the West, the Occident. 동양 Eastern countries, the Orient

선생님 *n.* teacher; doctor [의사 선생님 is used to address or refer to a medical doctor]

설렘 *n.* fluttering; uneasy feeling. 설레다 (one's heart) flutters

설치다 *v.* to leave (it) half done, stop (work) halfway ¶잠을 설치다 to sleep badly

소화 *n.* digestion. 소화하다, 소화되다 to digest ¶야채는 소화가 잘 된다. Vegetables digest well.

스크류드라이버 *n.* screwdriver

시집가다 *v.* to marry into a man's family. 시집 one's husband's house ¶시집간 여자 married woman

시험지 *n.* test (examination) paper. 시험 test; ~지 paper

신랑 *n.* bridegroom; newlywed (husband)

쏴 붙이다 *v.* to retort; to yell (at); to talk back. 쏘다 to shoot, fire; 붙이다 to attach; to hit

아찔하다 *adj.* to feel dizzy, giddy; to be terrified ¶밑을 내려다보니 아찔했다. I felt dizzy when I looked down.

안내 *n.* guidance; conducting ¶안내(를) 하다 to show (a person) over (a place); to usher ¶안내(를) 받다 to be ushered

양반 *n.* adult male; husband ¶우리 집 양반 my husband

애 *adv.* contr. of 이 애 this child; you; there; hey

어떻게 해서 *adv.* in what way, how

어리둥절해하다 *v.* to become (feel) confused; to be stunned, be at a loss

어찌나 자랑을 하는지 boasted of (it) so much (that . . .)

영문 *n.* English writing; English version; English sentence

외식 *n.* eating (dining) out. 외식하다 to dine out

윈드스크린 *n.* windscreen

윈드실드 *n.* windshield

유머 = **우스갯소리** *n.* humor; joke. 우스개 jocularity; 우스갯짓 clowning ¶유머 감각 sense of humor ¶그따위 우스갯소리에 누가 웃겠니? Who would laugh at such a joke?

익살 *n.* joke; humor

일요신문 *n.* Sunday newspaper

자두 *n.* plum; prune (= 오얏)

자랑하다 *v.* to brag, boast of

잠을 설치다 *v.* to sleep badly. 설치다 to stop halfway; to be rampant; to overrun

잠을 이루다 *v.* to get to sleep. 이루다 to achieve, attain, accomplish, complete

장수하다 *v.* to live long

재치 *n.* wit; tact ¶재치 있는 사람 tactful (witty) person

전혀 *adv.* entirely, totally, altogether; at all

정답 *n.* correct answer, correct solution. 정~ correct; 답 answer, reply, solution

정도 *n.* degree, measure, extent; grade; standard ¶정도 문제 a matter of degree ¶네 말에는 어느 정도 진리가 있다. There is a certain degree of truth in what you say.

정신없다 *adj.* to be absent-minded; to be distracted; to have a poor memory. 정신 mind, spirit, soul ¶정신을 잃다 to lose one's senses

조르다 *v.* to badger, press, urge ¶나는 아버지한테 비디오 카메라를 사 달라고 졸랐다. I badgered my father to buy me a video camera.

조심하다 *v.* to heed, be careful

중(에) *n., adv.* (in) the middle; during, while

지각하다 *v.* to be late ¶학교에 지각하다 to be late to school

지켜보다 *v.* to watch, keep an eye on, observe

지폐 *n.* paper money, bill ¶만 원짜리 지폐 a ten-thousand won bill

쪽지시험 *n.* quiz (= 퀴즈). 쪽지 slip of paper

채점하다 *v.* to mark, grade, score, mark examination papers

처녀 *n.* maiden, young woman, virgin

척 *n.* pretense, make-believe (= 체). ¶못들은 척하다 to ignore, overlook; to pretend not to hear

출판하다 *v.* to publish; to issue, put out. 출판 publication; publishing; issue; 출판되다 to be published ¶출판의 자유 freedom of the press ¶출판물 a publication ¶출판사 publisher

치르다 *v.* to pay (= 지불하다); to take (an examination) ¶물건 값을 치르다 to pay for an article

탈나다 *v.* to have trouble; to be sick. 탈 a hitch, trouble; 나다 to appear, occur, happen ¶탈없이 without a hitch, safely; in good health ¶(저는) 배탈이 났어요. I have stomach trouble. ¶저 집에 큰 탈이 났다. The worst possible trouble has happened in that house.

통하다 *v.* to be known (as), pass; to lead to; to be on the line; to go through ¶~으로 통하다 to be known as

포장되다 *v.* to be packed, packaged. 포장 packing; 포장하다 to pack, package, wrap (in) ¶그 소포는 포장이 잘 되어 있었다. The parcel was well packed.

풍자 *n.* satire; sarcasm; innuendo; irony

하면 *adv.* contr. of 그러하면 then, and

하지만 *adv.* but, however ¶(그렇기는) 하지만 나는 찬성할 수 없어요. (It is true,) but I cannot agree with you.

한국경제신문 *n. Korean Economy Daily*

한국일보 *n. Han'guk Daily*

해학 *n.* humor; a joke

환자 *n.* patient

횡재 *n.* windfall, unexpected financial gain. 횡재하다 to have an unexpected financial gain ¶저의 아버지는 복권에 당첨되어 크게 횡재했어요. Winning the lottery gave my father a windfall.

혼해 빠지다 *v.* a dime a dozen [derogatory]. 혼하다 to be commonplace, usual, ordinary ¶혼해 빠진 얘기 a well-known story ¶그 따위는 혼해 빠졌다. Such things are by no means uncommon.

Useful Expressions

4.1 ~을/를 통하여 through(out), by (way of), via

~을/를 통하여, which contains the transitive verb 통하다 'to go through, lead to' literally means 'by going through' or 'by leading to.' It is used like a suffix to mean 'through, via.' Thus, 동서고금을 통하여 means 'through all times and places' (*lit.,* 'through the east, the west, ancient times, and modern times'), 전국을 통하여 means 'all over the country,' and 라디오를 통하여 means 'by radio.'

4.2 (이)란 entitled; called; named

(이)란 is a contraction of (이)라는, which in turn is a contraction of the quotative construction (이)라고 하는 'which (one) calls that' where (이) is the copula, 라 a statement ending, 고 the quotative particle, and 하 'do, say, call.' (이)란, (이)라는, and (이)라고 하는 all have the same meaning. They differ only in their degree of formality. (이)란 is the most casual.

「유머 인생」 **이란** (이라는, 이라고 하는) 책   a book called *A Life of Humor*
최불암**이란** (이라는, 이라고 하는) 사람   a person named Ch'oe, Puram

4.3 달라고 하다 to ask (someone) to give (something) to oneself

The verb stem 달~ is a variant form of 주 'give.' It occurs only before ~라고 하다, where ~라 is a command ending, 고 the quotative particle, and 하다 means 'to do; to say; to request.' Unlike 주라고 하다, which is used when the recipient is not the subject, 달라고 하다 is used only when the recipient is the subject. Compare these examples of the two expressions.

형은 그 책을 미아에게 **주라고 했어요**.
My brother asked me to give the book to Mia (a third person).
형은 그 책을 (자기에게) **달라고 했어요**.
My brother asked me to give the book to him (the quoted speaker).

선생님은 저에게 영수를 도와 **주라고 하셨어요**.
The professor asked me to help Young-Soo (a third person).

선생님은 저에게 도와 **달라고 하셨어요**.

The professor asked me to help him (the quoted speaker).

4.4 ～고 나서(는) after; and then

This phrase is composed of the suffix ～고 'and,' the verb stem 나 'appear, come out,' the suffix ～서 'and (then),' and the optional topic particle 는 'as for.' Together, these elements mean 'after (doing)' or '(do) and then.' Only verbs occur before ～고 나서(는). This pattern is equivalent to ～(으)ㄴ 뒤에 'after ～,' as in 밥을 먹고 나서 'after having a meal' (= 밥을 먹은 뒤에), and 꽃을 주문하고 나서 'after ordering flowers' (= 꽃을 주문한 뒤에). (See 3.2.)

집사람은 늦잠을 **자고 나서**는 미장원으로 갔어요.

My wife slept late in the morning and then went to the beauty salon.

숙제를 **끝내고 나서** 친구들하고 테니스 쳤어요.

After having finished my homework, I played tennis with my friends.

그리고 나서 끌과 망치를 찾았다.

After (doing) that, he called for a chisel and a hammer.

4.5 거예요 it is that; the fact is that

거 is a colloquial form of 것, as in 것이다/거다, 것이지요/거죠, 그것을/그걸, 것이에요/거예요, and 그것이/그게. It has a wide variety of meanings, among them 'a thing; an affair; the fact that; the one that; the doing; the being; the probable fact; the obligation; that.' 거 has different functions depending on what precedes and follows it. For instance, the prospective modifier suffix ～(으)ㄹ + 거 + copula (as in ～(으)ㄹ 거다/것이다/거야/것이야/거예요/것이에요) denotes a speaker's (in statements) or listener's (in questions) prediction or mild intention, as in 비가 올 거예요 '(I predict that) it will rain,' 나는 공부할 거예요 'I would like to study; I'm going to study,' and 잘 거예요? 'Would you like to sleep?' When the past modifier suffix ～(으)ㄴ or the non-past modifier suffix ～는 precedes 거 + copula, the basic meaning is 'it is that; the fact is that,' as in the following examples.

그게 어떻게 도움이 되었다는 **거예요**?　　How did that help?

　　　　　　　　　　　　　　　　　　(*lit.,* 'How is it that you say that helped?')

A: 어디가 탈난 **거예요**?　　　　　　　Where is it that he feels sick?

B: 배가 탈난 **거예요**.　　　　　　　　It's his stomach.

4.6　어쩌나 ~는지/(으)ㄴ지 so ~ that ~; too ~ to ~

The adverb 어쩌나 'too; so' + verb or adjective + modifier suffix ~는지/(으)ㄴ지 'whether; (so) . . . that; wondering about; not certain of' mean 'so ~ that ~' or 'too ~ to ~.'

나는 **어쩌나 기뻤던지** 눈물이 났다.
My joy was so great that I cried.

어쩌나 자랑을 **하는지** 듣기가 싫었다.
(He) boasted so much that I hated to hear about it.

이 책은 **어쩌나 어려운지** 읽을 수가 없어요.
This book is too difficult for me to read.

4.7　~다 못해(서) (being) unable to continue to . . .

This compound suffix follows a verb stem. It derives from the suffix ~다(가) 'while (doing),' the negative adverb 못 'unable,' 하 'do,' and ~어/아(서) 'and so, and then.' Literally, it means 'while continuing to do something, one becomes unable to do it anymore.' This construction is used when the speaker's reaction becomes so intense that (s)he cannot continue as (s)he was any longer.

아내가 **듣다 못해(서)** 쏴 붙였다.
Unable to continue to listen, his wife finally retorted.

언니는 **참다 못해(서)** 울음을 터뜨리고 말았어요.
Unable to bear it any longer, my older sister burst into tears.

4.8　~어/아 빠지다 extremely [derogatory]

~어/아 빠지다 is used to describe an aggravated state with a negative (or derogatory) connotation. Thus, 늙어 빠지다 is acceptable, but 젊어 빠지다 is not used because there is hardly any situation where to be young is interpreted in a negative or derogatory way. When independently used, 빠지다 is a verb meaning 'to fall into.' In this construction, 빠지다 acts as a suffix.

미국에는 **흔해 빠진** 게 부사장이래요.
Vice presidents are a dime a dozen in America.

우리 아들은 게을러 **빠졌어요**.
My son is extremely lazy.
이 동네 개들은 늙어 **빠져서** 잘 짖지를 않아요.
The dogs in this neighborhood are very old and so rarely bark.

4.9 ~(스)ㅂ디다 (past experience/observation)

~(스)ㅂ디다 is a deferential sentence ending indicating the speaker's (in statements) or listener's (in questions) own past experience or observation of an event, action, or state. Although deferential in form, this is not a form to use to a senior. Because it implies a strong assertion of one's own experience or a strong question of the listener's experience, it has an impolite connotation. In a sentence with this ending, the subject of the clause preceding this ending must not be in the first person in a statement or in the second person in a question. For example, 저는 행복합디다 'I was happy' is ungrammatical.

자두 담당 부사장도 **있습디다**.
(I witnessed) there was even a vice president in charge of prunes.
거리에 사람이 **많습디다**.   I saw many people on the street.
모두 다 교회에 **갑디다**.   I saw all of them going to church.

4.10 ~다며 saying that

This suffix is a contraction of ~다면서, which is itself a contracted form of ~다고 (말)하면서 'saying that.' All these forms are used interchangeably.

윈드실드라고 해야 **한다며/한다면서/한다고 하면서** 바로잡아 주었다.
(He) corrected (him), saying that it must be called a 'windshield.'
마이클은 급한 일이 **있다며/있다면서/있다고 하면서** 방금 떠났어요.
Michael left just now, saying that he had urgent business to do.

4.11 ~어/아 가지고 with; by doing/being; for the reason that

~어/아 가지고 is an emphatic, colloquial counterpart of ~어서/아서. Both this pattern and ~어서/아서 indicate a way or a reason.

남편을 **졸라 가지고** (졸라서) 외식을 했다.

(She) pressed her husband to dine out. (*lit.,* (she) dined out by pressing her husband.)

우리는 기분이 너무 **좋아 가지고** (좋아서) 춤을 췄어요.

We were so happy that we danced.

형은 돈을 많이 **벌어 가지고** (벌어서) 집으로 돌아왔어요.

My older brother came back home with all the money he had made (*lit.,* by earning a lot of money).

어젯밤 불이 **꺼져 가지고** (꺼져서) 공부를 못 했어.

The lights were out last night, so I was unable to study.

4.12 ～구만; ～구먼 well; I see; so it is

The intimate sentence endings ～구만 (used by younger speakers) and ～구먼 (used by older speakers), which occur only in statements, indicate the speaker's sudden discovery, spontaneous realization, and/or confirmation (frequently with surprise) of something. (Another form with the same meaning and function is ～군.) Their plain counterpart is ～구나, and polite counterparts are ～군요, ～구만요, and ～구먼요. Immediately after a verb stem, the modifier suffix ～는 is inserted before ～구만, ～구먼, ～군, and ～구나, as in 먹는구먼 and 가는군요.

정신없는 놈이구먼.	(He) must be a lunatic!
비가 오겠구만.	I see it's going to rain!
그것하고 똑 같구만.	Why, it looks just like it!
저기 수미가 오는구먼요.	Sumi is coming over here!

Exercises

1. 관련된 단어들끼리 연결하여 문장을 만들어 보세요.

    (1) 잠   •   • 설치다 _____

    (2) 탈   •   • 피우다 _____

    (3) 전화   •   • 채점하다 _____

    (4) 시험지   •   • 나다 _____

    (5) 담배   •   • 걸다 _____

2. 아래의 설명과 맞는 단어나 표현을 본문에서 찾아 쓰세요.

(1) 정해진 시간보다 늦게 도착하다: _____

(2) 병이 생기다: _____

(3) 책임을 지고 맡다: _____

(4) 몸이 지쳐 기운이 빠져 있다: _____

(5) 오래 살다: _____

3. 보기에서 적당한 말을 골라 빈칸을 채우세요.

> 보기: 통하여, 받은, 하는지, 한다며

(1) 유머는 동서고금을 _____ 어느 사회에나 있습니다.

(2) 환자의 방으로 안내를 _____ 의사는 몇 분 후 스크류드라이버를 달라고 했다.

(3) 새로 부사장이 된 사람이 어찌나 자랑을 _____ 아내가 듣다 못해 쏴 붙였다.

(4) 미국 사람은 윈드스크린이 아니라 윈드실드라고 해야 _____ 바로 잡아 주었다.

4. 밑줄 친 말과 가장 관계 <u>없는</u> 단어나 표현을 보기에서 고르세요.

(1) 유머는 우습고 재미있고 소화까지 돋구며 보약 <u>구실</u>까지 한다고 합니다.
　　 a. 역할　　　　　　　b. 기능　　　　　　　c. 이유

(2) 자니야, 너 <u>어째서</u> 지각했지?
　　 a. 왜　　　　　　　　b. 무슨 이유로　　　　c. 어떻게

(3) 영국 사람은 자동차의 윈드스크린을 <u>청소해야겠다</u>는 이야기를 했다.
　　 a. 깨끗이 해야겠다　　b. 소제해야겠다　　　c. 고쳐야겠다

(4) 게을러 빠져 가지고 매일 아침 늦잠을 자고 나서는 <u>노상</u> 미장원에서 시간을 보낸대요.
　　 a. 가끔　　　　　　　b. 늘　　　　　　　　c. 항상

5. 보기와 같이 주어진 말이 들어가는 단어를 3개 이상 써 보세요.

> 보기: 친 (親, friendly, parents): 친지, 양친, 친척, 친구, 친절

  (1) 약 (藥, medicine): _____

  (2) 사 (師, teacher, master): _____

  (3) 부 (副, vice, deputy, assistant; accompany): _____

  (4) 원 (院, public place or building): _____

6. "~를/을 통하여"를 사용하여 문장을 만드세요.

  (1) _____

  (2) _____

7. "(이)란"을 사용하여 다음 영문을 한국말로 말하세요.

  (1) A while ago, a student named Yong-ho Kim visited you.

  _____

  (2) Pearl Buck wrote a novel entitled *The Good Earth* (대지).

  _____

  (3) A Pacific island called Nauru is a rich country.

  _____

8. "~고 나서"를 사용하여 보기처럼 대화를 만들어 보세요.

> 보기: A: 언제 발렌타인 데이 선물 사러 가시겠어요?
>   B: 점심을 먹고 나서요.

  (1) A: _____

      B: _____

  (2) A: _____

B: _____

(3) A: _____

B: _____

9. 보기와 같이 문장을 완성하세요.

> 보기: 숙제를 끝내고 나서 친구들하고 테니스 쳤어요.

(1) 저녁을 먹고 나서 _____

(2) 친구와 약속하고 나서 _____

(3) 이 약을 먹고 나서 _____

10. 맞는 말에는 ○표를 하고 틀린 말에는 ×표를 하세요.

(1) 할아버지는 머리가 아파서 약을 주라고 하셨어요. (   )

(2) 미아는 오빠에게 돈 좀 달라고 했어요. (   )

(3) 아버지는 그 편지를 선생님께 전해 드리라고 하셨어요. (   )

(4) 나는 마이클한테 나를 좀 도와 주라고 했어요. (   )

11. "~라고 하다"를 이용해서 보기와 같이 문장을 만드세요.

> 보기: 선생님: 마이클 한국어 숙제를 도와 주겠니?
> 원식: 네, 그러겠습니다.
> 사라: 선생님께서 뭐라고 하셨어?
> 원식: 마이클 한국어 숙제를 도와 주라고 하셨어.

(1) 마크: 이 사전을 미아한테 전해 주겠니?

사라: 응.

〔잠시후〕

원식: 마크가 뭐라고 했니?

사라: _____

(2) 어머니: 소영아 학교 가기 전에 꼭 꽃에 물을 줘라.

소영: 네.

〔잠시후〕

소영 오빠: 어머니께서 뭐라고 하셨어?

소영: _____

(3) 마이클: 경제학 리포트 쓰는 것 좀 도와 줄래?

원식: 그래. 수업 끝나고 나서 만나자.

〔잠시후〕

소영: 마이클이 뭐라고 했어?

원식: _____

12. "어찌나 ~는지/(으)ㄴ지"를 사용하여 다음 영문을 한국말로 말하세요.

(1) Michael drove the car so fast that I was scared.

_____

(2) The kimchi was so hot that I was unable to eat it.

_____

(3) My younger brother bothered (귀찮게 하다) me so much that I could not study.

_____

13. "~다 못해(서)"를 사용하여 다음 영문을 한국말로 말하세요.

(1) Unable to continue to eat all the food, we gave it to the birds.

_____

(2) Being unable to bear hunger, the man began to commit theft.

_____

(3) Being not satisfied with hating the child, he even beats him.

_____

14. "~어/아 빠지다"를 사용하여 밑줄 친 곳을 채우세요.

> 보기: 그 자동차는 낡아 빠져서 버렸어요. (낡다)

(1) _____ 개 한 마리가 집을 지키고 있었다. (늙다)

(2) 그 꽃나무는 _____ 때문에 뽑아 버렸어요. (시들다)

(3) 그 애는 항상 _____ 청바지를 입고 다닌다. (닳다 to wear out)

15. 다음 영어 유머를 읽고 한국말로 바꿔 쓴 후, 교실에서 발표하세요.

(1) A: Do you know what are two most popular things (좋아하는 것) full of germs (세균, 병균)?

B: I don't know. What are they?

A: Kisses and money.

(2) A: So you taught your wife to play poker?

B: Sure, and it was a great idea. Last Saturday night I won back (이겨서 되찾다) nearly a third of my salary.

16. "～구먼(요)"를 사용해서 다음 영문을 한국말로 바꾸세요.

(1) My, there are a lot of monkeys in this zoo!

_____

(2) This is certainly a nice book!

_____

(3) Hey, they close the gate at 6 o'clock!

_____

(4) In the country I found that parents still arrange (decide) their children's marriages!

_____

(5) Well, I see we have no choice but to eat the fixed meal (정식) in this restaurant!

_____

Discussion and Composition

1. 아래 글을 읽고 무엇이 유머 감각을 일으키는지를 교실에서 말해 보세요.

> 최불암이란 사람이 약국을 하고 있었다. 어느 날 토끼가 찾아왔다.
>
> 토끼: 아저씨, 당근 있어요?
> 최불암: 없어.
>
> 그 다음날 토끼가 또 찾아왔다.
>
> 토끼: 당근 있어요?
> 최불암: 없다니까! 아이참, 너 한번만 더 찾아오면 가위로 네 큰
>   귀를 싹둑 잘라 버릴 테다.
>
> 그 다음날 토끼가 또 찾아와서는
>
> 토끼: 아저씨, 가위 있어요?
> 최불암: 없어!
> 토끼: 그럼, 당근 있어요?
>
> （「새국어 생활」1992. 2. 2. pp. 115-116）

2. 여러분이 알고 있는 재미있는 이야기를 하나 글로 써 보세요.

Further Reading

1. 논리적인 이야기가 되도록 순서를 쓰세요.

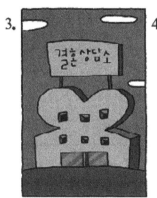

「광수 생각」 (Kwangsoo Reflects), 박광수, 소담출판사, 1999

(3), (   ), (   ), (   ), (   )

2. 다음을 읽고 질문에 답하세요.

미인을 업은 스님

두 스님이 절로 돌아가는 길에 어떤 시내를 건너게 되었는데 시냇가에 한 아름다운 여자가 서 있었다. 그 여자도 역시 시내를 건널 참이었으나 주저하고 있던 중이었다. 그 시내는 깊고 물살이 셌다.

한 스님이 여인을 못 본 척하고 혼자서 물을 건너기 시작했다. 그러나 다른 스님은 여인에게 등을 들이대며 말했다.

"업히시지요. 건네 드리겠습니다."

이렇게 하여 그 스님은 여인을 시내 저쪽에 내려 놓았다.

두 스님은 다시 길을 걸었다. 그런데 조금 전에 여인을 업지 않았던 스님이 화난 목소리로 말했다.

"스님으로서 여자의 몸에 손을 대고 부끄럽지도 않은가?"

여자를 업었던 스님은 아무 대답도 하지 않았다. 다른 스님은 더욱 화가 나서 여자를 업었던 스님을 계속해서 꾸짖었다. 여자를 업었던 스님은 한 두어 시간쯤 꾸지람을 듣고 나서, 더 이상 참을 수 없다는 듯이 껄껄 웃으며 말했다.

"이 사람아, 나는 벌써 두어 시간 전에 그 여자를 냇가에 내려 놓고 왔는데, 자네는 아직도 업고 있군."

「철학하는 바보」(1996), 이명수 편저, 보성출판사

건네다 to carry across, take over; 계속해서 continuously; 껄껄 ha-ha; 꾸지람 scolding, rebuke; 꾸짖다 to scold; 두어 시간 a couple of hours; 들이대다 to thrust (a thing); 등 the back; 물살 current of water; 미인 a beauty; 스님 Buddhist priest; 시내 stream, brook; 업다 to carry on one's back; 업히다 to ride on (someone's) back; 역시 also; ~으로서 as, for; 이 사람아 you! 주저하다 to hesitate; 참 at the point of, just when

---

1. 아름다운 여자는 왜 주저하고 있었습니까?

2. 한 스님은 왜 그냥 가고 한 스님은 왜 여자에게 등을 들이댔습니까?

3. 여자를 업지 않았던 스님은 왜 화가 났습니까?

4. 여자를 업은 스님은 꾸지람을 듣고 나서 뭐라고 했습니까?

5. 이 이야기 가운데서 어디가 가장 유머가 있다고 생각합니까? 그 이유를 말해 보세요.

6. 두 스님은 친구 사이일까요, 아니면 선후배(senior-junior) 사이일까요? 두 스님의 관계를 어떻게 알 수 있습니까?

LESSON 4. A LIFE OF HUMOR

Humor is funny, interesting, even aids appetite, and is said to act as a tonic as well. That is why humor is ubiquitous in society. Here we introduce a selection of Western humor included in a book called *A Life of Humor* (1994) published by *Korean Economic Newspaper* in Seoul and a selection of Korean humor included in Sunday papers of the *Han'guk Daily.*

A Windfall

Teacher: Now, Johnny, why are you late?
Johnny: Well, there was a man who had lost a dollar bill.
Teacher: And you were helping him look for it?
Johnny: No, I was standing on it.

Suspense

A doctor was taken into a patient's room, and in a few minutes he called for a screwdriver. A few minutes later he called for a chisel and a hammer. The patient's wife was terrified.

Patient's wife: Doctor! What is wrong with him?
Doctor: Don't know yet. I can't get my bag open.

Vice President

A man who had just been promoted to vice president boasted of it so much to his wife that she finally retorted:

Wife: Vice presidents are a dime a dozen. Why, in the supermarket they even have a vice president in charge of prunes.

Furious, the husband phoned the supermarket in the expectation of refuting his wife. He asked to speak to the vice president in charge of prunes.

Clerk: Which kind? Packaged or bulk?

The Root

The visiting American and his English friend were driving through London when the latter mentioned that his windscreen needed cleaning. "Windshield," the American corrected him.

Englishman: Well, over here we call it a windscreen.

American: Then you're wrong. After all, we Americans invented the automobile, and we call this a windshield.

Englishman: That's all very well, old boy, but who invented the language that Americans use?

A Daughter and a Daughter-in-law

First woman: What kind of boy did your daughter marry?

Second woman: Oh, he's wonderful. He lets her sleep late, wants her to go to the beauty parlor every day, won't let her cook, and insists on taking her out to dinner every night.

First woman: That's nice. And your son, what kind of girl did he marry?

Second woman: Oh, I'm not so happy there. She's lazy, sleeps late every morning, spends all her time at the beauty parlor, won't cook, and makes him take all their meals out.

You're Wrong!

A teacher was reading her students the correct answers for a multiple-choice exam taken the day before. The teacher, who had graded exams until late at night, was so tired that she mistakenly gave an incorrect answer for the third question. She said 1, instead of the correct answer, 2.

Most of the students in the class were very surprised, and confusedly called out, "Teeeacherrrrrr!"

But the voice of Ch'oe Pulam was heard from the very back of the classroom, "Wow! I got one right!"

The Absent-minded Old Man

An old man was driving down the highway on the way to his son's house when a phone call came from his son.

"Dad, are you on the highway now?"

"Yes, why?"

"The news just reported a car driving down the highway going in the opposite direction. Please be careful!"

The old man answered, "He certainly must be absent-minded! But it's not just one car, you know—why, there are hundreds of cars going in the wrong direction!"

Try It My Way!

A woman walking down the street spotted an old man sitting in a chair on his porch. She approached him, and smilingly called to him,

"What's your secret for a long and happy life?"

"I smoke three packs of cigarettes a day, drink a bottle of wine, eat lots of greasy food, and I never exercise!"

"I can't believe that! How old will you be this year?"

"Uhh, twenty-six."

Let's Go, Young Lady!

An old woman was passing by a road in her neighborhood. From behind her she heard a man calling out, *"Kach'i ga ch'ŏnyŏ!"* ("Come along with me, young lady!") The old woman went home, pretending she hadn't heard anything. But in her heart she was so excited that she still looked like a young lady, she could not sleep a wink.

The next day, of course, she passed by the same place, and she heard the same man's voice again, saying *"Kach'i ga ch'ŏnyŏ!"*

That night again, the old woman could not sleep for excitement.

The next day, she passed by the spot again, having firmly made up her mind to answer the man's call.

She heard the man's voice from behind. On listening more closely, however, she found out what he was really saying:

"Kalch'iga ch'ŏn wŏn!" ("A thousand wŏn for hair-tail [a kind of fish]!")

제5과 문화 유산

(Lesson 5: Cultural heritage)

PRE-READING QUESTIONS

1. 위의 그림들은 무엇입니까?

2. 한국의 문화 유산은 어떤 것이 있을까요?

3. 여러분의 나라의 대표적인 문화 유산은 어떤 것이 있나요?

GAINING FAMILIARITY

1. 문화재, 유형 문화재, 무형 문화재, 인간 문화재

2. 경주, 불국사, 석굴암, 천마총, 첨성대, 경주 국립 박물관

3. 서울의 4대문, 경복궁, 광화문

4. 택견도, 판소리, 강강술래, 춘향전

한국의 문화재

씨름

한국인의 조상들이 남긴 문화적 유산 가운데, 문화적 가치가 두드러져서 길이 보존할 만한[5.1] 것을 문화재라고 한다. 문화재는 특별히 법으로 보호를 받는다. 문화재에는 유형 문화재와 무형 문화재와 인간 문화재가 있다. 유형 문화재란[5.2] 일정한 형태가 있는 문화재인데 서울의 남대문과 동대문, 경주의 첨성대와 에밀레종 등은 모두 중요한 유형 문화재이다. 무형 문화재란 일정한 형태가 없는 문화재를 말한다. 춘향전 같은 연극, 판소리 같은 음악, 강강술래 같은 춤, 씨름이나 그네뛰기 같은 민속 놀이, 택견도 같은 전통 무술 등이 무형 문화재이다. 인간 문화재는 꼭 지켜야 할 전통 예술의 뛰어난 기능을 가지고 있는 사람을 말한다. 한국 정부에서는 현재 180여 명을 인간 문화재로 지정하고 있다.

유형 문화재 중에는 국보와 보물이 있는데 국보는 한국 민족의 우수성과 독창성을 뽐낼 수 있는 문화재이고, 보물은 국보만 못하지만[5.3] 한국 민족의 지혜가 담긴 문화재를 가리킨다. 서울 남대문은 국보 제1호이다. 조선을 세운 태조 이성계가 개성에서 서울로 도성을 옮기고

남대문

도성 주위에 대문을 세우기 시작했다. 도성 남쪽에 세운 남대문은
태조가 왕위에 오른 지 7년째가 되던 해(1398년)에 완성되었고, 그
뒤 세종대왕 때 다시 보수 공사를 했다. 도성 동쪽에 세운 동대문
은 보물 제1호로, 남대문과 같은 때인 1398년에 완성되었다. 동대
문은 1869년에 크게 보수 공사를 했다.

　수많은 국보와 보물이 전국 곳곳에 있다. 또한 많은 국보와 보
물이 일본, 미국, 영국 등 해외 여러 나라에 산재해 있기도 하다.
예를 들면[5.4] 경주 불국사에 있는 다보탑(국보 제20호)에는 원래 돌
사자가 네 마리 있었는데 그 중 세 마리가 없어지고 지금은 한 마
리만 남아 있다. 없어진 세 마리 중 두 마리는 일본에 있고 나머지
한 마리는 영국 대영 박물관에 있다고 한다.

동대문　　　　　　　　　　　다보탑

대화

1

(여행을 좋아하는 남원식 교수는 미국인 영어 선생 네드 슐츠 씨를 식당에서 만났다.)

원식: 한국에 오신 지 몇 년이나 되셨어요?

네드: 한 삼 년쯤 됐는데요.

원식: 그럼 그동안 한국에서 여행 많이 하셨겠네요.[5.5]

네드: 별로요. 올 봄에 경주에 2박 3일로[5.6] 가 본 것 말고는[5.7] 그동안 시간도 없고 돈도 없고 해서[5.8] 여행 많이 못했어요.

원식: 경주에서는 어디 어디 구경하셨어요?

네드: 불국사, 석굴암, 안압지, 천마총, 첨성대, 경주 국립 박물관 등 유명하다는 데는 모두 다 가 봤어요. 정말 많은 걸 배웠다고 생각해요.

원식: 뭐가 가장 인상적이었다고 생각하세요?

네드: 모두 다요.

원식: 그 중에서도 특별히 뭐가 좋았어요?

네드: 특별히 천마총하고 경주 박물관이 좋더라구요.[5.9] 박물관에는 한국에서 제일 큰 에밀레종이 있고 국보, 보물 등 문화재가 12,000여 점이나 전시되어 있었어요.

원식: 그래서 신라의 예술이나 문화를 알고 싶으면 경주 박물관을 꼭 가 봐야 한다지 않아요.

네드: 저도 동감이에요. 저도 그렇게 생각했거든요.

2

(수현이는 한국어 수업 시간에 한국의 문화재에 관해 발표를 하고 있다. 문화재에 관한 슬라이드를 보여 주면서 질문을 받고 있다.)

마이클: 저기 뒤쪽에 보이는 저게 광화문이죠?

수현:　맞습니다. 광화문은 그 뒤에 있는 경복궁의 남쪽 문이지요. 경복궁 문은 동서남북에 각각 하나씩 있거든요.

마이클: 광화문은 그동안 수난을 많이 당했다고 알고 있는데요.

수현:　그렇죠. 14세기에 세운 원래의 광화문은 임진왜란 때에 불에 타 버렸고, 그 뒤 400년 동안 흉칙한 모습으로 버려져 있었대요.

마이클: 그러면 저것이 진짜 광화문이 아니겠네요.

수현:　진짜는 진짜지요.[5.10] 19세기에 대원군이 경복궁을 다시 지을 때 광화문도 다시 제 모습으로 지었으니까요.

마이클: 그렇지만 제가 본 옛날 서울 사진에는 저 자리에 저런 문이 없던대요.

수현:　그건[5.11] 일본이 한국을 지배할 때 경복궁 앞뜰에다 총독부 건물을 짓고 광화문은 눈에 안 띄는 경복궁 북쪽으로 옮겨 버렸기 때문이에요.

마이클: 세상에 그럴 수가![5.12]

수현:　그랬다가 1968년에 와서야[5.13] 원래의 자리로 옮겨졌대요.

마이클: 그랬군요. 몇 년 전에 한국 정부에서 총독부 건물을 헐어 버렸다고 들었는데요.

수현:　그래요. 총독부 건물을 헐어 버리고 나니 경복궁과 광화문의 옛 모습이 살아 난 거예요.

마이클: 역사가 한바퀴 되돌아오는 데 그렇게도 많은 세월이 흘렀군요.

수현:　그러게 말이에요. 그 동안 정말 많은 수난을 당한 거예요.

Comprehension Questions

1. **Reading Comprehension.** "한국의 문화재"를 읽고 맞고(Ⓣ) 틀린 (Ⓕ) 것을 지적하거나 질문에 대답해 보세요.

    (1) 판소리는 민속 놀이의 하나다.   Ⓣ   Ⓕ

    (2) 춘향전은 유형 문화재이다.   Ⓣ   Ⓕ

    (3) 서울의 남대문은 보물 제1호이다.   Ⓣ   Ⓕ

    (4) 동대문은 1398년에 크게 보수 공사를 했다.   Ⓣ   Ⓕ

    (5) 불국사에 있는 다보탑의 돌사자 네 마리는 지금 일본과
        영국에 있다.   Ⓣ   Ⓕ

    (6) 문화재에는 어떤 종류가 있습니까?

    (7) 유형 문화재란 무엇입니까?

    (8) 무형 문화재에는 어떤 것이 있는지 아래에 적어 보세요.

    _____

    _____

    _____

    (9) 인간 문화재란 무엇입니까?

  (10) 국보와 보물은 어떻게 다릅니까?

  (11) 서울은 언제부터 한국의 수도가 되었습니까? 서울이
       한국의 수도가 되기 전에는 어느 도시들이 옛날 한국의
       수도였나 알아보세요.

  (12) 신라의 예술이나 문화를 알고 싶으면 어디를 가 봐야
       합니까? 왜 그렇습니까?

  (13) 많은 한국의 국보와 보물이 왜 해외에도 있다고 생각합니까?

2. **Listening Comprehension.** 대화를 듣고 맞고(Ⓣ) 틀린(Ⓕ) 것을 지적하거 나 질문에 대답해 보세요.

대화 1

(1) 네드는 석굴암과 천마총을 제일 좋아했다. ⊤ Ⓕ

(2) 네드는 신라의 예술과 문화를 알고 싶으면 경주 박물관에
가 봐야 한다고 생각한다. ⊤ Ⓕ

(3) 네드는 왜 여행을 많이 못 했습니까?

(4) 네드는 한국에 간 지 몇 년이 되었습니까?

(5) 다음 중 네드가 경주에서 방문한 곳에 ○표를 하세요.

불국사 _____ 석굴암 _____ 안압지 _____

천마총 _____ 첨성대 _____ 경주 국립 박물관 _____

대화 2

(1) 1968년에 광화문을 다시 지었다. ⊤ Ⓕ

(2) 20세기에 대원군이 경복궁과 광화문을 지었다. ⊤ Ⓕ

(3) 경복궁의 문은 몇 개가 있습니까?

(4) 마이클은 언제 서울의 옛날 사진을 보았습니까?

(5) 일본이 한국을 지배할 때 광화문은 어떤 수난을 당했습니까?

New Words

가리키다 *v.* to indicate, denote, point to

가치 *n.* value; worth; merit

곳곳 *n.* various places; here and there ¶시내 곳곳이 침수되었다. The city was flooded in several places.

관측 *n.* observation, survey. 관측하다 to observe; 관측되다 to be observed ¶이제까지 관측되지 않았던 별 a star so far unobserved

국보 *n.* national treasure ¶국보로 지정되다 to be designated a national treasure

그랬다가 *contr.* of 그러했다가 such was the case; and then

기능 *n.* technical skill; ability ¶기능을 습득하다 to learn the skill (of)

길이 *adv.* for a long time; forever, eternally. 길다 to be long; ～이 (adverbial suffix) ¶길이 보존하다 to preserve or cherish forever

농사 *n.* farming, agriculture ¶농부들이 농사를 짓는다. Farmers engage in agriculture.

다보탑 *n.* Tabo (*lit.,* many treasures) Tower

담기다 *v.* to be filled; to be put in; to be dished up. 담다 to put in; ~기 (passive suffix)

대영 박물관 *n.* the British Museum

대원군 *n.* Lord Taewŏn, father of Kojong (the Chosŏn dynasty's 26th king), who acted as regent for his son from 1864 to 1873

도성 *n.* castle town; capital city (in old Korea)

독창성 *n.* originality ¶독창성이 없는 unoriginal

돌사자 *n.* stone lion

동감이다 *adj.* to be in agreement, agree. 동감 the same sentiment; sympathy ¶저도 동감이에요. I agree with you.

두드러지다 *adj.* to be conspicuous, prominent, marked ¶그의 한국어 실력이 두드러지게 늘었다. He showed marked improvement in his Korean.

띄다 *v.* (= 뜨이다) to catch sight of; to meet the eye. 뜨다 to rise, float; ~이 (passive suffix) ¶눈에 띄다 to catch (meet) one's eye, come to one's notice, attract one's attention

무술 *n.* martial arts

무형 *n.* (being) intangible; formless(ness) ¶무형 문화재 intangible cultural assets

문화재 *n.* cultural assets, cultural properties ¶중요 문화재로 지정되다 to be registered as an important cultural property

버려지다 *v.* to be abandoned, marooned. 버리다 to throw away; 지다 to get, become ¶흉칙한 모습으로 버려져 있었다. It was abandoned in terrible shape.

법 *n.* law ¶법을 지키는 시민 law-abiding citizen

별로 *adv.* (not) particularly, (not) especially ¶별로예요. (It) is so-so; (It) is not particularly good.

보물 *n.* treasure, valuables ¶이것은 대대로 내려오는 보물이다. This is an heirloom handed down from our ancestors.

보수 공사 *n.* repair works. 보수하다 to repair, mend

보존하다 *v.* to preserve, conserve, maintain ¶이 책은 잘못 보존되었다. This book has been poorly preserved.

보호 *n.* protection. 보호하다 to protect ¶경찰에 보호를 요청하다 to apply to the police for protection

불국사 *n.* Pulguk Temple (a Silla dynasty Buddhist temple built in Kyŏngju in the eighth century by the chief minister of the time, Kim Tae-sŏng)

뽐내다 *v.* to take pride (in), brag, boast

사다리 *n.* ladder ¶내가 올라가 있는 동안 사다리를 붙들고 있어 줘. Steady the ladder while I'm on it.

산재하다 *v.* to be scattered around· ¶졸업생들은 전국에 산재해 있다. The graduates are scattered all over the country.

석굴암 *n.* Sŏkkuram Cave Temple (a manmade grotto located on Mt. T'oham, Kyŏngju and noted for its architectural beauty)

세기 *n.* century. 21세기 the twenty-first century

세월 *n.* time and tide; time; years ¶많은 세월이 흘렀다. Many years have gone by.

수난 *n.* suffering; ordeals; disasters, catastrophes ¶한국 민족은 오천 년 역사 동안 많은 수난을 겪었다. The Korean people have suffered great ordeals during their five thousand years' history.

안압지 *n.* Anapchi (manmade lake in Kyŏngju)

앞뜰 *n.* front yard (court). 뜰 yard

에밀레종 *n.* Emille Bell (Cast in 771 to honor King Sŏngdŏk posthumously, the bell was originally located at Pongdŏk-sa Temple, but is now in the national museum in Kyŏngju. It measures seven feet six inches [2.27 meters] in diameter and is eleven feet [3.3 meters] high.)

연극 *n.* a play; a drama ¶나는 연극을 별로 보러 가지 않는다. I am not much of a playgoer.

오르다 *v.* to ascend, climb up ¶태조는 1392년에 왕위에 올랐다. T'aejo ascended to the throne in 1392.

올 *n.* (= 올해) this year ¶올 봄 this year's spring ¶올 여름 휴가 this year's summer vacation

완성 *n.* completion; perfection. 완성하다 to complete; 완성되다 to be completed ¶이 일이 완성되려면 아직 멀었다. This work is far from (being) complete(d).

왕위 *n.* throne; crown; kingship ¶왕위에 오르다 to ascend to the throne

왕조 *n.* dynasty ¶조선 왕조 the Chosŏn dynasty

우수성 *n.* superiority; excellence

원래 *adv.* originally; primarily; essentially ¶삶과 죽음은 원래 동일한 것이다. Life and death are essentially one and the same.

유명하다 *adj.* to be famous, well known ¶유명하다는 데 (= 유명하다고

[말]하는 데) famous places (*lit.,* places said to be famous)

유산 *n.* heritage; legacy; inheritance, property left by a deceased person
    ¶문화(적) 유산 cultural heritages ¶그 여자는 자기 할아버지로부터 많은
    유산을 받았다. She received a large inheritance from her grandfather.

유형 *n.* concreteness; (being) tangible ¶유형 문화재 tangible cultural
    properties (assets)

인간 문화재 *n.* living cultural treasures; people who have exceptional skills
    in traditional artforms

일정한 *pre-n.* definite; fixed, established, set ¶일정한 수입 a regular (fixed)
    income

임진왜란 *n.* Imjinwaeran. Japanese invasion of 1592 (After unifying Japan,
    Toyotomi Hideyoshi invaded the Korean peninsula. The war lasted
    seven years, with the Japanese retreating only in 1598.)

전시 *n.* exhibition, display. 전시하다 to exhibit; 전시되다 to go on display,
    be exhibited

지배하다 *v.* to occupy; to control; to govern ¶그 때 일본은 군인들이 지배하고
    있었다. At that time Japan was controlled by militaristic hands.

지정하다 *v.* to appoint, designate, assign ¶지정된 시간까지 by the appointed
    time

지혜 *n.* wisdom, sagacity; intelligence

진짜 *n.* the genuine article, the real thing. 가짜 false one, imitation, phony

천마총 *n.* Ch'ŏnmach'ong, name of one of the tombs of the Silla kings. 천마
    a flying horse, ~총 a tomb. (The tomb was named 천마총 because it
    contained equestrian paraphernalia with flying horses engraved on it.)

첨성대 *n.* Ch'ŏmsŏngdae (observatory built sometime between 632 and 647
    to conduct basic astronomical observations)

총독부 *n.* Japanese government in Seoul during the colonial period
    (1910-1945). 총독 governor-general; ~부 prefecture; mansion; center

탑 *n.* tower; pagoda; steeple

태조 *n.* first king of a dynasty

택견도 *n.* t'aekkyŏndo, a Korean sport in which one kicks and trips an
    opponent

특별히 *adv.* specially, especially, particularly

판소리 *n.* p'ansori, a long Korean epic song

한다지 않아요 contr. of 한다고 하지 않아요

한바퀴 *n.* one cycle

헐다 *v.* to demolish, destroy, flatten out ¶낡은 집을 헐어 버렸다. We demolished the old house.

형태 *n.* form, shape

흉칙하다 *adj.* to be very ugly

Useful Expressions

5.1 ~(으)ㄹ 만하다 to be worth (doing); to deserve

When the adjective 만하다 'to be as big/much/little as; to be the size of' is preceded by a verb with the modifier suffix ~(으)ㄹ, it means 'to be well worth (doing), to deserve, to be sufficient to (do), to be at the point of (doing).' Examples include 읽을 만하다 'to be readable, worth reading,' 믿을 만하다 'to be trustworthy,' 먹을 만한 음식 'food worth eating,' 쉴 만한 공원 'a park (that is a) good (place) to relax in,' and 일을 할 만한 나이에 'at the age when one can work.'

5.2 (이)란 as for

(이)란 consists of the copula 이 'to be' (omitted after a vowel) + ~란. ~란 is a contraction of ~라고 하는 것은, in which ~라 is a statement ending, 고 the quotative particle, 하 'call, say,' 는 a modifier suffix, 것 'thing, fact,' and 은 a topic particle 'as for.' Literally, it means '(as for) something that is called' or '(as for) what is called.'

수수께끼**란** 무엇인가? = 수수께끼라고 하는 것은 무엇인가?

구비 문학(literature of oral tradition)**이란** 말로 전해 온 문학이다.
= 구비 문학이라고 하는 것은 말로 전해 온 문학이다.

5.3 ~만 못하다 not to be as good as

The adjective 못하다 means 'to be inferior, worse, not on a level (with), below.' The particle 만 seems to have developed from 만큼 '(to) the extent (degree, measure) of.' The pattern ~만 못하다 means 'not to be as good as,' as in:

존은 한국말이 네드**만 못해요**.
John's Korean is not as good as Ned's.

이 꽃이 저기 있는 저 꽃만 **못해요**.
This flower is not up to that one over there (in beauty).

5.4 예를 들면 for example

This frequently used pattern literally means 'if one holds up (presents, gives, takes) an example.' Other forms with the same meaning and usage are 예를 들자면 and 예컨대.

5.5 ~겠네요 I guess (he/she/it/they/you) probably . . .

The pattern ~겠네요 has two parts, a suffix and a sentence ending. The suffix ~겠 denotes the speaker's conjecture based on circumstantial evidence. It may be translated as 'may, maybe, probably, must.' The sentence ending ~네(요) expresses the speaker's spontaneous emotive reaction (surprise, admiration, sympathy, puzzlement, and so forth) to something he or she observes or hears. The pattern ~겠네요 expresses the speaker's conjecture in a mild tone of voice. It is less assertive, and thus more polite, than ~겠어요, which is a more straightforward expression of the speaker's conjecture.

날씨가 흐린 걸 보니 비가 곧 **오겠네요**.
Judging from the overcast sky, I guess it will rain very soon.

5.6 2박 3일 two nights and three days (of a trip)

~박 is a Sino-Korean suffix meaning 'stay.' It is used to indicate the number of nights spent or to be spent for a trip, as in 4박 여행 'an excursion covering four nights' and 1박하다 'to stay overnight.' More frequently, it is followed by the number of days, as in 1박 2일, 3박 4일, 5박 6일, and so on.

5.7 말고는 other than, except

While 말고 means both 'not . . . but' and 'instead of, except,' 말고는 means only 'instead of' or 'except.'

이것 **말고** 더 좋은 것을 주세요.　　Please give me something better than this.
너 **말고(는)** 누가 거기를 갈 수 있겠니?　Who would be able to go there but you?

5.8 ~고 해서 because . . . and the like; and such, so

This phrase, which consists of the suffix ~고 'and,' 해 'do, be,' and 서 'and so,' is equivalent to and interchangeable with ~고 그래서 'and therefore; and the like, so.' It can occur after a verb or adjective stem.

지난번에 신세진 것도 있고 **해서** 저녁을 한번 살까해요.
I'd buy you dinner because I am indebted to you [for the] last time and such.
식욕도 없고 기분도 울적하고 **해서** 친구들하고 노래방에 갔어요.
I didn't have any appetite, felt depressed, and so on, so I went to a *noraebang* with friends.
민호는 열심히 공부하고 **해서** 의사가 되었어.
Minho studied hard and such, and as a result he became a (medical) doctor.

5.9 ~더라구요 I saw/witnessed/felt that; you know

This and its variant ~더라고요 are the most frequently used sentence endings in conversation. This ending is used when the speaker casually reports, though in a polite manner, his or her past observation of an event or past experience of an emotional or sensory state. The suffix ~더 carries the meaning of the speaker's past observation or experience, while the statement suffix ~라 and the quotative particles 고/구 convey the idea of reporting.

A: 너 우산 찾았니?
   Did you find your umbrella?
B: 있을 만한 곳은 다 찾아 보았는데 없더라고.
   I hunted in all the likely places, but couldn't find it, you know.

5.10 N는/은 N이다 it is N, if anything

Literally, this espression means 'as for N, it is N' or 'talking about N or not, it is N.' The meaning of 진짜는 진짜지요 is 'talking about a genuine one (or not), it is a genuine one,' or something like 'it is real, if anything.' Similarly, 학생은 학생이에요 means '(he) is a student, if anything.' This pattern is used when the speaker admits a certain fact, but with slight reservation. This pattern is similar to verb or adjective expressions like 가기는 간다, 먹기는 먹는다, 좋기는 좋다, and the like.

5.11   그건 . . . 때문이에요 that is because . . .

그건 (or 그것은) in this construction refers to the entire content of the immediately preceding sentence. It functions as the subject of the sentence in which the reason is given, using 때문이에요.

5.12   세상에 그럴 수가! how could such things happen in the world!

This is an expression often heard when someone is amazed, stunned, or dumb-founded. It is a contraction of something like 어떻게 세상에 그럴 수가 있겠어요? 'How could such things happen in the world?' 그럴 수 (or its full form 그러할 수) means 'such things,' 'such occasions,' or 'such possibilities.'

5.13   ~어서야/아서야 only when; not until

This pattern is composed of the suffix ~어서/아서 which indicates cause 'as, because' or temporal sequence 'when, since' and the suffix ~야, which indicates exclusivity: 'if only.' The complete construction means 'only when.' The difference between 1968년에 와서 and 1968년에 와서야 is that the first means simply 'in 1968' (*lit.,* 'when we came to 1968'), while the second means 'only in 1968' or 'not until 1968' (*lit.,* 'only when we came to 1968').

Exercises

1. 아래의 설명과 맞는 단어나 표현을 본문에서 찾아 쓰세요.

    (1) 혼자서 새로운 것을 생각해 내거나 만들어 내는 능력: _____

    (2) 서울, 수도의 옛말: _____

    (3) 건물의 부서진 부분을 고치는 일: _____

    (4) 생각이나 느낌이 같다: _____

    (5) 이곳 저곳에 흩어져 있다: _____

    (6) 특별한 자격이 주어지도록 정하다: _____

2. A, B, C의 관계되는 단어에 줄을 그으세요.

	A	B	C
(1)	문화적	세월이	옮겼다
(2)	흉칙한	보존해야 할	두드러지다
(3)	도성을	모습으로	산재해 있다
(4)	우수성과	가치가	뽐내다
(5)	많은	여러 나라에	버려져 있다
(6)	태조가	서울로	흘렀다
(7)	길이	왕위에	문화재
(8)	보물이	안 띄는	올랐다
(9)	눈에	독창성을	자리

3. 밑줄 친 말과 가장 비슷한 단어나 표현을 보기에서 고르세요.

   (1) 한국인의 조상들이 남긴 문화적 유산 <u>가운데</u>, 문화적 가치가 두드러져서 길이 보존할 만한 것을 문화재라고 한다.

      a. 속에서   b. 중에서

      c. 이거나   d. 이지만

   (2) <u>수많은</u> 국보와 보물이 전국 곳곳에 있다.

      a. 매우 적은   b. 매우 많은

      c. 많지 않은   d. 적지 않은

   (3) 많은 국보와 보물이 일본, 미국, 영국 등 해외 여러 나라에 <u>산재해 있다</u>.

      a. 잘 알려져 있다   b. 잘 보존되어 있다

      c. 이곳저곳에 흩어져 있다   d. 산에 쌓여 있다

   (4) 몇 년 전 한국 정부에서 총독부 건물을 <u>헐어</u> 버렸다고 들었는데요.

      a. 무너뜨려   b. 다시 지어

      c. 버려   d. 만들어

4. 보기에서 적당한 말을 골라 빈칸을 채우세요.

보기: 길이, 다시, 꼭, 원래, 특별히, 곳곳에

(1) 문화적 가치가 두드러져서 _____ 보존할 만한 것을 문화재라고 한다.

(2) 문화재는 _____ 법으로 보호를 받는다.

(3) 남대문은 태조가 왕위에 오른 지 7년째가 되던 해(1398년)에 완성되었고, 그 뒤 세종대왕 때 _____ 보수 공사를 했다.

(4) 수많은 국보와 보물이 전국 _____ 있다.

(5) 경주 불국사에 있는 다보탑에는 _____ 돌사자가 네 마리 있었는데 그 중 세 마리가 없어지고 지금은 한 마리만 남아 있다.

(6) 신라의 예술이나 문화를 알고 싶으면 경주 박물관을 _____ 가 봐야 한다지 않아요.

5. 보기와 같이 주어진 말이 들어가는 단어나 표현을 3개 이상 써 보세요.

보기: 친 (親, friendly, parents): 친지, 양친, 친척, 친구, 친절

(1) 문화 (文化, culture): _____

(2) 전통 (傳統, traditional): _____

(3) 공사 (工事, construction work): _____

(4) 형 (形, shape, form): _____

(5) 동 (同, same, similar): _____

6. Translate into Korean using ~(으)ㄹ 만하다.

(1) These clothes are still well worth wearing.

_____

(2) Do you have any Korean books worth reading?

_____

(3) His father may well be proud of his son.

_____

7. "(이)란"을 사용해서 문장을 만들어 보세요.

> 보기: 인간이란 누구나 다 죽게 마련이다.
> 'Human beings are doomed to be mortal.'

(1) 남자란 _____

(2) 사랑이란 _____

(3) 웃음이란 _____

8. Make up sentences using ～만 못하다.

(1) _____

(2) _____

9. Write a paragraph in which 예를 들면 occurs.

_____

_____

_____

_____

_____

10. "～고 해서"를 사용하여 밑줄 친 곳에 알맞은 말을 쓰세요.

(1) A: 어제 학교에 왜 안 나왔어요?
   B: _____ 집에서 쉬었어요.

(2) A: 어제 영화 보셨지요? 어땠어요?
   B: 사실은 피곤하기도 하고 _____ 중간에 나왔어요.

(3) A: 지난 주말에 노트북 컴퓨터 사셨지요? (가격이 비싸다)
   B: 아니오. _____ 안 샀어요.

(4) A: 영호오빠가 과 대표가 되었다면서요? (인기가 있다)
   B: 응. 유머가 있고 _____ 과 대표로 뽑혔어요.

11. Translate into Korean, using ～어서야/아서야.

(1) It was not until late at night that Father returned home.

_____

(2) I came to know the blessing of health only when I became an adult.
(건강의 고마움 blessing of health)

_____

Discussion and Composition

1. (Pair work) 여러분이 여행한 곳 중에서 가장 인상 깊은 곳에 관해 서로 대화를 해 보세요. 대화를 할 때는 다음 표현을 사용해 보세요.

> • ～박 ～일
> • ～고 해서
> • ～는 어디 어디 구경했어요(?)
> • ～더라구요
> • ～겠네요
> • ～가 가장 인상적이었어요(?)
> • 그 중에서도 특별히 ～가/이 좋았어요(?)
> • 저도 동감이에요

2. (Group work) 대화가 끝난 후 네 명이 한 조가 되어 여러분의 파트너가 여행한 곳 중에 가장 인상 깊은 곳에 관해 이야기해 보세요.

3. 봄방학 여행 계획(travel itineraries)을 세워 보세요. 계획을 세운 후 여러분의 여행에 관해 대화를 만들어 보세요. 대화를 만들 때는 다음의 표현을 사용해 보세요.

> • ～박 ～일
> • ～고 해서

> • ~(으)ㄹ 계획/생각이에요
> • ~는 어디 어디 구경할 거예요(?)
> • ~더라구요
> • ~겠네요
> • 그 중에서도 특별히 ~
> • 저도 동감이에요

4. (발표하기) 다음의 문화재가 무엇인지 알아보세요. 이 중 하나를 골라서 수업 시간에 발표하세요.

   (1) 천마도 _____

   (2) 고려 자기 _____

   (3) 훈민정음 _____

   (4) 팔만 대장경 _____

   (5) 혜원의 풍속도 _____

5. 서울에는 많은 궁전(palace)들이 있습니다. 어떤 궁전들이 있는지, 또 이 궁전들을 누가 언제 지었는지 한 페이지의 글로 써 보세요.

6. 한국에는 불국사 이외에도 많은 유명한 절들이 있습니다. 어떤 절이 어디에 있을까요? 조사해 보고 한 페이지의 글로, 써 보세요.

Further Reading

불국사, 석굴암, 첨성대

서울 강남 고속 버스 터미널에서 버스를 타고 남쪽으로 5시간쯤 가면 신라 천년의 수도였던 경주에 이른다. 경주와 경주 부근에는 고적과 유물 등 수많은 문화재가 있다. 경주에는 웅장한 경주 박물관이 자리잡고 있는데 여기에는 신라의 많은 유물이 전시되어 있고 박물관 뜰에는 슬픈 전설의 에밀레종이 있다. 경주에서 동남쪽으로 16킬로쯤 가면 불국사가 있고 불국사를 돌아서 조금 올라가면 토함산 꼭대기 가까운 곳에 석굴암이 있다. 불국사와 석굴암은 지금으로부터 1,200여 년 전에 신라 35대 경덕왕(재위 742-765) 때 재상 김대성이 짓기 시작하였는데 774년 김대성이 죽은 후에 완성되었다. "불국"이란 부처님이 계신 나라라는 뜻이다. 불국사의 대웅전 앞뜰에는 국보 20호인 다보탑과 21호인 석가탑이 각각 동쪽과 서쪽에 자리를 잡고 있다. 국보 24호인 석굴암은 가장 섬세하고 정확하게 만들어진 석굴이다. 굴 한가운데에는 커다란 돌 부처님이 너그러운 미소를 지으면서 앉아 있고 벽 둘레에는 11명의 자비스러운 보살이 돌에 섬세하게 새겨져 있다. 석굴암은 동해의 해맞이로도 유명하다. 여기서 아침 일찍 동해에서 솟아오르는 붉은 해를 볼 수 있기 때문이다.

에밀레종   불국사   석굴암

첨성대

또 경주에 있는 첨성대는 국보 제31호로, 지금부터 1300여 년 전인 신라 27대 선덕여왕(재위 632-647) 때 별을 관측하기 위해 쌓았다. 첨성대는 높이 8.17미터인데, 처음에는 별의 모양을 보고 나라나 왕조의 운명을 점쳤다. 그러다가 세월이 흐르면서, 농사와 관계 있는 자료를 얻기 위해 이용했다고 한다. 옛날 사람들은 1년이 362일이라고 믿었기 때문에 첨성대도 362개의 돌로 쌓았다. 사람들은 사다리를 놓고 첨성대 가운데에 있는 구멍으로 들어가 별을 관측했다고 한다.

강남 Kangnam (*lit.,* south of the Han River); 고적 historic site; 관측하다 to observe, survey; 구멍 hole; 꼭대기 top, summit; 너그럽다 to be generous, magnanimous; 농사 farm work; 대 generation (35대 왕 'the 35th king'); 대웅전 main building of a temple; 동해 East Sea (Sea of Japan); 미소를 짓다 to wear a smile; 벽 둘레 around a wall; 보살 Buddhist saint; 부근 vicinity; 부처님 Buddha; 사다리 ladder; 새겨지다 to be carved; 석굴 stone cave, grotto; 섬세하다 to be delicate; 솟아오르다 to rise up, soar, shoot up; 수도 capital; 쌓다 to heap up, build; 운명 destiny, fate; 웅장하다 to be stately, grand; 유물 relic; 이용하다 to use; 자료 data, materials; 자리(를) 잡다 to take a seat, be seated; 자비스럽다 to be merciful; 재상 minister of state (in old Korea); 재위 reign; 전설 legend; 점치다 to divine, tell fortunes; 해맞이 viewing the rising sun (*cf.* 달맞이)

1. 서울에서 경주까지 고속 버스로 얼마나 걸립니까?

2. 경주 박물관에는 무엇이 전시되어 있나요?

3. 불국사와 석굴암은 언제 누가 지었습니까?

4. 불국사에는 무슨 탑이 있습니까?

5. 첨성대는 언제 무슨 목적으로 만들었습니까?

6. 첨성대가 362개의 돌로 만들어진 이유는 무엇입니까?

LESSON 5. CULTURAL HERITAGE

Korea's Cultural Treasures

Among the cultural legacies left by the ancestors of the Korean people, those possessing outstanding value and meriting long-term preservation are called "cultural treasures" (or "cultural assets"). Cultural treasures are given special protection by law. There are three kinds of cultural treasures: tangible, intangible, and living.

Tangible cultural treasures are those with a concrete form. The South and the East Gates in Seoul, the astronomical observatory in Kyŏngju, the *Emille* Bell, and so forth, are important tangible cultural treasures.

Intangible cultural treasures are those without concrete form. Dramas like *The Tale of Ch'unhyang,* music like *p'ansori,* dances like the *kanggang sullae,* folk games like Korean-style wrestling and the traditional swing (*kŭne*), traditional martial arts like *t'aekkyŏndo,* and so on, are intangible cultural assets. Living cultural treasures are people who have exceptional skills in traditional artforms that must be preserved. The Korean government has designated more than 180 people as living cultural treasures (*lit.,* with this title).

There are two categories of tangible cultural treasures: national treasures (*kukpo*) and regular treasures (*pomul*). National treasures are those that testify to the excellence and the creativity of the Korean people. Regular treasures do not qualify to be national treasures, but are (still) pointed to as (cultural treasures) embodying the wisdom of the Korean people. The South Gate in Seoul is national treasure no. 1. When King T'aejo (Yi Sŏng-gye), the founder of the Chosŏn dynasty, moved the Korean capital (or "castle town") from Kaesŏng to Seoul, he began building gates around the new capital city. The South Gate, erected in the southern area of the capital, was completed in 1398, the seventh year of T'aejo's reign. It was repaired during King Sejong's reign. The East Gate, built in the eastern area of the capital, is regular treasure no. 1. It was completed in the same year as the South Gate (1398), and it underwent major repairs in 1869.

Many of Korea's national and regular treasures are found throughout the country, but others are scattered overseas, in countries like Japan, the United States, England, and elsewhere. The Tabo Tower in Kyŏngju's Pulguk Temple (National Treasure #20), for example, was originally surrounded by four stone lions, three of which have been lost. It is said that two of the three missing lions are in Japan, and one is in the British Museum.

CONVERSATION

1

(Professor Nam Wŏn-shik, who enjoys traveling, meets Ned Schultz, an American teacher of English, in the cafeteria.)

Wŏn-shik: How many years has it been since you came to Korea?

Ned: It has been about three years.

Wŏn-shik: (Then) You must have traveled a lot in Korea during that time.

Ned: Not really, except for a three-day trip to Kyŏngju last spring. I don't have the time or the money to travel much.

Wŏn-shik: Where did you go in Kyŏngju?

Ned: I saw all the famous places: Pulguk Temple, Sŏkkul Cave, Anapchi, the Ch'ŏnmach'ong Tomb, Ch'ŏmsŏngdae Observatory, the National Museum of Kyŏngju, and so on. I really learned a lot.

Wŏn-shik: Which did you find most impressive?

Ned: Everything.

Wŏn-shik: What did you like the most?

Ned: I especially liked the Ch'ŏnmach'ong Tomb and the National Museum. The museum houses the biggest bell in Korea and has more than 12,000 cultural treasures (both national and regular) on display.

Wŏn-shik: That's why they say that if you want to know about Silla art and culture, you have to go to the National Museum in Kyŏngju.

Ned: Yes, I had the same thought!

2

(Suhyŏn gives a presentation about Korea's cultural treasures in Korean class. She answers questions while showing slides about cultural properties.)

Michael: That's Kwanghwa Gate over there, isn't it?

Suhyŏn: That's right. It's the southern gate leading to Kyŏngbok Palace, which lies behind it. There is one gate in each direction from the palace.

Michael: I know that Kwanghwa Gate has met with many catastrophes over the years.

Suhyŏn: That's right. The original structure, built in the fourteenth century, was burned during the Japanese invasion of 1592. It was an awful sight for more than four hundred years.

Michael: So that's not the real Kwangwha Gate, I suppose.

Suhyŏn: It's real. When Taewŏngun rebuilt Kyŏngbok Palace in the nineteenth century, he also restored Kwanghwa Gate to its original appearance.

Michael: But in old pictures of Seoul, there is no gate in that spot.

Suhyŏn: Well, that's because when Japan occupied the country, they put up a building for the Japanese governor-general in the front yard of Kyŏngbok Palace, then moved Kwanghwa Gate to the north of the palace, an inconspicuous place.

Michael: How in the world. . . ?

Suhyŏn: Only in 1968 was the gate moved back to its original location.

Michael: I see. I heard that the Korean government tore down the governor-general's quarters several years ago.

Suhyŏn: Yes. Now that we've torn it down, the original view of the palace and the gate has been restored.

Michael: Lots of time passed before history came full circle.

Suhyŏn: That's right. It [the gate] sure suffered many disasters in between.

제6과 플루트 연주자

(Lesson 6: The flutist)

PRE-READING QUESTIONS

1. 하모니가 중요한 조직체(organization)에는 어떤 것이 있다고 생각합니까? 두 명씩 짝을 지어 이야기해 보세요.

2. 여러분이 좋아하는 교향곡에 대해 이야기해 보세요. 어떻게 그 교향곡을 알게 되었는지 그리고 좋아하는 이유는 무엇인지 이야기해 보세요.

GAINING FAMILIARITY

1. 오케스트라/관현악단, 콘서트/연주회, 심포니/교향곡, 심포니 오케스트라/교향악단, 베토벤 교향곡, 전원 교향곡

2. 악기 이름
   색소폰, 클라리넷, 트럼펫, 트럼본, 하모니카, 플루트, 팀파니, 피아노, 바이올린, 비올라, 첼로, 오보에, 바수운

플루트 연주자

지은이: 피천득

바통을 든 오케스트라의 지휘자는 찬란한 존재다. 토스카니니 같은 지휘자 밑에서 플루트를 분다는 것은 또 얼마나 영광스러운 일인가.[6.1] 그러나 다 지휘자가 될 수는 없는 것이다. 다 콘서트 마스터가 될 수도 없는 것이다.

오케스트라와 같이 하모니를 목적으로 하는 조직체에 있어서는 일원이 된다는 것만도 참으로 행복한 일이다. 그리고 각자의 맡은 바[6.2] 기능이 전체 효과에 종합적으로 기여된다는 것은 의의 깊은 일이다. 서로 없어서는 안 된다는[6.3] 신뢰감이 거기에 있고, 칭찬이거나 혹평이거나, '내'가 아니고 '우리'가 받는다는 것은 마음 든든한 일이다.

자기의 악기가 연주하는 부분이 얼마 아니 된다 하더라도,[6.4] 그리고 독주하는 부분이 없다 하더라도 그리 서운할 것은 없다. 남의 파트가 연주되는 동안 기다리고 있는 것도 무음의 연주를 하고 있는 것이다.

야구팀의 외야수와 같이 무대 뒤에 서 있는 콘트라베이스를 나는 좋아한다. 베토벤 교향곡 제5번 '스켈소'의 악장 속에 있는 트리오 섹션에도, 둔한 콘트라베이스를 쩔쩔매게 하는 빠른 대목이 있다. 나는 이런 유머를 즐길 수 있는 베이스 연주자를 부러워한다.

전원 교향악 제3악장에는 농부의 춤과 아마추어 오케스트라가 나오는 장면이 묘사되어 있다. 서투른 바수운이 제때 나오지를 못하고 뒤늦게야 따라 나오는 대목이 몇 번 있다. 이 우스운 음절을 연주할 때 바수운 연주자의 기쁨을 나는 안다.

팀파니스트가 되는 것도 좋다. 하이든 교향곡 94번의 서두가 연주되는 동안은 카운터 뒤에 있는 약방 주인같이 서 있다가, 청중이 경악하도록 갑자기 북을 두들기는 순간이 오면 그 얼마나 신이 나겠는가? 자기를 향하여 힘차게 손을 흔드는 지휘자를 쳐다볼 때, 그는 자못 무상의 환희를 느낄 것이다.

  어렸을 때 나는 공책에 줄치는 작은 자로 교향악단을 지휘한 일이 있었다. 그러나 그후 지휘자가 되겠다는 생각을 해 본 적은 없다. 토스카니니가 아니라도[6.5] 어떤 존경받는 지휘자 밑에서 무명의 플루트 연주자가 되고 싶은 때가 가끔 있었다.

「인연」(1996), 피천득, 서울 샘터사

대화

1

(학교 신문사 기자인 이현주가 새로운 동아리 "국악사랑"의 회장인 김상원을 인터뷰하고 있다.)

현주: 저를 포함한 요즘 세대 젊은이들은 국악을 하면 지루하다고 생각하고 있는데, 어떻게 국악에 관심을 갖게 되셨어요?

상원: 예, 저도 예전에는 막연하게 국악은 참 지루하다고만 생각했습니다. 그런데 제 친구 초대로 사물놀이 공연에 한번 가게 됐는데, 제가 알고 있는 어떤 음악보다 힘차고 스피드가 있더라고요. 전 원래 비트가 강한 음악을 좋아하거든요.

현주: 아 그러셨군요.

상원: 그후 국악에 매료되어서 콘서트에 많이 쫓아다니고 나름대로 공부도 하다 보니까[6.6] 정말 새로운 보물을 찾은 기분이었습니다. 제가 경험한 것을 여러 사람들과 나누고 싶기도 하고 또 같이 공부도 할 수 있었으면 하는[6.7] 생각이 들더군요. 그래서 국악 동아리를 시작하게 되었습니다.

현주: 네에. 다음달 초에는 교내 노천 극장에서 국악 콘서트도 계획하고 계시죠? 제목이 국악과 가요의 만남이던데 . . . 일종의 퓨전 콘서트인가요?

상원: 네, 그렇습니다. 처음 교내에서 열리는 국악 콘서트라,[6.8] 요즘 학생들에게 친근한 가요하고 접목시켜 보고 싶었어요. 그렇게 해서 국악에 대한 거리감을 없애 보려고 기획하였습니다. 물론 정통 국악도 많이 선보이지요. 현주 씨도 꼭 오십시오.

현주: 네에 그래야지요. 오늘 인터뷰에 응해 주셔서 감사합니다.

2

(김상원이 종로에 있는 외국어 학원 로비에서 우연히 현주를 만났다.)

상원: 현주 씨 아니세요? 이 학원 다녀요?

현주: 어, 상원 씨. 안녕하세요? 여기가 일본어를 잘 가르친다고
해서 한번 본격적으로 배워 보려고요.[6.9] 참, 지난번 콘서트는
너무 좋았어요. 표를 네 장이나 보내 주셔서 제 친구들하고
갔는데 다들 너무 좋았다고[6.10] 다음 공연은 언제냐고 물어
보던데요.

상원: 다음 공연은 아직 일정이 잡혀 있지 않은데, 내년 이맘때쯤
으로 생각하고 있습니다.

현주: 네에. 언제 그렇게 홍보를 하셨던지[6.11] 그 넓은 공연장이 다
찼던데요.

상원: 예. 준비 기간도 짧고 공연일이 평일이라서 걱정했는데, 생
각보다 관객이 많아서 다행이었습니다.

현주: 그렇지 않아도 연락 드리려고 했는데. 제가 마침 남북 교향
악단 합동 연주회 표가 생겼거든요.

상원: 어, 그 구하기 힘든 표를 어떻게 구하셨어요? 판매 시작 여
섯 시간만에 매진됐다고 들었는데.

현주: 저희 집이 예술의 전당 바로 앞이잖아요. 저희 언니가 소프
라노 조수미 씨랑 첼리스트 장한나 양 팬이어서, 판매 시작
하는 날 아침에 일어나자마자 예술의 전당으로 뛰어가서 샀
어요. 근데 오늘 갑자기 회사에서 중요한 회의가 있어서 못
갈 것 같다고 저한테 표를 줬거든요. 시간 있으시면 같이
가실래요?

상원: 시간이 있다마다요.[6.12] 오늘 뭔가 좋은 일이 생길 것 같았거
든요. 감사합니다.

Comprehension Questions

1. **Reading Comprehension.** "플루트 연주자"를 읽고 맞고(Ⓣ) 틀린(Ⓕ) 것을 지적하거나 질문에 대답해 보세요.

    (1) 지은이는 훌륭한 지휘자 밑에서 플루트를 부는 것이 영광스럽다고 생각한다.   Ⓣ   Ⓕ

    (2) 지은이의 꿈은 교향악단을 지휘하는 존경받는 지휘자가 되는 것이다.   Ⓣ   Ⓕ

    (3) 지은이는 오케스트라의 일원이 된다는 것이 왜 행복한 일이라고 생각합니까?

    (4) 지은이가 오케스트라에서 자기의 악기가 연주하는 부분이 얼마 되지 않는다 하더라도 서운할 것이 없다고 생각하는 이유는 무엇입니까?

    (5) 지은이는 오케스트라의 콘트라베이스와 야구의 어떤 선수와 같다고 했습니까?

    (6) 지은이는 오케스트라에서 연주하는 부분이 얼마 안 되지만 조직체의 일원이 되는 것으로 어떤 악기를 예로 들었습니까?

2. **Listening Comprehension.** 대화를 듣고 맞고(Ⓣ) 틀린(Ⓕ) 것을 지적하거나 질문에 대답해 보세요.

대화 1

    (1) 현주는 다음달에 있는 국악 콘서트에 갈 생각이다.   Ⓣ   Ⓕ

    (2) 현주는 신세대 젊은이들은 국악에 관심이 많다고 생각한다.   Ⓣ   Ⓕ

    (3) 상원이는 어떤 음악을 좋아합니까?

    (4) 상원이는 어떻게 국악에 관심을 갖게 되었습니까?

    (5) 상원이가 퓨전 콘서트를 기획한 이유는 무엇입니까?

대화 2

(1) 현주는 친구 네 명과 상원이가 계획한 콘서트에 갔다.   T F

(2) 상원이는 현주와 함께 남북 교향악단 공연에 갈 것이다.   T F

(3) 현주는 소프라노 조수미 씨와 첼리스트 장한나 양의 팬이다.   T F

(4) 현주는 어떻게 남북 교향악단 공연 표를 구했습니까?

(5) 상원이가 콘서트에 관객이 적게 올 것 같아 걱정한 이유는
    무엇입니까?

New Words

각자 *n.* each person ¶민주주의는 시민 각자의 의견을 존중하는 제도이다.
    Democracy is a system in which each citizen's opinion is highly
    valued.

거리감 *n.* sense of distance. 감 sense, feeling, sensation, impression

경악하다 *v.* to be astonished, shocked, frightened ¶그 소식을 듣고
    경악하였다. The news gave me a great shock.

경험하다 *v.* to experience, go through, undergo

공연 *n.* a public performance ¶공연일 performance day

공연장 *n.* place where a performance is presented

관객 *n.* audience, onlookers, spectators

관심을 갖다 *v.* to be interested in; to be concerned about. 관심 interest,
    concern

교내 *n.* (inside) the school; (on) the campus; intramural

교향곡 *n.* symphony ¶베토벤은 9개의 교향곡을 남겼다. Beethoven left nine
    symphonies.

교향악단 *n.* symphony orchestra

구하다 *v.* to get, buy, purchase; to seek ¶사전을 어디서 구하셨어요? Where
    did you get the dictionary?

그리 *adv.* (not) so; (not) to that extent (= 그다지) ¶그리 크지 않다. It is
    not so big.

기간 *n.* period, duration ¶준비 기간 preparatory period

기능 *n.* function ¶기능이 우수하다 to be highly skilled (in)

기여되다 *v.* to be contributed. 기여 contribution; service (= 공헌)

기자 *n.* journalist, newspaper reporter

기획하다 *v.* to (make a) plan, work out a scheme. 기획 planning, plan, project

나누다 *v.* to share (with), distribute ¶기쁨을 나누다 to share one's joy

나름대로 *adv.* in one's own way; after one's kind

남북 교향악단 *n.* the South-North Symphony Orchestra. 교향악 symphony; 단 group

노천 극장 *n.* open-air theater. 노천 the open air, the open

농부 *n.* farmer

다행이다 *adj.* to be lucky, fortunate, blessed ¶다행히도 그를 만났다. I was lucky enough to meet him.

대목 *n.* most important occasion, vital moment, portion, part, passage ¶이제부터가 가장 어려운 대목이다. Now we have come to the most difficult part of the work.

독주하다 *v.* to play solo, play alone

두들기다 *v.* to beat, hit, knock

둔하다 *adj.* to be slow, dull, slow-witted, thick ¶트럼본은 둔한 소리를 낸다. Among musical instruments, the trombone has a thick, dull sound.

뒤늦게 *adv.* belatedly

마음 든든하다 *adj.* to feel confident; to feel safe. 든든하다 to be strong, firm, safe ¶네가 옆에 있어 주면 마음이 든든하다. Your presence will inspire me with confidence.

막연하다 *adj.* to be vague, obscure, dim, hazy ¶나는 막연하게 그 일을 기억한다. I have a faint remembrance of it.

매료되다 *v.* to be fascinated, charmed, entranced, spellbound

매진되다 *v.* to be sold out. 매진 selling out, sellout

목적 *n.* aim, purpose, goal

묘사하다 *v.* to depict, delineate, portray, describe

무대 *n.* stage ¶무대에 서다 to appear on the stage ¶무대를 장치하다 to set the stage

무명 *n.* namelessness, anonymity. 무명의 nameless

무상 *n.* supreme, greatest, highest ¶무상의 영광 the highest honor ¶무상의 행복 consummate happiness; ultimate joy

무음 *n.* soundlessness, muteness ¶대부분의 텔레비전에는 무음(mute) 기능이 있다. Most television sets have a mute function.

바라다 *v.* to desire, want, wish, seek. 바람 a desire; a wish ¶행복을 바라다 to wish for happiness

바수운 *n.* bassoon ¶바수운 연주자 bassoonist

바통 *n.* baton

보물 *n.* treasure, highly prized article

본격적으로 *adv.* in earnest, on a full scale. 본격적 full-scale, genuine, earnest, serious ¶비가 본격적으로 내리고 있다. It is raining in earnest.

부러워하다 *v.* to envy, be envious

부분 *n.* part, section ¶전체는 부분의 합이다. The whole is the sum of its parts.

북 *n.* drum ¶북을 치다 to beat a drum ¶북 치는 사람 a drummer

비트 *n.* beat

사물놀이 *n. samulnori,* traditional Korean music using four percussion instruments

서두 *n.* beginning, introduction, prologue ¶글의 서두에서는 독자의 흥미를 유도한다. In the introduction, writers try to engage readers' interest.

서운하다 *adj.* to feel regretful, be sorry ¶이별이 서운하다 to be sorry to part from a person

서투르다 *adj.* to be poor (at) ¶서투른 영어로 말하다 to speak in poor English

선보이다 *v.* to introduce, present (for the first time). 선 interview between the prospective bride and groom; 선(을) 보다 to see each other with a view to marriage

세대 *n.* generation

신뢰감 *n.* sense of trust; trust. 신뢰 confidence, trust, faith; 감 feeling ¶이제 남북한간에는 신뢰감이 조성되고 있다. We can sense trust between South and North Korea.

신문사 *n.* newspaper publishing company; newspaper office

아니 *adv.* not (= 안) (아니 is used only in writing)

악기 *n.* musical instrument ¶사물놀이에 쓰이는 악기로는 꽹과리, 징, 장구, 북이 있다. *Samulnori* consists of four musical instruments: the small gong (*kkwaenggwari*), the gong (*ching*), the hourglass drum (*changgu*), and the drum (*puk*).

악장 *n.* movement (of music); chapter ¶베토벤의 소나타 '월광'은 1악장이 아름답다. The first movement of Beethoven's "Moonlight" sonata is beautiful.

야구 *n.* baseball

연락드리다 *v.* (honorific of 연락하다) to contact, inform, notify, communicate to (a senior person)

연주하다 *v.* to play, perform ¶밴드는 신나는 곡을 연주하기 시작했다. The band struck up a sprightly air.

연합회 *n.* united association, union

영광스럽다 *adj.* to feel honored; to be glorious

예술의 전당 *n.* Yesul-ŭi Chŏndang (an art hall in Seoul). 전당 palace; temple; hall ¶학문의 전당 sanctuary of learning

예전 *n.* former days, former times

외야수 *n.* outfielder. 외야 the outfield; ~수 player, person

음절 *n.* (musical) measure, bar; syllable

응하다 *v.* to comply with, accept, accede to

의의 깊다 *adj.* to be meaningful, significant. 의의 meaning; significance (= 의미) ¶남북한 정상의 만남은 역사적으로 의의 깊은 일이었다. The summit talk between the two Korean leaders was very significant.

이맘때 *n.* about this time; this time of day (night, year) ¶내일 저녁 이맘때 또 오겠습니다. Tomorrow evening at this time I'll come again.

일원 *n.* member ¶일개미는 전체 개미 사회의 한 일원이다. A worker ant is a member of the entire ant society.

일정 *n.* agenda; schedule

자 *n.* ruler; rule; measure

자못 *adv.* very, very much, exceedingly, greatly, not a little ¶그 일은 자못 어렵다. It is an exceedingly hard job.

잡히다 *v.* to be fixed, determined; to be caught. 잡다 to catch, get, capture; to fix, decide ¶날짜를 잡다 to fix the date (for) ¶일자리를 잡다 to get a job

장면 *n.* scene; situation

전원 *n.* the country; fields and gardens; rural districts ¶전원 교향악 the *Pastoral Symphony;* a pastorale

접목 *n.* graft (splicing two plants together). 접목하다, 접목시키다 to graft together, graft onto

정통 *n.* orthodoxy; legitimacy. 정통(의) legitimate, orthodox ¶정통극 legitimate drama ¶정통적인 방법 the orthodox approach

제때 *n, adv.* (at) the proper time, (at) the right time, (at) the right moment ¶김장은 제때에 담가야한다. You have to make *kimchi* at the right season.

조직체 *n.* organization; structure

존재 *n.* presence; existence; figure ¶작가 박경리는 한국 문학계에서 귀중한 존재이다. The writer Pak Kyŏngni is a very important figure in the Korean literary world.

종합적으로 *adv.* comprehensive; all-embracing, from all sides; synthetically. 종합적 synthetic, composite, comprehensive ¶중요한 결정을 내릴 때는 종합적으로 판단하라. Try to give (the matter) comprehensive consideration before making an important decision.

줄치다 *v.* to draw a line; to rule paper

즐기다 *v.* to enjoy, enjoy oneself, have a good time (of it) ¶독서를 즐기다 to enjoy oneself by reading

지루하다 *adj.* to be boring, tedious, tiresome, wearisome

지은이 *n.* writer, author

지휘자 *n.* conductor (music) ¶그 지휘자는 음악회에서 바통을 휘둘렀다. The conductor wielded the baton at the concert.

지휘하다 *v.* to conduct, direct, lead. 지휘 command, supervision

쩔쩔매다 *v.* to be confused, bewildered, perplexed, at a loss ¶쩔쩔매게 하다 to make (a person) confused, perplexed ¶그는 질문을 받고 쩔쩔맸다. He was very much confused by the question.

차다 *v.* to become full (of), be filled up (with), be jammed ¶방에 사람이 가득 차 있다. The room is jammed with people.

찬란하다 *adj.* to be brilliant; to be magnificent ¶세종대왕은 한글 창제라는 찬란한 업적을 남겼다. King Sejong left the magnificent legacy of (having created) the Korean alphabet, Han'gŭl.

청중 *n.* audience

친근하다 *adj.* to be close, intimate, familiar

칭찬 *n.* praise; compliment ¶아이들은 칭찬으로 자란다. Praise raises children.

콘트라베이스 *n.* contrabass. 베이스 연주자 contrabassist

팀파니 *n.* timpani. 팀파니스트 timpanist

파트 *n.* part

판매 *n.* sale, selling, marketing ¶판매되고 있다 to be on sale, be on the market

팬 *n.* fan, fanatic, enthusiastic admirer

평일 *n.* weekday; ordinary days

포함하다 *v.* to include; to contain

퓨전 콘서트 *n.* fusion concert

학원 *n.* (educational) institute; academy; school; cram school ¶자동차 학원 driver's school

합동 연주회 *n.* joint concert. 합동 combination, union

혹평 *n.* harsh criticism

홍보 *n.* publicity; advertisement; public information

환희 *n.* joy; delight; ecstasy ¶삶의 환희를 맛보려면 노동하라. Work to enjoy the ecstasy of life.

회장 *n.* president (of a society); chairman; grandee

효과 *n.* effect; effectiveness; efficiency ¶전체 효과 overall effect

힘차다 *adj.* to be powerful, energetic ¶힘찬 연설 a powerful speech

Useful Expressions

6.1 (그) 얼마나 . . . ~가/까 how/what. . . !

This pattern, in which the (optional) pre-noun 그 'that,' the adverb 얼마나 'how, how much, to what extent, what,' and the interrogative suffix ~가 or ~까 occur, is used for exclamations, as in 얼마나 영광스러운 일인가 'How honorable it is!,' 얼마나 괴로웠겠는가 'What he has suffered!' More examples:

그 사람들은 **얼마나** 기쁠**까**.	How glad they must be!
그 **얼마나** 신이 나겠는**가**.	How exciting it will be!
얼마나 마음 아프십니**까?**	I can well imagine your grief.

6.2 바 what (one does)

Although its usual meaning is 'what (one does)', the noun 바 has many additional meanings such as 'thing, means, extent, and (then).' It cannot stand alone, but must be preceded by a relative clause, as in 맡은 바 'what one takes charge of,' 맡은 바(의) 기능 '(their) functions as assigned to (them),' 내가 아는 바로는 'from what I know,' and 위에서 말한 바와 같이 'as mentioned above.' It can often be replaced by 것. More examples:

그것은 내가 바라던 **바다**.	That's just what I (have) wished for.
어찌할 **바를** 모르겠어.	I am at a loss [as to] what to do.

적어도 맡은 **바** 일은 끝까지 책임을 져야 한다.

We should at least take responsibility for our allotted work.

3월 5일에 서울 교향악단의 연주회가 있었던 **바** 대성공이었다.

On March 5, [a performance by] the Seoul Symphony Orchestra was held with great success.

6.3 없어서는 안 되다 to be indispensable

The literal meaning of this construction is 'it won't do if (one) does not exist.' For example, 서로 없어서는 안 된다는 신뢰감 literally means 'the sense of trust that each member is indispensable.'

6.4 ~다/라 하더라도 even if (it is the case that); granting that

The literal meaning of this form is 'even if one says that,' and this meaning holds in certain contexts. Frequently, however, the meaning becomes 'even if it is the case that' or simply 'even if' or 'granting that.' The extended meanings of the construction are very similar to the meaning and function of ~더라도 'even if,' except that ~다/라 하더라도 is slightly more emphatic than ~더라도.

독주하는 부분이 **없다 하더라도**	even if (it is the case) that you don't take any solo part
독주하는 부분이 **없더라도**	even if you don't take any solo part
그것이 사실이(**라 하)더라도**	granting that it is true
무엇을 먹(**는다 하)더라도**	no matter what one eats

6.5 (이)라도; 아니라도 even if/though (it is); even if/though (it is) not; any ~

This concessive form, which contains the copula (이)다/아니다, occurs only after a nominal construction, as in 지금이라도 'even now' and 토스카니니가 아니라도 'if not T; even if it is not T.' When the nominal before (이)라도 is a question or indefinite word such as 누구, 무엇, 언제, 어디, 아무, 아무것, 아무때, 아무데, 어느 분, 어느 곳, 어떤 사람, or 어떤 집, (이)라도 can best be translated as 'any ~' or '~ever,' as in 누구라도 'anybody; whoever (he/she is),' 무엇이라도 'anything, whatever (it is),' 언제라도 'anytime, whenever (it is),' and so on. More examples:

어린애**라도** 그건 알아요.   (Even) a mere child knows it.

아무것**이라도** 좋아하는 것을 드세요.   Please help yourself to anything you like.

동생은 그 돈을 전부는 **아니라도** 반 이상이나 써 버렸다.

My younger brother has spent more than half the money, (even) if not all.

6.6   ~다(가) 보니(까) while one kept (doing), (as a result) . . .

The extended meaning of this pattern has developed from its literal meaning, which is 'when (one) looked while doing something.' Thus, 날마다 놀다 보니까 바보가 되어 버렸어요 'As a result of playing around every day, I ended up being a fool' and 공부를 하다 보니까 새로운 보물을 찾은 기분이었어요 means 'While I kept studying about it, I felt as if I were finding a treasure.'

6.7   ~었으면/았으면 하다 to wish to; to wish that it would

This pattern is a short form of ~었으면/았으면 좋겠다고 생각하다 'to think it would be good if it would.' Thus, 비가 왔으면 해요 'I wish it would rain' is equivalent to 비가 왔으면 좋겠다고 생각해요. Similarly, 형을 만났으면 했는데 여기서 잘 만났군요 'I wished to meet you, so it's nice to see you here' is equivalent to 형을 만났으면 좋겠다고 생각했는데 여기서 잘 만났군요. Notice that the past-tense form of ~었으면/았으면 indicates a strong wish on the part of the speaker.

6.8   (이)라(서) as, because

This pattern is equivalent to (이)기 때문에, as in 처음 콘서트라(서) 'as/because it is the first concert' (= 처음 콘서트이기 때문에); 학생이라(서) 'as/because (s/he) is a student' (= 학생이기 때문에); 바다라(서) 'as/because (it) is a sea' (= 바다이기 때문에). 이라(서) occurs after a consonant, 라(서) after a vowel. 서 can be omitted with no change in meaning.

일요일**이라(서)** 차가 막히지 않아요.

As it is Sunday, the traffic is smooth.

그 애는 어린아이**라(서)** 부모의 마음을 이해하지 못해요.

Because he is a child, he is unable to understand his parents.

공연일이 평일**이라(서)** 걱정했어요.

I was worried because the day of the performance was a weekday.

6.9 ~(으)려고요 because one intends to

The suffix ~(으)려고 indicates the subject's intention ('intending to; in order to'), as in 먹으려고 산다 'We live (in order) to eat.' Its colloquial form is ~(으)ㄹ려고, as in 먹을려고 산다. When it acts as a sentence ending, it gives the reason or purpose for the action indicated or implied in the immediately preceding clause or sentence.

오늘 학교에 안 갈래요. 그 대신 집에서 공부**하려고요** (or 공부할려고요).
I am not going to go to school. (Because) I intend to study at home instead.

A: 지금 부엌에서 뭐하고 계세요?
   What are you doing in the kitchen?
B: 배가 고파서 밥 좀 먹**으려고요** (or 먹을려고요).
   I am hungry and I want to have something to eat. (That's why.)

6.10 ~다고/라고 (saying) that

~다고/라고 consists of the statement ending ~다 or ~라 (following the copula) and the quotative particle 고. The indirect quotation is usually followed by a verb of saying, such as 말하다 or 하다 'to say,' as in ~다고/라고 (말)해요 'say that.' In conversation, the verb of saying is frequently omitted, but its meaning is understood because of the presence of the particle 고. Thus, the (말)하면서 part of ~다고/라고 (말)하면서 'while saying that' is often left out. For example, in 콘서트가 좋았다고 다음 공연은 언제냐고 물었어요 'Saying that the concert was good, they asked me when the next one would be performed,' 좋았다고 is equivalent to 좋았다고 하면서 'saying that it was good.' Similarly, in 자기는 못 갈 것 같다고 저한테 표를 줬어요 'Saying that she would be unable to go, she let me have the tickets,' 못 갈 것 같다고 is equivalent to 못 갈 것 같다고 말하면서. More examples:

소매치기는 경찰한테 잘못했**다고** (하면서) 싹싹 빌었어요.
With his hands pressed together, the pickpocket begged the policeman's pardon.
학생들은 내일부터 방학이**라고** (하면서) 모두 좋아해요.
The students are all happy (saying) that the vacation starts tomorrow.
용호는 미아를 만나야 한**다고** (하면서) 학교로 갔어요.
Yongho headed toward the school, saying that he should see Mia.

곧 시험이**라고** 공부해야 한대요

Saying that he had an exam soon, he said he had to study.

6.11 ～는지/(으)ㄴ지 I don't know [question word]. . . , but; probably because

One of the uses of the noun 지 'whether' when preceded by a modifier suffix is to indicate a probable reason. This use of ～는지/(으)ㄴ지 is assumed to have developed from ～는지/(으)ㄴ지 몰라도 'although I am not sure whether' with the omission of 몰라도 'although I am not sure.' This deleted part and 'whether' have come to mean 'I don't know [whether, when, who, what, where, etc.]. . . , but' when a question word is involved, and 'probably because' when no question word is involved.

아무도 없는**지** 집안이 조용하다.

Probably because nobody is in, (the inside of) the house is quiet.

언제 그렇게 홍보를 하셨던**지** 공연장이 다 찼대요.

(I am not sure when) you publicized it so much that the concert hall was completely filled.

일요일이라 그런**지** 차가 안 막히네요.

The traffic is probably OK because it is Sunday.

미아가 마음이 변했는**지** 나를 피하기 시작했어요.

Mia probably began to avoid me because she doesn't like me (*lit.,* she has changed her mind).

6.12 ～다마다요 of course, certainly, indeed, to be sure

～다마다요 is equivalent to and interchangeable with ～고말고요 'of course, certainly, to be sure.' The stem form of a verb or adjective occurs before both ～다마다요 and ～고말고요. The pattern ～다마다요 contains the statement ending ～다 and the obsolete verb 마다 'to refuse, decline, dislike' (as in 마다할 수 없다 'to be unable to refuse it'). Since the ending ～다 implies acceptance and ～마다 implies refusal, the underlying idea in the pattern is 'How can I say yes or no? Of course, yes.' For example, 시간이 있다마다요 means 'Of course I have time.'

A: 망고 좋아하세요?　　　　　　Do you like mangos?
B: 좋아하**다마다요**.　　　　　　Sure I do.

A: 덕수궁 가 보셨어요?   Have you been to Tŏksugung?
B: 가 **보다마다요**. 다섯 번이나   Of course, I have visited it five times,
   가 **봤는걸요**.   you know.

Exercises

1. 관련된 단어들끼리 연결하여 문장을 만들어 보세요.

   (1) 신   •   • 되다   _____

   (2) 의의   •   • 나다   _____

   (3) 일원   •   • 깊다   _____

   (4) 북   •   • 느끼다   _____

   (5) 환희   •   • 두들기다   _____

   (6) 인터뷰   •   • 응하다   _____

   (7) 선   •   • 보이다   _____

2. 아래의 설명과 맞는 단어나 표현을 본문에서 찾아 쓰세요.

   (1) 교향악을 연주하는 대규모의 관현악단: _____

   (2) 한 단체를 이루는 한 사람: _____

   (3) 음악을 연주할 때 쓰이는 기구: _____

   (4) 일이 바라는 대로 되지 않아서 속상하다: _____

   (5) 남의 좋은 것을 보고 남과 같이 되고 싶어 하다: _____

   (6) 같은 상태가 계속되어 싫증나고 따분하다: _____

   (7) 휴일이 아닌 보통의 날: _____

3. 보기에서 적당한 말을 골라 빈칸을 채우세요.

   > 보기: 참으로, 혹평, 기여된다, 서운할 것은 없다, 힘차게,
   >   자못, 가끔

(1) 오케스트라와 같이 하모니를 목적으로 하는 조직체에 있어서는 일원이 된다는 것만도 _____ 행복한 일이다.

(2) 칭찬이거나 _____이거나, '내'가 아니고 '우리'가 받는다는 것은 마음 든든한 일이다.

(3) 각자의 맡은바 기능이 전체 효과에 종합적으로 _____는 것은 의의 깊은 일이다.

(4) 그리고 독주하는 부분이 없다 하더라도 그리 _____.

(5) 자기를 향하여 _____ 손을 흔드는 지휘자를 쳐다볼 때, 그는 _____ 무상의 환희를 느낄 것이다.

(6) 토스카니니가 아니더라도 어떤 존경받는 지휘자 밑에서 무명의 플루트 연주자가 되고 싶은 때가 _____ 있었다.

4. 밑줄 친 말과 가장 비슷한 단어나 표현을 보기에서 고르세요.

(1) 바통을 든 오케스트라의 지휘자는 찬란한 존재다.

    a. 매우 힘있고 똑똑한   b. 매우 존경스럽고 자랑스러운
    c. 매우 부드럽고 친근한   d. 매우 아름답고 훌륭한

(2) 그러나 다 지휘자가 될 수는 없는 것이다.

    a. 끝까지   b. 모두
    c. 거의   d. 아주

(3) 각자의 맡은 바 기능이 전체 효과에 종합적으로 기여된다는 것은 의의 깊은 일이다.

    a. 도움이 된다   b. 노력한다
    c. 기억된다   d. 계획된다

(4) 국악에 매료되어서 콘서트에 많이 쫓아다니고 나름대로 공부도 하다 보니까 정말 새로운 보물을 찾은 기분이었습니다.

    a. 매달려서   b. 마음이 사로잡혀서
    c. 매어   d. 마음이 흔들려서

(5) 판매 시작 여섯 시간만에 매진됐다고 들었는데.

    a. 매매됐다고   b. 매매된다고
    c. 전부 팔렸다고   d. 전부 판다고

5. 보기와 같이 주어진 말이 들어가는 단어를 3개 이상 써 보세요.

> 보기: 친 (親, friendly, parents): 친지, 양친, 절친, 친척,
> 친구, 친절, 친하다

(1) 자 (者, person): _____

(2) 청 (聽, listen): _____

(3) 대 (代, substitute, generation): _____

(4) 평 (平, ordinary, common, peaceful): _____

6. "(그) 얼마나 . . . ~가/까"를 사용하여 보기처럼 문장을 만드세요.

> 보기: A: 마크 씨가 다음 달에 결혼한대요.
> B: 얼마나 좋을까.

(1) A: 미아가 이번에 대학 수학 능력 시험(SAT)에서 전국 일등을 했대요.
   B: (기쁘다) _____

(2) A: 수잔 씨가 복권에 당첨되어 100만 불을 받는대요.
   B: (신이 나다/기쁘다) _____

(3) A: 민지 씨 어머님이 어제 돌아가셨대요.
   B: (마음 아프다) 민지 씨가 _____

7. "없어서는 안 되다"를 사용하여 문장을 만드세요.

> 보기: 가족들 간에는 사랑이 없어서는 안 된다.

(1) _____

(2) _____

(3) _____

8. "~다/라 하더라도"를 사용하여 대화를 완성하세요.

  (1) A: 음식이 맛있어서 저녁을 너무 많이 먹었어요.

      B: _____ 적당히 드셔야지요.

  (2) A: 머리가 좋은 사람은 시험 공부 안 해도 되겠지.

      B: 머리가 _____ 시험 공부는 해야지요.

  (3) A: 두 사람이 서로 때리면서 싸웠어요.

      B: (화가 나다) _____ 남을 때려서는 안 되지요.

9. "~다(가) 보니(까)"를 사용하여 보기처럼 문장을 만드세요.

> 보기: A: 몇 시예요?
>
>   B: 7시예요. 놀다 보니까 시간이 금방 갔어요.

  (1) A: 더 드세요. (먹다)

      B: 그만 먹을 거예요. _____ 배가 불러요.

  (2) A: 어디 나가세요? (집에만 있다)

      B: _____ 갑갑해서 바람 쐬러 나가요.

  (3) A: 왜 이렇게 늦었어요? (이야기하다)

      B: _____ 시간 가는 줄 몰랐어요.

10. "~(으)려고"를 사용하여 다음 대화를 완성하세요.

> 보기: A: 부엌에서 뭐 하고 계세요?
>
>   B: (밥 좀 먹다) 밥 좀 먹으려고.

  (1) A: 아니 웬 가래떡(bar rice cake)을 그렇게 많이 샀어?

      B: (떡볶이를 만들다) _____

  (2) A: 동전을 왜 그렇게 많이 바꾸니?

      B: (전자 오락을 하다) _____

  (3) A: 오늘은 왜 이렇게 일찍 퇴근하세요?

      B: _____

11. 왼편 말에 "~라(서)"를 붙여서, 적절한 오른편 말과 연결시키세요.

(1) 노인이다.   입맛도 없고 기운도 없어요.

(2) 봄이다.   모두가 여행을 떠났어요.

(3) 친한 친구가 아니다.   버스에서 자리를 양보했어요.

(4) 여름방학이다.   그 일을 부탁하기 어려워요.

12. 보기처럼 대화를 완성하세요.

> 보기: 마크: 용호는 왜 술을 안 마셔요? (배가 아프다)
> 민지: 배가 아프다고 술을 안 마셔.

(1) 마크: 용호가 왜 저렇게 울고 있어요? (고양이가 죽었다)
    민지: _____

(2) 마크: 미아는 왜 안 왔어요? (시험 중이다)
    민지: _____

(3) 마크: 민지 씨 동생은 공부하지 않고 왜 저렇게 놀기만 하지요? (대학에
    안 가겠다)
    민지: _____

(4) 마크: 저 애는 왜 저렇게 좋아서 야단이지? (취직 시험에 합격했다)
    민지: _____

13. "~는지/(으)ㄴ지"를 사용하여 보기처럼 대화를 완성해 보세요.

> 보기: A: 차가 안 막히네요.
> B: 네. 일요일이라서 그런지 하나도 안 막혀요.

(1) A: 졸려요? (잠을 못 자다)
    B: 네. _____ 자꾸 하품이 나고 졸려요.

(2) A: 마크가 연락했어요? (바쁘다)
    B: _____ 몇 달째 연락이 없어요.

(3) A: 안색이 창백(pale)해요. 어디 아파요?

　　B: _____

14. "~다마다요"를 사용하여 보기처럼 문장을 만드세요.

> 보기: A: 그 영화 좋아하세요?
> 　　　B: 좋아하다마다요. 네 번이나 봤는데요.

(1) A: 저분 누구신지 아세요?

　　B: _____

(2) A: 민지 만나 봤니?

　　B: _____

(3) A: 오늘 시험 잘 봤니?

　　B: _____

15. Partner와 함께 대화 1과 2를 자연스럽게 따라 해 보세요.

Discussion and Composition

1. "나의 꿈"이라는 제목으로 한 페이지의 글을 지어 보세요.

2. (인터뷰하기) 선생님께서 나누어 주신 반 친구들의 글 "나의 꿈"을 읽으세요. 친구들의 글을 읽고, 인터뷰를 할 때 무슨 질문을 할 것인지 써 보세요. 여러분이 신문 기자라고 생각하고 친구들을 인터뷰해 보세요.

Further Reading

아주 특별한 만남 . . . 겨울
3인 3색의 매혹적인 무대

아주 특별한 아티스트들과의 만남
국내 최고의 첼리스트 양성원, 무대 위의 카리스마 소프라노
박미혜, 그리고 영원한 대중 음악계의 가수 이문세. 이 세
명의 아티스트가 '아주 특별한 만남-겨울'을 위해 모였다.
좀처럼 한 무대에서 만나질 것 같지 않은 . . .

아주 특별한 음악으로 분위기 연출
세 명의 아티스트가 클래식 음악을 최고의 오케스트라 서울
시향(지휘 김봉)과 협연한다.

Program

1부

서울시향	재즈 모음곡 중 왈츠2번/쇼스타코비치
박미혜 협연	모차르트 콘서트 아리아/모차르트
양성원 협연	헝가리안 랩소디/포퍼

2부

양성원과 8대의 첼로와 박미혜	브라질풍의 아리아/빌라 로보스
양성원 박미혜 듀오	카니발의 아침/안토니오 카를로스 조빔
서울시향	Cheek to Cheek/어빙 벌린
박미혜 협연	보헤미안 걸 중 I Dreamed I Dwelt in Marble Halls
양성원 협연	Tango Apasionado/아스토르 피아졸라
이문세 협연	광화문 연가/이영훈
박미혜 이문세 듀오 협연	When I Fall in Love

일 시:　2000년 12월 12일(화) 오후 7시 30분
장 소:　예술의 전당 콘서트홀
출 연:　양성원(첼로) 박미혜(소프라노) 이문세(보컬)
주 최:　예술의 전당, 월간 「객석」
공연문의: 월간 「객석」 공연부 3673-2162 오영민, 이은주
입장권:　커플석 5만원, R석 4만원, S석 3만원, A석 2만원, B석 1만원
티켓예매: 티켓 링크 1588-7890

(월간 객석 2000년 11월)

공연부 department of public performance (~부 department, division); 대 (classifier of car, cart, plane; 대중 음악계 popular music circles(~계 community, circle, world); 매혹적인 charming, bewitching; 모음곡 medley; 분위기 atmosphere; 삽입되다 to be inserted; 서울 시립 교향악단 Seoul City Symphony Orchestra (*cf.* 시립[의] municipal); 서울시향 contracted form of 서울 시립 교향악단; ~석 seat; 연가 love song, poem; 연출 production, presentation; 영원하다 to be eternal; 예매 advance purchase; 월간 객석 monthly magazine *Wŏlgan Kaeksŏk* (*lit.,* "Monthly Guest Seats"); 일시 day (date) and time; 입장권 admission (ticket); 좀처럼 rarely; 주최 sponsorship, promotion; 지휘 conducting; 출연 appearance on stage; 커플석 seat for a couple (*cf.* ~석 seat, place); 풍 mode, style; 협연하다 to perform music or give a recital with other musicians

1. 이 공연의 제목이 "아주 특별한 만남"인 이유는 무엇일까요?

2. 당신은 이 공연을 보러 가고 싶습니다. 그런데 공연이 있는 날 친구의 집들이 (housewarming)가 있습니다. 마침 친구 집이 예술의 전당 근처라서 공연이 늦게 끝나지 않으면 공연을 보고 친구 집에 갈 수 있을 것 같습니다. 공연이 끝나는 시간을 알아보기 위해서는 어디에 연락을 해야 할까요?

3. 당신의 선생님인 김지연 선생님에게서 온 다음의 이메일을 읽고 답장하는 이메일을 써 보세요.

수신인: ○○○○○
발신인: 김지연
주제:　콘서트 정보

지난번에 통화할 때 이야기한 "아주 특별한 만남 콘서트"에 관해 물어 보려고 메일을 보내. 콘서트 광고지가 있다고 생각했는데 아무리 찾아도 찾을 수가 없어. 아마 어머니께서 청소하시면서 버리신 모양이야. 미안하지만 정확한 콘서트 정보 좀 알려 줄래? 콘서트가 언제 어디서 열리는지, 어떤 음악가가 나오는지, 입장권 가격은 얼마인지, 그리고 티켓은 어디에서 살 수 있는지 좀 알려줘. 고마워.

김지연

LESSON 6. THE FLUTIST

The Flutist
P'i Ch'ŏn-dŭk

An orchestral conductor holding his baton is a dazzling figure. What an honor it would be to play the flute under a conductor like Toscanini! But we cannot all become conductors or concert masters.

It is truly a blessing to be a member of an organization whose purpose is to create harmony. Each person in the group contributes to the entire effort by carrying out her own assigned function, and this fact carries with it a deep significance. (There develops a trust that) Each member is indispensable. Whether praised or criticized, the object is not "me," but "us"; and knowing this gives the members confidence.

It does not matter how small the part played on one's own musical instrument, or if one does not take any solo part. Waiting while others play their parts is itself a kind of mental performance.

I like the contrabass. He lurks behind the scene much like an outfielder in baseball. In the trio section in the scherzo from Beethoven's Fifth Symphony, there is a rapid passage where the dull-sounding contrabass is made to play a flurry of notes. I envy the contrabassist who is able to enjoy such humor.

The third movement of the Pastoral Symphony describes a scene in which farmers are dancing and an amateur orchestra is playing. There are several passages in which the clumsy bassoonist fails to make his entrances on time, but follows along behind the beat. I am sure the bassoonist is happy when playing these humorous bars of music.

It is also nice to be a timpanist. When playing the introduction to Haydn's 94th Symphony, the timpanist stands like a pharmacist behind a counter. Then how exciting when the moment comes to surprise the audience by striking the drum! When he looks up at the conductor waving his baton furiously toward him, he must feel a high degree of pleasure.

When I was young, I once conducted an orchestra with a small ruler used for drawing lines in my notebook. Though I never thought I would become a conductor, I sometimes thought I would like to be an anonymous flutist under a respected conductor—even if not Toscanini.

Inyŏn, P'i Ch'ŏn-dŭk, Seoul: Saemt'ŏsa, 1996

CONVERSATION

1

(Yi Hyŏn-ju, a reporter for the school newspaper, is interviewing Kim Sang-wŏn, president of a newly formed club for the appreciation of Korean classical music.)

Hyŏn-ju: Young people of this generation, including myself, find Korean classical music boring. How did you become interested in it?

Sang-wŏn: I used to have only vague impressions about Korean classical music. I thought it must be boring. Then a friend invited me to a *samulnori* (traditional percussion quartet) performance. It was stronger and faster than any music I knew. I have always liked music with a strong beat.

Hyŏn-ju: Oh, I see.

Sang-wŏn: Afterward I really got into Korean classical music and attended lots of concerts. When I looked more deeply into the subject I felt as if I had uncovered a new treasure. Because I wanted to share my experience with others, and learn more about Korean classical music with them, I started the Korean classical music club.

Hyŏn-ju: Hmmm. Early next month you are planning an outdoor concert on campus, isn't that right? The theme is the meeting of classical and popular music . . . is it a kind of fusion concert?

Sang-wŏn: That's right. Because it's our first concert on campus, we've planned to try grafting Korean classical music onto the songs students are familiar with nowadays, to make them comfortable with Korean classical music. Of course we'll introduce them to lots of Korean classical music. Be sure to come!

Hyŏn-ju: Yes, I will. Thanks for participating in the interview today.

2

(Kim Sang-wŏn encounters Hyŏn-ju in the lobby of the foreign language *hagwŏn* in Chongno.)

Sang-wŏn: Aren't you Hyŏn-ju? Do you study in this *hagwŏn*?

Hyŏn-ju: Hi, Sang-wŏn! They say they teach Japanese well here. I've decided to try learning it in earnest for once. By the way, that concert was really great. Thanks for sending me those four tickets. I went with friends, and everyone loved it! They were asking when the next concert would be.

Sang-wŏn: The next performance date hasn't been set yet. It will probably be about this time next year.

Hyŏn-ju: Hmmm. How were you able to get such a big crowd? You must have really advertised the concert well!

Sang-wŏn: Well, we were worried because we didn't have much preparation time, and the concert was on a weekday. The surprisingly large turnout made us very happy.

Hyŏn-ju: By the way, I was trying to contact you. I have tickets to the South-North Joint Orchestral Concert.

Sang-wŏn: Gee, how did you get those? I heard they sold out six hours after they went on sale.

Hyŏn-ju: Our house is in front of the *Yesul-ŭi Chŏndang* Art Hall. My sister is a fan of the soprano Cho Su-mi and the cellist Chang Hanna. The day the tickets went on sale, she rushed over first thing in the morning and bought them. But she has an important meeting today, and can't go [to the concert], so she let me have them. How about going with me, if you have the time?

Sang-wŏn: Of course I have the time! It looks like my lucky day today. Thank you!

제7과   철학하는 바보

(Lesson 7: A philosophizing fool)

PRE-READING QUESTIONS

1. (그룹으로 이야기하기) 여러분이 읽은 책 중 가장 교훈적인 책에 대해 이야기해 보세요.

2. 여러분은 어디에서 책을 구입합니까? 서점에서 삽니까? 아니면 인터넷을 통해서 삽니까? 그 장점과 단점을 이야기해 보세요.

3. 여러분의 친구한테 책을 선물한다면 어떤 책을 선물하고 싶습니까? 그 이유는 무엇입니까?

GAINING FAMILIARITY

1. 서점에서 책 찾기
   베스트셀러, 새로 나온 책, 추천 도서, 한국 도서, 서양 도서

2. 분야별 도서
   경제/경영, 공학, 관광, 교육학, 문학, 미술/사진, 사전, 수험서, 순수 과학, 스포츠, 어린이, 어학, 여성, 역사/전기, 연극/영화, 음악, 의학, 잡지, 종교, 중고 학습서, 철학, 컴퓨터

거위와 보석

옛날 한양 근처 어느 고을에 한 부자가 있었는데, 어느 날 해질 무렵 나그네 한 사람이 들렀다. 주인은 나그네를 사랑채에 머물게 하고 하인을 시켜 저녁을 대접했다.

나그네는 저녁을 먹은 뒤 무심코 안마당을 내다보니 마당 한쪽에서 무언가 반짝 빛나는 것이 눈에 띄었다. 나그네가 좀더 자세히 보려고 안마당 쪽으로 몸을 내미는 순간, 마당을 거닐던 거위 한 마리가 그것을 그만 쪼아 먹고 말았다.[7.1] 나그네는 곧 그에 대한 생각을 잊고 조용히 잠들었다.

그런데 잠시 후 갑자기 안마당 쪽에서 시끄러운 소리가 들리더니 곧 하인 몇 사람이 사랑채로 들어왔다.

하인들은 한마디 말도 없이 나그네를 꽁꽁 묶어서 주인 앞에 끌어다 놓고[7.2] 소리쳤다.

"네 이놈, 어서 네 죄를 바른 대로 말씀드려!"

"아니, 이게 무슨 짓이오? 무엇 때문에 이러는 것이오? 나는 다만 길 가는 나그네일 뿐이오."

나그네는 영문을 몰라 주인에게 묻자 주인은 이렇게 말했다.

"내 집에는 아주 귀한 보석이 하나 있었어. 그런데 오늘 저녁 갑자기 그것이 없어졌어. 당신이 아니면 누가 가져갔겠는가?"

주인의 말을 들은 나그네는 잠시 생각하더니 말했다.

"그러니까 댁의 보석을 찾아 주기만 한다면 나는 풀려 날 수가 있겠군요. 그야 어렵지 않은 일이지만. . . ."

나그네의 말에 주인과 하인들은 당장 보석을 내놓으라고 아우성치며 나그네의 몸과 봇짐을 샅샅이 뒤졌다.

"아무리 찾아도 내게는 그 보석이 없어요. 그러나 내일 아침까지는 그 보석을 찾아 드리겠어요. 그런데 한 가지 조건이 있어요. 댁에서 기르고 있는 거위가 한 마리 있을 텐데 그것을 내 곁에 데려다 주세요."

집주인은 나그네의 말이 이상스럽게 들렸지만 달리 방법이 없었기 때문에 시키는 대로 했다.

나그네는 그날 밤 몸을 묶인 채 추녀 밑에서 새우잠을 자게 되었다. 나그네의 곁에는 거위도 묶여 있었다.

다음날 아침 집주인과 하인들이 나그네에게로 모여들었다.

"자아, 저기에 그 보석이 있으니 집어 가세요."

나그네는 밤 사이에 거위가 눈 똥을 가리켰는데, 거위의 똥에 섞여 있는 보석을 본 주인과 하인들은 깜짝 놀랐다.

보석을 찾은 주인은 대단히 기뻐하면서 나그네에게 어찌 된 영문인가를 묻자, 나그네는 어젯밤 자기가 본 일을 이야기했다.

"아니, 그렇다면 진작 거위가 먹었다고 말씀을 하시지요. 그랬다면 저희가 이런 실례를 하지는 않았을 것을. . . ."

주인이 이렇게 말하자, 나그네가 대답했다.

"내가 하룻밤 불편하게 지내면 자연히 일이 해결될 것을[7.3] 만일 어젯밤에 그 말씀을 드렸다면 저 거위는 나 때문에 목숨을 잃었을 게 아닙니까?"

나그네의 말에 집주인은 크게 감동하였고, 그 나그네가 보통 사람이 아님을 알고 극진히 대접했다.

「철학하는 바보」(1996), 이명수 편저, 서울 보성출판사, pp. 134-136

대화

1

(같은 회사에서 일하는 이승희 씨와 한영국 씨가 교보문고에서 만났다.)

승희: 어머. 영국 씨 여기 웬일이세요?

영국: 어, 승희 씨. 안녕하세요?

승희: 아직 결혼도 안 하신 분이 아동 서적 코너에서 뭐 하고 계세요?

영국: 아, 예. 내일이 어린이날이잖아요. 그래서 조카들한테 뭘 좀 선물하고 싶은데 마땅한 게 생각이 안 나서 동화책을 사주려고요.

승희: 자상도 하셔라.[7.4]

영국: 근데, 책이 너무 많아서 고르기가 힘드네요. 저 어렸을 때는 콩쥐 팥쥐, 백설공주 등 손에 꼽을 정도였는데, 이렇게 아동 서적이 많은 줄 몰랐어요.

승희: 신간 서적이 계속해서 나오고, 특히 요즘 창작 동화집이 아주 많이 나와요.

영국: 아 그래요. 승희 씨는 책에 대해 많이 아시네요.

승희: 저는 원래 독서가 취미잖아요. 참, 영국 씨 조카가 몇 살이에요?

영국: 큰 조카는 초등학교 6학년이고, 작은 조카는 3학년이에요.

승희: 그럼 웬만한 책은 많이 읽었겠네요.

영국: 그렇지요. 특히 제 큰 조카는 책을 좋아하긴 하는데, 제 누나가 아주 골치 아파해요.

승희: 책 많이 읽으면 좋은데, 왜 골치에요? 눈 나빠질까봐요?

영국: 아니오. 책 중에서도 하필 만화책을 너무 좋아해서요.

승희: 어머, 만화책도 좋은 게 많이 나오는데. . . .

영국: 좋은 만화책도 많지만, 요즘 폭력 만화가 많아서요. 그리고

만화책도 텔레비전하고 비슷해서 너무 많이 읽으면 상상력
이 떨어진대요.

승희: 하긴, 아이들은 좋은 책과 나쁜 책을 분별하는 능력이 떨어
지니까, 부모님들께서 신경을 쓰셔야겠군요. 장가도 가시기
전에 아버지 연습 톡톡히 하시는군요.

영국: 뭘요.[7.5]

2

영국: 승희 씨, 혹시 시간 있으세요?

승희: 왜요?

영국: 시간 있으시면, 책 고르는 거 도와 주실 수 있으신가 해서요.[7.6]

승희: 어머. 그러지요.

(이승희 씨와 한영국 씨, 동화책을 고르고 있다.)

승희: 영국 씨, 이 책 어때요? 제가 지금 잠깐 훑어봤는데, 재미도
있고 교훈적인 것 같아요.

영국: 제목이 뭔데요?

승희: 「철학하는 바보」예요.

영국: 책 제목이 재미있군요. 제가 잠깐 봐도 될까요?

승희: 네. 그러세요.

(한영국 씨 책을 훑어본다.)

영국: 네. 정말 재미있고 교훈적인 것 같네요. 삽화도 예쁘고요.
제 큰 조카가 아주 좋아하겠는데요. 하나는 이걸로 해야겠
어요.

승희: 이제 작은 조카 것 한 권만 더 고르면 되겠네요.

영국: 승희 씨 덕분에 "삼촌 최고"라는 소리 듣겠네요. 정말 감사
합니다.

승희: 뭘요. 그까짓 것 가지고.[7.7]

Comprehension Questions

1. **Reading Comprehension.** "거위와 보석"을 읽고 맞고(Ⓣ) 틀린(Ⓕ) 것을 지적하거나 질문에 대답해 보세요.

(1) 거위는 안마당을 거닐면서 똥을 누었다.   Ⓣ   Ⓕ

(2) 하인들은 나그네도 묶고 거위도 묶었다.   Ⓣ   Ⓕ

(3) 나그네의 몸과 봇짐에 보석이 없었던 이유는 나그네가
보석을 다른 곳에 잘 숨겨 두었기 때문이다.   Ⓣ   Ⓕ

(4) 나그네는 어디에서 저녁을 먹었습니까?

(5) 주인의 보석은 어디에서 발견되었습니까?

(6) 주인은 왜 나그네가 보석을 훔쳐 갔다고 생각했습니까?

(7) 주인은 왜 나그네가 보통 사람이 아니라고 생각했습니까?

(8) 나그네가 거위가 보석을 먹었다는 말을 미리 하지 않은
이유는 무엇입니까?

2. **Listening Comprehension.** 내화를 듣고 맞고(Ⓣ) 틀린(Ⓕ) 것을 지적하거나 질문에 대답해 보세요.

대화 1

(1) 영국이의 취미는 책을 읽는 것이다.   Ⓣ   Ⓕ

(2) 승희와 영국이는 교보문고에서 만나기로 약속을 했다.   Ⓣ   Ⓕ

(3) 영국이의 누나는 조카들 눈이 나빠질까봐 조카들이 만화책
읽는 것을 좋아하지 않는다.   Ⓣ   Ⓕ

(4) 영국이는 왜 책을 고르기가 힘들다고 합니까?

(5) 영국이는 왜 조카들한테 선물을 하려고 합니까?

대화 2

(1) 영국이는 왜 승희에게 시간이 있는지 물어 봤습니까?

(2) 영국이는 「철학하는 바보」라는 책을 누구에게 선물하려고 합니까?

(3) 승희가 「철학하는 바보」라는 책을 영국이에게 추천한(recommend)
   이유는 무엇입니까?

New Words

감동 *n.* (deep) emotion; impression; sensation. 감동하다 to be (deeply) impressed, moved ¶그녀의 정성에 그는 감동하였다. Her sincerity touched his heart.

거위 *n.* goose

고르다 *v.* to choose ¶좋은 책은 고르기가 힘들다. It is hard to choose a good book.

고을 *n.* village; town (old usage; currently 마을, 읍내, 고장)

골치다 *adj.* contr. of 골치이다 to have a headache (= 골치가 아프다; 골치를 앓다)

교보문고 *n.* Kyobo Book Center (located at the Sejong-no intersection in the center of Seoul). 문고 bookstore

교훈적이다 *adj.* to be instructive, educational. 교훈 teaching; instruction; precept; moral

그까짓 *pre-n.* that kind of; so trifling (trivial, slight) ¶그까짓 짓을 누가 하겠어요? Who would do that sort of thing?

그야 contr. of 그거야, 그것이야 as for that; so far as that is concerned

극진히 *adv.* cordially, heartily, very kindly ¶극진히 대접하다 to give (a person) a cordial reception. 극진 cordiality; utter devotion; 극진하다 to be cordial

꽁꽁 *adv.* tightly; hard; thickly ¶꽁꽁 묶다 to tie up tightly ¶길이 꽁꽁 얼어붙어 있다. The road is frozen hard.

끌어다 놓다 *v.* to drag and put

나그네 *n.* traveler, tourist, wayfarer

누다 *v.* to evacuate, let out (urine or excrement) ¶오줌을 누다 to urinate ¶똥을 누다 to evacuate

달리 *adv.* particularly, in particular; differently; separately ¶달리 볼일이 없으면 함께 갑시다. Please come with me, if you are not otherwise engaged (=

if you don't have something in particular) ¶어머니와는 달리 그녀는 미인이다. Unlike her mother, she is very pretty.

댁 *n.* home (honorific form of 집); your house; you (addressed to a stranger adult) ¶박 선생님 댁에 계십니까? Is Mr. Pak at home? ¶이건 댁의 것입니까? Is this yours?

독서 *n.* reading ¶그는 독서를 즐긴다. He enjoys reading.

동화 *n.* nursery story, fairy tale ¶동화집 a collection of fairy tales ¶동화책 book of fairy tales; book of juvenile stories

뒤지다 *v.* to ransack, fumble (in), search (= 찾다) ¶샅샅이 뒤지다 to search thoroughly (for) ¶호주머니를 뒤지다 to fumble in one's pocket

들르다 *v.* to drop in (at), stop off in (at), stop over (at) ¶부산에 이틀간 들렀어요. (I) stopped two days at Pusan ¶잠깐 저희 집에 들르시지 않겠어요? 'Won't you come in for just a moment?'

똥 *n.* feces, droppings, dung

마땅하다 *adj.* to be suitable, appropriate ¶마땅한 것 suitable thing

만화책 *n.* comic book. 만화 caricature; cartoon; comic strip

모여들다 *v.* to gather (together), assemble

목숨 *n.* life ¶귀한 목숨 one's most precious life

무렵 *n.* time; about the time (when), around ¶그 무렵에 in those days; at that time ¶해질 무렵에 at sunset

무심코 *adv.* involuntarily; by chance, accidentally; casually. 무심하다 to be unconcerned, heartless, careless ¶나는 무심코 뒤를 돌아다보았다. I happened to look behind me. ¶나는 무심코 그 말을 하고 말았다. The word slipped out of my mouth.

묶이다 *v.* to be bound, tied up. 묶다 to bind, bundle, tie up, chain

바른 대로 *adv.* truthfully; correctly

방법 *n.* method; alternative

백설공주 *n.* Snow-White (fairy tale). 백설 white snow; 공주 princess

보석 *n.* jewel

봇짐 *n.* bundle; backpack

분별하다 *v.* to distinguish, separate, differentiate. 분별 division; separation; distinction

뿐 *n.* only; all ¶이것 뿐이에요. This is all I have. ¶나는 의무를 다 했을 뿐이에요. I have done nothing but my duty.

사랑채 *n.* a detached building used for parties (or as a guest room). 사랑

reception room for male guests or party; 채 chamber, wing, building

삼촌 최고 "My uncle is the best" (children's expression). 삼촌 uncle; 최고 best ¶우리 아빠 최고. My father is no. 1.

삽화 *n.* illustration; a cut ¶책에 삽화를 그리다 to illustrate a book

상상력 *n.* imaginative power. 상상 imagination ¶상상력이 떨어진다. The imaginative powers are reduced.

샅샅이 *adv.* all over, thoroughly. 샅 crotch, groin ¶샅샅이 뒤지다 to look in every nook and corner

새우잠 *n.* (*lit.,* shrimp sleep) sleeping all curled up (in a fetal position) ¶새우잠을 자다 to sleep curled up

손에 꼽다 *v.* to count on one's fingers

신간 서적 *n.* newly published book. 신간 new publication

신경 쓰다 *v.* to care about. 신경 nerve; sensitivity; 쓰다 to use ¶동생 일에 신경을 써라. Look after your younger siblings.

아동 서적 코너 *n.* children's book section (*lit.,* corner). 아동 children; 서적 books

아우성 *n.* shout; outcry; clamor. 아우성치다 to clamor, shout out ¶왜 그리 아우성이냐? What are you shouting at?

안마당 *n.* courtyard, inner yard (= 안뜰)

어린이날 *n.* Children's Day. 어린이 child

어머! *adv.* Oh! O my! Dear me! Good heavens! (women's speech) ¶어머, 이게 누구야? O my! Who is this?

어찌 *adv.* why, for what reason; how (= 어떻게) ¶나는 어찌 해야 좋을지 몰랐어. I was at a loss what to do. ¶넌 어찌 왔니? What has brought you here? ¶어찌 된 일이니? (= 어떻게 된 일이니?) How did it happen?

영문 *n.* circumstances, situation, state of affairs; reason ¶그가 왜 화내고 있는지 영문을 모르겠다. I don't know why he is angry.

원래 *adv.* originally; from the first; by nature

웬만하다 *adj.* to be O.K., tolerable, acceptable, satisfactory ¶웬만한 책 fairly good books ¶웬만하면 차 한잔 마십시다. Let's have a cup of tea, if you don't mind. ¶내 수입은 웬만해. I have a handsome income.

자상하다 *adj.* to be considerate, detailed; to be cautious and careful, attentive, considerate

자연히 *adv.* naturally; spontaneously

잠들다 *v.* to fall asleep, drop off to sleep ¶깊이 잠들다 to sink into a sound sleep

장가를 가다 *v.* to get married; to take a wife ¶장가를 늦게 갔다. He married late in life.

조건 *n.* condition; term; qualification ¶그것을 승낙하는 데 한 가지 조건이 있다. I agree to it on one condition. ¶그는 유리한 조건으로 채용되었다. He was employed on favorable terms.

조카 *n.* nephew ¶조카딸 niece

죄 *n.* crime, sin

진작 *adv.* then and there; on the spot; earlier

짓 *n.* behavior, activity, conduct ¶손짓 hand signal ¶눈짓 eye-signal ¶이게 무슨 짓이냐? Where are your manners? ¶또 그 짓이야! The same old game!

쪼다 *v.* to peck ¶닭들이 옥수수를 쪼아 먹었다. The chickens pecked at the corn.

참 *adv.* by the way; oh; well ¶참 오늘이 목요일 아냐? Oh, it's Thursday, isn't it?

창작 동화집 *n.* collection of original fairy tales. 창작 creation; original work

철학하는 바보 *n. A Philosophizing Fool* (title of a book). 철학하다 to study philosophy, philosophize

청하다 *v.* to ask, request; to invite, send for ¶그들은 나에게 노래 한 곡을 청했다. They asked for a song from me. ¶나는 친구들을 생일 파티에 청했다. I invited friends to my birthday party.

추녀 *n.* protruding corners of Korean eaves; angle rafter

콩쥐 팥쥐 *n. K'ongjwi P'atchwi* (a children's novel of the Chosǒn dynasty in which a girl named 콩쥐 was harassed by her stepsister 팥쥐 and stepmother, but eventually got over all hardships, thanks to a fairy's help)

톡톡히 *adv.* much, a lot, a great deal ¶우리 형은 이번에 돈을 톡톡히 벌었어요. My older brother made quite a lot of money.

폭력 *n.* violence, force ¶폭력 만화 violent cartoon ¶폭력을 쓰다 to use (resort to) violence

풀려 나다 *v.* to be released, freed. 풀다 to untie; 풀리다 to come untied, get loose; to be solved; 나다 to come out

하긴 *contr.* of 하기는 in fact, indeed ¶하긴 그것은 그렇게 되어야 해요. Indeed, it has gotten to be that way.

하인 *n.* servant

하필 *adv.* of all occasions (things, places, persons) ¶왜 하필 내가 가야

하니? Why should I go of all things? ¶하필 미아가 올 줄은 몰랐어.
Mia was the last person of all that I expected to come.

한양 *n.* Hanyang (old name for Seoul, used in the Chosŏn dynasty)

해결 *n.* solution; settlement. 해결하다 to solve, settle; 해결되다 to be solved, settled

해지다 *v.* the sun sets/goes down/sinks

훑어보다 *v.* to give a searching glance at, scrutinize, scan. 훑다 to thresh, hack ¶형사는 나를 위 아래로 훑어보았다. The police detective took a careful look at me.

Useful Expressions

7.1 ~고 말다 to end up doing; to get around to doing

The auxiliary verb 말다 'to end up with' developed from the verb 말다 'to stop doing.' As an auxiliary, it occurs after a verb + the suffix ~고 'and.'

거위가 보석을 쪼아 먹고 **말았다**.
A goose (pecked at and) ended up eating the jewel.
싸움이 벌어지고 **말겠다**.
I am afraid they will end up fighting.
그 도둑이 마침내 잡히고 **말았다**.
The thief finally got around to being arrested.

7.2 ~어다/아다 (놓다, 두다, 가두다, etc.) to carry (something) from one place to another

The suffix ~어다/아다 (contraction of ~어다가/아다가) 'and then' indicates that a person or thing (놓다, 두다, 가두다, etc.) is taken from one place to another. In the sentence 그 도둑을 잡아다 감옥에 가두었다 'They arrested the thief and put him in jail,' for example, the meaning is that the thief was caught at some place other than the jail (감옥).

하인들은 나그네를 주인 앞에 잡**아다** 놓**았다**.
The servants caught the wayfarer and set him before their master.

나는 그 무거운 돌을 마당에 들**어다 놓았다.**
I carried the heavy rock and put it down in the yard.

7.3 ~(으)ㄹ 걸/것을 with a thing/fact that; but instead

~(으)ㄹ 걸/것을 is a contraction of ~(으)ㄹ 걸/것을 가지고, which means 'with a thing/fact that,' 'for a thing/fact that,' or 'but instead.'

용호를 보냈어야 **할 걸 (가지고)** 사라를 보냈어요.
I should have sent Yongho, but I sent Sarah instead.
내일이면 모두에게 다 알려**질 걸 (가지고)** 왜 지금 말해 주지 않는지 모르겠어.
I don't understand why he does not want to tell us anything for a fact that will be revealed to everybody tomorrow.
나만 고생하면 해결**될 걸 (가지고)** 다른 사람들까지 고생시키고 싶지는 않았어요.
I didn't want to trouble other people with/for a thing that would be solved if I suffered alone.

7.4 ~어라/아라 oh! (interjection)

A verb followed by ~어라/아라 is a plain-style command, but an adjective followed by ~어라/아라 is an exclamation. Adjectives expressing sensation or emotion are particularly common with this pattern. If there is a noun, the particle 도 'also, indeed' often follows the noun.

아이고 더**워라.**	Oh! It's very hot!
아이 추**워라.**	Ah, it's very cold!
달도 밝**아라.**	The moon is certainly bright.
자상도 하**셔라.**	How considerate you are (he/she is)!

7.5 뭘(요) not really

뭘 is a contraction of 무엇을 (무엇 'what' + object particle 을). Its idiomatic meaning 'not at all, not really' occurs only when it is used alone to negate, out of courtesy, another's praise, appreciation, and so on. It is somewhat similar to 천만에요 'not at all,' but is less emphatic. 뭘 is the intimate form; 뭘요 is polite.

A: 선생님댁 참 좋네요.   Your house is really good, Professor.
B: **뭘**. 별로야.   Not really. It's so so.

A: 도와 주셔서 정말 감사합니다.   Thank you indeed for helping us.
B: **뭘요**.   Not at all.

7.6   ~는가/(으)ㄴ가/(으)ㄹ까 해서 wondering if ~; thinking that ~

The phrase ~는가/(으)ㄴ가/(으)ㄹ까 해서 is composed of 가 or 까 'whether, if'
preceded by a modifier suffix (~는 after a verb, ~[으]ㄴ after an adjective, or
~[으]ㄹ) and followed by the verb stem 해 'do; think' and the suffix ~서 'and, as,
because.' Similar expressions are ~는가/(으)ㄴ가/(으)ㄹ까 하고 and 는지/(으)ㄴ지
/(으)ㄹ지 해서/하고.

도와 주실 수 있으**신가 해서**요.
(I am) just wondering if you can help me.
용호가 수술을 받았**는가 해서** 병원에 전화해 봤어요.
I called the hospital, wondering if Yongho had undergone the surgery.
추울**까 해서** 스웨터를 가져왔어요.
Thinking that it would be cold, I brought my sweater.

7.7   가지고 with, for, about

가지고 has developed from the verb 가지다 'to have, own, take' and the suffix
~고 'and.' It can be preceded by the object particle 을/를. Its literal meaning is
'having . . .'

무엇(을) **가지고** 그렇게 싸우니?
What are you quarrelling about?
그까짓 걸 **가지고** 그렇게 걱정했니?
Were you worried so much for such a trifling matter?

Exercises

1. 관련된 단어들끼리 연결하여 문장을 만들어 보세요.

   (1) 깜짝   •   • 생각하다 _____

   (2) 꽁꽁   •   • 빛나다 _____

   (3) 반짝   •   • 뒤지다 _____

   (4) 잠시   •   • 말하다 _____

   (5) 톡톡히   •   • 묶다   _____

   (6) 무심코   •   • 놀라다 _____

   (7) 샅샅이   •   • 하다   _____

2. 아래의 설명과 맞는 단어나 표현을 본문에서 찾아 쓰세요.

   (1) 집을 떠나 여행 중에 있는 사람: _____

   (2) 형제 자매의 아들이나 딸: _____

   (3) 어린이가 듣거나 읽고 즐기는 이야기: _____

   (4) 한 끝에서 다른 끝까지 쭉 살펴보다: _____

   (5) 도움이 되거나 따를 만한: _____

   (6) 글의 내용을 쉽게 이해할 수 있도록 그린 그림: _____

3. 보기에서 적당한 말을 골라 빈칸을 채우세요.

   > 보기: 아우성, 신경, 손, 방법, 대접, 영문

   (1) 주인은 나그네를 사랑채에 머물게 하고 하인을 시켜 저녁을 _____했다.

   (2) 나그네의 말에 주인과 하인들은 당장 보석을 내놓으라고 _____치며 나그네의 몸과 봇짐을 뒤졌다.

   (3) 집주인은 나그네의 말이 이상스럽게 들렸지만 달리 _____이 없었기 때문에 시키는 대로 했다.

(4) 저 어렸을 때는 아동 서적이 콩쥐 팥쥐, 백설공주 등 _____에 꼽을 정도였어요.

(5) 아이들은 좋은 책과 나쁜 책을 분별하는 능력이 떨어지니까, 부모님들께서도 _____을 쓰셔야겠군요.

(6) 나는 _____도 모르고 그를 따라 웃었다.

4. 밑줄 친 말과 가장 비슷한 단어나 표현을 보기에서 고르세요.

(1) 마당 한쪽에서 무언가 반짝 빛나는 것이 <u>눈에 띄었다</u>.

    a. 우연히 보였다   b. 찬란하게 보였다

    c. 눈에 나타났다   d. 똑똑히 보였다

(2) 나그네는 <u>영문</u>을 몰라 주인에게 묻자 주인은 이렇게 말했다.

    a. 영어   b. 이유

    c. 영화   d. 이웃

(3) 그러니까 <u>댁</u>의 보석을 찾아 주기만 한다면 나는 풀려날 수가 있겠군요.

    a. 가정   b. 집

    c. 부인   d. 당신

(4) 저 거위는 나 때문에 <u>목숨을 잃었을</u> 게 아닙니까?

    a. 자살했을   b. 목숨을 끊었을

    c. 죽었을   d. 목숨을 건졌을

(5) 조카들한테 뭘 좀 선물하고 싶은데 <u>마땅한</u> 게 생각이 안 나서 동화책을 사주려고요.

    a. 당연한   b. 적당한

    c. 옳은   d. 작은

(6) <u>장가도 가시기</u> 전에 아버지 연습 톡톡히 하시는군요.

    a. 시집도 가시기   b. 아이도 낳으시기

    c. 결혼도 하시기   d. 약혼도 하시기

5. 보기와 같이 주어진 말이 들어가는 단어나 표현을 3개 이상 써 보세요.

> 보기: 친 (親, friendly, parents): 친지, 양친, 친척, 친구, 친절

(1) 죄 (罪, crime, sin): _____

(2) 법 (法, law, method): _____

(3) 교 (敎, education, teaching): _____

(4) 서 (書, book, writing): _____

6. "Adjective~어(라)/아(라)"를 사용하여, 아이고 무서워(라) 'Oh! Am I scared!' 처럼 연습하세요.

> 무겁다 'to be heavy,' 뜨겁다 'to be hot' (temperature), 맵다 'to be hot' (taste), 더럽다 'to be dirty,' 귀찮다 'to be annoying,' 피곤하다 'to be tired,' 고맙다 'to be thankful,' 예쁘다 'to be beautiful'

(1) _____   (2) _____

(3) _____   (4) _____

(5) _____   (6) _____

(7) _____   (8) _____

7. "뭘(요)"를 사용하여 보기처럼 대화를 완성하세요.

> 보기: A: 어제는 오후 늦게까지 실례가 많았습니다.
>   B: 뭘요. 저도 아주 즐거웠습니다.

(1) A: 차 예쁜데. (작다)

    B: _____

(2) A: 선생님 강연 정말 잘 들었습니다. (도움이 되다)

   B: _____

(3) A: 따님이 그렇게 공부를 잘 한다면서요? (수학을 잘 못한다)

   B: _____

8. "~는가/(으)ㄴ가/(으)ㄹ까 해서"가 쓰일 수 있도록 보기처럼 대화를 만들어
   보세요.

   ┌───┐
   │ 보기: A: 이 떡 왜 가져왔니?   │
   │   B: 모두가 좋아할까 해서요.   │
   └───┘

   (1) A: 오늘은 아침 일찍 출근하시네요?

      B: _____

   (2) A: 우산은 왜 가지고 오시는 거지요?

      B: _____

   (3) A: 신문에 난 자동차 광고를 왜 그렇게 유심히 보세요?

      B: _____

9. "가지고"를 사용하여 보기처럼 대화를 완성하세요.

   ┌───┐
   │ 보기: A: 지금 무슨 문제로 토론하고 있나요?   │
   │   B: 한국 경제 문제 가지고 토론하고 있어요. │
   └───┘

   (1) A: 누구를 지금 놀려대고 있니?

      B: _____

   (2) A: 저 애들이 무엇 때문에 싸우고 있는 거예요?

      B: _____

   (3) A: 김 선생님이 무슨 일로 고민하고 계세요?

      B: _____

10. 다음 문장들을 "~고 말다"의 형태로 바꾸세요.

   (1) 이 일을 꼭 해 놓겠습니다.

      → _____

   (2) 그 개가 그 동안 많이 아팠는데 오늘 아침 마침내 죽었어요.

      → _____

   (3) 그 회사는 빚이 많아서 사업이 잘 되지 않았었는데 드디어 망했어요.

      → _____

11. 보기처럼 "~어다/아다"를 사용해서 문장을 만드세요. "~어다/아다"앞에
   올 동사(verb)는 아래에서 고르세요.

   ┌───┐
   │ 싣다 'to load,' 물다 'to bite,' 받다 'to receive,' 밀다 │
   │ 'to push,' 묶다 'to tie,' 끌다 'to drag,' 빨다 'to wash │
   │ (clothes),' 꺾다 'to break,' 집다 'to pick up'   │
   └───┘

   ┌───┐
   │ 보기: 나는 할아버지 신을 닦아다 드렸다.   │
   │   용호는 그 많은 짐을 공항에서 실어다 기숙사   │
   │   방에 내려 놓았다.   │
   └───┘

   (1) _____
   (2) _____
   (3) _____
   (4) _____

12. 영어로 말해 보세요.

   (1) 3일이면 끝나 버릴 걸 (가지고) 그렇게 모두 걱정하고 있었어요.

   (2) 그 사람이 그렇게 빨리 풀려 날 걸 (가지고) 신문에서는 그 사람이 사
      형당할(to be punished with death) 것으로 보도되었어요.

   _____

Discussion and Composition

1. (Group work) "거위와 보석"의 내용에 맞게 간단한 연극(mini-drama)을 꾸며서 교실에서 발표하세요. 우선 학생들은 감독(피디 'producer')을 한사람 뽑고 감독과 의논해서 다음 역할(part)을 맡으세요.

    a. 해설자 (narrator)

    b. 나그네

    c. 부자

    d. 하인들

    e. 거위

  (1) 감독과 의논하여 모두 같이 시나리오를 쓰세요.

  (2) 감독은 각 역할을 맡은 학생들에게 시나리오를 나눠 주고 함께 연습하세요.

2. (Pair work) 다음의 상황에서는 A가 요청하거나 부탁을 해야 합니다. 다른 사람에게 요청하거나 부탁을 할 때는 공손한 표현을 쓰는 것이 중요합니다. 다음 상황을 잘 읽고 대화를 만들어 보세요. 대화를 만들 때는 다음 표현을 사용해 보세요.

• 죄송하지만	• 혹시 ~ 있으세요?
• ~도 될까요?	• ~가 해서요
• ~덕분에 ~네요	• 정말 감사합니다
• 뭘요, ~가지고.	• 정말 죄송합니다만/미안합니다만

〔상황 1〕

A는 방학이 시작해서 내일 집으로 갑니다. 내일 아침 8시에 친구 C가 공항까지 데려다 주기로 했는데, 저녁 7시에 C로부터 전화가 왔습니다. 자동차

에 갑자기 문제가 생겨서 내일 공항에 못 나갈 것 같다고 합니다. 공항 서틀은 24시간 전에 예약을 해야 하기 때문에 서틀 버스를 이용할 수는 없고, 택시는 대학생이 이용하기에 너무 비쌉니다. A는 친구 B에게 공항까지 데려다 달라고 전화를 합니다.

B는 매일 오전 9시에서 12시까지 학교 서점에서 아르바이트를 합니다. B는 보통 일찍 일어나는 편이라 7시에 일어나서 7시 30분에서 8시 30분까지 학교 수영장에서 수영을 하거나 취미인 웹페이지 디자인을 합니다.

〔상황 2〕

A는 내일 중요한 경제학 시험이 있습니다. 지난달 그는 감기에 심하게 걸려서 경제학 수업에 몇 번 결석을 했습니다. 경제학 수업이 끝나고 B한테 경제학 노트를 빌려 달라고 부탁을 합니다.

B는 지난달에 자신이 기르는 강아지가 많이 아파서 동물 병원에 가느라고 경제학 수업에 몇 번 결석을 해서 자기도 노트를 빌려야 합니다.

3. 여러분이 가장 감명깊게 (impressively) 읽은 책은 무엇입니까? 그 책의 줄거리(plot)와 감명깊었던 점에 대해서 이야기하고 한 페이지 정도의 글로 써 보세요.

4. 여러분은 어렸을 때 만화책을 좋아했습니까? 많은 부모님들과 선생님들은 만화책이 어린이들에게 좋지 않다고 생각합니다. 만화책이 어린이에게 좋은지, 좋지 않은지 이야기해 보세요. 어야기한 내용을 간단히 (반 페이지 정도) 글로 써 보세요.

Further Reading

상술

어느 시장에 골동품 가게가 두 군데 있었다. 한 군데는 오래 전부터 그곳에서 장사를 했고 또 한 군데는 겨우 2년 전에 가게를 열었을 뿐이다. 그런데 놀랍게도 오래된 가게에는 손님이 줄어들고 새로 연 가게는 날로 손님이 많아졌다.

그때 마침 새 가게의 종업원이 그만두게 되었다. 오래된 가게의 주인은 그 젊은이를 고용했다. 주인은 어떻게 해서 상대방 가게가 장사가 잘 되는지를 물었다.

젊은이는 이렇게 대답했다. "그 가게가 손님이 많은 이유는 주인의 귀가 먹었기 때문이에요. 정말로 귀가 먹었는지 아닌지는 저도 잘 모릅니다. 주인 아줌마는 항상 사무실에서 일을 하고 가게에는 주인 아저씨가 나와 있습니다. 손님이 들어와서 쇼 윈도에 있는 골동품이 얼마냐고 물으면 주인 아저씨는 사무실을 향하여, '쇼 윈도에 있는 골동품이 얼마지?'하고 아줌마에게 묻습니다. 그러면 주인 아줌마가 '그 골동품은 380만원이에요.'라고 대답을 하지요. 귀가 먹은 주인 아저씨는 손님에게 이렇게 말한답니다. '들으셨지요. 180만원입니다.' 그렇게 하면 손님이 골동품을 사지 않을 수가 없지요."

「철학하는 바보」(1996), 이명수 편저, 보성출판사, pp. 28-30

고용하다 to hire; 골동품 가게 curio (antique) shop; 귀(가) 먹다 to become deaf; 그만두다 to quit a job; 사무실 office; 상대방 the other party; 상술 trick of the trade; 시장 market; 젊은이 young man; 종업원 employee; 줄어들다 to shrink, decrease; 향하여 facing

---

1. 새로운 가게와 오래된 가게 중, 어느 가게에 손님이 더 많았나요?

2. 새로운 가게는 언제 문을 열었나요?

3. 오래된 가게의 주인은 왜 새로운 가게의 종업원을 고용했을까요?

4. 왜 새로운 가게에 손님이 많이 갔을까요?

LESSON 7. A PHILOSOPHIZING FOOL

The Goose and the Jewel

Long ago, in a village near Seoul, there was a wealthy man. One day, just before sundown, a wayfarer came along. The host gave him lodging in a separate house and had his servants treat him to dinner.

After dinner the wayfarer casually looked out into the inner courtyard when something bright in the corner of the yard caught his eye. But the moment he turned (*lit.*, his body) toward the inner courtyard to get a closer look, a goose walking across the yard (just) pecked and ate it. The wayfarer soon forgot the matter (*lit.*, about it) and quietly went to sleep.

But a little later, a sudden clamoring sounded from the inner courtyard, and soon several servants entered the house. Without a word the servants bound the wayfarer tightly, dragged him before the host, and shouted,

"You scoundrel, confess your crime truthfully and quickly!"

"Why, what is this? Why are you doing this? I'm only a traveling wayfarer."

When the wayfarer asked the host for an explanation (*lit.*, not knowing the reason), the host replied thus: "I had a very precious jewel in my house. But tonight it has suddenly disappeared. Who would have taken it if not you?"

After hearing the host's words, the wayfarer thought for a while and spoke. "Then I'll be freed once I recover your jewel. That's not a difficult task, but. . . ."

At the wayfarer's words, the host and the servants shouted, demanding that the jewel be given up. They thoroughly searched the wayfarer's body and his bundle.

"No matter how much you search, I do not have that jewel. However, I'll find that jewel for you by tomorrow morning. But I have a condition. You probably have a goose that you are raising—please bring it (*lit.*, next) to me." Although the wayfarer's request sounded strange to the host, he did as asked, for there were no other alternatives.

That night, the wayfarer slept curled up under the protruding corners of the eaves, his body bound. The goose was (also) tied next to him.

The next morning, the host and his servants gathered around the wayfarer.

"There, the jewel is over there, so take it."

When the wayfarer pointed to the excrement passed by the goose during the night, the host and servants, (upon) seeing the jewel in the excrement, were surprised. The host, overjoyed at recovering the jewel, asked how the matter had come about. The wayfarer told what he had seen the night before.

"You could have told us earlier that the goose had eaten it. Then we wouldn't have made such a blunder. . . ."

As the host spoke (thus), the wayfarer replied, "By my spending one night uncomfortably, the matter would come to a natural solution. But if I had told you the story last night, wouldn't the goose have lost its life because of me?"

The master of the house was deeply touched by the wayfarer's words. Realizing that the wayfarer was no ordinary character, he treated him very kindly.

A Philosophizing Fool, compiled by Yi Myŏng-su (Seoul: Posŏng, 1996, 134-136)

CONVERSATION

1

(Seung-hee Lee and Yŏng-guk Han, who work at the same company, meet at the Kyobo Book Center.)

Seung-hee:	Hey, Yŏng-guk, what brings you here?
Yŏng-guk:	Oh, Seung-hee. How are you?
Seung-hee:	What is a single person doing in the children's book section?
Yŏng-guk:	Oh, well. As you know, tomorrow is Children's Day. I'd like to give a little something to my nephews, but I couldn't think of anything appropriate, so I am thinking of getting them books of fairy tales.
Seung-hee:	How thoughtful of you (*lit.,* meticulous you are).
Yŏng-guk:	But there are so many books that it is difficult to choose (*lit.,* from them). When I was young there were only a handful, like *K'ongjwi P'atchwi* and *Snow White Princess.* I didn't know there were this many children's books.
Seung-hee:	Newly published books continue to come out, and especially nowadays, collections of creative fairy tales come out a lot.
Yŏng-guk:	Is that so? You know a lot about books.
Seung-hee:	Reading has always been my hobby. By the way, how old are your nephews?
Yŏng-guk:	The older nephew is a sixth grader in primary school, and the younger nephew is a third grader.
Seung-hee:	Then they must have read a lot of fairly good books.
Yŏng-guk:	Yes, that's right. My older nephew, in particular, enjoys books, but he gives my older sister a real headache.

Seung-hee:	It's good to read a lot, so why does she feel that he's a headache? [Is she worried] that his eyes will go bad?
Yŏng-guk:	No. It's because he loves comic books, of all books.
Seung-hee:	Actually, there are lots of good comic books, too.
Yŏng-guk:	There are many good comic books but these days there are too many violent ones. Also, it's been said that because comic books are similar to TV, if you read too many of them, it stunts your imagination.
Seung-hee:	It is true that children can't distinguish good from bad books, and parents must pay [close] attention. You are (certainly) practicing to be a father even before you are married.
Yŏng-guk:	Not really.

2

Yŏng-guk:	Would you happen to have some time?
Seung-hee:	Why?
Yŏng-guk:	Well, I was wondering if you could help me choose books, if you had time.
Seung-hee:	Oh, sure.

(They browse through the books.)

Seung-hee:	How about this book? I've just glanced at it (now), and it seems interesting and educational.
Yŏng-guk:	What's the title?
Seung-hee:	It's *A Philosophizing Fool.*
Yŏng-guk:	That's an interesting title. May I take a look at it (*lit.,* a little)?
Seung-hee:	Yes, please do.

(Yŏng-guk leafs through the book.)

Yŏng-guk:	Yes, it seems to be interesting and educational. The illustrations are pretty, too. I think my older nephew will really like it. I'll take this, for one.
Seung-hee:	Now all we have to do is choose one for your younger nephew.
Yŏng-guk:	Thanks to you, I'll be hearing, "My uncle is the best." I really appreciate it.
Seung-hee:	Not at all. This is nothing.

제8과 미국인이 본 한국인

(Lesson 8: The American's view of the Korean)

PRE-READING QUESTIONS

1. (Icebreakers) 여러분은 처음 만난 사람과 어떻게 대화를 시작합니까? 처음 만난 사람에게 보통 무엇을 물어 봅니까? 처음 만난`사람들한테서 받는 질문은 어떤 것들이 있습니까?

2. (Group work) 한국의 음식 예절에 대해 무엇을 알고 있나요? 한국의 음식 예절과 서양의 음식 예절은 어떤 차이가 있는지 이야기해 보세요.

3. 언어 사용으로 인한 문화적 충격(culture shock)을 경험한 적이 있습니까? 있다면 그 경험을 이야기해 보세요.

GAINING FAMILIARITY

1. 여러분은 무슨 띠입니까?
   쥐, 소, 호랑이, 토끼, 용, 뱀, 말, 양, 원숭이, 닭, 개, 돼지

2. 사적인 일, 초면, 사고 방식, 대면, 발표, 토론, 토의, 질문, 지적

몇 살입니까?

한국 사람은 상대방의 나이를 알고 싶어하는 것 같다. 처음 만난 사람에게 몇 살이냐고 묻는 것이 보통이다. 불쑥 나이를 물어 오는 질문에 처음에는 사적인 일에 관심도 많다 싶어[8.1] 이상하고 별로 기분 좋은 일이 아니었다.

초면 인사와 함께 나이를 묻는 것은 "어른을 공경하라"는 유교적인 사고 방식과 한국어 구조 때문이란 것을 곧 알게 되었다. 대화하는 상대의 나이에 따라 말을 올리고 내려 써야 하기 때문에 상대의 나이를 알아야 한다.

처음 만난 사람들끼리 나이를 알아내는 방법도 다양한 것 같다. 상대방의 나이가 눈에 띄게 차이가 있을 때는 물어 볼 필요도 없이 나이가 적은 사람이 나이가 많은 사람에게 존댓말을 쓰고 나이가 비슷하게 보일 때, 단박에 몇 살이냐고 묻기보다는[8.2] 무슨 띠냐고 물어서 순위를 파악하는 것 같다. 만약에 똑같은 띠일 때, 생일이 언제냐고 묻는 것 같다.

나와 나이가 비슷한 미스터 유와의 첫 대면에서였다. 그는 서울에서 나는 미국에서 충청북도의 작은 마을에 있는 중학교 영어선생으로 부임했다. 처음 만나자마자 미스터 유는 대뜸 내게 물었다.

"무슨 띠지요?" ("What is your sign?")

"무슨 띠라니요?"[8.3] ("What do you mean, my sign?") 나는 어리둥절하여 물었다.

"나는 1949년에 태어났으니까, 소띠인데요."하고 미스터 유가 설명하였다.

나는 그제야 내가 어느 해에 태어났느냐고 묻는 것을 알았다. "나도 1949년에 태어났어요. 그러니까 나도 소띠인가 봐요."하고 대답했다.

　　우리는 교정을 걸으면서 학교를 구경하였던 것 같다. 앞서 가던 미스터 유가 갑자기 돌아서면서 "생일날이 언제지요?"하고 물었다. 나는 속으로 왜 이 사람이 나의 생일을 이토록 알고 싶어하는지 참 이상하다고 생각하였다. 가까운 친구들 중에서도 내 생일을 그처럼 알고 싶어 생년월일을 물었던 사람은 내 기억에 없었기 때문이었다. "크리스마스 이브에 태어났는데요. 그래서 내 이름이 크리스지요."라고 말해 주었다.

　　미스터 유는 활짝 웃으면서 "나는 11월에 태어났는데."하며 손뼉을 쳤다. 이 사람이 왜 갑자기 이렇게 좋아하나 하며 어리둥절했었다.

　　나의 심드렁한 반응에 실망한 표정으로 미스터 유는 자기가 나보다 한 달 더 먼저 태어났으니 자기가 나의 형님이라는 것을 강조하였다. 그가 무슨 소리를 하는지 그때에 이해를 하지 못했다. 젊음을 선호하는 미국에서 자란 나의 관념 속에서는 나이가 나보다 많다고 좋아하는 미스터 유를 이해하지 못했던 것이다.

　　미스터 유가 손뼉을 치며 기뻐하였던 이유를 그의 설명을 통해 알게 되었다. 그가 나보다 나이가 많기에[8.4] 나는 그에게 존댓말을 써야 하고 그가 시키는 대로 해야 한다는 한국 풍습이 이해가 되질 않았던 것은 물론이고[8.5] 거부감마저[8.6] 들었다. 나의 형도 이름을 부르고, 심지어는[8.7] 선생님도 이름을 부르는 데 익숙했던 나는 미스터 유의 요청을 정중히 거절하여 형이라고 부르질 않았다.

　　한국에 사는 동안 나이 차이로 일어났던 재미있는 에피소드들도 있다. 내가 하숙하고 있었던 집에 쌍둥이 형제가 있었다. 같은 날 태어난 형제끼리인데도, 27분 늦게 태어난 아이가 먼저 태어난 아이에게 "형"이라고 불렀다. 미국 사람에게는 쉽게 이해가 안 되는 관념이다.

크리스 포오먼, 샌프란시스코주립대 교수, "한국일보 오피니언"
2000년 4월 20일 수요일

대화

1

(마이클이 한국어 수업 시간에 문화 충격이라는 제목으로 발표를 한다.)

마이클: 여러분 갈비 다들 좋아하시죠?

반 친구들: 네.

마이클: 저는 갈비에 관해[8.8] 있었던 일에 대해서[8.8] 발표하겠습니다. 저는 지난 여름 방학에 한국에 있는 제 친구네 집에 놀러 갔었습니다. 제 친구네 집에 갔을 때가 저녁 때쯤이었는데, 제 친구 어머니께서 저녁 식사를 했냐고 물어 보셨어요. 그래서 아직 안 했다고 하니까, 마침 갈비찜을 해 놨다고 좀 먹고 가라고 하시는 거예요. 그래서 저는 괜찮다고 그랬더니 그래도 저녁 시간인데 먹고 가라고 하시면서 상을 차려 주셨습니다. 갈비찜하고 밥을 주셔서 아주 맛있게 먹었어요. 근데 갈비찜 한 접시를 다 먹고 나니까 한 접시를 더 주시는 거예요. 그래서 배가 몹시 불렀지만 두 번째 갈비찜을 겨우 먹었죠. 근데 두 번째 접시를 비우자마자 또 다시 좀 더 먹겠느냐고 물어 보시는 거예요. 배가 너무 불러서 아니라고 했죠. 그런데도 많이 먹으라고 하시면서 세 번째 갈비찜을 가지고 오시는 거예요. 그래서 아픈 배를 움켜쥐고 세 번째 갈비찜을 겨우 겨우 먹었어요. 그날 하도 갈비찜을 많이 먹어서, 전 이제 한 일 년 동안 갈비는 못 먹을 것 같아요.

선생님: 마이클 씨 발표 잘 들었어요. 여러분 중에도 비슷한 경험이 있는 사람이 많을 것 같아요. 마이클 씨의 발표에 대해 토론을 해 봅시다.

2

(마이클이 발표를 끝낸 후 토론을 하고 있다.)

마이클: 나중에 제 친구한테 들은 얘긴데요, 제 친구 어머님께서
          저처럼 한자리에서 갈비를 많이 먹는 사람은 처음 봤다
          고, 저를 갈비 대장이라고 부르셨대요.

선생님: 한국에서 식사할 때 더 못 먹겠으면 음식을 약간 남기던
          지 아니면 더 준다고 할 때 "아니에요"라고 해서 의사를
          분명하게 밝혀야 해요.

마이클: 전 어려서부터 음식을 남기면 안 된다고 배워서 음식을
          아주 깨끗하게 먹거든요. 그리고, "아니에요"라고 했는데요.

선생님: 한 번만 "아니에요"라고 하면 더 먹고 싶은데 그냥
          예의로 그런 줄 안다구요.[8.9] 그리고 접시를 하도 깨끗하게
          비우니까 마이클 씨 친구 어머님께서는 마이클 씨가 아직
          도 시장한가 해서 계속 갈비를 주신 거예요.

마이클: 아, 그랬군요.

데비: 음식을 남기지 않는 청교도적 사고 방식과 한국의 예의
          범절 때문에 생긴 에피소드 같네요.

선생님: 그렇죠. 아주 좋은 지적이에요.

마이클: 아아. 이제야 수수께끼가 풀린 것 같네요. 한국에 가기 전
          에 진작 이런 문화 차이에 대해 배웠으면 그런 일이 없었
          을 텐데.

루시: 마이클 씨 덕분에 한국식으로 거절하는 법을 잘 배웠으니
          저희들 모두 다음에 한국 분한테 초대받았을 때 음식을
          너무 많이 먹어서 배탈이 나는 일은 없겠네요.

크리스 포오먼, 한국일보 칼럼에서 발췌하고 내용을 고침

Comprehension Questions

1. **Reading Comprehension.** "몇 살입니까?"를 읽고 맞고(Ⓣ) 틀린(Ⓕ) 것을 지적하거나 질문에 대답해 보세요.

   (1) 초면 인사와 함께 나이를 묻는 것은 "어른을 공경하라"는
       유교적인 사고 방식과 관계가 있다.   Ⓣ Ⓕ

   (2) 처음 만난 사람이 나이가 눈에 띄게 차이가 있을 때는
       무슨 띠냐고 물어서 나이를 파악한다.   Ⓣ Ⓕ

   (3) 한국에서는 쌍둥이라도 늦게 태어난 아이가 먼저 태어난
       아이에게 "형"이라고 부른다.   Ⓣ Ⓕ

   (4) 한국 사람이 상대방의 나이를 알고 싶어 하는 이유는
       무엇입니까?

   (5) 처음 만난 사람끼리 나이를 알아내는 방법은 어떤 것이
       있습니까?

   (6) 미스터 유가 크리스에게 생일이 언제인지 물은 이유는
       무엇입니까?

   (7) 미스터 유가 크리스의 생일을 알고 좋아한 이유는
       무엇입니까?

2. **Listening Comprehension.** 대화를 듣고 맞고(Ⓣ) 틀린(Ⓕ) 것을 지적하거나 질문에 대답해 보세요.

   대화 1
   (1) 마이클은 원래부터 갈비를 많이 먹는 갈비 대장이다.   Ⓣ Ⓕ
   (2) 마이클은 저녁 식사에 초대받아서 친구네 집에 가게 되었다.   Ⓣ Ⓕ
   (3) 마이클은 친구네 집에서 갈비를 얼마나 먹었습니까?

   대화 2
   (1) 마이클의 발표는 청교도적 사고 방식과 음식을 남기지 않는

한국의 예의 범절에 관한 것이다.   Ⓣ Ⓕ

(2) 마이클이 음식을 남기지 않은 이유는 무엇입니까?

(3) 마이클 친구의 어머니께서 마이클에게 갈비를 계속 준
이유는 무엇입니까?

(4) 마이클 친구의 어머니께서는 왜 마이클을 갈비 대장이라고
불렀습니까?

(5) 선생님께서는 한국에서 음식을 먹고 싶지 않을 때 어떻게
하라고 말씀하셨습니까?

New Words

갈비찜 *n. kalpitchim,* steamed ribs. 찜 steamed dish; 닭찜 steamed chicken

강조하다 *v.* to stress, put emphasis on ¶맹자는 사람이 본래 선하다는 점을 강조했다. Mencius reiterated that human beings are innately virtuous.

거부감 *n.* feeling of rejection or disapproval ¶한약에서 나는 고약한 냄새는 환자들에게 거부감을 일으켰다. The unpleasant smell of herbal medicine put off the patients.

거절 *n.* decline; reject. 거절하다 to decline, reject ¶거절해도 그 사람은 듣지 않는다. He will take no refusal.

겨우 *adv.* barely, narrowly, with difficulty, only ¶그는 겨우 살아간다. He manages to earn his living.

공경하다 *v.* to respect, revere ¶윗사람을 공경하는 것이 한국의 예절이다. It is Korean etiquette to revere one's elders.

관념 *n.* notion, idea, conception

교정 *n.* schoolyard; campus ¶봄 축제에는 아름다운 교정을 보려고 많은 시민들이 방문하였다. During the spring festival, many people visited the school to see the beautiful campus.

구조 *n.* structure ¶한국어 구조 structure of Korean

그런데도 *adv.* and yet; still; in spite of that; for all that; nevertheless

그제야 *adv.* only then; for the first time; not . . . until

근데 *adv.* contr. of 그런데 but, however, for all that

남기다 *v.* to leave (behind)

다양하다 *adj.* to be various, diverse, manifold ¶내 동생은 취미가 다양하다.

My younger brother has diverse interests (hobbies).

단박에 *adv.* at once, immediately, instantly ¶단박에 그는 상황을 알아차렸다. He grasped the situation at once.

대뜸 *adv.* outright; without reservation; openly ¶대뜸 한다는 말이 "사랑해"였다. He said, "I love you" openly.

대면 *n.* facing; meeting. 대면하다 to face, meet ¶나는 그들과 대면한 적도 없었다. I never met them.

대장 *n.* general; admiral; head; boss

동료 *n.* colleague; associate; co-worker; companion

띄다 *v.* to be seen; to be found; to be prominent (= 뜨이다) ¶눈에 띄게 remarkably; conspicuously; definitely; surely; markedly; noticeably ¶그녀는 눈에 띄게 야위었다. She became markedly thin.

띠 *n.* Chinese animal sign under which one was born

마침 *adv.* just in time, at the right moment, in the nick of time; fortunately

문화 차이 *n.* cultural difference

물어 오다 *v.* to ask the speaker (The auxiliary verb 오다 indicates direction toward the speaker.)

반응 *n.* reaction, response

밝히다 *v.* to make (a matter) clear, clear up ¶태도를 밝히다 to clarify one's attitude

부르다 *v.* to be full ¶배부르게 먹다 to eat heartily, eat one's fill ¶이젠 배가 불러요. I have my stomach full.

부임하다 *v.* to start (assume) a new post ¶새로 부임해 오신 선생님 a newly arrived teacher

불쑥 *adv.* suddenly; unexpectedly ¶불쑥 질문을 던졌다. A question was asked suddenly.

비우다 *v.* to empty; to clear; to exhaust ¶병을 비우다 to empty a bottle

사고 방식 *n.* way of thinking ¶올바른 사고 방식은 건강한 삶을 가져다 준다. A sound way of thinking brings a sound life.

사적이다 *adj.* to be private ¶초면에 남의 사적인 일을 캐묻는 것은 실례야. It is not good/proper etiquette to ask about private matters at the first meeting.

상대방 *n.* opposite party, other person ¶상대방을 생각하세요. Give consideration to other people.

생기다 *v.* to happen, come to pass, occur, come about

생년월일 *n.* date (and year) of birth. 생년 the year of one's birth ¶생년월일을 알려 주세요. Let me know your birthdate.

선호하다 *v.* to have preferences, prefer, have more of a taste for something ¶선호하는 음식은 무엇인가요? What is your favorite food? What food do you prefer?

소띠 *n.* cow sign of Korean zodiac; year of the cow

속으로 *adv.* in the back of one's mind (= 마음 속으로)

손뼉 *n.* flat or palm of the hand ¶청중들은 손뼉을 치며 환호했다. The audience cheered and clapped their hands.

수수께끼 *n.* riddle, conundrum, puzzle, mystery

순위 *n.* order, ranking, standing

시장하다 *adj.* to be hungry, feel empty

실망하다 *v.* to be disappointed ¶계약이 취소되자 김 사장은 크게 실망한 듯 했어요. President Kim seemed very disappointed when the contract was canceled.

심드렁하다 *adj.* to be uninterested (in doing), indisposed (to do) ¶그녀는 불만에 차서 심드렁한 표정을 지었다. Her face showed a lack of interest because she was unhappy about something.

쌍둥이 *n.* twin

알아내다 *v.* to find out, discover

앞서 가다 *v.* to go before, go ahead (of), precede

어리둥절하다 *adj.* to be stunned, bewildered ¶나는 갑자기 질문을 받고 어리둥절했다. I was bewildered by the sudden question.

에피소드 *n.* episode; anecdote

예의 범절 *n.* rules of etiquette. 예의 courtesy, manners; 범절 etiquette; proprieties; decorum

요청 *n.* request; demand ¶대통령은 국회의 해산을 요청하였다. The President requested the dissolution of the National Assembly.

움켜쥐다 *v.* to grip, clutch, clench, hold tightly

유교적 *n.* (being) Confucian; (being) related to Confucianism ¶조선 시대의 삶은 유교에 기초한 유교적인 삶이었다. Life during the Chosŏn Dynasty was based on the Confucian way.

의사 *n.* mind; intention; idea; thought

이토록 *adv.* to this extent, this much; like this ¶이토록 나에게 잘 해준 사람은 없어요. There is no one who takes good care of me like him.

익숙하다 *v.* to get used to ¶너는 곧 내 말씨에 익숙해질 거야. You will soon get used to my way of speaking.

젊음 *n.* youth; youthfulness

정중히 *adv.* gentlemanly; polite, courteous ¶너의 잘못을 인정한다면 정중히 사과해야 해. If you admit your mistake, you must make a polite apology.

존댓말 *n.* honorific expressions. 존대 treatment with respect ¶어른들께는 존댓말을 쓰는 것이 당연하다. It is natural for people to use honorifics to their elders.

지적 *n.* pointing out, indication

진작 *adv.* earlier; then and there ¶내가 진작 갔어야 했어요. I should have gone earlier.

차리다 *v.* to prepare, make ready; to arrange ¶저녁상을 차리다 to get supper ready, fix supper

청교도적 *n.* (being) puritanical

초면 *n.* first meeting (with) ¶초면일 때는 서로가 어색하게 마련이에요. It is natural for people to be awkward and uneasy at first meeting.

충청북도 *n.* North Ch'ungch'ŏng Province

파악하다 *v.* to grasp, get hold of, grip. 파악 grasp; hold; grip

표정 *n.* (facial) expression ¶연극 배우들은 다양한 표정 연기를 연습한다. Actors and actresses practice various facial expressions.

풀리다 *v.* to be solved, worked out, unraveled ¶그 어려운 문제가 풀렸다. The difficult problem was solved.

풍습 *n.* custom; manners ¶이 지방에는 아직 옛날 풍습이 남아 있어요. Some old customs still prevail in this part of the country.

하도 *adv.* very much indeed ¶하도 기뻐서 in the excess of one's joy

혼나다 *v.* to have a bitter experience, have an awful time, have a hard time ¶시험 치르느라 혼나다 to sweat out an exam

활짝 *adv.* (to smile) radiantly, brightly, happily ¶아이는 활짝 웃었다. The child smiled radiantly.

Useful Expressions

8.1 ~다 싶다 it appears that

The adjective 싶다 usually appears after ~고 or ~(으)면 to mean 'to want to, wish to, hope to, desire to,' as in 나도 가고 싶었어 'I wished I had been there' and 내일은 날씨가 좋았으면 싶어요 'I hope it will be fine tomorrow.' When it occurs after the plain statement ending ~다 or the indirect question ending ~(느)ㄴ가 or ~(으)ㄹ까, however, it means 'to appear, seem, be likely.'

용호가 올**까 싶**지 않다.
It is not likely that Yongho will come.

형은 돌아오지 않겠**다 싶**었어요.
It appeared that my brother would not come back.

사적인 일에 관심도 많**다 싶**어 이상했다.
I felt strange because he appeared to be too interested in others' personal matters.

8.2 ~기보다는 rather than

보다는 'rather than' is an emphatic form of the comparative particle 보다 'than.' Both forms occur after a noun, a pronoun, or a predicate stem nominalized by ~기.

요즘 아이들은 떡**보다는** 빵이 맛있다고 한다.
Children of today say they like bread, rather than rice cake.

새 일을 시작하**기보다는** 하던 일을 먼저 끝내지요.
Let's finish up the work we have been doing rather than starting a new work.

사람들은 보통 몇 살이냐고 직접 묻**기보다는** 무슨 띠냐고 묻는다.
People usually ask the other's sign rather than asking directly about their age.

8.3 ~라니요/다니요? What do you mean? What are you talking about?

The speaker uses this sentence ending to request clarification in surprise when the interlocutor makes a remark that is not clear, unexpected, or doubtful to him or her. It is attached to the portion of the interlocutor's remark that needs clarification. ～라니요? occurs with the copula stem (이), while ～다니요? occurs elsewhere.

A: 방금 사고가 났어요.
   There was an accident just now.
B: 사고**라니요?** (or 사고가 났**다니요?**) 누가요? 어디서요?
   What do you mean, an accident? (*or* What do you mean, there was an accident?) Who? Where?

A: 선생님이세요?
   Are you a teacher?
B: 선생님이**라니요?** 아니에요. 학생이에요.
   What are you talking about? No, I am a student.

A: 여행하는 동안 배가 아파서 혼났어요.
   I had a hard time with stomach trouble during my trip.
B: 배가 아팠**다니요?** 뭘 잘못 먹었는데요?
   What do you mean, you had stomach trouble? What kind of wrong food did you eat?

8.4 ～기에 (= ～기 때문에) as, because

～기에 (nominalizer suffix ～기 + particle 에 'at, in') and ～기 때문에, as well as ～(으)니까, denote reason. Both ～기에 and ～기 때문에 are used only in statement and question sentences, and cannot be used in command or proposal. Thus, 방이 덥기에 (or 덥기 때문에) 창문을 열어라/열자 'Please/Let's open the windows as the room is hot' is not grammatical. In sentences of command and proposal, the suffix ～(으)니까 'because' is used to indicate reason, as in 방이 더우니까 창문을 열어라/열자. Unlike ～기 때문에, however, ～기에 normally occurs in statement sentences and requires the subject of the main clause to be the speaker (first person). Thus, in 책이 싸기에 한 권 샀어요 'As the book was cheap, I bought a copy,' the understood subject is the speaker. Also unlike ～기 때문에, ～기에 requires the main clause predicate to be a verb, and not an adjective. A more colloquial form of ～기에 is ～길래.

비가 오겠**기에** 우산을 가지고 왔어요.
I brought my umbrella, expecting rain.

그가 나보다 나이가 많았**기에** 나는 그에게 존댓말을 써야 했다.

I had to use an honorific speech because he was older than I.

8.5 것은 물론(이고) not only. . . , but also

것은 물론이다, in which 물론 is an adverb with such meanings as 'of course, no doubt, without question,' means 'there is no doubt that,' 'it goes without saying that,' or 'it is a matter of course that.' When this construction is used as a clause ending with ~고 'and,' it has the meaning 'not only. . . , but also; let alone. . . .' In such cases, 이고 may be omitted.

인도의 지진 때문에 많은 사람이 죽은 **것은 물론(이고)** 여러 가지 전염병마저 퍼졌다.

Because of the earthquake in India, not only were many people killed, but also various infectious diseases became prevalent.

8.6 ~마저 even, also

Attached to a noun or pronoun, the particle ~마저 means 'even, also, so far as.' It connotes 'on top of, in addition to, or as well as something else' or 'with everything else, with all the rest.' Its meaning and use are similar to those of the particle 까지도 'even, so far as.'

추운데다가 바람**마저** 세게 불었어요.

It was very cold. Also, it was very windy.

그 사람은 집**마저** 팔았어요.

He went so far as to sell his house.

저**마저** 데려가 주세요.

Take me with you, too (since everyone else is going).

The particle ~마저 has developed from the adverb 마저 'also, too, all the way, going to the extreme.' The latter appears in sentences like 이것까지 마저 잡수세요 'Please eat this last one up, too' and 나는 읽던 책을 마저 읽어 버렸어 'I have completely finished reading the book that I was reading.'

8.7 심지어(는) on top of (all) that; what is more (worse)

The Sino-Korean adverb 심지어 literally means 'at its extreme.' This word can be followed by the topic particle 는 when emphasis is intended. Its usual meaning is 'on top of (all) this/that,' 'what is more,' 'what is worse.'

그 여자는 돈이 필요해서 이것 저것 다 팔고 나서 **심지어는** 결혼 반지까지 팔아 버렸어.
In great need of money, the woman sold various things and then (even) went so far as to sell her wedding ring.
비가 오더니 **심지어** 눈까지 오기 시작했어요.
It rained, and what was worse, it started to snow.

8.8   ~에 관해(서)/대해(서) on, about, in regard to, in relation to

These two idiomatic expressions are used interchangeably with the same meanings, although one contains the verb 관하다 'to be about, be concerned (with)' and the other the verb 대하다 'to face, confront.' Both forms may be followed by the topic particle 은/는 'as for' for emphasis. The corresponding adnomial forms are ~에 관한 and ~에 대한 'regarding, concerning, related to' as in 갈비에 관한/대한 발표 'a report on *kalbi*.'

저는 골프에 **관해서는/대해서는** 아는 것이 없어요.
Regarding golf, I don't know anything about it.
오는 수요일 저녁에는 김 박사님이 정신 건강**에 관해(서)/대해(서)** 강연하실 거예요.
In the coming Wednesday evening, Dr. Kim will deliver a lecture on mental health.

8.9   ~다구(요)/라구(요) you know, you see

The sentence-final ~다구(요)/라구(요), in which ~다 and ~라 (after the copula stem) are statement endings and 구(or 고) is a quotative particle, has derived from the quotative construction ~다고/라고 해(요) 'they say that ~' with truncation of the verb 하다 'to say.' ~다구(요)/라구(요) indicates a speaker's mild assertion and is equivalent to 'you know' or 'you see.'

저는 아직 학생이**라구요**.   I am still a student, you see.
김치도 조금 밖에 안 준**다구요**.   They give only a little kimchi, you know.
나를 도와주는 사람은 아무도 없**다구요**. There's nobody who helps me, you see.

Exercises

1. 관련된 단어들끼리 연결하여 문장을 만들어 보세요.

   (1) 배를   •   • 좋지 않다 _____

   (2) 활짝   •   • 묻다   _____

   (3) 손뼉을 •   • 치다   _____

   (4) 별로   •   • 움켜쥐다 _____

   (5) 대뜸   •   • 웃다   _____

2. 아래의 설명과 맞는 단어나 표현을 본문에서 찾아 쓰세요.

   (1) 상대가 되는 사람: _____

   (2) 개인에 관계되는: _____

   (3) 단 한번에 곧바로, 금방: _____

   (4) 학교의 넓은 뜰: _____

   (5) (사실, 생각, 일을) 공개적으로 널리 알리다: _____

3. 보기에서 적당한 말을 골라 빈칸을 채우세요.

> 보기: 하도, 불쑥, 진작, 마침, 심지어, 단박에, 그제야

   (1) 초면에 _____ 결혼했느냐는 질문을 받으면 기분이 안 좋다.

   (2) 그는 다니던 회사가 망하자 _____ 거지가 되었다.

   (3) 초등학생들은 물론 _____ 유치원생들도 컴퓨터를 할 줄 안다.

   (4) 부모님께서 무사히 한국에 도착하셨다는 전화를 받고 _____ 나
       는 안심이 되었다.

   (5) 내 동생이 _____ 운동을 잘 해서 여학생들 사이에 인기가 많아요.

   (6) 그동안 그렇게 배가 아팠으면 _____ 병원에 갔어야지.

   (7) _____ 점심을 먹으려고 하는데, 같이 좀 드시지요.

4. 밑줄 친 말과 반대되는 단어나 표현을 쓰고 그 단어나 표현을 사용하여 문장을 만들어 보세요.

(1) 나이를 물어 오는 질문에 처음에는 <u>사적</u>인 일에 관심도 많다 싶었어요.

_____: _____

(2) 어떤 한국 사람이 <u>초면</u> 인사와 함께 나이를 물었어요.

_____: _____

(3) 한국에서는 나이가 적은 사람이 나이가 많은 사람에게 <u>존댓말</u>을 쓴다.

_____: _____

5. 밑줄 친 말과 가장 비슷한 단어나 표현을 보기에서 고르세요.

(1) 나는 속으로 왜 이 사람이 나의 생일을 <u>이토록</u> 알고 싶어하는지 참 이상하다고 생각하였다.

    a. 이러한   b. 이렇게

    c. 이제야   d. 이튿날

(2) 한국 풍습이 이해가 되질 않았던 것은 물론이고 <u>거부감</u>마저 들었다.

    a. 긍정적인 마음   b. 큰 부자가 된 것 같은 마음

    c. 좋아하는 마음   d. 싫어하는 마음

(3) 어머니, 할머니께서 <u>시장하다</u>고 하셨어요.

    a. 배가 고프다   b. 배가 아프다

    c. 시장에 간다   d. 시작한다

6. 보기와 같이 주어진 말이 들어가는 단어나 표현을 3개 이상 써 보세요.

보기: 친 (親, friendly, parents): 친지, 양친, 친척, 친구, 친절

(1) 초 (初, beginning): _____

(2) 감 (感, feeling): _____

(3) 식 (式, style): _____

7. 다음 문장들을 "~다 싶다"(it appears that ~)의 형태로 바꾸세요.

(1) 이 일이 잘 되겠다.

→ _____

(2) 잠깐이면 다녀오겠다.

→ _____

(3) 친한 친구가 입원했으니 그 병원에 가 봐야겠다.

→ _____

8. "것은 물론이고"를 사용하여 보기처럼 대화를 완성하세요.

> 보기: A: 미아가 TV 방송에 나갔다구요?
>
>   B: 방송에 나간 것은 물론이고, 유명해졌어요.

(1) A: 태풍 때문에 가게들이 문을 닫았다. (학교도 쉰다)

B: _____

(2) A: 차 사고가 나서 사람이 다쳤대요. (길도 막혔어요)

B: _____

(3) A: 새 직장이 좋아요. (봉급도 많아요)

B: _____

9. "심지어(는)"를 사용하여 주어진 두 문장을 하나로 연결하세요.

> 보기: 친구가 없어요. 가족도 없어요.
>
>   → 친구도 없고 심지어는 가족도 없어요.

(1) 두 사람이 말다툼을 한다. 두 사람이 주먹으로 싸운다.

→ _____

(2) 동생이 자기 피자를 먹었다. 내 피자도 먹었다.

→ _____

(3) 직장이 없어요. 저축한 돈도 없어요.

→ _____

10. "~다구(요)"를 사용하여 다음 대화를 완성하세요.

> 보기: A: 학교 식당 밥이 그렇게 맛이 없다면서?
>
>   B: (김치도 조금 밖에 안 준다) 김치도 조금 밖
>   에 안 준다구요.

(1) A: 컴퓨터에 무슨 문제가 있으세요?

   B: (한글이 깨져서 나온다) _____

(2) A: 죄송하지만 방금 뭐라고 하셨어요.

   B: (하와이에서 콘서트가 열리다) _____

(3) A: 다음 학기에 무슨 과목 듣는다고 하셨죠?

   B: _____

11. "~라니요?/다니요?"를 사용하여 보기처럼 대화를 완성하세요.

> 보기: A: 한국어 배우는 학생이세요?
>
>   B: 학생이라니요? 저는 한국어 가르치는 선생님이에요.

(1) A: 다음 주에 이사 간다고 하던데 사실이에요?

   B: _____ 아니에요. 저는 계속 이 집에서 살아요.

(2) A: 주말에 아파서 병원에 갔다면서요?

   B: _____ 아니에요. 저 안 아팠어요.

(3) A: 저 사람이 범인(criminal)이에요?

   B: _____ 그 사람은 목격자(witness)예요.

12. "~마저"를 사용하여 주어진 두 문장을 하나로 연결하세요.

> 보기: 날씨가 추워요. 바람도 불어요.
>
>   → 날씨가 춥고 바람마저 불어요.

(1) 그 고양이는 늙었어요. 걸음도 못 걸어요.

→ _____

(2) 그는 한글 쓰기를 잘 못해요. 이름도 못 써요.

→ _____

(3) 가족이 없어요. 친구도 없어요.

→ _____

13. "～에 관해서"나 "～에 대해서"를 사용하여 보기처럼 대화를 완성하세요.

> 보기: A: 김 박사님, 강연(lecture)의 주제(topic)가 뭐예요?
> 　　　B: 21세기 환경보호에 관해서예요.

(1) A: 저 다큐멘터리(documentary)는 무슨 내용이에요? (코끼리의 이동)

　　B: _____

(2) A: 이 논문은 무슨 내용이에요? (인구와 경제 발전의 관계)

　　B: _____

Discussion and Composition

1. (Group work) 문화적 충격

　　Step 1. 한국인과 대화하면서 혹은 한국을 방문했을 때 문화적 충격을 받은 적
　　　　　　이 있습니까? 네 명이 그룹을 지어 자신의 경험을 이야기해 보세요.

　　Step 2. 한 가지 이야기를 골라서 짧은 연극(skit)을 만들어 보세요.

　　Step 3. 만든 연극을 발표하세요.

2. 문화 차이로 인한 오해(cross-cultural misunderstanding)를 경험한 적이 있습
　니까? 자신의 경험을 발표해 보세요. 발표할 때는 다음의 표현을 써 보세요.

> • ～더라구요　　　　　　• ～는 거예요/겁니다
>
> • ～라고 했어요/했습니다　• ～에 관해 발표하겠습니다

3. 문화 차이 때문에 생긴 오해를 어떻게 극복할(overcome) 수 있는지에 관해 자신의 경험을 바탕으로(on the basis of), 반 페이지 정도의 글을 써 보세요.

4. 한국어에서는 언제 존댓말을 씁니까? 영어에서도 한국어와 비슷한 존댓말이 있다고 생각합니까? 한국어와 영어의 존댓말의 차이는 무엇입니까? 여러분의 의견을 정리하여 한국어와 영어의 존댓말의 차이에 대해 짧은 글을 써 보세요.

5. "유교적인 사고 방식"은 무엇인지 조사하여 반 페이지 정도의 글로 써 보세요.

Further Reading

(1) **제목:** _____

한국 사람으로부터 처음 느끼는 것 중에 하나가 후한 인심이다. 특히 식당에서 친구들끼리 서로 돈을 내겠다고 싸우다시피 하는 모습은 매우 인상적인 광경이었는데 이러한 한국 문화가 처음에는 이해가 되지 않았다.

동료 영어 선생님의 초청으로 다방에 갔는데, 찻 값을 자기가 내겠다고 하여 다음에는 내 차례라고 하며 커피를 마셨다. 다음날 그 친구와 다방에 다시 갔는데 내 차례로 정해진 약속을 깨뜨리고 자기가 내겠다고 하면서 돈을 냈다. 그 후에도 내가 찻 값을 내려고 하면 번번이 그 친구는 손을 내저으면서 자기가 내겠다고 하여 어리둥절하였다. 그 친구의 친절이 혼돈이 되었다.

나중에 한국 문화 워크샵에서 한국식 에티켓을 배우면서 한국 사람이 돈을 내기 위해서 서로 다투는 것이 예의라는 것을 알게 되었다. 워크샵 강사가 "예의"를 시범으로 보이면서 가르쳤다. 세 번 이상 거절하는 것이 예의라 하였다. 식탁에 앉을 때 "내가 낼 테니 많이 잡수세요"라고 말하라 하였다. 그러면 상대방이 "내가 낼게요"하고 우길 것이라고 하였다. 식사가 끝나고 지갑을 꺼내면서 "내가 낸다"고 말하라고 하였다. 마지막으로 캐시어 앞에 와서 돈을 캐시어에게 먼저 주는 사람이 돈을 내는 사람이라고 하였다.

워크샵에서 정보를 얻은 후 빚을 갚기 위해 친구에게 식당에 가자고 초청하였다. 워크샵에서 배운 대로 실험을 하였더니 효과가 있어 밥 값을 낼 수 있었지만, 그 절차가 너무 복잡하고 세 번씩이나 내가 낸다고 말하는 것이 힘들었던 기억이 난다.

미국에서 (2) _____ 이러한 방법으로 자기 것은 자기가 내는 것을 (3) _____ 라고 한다.

(크리스 포오먼, 샌프란시스코 주립대 교수, "한국일보 오피니언"
2000년 9월 13일 수요일)

거절 refusal; 광경 scene, sight, spectacle; (돈을) 내다 to pay; 내젓다 to wave (hands), to swing (arms); 다방 tea room, cafe; 다투다 to argue, quarrel; 동료 colleague, co-worker; 번번이 always, every time;

> 빚을 갚다 to pay one's debts; 시범 showing an example; 싸우다시피
> as though someone is fighting, like real fighting; 약속을 깨뜨리다 to
> break a promise; 예의 manners, etiquette; 우기다 to insist; 인상적인
> impressive; 인심 the human mind, hospitality; 절차 procedure; 정보
> information; 정해진 fixed, established; 차례 order; 초청 invitation;
> 혼돈 chaos, confusion; 효과 effect; 후한 affluent, enough

1. 윗글을 읽고 (1)에 알맞은 제목을 써 넣으세요.

2. 다음 빈칸에 윗글 (2)에 들어갈 내용을 써 보세요.

_____

_____

_____

3. 밑줄 친 (3)에 적당한 표현을 영어로 써 넣으세요.

LESSON 8. AMERICANS' VIEW OF KOREANS

How Old Are You?

Koreans seem to be curious about other people's ages. They normally ask people their age when meeting them for the first time. When people abruptly ask me how old I am, my first thought is that they are being too inquisitive about my private life, and so [at first] I felt strange and uncomfortable.

I soon found out that asking another's age at first meeting comes from the structure of the Korean language and the Confucian way of thinking about respect for elders. Speech forms are raised or lowered depending on the age of the other person, so it is necessary to know the age of the person with whom you are speaking.

There are various ways to find out the age of someone you have just met. If someone is visibly older than you are, there is no need to ask. The younger person uses respectful language to the older person. When both people seem to be about the same age, they can find out their birth order by asking the other's sign [in the Chinese cycle of years] rather than asking directly about age. If the two share the same sign, they ask the birthday.

I remember when I met Mr. Yu for the first time. We were about the same age. He was from Seoul, and I was an American working as a middle-school English teacher in a small village in North Ch'ungch'ŏng province.

As soon as we met, he asked me outright, "What is your sign?"

"What do you mean, my sign?" I asked confusedly.

"I was born in 1949, the Year of the Cow," he explained.

I knew then that he was asking me the year of my birth. "I was also born in 1949, so I am a Cow, too," I answered.

While we were walking and having a look around campus, Mr. Yu, who walked ahead of me, turned to me and asked, "When is your birthday?" Inwardly, I found it very strange that this man wanted to know so much about my birthday. I could not remember even my close friends ever wanting to know my birthday, or asking for the year and date of my birth. I told him, "I was born on Christmas Eve. That's why my name is Chris."

Mr. Yu beamed and clapped his hands. "I was born in November!" I was confused as to why this person was suddenly so happy.

Disappointed by my lack of interest in his response, Mr. Yu explained, emphasizing that because he was a month older than I, he was therefore my "older brother." At the time, I didn't know what he was talking about. As one who grew up in America, where youth is celebrated, I could not understand Mr. Yu's happiness at being older.

When he gave me an explanation, I came to understand why Mr. Yu clapped his hands happily. Of course I did not understand the Korean custom according to which I had to use respectful language to him because he was older, or that I had to do what he told me to do. In fact, I hated it. I was accustomed to calling my older brother by his first name, and even calling teachers by their first names. I courteously declined Mr. Yu's request and did not call him "older brother."

I have heard some interesting stories about age difference. There were twin boys at the boardinghouse where I lived. Even though they were both born on the same day, the brother born twenty-seven minutes later called his earlier-born sibling "older brother." This is not an easy concept for Americans to fathom.

Chris Foreman, *Han'guk Ilbo,* 13 September 2000, Opinion column.

CONVERSATION

1

(Michael is making a class presentation on the subject of culture shock.)

Michael: All of you like *kalbi*, don't you?

Classmates: Yes, we do!

Michael: Let me talk about an episode related to my experience with *kalbi*. During the last summer break, I visited my friend's house in Korea. When I went to her house, it was about dinnertime. Her mother asked me if I'd eaten dinner. I said I hadn't. Then she said she had made steamed ribs, and told me to have some before leaving. I said that wouldn't be necessary, but she set the table, insisting that I stay and eat. She gave me steamed ribs and a bowl of rice. It was delicious. And after I ate one plate of ribs, she brought me another. I was already full, but I managed to eat the second plate. Alas, as soon as I finished the plate, she asked me if I wanted a little more. I said no because I was so full. But she told me to "fill up," and she brought me a third plate of ribs. Clasping my full stomach, I just barely managed to eat the third plate. I ate so many steamed ribs that day, I won't be able to eat them again for a whole year.

Teacher: I enjoyed Michael's talk. I guess perhaps some other students have had similar experiences. Now, let's discuss Michael's presentation.

2

(Discussion follows Michael's presentation.)

Michael: Later I heard from my friend that her mother said she'd never seen anyone eat so many ribs at one sitting, so she called me "General Ribs."

Teacher: When you have meals in Korea, you should make it clear when you have had enough, either by leaving a little food on your plate or by saying no when they offer more.

Michael: I learned from childhood not to leave food on my plate. I always clean my plate. And I did say no.

Teacher: If you say no just once, it means you want to eat more. They think you are refusing out of politeness. And because you completely emptied your plate, your friend's mother thought you

	were still hungry, and kept giving you more.
Michael:	Oh, I see.
Debby:	That (seems to have) happened because of the difference between the Puritan idea of not wasting food, and Korean etiquette.
Teacher:	That's right. You made a good point.
Michael:	Ah, it seems like the riddle has been solved! If I had heard from you about this kind of cultural difference before I went to Korea, it never would have happened.
Lucy:	Now that we have learned how to decline in the Korean way, we certainly won't have stomach trouble from overeating next time we are invited by Koreans.

Excerpted and changed from Chris Foreman, *Han'guk Ilbo,* Opinion column.

제9과 거북선과 콜라 병

(Lesson 9: The turtle boat and coca-cola bottle)

PRE-READING QUESTIONS

1. 세계를 바꾼 가장 위대한(great) 발명품(an invention)은 무엇이라고 생각합니까?

2. "필요는 발명의 어머니"라는 말은 무슨 뜻입니까?

3. 여러분이 무엇이든 발명할 수 있다면 어떤 것을 발명하고 싶은지 이야기해 보세요.

GAINING FAMILIARITY

1. 숫자 읽기

   ⅔ 〔삼분의 이〕, 1½ 〔일과 이분의 일〕, 0.51 〔영점 오일〕

2. 콜라 병, 유리 병, 제조업자, 특허, 성공

3. 거북선, 임진왜란, 전투함, 이순신 장군, 철갑, 측면, 뱃머리, 후미, 포 구멍, 송곳

애인의 치마를 닮은 코카콜라 병

허리가 잘록하게 들어가고 굴곡이 있는 코카콜라 병은 어떻게 해서 만들어졌을까?

바로 이 콜라 병을 만든 주인공은 미국의 얼 딘이라는 사람이다. 콜라 병을 만들어 내기 전, 그는 병을 만드는 한 평범한 제조업자에 지나지 않았다.[9.1] 하지만 그에게는 남다른 데가 있었다. 특히 그는 이상한 병을 만들어서 맘에 들지 않을 때는 그 자리에서 깨 버렸다. 그래서 주위 사람들은 그를 미치광이라고 놀려대곤 했다.[9.2]

"미끄러지지 않고 내용물이 많이 들어 있는 것처럼 보이는 병을 만들 수 있다면 얼마나 좋을까?"

사람들의 비웃음 속에서도 그는 늘 새로운 병을 만들기 위해 끝없이 노력했다. 어느 날, 얼 딘의 작업실로 애인이 찾아왔다. 애인은 그 무렵 유행하는 항아리처럼 생긴 치마를 입고 있었는데, 그 모습이 무척 예뻤다. 엉덩이 선이 유난히 아름답고 무릎이 있는 곳이 좁은 그 치마를 보는 순간, 얼 딘의 머리에 반짝 아이디어가 떠올랐다.

'그래, 바로 저거야! 저렇게 생긴 병을 한번 만들어 보자.'

애인을 보낸 뒤 얼 딘은 당장 작업실로 돌아와 애인의 주름치마를 응용하여 병을 만들기 시작했다. 얼 딘은 며칠 밤을 새워 병을 만드는 데 성공했고, 곧 그 병으로 특허를 받았다.

얼 딘은 그 병을 가지고 코카콜라 사장을 찾아갔다. 사장과 마주앉은 그는 자기가 만든 병의 장점을 열심히 설명했다. 그런데 코카콜라 사장은 고개를 저었다. 얼 딘은 크게 실망했다.

그러나 얼 딘은 굴하지 않고 이튿날 다시 코카콜라 사장을 찾아갔다. 그의 손에는 자기가 만든 병과 평범한 병, 그리고 작은 주전자가 들려 있었다. 얼 딘은 코카콜라 사장이 보는 앞에서 자기가 만든 병에 물을 부었다.

"사장님, 잘 보십시오. 어느 병에 물이 더 많이 들어가겠습니까?"

"물론, 이 병에 더 많이 들어가겠지." 사장은 얼 딘이 새로 만든 병을 가리켰다.

"아닙니다, 사장님. 잘 보십시오. 제가 만든 병에 담겨 있는 물을 이 평범한 병에 부어 보겠습니다. 자, 보십시오. 다 부었는데도 평범한 병은 3분의 2밖에 차지 않았습니다."

사장은 얼 딘의 설명에 고개를 끄덕였다. 그제서야 얼 딘이 발명한 병의 장점을 알아냈던 것이다.[9.3] 사장은 당장 계약을 하자고 했다. 평범한 유리 병 제조업자인 얼 딘은 마침내 자신의 끊임없는 노력에 대한 대가로 크게 성공했던 것이다.

「세상에서 가장 금쪽같은 이야기」 (1996), 정임조 엮음, 동쪽나라, pp. 154-157

대화

1

(덕수궁 현대 미술관, 거북선 모형이 전시된 곳에서)

사라: 어머, 영호 오빠, 저것이 거북선 모형인가 봐요? 진짜 거북이
       하고 똑같이 생겼어요.

영호: 그렇지? 거북의 모습을 본떠서 만들었다니까.

사라: 이게 일본이 한국을 침입했던 임진왜란 때 사용한 전투함
       이었지요?

영호: 응, 아마 임진왜란 1년 전에 만들었다지.[9.4]

사라: 그랬군요. 이 배를 만든 장군이 이순신 장군이죠?

영호: 응, 그 당시 이순신 장군이 전라도 해안 경비를 맡고 있었지.

사라: 그런데 이렇게 생긴 배로 어떻게 일본하고 전투를 했지요?

영호: 응, 잘 봐. 거북의 딱딱한 등 껍질을 본떠서 배 위를 철갑
       으로 덮었잖아.

사라: 아, 그러면 적군이 위로 들어갈 수가 없겠네요.

영호: 그렇지. 그런데 철갑 위에 다시 송곳을 꽂아서 적군의 접근
       을 철저히 막을 수 있도록 되어 있어.

사라: 그래요? 그럼 공격은 어떻게 해요?

영호: 여기 측면을 잘 봐, 구멍이 죽 나와 있지? 여기로 포를 쏘
       는 거지. 그리고 측면만 아니라 여기 이 거북선의 뱃머리와
       후미를 봐. 이것들이 또 포 구멍이야.

사라: 그러니까 전후좌우에서 공격을 할 수 있도록 만들어져 있
       군요. 거북을 본떠서 이런 전투함을 만들었다는 게 정말 신
       기하네요.

영호: 그러게 말야.[9.5] 이게 세계 최초의 철갑선이래.[9.6]

사라: 네, 그렇군요.

2

(덕수궁 현대 미술관 앞 분수대에서 사라와 영호가 이야기를 하고 있다.)

사라: 거북선을 보면 발명이라는 게 무에서 유를 만든다기보다
       모방에서 시작되는 것 같아요.

영호: 그렇지. 세계의 유명 발명가인 레오나르도 다빈치도 새의
       비행을 연구해서 비행기를 설계했잖아.

사라: 그리고 또 발명은 필요에서 오는 것 같아요. 필요하지 않으
       면 동기가 생기지 않으니까요.

영호: 그래. 그래서 필요는 발명의 어머니라고 하잖아. 며칠 전
       신문에서 보니까 한 중학교 여학생이 편찮으신 할머니를
       위해서 '장애인용 도우미 의자'를 발명해서 발명상을 탔대.
       그 학생은 몇 년 전 할머니께서 중풍으로 쓰러지셨는데, 할
       머니께서 쉽게 이동하고 화장실 이용도 쉽게 할 수 있도록
       의자를 만들었대.

사라: 와, 정말 효녀 발명가네요.

영호: 또 실패에서 생긴 발명품도 있지. 너 포스트잇이 어떻게 발
       명되었는지 아니?

사라: 아니오.

영호: 원래 쓰리엠이 접착용 풀을 만드는 회사였는데 한 사원이
       실수를 해서 풀의 원료를 잘못 섞었대. 그래서 접착력이 없
       어지는 바람에 붙여 놓으면 떨어지고 붙여 놓으면 떨어지
       고 해서[9.7] 만들어 놓은 풀을 다 버려야 할 판이었지.

사라: 그래서요?

영호: 근데, 마침 한 사원이 메모지에 실패한 풀을 붙여 판매하자
       고 아이디어를 냈어. 메모지를 책에 붙였다가 흔적 없이 떼
       어 낼 수 있기 때문이었지.

사라: 아, 그렇게 해서 포스트잇이 히트 상품이 되었군요.

Comprehension Questions

1. **Reading Comprehension.** 본문을 읽고 맞고(Ⓣ) 틀린(Ⓕ) 것을 지적하거나 질문에 대답해 보세요.

    (1) 얼 딘은 병을 만들면 언제나 깨 버렸다.   Ⓣ   Ⓕ

    (2) 얼 딘이 본 애인의 주름치마는 넓고 길었다.   Ⓣ   Ⓕ

    (3) 얼 딘은 자신이 만든 콜라 병에 대한 장점을 사장에게 알리는 데 실패했다.   Ⓣ   Ⓕ

    (4) "고개를 젓다"의 반대말은 무엇입니까?

    (5) 새로 만든 콜라 병의 장점은 무엇입니까?

    (6) 얼 딘이 새로운 병을 만들게 된 동기는 무엇입니까?

    (7) 주위 사람들은 얼 딘을 왜 미치광이라고 불렀습니까?

    (8) 얼 딘은 어떻게 자신이 만든 새 콜라 병의 장점을 증명해 보였습니까?

2. **Listening Comprehension.** 대화를 듣고 맞고(Ⓣ) 틀린(Ⓕ) 것을 지적하거나 질문에 대답해 보세요.

대화 1

    (1) 거북선은 앞쪽으로만 공격을 할 수 있게 만들었다.   Ⓣ   Ⓕ

    (2) 거북선은 미국의 군함을 보고 만들었다.   Ⓣ   Ⓕ

    (3) 거북선의 등은 철로 덮여서 적군이 올라갈 수가 없다.   Ⓣ   Ⓕ

    (4) 거북선의 장점은 무엇입니까?

    (5) 거북선은 무엇을 본떠서 만들었습니까?

    (6) 거북선의 등은 어떻게 만들어졌습니까?

    (7) 거북선이 만들어진 동기는 무엇입니까?

    (8) 임진왜란과 이순신 장군에 관해서 이야기해 봅시다.

대화 2

(1) 포스트잇은 모방에서 만들어진 발명품이다.　　　T　F

(2) 쓰리엠은 포스트잇을 만들려고 오랫동안 연구를 했었다.　　T　F

(3) 모방에서 만들어진 발명품의 예를 들어보세요.

New Words

가리키다 *v.* to point to, indicate

거북 *n.* turtle; tortoise (= 거북이)

거북선 *n.* the "Turtle Boat," an ironclad warship shaped like a turtle

경비 *n.* defense; guard. 경비하다 to defend, guard

계약 *n.* contract, compact. 계약하다 to contract ¶계약을 취소하다 to cancel a contract

고개 *n.* nape (of the neck); head; ridge; peak; pass (of a mountain) ¶고개를 들다 to raise one's head ¶고개를 숙이다 to droop one's head ¶고개를 끄덕이다 to nod one's head (for approval) ¶고개를 젓다 to shake one's head; to say "no"

공격하다 *v.* to attack; criticize. 공격 attack, assault; 공격적인 offensive, aggressive ¶적을 공격하다 to attack the enemy

굴곡 *n.* bends, windings, twists ¶굴곡이 진 winding, crooked ¶한국의 남해안은 굴곡이 심하다. The southern coast of Korea winds in and out.

굴하다 *v.* to yield, submit ¶~에 굴하지 않고 in spite of, in defiance of

껍질 *n.* skin; bark; shell

끄덕이다 *v.* to nod, nod approval ¶고개를 끄덕이다 to nod the head

끊임없다 *adj.* to be endless. 끊임없는 endless. 끊임없이 endlessly

남다르다 *adj.* to be peculiar, be different from others ¶남다른 노력 a great effort ¶그는 어딘지 남다른 데가 있다. He has something uncommon.

내다 *v.* to put forth

내용 *n.* content(s). 내용물 the contents

놀리다 *v.* to tease, make fun of. 놀려대다 to keep teasing

당시 *n.* in those days (times) ¶당시 나는 아이였다. I was a child then.

당장 *adv.* at once, right now; immediately ¶당장 학교로 가자. Let's go to school immediately.

대가 [대까] *n.* price, cost ¶대가를 치르다 pay the price ¶어떤 대가를 치르더라도 at any price

덕수궁 현대 미술관 *n.* Tŏksu Palace Modern Art Museum

도우미 *n.* helper. (derived from 도움 help, assistance and ～이 person)

동기 *n.* motive, motivation

떼어 내다 *v.* to remove, take off. 떼다 to take off; 내다 to put out, take out

마침내 *adv.* at last; in the long run ¶마침내 방학은 끝났다. Vacation has ended at last.

막다 *v.* to defend, check; to stop up ¶적을 막다 to hold the enemy off ¶구멍을 막다 to block up a hole

메모지 *n.* notepad, scratch paper. 메모 memo; 메모하다 to take a memo; 지 paper

모방 *n.* imitation, copying, mimicry. 모방하다 to imitate, model ¶～을 모방하여 after the model of ¶우리는 모방에 의해서 많은 것을 배워요. We learn many things by imitation.

모습 *n.* shape; (outward) look; state

모형 *n.* model; dummy; pattern ¶모형을 뜨다 to make a model (of)

무 *n.* nothing, none, nonexistence, naught ¶무에서 유는 못 만든다. Out of nothing, nothing comes.

무릎 *n.* knee; lap ¶무릎을 꿇다 to kneel down

미끄러지다 *v.* to slide, glide, slip ¶미끄러져 넘어지다 to slip and fall ¶빙판에서 미끄러져 넘어지다 to slip on the ice

미치광이 *n.* madman, lunatic, eccentric

바람 *n.* wind; motive; result ¶～는 바람에 because of

반짝 *adv.* sparkling, glittering, in flashes. 반짝이다 to glitter, flash, twinkle

발명 *n.* invention. 발명하다 to invent ¶발명의 천재 inventive genius

발명가 *n.* inventor. ～가 person

발명상 *n.* award for the best invention. 상 award

발명품 *n.* invention. ～품 item

뱃머리 *n.* bow (of a boat), prow; head

버리다 *v.* to throw away, finish, get through, do completely ¶다 써 버리다 to use up ¶음식을 다 먹어 버리다 to eat up the food

본뜨다 *v.* make a copy of. 본 example, model, pattern; 뜨다 to copy, imitate

분수대 *n.* fountain (base). 분수 fountain, jet of water; ～대 stand, base

붓다 *v.* to pour (into, out), put (water in a bowl) (= 따르다)

비웃음 *n.* derisive smile, sneer, jeer, ridicule. 비웃다 to ridicule, deride, sneer (at)

비행 *n.* aviation, flying; flight

사실 *n.* fact, reality, actuality, truth

상 *n.* prize ¶상을 타다 to win a prize, be awarded a prize

새우다 *v.* to stay up all night ¶공부로 밤을 새우다 to study all night long ¶밤을 새워 끝내다 to finish something by working all night

설계하다 *v.* to design, plan, make a plan for. 설계 plan, design ¶설계 중인 in the planning stages ¶정원을 설계하다 to lay out a garden design

성공하다 *v.* to succeed, be successful. 성공 success, accomplishment

송곳 *n.* gimlet; auger; awl; drill

신기하다 *adj.* to be marvelous, miraculous. 신기한 marvelous

실망하다 *v.* to be disappointed ¶그 결과에 실망하다 to be disappointed at the result

실패하다 *v.* to fail, go wrong, be unsuccessful. 실패 failure, blunder ¶사업에 실패하다 to fail in one's business

쓰리엠 *n.* 3M (corporation)

아이디어 *n.* idea

엉덩이 *n.* buttocks, hips ¶엉덩이 선 hipline

원료 *n.* raw material ¶원료가 부족한 나라 a country lacking raw materials

유 *n.* existence, being

유난히 *adv.* unusually; exceptionally

유행하다 *v.* to be in fashion, become popular ¶유행이 지나다 to go out of fashion ¶골프가 한창 유행하고 있다. Golf is all the rage.

응용하다 *v.* to apply; to put knowledge to practical use ¶배운 것을 응용하세요. Please put to use what you have learned.

이순신 장군 *n.* Admiral Yi Sunsin. 장군 general; commander-in-chief; admiral

이동하다 *v.* to move (around). 이동 movement

임진왜란 *n.* Imjinwaeran (Japanese invasion of Korea in 1592)

작업실 *n.* workroom. 작업 work, operation; ～실 room; 작업하다 to work

잘록하다 *adj.* to be slender; to be narrow ¶잘록한 허리 a slender waist

장군 *n.* military general

장애인 *n.* disabled person (= 신체 장애자). 장애 obstacle, handicap, hindrance, hitch; ～인 person

장점 *n.* strong point; advantage *ant.* 단점 weak point; disadvantage ¶~라는 장점이 있다 to have the advantage over

적군 *n.* enemy force (troops, army)

전라도 *n.* Chŏlla Province

전시되다 *v.* to be displayed, exhibited. 전시 display, exhibition; 전시하다 to display, exhibit

전투 *n.* battle, fight, combat. 전쟁 war; 전투하다 to fight, battle

전투함 *n.* battleship (= 전함)

전후좌우 *n.* in every direction (*lit.,* before and behind, left and right)

접근 *n.* approach; access. 접근하다 to draw near, approach, come close

접착용 *n.* for adhesion. 접착 adhesion; ~용 for (the use of)

젓다 *v.* to stir, row, shake ¶고개를 저었다. He shook his head (said no).

제조업 *n.* manufacturing industry. 제조 making, manufacture; 업 business ¶제조업자 manufacturer

주름치마 *n.* hobble skirt, pleated skirt. 주름 wrinkles, pleat, creases

주위 *n.* the circumference, the surroundings, the environs, the neighborhood. 주위의 surrounding ¶주위(의) 사람들 those around one

주인공 *n.* master; protagonist; hero/heroine; central character

주전자 *n.* teakettle

죽 *adv.* in a row (line) ¶죽 서다 to stand in line

중풍 *n.* palsy; paralysis

철갑선 *n.* ironclad ship. 철갑 iron covering; ~선 ship

철저히 *adv.* thoroughly; completely. 철저하다 to be thorough, complete

측면 *n.* side; profile ¶건물의 측면 the side of a building

침입하다 *v.* to invade. 침입 invasion, aggression

타다 *v.* to receive; to be awarded ¶상을 타다 to win a prize ¶졸업장을 타다 to receive a graduation certificate

특허 *n.* patent ¶특허권 patent right ¶특허 소유자 patentee ¶특허를 받다 to obtain a patent

판 *n.* scene; situation; circumstances; state of affairs; situation; moment (= 지경) ¶이러한 판에 at this juncture ¶음식을 다 버려야 할 판이었다. It was a situation where all of the food had to be disposed of.

판매하다 *v.* to sell; to merchandise. 판매 sale, selling, marketing

편찮다 *adj.* to be sick; to be uncomfortable. 아프다 to be sick ¶몸이 편찮아서 on account of illness

평범하다 *adj.* to be common, ordinary, mediocre, featureless ¶평범한 얼굴 featureless face ¶평범한 문장 ordinary composition

포 *n.* cannon; gun (= 대포)

포 구멍 *n.* cannon bore. 포 cannon; 구멍 hole

포스트잇 *n.* Post-it note

풀 *n.* glue ¶풀로 붙이다 to paste

필요 *n.* necessity, need, requirement. 필요하다 to be necessary ¶그는 휴식이 필요하다. He needs rest.

항아리 *n.* jar, earthenware pot ¶물 항아리 water jar

해안 경비 *n.* coastal defense. 해안 coast; 경비 defense, guard

효녀 *n.* dutiful daughter; a filial female

후미 *n.* the tail (end); the very end

혼적 없이 *adv.* without leaving trace. 혼적 traces, marks, vestiges

히트 상품 *n.* new, popular product. 히트 hit; 상품 product

Useful Expressions

9.1 ~에 지나지 않다 to be nothing but, to be no more than, merely

지나지 않다 literally means 'do not go beyond' or 'do not exceed.' Note that in the idiomatic meaning of the phrase, the particle 에 'at' must be used, not the object particle.

나는 평범한 학생에 지나지 않는다.
I am nothing but a common student.
얼 딘은 한 평범한 제조업자에 지나지 않았다.
Earl Dean was no more than an ordinary manufacturer.

9.2 ~곤/고는 하다 to do habitually; to do occasionally

~곤 and its uncontracted form ~고는 have developed from the suffix ~고 'and' and the particle 는 'as for.' The pattern ~곤/고는 하다 indicates an action habitually or occasionally done at present or in the past.

우리 아버지는 토요일이면 등산하시곤 **해요.**

My father occasionally goes mountain climbing on Sundays.

나는 어렸을 때 집 가까이 있는 호수에서 낚시질을 하곤 **했다.**

I used to fish at the lake near our house.

9.3 ~던 것이다 the fact is that (someone/something) did ~

~던 것이다 emphasizes a past fact, state, or event. 것 is 'fact; thing,' and 이다 is a copula. This pattern is usually used in formal speech and in writing.

사장은 얼 딘이 발명한 병의 장점을 알아냈던 **것이다.**

The fact is that the company president realized the strength of the bottles Earl Dean had invented. (emphatic)

Cf. 사장은 얼 딘이 발명한 병의 장점을 알아냈다.

The company president realized the strength of the bottles Earl Dean had invented. (non-emphatic)

얼 딘은 자신의 노력에 대한 대가로 크게 성공했던 **것이다.**

The fact is that Earl Dean succeeded greatly as a result of his efforts. (emphatic)

Cf. 얼 딘은 자신의 노력에 대한 대가로 크게 성공했다.

Earl Dean succeeded greatly as a result of his efforts. (non-emphatic)

9.4 ~지(요) (sentence ending)

In the dialogues in this and many previous lessons, several uses of the sentence ending ~지(요) have been illustrated. While sentences ending ~어(요)/아(요) make straightforward statements, questions, suggestions, or commands, sentences ending ~지(요) indicate the speaker's feelings and attitudes, including the following.

1. Assuring in a casual or friendly manner ('I'm sure'; 'I assure you'), in statements with falling intonation.

이순신 장군이 해안 경비를 맡고 있었지.

Admiral Yi Sunsin was in charge of the coastal defense.

여기로 포를 쏘는 거지.

They fired the cannon through this (hole).

실패에서 생긴 발명품도 있지요.
There surely are inventions derived from failure.

2. Asking about something that the speaker wonders about and believes the listener knows. Used in question-word questions with rising intonation.

저 학생이 누구지요? ↗
Who is that student? (I wonder.)

Cf. 저 학생이 누구예요? ↘
Who is that student?

이렇게 생긴 배로 어떻게 전투를 했지요? ↗
How did they fight in a boat shaped like this? (I wonder.)

Cf. 이렇게 생긴 배로 어떻게 전투를 했어요? ↘
How did they fight in a boat shaped like this?

3. Seeking agreement (equivalent to English tag questions like 'is[n't] it? do[n't] they? is that right?'). Used in yes-or-no questions with rising or rising-falling intonation.

이게 임진왜란 때 사용한 전투함이었지요? ↗ or ↗↘
This is a battleship used during the Japanese invasion of 1592, isn't it?

이 배를 만든 장군이 이순신 장군이죠? ↗ or ↗↘
The admiral who invented this boat is Admiral Yi Sunsin, isn't he?

4. Supposition ('I suppose [think] that ~'); in statements with a level intonation. Frequently, an adverb of probability, for example, 아마 also occurs.

임진왜란 1년 전에 만들었다지 (아마). →
I suppose they say that it was (probably) made a year before the Japanese invasion of 1592.

아마 그 도둑은 잡히고 말았지요. →
I suppose the thief (probably) ended up being caught.

5. Suggestion ('how about ~'; 'would you please ~?'), in commands.

들어오시지요.　　　　　　Would you come in, please?

Cf. 들어오세요.	Please come in.
먼저 떠나시지요.	How about leaving first?
Cf. 먼저 떠나세요.	Please leave first.

9.5 그러게 (말이다) I agree; that's right

그러게 (말이다) is a frequently used pattern indicating agreement with what has just been said. 그러게 alone, which is equivalent to 그러게 말이야, is used only at the intimate level. To make the pattern polite, 말이에요 or 말입니다 must be added. For the plain form, 말이다 is used.

A: 바퀴에 체인을 감아도 소용이 없더라구.	I chained the tires, but it didn't help.
B: 그러게 말야.	That's right.
A: 오늘 정말 바람이 세요.	It's very windy today.
B: 그러게 말이에요.	That's right.
A: 어두워지기 전에 집에 들어가는 게 좋은데.	We better go home before dark.
B: 그러게.	I agree.

9.6 (이)래 it is said that ~

이래 is a contraction of 이라고 해, where 이 is the copula and ~라 is a statement ending (equivalent to ~다) that occurs after the copula stem and before the quotative particle 고. When the ending ~다고 해 'it is said that' is expected, its contracted form ~대 is used.

이게 세계 최초의 철갑선이래.
It is said that this is the world's first ironclad boat.
마이클은 아주 열심이래.
Michael is said to be very diligent.

Cf. 이게 세계 최초의 철갑선이었대.
It is said that this was the world's first ironclad boat.
Cf. 그 여학생이 발명상을 탔대.
That female student is said to have received a prize for her invention.

9.7 ~고 ~고 하다 (repeated action)

~고 ~고 하다 is used when the same or parallel actions are repeated.

붙여 놓으면 떨어지고 붙여 놓으면 떨어지고 **한다**.
It falls off when pasted over and over.

그는 날마다 먹고 자고만 **한다**.
He eats and sleeps every day.

Exercises

1. 관련된 단어들끼리 연결하여 문장을 만들어 보세요.

   (1) 특허   •   • 떠오르다   _____

   (2) 아이디어 •   • 받다   _____

   (3) 고개   •   • 입다   _____

   (4) 계약   •   • 끄덕이다   _____

   (5) 치마   •   • 하다   _____

2. 아래의 설명과 맞는 단어나 표현을 본문에서 찾아 쓰세요.

   (1) 함부로 남의 나라에 들어오다: _____

   (2) 뛰어나거나 특별한 점이 없다: _____

   (3) 남과 많이 다르다: _____

   (4) 조금도 소홀히 하는 것이 없이 완전하게: _____

   (5) 어떠한 사고가 나지 않도록 살피고 지키는 일: _____

   (6) (원리, 지식, 기술을) 다른 일을 하는 데에 쓰다: _____

3. 보기에서 적당한 말을 골라 빈칸을 채우세요.

   > 보기: 크게, 끝없이, 정말, 반짝, 철저히, 당장

   (1) 그는 늘 새로운 병을 만들기 위해 _____ 노력했다.

   (2) 그 치마를 보는 순간, 얼 딘의 머리에 _____ 아이디어가 떠올랐다.

(3) 얼 딘이 발명한 병의 장점을 알아내자, 사장은 _____ 계약을 하자고 했다.

(4) 자신의 끊임없는 노력에 대한 대가로 _____ 성공했던 것이다.

(5) 거북이를 본떠서 이런 전투함을 만들었다는 게 _____ 신기하네요.

(6) 철갑 위에 다시 송곳을 꽂아서 적군의 접근을 _____ 막을 수 있도록 되어 있어요.

4. 밑줄 친 말과 가장 비슷한 단어나 표현을 보기에서 고르세요.

(1) 사람들의 <u>비웃음</u> 속에서도 그는 늘 새로운 병을 만들기 위해 끝없이 노력했다.
　　a. 조롱　　　　　　　　b. 큰 웃음
　　c. 조사　　　　　　　　d. 미소

(2) 여기 <u>측면</u>을 잘 봐, 구멍이 죽 나와 있지?
　　a. 옆면　　　　　　　　b. 앞면
　　c. 뒷면　　　　　　　　d. 아래면

(3) 허리가 <u>잘록하게</u> 들어가고 굴곡이 있는 코카콜라 병은 어떻게 해서 만들어졌을까?
　　a. 홀쭉하고 가늘게　　　　b. 홀쭉하고 짧게
　　c. 가늘고 짧게　　　　　　d. 가늘고 두껍게

(4) 얼 딘은 <u>굴하지 않고</u> 이튿날 다시 코카콜라 사장을 찾아갔다.
　　a. 뜻을 굽히지 않고　　　　b. 실망하지 않고
　　c. 뜻을 따라서　　　　　　d. 실망해서

5. 보기에서 적당한 말을 골라 빈칸을 채우세요.

> 보기: 하지만, 그래서, 특히, 바로

허리가 잘록하게 들어가고 굴곡이 있는 코카콜라 병은 어떻게 해서 만들어졌을까? _____ 이 콜라 병을 만든 주인공은 미국의 '얼 딘'이라는 사람이다.

　　콜라 병을 만들어 내기 전, 그는 병을 만드는 한 평범한 제조업자에 지나지 않았다. _____ 그에게는 남다른 데가 있었다. _____ 그는 이상한 병을 만들어서 맘에 들지 않을 때는 그 자리에서 깨 버렸다. _____ 주위 사람들은 그를 미치광이라고 놀려대곤 했다.

6. 보기와 같이 주어진 말이 들어가는 단어나 표현을 3개 이상 써 보세요.

> 보기: 친 (親, friendly, parents): 친지, 양친, 친척, 친구, 친절

　　(1) 가 (價, price, value): _____

　　(2) 명 (名, name, famous): _____

　　(3) 품 (品, item, article): _____

　　(4) 군 (軍, military): _____

7. "~어요/아요" 문장을 밑줄 친 곳에 "~지(요)" 문장으로 바꾸고 "~지(요)"의 뜻을 괄호 안에 적으세요. "~지(요)"의 뜻에는 assurance/casualness (AC), question/wondering (QW), seeking agreement (SA), supposition (SP), and suggestion (SG) 등이 있습니다.

　　(1) A: 어디 가세요? _____ (　　)
　　　　 B: 시장에 좀 가요.

　　(2) A: 밖에 비가 와요? _____ (　　)
　　　　 B: 네, 지금 비가 오고 있어요.

　　(3) A: 언제 결혼하세요?
　　　　 B: 아마 내년에는 할 거예요. _____ (　　)

　　(4) A: 어서 들어오세요. _____ (　　)
　　　　 B: 감사합니다.

　　(5) A: 우리는 여름마다 하와이에 가요. _____ (　　)
　　　　 B: 그러세요?

8. "그러게 말이다"를 사용하여 다음 대화를 완성하세요.

> 보기: 마크: 요즘 날씨가 왜 이리 덥지요?
>   민지: 그러게 말이에요. 엘리뇨 현상인가 봐요.

(1) 마크: 오늘 서울에서만 교통 사고가 열 군데서 났다더군요.
    민지: _____

(2) 마크: 오늘 밤에는 별이 유난히 반짝이네요.
    민지: _____

(3) 마크: 강원도에 폭설이 내린다지요?
    민지: _____

9. "(이)래(요)"를 사용하여 다음 대화를 완성하세요.

> 보기: A: 저 분은 누구신가요? (김민수 교수)
>   B: 김민수 교수시래요.

(1) A: 거북선은 어떤 배인가요? (세계 최초의 철갑선)
    B: _____

(2) A: 마이클은 열심히 공부한대요? (아주 열심이다)
    B: 네, _____

10. "~곤/고는 하다"를 사용하여 대화를 완성하세요.

> 보기: A: 토요일에 보통 뭐 하세요?
>   B: 집 가까이에 있는 호수 가에서 낚시를 하곤 해요.

(1) A: 시험 때 주로 어디에서 공부하세요?
    B: _____

(2) A: 수업이 끝나고 나면 주로 뭐 하세요?
    B: _____

(3) A: 차를 사기 전에는 어떻게 학교에 다녔어요?
    B: _____

11. "~에 지나지 않다"를 사용하여 말을 만드세요.

 (1) A: 어제 만난 사람은 어떤 사람이에요?

  B: _____

 (2) A: 얼 딘은 부자가 되기 전에 어떤 사람이었어요?

  B: _____

 (3) A: 남편께서는 뭐 하시는 분이세요?

  B: _____

Discussion and Composition

1. (Role play) 선생님께서 나누어 주시는 role card를 보고 role play를 하세요.

2. (In-class presentation) 한국에는 거북선 이외에도 해시계, 물시계, 금속 활자 등 여러 가지 발명품이 있습니다. 한국의 발명품 중에서 하나를 골라 조사를 한 다음 수업 시간에 5분 정도 발표를 하세요.

3. "내가 가장 중요하다고 생각하는 발명품"에 대해 이야기하세요. 이야기한 내용을 정리하여 introduction, body, conclusion 있는 한 페이지 정도의 글을 써 보세요. 글을 쓸 때는 다음의 연결어(connectives)를 사용해 보세요.

> 그리고, 하지만, 그러나, 특히, 그래서, 그런데,
> 그러면, 그러므로

Further Reading

곰

지리산 어느 골짝에는 유난히 감이 많은데, 이 감은 겨울에

먹이가 적은 곰들에게는 좋은 간식 거리가 된다. 마을 사람
들은 감을 이용하여 별 힘을 들이지 않고 아래와 같이 곰을
잡는다.
　(1) ＿＿＿＿＿＿ 자갈을 가득 넣은 가마니와 솜을 가득 넣
은 가마니를 각각 준비한다. (2) ＿＿＿＿＿＿ 솜을 넣은 가마
니를 산에 있는 감나무에 매달고는 마구 머리로 박는다. (3) ＿＿＿＿＿＿ 감을 그
렇게 따는 것 같이 한다. 그때 누군가가 위에서 감을 던져 준다. (4) ＿＿＿＿＿＿
곰의 눈에는 가마니에 박치기를 하기 때문에 감이 떨어지는 것으로 보인다.
　그 모습을 숨어서 지켜본 곰은 다음날 사람이 없는 틈을 타서 사람이 하던
것과 똑같은 행동을 하기 시작한다. (5) ＿＿＿＿＿＿ 처음 박치기를 한 곰은 머리
가 무척 아프다. 곰은 다시 한번 더 힘껏 박치기를 하지만, 가마니는 별로 움
직이지 않고 감도 떨어지지 않는다. 자기 머리만 더 아플 뿐이다. 사실 곰이
박치기를 하고 있는 가마니는 (6) ＿＿＿＿＿＿ 가마니가 아니라, (7) ＿＿＿＿＿＿
가마니이기 때문이다.
　그 사실을 모르는 미련한 곰은 더욱 세게 박치기를 한다. 곰은 나무에 매
달린 맛좋은 감을 따기 위해서 그렇게 계속 박치기를 한다. 곰은 결국 까무러
치고 만다. (8) ＿＿＿＿＿＿ 숨어서 지켜보던 사람들이 우르르 몰려나와 곰을 잡아
간다.

　　　　　　　「세상에서 가장 금쪽같은 이야기」 (1996), 정임조 엮음, 동쪽나라

~(으)ㄹ 뿐이다 only, just; ~고 말다 it ends up; 가득 full; 가마니
straw bag; 간식 거리 between-meal refreshments, snacks; 감
persimmon; 거치다 to go through; 결국 finally; 골짝 valley; 그토록 to
that extent; 금쪽 something as precious as a piece of gold
(figurative); 까무러치다 to faint away; 끝에 at last, in the end; 누군가
someone; 단계 steps; a stage; 단지 only, just; 던져 주다 to throw;
따다 to pick; 마구 recklessly, carelessly; 매달다 to hang up; 먹이 food;

몰려나오다 to turn out en masse; 무려 as much/many as; 무척 very much, extremely; 미련하다 to be stupid, dull; (머리를) 박다 to butt; 박치기 butt with the head; 발명하다 to invent; 별 contracted form of; 별로 not very, not much; 성공하다 to succeed; 세게 strongly; 솜 cotton; 수없이 countless; 실패하다 to fail; 실험 experiment; (책) 엮음 compilation (of a book); 우르르 in droves; 이용하다 to use, utilize; 자갈 pebble; 잡아가다 to take; 전구 lightbulb; 준비하다 to prepare; 지켜보다 to keep watch; 틈을 타다 to watch for a chance, take advantage of; 행동 action; 힘껏 with full force; 힘을 들이다 to exert one's power

1. 위 글의 밑줄 친 곳에 가장 적당한 표현을 고르세요.

(1) a. 그때
    b. 그리고
    c. 먼저

(2) a. 그런 다음
    b. 그러면
    c. 그러나

(3) a. 그리고 나서
    b. 말하자면
    c. 그러나

(4) a. 그리고
    b. 그러면
    c. 그러나

(5) a. 그러면
    b. 말하자면
    c. 그러나

(6) a. 솜
    b. 자갈
    c. 좋은

(7) a. 솜
    b. 자갈
    c. 나쁜

(8) a. 그때
    b. 말하자면
    c. 그러나

2. 다음 만화를 읽고 뜻을 영어로 말하세요.

("광수 생각" [Kwangsoo Reflects], 조선일보, 1998년 7월 22일)

LESSON 9. THE TURTLE BOAT AND THE COCA-COLA BOTTLE

Coca-Cola Bottle that Resembles Girlfriend's Skirt

How was the Coca-Cola bottle, with its slender waist and unevenness, made?

The central character who made this cola bottle is America's (*lit.,* person named) "Earl Dean." Before he made the Coca-Cola bottle, he was no more than an ordinary bottle manufacturer. Yet, there was something different (*lit.,* from others) about him. In particular, when he was not pleased with an unusual bottle he made, he broke the bottle on the spot. People around him teased him, calling him an eccentric.

"How wonderful it would be to make a bottle that did not slip and looked as if it held a lot?"

Even though people ridiculed him, he struggled endlessly (to continue) to make new bottles. Then, one day, Earl's girlfriend came to his workroom. She was wearing a fashionable hobbleskirt that looked like a jar. Its appearance was quite pretty. The moment Earl saw the skirt with the (especially) beautiful hipline and the tight hemline, an idea flashed into his head.

"Yes, that's it! Let's try to make a bottle that looks like that."

After he sent his girlfriend away, Earl immediately returned to his workroom and began making a bottle based on (*lit.,* utilizing) her hobbleskirt. After several nights, Earl succeeded in making the bottle. He immediately obtained a patent for it.

With this bottle [in hand], Earl sought out the president of Coca-Cola. Sitting across from the president, Earl eagerly (*lit.,* strenuously) explained the advantages of the bottle he had made. But the Coca-Cola president shook his head. Earl was terribly (*lit.,* largely) disappointed.

But Earl was [also] undaunted, and the next day, he sought out the president of Coca-Cola again. In his hand he held the bottle he had made, an ordinary bottle, and a small teapot. In plain sight of the president of Coca-Cola, Earl poured water into the bottle he had made.

"President, please look carefully. Which bottle do you think will hold more water?"

"Of course, this bottle will hold more." The president pointed to the bottle that Earl had recently made.

"Not so, president. Look carefully. I shall pour the water from the bottle that I made into this ordinary bottle. Here, look. Although I poured it all out, only two-thirds of the ordinary bottle is filled."

The president nodded in response to Earl's explanation. At last he understood (*lit.,* came to understand) the advantages of the bottle invented by Earl. The president immediately offered Earl a contract. In return for his endless striving, a common bottlemaker, Earl, succeeded greatly.

Sesang esŏ Kajang Kŭmtchok Kat'ŭn Iyagi, compiled by Ch'ŏng Im-Cho. Seoul: Tongtchok Nara, 1996, 154−157

CONVERSATION

1

(At the model Turtle Boat exhibit in the Tŏksu Palace Modern Art Museum)

Sarah: Oh my (*lit.,* older brother), Yŏng-ho, that must be the model Turtle Boat. It really looks exactly like a tortoise.

Yŏng-ho: Doesn't it? That's because it was built in the image of a tortoise.

Sarah: This was the battleship used in the Japanese invasion of Korea in 1592, right?

Yŏng-ho: Uh-huh. Probably built one year before the Japanese invasion of Korea (*lit.,* so they say).

Sarah: I see. The admiral who built this boat was (*lit.,* Admiral) Yi Sunsin, right?

Yŏng-ho: Yes. At that time, Admiral Yi Sunsin was in charge of the Chŏlla coastal defense.

Sarah: But how did they fight Japan with boats that looked like this?

Yŏng-ho: Well, look carefully. See that the boat's top (*lit.,* back) is covered with iron, just as the tortoise's back is made of hard shell.

Sarah: Ah, then the enemy cannot enter through the top.

Yŏng-ho: Right. In addition, they staked gimlets on top of the iron covering so that the enemy's attack could be completely blocked.

Sarah: Really? Then how do you [launch an] attack [from this ship]?

Yŏng-ho: Look carefully at the side here. See these holes in a row? You shoot the cannon through here. In addition to the side, look here at the boat's head and the tail end. These are also cannon holes.

Sarah: So the boat (*lit.,* it) was made to attack from every direction. It's really amazing that battleships like this were made in the likeness of a tortoise.

Yŏng-ho: Don't I know it. This is the world's first ironclad ship.

Sarah: Yes, I see.

2

(Sarah and Yŏng-ho are talking by the fountain in front of Tŏksu Palace Modern Art Museum.)

Sarah: When I see the Turtle Boat, I think that invention arises not by making something from nothing, but rather through imitation.

Yŏng-ho: Of course. Even the world-famous inventor Leonardo da Vinci designed the airplane by studying the flight of birds.

Sarah: Also, I think that invention comes out of necessity. If something is not needed, there is no (*lit.,* creation of) motivation for it.

Yŏng-ho: Right. That's why they say necessity is the mother of invention. I read in the newspaper a few days ago that a female student at an intermediate school won an inventor's award for inventing a "disabled person's helper-chair" for her ailing grandmother. Yes. Her grandmother became prostrate with paralysis several years ago, so the girl built a chair to help her move around and use the restroom easily.

Sarah: Wow, what a truly filial inventor.

Yŏng-ho: There are also inventions that came from failure. Do you know how Post-its came to be invented?

Sarah: No.

Yŏng-ho: 3M was originally a company that produced adhesives. An employee of the company made a mistake and incorrectly mixed the raw materials for the glue. Without the proper adhesive quality, the glue came off when pasted repeatedly, resulting in a situation where all of the glue had to be disposed of.

Sarah: Really?

Yŏng-ho: But luckily an employee presented an idea to sell memo pads pasted with the failed glue. He reasoned that there might be people who needed memo pads that could be pasted to a book and removed without a trace.

Sarah: Oh, so that's how Post-its became a hit product.

Useful Expressions

L = lesson, C = conversation, N = narration, U = useful expression

Item	Meaning	Lesson	
2박 3일	two nights and three days (of a trip)	L5C1	U5.6
modifying clauses		L2C2	U2.10
N는/은 N이다	it is N, if anything	L5C2	U5.10
N에다(가)	at, on, in, onto, to N	L16C2	U16.8
N하면	if (when) one does (says, thinks) about N; speaking of N	L3N	U3.3
omission of the copula		L17N	U17.3
[time word]~이/가 되다	to come; to be	L3N	U3.4
~(느)ㄴ 데에는	(in the circumstance) that; in doing/being	L13N	U13.2
~(스)ㅂ디다	(past experience/observation)	L4N	U4.9
~(으)ㄴ 만큼	as, since, now that	L14N	U14.2
~(으)ㄹ건데(?)	(elaboration on the background)	L14C1	U14.5
~(으)ㄹ걸	I guess, maybe, I wish	L12C2	U12.6
~(으)ㄹ 거라는 생각이 들다	to feel that	L11N	U11.3
~(으)ㄹ 걸/것을	with a thing/fact that; but instead	L7N	U7.3
~(으)ㄹ 만하다	to be worth (doing); to deserve	L5N	U5.1
~(으)ㄹ 뿐더러	not only . . . but (also)	L14N	U14.3
~(으)ㄹ 수밖에(요)	can't help ~ing; have no other way but to	L15C1	U15.8
~(으)ㄹ 텐데	be supposed to do/be, and/but/so	L3C1	U3.5
~(으)라	(non-interactional imperative)	L15N	U15.2
~(으)라는	(ordering) that . . .	L13N	U13.3
~(으)라잖니	you know, A tells B to do; as they say, one should do	L14C1	U14.6
~(으)려고요	because one intends to	L6C2	U6.9
~(으)려는/(으)려던 참	(at) the point of (doing); just when	L18N	U18.2
~(으)리(라)	I/(s)he/it will	L2C2	U2.9
~이/가 그러는데	according to (a person)	L10C1	U10.7
~거나 ~거나 하다	to do/be ~ or ~	L16N	U16.1
~거늘	(archaic) now that, since, given that; though, while	L18N	U18.9
~거든요	because, since, as, indeed	L1C1	U1.5

~건/거나 . . .	whether . . . or; either . . . or; and;		
~건/거나	regardless of	L2N	U2.1
~게 생기다	it appears (seems) that ~	L12C2	U12.7
~게/기 마련이다	it is natural that ~; to be bound to	L10N	U10.3
~겠네요	I guess (he/she/it/they/you) probably . . .	L5C1	U5.5
~고	and also, please (why don't you)	L3C1	U3.7
~고 ~고 하다	repeated action	L9C2	U9.7
~고 그러다/그렇다	and the like	L12C1	U12.2
~고 나다	to have just finished (doing)	L3N	U3.2
~고 나서(는)	after; and then	L4N	U4.4
~고 말다	to end up doing; to get around to doing	L7N	U7.1
~고 해서	because . . . and the like; and such, so	L5C1	U5.8
~고(요)	and . . . (afterthought)	L17C2	U17.6
~고서는	(in negative constructions) without		
	doing ~; unless one does ~, if not ~	L15N	U15.1
~곤/고는 하다	to do habitually; to do occasionally	L9N	U9.2
~구만; ~구먼	well, I see; so it is	L4N	U4.12
~기(가) 일쑤이다	always to be doing (something unpleasant)	L1C2	U1.10
~기는 (or 긴) 하다	it is true that ~ (but)	L2C1	U2.5
~기보다는	rather than	L8N	U8.2
~기에 (= 기 때문에)	as, because	L8N	U8.4
~길래 = ~기에	as, since, because	L12C2	U12.4
~나?	I wonder (self-addressed question)	L11C1	U11.6
~느라(고)	while doing ~, (in) doing	L13N	U13.1
~는 게 아니겠어요!	alas!	L18N	U18.3
~는가/(으)ㄴ가 싶다 or			
~(으)ㄹ까 싶다	to think (wonder, feel) that ~	L11N	U11.2
~는가요/(으)ㄴ가요?	(polite question form)	L1C1	U1.4
~는/(으)ㄴ지	I don't know [question word]. . . , but;		
	probably because	L6C2	U6.11
~는가/(으)ㄴ가 보다	it seems; it looks; I guess	L15C1	U15.6
~는가/(으)ㄴ가/(으)ㄹ까			
해서	wondering if ~; thinking that ~	L7C2	U7.6
~다 못해(서)	(being) unable to continue to . . .	L4N	U4.7
~다 싶다	it appears that	L8N	U8.1
~다(가) ~다(가) 하다	alternation of actions or states	L1C1	U1.8
~다(가) 말다	to leave off ~ing	L15C2	U15.9
~다(가) 보니(까)	while one kept (doing), (as a result) . . .	L6C1	U6.6

~다(가) 보면	if one keeps doing; while doing	L10N	U10.2
~다/라 하더라도	even if (it is the case that); granting that	L6N	U6.4
~다가는	to do and then; if . . . (with negative consequence)	L17N	U17.4
~다고/라고	as it is said that	L10C3	U10.9
~다고/라고	(saying) that	L6C2	U6.10
~다고/라고 해서	be called (entitled or known as) ~ and (so/then)	L13C1	U13.5
~다구(요)/라구(요)	you know, you see	L8C2	U8.9
~다구(요)?/라구(요)?	are you saying that . . . ? (echo-question)	L12C	U12.5
~다는 겁니다	it is/was said/reported/found that	L1N	U1.2
~다더니/라더니	I heard that ~, and	L10C1	U10.8
~다마다요	of course, certainly, indeed, to be sure	L6C2	U6.12
~다며	saying that	L4N	U4.10
~다면서	indicating that	L17N	U17.1
~다시피	as	L13C2	U13.6
~다시피 하다/되다	nearly do ~; to do as if ~	L10C1	U10.6
~다지/라지 뭐예요	indeed, it is said	L15C1	U15.7
~대로	as, like, in accordance with, as it is	L16C2	U16.9
~댄다	(they/he/she) say(s) that	L3C1	U3.6
~더니	[speaker] observed/experienced ~, but/and now	L16N	U16.2
~더라구요	I saw/witnessed/felt that; you know	L5C1	U5.9
~더러	specialized indirect object marker	L2C1	U2.7
~던 것이다	the fact is that (someone/something) did ~	L9N	U9.3
~도 (말고) ~도 말고	neither. . . nor. . ., but	L3N	U3.1
~도록 하다	to (decide to) do; be sure to do	L13C2	U13.8
~든(지) ~든(지)	whether ~ or ~; regardless	L15C1	U15.5
~들	indicates a plural subject	L11C2	U11.10
~듯(이)	as if, like, as, as . . . as	L16C1	U16.6
~라니요?/다니요?	what do you mean? what are you talking about?	L8N	U8.3
~마저	even, also	L8N	U8.6
~만 못하다	not to be as good as	L5N	U5.3
~만 해도	even; at least	L11N	U11.1
~어/아 가지고	with; by doing/being; for the reason that	L4N	U4.11
~어/아 놓다, ~어/아 두다	to do something for later; to do something and keep it that way (or for future use)	L3C1	U3.8

~어/아 보세요	supposing (that) ~; provided that	L15C2	U15.11
~어/아 빠지다	extremely [derogatory]	L4N	U4.8
~어/아 마땅하다	to deserve to	L18N	U18.8
~어다/아다 (놓다, 두다, 가두다, etc.)	to carry (something) from one place to another	L7N	U7.2
~어도/아도 너무 ~	to do/be too (much)	L17C1	U17.5
~어도/아도 되다; ~(으)면 되다	to be all right	L11C1	U11.7
~어라/아라	oh! (interjection)	L7C1	U7.4
~어라/아라	exclamation	L13C2	U13.7
~어서야/아서야	only when; not until	L5C2	U5.13
~어야/아야 하느니라	(archaic) one should; one is supposed to; one is to	L18N	U18.10
~어야지(요)/아야지(요)	I suppose/suggest one must	L3C1	U3.9
~어야겠다/아야겠다	I think (it/one) should ~	L13C1	U13.4
~어하다/아하다	changes an emotive adjective to a verb	L10N	U10.4
~었으면/았으면 하다	to wish to; to wish that it would	L6C1	U6.7
~에 관해(서)/대해(서)	on, about, in regard to, in relation to	L8C1	U8.8
~에 따르면	according to	L2N	U2.2
~에 지나지 않다	to be nothing but, to be no more than, merely	L9N	U9.1
~에다(가)	in addition to	L12C1	U12.3
~은/는 물론이다	there is no doubt that, it goes without saying that, it is a matter of course that	L2N	U2.3
~은(요)/는(요)	not at all, far from it, not really	L11C2	U11.9
~을/를 대상으로	taking (something/someone) as a (research) subject	L1N	U1.1
~을/를 두고	in regard to; on; about	L12N	U12.1
~을/를 통하여	through(out); by (way of); via	L4N	U4.1
~의 경우	in case (event) of	L14N	U14.4
~자고?	are you suggesting (asking) that we do ~?	L2C1	U2.4
~지 못할까!	can't you . . . ?!	L18N	U18.4
~지(요)	sentence ending	L9C1	U9.4
가지고	with, for, about	L7C2	U7.7
거	contraction of 것	L16C1	U16.4
거겠지(요)	it may be that ~; I guess that ~	L15C2	U15.10
거예요	it is that; the fact is that	L4N	U4.5

것은 물론(이고)	not only. . . , but also	L8N	U8.5
(그) 얼마나 . . . ~가/까	how/what. . . !	L6N	U6.1
그건 . . . 때문이에요	that is because . . .	L5C2	U5.11
그래야	only then; only if it is so (that way)	L15N	U15.3
그러게 (말이다)	I agree; that's right	L9C1	U9.5
그렇고 말고(요)	of course, that is true	L18N	U18.6
그렇지 않아도 (=			
그러잖아도)	as a matter of fact	L1C1	U1.6
기왕이면 (= 이왕이면)	while one is at it; things being what		
	they are	L18N	U18.5
내 정신 좀 봐	I completely forgot about it.	L1C2	U1.12
넘게	more than	L3C2	U3.10
누군가	someone	L10N	U10.1
다시 말해서	in other words	L1N	U1.3
달라고 하다	to ask (someone) to give (something)		
	to oneself	L4N	U4.3
두말할 것도 없다	it is obvious (needless to say) that ~	L16N	U16.3
마	'don't (do)'	L12C2	U12.8
마침 잘 됐다	perfect timing!	L3C2	U3.11
말고는	other than, except	L5C1	U5.7
말씀 낮추세요	Please lower your speech (level).	L1C1	U1.7
말씀 도중 실례지만	excuse me for interrupting, but	L1C2	U1.11
말이다	I mean; you know	L3C2	U3.12
못지않게	no less (than); equally	L14N	U14.1
뭐라고(요)?!	what?! what are you talking about?!	L18N	U18.1
뭘 사 가야 할지			
고민이에요	I am worried about what to take	L16C1	U16.5
뭘(요)	not really	L7C1	U7.5
바	what (one does)	L6N	U6.2
세상에 그럴 수가!	how could such things happen in		
	the world!	L5C2	U5.12
손꼽아 기다리다	to look forward to; to wait eagerly for	L18N	U18.7
심지어(는)	on top of (all) that; what is more (worse)	L8N	U8.7
아무래도	I guess, in any case, anyway	L11C1	U11.5
어디	well (now); let me see	L14C2	U14.8
어떻게 해서든(지)	by any means	L15C2	U15.12
어찌나 ~는/(으)ㄴ지	so ~ that ~; too ~ to ~	L4N	U4.6
얼마 안 가면	before long	L11C1	U11.8

얼마나 ~던지	to be so very (much) ~	L16C1	U16.7
없어서는 안 되다	to be indispensable	L6N	U6.3
여기, 저기, 거기	this person, that person (over there), that person (near you)	L1C2	U1.9
예를 들면	for example	L5N	U5.4
(이)라(서)	as; because	L6C1	U6.8
(이)라도; 아니라도	even if/though (it is); even if/though (it is) not; any ~	L6N	U6.5
(이)란	as for	L5N	U5.2
(이)란	entitled, called, named	L4N	U4.2
(이)래	it is said that ~	L9C1	U9.6
(이)면	after, in (after a time word)	L14C1	U14.7
이자	both . . . and; and at the same time	L11N	U11.4
제일가다/일등가다/ 첫째가다	to be best, to be first-rate	L2C2	U2.8
족	a group of people	L17N	U17.2
하기는 그래(요)	that is certainly true	L2C1	U2.6
할 것 없이	irrespective of; regardless of; including	L15C1	U15.4
할 수 없지요	it can't be helped	L10N	U10.5

Korean–English Glossary

1.5세 교포   1.5 generation Korean; Korean resident in a foreign country

18번   favorite song

가곡   song in the classical style

가난뱅이   pauper, poor man

가늘다   to be thin, slim, slender

가령   for example; in case; supposing that

가루   flour; powder

가리키다   to denote, indicate, point to

가수   singer; vocalist

가여워하다   to be sympathetic to, pity

가요   ballad; song

가요곡   folk song; popular song

가을날   an autumn day

가정의학과   family medicine

가치   merit, value, worth

가치관   sense of values

가톨릭   Catholic

각자   each person

간밤   last night

간호사   nurse

간히다   to be confined, imprisoned, shut up

갈등   complications; conflict; discord

갈라 잡다   to hold (two swing ropes) with each hand

갈라지다   to split, crack

갈비찜   steamed short ribs

갈치   scabbard fish

감   material, stuff

감각   feeling; touch

감동   (deep) emotion; impression

감정   emotion, feeling, sentiment

갑   box, case; packet

강강수월래 (= 강강술래)   *kangkang suwollae* (Korean circle dance)

강남역   Kangnam subway station

강변   riverside, riverbank

강산   landscape, scenery; rivers and mountains

강연   address; lecture

강조하다   to put emphasis on, stress

개방하다   to open (doors)

개별적으로   individually; separately

개봉관   first-run movie theater

개인   individual

개인주의   individualism

개조하다   to rebuild, remodel, reorganize

거꾸로   headlong; inside out, inversely, upside down

거들떠 보다   to pay attention to, take notice of

거룩하다   to be great; to be holy, sacred

거르다   to omit, skip (over)

거리감   sense of distance

거부   denial, refusal, rejection

거부감   feeling of disapproval or rejection

거북(이)   tortoise; turtle

거북선   turtle boat (ironclad warship shaped like a tortoise)

거위   goose

거절   decline, reject

거절하다   to refuse, reject, turn down

거참   (contr. of 그것 참) that really

거품	bubble; foam
건너	other (opposite) side of, over there
건넌방	opposite room, room on the opposite side
건전하다	to be healthy, sound
건지다	to pick up, take out of
건축	architecture
걸려 있다	to be dependent (on), hinge (on)
걸인	beggar
검사	examination, inspection, test
겁탈하다	to plunder, loot, rape, rob
게다가	besides, furthermore, in addition
게시	notice, bulletin
게시판	bulletin board
게으름뱅이	idler, lazybones, sluggard
게을러 빠지다	to be intolerably lazy [derogatory]
겨냥하다	to aim for
겨우	barely, narrowly, only, with difficulty; barely manage to
격식	established form, protocol
견디다	to bear up, endure
결과	result
결국	after all, eventually, in the end
결론	conclusion
결산	balancing of accounts; settlement of accounts
결합	combination; union
결혼식	wedding ceremony
겸손	humility; modesty
겸하다	to combine one thing with another; to serve both as
경비	defense, guard
경악하다	to be astonished, frightened, shocked
경영대	college of business administration
경우	case, situation
경쟁	competition
경제권	economic power
경제학과	economics
경제학사	history of economics
경치	scenery; scenic beauty
경향	current, tendency, trend
경험하다	to experience, go through, undergo
계산하다	to calculate; to pay
계속	continuation
계속해서	continuously, uninterruptedly
계약	contract, compact
계절	season, time of year
계집	female; woman [derogatory]
계획	plan
계획하다	to intend, plan, project
고개	nape (of the neck); head; peak; pass (of a mountain)
고객	client, customer, patron
고구마	sweet potato
고르다	to be equal, even, uniform
고르다	to choose, single out, select
고민	anguish, agony; worry
고백하다	to admit, confess
고생하다	to be in straitened circumstances, undergo hardships
고속 도로	highway
고을	town, village, county (old usage) (currently 마을, 읍내, or 고장)
고적지	ancient landmark; historic site
고집이 세다	to be obstinate, pigheaded, stubborn
곡	melody, tune
골치	bother, nuisance, trouble

골치다	to have a headache (= 골치가 아프다, 골치를 앓다)	교대역	Kyodae subway station
		교도관	jailer
골칫덩이	"headache," nuisance	교보문고	Kyobo book center
곱다	to be beautiful, good-looking, lovely, nice, refined	교정	campus, schoolyard
		교통 체증	traffic jam
		교통로	traffic route
		교향곡	symphony
곳곳	here and there; various places	교향악단	symphony orchestra
		교환 학생	exchange student
공격하다	to attack, criticize	교환하다	to exchange
공경하다	to respect, revere	교훈적이다	to be educational, instructive
공급	supply		
공연	public performance	구걸	begging
공연장	hall; place where a performance is presented	구걸하다	to beg (one's bread)
		구두쇠	tightwad, miser
공예	industrial arts	구렁이	big snake, boa, huge serpent
공통점	common feature		
과로	overwork, overexertion	구미	Europe and America, the West
과연	as expected, indeed, sure enough		
		구상하다	to conceive, formulate a plan
과장	exaggeration, overstatement		
		구슬	bead; gem
과정	course, curriculum, course of study, program	구실	duty; function, role
		구조	structure
과하다	to be excessive, too much	구체적으로	concretely
		구하다	to ask for, look for, seek; to buy
관객	audience; onlookers; spectators		
		국경 지대	border area
관념	idea, conception, notion	국교	state religion
관리	administration, charge, control; management	국보	national treasure
		국산품	domestic goods, products of domestic industry
관심	concern; interest		
관심을 갖다	to be interested in, concerned with	국악	Korean classical music
		군수	county administrator
관청	government office	군인	soldier
관측	observation, survey	굳다	to harden
광고	advertisement; announcement; notice	굳이	firmly; on purpose
		굴곡	bends, twists, windings
광고주	advertisement client, sponsor	굴하다	to submit, yield
		굶다	to starve, go hungry, go without food (eating), be famished
광고하다	to advertise, announce		
굉장히	exceedingly; splendidly		
교내	(on) campus, intramural, (in) school	굽	heel; hoof
		귀공자	young noble

규칙적	orderly, regular
그까짓	(so) trifling (trivial, slight); that kind of
그냥	free, at no charge, gratis, just
그네	swing
그네 뛰기	swinging (on a swing)
그대	you (archaic; used in songs, novels, etc.) (= 당신)
그래	by the way, so, well
그래 맞아	that's right
그랬다가	(contr. of 그러했다가) such was the case, and then
그나 저나	(contr. of 그러나 저러나) anyhow, anyway, at any rate, in any case
그러니까	namely, that is
그러다(가)	in that manner, like that
그러자	and (just) then
그러지 뭐	(contr. of 그렇게 하지 뭐) let's do so
그러지요	(contr. of 그렇게 하지요) I will do so
그런데	but, however, for all that
그런데도	and yet, in spite of that, still, nevertheless
그럴듯하다	to be plausible
그럼	(contr. of 그러면, from 그렇게 하면 'if you do so, then')
그리	(not) so, (not) to that extent (= 그다지)
그리고 나서	(contr. of 그리하고 나서) and then, after that, after doing that
그립다	to miss dearly
그만두다	to discontinue, end, give up, quit
그만하다	to be about the same; to be appropriate
그야	(contr. of 그거야, 그것이야) as for that, so

	far as that is concerned
그저	without doing anything
그제야	at last, not . . . until, only then
극적	(being) dramatic
극진히	cordially, heartily, very kindly
극히	exceedingly, extremely
근데	contr. of 그런데
근무	duty, service, work
근본	basis, foundation, root
근처	nearby; neighborhood, vicinity
글 짓다	to compose a piece, write a composition
금강산	Mt. Kŭmgang (lit., Mt. Diamond)
금년	this year
금방	in a moment, at once, immediately
금은보화	money and valuables, treasures, worldly goods
금지하다	to forbid, prohibit
급변하다	to change rapidly
기(가) 막히다	to be amazed, dumbfounded, stunned
기간	period, duration
기관	institution, organization; organ
기금	endowment; fund
기능	ability, technical skill; faculty; function
기대	anticipation, expectation
기대하다	to expect, look forward to
기록	record
기본	foundation, basis, basic
기본 색상	(basic) color tone
기분	feeling, mood
기생	Korean geisha
기술	ability, skill, talent; technique
기악과	department of

	instrumental music	끊어지다	to be broken (down); to be terminated
기억	memory, recollection		
기업	business, company, corporation, enterprise	끊임없다	to be endless
		끊임없이	constantly, continually; successively
기여되다	to be contributed		
기왕	already; past; since	끌	chisel
기원하다	to pray, wish	끌어 안다	to embrace tightly, hug
기자	journalist	끌어다 놓다	to drag and put
기적	miracle	끌어들이다	to bring into; to induce
기적	steam whistle	끼리	among themselves
기획	planning, project		
기획하다	to (make a) plan, work out a scheme	나귀	donkey
		나그네	traveler, tourist
길이	eternally, forever; for a long time	나누다	to distribute, share (with)
		나름대로	after one's kind, in one's own way
김	chance, occasion		
까다롭다	to be complicated; to be fastidious, particular	나머지	rest, remainder
		나무꾼	lumberjack, woodcutter, woodsman
깔끔하다	to be neat and tidy; to look sharp		
		나일론 옷감	nylon (cloth)
깜빡이다	to flicker, twinkle, wink (= 깜빡(깜빡)거리다; 깜빡(깜빡)이다/거리다)	난방	heating
		날개	wing
		날쌔다	to be nimble, quick
깜찍하다	to be clever; to be cute	남기다	to leave (behind)
깨	sesame	남다르다	to be peculiar, be different from others
꺼내다	to take out, bring out		
꺼리다	to avoid, keep aloof from; to dislike	남방	south side
		남북 교향악단	the South-North Korea symphony orchestra
껍질	bark; shell; skin		
꼭	firmly, tightly	남행 열차	southbound train
꼽다	to count (on one's fingers); to take (something as an example)	낯설다	to be unfamiliar
		내과	internal medicine
		내다	to put forth
		내디디다	to advance, step forward
꽁꽁	hard; tightly	내외	husband and wife, married couple
꽃답다	to be beautiful, lovely (pretty) as a flower		
		내용	content(s)
꽤	fairly, pretty, considerably	내의	undergarment (= 속옷)
꾀꼬리	Korean nightingale; oriole	너나(할것)없이	everybody, all alike
꾸다	to borrow	너머로	beyond; over; through
꾸미다	to decorate; to disguise oneself	너무	awfully; too
		넉넉하다	to be enough, plenty
꿀꺽	in great gulps	넘어가다	to go across
끄덕이다	to nod, nod approval	넘치다	to overflow

Korean	English
노동자	laborer
노랑벌	yellow bee
노래방	*noraebang* (similar to Japanese *karaoke*)
노상	all the time, always, habitually (= 항상, 늘)
노인	old person
노천 극장	open-air theater
노트 정리	arranging one's class notes
녹죽	green bamboo
놀랍게도	surprisingly (enough)
놀려대다	to keep teasing
놀리다	to make fun of, tease
놈	fellow; guy [derogative]
농담	joke; pun
농부	farmer; peasant; peasantry
농사	agriculture, farming
농악	instrumental music of peasants
농장	farm; plantation
뇌 활동	brain (mental) activity
누군가	someone
누다	to evacuate, let out (urine or excrement)
누비다	to thread one's way through the crowd
눈(이) 멀다	to be blind
눈물	tears
눈에 띄게	definitely, markedly
뉴욕제과	New York bakery
늘	always, all the time
늦장가를 들다	to take a wife late in life
니트	knit
다가가다	to approach, step (go) near
다가 오다	to come up to
다녀가다	to drop in for a short visit and then go
다름(이) 없다	not to be different
다보탑	Tabot'ap (*lit.,* many treasures tower)
다양하다	to be diverse, various
다양해지다	to become varied
다지다	to consolidate, harden, strengthen, solidify
다행	luck, good fortune
다행이다	to be blessed, fortunate, lucky
다행히	fortunately, luckily
단골	customer, patron
단김에	at a breath, at a stretch
단단히	firmly, solidly, strongly
단단히 마음 먹다	to be determined, make a firm resolution
단둘이	only two persons
단말기	computer terminal
단박(에)	at once, immediately, instantly
단오	Tano festival (fifth day of the fifth lunar month); May Day
단정하다	to be decent, neat, proper
달다	to become hot
달라고 하다	to ask (someone) to give (something) to him/her
달리	in particular; particularly; separately
닮다	to be (look) like, resemble
담기다	to be filled, put in
담당하다	to be responsible for, take charge of
담뱃대	tobacco pipe; pipe
담뱃불	lighting a cigarette
답례	return courtesy; return salute
답을 맞추다	to check answers
당분간	for the time being
당시	in those days (times)
당장	at once, immediately
닿다	to touch, come in contact with
대	rest; stand
대가	cost, price

대궐	(royal) palace	덕수궁	
대그룹	large-scale conglomerate	현대미술관	Tŏksu Palace Modern Art Museum
대뇌	cerebrum		
대뜸	openly, without reservation	덕택	grace; help; indebtedness; patronage
대면	facing; meeting	덕택으로	thanks to
대목	most important occasion, vital moment; portion, part	덜	incompletely; less; little
		덜하다	to decrease; to be less
		덤	extra
대부분	majority, great (large, major) portion (of); for the most part, mostly	덩굴	runner (creeper), tendril, vine
		덩실덩실	(dancing) cheerfully, joyfully
대상	object; subject; target		
대수롭지		덮치다	to attack, fall on, raid
않다	to be of little importance, trivial	데리다	to be accompanied by
		도깨비	apparition; goblin; hobgoblin
대영 박물관	British Museum		
대원군	Lord Taewŏn, father of Kojong (Chosŏn dynasty's 26th king)	도대체	at all; in the world; on earth
		도리	duty; justice; reason; truth
대인 관계	interpersonal relations		
대장	admiral, general; head, boss	도매장	wholesale market
		도미노 현상	domino effect
대장부	manly man	도성	capital city (castle town in the old Korea)
대조적이다	to be comparative, contrastive		
		도움 되다	to be helpful
대중 가요	popular song	도우미	helper
대중 음악	popular music	도전	challenge; defiance
대추	Chinese date; jujube	도중	in the middle of; on the way
대충	roughly, loosely, approximately		
		독무대	master of the stage
대표적이다	to be representative	독서	reading
대표하다	to represent	독주하다	to play alone, solo
대학 입시	college entrance examination	독창성	originality
		돋구다	to raise, stimulate; make (a degree or standard) higher (= 돋우다)
대학원	graduate school		
대형	large size		
대형 할인점	(huge) discount market	돌사자	stone lion
대화	chat, conversation	동감이다	to agree with, feel the same way (as)
댁	you (honorific form); one's house, residence (honorific form)		
		동갑	same age; person of the same age
더러	to (indirect object marker)	동고동락하다	to share one's joys and

	sorrows (with)
동기	motive; motivation
동네	neighborhood; village
동등하다	to be equal, of the same rank
동료	associate, colleague
동서고금	all places and times
동시	children's verse; nursery rhymes
동시대	same period, contemporary
동아리	group; school organization, (social) club
동여매다	to bind (= 묶다)
동요	children's song; nursery rhyme
동원하다	to mobilize
동의하다	to approve of, consent to
동화	children's story; fairy (nursery) tale
동화책	book of fairy tales
되겠다	it will be good (fine, O.K.)
두다	to have, keep, place
두드러지다	to be marked, conspicuous
두들기다	to beat, hit, knock
두들겨 맞다	to be struck hard
두루	all around, throughout; extensively, far and wide
둔하다	to be dull, slow, thick
둘러앉다	to sit in a circle, sit around (the table)
둥지	nest
뒤늦게	belatedly
뒤떨어지다	to fall behind
뒤지다	to fumble, rummage, search
뒤집히다	to be turned inside out
드나들다	to come and go; to visit
드물다	to be few, rare, scarce
든든하다	to be robust, strong
듣다못해	(being) unable to continue to listen to
들다	to enter

들다	to hold (up), raise; to enumerate, mention
들뜨다	to be unsteady; to grow restless
들르다	to drop in (at)
들어서다	to step in
들어차다	to be packed, fill (with)
들춰보다	to raise and see; to skim
등	and the like, etc.
디디다	to step on, tread on
디지털 방식	digital (mode)
따르다	to pour water into a bowl
따습다	to be comfortably warm
따지고 보면	after all
딴	another; different, other
때아닌	out of season; unseasonable; untimely
때우다	to fill in, solder; to substitute
떠나 보내다	to send one off
떨어지다	to fall, drop; to run out of
떼어 내다	to remove, take off
똥	droppings, dung
뚝	with a snap, abruptly
뛰어나게	by far, preeminently
뜨다	to rise; to float
뜨뜻하다	to be warm
뜰	garden, ground, yard
뜻	intent; want, wish
띄다	(= 뜨이다) to be seen; to catch sight of, meet the eye
띠	Chinese animal sign under which one was born
레스토랑	restaurant
리모콘	remote control
리어커	handcart; pushcart
마감 날짜	closing date; deadline

마당	court, garden, yard	매진	selling out
마땅하다	to be suitable, appropriate	매진되다	to be sold out
마무리 짓다	to finish off, give the final touches to	맨	extreme, very
		맨날	always
마음	heart, mind	맹세하다	to take an oath, pledge
마음 든든하다	to feel confident, safe	맹인	blind person; the blind
마음(을) 먹다	to intend to, think of	맺다	to conclude; to form (a relationship); to knot, tie
마음껏	as one wishes, to the heart's content, with the whole heart	머리	brain, head, intellect
		먹히다	to be consumed
마저	even; so far as (= 까지도)	멀리	(from) afar, far (off)
		메모	memo
마주 앉다	to sit face-to-face	메모지	notepad
마주치다	to come across, run into	멥쌀	non-glutinous rice
마지막 회	final round	명령	bidding, command
마침	at the right moment; fortunately, just in time	명소	famous place, sight(s) to see
마침내	at last, finally; in the end, in the long run	명예	credit; dignity; fame
		명절	major holiday(s), festival(s), national holidays
막다	to check, defend		
막연하다	to be dim, hazy, obscure, vague	몇몇	few, several, some
만	as much as, just, only	모금	fund raising
만나리(라)	will meet (him/her) (archaic; = 만나겠다)	모녀	mother and daughter
		모방	copying, imitation
만복	all kinds of good luck; great happiness	모습	appearance, looks; figure, shape
만화책	comic book	모시다	to accompany (a senior person)
말을 붙이다	to address, speak to		
망령 나다	to be in one's dotage	모임	gathering, meeting
망치	hammer	모친	one's mother
망하다	to die out, perish	모형	dummy; model, pattern
맞다	to be correct	목숨	life
맞벌이	working together (for a living), two-income (family)	목적	aim, purpose
		몰래	furtively, secretly
		몽땅	all, completely
맞추다	to adapt, adjust, fit, assemble, check	묘사하다	to delineate, describe
		묘약	golden remedy, wonder (miracle) drug
맡기다	to entrust		
맡다	to obtain, take charge of, undertake	무	none, nothing
		무궁무진하다	to be infinite, unlimited
매료되다	to be charmed, fascinated	무기질	inorganic substance; mineral
매이다	to be bound up, tied		
매장	shop, store	무난하다	to be safe, free from

	danger
무너지다	to collapse, fall down
무늬	design; figure; pattern
무당	(female) necromancer, sorceress, witch
무대	stage
무드	mood
무럭무럭	rapidly; well
무렵	about, around
무르익다	to become mature, ripe
무릎	knee; lap
무명	anonymity, namelessness
무사하다	to be safe
무상	greatest, highest, supreme (*lit.,* "lack of an above")
무술	martial arts
무시하다	to disregard, ignore
무식하다	to be ignorant, illiterate
무심코	accidentally, casually
무용	dancing
무음	muteness
무지개	rainbow
무척	exceedingly, very
무턱대고	for no good reason
무표정하다	to be blank, expressionless
무형	(being) intangible; formless(ness)
묵묵히	mutely, silently
묶다	to bind
문명	civilization
문명 사회	civilized society
문안 드리다	to ask after the health of (a senior person)
문화	culture
문화권	cultural sphere
문화재	cultural assets
문화 차이	cultural difference
물다	to bite; to hold in one's mouth
물동이	water jar
물려주다	to bequeath (property) to (someone); to transfer
물어 오다	to ask the speaker

물어다 주다	to carry in one's mouth and give it
뭐니뭐니해도	after all, all things considered together
미각	sense of taste
미끄러지다	to glide, slide, slip
미술	fine art
미식가	epicure, gourmet
미장원	beauty salon
미치광이	lunatic
미치다	to become insane, go crazy
민감하다	to be sensitive, susceptible
민속 놀이	folk game, folk sport
민요	ballad, folk song
민화	folk story, folktale
믿음	beliefs
믿음직하다	to be authentic, reliable, trustworthy
밀리다	to lag behind; to be pushed, shoved
밀집 지역	densely populated area
밑지다	to lose, suffer loss
바가지 (= 박)	calabash; gourd (dipper)
바꿔드리다	to barter, exchange, replace; (in telephone calls) to put (someone) on
바뀌다	to be altered, changed
바라다	to desire, seek, want
바람	desire, wish; motive
바람직하다	to be advisable, desirable
바로잡다	to care; to correct, remedy
바르다	to be correct; to be straight
바른 대로	correctly; truthfully
바수운	bassoon
바통	baton
박사	Ph.D. (degree)
박히다	to be nailed; to be stuck in

Korean	English
반기다	to welcome
반복되다	to be reiterated, repeated
반영하다	to reflect
반응	reaction, response
반죽하다	to knead
반증하다	to prove the contrary
반지르르하다	to be glossy, lustrous, sleek
반짝	glittering, sparkling
반항하다	to disobey, resist
받아 주다	to accept, comply with, heed
발 디딜 틈	space to step on
발달하다	to develop, progress
발등의 불	"fire on the foot," urgent business
발렌타인 데이	Valentine's Day
발명	invention
발명가	inventor
발명상	award for best invention
발명품	invention
발명하다	to invent
발을 구르다	to stamp the feet; to push (a swing)
발표하다	to announce, report
발표회	exhibition; presentation
밝히다	to clarify, explain
밥상	dining table
밤늦다	to be late at night
방	room
방망이	club, cudgel, mallet
방법	alternative; device; method; scheme
배	double; -fold; times; twofold (= 2배)
배불리	(eat) heartily
백과사전	encyclopedia
백만장자	millionaire
백설공주	Snow White
백성	common people; people
뱃머리	bow, prow; head of a boat
버들	willow
버려지다	to be abandoned, marooned
버리다	to throw away
벌리다	to open; to widen
벌벌	trembling, shivering
벌어지다	to arise, happen; to open
법	law; rule
법대	law school
법령	law, ordinance
벗어나다	to get out of; to miss the mark
베	hemp cloth
베란다	veranda, porch
벽보	wall newspaper; poster
변화	change, variation
별로	particularly, especially
별안간	in the blink of an eye
보건소	health center
보디가드	bodyguard
보름	fifteen days, two weeks; half month
보름달	full moon (fifteenth night of a lunar month)
보물	highly prized article, treasure
보석	jewel
보수 공사	maintenance work, repair work
보수하다	to repair, mend
보약	restorative, tonic
보장하다	to guarantee, secure
보존하다	to conserve, maintain, preserve
보충하다	to fill up; to supplement
보태다	to add, supplement
보호	protection
보화	prized article, precious things, treasure
복무	public service
본	example, model
본 뜨다	to copy
본격적으로	in earnest; on a full scale
본체	body; computer harddrive, CPU
봇짐	backpack, bundle

봐주다   to give special consideration, go easy on

부담   burden

부담없이   without a burden, without any inconvenience

부드럽다   to be soft, smooth, tender

부러워하다   to be envious

부러뜨리다   to break off, snap

부르다   to call; to sing

부르다   to be full (of one's stomach)

부리다   to manage; to play

부분   part; section

부사장   vice president

부산을 떨다   to be busy, restless

부임하다   to assume (start) a new post

부친   one's father

부하   follower, subordinate

북   drum

분노하다   to fly into a rage

분별하다   to differentiate, distinguish

분부   command, order

분수대   fountain (stand)

분위기   atmosphere; mood

불가능하다   to be impossible

불과   merely, only

불국사   Pulguk Temple (a Silla dynasty Buddhist temple)

불균형   disproportion, imbalance

불균형하다   to be out of balance

불러 오다   to summon

불리다   to be called, named

불쑥   suddenly; unexpectedly

불쑥불쑥   here and there; one after another

불쾌감   discomfort, unpleasantness

불타다   to blaze

붐비다   to be crowded with

붓다   to pour

비결   key; secret; mysteries

비공식   being unofficial; informality

비길 데 없다   to be unparalleled, have no comparison

비단 옷   silk dress

비만   obesity

비밀   privacy, secrecy, secret

비비다   to chafe, rub

비상   crisis, emergency

비상용   for emergencies

비우다   to clear, empty, exhaust

비웃다   to ridicule, deride

비웃음   derisive smile, jeer, sneer

비워 두다   to leave vacated

비유적이다   to be figurative, metaphorical

비율   ratio, percentage, proportion

비추다   to shed light on

비트   beat

비행   aviation, flight, flying

빈손   empty hand(s)

빌다   to pray; to beg pardon

빗물   rainwater

빚다   to brew (rice wine), knead dough (만두, 송편, etc.); to cause

빠지다   to go deep into; to skip, miss out

빻다   to grind

뺏기다   to be deprived of, be taken away

뽐내다   to brag, take pride (in)

뽑다   to uproot, pull out, draw; to sing

뿌리   root

뿐   only

뿐(만) 아니라   not only

삐삐   cordless beeper (= 무선 호출기)

사 가다   to buy and take

사고 방식   way of thinking

사랑채   detached building used as a party room or guest room

사로잡다	to capture, take alive	샅샅이	thoroughly, all over
사물놀이	traditional Korean music using four percussion instruments	새내기	freshman, new student; newcomer
사실	fact, reality	새옹지마	horse of an old man on the frontier
사이좋게	on good terms; in peace	새우다	to stay up all night
사용료	fee, charge, rate	새우잠	sleeping curled up (in a fetal position) (*lit.,* shrimp sleep)
사원	employee		
사적인	private		
사제	pastor; priest	색깔	color
사치품	luxuries	색상	hue
사형	death penalty	생각 중이다	to be in the middle of thinking
사회	community, society		
사회적으로	socially	생기	animation, life, vitality
산더미	mountain (of), huge amount, pile	생기다	to appear, seem; to come about, happen, occur
산부인과	obstetrics and gynecology	생년월일	date of birth
산소	ancestral burial ground; grave; tomb	생시	(one's) lifetime
		생일 잔치	birthday party
산실	delivery room	생일 축하	
산재하다	to be scattered around	노래	"Happy Birthday" (song)
살림	household; housekeeping; livelihood	생활 양식	lifestyle, mode of living
		서두	beginning, introduction
살펴보다	to examine, observe	서명	autograph, signature
삼남 이녀	three sons and two daughter	시성거리다	to hang around, loiter
		서스펜스	suspense
삼삼하다	to be unforgettably vivid	서슴없이	without hesitation, unreservedly
삽화	cut; illustration		
상	prize	서양	the West, Western countries
상가	arcade; business center; shopping mall		
		서운하다	to be sorry, feel regretful
상담	consultation; counsel	서투르다	to be poor at, bad at
상대방	the other (opposite) party; the other side (= 상대편)	석굴암	Sŏkkuram Cave Temple (a manmade grotto on Mt. T'oham, Kyŏngju)
상반기	first half of the year	석사	M.A. (degree)
상사	higher office; (one's) superior, senior official	선	interview with the prospective bride and groom
상상력	imagination		
상상하다	to imagine, suppose	선고하다	to announce, pronounce
상영하다	to be on show (of a film)	선교사	missionary
상인	merchant	선녀	fairy, nymph
상표	brand, label, trademark	선물 가게	gift shop
상품	commodity, merchandise	선배	elder, senior, superior

선(을) 보다	to see each other with a view to marriage	세상	life; society; world
선보이다	to introduce, present	세월	time, time and tide, years
선생님	doctor; teacher	세일	sale
선전	advertisement, propaganda	소띠	cow sign in the Korean zodiac, year of the cow
선진국	advanced nation	소모	dissipation, exhaustion
선택하다	to choose, select	소문	hearsay, rumor; news
선호하다	to prefer	소용이 없다	to be useless
설	first day of the year, New Year's Day (= 설날)	소원	desire, wish
		소중하다	to be precious, valuable
		소화	digestion
		소화 기능	digestive function
설계	plan, design	속성	attribute, generic character
설계하다	to design, plan		
설득력이 있다	to be persuasive	속속	one after the other, successively
설렘	uneasy feeling; fluttering		
설마	(not) by any means, hardly	속으로	in one's mind (= 마음속으로)
설치다	to leave halfdone; to spoil	손때	dirt from the hands; thumb (finger) marked
설화	narration, story, tale		
섬기다	to be devoted to (one's master); to serve	손뼉	flat of the hand
		손에 꼽다	to count on one's fingers
성	family name	손윗사람	senior, superior
성	St., sage, saint	손해	damage; loss
성격	character, personality	솟아나다	to spring out
성공(의) 비결	secret to success	송곳	auger, awl, drill, screw
성공하다	succeed	송이	blossom, bunch, cluster
성냥	matches	송편	songp'yŏn (rice cake steamed on a layer of pine needles)
성능	capacity, efficiency; power		
성묘	visit to the ancestral grave	쇠뿔	bull's horn
		수	means, way; likelihood, possibility
성실성	fidelity, honesty, sincerity		
성자	holy man, saint	수	piece (of poetry); poem
성장	growth	수난	ordeals, sufferings
성장기	period of growth	수능 시험	Scholastic Aptitude Test
성품	disposition, nature, temperament	수수께끼	conundrum, mystery, puzzle
성함	name (honorific)	수입 상품	imported goods
성형 수술	plastic surgery procdure	수직 문화	hierarchy-oriented culture
성형 외과	plastic surgery	수차	several times, again and again
세기	century		
세대	generation	수천	several thousand
세련되다	to be polished, refined	수평 문화	equality-oriented culture

수호신	guardian angel, protective deity	신경을 쓰다	to care about
순간	instant, moment	신기하다	to be marvelous, miraculous, novel, original
순교	martyrdom	신랑	bridegroom; newlywed husband
순교자	martyr, martyress		
순서	order, sequence	신령	divine spirit, soul
순수하다	to be pure	신령님	guardian spirit
순위	order, rank, standing	신뢰감	trust
술상	drinking table, bar table	신문사	newspaper office; newspaper publishing company
쉬	easily, readily		
스카프	scarf		
스크류		신발장	shoe chest
드라이버	screwdriver	신분	identity; social position
슬근슬근	rubbing gently together	신비롭다	to be mysterious, mystical
슬피	sadly, sorrowfully		
습관	custom, habit	신선하다	to be new, unripe
승인하다	to acknowledge, admit	신속히	promptly; quickly, swiftly
승진	promotion	신어	new word
승진하다	to be promoted	신입생 환영회	welcoming party (reception) for new students
시각	sense of sight, vision		
시각적이다	to be visual, of vision		
시기	period, season, time	신청하다	to propose, request, apply
시다	to be sour, tart; to feel a dull pain	신체	body; physical system
		신촌 일대	whole of Sinch'on district
시대	age, era, period	신통하게	admirably; marvelously
시도하다	to attempt, try out, test	신화	myth; mythology
시들다	to wither	실	line; string, thread; twine
시력	eyesight	실내 연습장	indoor gym; indoor sports complex
시리다	to be cold, chilled		
시범	example, model	실력	ability, competence
시범적으로	by showing an example; experimentally	실망하다	to be disappointed
		실수하다	to make a mistake
시스루	see-through	실시하다	to carry out, put into practice
시장	empty stomach; hunger		
시장	mayor	실용주의	pragmatism
시장하다	to be hungry, feel empty	실직자	jobless person; the unemployed
시절	occasion, season, time		
시집가다	to marry (a man)	실패하다	to fail, go wrong
시험장	testing site	실현되다	to be realized
시험지	test (examination) paper	심드렁하다	to be indisposed (to do), uninterested (in doing)
식욕	appetite		
식후경	sightseeing after a meal	심리	mentality, mind, psychology
신간 서적	newly published book		
신경	nerve; sensitivity	심술을 부리다	to be cross with

심야	dead of night, midnight		the Silla dynasty)
심하다	to be extreme, harsh, severe	안절부절 못하다	to be anxious, fidgety
십중팔구	eight or nine out of ten; most likely	안주	appetizers served with drinks
싸움터	battlefield, battleground	안팎	more or less
싹	bud, shoot, sprout	알아내다	to find out, discover
쌀	(any) hulled grain; (raw, uncooked) rice	알아보다	to examine, inquire, search; to notice, recognize
쌍둥이	twin		
쏴 붙이다	to retort, talk back, yell (at)	앞뜰	front yard (court)
		앞서 가다	to go ahead, go before
쏟아지다	to pour (out, down)	애원	appeal, entreaty
쓰리엠	3M (corporation)	야간	nighttime
		야간진료	nighttime medical treatment
아니	not (= 안; used only in writing)	야구	baseball
아동 서적		야근하다	to work the night shift
코너	children's book section (lit., corner)	야상곡	nocturne
		야찬	late-night snack; nighttime meal (= 밤참)
아르바이트	part-time job		
아부	flattery	양반	male adult; one's husband; the two upper classes (civil and military) of old Korea
아시다시피	as you know		
아예	from the outset		
아우	man's younger brother; woman's younger sister		
		양복	Western style clothes, suit
아우성	clamor, outcry; shout	애	hey; there; you
아이디어	idea	어떡하나	what shall I do?
아찔하다	to feel dizzy, giddy; to be terrified	어떨까 하다	I am wondering how it will be (if ~)
아파트촌	apartment complex	어떻게 해서	how, in what way
악기	musical instrument	어른	adult; elder
악장	chapter; movement (of music)	어리둥절하다	to be at a loss, bewildered, (feel) confused, stunned
안건	case; item (in an agenda)		
안내	conducting; guidance	어린이날	Children's Day
안내하다	to act as a guide, guide, usher in	어머!	Dear me! Good heavens! O my! (used by females) (= 어머나!)
안마당	courtyard		
안목	appreciation; appreciative eye	어미	mother (vulgar); mother animal
안부	safety; regard	어이	hey! (used to an inferior)
안압지	Anapchi, manmade lake in Kyŏngju (capital of	어질다	to be considerate, gentle, wise

어쩌다(가)   by chance; by doing what, how

어찌   by what means, in what way, how

어찌나 자랑을
하는지   boasted of (it) so much (that . . .)

억울하다   to be mistreated, feel victimized, suffer unfairness

언어 사용   language use

얻어 가다   to get something free

얻어먹다   to beg

얼떨결에   in a moment of bewilderment

얼른얼른하다   to glisten

얽매이다   to be bound, restricted

엄벌   severe punishment

업무   business, work; duty

엇갈리다   to be controversial

엉덩이   buttocks, hips

엎드리다   to lie on the ground

에밀레종   *Emille* Bell (cast in 771 to honor King Sŏngdŏk posthumously)

에피소드   anecdote; episode

여기   here, this place; this person

여성관   view of womanhood

여전히   as ever, as before, as it used to be

여쭙다   to inquire

여학생   female student

여학생 회관   sorority (house)

여행사   travel agency

역사   history

역시   after all, as well, too

역효과   opposite effect

연결   connection, linking

연결하다   to attach, connect

연구   investigation; research, study

연극   drama, play

연기   postponement

연락드리다   to communicate (with), contact, notify (honorific of 연락하다)

연락하다   to contact, communicate (with), inform

연분   bond; fate; relation

연속   continuation, succession

연유   cause, origin, reason

연인   sweetheart

연주하다   to perform, play

연출   presentation, production; representation

연합회   united association, union

영감   elderly man; husband (of an elderly woman)

영광스럽다   to be glorious; to feel honored

영문   circumstances; reason

영문   English writing; English sentence; English version

영문과   department of English literature

영양   nourishment; nutrition

영양실조   malnutrition

영양분   nutrients

영양소   nutrient

영양식   nourishing meal

영향   effect, influence

예상   anticipation, expectation; forecast

예술의 전당   Yesul-ŭi Chŏndang concert hall

예술적이다   to be artistic

예약하다   to reserve

예외   exception

예의   courtesy, manners

예의 범절   etiquette

예전   former days, former times

예절   courtesy, etiquette, manners

예절 바르다   to have good manners

옛날   ancient times; remote antiquity

오곡	all kinds of grains (cereals); five grains
오락가락	coming and going; milling (mimetic word)
오랑캐	barbarian, savage
오래가다	to last a long time
오랜만	after a long time
오르다	to accede (to a throne); to ascend, climb up
오복	five blessings (longevity, wealth, health, virtue, and peaceful death)
옥	jail, prison
온갖	all manner of; all sorts of; every kind of
온돌	*ondol* (hot floor)
온통	totally, wholly
올	this year (= 올해)
올빼미	owl
올빼미족	night owls
옷감	cloth, material; texture
옷차림	attire, manner of dressing
와이셔츠	dress shirt (for man)
완성	completion; perfection
완전히	completely; perfectly
왕위	crown, kingship, throne
왕조	dynasty
외국계	being related to a foreign country, foreign
외래	foreign, from abroad
외래어	loanword, word of foreign origin
외식	eating (dining) out
외야수	outfielder
외제	foreign goods
외치다	to call out, cry out
요금	charge, cost, fare
요새	nowadays; recently
요소	constituent, element
요술	black magic, sorcery, witchcraft; tricks
요청	demand; request
욕심	avarice, covetousness, greed

욕심쟁이	avaricious (grasping) person
용량	capacity; content; volume
용서	pardon, forgiveness
우선	before everything, first of all
우선	preference; priority
우수성	excellence; superiority
우연하다	to be accidental, incidental
우편함	mailbox
우화	allegory, fable
울렁거리다	to beat, pound, throb
움켜쥐다	to clench, clutch, grip
워낙	by nature; from the first; really
원	circle
원래	by nature; from the first, originally
원료	raw material
원만하다	to be harmonious; to be satisfactory
원망	grievance, grudge, resentment
원숭이	ape, monkey
원시 사회	primitive society
웬만하다	to be acceptable, tolerable
위로하다	to comfort, console
위치	location, place, position; situation
위치하다	to be located
윈드스크린	windscreen
윈드실드	windshield
유	existence
유교적	(being) Confucian; related to Confucianism
유교적이다	to be Confucian
유난히	exceptionally, particularly, uncommonly, unusually
유머	humor; joke (= 우스갯소리)
유명하다	to be famous
유물	relic, remains
유부남	married man

유부녀	married woman	의식주	food, clothing, and shelter; essentials
유산	heritage, inheritance, legacy	의심	distrust; doubt
유산	inheritance, legacy	의의 깊다	to be meaningful, significant
유심히	attentively, carefully, cautiously	이것으로	here; now; with this
유용하다	to be useful	이기	convenience; device
유전	heredity, transmission	이동	movement
유전되다	to be inherited; to be transmitted	이동 통신 시대	age of mobile communication
유지	maintenance; preservation		
유지하다	to keep up, maintain	이동하다	to move (from one place to another) (= 옮기다)
유창하다	to be fluent		
유치하다	to be childish, immature	이듬해	next (following) year
유학 오다	to come (to Korea) for study	이따(가)	a little later
		이르다	to arrive, reach
유행	fashion, style	이맘때	about this time
유행가	popular song	이민을 가다	to emigrate to
유행하다	to be in fashion, become popular	이번	this time
		이순신 장군	Admiral Yi Sunsin
유형	concreteness	이야말로	indeed, precisely, the very
육체	body	이어 오다	to inherit; to uphold
윷놀이	playing *yut* (four-stick game)	이용객	customer
		이윽고	after a while, before long
음력	lunar calendar	이토록	like this, this much
음절	measure, bar (of music); syllable	이후	after, henceforth
		익살	humor, joke
음향	noise; sound	익숙하다	to be acquainted with, get used to
응답기	answering machine		
응용하다	to apply, put knowledge to practical use	익히다	to acquaint oneself with, become familiar with; to gain skill in, learn
응하다	to accept, comply with, meet		
		인간	human being(s), mankind
의견	opinion	인간 관계	human relations
의논하다	to confer, consult	인간 문화재	people who have exceptional skills in traditional artforms
의류	clothing		
의류 상가	shopping mall selling only clothes		
		인근	vicinity
의미하다	to connote, mean	인물	character, figure
의복	clothes, dress; suit	인생	life
의사	idea; intention	인연	bond, fate, karma
의상학과	department of fashion study	인정하다	to acknowledge, admit
		일단	for the moment; once
의식	awareness, consciousness	일반 대중	general public, masses

일반화	being common, generalization	자유 경쟁	free competition
일부	part, portion, section	자제	children; sons
일상	daily, everyday	자존심	pride; self-respect
일상 대화	daily conversation	자주색	maroon, purple, violet color
일상 말	everyday language	자체	itself
일석이조	two birds with one stone	자택	one's own house (home)
일쑤	habitual practice	자택 근무	home transaction of office business
일요 신문	Sunday newspaper		
일원	member	작곡	(musical) composition
일정	agenda, schedule	작별하다	to part, say good-bye
일정하다	definite, fixed, set	작사	songwriting
임	lover, sweetheart	작업실	workroom
임진왜란	Japanese invasion of 1592	작품	product; (piece of) work
입증하다	to attest to, prove	잘록하다	be slender, narrow
입학식	entrance ceremony	잠들다	to fall asleep, drop off to sleep
잇다	to connect, join, link		
잇몸	gums (in mouth)	잠을 설치다	to sleep badly
있잖아	you know (what)	잠을 이루다	to get to sleep
		잡다	to catch; to fix
자	ruler; measure	잡화	miscellaneous items
자그마치	a few, a little, as much (many, long) as	잡히다	to be fixed, determined; to be caught
자극적이다	to be exciting, stimulating	잣	pine nuts
		장가를 가다	to get married, take a wife
자극하다	to excite, stir up		
자꾸만	frequently, repeatedly	장군	(military) general
자네	you; your (familiar level)	장기	long time
자녀	children	장면	scene; situation
자두	plum; prune (= 오얏)	장모	man's mother-in-law
자라	snapping (mud, soft-shelled) turtle	장(을) 보다	to go grocery shopping
		장소	place, position, site
자랑하다	to brag, boast (of)	장수하다	to enjoy longevity, live a long time
자리잡다	to establish oneself, settle down		
		장식	decoration, ornament
자못	greatly, not a little, very (much)	장애	obstacle, handicap
		장애인	disabled person (= 장애자)
자문	consultation; inquiry	장점	advantage, strong point
자본	capital; funds	쟁쟁하다	to be clear, resonant, sonorous
자본주의	capitalism		
자상	details; meticulousness	저항	defiance, resistance
자세히	in detail, in full	적군	enemy troops
자연히	naturally, spontaneously	적당하다	to be adequate, suitable, temperate
자유	freedom		

적응	adaptation	점포	shop, store
~전	legend; life; story	접근	approach
전교	whole school	접대하다	to entertain, receive a guest
전국	whole country		
전단	leaflet	접목	graft
전라도	Chŏlla province	접착용	for sticking, gluing
전래	introduction; transmission	접촉	contact, touch
전문점	specialty shop	젓다	to shake, stir
전설	legend, tradition; legendary	정기	fixed time; regular period
		정기 모임	regular meeting
전승	tradition; transmission	정답	correct answer
전시	display, exhibition	정도	degree, extent, standard
전시되다	to be displayed, exhibited	정문	front gate
전열등	electric light	정보	information, intelligence
전원	country; fields and gardens; rural districts	정성껏	elaborately; with the utmost sincerity, wholeheartedly
전자 우편	e-mail		
전 재산	one's whole property (fortune)	정신	mind, soul, spirit
		정신없다	to be absent-minded, distracted, have a poor memory
전쟁	battle; war		
전체	the whole		
전체적으로	generally, on the whole	정월 대보름	January full moon day (January 15 by the lunar calendar)
전통	convention, tradition		
전통 가요	old-style Korean pop song		
전통 사회	traditional society	정장	formal dress, full dress
전통 음악	traditional music	정중히	politely, with courtesy
전투	battle, combat, fight	정크 메일	junk mail
전투함	battleship	정통	legitimacy; orthodoxy
전하다	to convey, impart, pass	정하다	to decide; to fix
전혀	altogether, at all, entirely	제	one's own; oneself
전후좌우	in every direction (*lit.*, before and behind, right and left)	제대로	as it is; properly, well
		제때	(at) the proper time, (at) the right moment
절경	fine scenery, magnificent view	제모 수술	hair removal surgery
		제비	swallow
절룩거리다	to hobble, limp, walk lame	제일가다	to be the best, leading
		제조업	manufacturing industry
절름발이	lame person, cripple	제품	manufactured goods, product(s)
절반 이상	more than half		
절벽	cliff, precipice	조르다	to press, urge, ask (a person) to do
절약	economy, thrift		
절약되다	to be saved	조사하다	to examine, research
젊음	youth, youthfulness	조상	ancestor, forefather, ancestry

조선	Korea (in North Korea only); Chosŏn dynasty (1392–1910)	줄치다	to draw a line; to rule paper
조직체	organization, structure	중(에)	in the middle; during, while
조카	nephew	중시	serious consideration
조카딸	niece	중시하다	to attach importance to
존대법	rules of honorifics	중요성	importance
존댓말	honorific expressions	중풍	palsy; paralysis
존재	existence; presence	즐기다	to enjoy
졸업반	graduating class	지각하다	to be late
종달새	lark, skylark	지각하다	to perceive
종합	synthesis	지경	(miserable) condition
종합 병원	general hospital	지구촌	global village
종합적으로	all-embracing, comprehensively	지껄이다	to chatter, gabble
		지나치게	too much
좌석 버스	bus with seats, coach bus	지도 교사	instructor, teacher; academic adviser
죄	crime; offense; sin	지루하다	to be boring, tedious
죄수	convict, prisoner	지방	fat, grease
주고받다	to exchange	지배하다	to control, govern
주관적이다	to be subjective	지은이	author, writer
주렁주렁	in abundance, in clusters	지적	indication
주로	chiefly, mainly, mostly, principally	지적이다	to be intellectual
		지정하다	to assign, designate
주름	wrinkles, plait	지진	earthquake
주름 치마	pleated skirt	지켜보다	to keep an eye on
주문	order	지퍼	zipper
주부	housewife	지폐	bill; paper money
주요	main	지하	basement, cellar
주위	circumference; the environs	지혜	intelligence, wisdom, wits
		지휘	command, supervision
주의	ism	지휘자	conductor
주인	head of a family; host, hostess	지휘하다	to conduct, direct, lead
		직설적이다	to be straightforward (in talking)
주인공	hero/heroine, protagonist; master	직장인	employee, worker
		진입하다	to enter
주장	assertion, insistence, contention	진작	at once, then and there
		진짜	genuine article
주장하다	to assert, claim, insist on	질기다	to be tough
주전자	teakettle	질투심	(feelings) of envy, jealousy
주차난	parking difficulties		
주파수	frequency	집단주의	collectivism
죽	in a row (line)	집안	family; household
줄무늬	stripe		

집행	enforcement; execution		no change
집행되다	to be executed	채점하다	to grade (exams)
짓	behavior, activity, conduct	책상다리하다	to sit cross-legged
짙다	to be dark; to be deep; to be rich	챙기다	to put (things) in order; to collect
		처녀	maiden, virgin, young woman
짜장면	*tchajang-myŏn* (noodles with black bean sauce)	처리	handling, treatment
짜증	annoyance, irritation	처리하다	to deal with, handle
짝	one of a pair; partner	처지	circumstance, condition
쩍	way or sound of ripping	처하다	to deal (with); to sentence
쩔쩔매다	to be at a loss, confused	척	pretense
쪼다	to peck	천	thousand
쪽지시험	quiz	천마총	Ch'ŏnmach'ong (one of the tombs of the Silla kings)
쫓겨나다	to be dismissed (from), evicted (from), get driven (out of)	천벌	divine punishment, heaven's judgment, nemesis
차다	to become full (of), be jammed	천지	heaven and earth, universe; world
차다	to kick	천하다	to be humble, low (in status)
차례	ancestor-memorial services (rites)	철갑	ironclad
차례	turn, order	철갑선	ironclad ship
차리다	to set the table; to arrange, make ready	철저히	completely, thoroughly
차림	outfit; preparation	첨단	cutting edge, spearhead; vanguard
차지하다	to hold, occupy; to consist of	첨단 과학 시대	age of cutting-edge science
차창	car window; train window	첨성대	Ch'ŏmsŏngdae (observatory built in 7th century to conduct basic astronomical observations)
차츰	gradually, little by little		
착하다	to be good, kindhearted		
찬란하다	to be brilliant, magnificent		
찬성	agreement; approval, endorsement		
찬송가	hymn, psalm	첫발	first step
참	by the way, oh, well	첫인상	first impression
창작 동화집	collection of original fairy tales	청각	auditory sense, hearing
		청개구리	green frog, tree frog, tree toad
찾다	to call on, visit		
찾아뵙다	to visit (a senior person)	청교도적	(being) puritan(ical)
채	intact; just as it is; with	청룡	blue dragon

청바지	blue jeans
청소년	teenagers; youth
청송	green pine, evergreen
청장년	people of mature age
청중	audience
청하다	to ask, request; to invite, send for
체조	gymastics
체조하다	to have gymnastics
체질	(physical) constitution
초	candle
초기	first stage
초년	the first year, younger years
초년생	beginner, novice
초면	first meeting (with)
초콜릿	chocolate
촉각	sense of touch
촛불	candlelight
총독	governor-general
총독부	*ch'ongdokpu,* Japanese government in Seoul during the colonial period (1910-1945)
최신 가요	up-to-date popular song
최후	last
추녀	angle rafter (protruding corners of Korean eaves)
추석	Ch'usŏk (Korean Thanksgiving), Harvest Moon Day
추세	trend; tendency
추수 감사절	Thanksgiving Day
축적	accumulation
출근	attendance at office
출근용	for the use of office work
출두	appearance, presence
출판사	publishing company
출판하다	to issue, publish
출품하다	to exhibit
충신	loyal subject, patriot
충청북도	North Ch'ungch'ŏng province

측	side
측면	side (face)
치과	dentistry
치다	to hit, pound, do, play, perform
치르다	to pay (= 지불하다); to take (an exam)
치솟다	to rise suddenly and swiftly, shoot up, skyrocket
치아	teeth (= 이)
치한	molester of women
친근하다	to be close, familiar, intimate
친정	married woman's parents' home
친지	acquaintance; friend
침	saliva
침 넘어가다	to whet the appetite
침입하다	to invade
칭찬	compliment, praise
칭찬하다	to admire, praise, speak highly of
칭칭	round and round tight
카네기재단	Carnegie Foundation
카피라이터	copywriter
캔디	candy
컴맹	computer illiterate
콘트라베이스	contrabass; contrabassist
콩	bean; pea; soybean
콩쥐 팥쥐	*K'ongjwi P'atchwi* (children's novel of the Chosŏn dynasty)
쾌적하다	to be comfortable, pleasant
클라우디우스	Emperor Claudius II (Gothicus)
키다	to mill, saw timber into boards
타다	to be awarded; to receive
타오르다	to blaze, burn up, burst into flame

탄수화물	carbohydrate	판단하다	to decide; to judge
탈나다	to be sick; to have trouble	판매	marketing, sale, selling
		판매하다	to sell
탑	pagoda; steeple; tower	판소리	*p'ansori* (a long Korean epic song)
태도	attitude, manner; behavior		
태조	first king of a dynasty	팝송	popular song
택견도	*t'aekkyŏndo* (Korean sport in which one kicks and trips an opponent)	팥	red bean
		패물	jewelry; things made of shell
터덜터덜	ploddingly (in a pedestrian manner)	팬	fan, enthusiastic admirer
		퍼지다	to broaden, spread out
테크놀로지	technology	페이저	radio pager
텔레파시	telepathy	편찮다	to be sick (honorific)
토끼	hare; rabbit	평가하다	to assess, evaluate, judge
톡톡히	a great deal, a lot, much	평균	average
톱질	sawing	평범하다	to be common, ordinary
통	entirely, wholly, utterly	평생	lifetime; throughout one's life
통신	communication		
통하다	to be known as; to be on the line, go through, lead to, pass	평안하다	to be peaceful; to be well
		평일	ordinary day(s), weekday(s)
통화	telephone conversation	포	cannon; gun
퇴근 길	way home after work	포 구멍	mouth of a cannon
퇴근하다	to go home from work, leave the office	포스트잇	Post-it
		포장되다	to be packed, packaged
툇마루	floor of a Korean veranda, porch floor	포함하다	to contain, cover, include
		폭력	force; violence
투자하다	to invest	폭발	explosion
트다	to sprout, bud	폭발적이다	to be explosive, to be tremendous
특별히	especially, particularly		
특이하다	to be peculiar, singular, unique	폭우	heavy rain, downpour
		표	coupon; ticket
특허	patent	표정	(facial) expression
틈	gap; space	표현	expression
팀장	head of a team	풀	glue
팀파니	kettledrum, timpani	풀	grass
		풀	swimming pool
파고들다	to come deeply (into)	풀다	to let out; to loosen, untie; to solve
파다	to dig		
파악하다	to get hold of, grasp, grip; to understand	풀려 나다	to be released, freed
		풀리다	to be unraveled; to be worked out, solved
파트	part		
판	circumstances, situation; scene	풀어 주다	to release, set free
		풋풋함	being fresh (new);

	freshness
풍년	bumper crop, good harvest; year of abundance
풍부하다	to be abundant, rich
풍성하다	to be abundant, affluent
풍자	innuendo; irony; sarcasm; satire
퓨전 콘서트	fusion concert
피로	exhaustion, fatigue
피부 스케일링	skin scaling
피서	summer retreat, trip to avoid hot weather
피투성이	being covered with blood
피해	damage; harm, injury
필	head (counter for horses and cows)
필수품	essentials, necessities
필요	need, requirement
하긴	(contr. of 하기는) in fact, indeed
하긴 그래	that's true indeed
하늘하늘하다	to be light and flimsy, buoyant
하다 보니까	while (one is) doing something
하도	very much indeed; ever so hard
하루아침에	overnight, all of sudden; in a single day
하면	(contr. of 그러하면) then, and
하숙집	boardinghouse
하이타이	High Tide (name of a detergent)
하인	servant
하지만	but, however
하직 인사	saying good-bye
하필	of all occasions (things, places, persons)
학사	B.A. (degree)
학생회관	student center
학원	cram school; (educational)

	institute; school
학정	despotism, tyranny
한	regret
한	about, approximately
한가위	Korean Thanksgiving Day (August 15 by the lunar calendar) (= 추석)
한국 문학	Korean literature
한국 경제신문	*Korean Economy Daily*
한국일보	*Han'guk Daily*
한국학 연구소	center for Korean studies
한데	at one place (= 한군데)
한마디로	in a word, in short
한바퀴	one cycle
한산하다	to be at leisure, off work; to be dull, inactive
한약	Chinese herbal medicine
한양	Hanyang, name of Seoul in Chosŏn dynasty
한없이	endlessly; extremely, greatly
한자리	one place
한자어	Sino-Korean word
한창	at the height of; height
할인	discount, reduction
할인점	discount store
함께	together
함부로	at random; for no good reason
합동 연주회	joint concert
합창	choral singing; ensemble
항아리	jar; pot
해결	settlement; solution
해버리다	to do completely, finish, get through
해안 경비	coast guard
해지다	the sun sets
해학	jest, joke
핸드폰	cellular (mobile) phone
햇곡식	new crop
햇과일	fresh fruits
행렬	parade
행사	event; function
향가	old Korean folk songs

	(ballads)		anger
향기	aroma, fragrance, scent	화려하다	to be gorgeous, splendid
향수	homesickness; nostalgia	환상	(day)dream, fantasy;
향악	(indigenous) Korean		illusion
	music	환상적이다	to be fantastic, wonderful
향학열	enthusiasm for learning	환영	welcome
허겁지겁	flustered	환자	patient
허둥지둥	all flustered	환희	delight, ecstasy, joy
허비하다	to waste	활동	activity, action, motion
헐다	to destroy, flatten	활동적이다	to be active, energetic
헷갈리다	to be confused, thrown	활짝	(to smile) brightly,
	off, distracted		happily, radiantly; widely,
혀를 차다	to click the tongue		extensively
혁명	revolution	황제	emperor
현대인	modern person, modern	회	game; round
	people	회계학 스타디	study on accounting
현대적	contemporary, modern	회관	hall
현대화	modernization	회장	chairman; president (of a
형상	appearance, form, shape		society)
형식주의	formalism	횡재	unexpected financial
형장	place of execution		gain(s), windfall
형태	form, shape	효과	effect, result; efficiency
혜택	benevolence, favor	효녀	filial (dutiful) daughter
호남선	Honam (Seoul-Cholla	후각	(sense of) smell
	province) railway line	후문	back gate
호롱불	(light of a) kerosene	후미	tail (end); very end
	lamp	후손	descendants, posterity
호리병	gourd bottle	훑어보다	to scan, scrutinize
호소	appeal, petition	훨훨	fluttering; in great flames
호소력 있다	to be convincing	휘두르다	to brandish, wield
호통	yell, shout, roar	휴가	leave of absence;
혹시	by any chance, possibly		vacation
혹평	harsh criticism	휴게실	lounge
혹하다	to become infatuated,	흉칙하다	to be very ugly
	fascinated, charmed	흐름	flowing; trend
혼나다	to have a hard time,	흔적	trace, mark
	have an awful time	흔적 없이	without a trace
혼자	alone, by oneself; one	흔해 빠지다	a dime a dozen
	person		[derogatory]
홀딱	completely; deeply	흔히	commonly, frequently
홀로	alone; single-handedly	흥	fun, pleasure
홍보	advertisement, publicity,	흥겹게	joyously, merrily
	public information	희뜩희뜩하다	to be very dizzy, giddy,
화(를) 내다	to flare up, give vent to		shaky

회망	hope, wish	흰나비	white butterfly
회미하다	to be dim, faint, vague	히트 상품	popular product
회생	sacrifice	힘차다	to be full of strength
회생하다	to sacrifice, victimize		

English-Korean Glossary

3M (company) 쓰리엠

abandoned 버려지다
ability 능력
about ~에 관하여; 쯤, 안팎
　~ this time 이맘때
absent-minded 정신 없다
abundant 풍부하다
acceptable 웬만하다
accompany 함께 가다
　~ (a senior) 모시다
　be/get ~ed by 데리고 가다/오다
accounts 은행 계좌
　balancing ~ 결산
accumulation 축적
accustomed 익숙하다
　get ~ to, (get)
　used to 익숙해지다
acoustic 음향의, 소리의
act as ~ ~ 노릇하다
adaptation 적응
adequate 적당하다
adjust 맞추다
admit 인정하다
adult 어른
advanced 진보하다
　~ nation 선진국
advantage 장점
advertise 광고하다
advertising
　client 광고주
advertisement 광고
adviser 조언자, 충고자
affluent 풍성하다

after 이후, 나중, 다음
　~ all 따지고 보면
　~ a long time 오랜만
　~ a while 이따(가)
　~ that 그리고 나서
age 나이
　same ~ 동갑
agenda 일정
agree 동감이다
agreement 찬성
　in ~, of the
　same opinion 동감이다
aim for 겨냥하다
all 전부, 전체, 온갖, 모든
　~ alike 너나(할것)없이
　~ kinds of 온갖
　~ of sudden 하루아침에, 갑자기
　~ places and
　　times 동서고금
　~ things taken
　　together 뭐니뭐니해도
　not at ~ 전혀, 통
allegory 우화
all-nighter 밤새껏 계속하는 것
　pull an ~ 밤 새우다
alone 혼자, 홀로
　live ~ 혼자 살다,
　　 독수공방하다
also, in addition 게다가
altered 바뀌다
always 늘, 항상
　almost ~ 십중팔구
among ~의 사이에
　~ themselves 끼리
ancestor 조상

~ -memorial services/rites	차례	artistic	예술적
ancestral	조상의	as	같이, 만큼, 처럼
~ burial ground	산소	~ for that	그야
~ god	조상신	~ it used to be	여전히
visit the ~ grave	성묘하다	~ much ~	자그마치
and the like	기타, 등	~ soon ~	~자 마자
angry	성나다, 화나다	~ well	역시
be/get ~	화(를) 내다	~ you know	아시다시피
announce	발표하다, 선고하다	ascend	오르다
anonymity	무명	ask	묻다, 달라고 하다
answer	답	~ for	구하다
correct ~	정답	assemble	모여들다, 모으다
~ing machine	자동 응답기	assertion	주장
anticipation	예상	assess	평가하다
apartment complex	아파트촌	astonished	경악하다
appear	생기다, 나타나다	at	에서, 에
appearance	모습	~ all	전혀
appetite	식욕	~ last	마침내
appetizers (served with drinks)	안주	~ leisure	한산하다
apply	신청하다; 응용하다, 실시하다	~ random	함부로
		atmosphere	분위기
appreciation	안목, 감상, 감사	attack	공격하다; 공격
approach	다가가다; 접근	attempt, try out	시도하다
appropriate	그만하다, 적당하다	attentively	유심히
approve	승인하다	attire	옷차림
approximately	~쯤, 안팎, 대충	attitude	태도
architecture	건축	attribute	속성
arise	벌어지다, 일어나다, 생기다	audience	관객, 청중
		author	지은이
around	무렵, ~쯤	autumn day	가을날
arranging class notes	노트 정리	average	평균
		avoid	꺼리다, 피하다
arrive	이르다, 도착하다	award	상; 상을 타다; 주다
art	예술	~ for the best invention	발명상
fine ~	미술		
		B.A. (degree)	학사
		backpack	봇짐

bad at, poor at	서투르다	bewilderment	당황, 어리둥절함
balance	균형	in a moment	
out of ~	불균형하다	of ~	얼떨결에
balancing accounts	결산	beyond	너머로
ballad	가요	bidding (of a	
old Korean ~s	향가	superior)	분부
bamboo	대나무	bill	지폐
green ~	녹죽	bind	묶다
barely	겨우	birthdate	생년월일
bark	껍질	birthday	생일
baseball	야구	~ party	생일 잔치
basement	지하	bite	물다
bassoon	바수운	blaze	불타다; 불꽃
baton	바통	blessing	복, 축복
battle	전투	blind	눈 멀다; 맹인
~ground	싸움터	blood-smeared	피투성이의
~ship	전투함	blue	푸른, 파란
bead	구슬	~ dragon	청룡
bean	콩	~ jeans	청바지
red ~	팥	bluff	허세
beat	두들기다; 비트	boa	구렁이
beauty salon	미장원	boardinghouse	하숙집
beef	쇠고기	boast	뽐내다; 자랑
beeper	호출기, 삐삐	boat	배
before	일찍, 전에	turtle ~	거북선
~ long	이윽고	body	육체
beg	얻어먹다, 구걸하다	~guard	보디가드
beggar	걸인	book	책
begging	구걸	~ of fairy	
beginning	시작	tales	동화책
from the ~	아예, 처음부터	newly	
behavior	행동, 짓	published ~	신간 서적
belatedly	뒤늦게	border (area)	국경 지대
belief	믿음	boring	지루하다
benefit	혜택	borrow	꾸다
bequeath	물려주다	boss	대장, 윗사람, 상사
best	제일가다; 최고(의)	bound	얽매이다
bewildered	쩔쩔매다	bow	뱃머리

brag	자랑하다	cannon	포, 대포
brain activity	뇌 활동	mouth of a ~	포 구멍
break	부러뜨리다	capacity	성능, 용량
bridegroom	신랑	capital	자본
brightly	활짝	~ism	자본주의
British Museum	대영 박물관	captivate	사로잡다
broken	망가지다, 부러지다	carbohydrate	탄수화물
bubble	거품	care about	신경을 쓰다
bull	황소	Carnegie	
~'s horn	쇠뿔	Foundation	카네기재단
bulletin board	게시판	car window	차창
bunch	무더기, 송이	case	경우
in a ~	무더기로	castle town	도성
burden	부담	catch sight of,	
without a ~	부담없이	glimpse	눈에 띄다
burn (up)	타오르다	Catholic	가톨릭
burning stubble	모닥불	cause	연유, 원인
bus with seats,		cel(lular) phone	핸드폰
coach bus	좌석 버스	center for Korean	
bustling	부산을 떨다	studies	한국학 연구소
butterfly	나비	century	세기
buttocks	엉덩이	cerebrum	대뇌
buy and take	사 가다	ceremony	식, 행사
by	옆에, 의하여	ancestor-	
~ doing what	어쩌다(가)	memorial ~	
~ the way	참	(service, rite)	성묘
		entrance ~	입학식
calculate	계산하다	challenge	도전
calculation	계산	chance	기회, 운
calendar	달력	by any ~	혹시
lunar ~	음력	change	변화
solar ~	양력	~ rapidly	급변하다
call out	불러 주다	charge	수수료, 요금; 책임,
campus	교내		비난; 청구하다
candle	초	take ~ of	담당하다
~light	촛불	chatter	지껄이다
candy	캔디	check	맞추다
cane	매를 치다; 지팡이	~ answers	답을 맞추다

childish	유치하다	cloth	옷감
children	자녀, 자제	clothing	의복
Children's Day	어린이날	club	동아리
chilly	시리다	clusters	송이, 한 덩어리
Chinese	중국의	in ~	주렁주렁
~ animal sign		coast guard	해안 경비
of the zodiac	띠	collapse	무너지다
~ date	대추	collect	챙기다, 모으다
~ noodles with		collectivism	집단주의
black bean		college	대학
sauce	짜장면	~ entrance	
~ herbal		examination	대학 입시
medicine	한약	~ of business	
chisel	끌	administration	경영대
chocolate	초콜릿	color	색깔
Cholla province	전라도	basic ~ tone	기본 색상
choose	고르다	combine	겸하다, 결합하다
chorus	합창	come	오다, 일어나다
Chosŏn	조선	~ across	마주치다
Ch'usŏk	추석	~ and go	드나들다
circle	원	~ deeply (into)	파고들다
Korean ~		~ for study	유하 오다
dance	강강수월래	~ing and going	오락가락
circumference	주위	~ to see	찾아오다
circumstance(s)	처지, 영문	comfort	위로하다; 위로
civilization	문명	comfortable	쾌적하다, 편하다
civilized society	문명 사회	comic book	만화책
claim	주장하다; 주장	command	지휘, 명령
classes	계급	commemorate	쇠다
the two upper		common	공통되다; 평범하다
~ (civil and		~ feature	공통점
military) of		~ly	흔히
old Korea	양반	~ people	백성
clear	밝은, 맑은, 명확한	communication	통신
make ~	밝히다	age of	
click the tongue	혀를 차다	mobile ~	이동 통신 시대
client	고객	competence	실력, 능력
cliff	절벽	competition	경쟁

free ~	자유 경쟁	be/get ~d	먹히다, 소비되다
completely	완전히	consumption, use	소모, 소비
compliment	칭찬	contact	연락하다
comply with	응하다	contemporary	현대적
compose	글 짓다	content	내용
comprehensively	종합적으로	continuation	계속; 연속
computer	컴퓨터	contrabass	콘트라베이스
~ illiterate	컴맹	contract	계약
~ terminal	단말기	contrary	반대의
conceive	구상하다	prove the ~	반증하다
concern	관심	contrastive	대조적
concert	연주회, 콘서트	contributed	기여되다
joint ~	합동 연주회	convenience	이기, 편리
conclusion	결론	conversation	대화
concretely	구체적으로	daily ~	일상 대화
concreteness	유형, 구체적임	telephone ~	통화
condition	조건	convict	죄수
conduct	지휘하다	convincing	호소력 있다
conductor	지휘자	copy	복사하다, 베끼다
confess	고백하다	~ing	모방
confident	자신 있다	make a ~ of	본 뜨다
feel ~	마음 든든하다	~writer	카피라이터
conflict	갈등	cordially	극진히
confront	대하다	corporation	기업
Confucian	유교적	correct	맞다, 바르다
confused	헷갈리다	~ answer	정답
connect	연결하다, 통하다	cost	대가
connote	의미하다	count	셈하다
consciousness	의식	~ on the	
consent	동의하다	fingers	손에 꼽다
consideration	고려	counter	반대; 계산대
serious ~	중시	~effect	역효과
consolidate	다지다	~ for horses	
conspicuous	두드러지다	and cows	필
constantly	끊임없이	country	나라, 국가
consult	의논하다	county	고을
consultation	상담, 자문	couple, husband	
consume	소비하다	and wife	내외

course	과정, 과목	decent	단정하다
courtesy	예절, 예의	decide	정하다
courtyard	안마당	decline	거절; 거절하다
co-worker	동료	decorate	꾸미다
crazy	미치다	decrease	덜하다
go ~	미치다	deed	소행, 행동
crime	범죄, 죄	defend	막다
criticism	비평	degree	정도, 계급, 도
harsh ~	혹평	make a ~	
cross-legged	다리를 포개다	higher	한 등급 올리다
sit ~	책상다리하다	deliberately,	
cross with	심술을 부리다	on purpose	굳이, 일부러
crowded with	붐비다	deliver	전하다; 낳다
cry out	외치다	~y room	산실
cultural	문화적인, 문화의	demolish	헐다
~ assets	문화재	dense	밀집한, 조밀한
~ difference	문화 차이	~ly populated	
culture	문화	area	인구 밀집 지역
customer	이용객, 손님, 고객	dentistry	치과
cut	끊어지다	department	부서, 과
cute	깜찍하다	~ of English	
cutting-edge	첨단	literature	영문학과
cycle	순환, 주기, 한 바퀴	~ of fashion	
		study	의상학과
daily	매일, 끊임없이	~ of	
~ conversation	일상 대화	instrumental	
damage	피해	music	기악과
dancing	무용	deprived of,	
dark	짙다, 어둡다	without	뺏기다
date	날짜; 대추	descendant(s)	후손
Chinese ~	대추	describe	묘사하다
day	날, 요일	design	설계하다
in a single ~	하루아침에	designate	지정하다
in those ~s	당시	desirable	바람직하다
deadline	마감 날짜	desire	바라다; 바람
deal with	처리하다	detail	세부, 상세
dear me!	어머나, 어머!	in ~	자세히
death penalty	사형	developed	발달되다

devised	창안되다	feel dizzy	아찔하다
difference	차이	documentary	다큐멘터리
cultural ~	문화 차이	domestic goods	국산품
different	딴	domino effect	도미노 현상
~ from others	남다르다	donkey	나귀
~ly	달리	doubt	의심
dig	파다	dough	가루 반죽; 연한
digestion	소화		덩어리
digestive function	소화 기능	make ~	빚다
digital mode	디지털 방식	downpour,	
dim	희미하다	heavy rain	폭우
dime a dozen	흔해 빠지다	drag and drop	끌어다 놓다
dining table	밥상	dragon	용
direction	방면	blue ~	청룡
in every ~	전후좌우	dramatic	극적
dirt	때, 먼지	draw a line, rule	줄치다
~ from the		dress	옷
hands	손때	formal ~	정장
disabled person	장애인	drill	송곳
disappointed	실망하다	drop	떨어지다
disapproval	거부(감)	~ by	들르다
discomfort	불편, 불쾌	~ in	들르다
discount	할인	~ in and then	
huge ~ store	대형 할인점	go	다녀가다
discover	알아내다, 발견하다	drum	북
disguise (oneself)	가장하다	dumbfounded	기(가) 막히다
dismissed	쫓겨나다	duty	도리, 업무
disposition	성품	dynasty	왕조
disregard	무시하다		
distance	거리	each	각각, 각자
sense of ~	거리감	earlier	진작, 일찍이
distinguish	분별하다	earnest	진지한, 열심인
distribute	나누다, 나누어 주다	in ~	본격적으로
divide	나누다	earth	흙, 땅, 지구
divided	엇갈리다	on ~	도대체
divine	신성한, 신의	earthquake	지진
~ spirit	신령	easily	쉬, 쉽게
dizzy	어지럽다	eat	먹다

~ heartily	배불리 먹다	enemy	적
~ing out	외식	~ troops	적군
economic power	경제권	energetic	활동적이다
economics	경제학과	enjoy	즐기다
ecstasy	환희	enter, make	
educational		one's way into	들다, 진입하다
institute	학원	entertain a guest	접대하다
effect	효과	enthusiasm for	
efficiency	효과, 능률	learning	향학열
eight or nine out		entirely	몽땅
of ten;		entrance ceremony	입학식
almost always	십중팔구	entreaty	애원
elaborately	정성껏	entrust	맡기다
elderly man	영감(님)	envy	부러워하다
electric light	전열등	episode	에피소드
element	요소	equal, of the	
elucidate	비추다; 설명하다	same rank	동등하다
e-mail	전자 우편	equality-oriented	
embrace	안다, 포옹하다	culture	수평 문화
~ tightly	끌어안다	era	시대
emergency	비상	especially	특별히
emigrate	이민을 가다	established	인정한
Emille bell	에밀레종	etiquette	예절
emotion	감정	rules of ~	예의 범절
emperor	황제	Europe and	
employee	종업원, 사원, 직원	America	구미
empty	비우다	even	고르다
feel ~	시장하다	event	행사
~ hand(s)	빈손	eventually	결국
~ stomach	시장	evergreen,	
leave ~,		green pine	청송
vacate	비워 두다	every	마다, 모두, 모든
encyclopedia	백과사전	almost ~ day	매일 같이
end	끝	~ kind of	온갖
~less	끊임없다	everyday	일상, 매일, 날마다
~lessly	한없이	~ language	일상어
very end	후미, 맨 끝	exaggeration	과장
endure	견디다	examination	검사, 시험

college		face-to-face	마주보다
entrance ~	대학 입시	sit ~	마주보고 앉다
~ paper	시험지	facial	얼굴의
take an ~	시험 치르다	~ expression	표정
example	모범, 보기, 예, 시범	facing	대면
for ~	가령, 예를 들면	fairly	꽤
exceedingly	지나치게	fairy	선녀
excellence	우수성	collection of	
exception	예외	original ~ tales	창작 동화집
excessive	과하다	~ tale	동화
exchange	교환하다, 바꾸다,	familiar (with)	익숙하다
	주고받다	family	가족, 가정
~ student	교환 학생	~ medicine	가정의학과
execute	집행하다	~ name	성
execution	집행	famish	굶다
exhibit	출품하다	fan	팬
exhibition	발표회, 전시	fantastic	환상적이다
existence	유, 존재	fantasy	환상
expect	기대하다	faraway	멀리
expectation	기대	fare	요금
experience	경험하다; 경험	farmer	농부
have bitter ~	혼나다	farming	농사
experimentally	시범적으로	fascinated	매료되다, 혹하다
expert	전문가	fashion	유행, 스타일, 패션
explosion	폭발	in an orderly ~	제대로
explosive	폭발적	fastidious	까다롭다
~ly	폭발적으로	fat	지방
expression	표정, 표현	fate, karma	인연
~less	무표정하다	fatigue	피로
extensively	두루	favorite song	18번; 좋아하는 노래
extent	정도	feature	특징
extra	덤	common ~	공통점
extreme	심하다	feces	똥
~ly	극히, 무척	fee	사용료
eye	눈	feel	느끼다
~sight	시력	~ confident	마음 든든하다
keep an ~ on	지켜보다	~ dizzy	아찔하다
		~ empty	시장하다

~ honored	영광스럽다	fluster	허둥지둥하다
~ing	감각	flustered	당황하다
~ing of		all ~	허둥지둥
disapproval	거부감	flutter	설렘
~ like going	갈 마음이 나다	~ingly	훨훨
~ sorry	서운하다	fly into a rage	분노하다
~ victimized	억울하다	folk	민속의
fellow	놈	~ game	민속놀이
female student	여학생	~ song	가요곡, 민요
fifteen days	보름	~tale	민화
figure	숫자; 모양; 인물	foot	발
good ~	맵시	for	~을 위하여; 용도의
filial daughter	효녀	~ adhesion	접착용
fill	차지하다, 채우다	forbid	금지하다
~ in	때우다	foreign	외래, 외국계
~ up	채우다	~ goods	외제
finish, get through	끝내 버리다	forever	길이
finish off	마무리 짓다	forgive	용서하다
firmly	단단히	form	맺다; 형태
first	처음, 최초, 먼저	formal	형식적인, 표면적인
~ half year	상반기	~ dress	정장
~ impression	첫인상	~ism	형식주의
~ king of a		~ity	격식
dynasty	태조	former times	예전
~ meeting	초면	fortunate	다행이다
~ of all	우선	~ly	다행히
~-run movie		fountain	분수대
theatre	개봉관	free	자유로운
~ step	첫발	~ competition	자유 경쟁
fish	생선, 고기	~dom	자유
scabbard ~	갈치	for ~, gratis	그냥
flattery	아부	~ from danger	무난하다
flicker	깜빡이다	~way	고속 도로
flight	비행	frequency	주파수
float	뜨다	frequent	출입하다
flowing	흐름	fresh	신선하다
fluent	유창하다	~ness	풋풋함
flurried	허겁지겁	fret	짜증

frog	개구리	get	얻다, 받다, 잡다
front	앞, 정면	~ something	
~ gate	정문	for free	얻어 가다
~ yard	앞뜰	~ through	버리다
fruit	과일	~ together,	
newly		meet	모이다
harvested ~,		~ used to	익숙해지다
fresh ~	햇과일	gift shop	선물 가게
full	부르다; 가득 차다	glimpse, catch	
~ of	들어차다; 가득찬	sight of	눈에 띄다
fun	놀이, 장난, 재미, 흥	glisten	얼른얼른하다
make ~ of	놀리다	glittering	반짝
function	기능	global village	지구촌
fund	기금	glossy, sleek	반지르르하다
~-raising	모금	glue	풀
fusion concert	퓨전 콘서트	go	가다, 출발하다
future	미래	~ ahead	앞서 가다
in the ~	장차	~ crazy	미치다
		~ easy on	봐주다
gain skill in	익히다	feel like ~ing	갈 마음이 나다
game	놀이, 경기, 게임	~ home from	
folk ~	민속 놀이	work	퇴근하다
gap	틈	~ing to work	출근
garden	마당; 뜰	~ wrong	실패하다
garments	의류	goal	목적
gate	문	goblin	도깨비
back ~	후문	good-bye	안녕
front ~	정문	say ~	작별하다
gathering	모임	goods	상품
general	일반의, 대체적인;	foreign ~	외제
	장군	imported ~	수입 상품
military ~	장군	manufactured ~	제품
generalization	일반화	miscellaneous ~	잡화
generally,		goose	거위
on the whole	전체적으로	gourd	박, 바가지
generation	세대	~ bottle	호리병
genuine	진짜의	gourmet	미식가
the ~ article	진짜	government	정부

~ office	관청	surgery	제모 수술
~ post	벼슬, 관직	hall	회관
governor-general	총독	hammer	망치
grade	채점하다; 학년; 성적	hand	손
gradually	차츰	flat of the ~	손바닥
graduate school	대학원	handcart	리어커
graduating class	졸업반	handicapped	장애인
graft	접목	handling	처리
grain	곡식	*Han'guk Daily*	한국일보
five ~s	오곡	Hanyang	한양
grasping person	욕심쟁이	happen	생기다
gratis, for free	그냥, 무료로	"Happy Birthday"	
grave	무덤	(song)	생일 축하 노래
weeding of a ~	벌초	hard	꽁꽁; 단단하다
greed	욕심	~drive	컴퓨터 본체
green	녹색의	harden	굳다
grieve	서러워하다	hardship(s)	고생, 고난
grind	빻다	undergo ~	고생하다
ground	땅, 지면; 근거	harmonious	원만하다
lie on the ~	엎드리다	harvest	수확, 추수
growth	성장	year of good ~	풍년
~ period	성장기	have	가지다
guarantee	보장하다; 보장	head	머리, 고개
guard	경비	~ of a team	팀장
guardian angel	수호신	headache	두통, 골칫덩이
guest room	사랑채, 객실	have a ~	골치다
guidance	안내	health center	보건소
guide	안내하다	heap	산더미
gulp	꿀꺽 삼키다	hearing	청각
in great ~s	단숨에, 한 입에	heart	마음; 심장; 가슴
gum	잇몸	in one's ~	내심
gymnastic		to one's ~'s	
exercises	체조	content	마음껏
have ~	체조하다	heartily	많이; 진심으로
		eat ~	배불리 먹다
habit, practice	습관, 일쑤	heat	달다; 열
hair	머리털, 털	~ing	난방
~ removal		heaven and earth	천지

heel	굽	parents' ~	친정
height	한창; 높이; 키	honor	명예
at the ~ of	한창	honored	명예롭다
help	돕다; 도움	feel ~	영광스럽다
~er	도우미	honorifics	존댓말
~ful	도움이 되다	rules of ~	존대법
helter-skelter,		hope	희망
in every direction	전후좌우	hospital	병원
hemp	베	general ~	종합 병원
here	여기	house	집
~after	이후	~hold	살림, 집안
~ and there	여기저기, 불쑥불쑥	one's own ~	자택
heredity	유전	~wife	주부
hero	주인공, 영웅	how, in what way	어떻게 해서
hesitation	주저, 망설임	human	인간의, 사람다운
without ~	서슴없이	~ being	인간
hey!	어이!	~ relationships	인간 관계
hierarchy-oriented		humanity, mankind	인류
culture	수직 문화	humble	천하다; 겸손하다
High Tide (soap)	하이타이 (= 세제)	humor	우스갯소리, 익살
highway	고속 도로	hungry	시장하다
hinge on	걸려 있다	husband (form	
hip	엉덩이	of address)	서방님
historic site	고적지	husband and wife	내외
history	역사	hymn	찬송가
~ of economics	경제학사		
hobble	절룩거리다	idea	아이디어
hold	잡다	"if you do so"	그럼, 그러면
~ (two ropes)		ignorant	무식하다
with each		illuminate	밝히다
hand	갈라 잡다	illustration	삽화
~ tightly	움켜쥐다	imagination	상상력
holiday(s)	휴일	imagine	상상하다
major ~	명절	immediately	당장, 단박에
holy	거룩하다; 거룩한	immense	대단하다
home	가정, 집	importance	중요성
married		imported goods	수입 상품
woman's		impossible	불가능하다

impression	감동; 인상	information	정보
first ~	첫인상	inherit	이어 오다
imprisoned	갇히다	inheritance	유산
in	안에, 중에, 속에	inherited	유전되다
~ any case	그러나 저러나	inquire	여쭙다, 알아보다
~ a row	죽	inside out	뒤집어, 샅샅이
~ a (single) day	하루아침에	turned ~	뒤집히다
~ a (single) word	한마디로	instant	순간
		~ly	단박, 별안간
~ clusters	주렁주렁	institute	연구소, 학원; 협회
~ detail	자세히	educational ~	교육기관, 학원
~ earnest	본격적으로	institution	기관
~ every direction	전후좌우	instructive	교훈적이다
		insufficiently	덜
~ the blink of an eye	별안간	intangible	무형(의)
		intellectual	지적이다
~ those days	당시	intend to	마음을 먹다
incidental	우연하다	intention	뜻, 의사
incite	자극하다	interested in	관심을 갖다
include	포함하다	internal medicine	내과
incomparable, have no comparison	비길 데 없다	intimate	가까워지다, 친근하다
		intolerably	참을 수 없이
		introduce	선보이다; 소개하다
indebtedness	덕택	invade	침입하다
indeed	과연, 하긴	invent	발명하다
individual	개인	~ion	발명품; 발명
individualism	개인주의	~or	발명가
individually	개별적으로	invest	투자하다
indoor sports complex	실내 연습장	investigate, look into	조사하다, 살펴보다
induce	끌어들이다	involuntarily	무심코
industrial arts	공예	ironclad	철갑
industry	제조업, 산업	~ ship	철갑선
infinite	무궁무진하다	~ism	주의
influence	영향	item (in an agenda)	안건
inform	연락하다, 알리다	itself	자체
informality	비공식		

jailor 교도관

January full
moon day 정월 대보름

jar 항아리

jealousy 질투심

jeans 진, 바지

blue ~ 청바지

jest 해학, 농담; 농담하다

jewel 보석

jewelry 패물

job 직업

jocularity, humor 익살

joint concert 합동 연주회

joke 농담; 농담을 하다

journalist 기자

joyfully (dancing) 덩실덩실

judge 판단하다

junk mail 정크 메일

just 만, 단지

~ as it is 채; 그대로

~ in time 마침

kalpitchim,
(steamed short
ribs) 갈비찜

kangkang
suwollae (dance) 강강수월래

Kangnam
subway station 강남역

karma, fate 인연

keep 두다

kerosene lamp 호롱불

kick 차다

kindhearted 착하다

king 왕

first ~ of
a dynasty 태조

kingship 왕위

knead 반죽하다

knee 무릎

knit 니트

knock 노크하다; 노크

Korean 한국의

~ classical
music 국악

~ *Economy*
Daily 한국 경제신문

~ literature 한국 문학

~ oriole 꾀꼬리

~ peasant
music 농악

~ Thanksgiving
Day 한가위

Kyobo book
center 교보문고

Kyodae subway
station 교대역

label 상표

laborer 노동자

ladder 사다리

lag (behind) 밀리다

lame person 절름발이

lamp (kerosene) 호롱불

language usage 언어 사용

last 마지막, 최후;
지속하다

~ long 오래가다

~ night 간밤

late 지각하다; 늦다

law 법

~ school 법대

lazy 게으르다

lead to 통하다

leaflet 전단

learning 배움, 학습

enthusiasm

   for ~   향학열

leave   남기다, 떠나다

   ~ behind   남기다

   ~ vacated,

      empty   비워 두다

lecture   강연, 강의

legend   전설

legitimacy   정통

lenient   관대하다

   be ~, go

    easy on   봐주다

less   덜

lie   눕다, 놓여 있다

   ~ down flat 나자빠지다

   ~ scattered

    around   산재하다, 흩어지다

life   목숨, 인생

   ~style   생활 양식

   ~time   평생, 생시

light   ① 가벼운; ② 빛, 불

   ~ and flimsy 하늘하늘하다

   electric ~   전깃불

   ~ of a

    cigarette   담뱃불

link   잇다, 연결하다

lion   사자

   stone ~   돌사자

live alone   독수공방하다

loanword   외래어

lobby   로비

located   위치하다

location   위치

loiter   서성거리다

long   오래

   last ~   오래가다

longevity   장수

long time   장기

look   찾다, 보다

   ~ for, search 찾아보다

   ~ into,

    investigate 살펴보다, 조사하다

Lord Taewǒn 대원군

lose   밑지다, 잃다

loss   손해

lounge   휴게실

lovely as a flower 꽃답다

loyal subject 충신

luck   행운, 다행

   all kinds of

    good ~   만복

lunar calendar 음력

lunatic   미치광이

luxuries   사치품

M.A. (degree) 석사

magic   요술

magnificent 찬란하다

   ~ view   절경

mail   우편

   ~box   우편함

   junk ~   정크 메일

main   주요

   ~ly   주로

maintain   유지하다

maintenance 유지

   ~ work   보수 공사

majority, more

   than half   대부분, 절반 이상

make   만들다, 하다, 벌다

   ~ a degree

    higher   돋구다

   ~ clear   밝히다

   ~ fun of   놀리다

   ~ one's way

    into   진입하다

male adult	양반; 남자 어른	family ~	가정의학과
mallet	방망이	meet, get together	모이다, 만나다
malnutrition	영양 실조	meeting	모임
management	관리	first ~	초면
manager	지배인	regular ~	정기 모임
mankind	인류	member	일원, 회원
manner	방법, 풍습, 예절	memory	기억
in that ~	그러다(가), 그렇게	mentality	심리
~s and customs	풍습	mention	들다, 언급하다
manufactured		merchant	상인
goods	제품	merely	불과; 단지
manufacturing		merrily	흥겹게
industry	제조업	metaphorical	비유적(인)
maple	단풍	method	방법
markedly	눈에 띄게	meticulousness	자상
married	결혼한	middle	중, 가운데
~ man	유부남	in the ~	
~ woman	유부녀	of thinking	생각 중이다
marry	결혼하다	millionaire	백만장자
~ a man	시집가다	mind	정신, 마음
~ a woman	장가가다	in one's ~	속으로
~ late in life		mineral	무기질
(of men)	늦장가를 들다	miracle	기적
martial arts	무술	miscellaneous	
martyrdom	순교	goods	잡화
marvelous	신기하다	miser	구두쇠
~ly	신통하게	miserable condition	지경
match(es)	성냥	miss dearly	그립다
mayor	시장	missionary	선교사
meal	식사, 간식	mistake	실수
after a ~	식후(에)	make a ~	실수하다
nourishing ~,		mobilize	동원하다
well-balanced ~	영양식	mock, make	
means	수단	fun of	놀리다
by what ~	어찌, 어떻게	mode of living	생활 양식
medicine	약	model	모형, 본
Chinese		modern person	현대인
herbal ~	한약	modernization	현대화

modesty	겸손	naturally	자연히
molester	치한	nearly	거의, 한
monkey	원숭이	neat and tidy	깔끔하다
mood	기분	neatly	단정하게
moon	달	necessity	필수품, 필요
full ~	보름달	nemesis	천벌
more or less,		nephew	조카
approximately	안팎, 약, 대충	nerve	신경
more than half	절반 이상	nervous	안절부절못하다
mostly, for the		nest	둥지
most part	대부분	nevertheless	그런데도
mother and		new	새로운
daughter	모녀	~ crop	햇곡식
mother-in-law		~ word	신어
(man's)	장모	~ Year's Day	설날
motivation	동기	~ York bakery	뉴욕제과
move	이동하다	newcomer	새내기
movement	이동; 악장 (in	newly	새로이
	music)	newspaper	신문
Mt. Kŭmgang	금강산	~ publisher	신문사
much, a great		next year	이듬해; 다음해
deal	톡톡히	niece	조카딸
music	음악	night	밤
indigenous		dead of ~	심야
Korean ~	향악	last ~	간 밤
popular ~	대중 음악	~ owls	올빼미족
traditional ~	전통 음악	~time	야간
musical	음악의	~time meal,	
~ composition	작곡	midnight	
~ instrument	악기	snack	야찬 (= 밤참)
muteness	무음	nimble	날쌔다
mysterious	신비롭다	noble	귀족; 고귀하다
myth	신화	young ~	귀공자
		nocturne	야상곡
name	성함, 이름	nod	끄덕이다
family ~	성	none	무
named as	불리다	nonetheless	하지만
national treasure	국보	non-glutinous rice	멥쌀

noodles	국수	office	사무실
Chinese ~		government ~	관청
with black		Oh! Indeed!	아이 참
bean sauce	짜장면	Oh my!	어머!
noraebang	노래방	Oh! Why!	어머나
nostalgia	향수	old	낡은, 늙은; 옛날의
not	아니	~ person	노인
certainly ~	설마	~ times	옛날
~ a little	자못	~-style	
~ at all	전혀, 통	Korean	
~ different	다름(이) 없다	pop song	전통 가요
~ only	뿐 아니라	on	위에, ~에 대해서
~ so	그다지 . . . 않다	~ purpose	굳이, 일부러
note pad	메모지	~ the spot	당장
notice	주목, 게시	~ the way	도중
take ~ of	거들떠 보다;	~ the whole	전체적으로
	주목하다	once	일단
notion	관념	at ~	단김에, 즉시
nourishing meal	영양식	*ondol* (hot floor)	온돌
nourishment	영양	one	하나, 어떤
novel	신기하다	~ after another	속속
novice	초년생	'~ Love' club	'한사랑' 동아리
nuisance	골치	one's	자신의
nurse	간호사	oneself	제, 자기
nursery	아이방, 육아실	only	뿐
~ rhyme(s)	동시	~ then	그제야
~ story	동화	~ two persons	단둘이
nutrient	영양소, 영양분	open	개방하다, 열다
nylon (cloth)	나일론 옷감	open-air theater	노천 극장
		opinion	의견
obesity	비만	of the same ~	동감이다
object	대상	opposite	반대의, 다른
observance	관측	~ party	상대방
obstetrics and		~ room	건넌방
gynecology	산부인과	orchestra	오케스트라
occasion	김; 경우	symphony ~	관현악단
occupy	지배하다, 차지하다	ordeal(s)	수난
of course	~다마다; 물론	order	명령, 주문; 순서

orderly	규칙적	patient	환자
in an ~ fashion	제대로, 순서대로	patron	단골
ordinance	법령	pattern	무늬
ordinary	평범하다	pauper	가난뱅이
organization	조직체, 단체	pay	치르다, 계산하다
origin	유래	payment	지불, 계산
originality	독창성	make a ~	지불하다
originally	원래	peaceful	평안하다
ornament	장식	peasant	농부
outcry	아우성	peck	쪼다
outfielder	외야수	peculiar	특이하다
outstandingly	뛰어나게	people	사람들, 국민
over	위쪽에, 넘어서	common ~	백성
~flow	넘치다	~ of mature	
~night	하루아침에	age	청장년
~ there	건너; 저기	perfection	완성
~time	시간외로, 초과 근무	perform	연주하다, 치다
~work	과로	~ing center	공연장
owl	올빼미	performance	공연
		public ~	공연
packed	포장되다	period	시기, 기간
packet	갑	regular ~,	
pager	페이저, 호출기	fixed ~	정기
pair	짝	perish	망하다
palace	대궐, 궁전	personage	인물
palpitate	울렁거리다	personal	개인적인
p'ansori	판소리	~ habit	버릇
parade	행렬	~ relations	대인 관계
paralysis	중풍	personality	성격
parking	주차	persuasive	설득력이 있다
~ difficulties	주차난	petition	호소
part	일부, 일부분	Ph.D. (degree)	박사
particularly	별로, 특별히	physical	신체의, 자연의
part-time job	아르바이트	~ constitution	체질
party	파티, 잔치	~ system	신체
welcome ~ for		pick	고르다, 취하다
new students	신입생 환영회	~ up	건지다, 줍다
patent	특허	pine	소나무

green ~,	
evergreen	청송
~ nuts	잣
pity	가여워하다
place	자리; 두다
one ~	한군데, 한자리
plan	계획, 기획
make a ~	계획하다
plantation	농장
plastic	플라스틱의
~ surgery	성형 외과
~ surgery	
procedure	성형 수술
plausible	그럴듯하다
play	연주하다; 연극
~ a solo	독주하다
~ing *yut*	윷놀이하다
pleated skirt	주름 치마
plenty, abundant	넉넉하다
plum	자두
point	끝, 점; 가리키다
~ing out	지적
~ to	가리키다
polite,	
well-mannered	예절 바르다
politely	정중히
poor at, bad at	서투르다
popular	대중적인, 인기 있는
~ music	대중 음악
~ product	히트 상품
~ song	대중 가요, 유행가,
	팝송
popularity	인기
portion	대목
position	위치
social ~	신분
possibility	수; 가능성
poster, wall	
newspaper	벽보
Post-it	포스트잇
postponement	연기
pounce on	달려들다
pour	따르다, 붓다,
	쏟아지다
powder	가루
pragmatism	실용주의
praise	칭찬하다
pray	기원하다, 빌다
prefer, have	
preferences	선호하다
preordained	
relationship	연분
prepare	차리다
presence	존재
presentation	연출
preserve	보존하다
president	회장
~ of a	
conglomerate	대그룹 회장
pretense	척
priest	사제
primarily	주로
primitive	원시의
~ society	원시 사회
printed	실리다, 인쇄되다
priority	우선
prison	옥, 감옥
private	사적인
prize	상
product	상품
popular ~	히트 상품
progress	발달하다; 발전
prologue	서두
promoted	승진; 진급하다
be/get ~	승진하다
promotion	선전, 승진

promptly	신속히	rape	겁탈하다
property	재산	rapidly	무럭무럭, 빠르게
one's whole ~	전 재산	rare	드물다
proprieties	예의, 예절	ratio	비율
protagonist	주인공	raw material	원료
protection	보호	reading	독서
protégé	부하	reality	사실, 현실
prove	입증하다, 증명하다	realized	실현되다
~ the contrary	반증하다	reason	이유
public	공적인; 대중	for no good ~	무턱대고; 특별한
general ~	일반 대중		이유 없이
~ performance	공연	for what ~	어찌, 어떻게
~ service	복무	rebel	반항하다
publish	출판하다	recently	요새
~ing company	출판사	recognize	알아보다
Pulguk temple	불국사	record	기록
purchase	사다, 구(입)하다	red bean	팥
pure	순수하다	refined	곱다, 세련되다
puritan	청교도	reflect	반영하다
put	두다, 놓다	refuse	거절하다
~ forth	내다	regard	안부
~ in	담기다	regret	한; 유감
~ into practice	실시하다	regular	규칙적인, 정기적인
~ on the screen	상영하다	~ meeting	정기 모임
		~ period	정기
quit	그만두다	rejection	거부
quiz	쪽지시험	relation	관계
		preordained ~	연분
rabbit	토끼	relative	친지
rage	격정, 분노	release, set free	풀어 주다
fly into a ~	분노하다	relic	유물
raid	덮치다	religion	종교
rain	비	state ~,	
~water	빗물	established ~	국교
rainbow	무지개	remainder	나머지
raise and see,		remedy	바로잡다
skim	들춰보다	remodel	개조하다
rank(ing)	순위	remote control	리모콘

repair	손질하다, 보수하다	ripe	무르익다, 익다
repeated	반복되다	rivers and	
repeatedly	자꾸만, 반복해서,	mountains	강산
	되풀이해서	riverside	강변
represent	대표하다	robust	건장하다
~ative	대표적이다	role	구실
request	요청; 청하다	room	방
research	연구	guest ~	사랑채, 객실
resemble	닮다	~ opposite the	
resentment	원망	main	
reservation	예약; 망설임, 삼감	bedroom	건넌방
without ~	대뜸	root	근본, 뿌리
reserve	예약하다	roughly	대충
residence	주거, 거주	round	회
one's ~	댁, 자택	final ~	마지막 회
resistance	저항	~ and ~	칭칭
resolution	결심, 해결	row	줄; 싸움; 배를 젓다
make a ~	마음을 먹다, 결심하다	in a ~	죽
respect	공경하다, 존경하다;	rub	비비다
	존경	rule	규칙; 지배; 줄 긋다
respond favorably	받아 주다	draw a ~ (line)	줄치다
response	반응	ruler	자; 지배자
restaurant	레스토랑, 식당	rummage	뒤지다
restless	안절부절못하다	rumor	소문
grow ~	들뜨다	run	달리기; 뛰다
result	결과	in the long ~	마침내
retort	쏴 붙이다, 반박하다	rural district(s)	전원
return courtesy,			
reciprocal		sacrifice	희생하다
courtesy	답례	sadly	슬피
reverse(ly), back	거꾸로	safe, free	
revolution	혁명	from danger	무난하다, 무사하다
rice	쌀	saint	성자
non-glutinous ~	멥쌀	sale	세일, 판매
riddle	수수께끼	same age,	
right	바른; 오른쪽의	contemporary	동갑, 동시대
that's ~	그래 맞아	satire	풍자
~ moment	제때	savage	오랑캐

saved	절약되다	dotage	망령 나다
saw	키다	senior	선배; 손윗사람
sawing	톱질	sense(s)	감각
scabbard fish	갈치	~ of distance	거리감
scan	훑어보다	~ of sight	시각
scarf	스카프	~ of smell	후각
scattered	흩어지다	~ of taste	미각
lie ~ around	산재하다	~ of trust	신뢰감
scene	장면, 판	sensitive	민감하다
scenery	경치	sentence	① 문장; ② 선고
scent	향기	English ~	영문
Scholastic		sequence	순서
Aptitude Test	수능 시험	seriously,	
school	학교	in earnest	본격적으로
whole ~	전교	servant	하인
~yard	교정	serve one's	
science	과학	master	(주인을) 섬기다
age of the		service	서비스
cutting-edge ~	첨단 과학 시대	public ~	군 복무
screen	스크린	sesame	깨
put on the ~	상영하다	set	두다, 놓다
screwdriver	스크류드라이버	~ free, release	풀어 주다
search, look for	찾아 보다	~ the table	(상을) 차리다
season	계절	settle (down)	자리 잡다
secrecy	비밀	several	몇몇
secret	비결, 비밀	~ thousands	수천
~ of success	성공(의) 비결	~ times	수차
section	부분	shaman	무당
children's		shape	형상, 형태
book ~	아동 서적 코너	share	나누다, 같이하다
see-through	시스루, 속이 비치는	~ joys	
select	선택하다	and sorrows	동고동락하다
self-respect	자존심	shed light on	비추다
sell	판매하다	shell	껍데기
~ing	판매	shiveringly	벌벌 (떨다)
~ing out	매진	shock therapy	쇼크 요법
send off	떠나 보내다	shoe chest	신발장
senile, in one's		shop	매장, 가게, 점포

gift ~	선물 가게	see	들춰 보다
specialty ~	전문점	skin scaling	피부 스케일링
shopping	쇼핑	skip	거르다, 빠지다
~ center,		skirt	스커트, 치마
~ mall	상가	pleated ~	주름 치마
~ mall for		skylark	종달새
clothes only	의류 상가	skyrocket	치솟다
sick	탈나다, 편찮다,	sleep	잠
	아프다	get to ~	잠을 이루다
side	측, 측면	~ poorly	잠을 설치다
south ~	남쪽	sleeping curled up	새우잠
sight	광경	slender	잘록하다, 날씬하다
sense of ~	시각	slide	미끄러지다
sights to see	명소	slim	가늘다
sightseeing (after		slow-witted	둔하다
a meal)	식후경	sluggard	게으름뱅이
sign	사인, 기호	smell	냄새
Chinese ~ of		sense of ~	후각
the zodiac	띠	sneer	비웃음
signature	서명	Snow White	백설공주
significant	의의 깊다	so	그래서, 그렇게, 워낙
silently	묵묵히	~ far as	마저; ~하는 한
simply	단순히	~ trifling	그까짓
sin	죄	socially	사회적으로
sincerity	성실성	social position	신분
sing	부르다, 뽑다	society	사회
~er	가수	primitive ~	원시 사회
Sino-Korean		traditional ~	전통 사회
character(s)	한자어	soft	부드럽다
sit	앉다	Sŏkkuram cave	
~ around	둘러앉다	temple	석굴암
~ cross-legged	책상다리하다	solar calendar	양력
~ face-to-face	마주 앉다	soldier	군인
site	장소	sold out	매진되다
situation	판, 처지, 입장	solo	혼자; 독주
skill	기술	play a ~	독주하다
technical ~	기능	solution	해결
skim, raise and		solve	풀다, 해결하다

song	노래
classical ~	가곡
favorite ~	18번; 좋아하는 노래
folk ~	가요, 민요
popular ~	대중 가요, 유행가, 팝
up-to-date	
popular ~	최신 가요
~ writing	작곡
sonorous	쟁쟁하다
sorority house	여학생 회관
sorry	미안하다
feel ~	서운하다
sound	건전하다; 음향
~ of ripping	쩍
sour	시다
south	남쪽
~bound train	남행 열차
~-North Korea	
symphony	
orchestra	남북 교향악단
~ side	남방
space to step on	발 디딜 틈
speak to	말을 붙이다
specialty shop	전문점
splendid	화려하다
~ly	굉장히
split	갈라지다
spread out	퍼지다
spring out	솟아나다
sprout, bud	싹; 트다
stage	무대; 시기
first ~	초기
stamp the feet	발을 구르다
stand	대
start a new job	부임하다
starve	굶다
state religion,	
established	

religion	국교
stay up all night	새우다
steam whistle	기적
step	걸음; 수단
first ~	첫발
~ forward	내디디다
~ in	들어서다
stimulate	자극하다
stir	젓다
store	점포
straightforward	직설적이다
strength	힘
full of ~	힘차다
stress	강조하다
stripe	줄무늬
strong	든든하다
structure	구조
~ of a room	방 구조
stubborn	고집이 세다
stuck in	박히다
student	학생
female ~	여학생
~ center	학생회관
study	공부
come for ~	유학 오다
~ of accounting	회계학 스타디
studying	글공부
stunned	어리둥절하다
subject	대상
subjective	주관적이다
sublet	하청 주다
submit	굴하다
succeed	성공하다
successively,	
one after another	속속
sufficiently	넉넉하게
suitable	마땅하다
summer retreat	피서

summon	불러 오다	~ out	꺼내다
(the) sun sets	해지다	tale	설화
Sunday paper	일요 신문	talent	재간, 재능
superior	위의, 높은; 윗사람	Tano festival	
one's ~	상사	(fifth day of	
supplement	보충하다	the fifth lunar	
supply	공급; 공급하다	month)	단오(날)
supreme	무상의, 최고의	taste	맛
surely	확실히	sense of ~	미각
~ not	설마	teacher	선생님
surprisingly		teakettle	주전자
(enough)	놀랍게도	team	팀
surrounding	주위	head of a ~	팀장
suspense	서스펜스	tear(s)	눈물
swallow	제비	tease	놀리다
swear	맹세하다	technical skill	기능
sweet	달콤하다, 달다	technology	테크놀로지
~heart	연인, 임	teeth	치아 (= 이)
~ potato	고구마	telecommuting,	
swing	그네	working at home	자택 근무
~ing on a		telepathy	텔레파시
swing	그네뛰기	telephone	
syllable	음절	conversation	통화
symphony	교향곡	tendency	경향
~ orchestra	교향악단	testing ground	시험장
synthesis	종합	Thanksgiving	
		Day	추수 감사절
table	탁자	thanks to	덕택으로
dining ~	밥상	then, in those	
set the ~	밥상 차리다	days	당시
Tabo tower	다보탑	therapy	요법
tactile sensation	촉각	therefore	그러니까
take	치르다, 얻다, 가지다	thereupon	그러자
~ an exam	시험 치르다	thin	가늘다
~ charge of	담당하다	this	이것, 이쪽, 여기
~ notice of	거들떠 보다;	~ time	이번
	주목하다	~ year	금년, 올해
~ off	떼다; 벗다	thoroughly	철저하게, 샅샅이

thousand	천	traffic jam	교통 체증
thread a way		train	기차
through a crowd	누비다	southbound ~	남행 열차
thrift	절약	transmission	전래, 전승
throw	버리다, 던지다	transmit	전하다
ticket	표	travel	여행; 여행하다
tie	맺다, 묶다	~ agency	여행사
tightly	꼭	~er	나그네, 여행자
time	시절; 시간	tread (on)	디디다
~ and tide	세월	treasure	보물, 보화
for the ~ being	당분간	national ~	국보
this ~	이번	trend	추세, 경향
times	회, 번	trifling	사소하다
several ~	수차	so ~	그까짓
timpani	팀파니	trivial	대수롭지 않다
to	까지, 쪽에, 으로	trudgingly,	
~ that extent	그리, 그만큼, 그	ploddingly	터덜터덜
	정도로	trust	신뢰
~ the heart's		sense of ~	신뢰감
content	마음껏	trustworthy	믿음직하다
~ the maximum	최고로	truthfully	바른 대로
(tobacco) pipe	담뱃대	try out, attempt	시도하다
together	함께	tune	곡
Tŏksu Palace		turned inside out	뒤집히다
Modern Art		turtle	거북(이)
Museum	덕수궁 현대미술관	~ boat	거북선
tonic	보약	snapping ~	자라
too, overly	너무	twin	쌍둥이
totally	온통	twine	실
touch	접촉; 닿다	two birds with	
tough	질기다	one stone	일석이조
tower	탑	twofold	배, 이 배
trace	혼적	two-income family	맞벌이
without a ~	혼적 없이		
tradition	전통	ugly	홍칙하다
traditional	전통의	unbalance	불균형
~ music	전통 음악	unbalanced	불균형하다
~ society	전통 사회	uncommonly	유난히

undergarment	내의, 속옷	view	경치, 관점, 봄
underground		magnificent ~	절경
passage	지하도	~ of values	가치관
understand	파악하다, 이해하다	~ of	
undertake	맡다, 착수하다	womanhood	여성관
unemployed	실직자	village	고을, 동네
unexpectedly	불쑥, 예상치 않게	vine	덩굴
unfamiliar	낯설다	violence	폭력
unfold	펼치다	virgin	처녀
uninterested	심드렁하다	vision	시력, 광경, 환상
union	결합, 연합회	sense of ~	시각
unpleasantness	불쾌감	visit	방문하다
unraveled	풀리다	~ (a senior)	찾아뵙다
untimely	때아닌	~ the ancestral	
unusually	유난히	grave	성묘
uproot	뽑다	visual	시각적
urge	조르다	vitality	생기
useful	유용하다		
useless	소용이 없다	wall newspaper,	
		poster	벽보
vacation	휴가	war	전쟁
vague	막연하다	warm	따스하다, 뜨뜻하다
Valentine's Day	발렌타인 데이	waste	허비하다
valuable	소중하다	watch,	
value	가치	keep an eye on	지켜보다
~ greatly	중시하다	water jar	물동이
varied	다양해지다	way	길; 방식; 습관
various	다양하다	in one's own ~	나름대로
~ places	곳곳, 여러 곳	in what ~	어떻게 해서
veranda	베란다	~ home after	
very	매우, 대단히	work	퇴근길
the ~	이야말로; 바로	~ of thinking	사고 방식
~ end	후미, 맨 끝	weeding (of a	
~ much indeed	하도; 정말	grave)	벌초
vice president	부사장	weekday	평일
vicinity	근처, 인근	welcome	반기다; 환영
victimized	희생되다	~ party for	
feel ~	억울하다	new students	신입생 환영회

well	잘, 능숙하게, 충분히	view of ~	여성관
~-known	유명하다	women writers'	
~-mannered	예절 바르다	literature	여성 문학
west	서양	wonder (miracle)	
whet		drug	묘약
(the appetite)	침이 넘어가다	woodcutter	나무꾼
whole	전체	word	단어
~ country	전국	in a (single) ~	한마디로
~ of Sinch'on		work	근무, 일, 작품;
district	신촌 일대		일하다
~ school	전교	~er	직장인
wholesale	도매	maintenance ~	보수 공사
~ market	도매장, 도매 시장	~ out a scheme	기획하다
widely	활짝, 넓게	~room	작업실
widen	벌리다	~ the nightshift	야근하다
wield	휘두르다	world	세상
willow	버들	worry	고민
wind	바람	wrong	잘못되다
~fall	횡재	go ~	실패하다
~screen	윈드스크린		
~shield	윈드실드	yard	뜰
winding(s)	굴곡	front ~	앞뜰
wing	날개	year	해, 년
wisdom	지혜	next ~	이듬해
wise and		this ~	금년, 올해
considerate	어질다	~ of good	
wish	소원; 소원하다	harvest	풍년
wit	재치	you	그대, 자네
wither	시들다	~ know	말이야, 있잖아
without	없이, 없으면	young noble	귀공자
~ a trace	흔적 없이	younger years	초년
~ doing		youth	젊음, 청소년
anything	그저, 아무것도 하지	yut	윷
	않고	playing ~	윷놀이하다
~ hesitation	서슴없이, 주저없이		
~ reservation	대뜸	zipper	지퍼
womanhood	여성, 여자다움	zone	구역

Photograph and Figure Credits

Han'guk Yumŏ Jŏng Jin-t'ae, Seoul: Posŏng, 1996—pp. 77a, 77b
Hello from Korea, Korean Overseas Information Service, 1994—p. 107b
http://flute.or.kr/—p. 151
http://manhwa.chosun.com/—p. 226
Korea Now, The Korea Herald, 2000—p. 124b; 2001—pp. 129a, 156
Korea: The Unexplored Orient, Tourist Section, Seoul Metropolitan Government, 1972—p. 105a
Korean Art Tradition, The Korea Foundation, 1993—p. 124a
Koreana, The Korea Foundation, 1996, Vol. 10, No. 4—p. 1
Kwangsoo Reflects, Pak Kwangsoo, Seoul: Sodam, 1999—p. 100
The Monthly Pictorial of Korea, HEK Communications, September 1996—p. 124c; September 1997—pp. 54a, 54b
Minsok Kyŏngki Haesŏljip, Seykye Hanminchok Ch'eychŏn Wiwŏnhoi, 1991—pp. 105b, 106a
Noraebang Taebaekkwa, Seoul: Seykwang Ŭmak Ch'ulp'ansa, 1995—p. 25
Pictorial Korea, Korean Information Service, July 2001—p. 180a; November 2001—pp. 129b, 180b
Seysang esŏ Kachang Kŭmtchok Kat'ŭn Iyagi, Chŏng Im-cho, Seoul: Tongtchok Nara, 1996—pp. 205, 224
Traveler's Korea, Korea National Tourism Organization, 1996—p. 125
www.knto.or.kr/Korean/K_indexb.html—p. 106b
www.metro.seoul.kr/kor2000/seoulguide/seoul_gallery/main.htm—p. 107a
www.sbs.co.kr/tv/index.html—p. 20

Contents

iii

Intravenous Infusion Therapy for Medical Assistants

AMERICAN ASSOCIATION
OF MEDICAL ASSISTANTS

Executive Editor

Nina Beaman, RNC, CMA, MS

Program Coordinator
Bryant and Stratton College, Richmond, Virginia
(804) 745-2444

Dianne L. Josephson, RN, MSN

Infusion Therapy Consultant, El Paso, Texas
Nursing Education Consultant Services, El Paso, Texas
(915)-855-6299

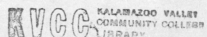

Australia   Canada   Mexico   Singapore   Spain   United Kingdom   United States

THOMSON

DELMAR LEARNING

Intravenous Infusion Therapy for Medical Assistants
by Dianne L. Josephson
The American Association of Medical Assistants
Executive Editor: Nina Beaman, RNC, CMA, M.S.

Vice President, Health Care Business Unit
William Brottmiller

Editorial Director
Matthew Kane

Acquisitions Editor
Rhonda Dearborn

Editorial Assistant
Debra S. Gorgos

Marketing Director
Jennifer McAvey

Marketing Channel Manager
Tamara Caruso

Marketing Coordinator
Kimberly Duffy

Production Director
Carolyn Miller

Production Manager
Barbara A. Bullock

Production Editor
Jessica McNavich

Library of Congress Cataloging-in-Publication Data
ISBN 1418033111

Josephson, Dianne L.
  Intravenous infusion therapy for medical assistants / Dianne L. Josephson, Nina Beaman.
     p. cm.
  Includes bibliographical references.
  ISBN 1-4180-3311-1
  1. Infusion therapy. 2. Medical assistants. I. Josephson, Dianne L. II. Beaman, Nina. III. Title.
  RM170.J67 2006
  615'.6--dc22

                       2005052925

NOTICE TO THE READER

DEDICATION

This book is dedicated to the versatile and hardworking certified medical assistants who were graduated from CAAHEP or ABHES accredited schools, who passed the prestigious CMA exam, and who continue their education to keep current in the everchanging world in which we live.

ACKNOWLEDGMENTS

I wish to express my sincere appreciation to Dianne Josephson, who authored *Intravenous Infusion Therapy for Nurses: Principles and Practice,* from which this text was redacted.

I would like to thank Bryant and Stratton College, especially Carl Newell and Beth Murphy, for generously funding my continuing education.

Certainly I wish to thank my daughters, Bonny Glidewell and Emily Blodgett, for meticulously proofreading the manuscript for me.

I would also like to acknowledge Debbie Benvenuto, BS, CRNI, Education Manager of the Infusion Nurses Society, Lynn Hadaway, Med, RNC, CRNI of Lynn Hadaway Associates, and Roxane Perruca, MSN, CRNI, IV Nurse Manager at Kansas University Medical Center who kept me current on my IV skills.

Above all, I would like to thank the Continuing Education Board of the American Association of Medical Assistants who saw the need for this book and supported me in my endeavor to create it.

Appreciation also goes to personnel at Thomson Delmar Learning, especially Rhonda Dearborn and Debra Gorgos, for their rapid and thorough production of this work.

The following companies deserve recognition for the clinical data, product information, and useful illustrations they provided.

Abbott Laboratories Hospital Products Division, Abbott Park, IL

AstraZeneca, Wilmington, DE

BARD Access Systems, Salt Lake City, UT

Baxter International, Inc., Round Lake, IL

BD Medical Systems, Sandy, UT

Block Medical, Carlsbad, CA

Braun Medical, Inc., Bethlehem, PA

Clintec Nutrition Company, Deerfield, IL

CONMED Corporation, Utica, NY

Delta Medical Specialties, Division of ARROW International, El Paso, TX

GESCO International, Norcross, GA

HDC® Corporation, San Jose, CA

Infusaid Corporation, Norwood, MA

IMED Corporation, San Diego, CA

Johnson & Johnson Endosurgery, McGaw, Inc., Irvine, CA

Menlo Care, Inc., Menlo Park, CA

Pall Biomedical Products Company, East Hill, NY

SIGMA International, Medina, NY

Deltec, St. Paul, MN

Smith and Nephew United, Inc., Largo, FL

SoloPak®, Boca Raton, FL

Strato/Infusaid, Inc., Norwood, MA

3 M Health Care, St. Paul, MN

United Ad Label, Inc., Brea, CA

Venetec, Venoscope, LLC, Lafayette, LA

VYGON Corporation, East Rutherford, NJ

Preface

Responding to a critical need for certified medical assistants to be educated in intravenous (IV) or infusion therapy, and knowing that the schools accredited by the Commission for the Accreditation of Allied Health Programs (CAAHEP) began teaching the theory of intravenous therapy in 2005, the Continuing Education Board (CEB) of the American Association of Medical Assistants (AAMA) commissioned that this book be created. While CMAs involved in infusion therapy should certainly read this text, it is appropriate for all CMAs who want to keep their knowledge of IV therapy current. It is also an excellent book for medical assisting educators to improve their understanding of infusion therapy in order to teach theory to students.

Indeed, infusion or IV therapy has long been part of the acute care of patients. However, more patients are receiving IV therapy at home, in emergent centers, at infusion centers, and in dialysis clinics. Thus, CMAs often find themselves needing at least to understand IV therapy, and sometimes to lay out the equipment, to monitor the patient, to assess the infusion site, to discontinue the infusion, and perhaps even to insert the IV. The purpose of this book is to help the CMA understand IV therapy, not to assure that the CMA has the manual skills to place an IV or the mathematical skills to calculate drip factors safely. Extra training beyond this publication would be needed for proficiency in those areas. Certifications are frequently available in the workplace to place and calculate IV therapy. Always check facility, local, and state requirements for delegation of therapy to unlicensed professionals before participating in IV therapy.

This text was developed by condensing a current text, *Intravenous Infusion Therapy for Nurses: Principles and Practice* by Dianne Josephson, RN MSN. Nina Beaman MS RNC CMA was commissioned to redact this text for publication for CMAs. Miss Beaman, herself both a CMA and RNC (certified in ambulatory women's health), recently completed a training course provided by infusion therapy nurses.

Miss Beaman has taught medical assisting since 1993, and is the Allied Health Program Coordinator for Bryant and Stratton College. Because IV therapy accounts for the largest number of accidental needlesticks, Nina (who is a health psychologist) hopes to protect CMAs by educating them about IV safety.

This essential publication deletes from the extensive text legal issues, basic principles of infection control, dosage calculations, blood transfusions, and IV placement. Instead, it focuses on what the CMA needs to know about intravenous therapy. Patient safety is paramount to the CMA, so the wise CMA understands the need for and complications of intravenous therapy. With patient safety in mind, risks, complications, and adverse reactions are discussed. Giving the correct medication is crucial to the CMA, so intravenous infusion preparations are compared and contrasted. Because the CMA may be asked to lay out equipment for someone placing an IV, equipment and supplies are illustrated and discussed. In some facilities, CMAs may insert IVs after receiving specialized training. This book will help those CMAs to understand the process of insertion. The CMA may be asked to maintain or discontinue infusion therapy, so the book addresses those issues as well.

Sidebars of Medical Assisting Alerts and Tips are distributed throughout the text to highlight key safety concerns and professional issues. Each chapter concludes with Review Questions and Activities to ensure that learning objectives have been met. A test appears at the end of the publication (Appendix A), which must be returned, completed, to the AAMA at 20 North Wacker Drive Suite 1575, Chicago, IL 60606 for continuing education unit credit.

The author welcomes feedback on www.nabeaman @bryantstratton.edu. Thank you for choosing this publication.

Nina Beaman MS RNC CMA

Note

References to certified medical assistants (CMAs) apply only to medical assistants who have passed the AAMA CMA Certification Examination, have kept the CMA current through retesting or continuing education, and have not had the CMA revoked because of violations of the Disciplinary Standards and Procedures for CMAs. "Certified medical assistant" (CMA) is not a generic phrase that can be used interchangeably with "medical assistant."

If you have purchased this product in order to receive continuing education credit from the AAMA, please complete the test that is highlighted in the Appendices and mail to David Knight, AAMA, 20 North Wacker Suite 1575, Chicago, Il 60606.

If neither test is highlighted, please contact the AAMA for further instruction at: 800/228-2262

ABOUT THE AUTHORS

Author

Dianne L. Josephson, RN, MSN

Dianne Josephson is a nurse educator and author, with clinical experience in medical-surgical nursing, infusion therapy, pharmacology, end of life care, and bereavement support. She is currently self-employed as a nursing education consultant and legal consulting expert. Her past employment experience includes Hotel Dieu Hospital in El Paso, Texas, where she worked as a nurse manager, supervisor, and patient/staff educator and the El Paso Community College where she served as a nursing faculty member and clinical mentor in the Health Occupations Division and was employed in the areas of curriculum development and instruction in the Division of Continuing Education for Health and Public Service. She developed and taught an extensive refresher course for inactive registered nurses and provided numerous infusion therapy courses for registered and licensed vocational nurses. Ms. Josephson has also worked as a Clinical Specialist at the University of Texas at El Paso College of Nursing and Health Sciences and has developed and presented numerous nursing education and training courses for hospitals and nursing agencies in the El Paso area. She is a faculty member at Tepeyac Institute, the international Roman Catholic formation center in the Diocese of El Paso, Texas where she presents programs on anticipatory grief and bereavement support. She has advanced training as a bereavement facilitator through the American Academy of Bereavement and is an active member of the Texas Partnership for End of Life Care.

Ms. Josephson is a graduate of Barry University in Miami, Florida where she received her B.S.N. She earned her M.S.N. from the University of Texas at El Paso College of Nursing and Health Sciences. She was selected as a participant in the Master Teacher Project at the El Paso Community College where she also received the Part-Time Faculty Award for Teaching Excellence. She is a member and past officer of the Delta Kappa Chapter of Sigma Theta Tau International Nursing Honor Society, the Intravenous Nurses Association, and is listed in *Who's Who in American Nursing*, *Notable Women of Texas*, *The National Dean's List*, and *The Society of Nursing Professionals*. She has been listed as a Sigma Theta Tau International Media Guide Expert in the areas of infusion therapy, pharmacology, and bereavement support since 1998.

Ms. Josephson is a published author and has been a textbook reviewer for Delmar Learning since 1991, has written articles for nursing journals, reviewed for a variety of publishing companies, and recently developed an interactive multimedia learning program on IV Therapy skills for Delmar Learning. Ms. Josephson is currently co-authoring a nursing pharmacology textbook.

Contributing Authors

Martha Yee-Nevárez, RN, MSN, C

Martha Yee-Nevárez is a Pediatric Critical Care Nurse Practitioner in El Paso, Texas. She is a graduate of the University of Texas at El Paso where she received her BSN and her MSN. She received her post-graduate certificate as a pediatric critical care nurse practitioner at the University of Pennsylvania in Philadelphia, PA. Ms. Yee-Nevárez has dedicated her career to critically ill children and has served as speaker for pediatric conferences at an international level. Ms. Yee-Nevárez would like to extend her gratitude to her parents, Martin and Emma Yee, her brother, sisters, nephews, niece, and her husband, M. Bernardo Nevárez for being an inspiration throughout her life.

Cerena Henderson Suarez, RN, MSN, FNP

Cerena Henderson Suarez is a Family Nurse Practitioner in El Paso, Texas. She is a graduate of West Texas State University in Canyon, Texas where she received her B.S.N. She earned her M.S.N. from the University of Texas at El Paso College of Nursing and Health Sciences. Ms. Henderson Suarez is a member of Sigma Theta Tau International, Delta Kappa Chapter. She is a published writer for various nursing journals and has presented nursing workshops and been a speaker for nursing seminars.

Executive Editor

Nina Beaman RNC CMA, MS

Nina Beaman RNC CMA, MS is the Allied Health Coordinator for Bryant and Stratton College in Richmond, Virginia. She holds dual credentials as a certified medical assistant (CMA) and registered nurse certified (RNC) in ambulatory women's health. Miss Beaman is the recipient of the American Association of Medical Assistants' 2004 Golden Apple Award. In addition to teaching college courses, she practices nursing working with brain-injured patients at the Arc of the Piedmont in Charlottesville, Virginia. She is a graduate of Capella University (MS), Randolph-Macon College (BA), Luther Rice College (AAS), and the University of Nice (DDEF), France. Miss Beaman earned her nursing degree from John Tyler Community College in Chester, Virginia. She is also a health psychologist and the author of numerous books and articles on current behavioral health issues, such as workplace violence and obesity reduction. She would like to thank her parents, Chester and Mary Beaman, for their support and inspiration, and her daughters Kayla, Bonny, Mary, Belle, and Emily and sons-in-law David Christianson and Troy Glidewell for their patience.

Chapter 1

Introduction to Intravenous Infusion Therapy

LEARNING OBJECTIVES

Upon completion of this chapter, the reader should be able to:

- List three indications for venipuncture and intravenous infusion therapy.
- State three advantages of intravenous infusion therapy.
- State three disadvantages of intravenous infusion therapy.

INTRAVENOUS INFUSION THERAPY

As technology rapidly advances, it affects all aspects of the health care industry. One area that has been greatly impacted involves the pharmacologic development of life-preserving fluids and medications, many of which are administered intravenously. Such products are ordered by the physician, but the responsibility for delivering them to patients may be delegated to the certified medical assistant (CMA). She or he may initiate infusion therapy, maintain it, monitor the patient, and may be responsible for discontinuing it.

Indications for Venipuncture and Intravenous Therapy

Although there are numerous risks associated with accessing the venous system, removing blood, or administering any product directly into the circulating blood, the intravenous route is often the best, or only, route of choice. It is indicated for situations when oral or other parenteral routes are not appropriate. The purpose of venipuncture is to access the venous circulation in order to draw blood for laboratory screens and diagnostic tests or to administer fluids, electrolytes, medications, blood, blood products, and nutritional supplements (Table 1-1).

Fluid Volume Maintenance

Fluid volume maintenance aims to preserve circulatory equilibrium by supplying the body's daily need for water, electrolytes, nutrients, vitamins, and minerals. In many situations, the patient's fluid volume is monitored and an infusion line kept in place to maintain the correct circulatory volume if needed. This is often the situation when a patient may have nothing by mouth (NPO) for a short period of time, such as during minor surgical and dental procedures or when undergoing certain diagnostic tests and procedures.

Fluid Volume Replacement

Whenever there is a loss of blood, body water, electrolytes, and nutrients, infusion therapy is indicated as a replacement regimen. Replacement is a critical factor during the life-threatening situations associated with shock, hemorrhage, and severe burns, where there is a drastic loss of fluid volume.

In cases of prolonged nausea, vomiting, and diarrhea, the replacement of both lost fluids and electrolytes is necessary. When there is any type of inflammatory bowel disease, infection, gastrointestinal obstruction, or stasis, intravenous fluid replacement is needed. It is also necessary for malabsorption syndromes or for people who have gastric or enteral tubes in place for decompression.

Medication Administration

Many medications cannot be given orally or by other routes without losing their potency or becoming denatured. These need to be administered directly into the vein over a short period of time or diluted in other infusates and given over several hours. Because of the health status of some patients who might have inconsistent absorption from the gastrointestinal system, medications are given intravenously to achieve consistent blood levels of the drug. Some medications are administered intermittently through a temporary port connected to a venous access device. Many chemotherapeutic agents are delivered by vein because they would be toxic, irritating, or rendered ineffective by other routes. For patients whose muscle mass is reduced because of disease or damaged from repeated injections, drugs that are normally given intramuscularly must be administered intravenously.

Blood and Blood Product Donation and Administration

Phlebotomy is the venipuncture and withdrawal of blood for the purpose of autotransfusion at a later time or for donation and transfusion to others. Although whole blood is rarely given anymore, blood and any one of its components must be administered directly into the circulatory system by special intravenous techniques.

Nutritional Support

When a state of negative nitrogen balance exists for any reason and the body is unable to assimilate oral nutrients, nutrition is supplied intravenously. This occurs with anorexia, burns, tumor growth, some malabsorption syndromes, and

Table 1-1	Intravenous Infusion Access and Therapy
Blood sampling for diagnostic tests	
Donor phlebotomy for transfusion	
Fluid volume maintenance	
Fluid volume replacement	
Medication administration	
Blood or blood product administration	
Nutritional supplementation	
To keep a vein open for emergency or special use	
Hemodynamic monitoring	

gastrointestinal disease, among others. High concentrations of dextrose or proteins, fats, electrolytes, vitamins, and minerals are given directly into one of the large veins of the body.

Advantages of Intravenous Infusion Therapy

The main advantage of intravenous infusion is that it provides an access route for medications, fluids, and anesthetics in emergency situations. It is also ideal for delivering a rapid, even supply of an infusate that can exert a systemic effect in a short period of time. Once a vein is accessed, an indwelling device can be inserted and the vein can be used numerous times. This alleviates the need for multiple punctures, which are uncomfortable and are a route for infections to develop as a result of breaks in the skin.

For persons who are unconscious or unable to take anything by mouth for long periods of time, the intravenous route is often used, especially when gastrointestinal intubation is contraindicated. It is the route of choice for any products that are irritating to body tissues or that are not absorbed orally or by the other parenteral pathways.

Because of new and improved equipment, the intravenous route provides a safe and efficient delivery system. It is convenient, especially with the availability of electronic infusion devices (Table 1-2).

Disadvantages of Intravenous Infusion Therapy

While the advantages far outweigh the disadvantages, there are several hazards associated with intravenous infusion therapy (Table 1-3). In some patients, it is difficult to access the vein, causing the patient discomfort and expense because of several cannulation attempts. Fluid overload is always a potential problem and allergic reactions can occur rapidly and without warning. While a medication administered by other routes takes longer to be absorbed and assimilated by the body, anything given intravenously exerts an immediate effect—a potentially fatal consequence if an incorrect drug or overdose is administered. As with any break in the body's skin barrier, the puncture of a vein can lead to a local or systemic infection and sepsis, especially if improper technique is used to initiate, maintain, or discontinue the infusion. There is always the possibility of venous thrombosis or embolism.

One of the greatest risks, for both the patient and the CMA, is the transmission of the hepatitis B, hepatitis C, or the human immunodeficiency virus (HIV) through blood contamination. Because blood is screened and tested prior to transfusion, the likelihood of exposure to these diseases through transfusion is minimal. The risk is greatest from inadvertent needlesticks or improper handling of blood and body fluids. (See Chapter 4 for risks and complications associated with intravenous therapy.)

Table 1-2 | Advantages of Intravenous Infusion Therapy
Provides a route for emergency access
Provides a route for the unconscious patient
Provides a route for the patient who cannot take anything by mouth
Provides a route during decompression of the stomach or bowel
Provides a route for the patient with inflammatory bowel disease
Provides a route to counteract the adverse reactions of other drugs or poisons
Faster absorption than other routes
Rapid distribution
Maximum bioavailability
Maintenance of controlled blood levels
Less discomfort for the patient
Saves time for the CMA

Table 1-3 │ Disadvantages of Intravenous Infusion Therapy

PROBLEM	DEFINITION
Local discomfort	Pain at site of needle or catheter insertion or in the vein from the infusate
Infiltration	The leakage of fluid outside the vein into the surrounding tissue
Needle or catheter displacement	Dislodgement of infusion device
Sepsis	Systemic circulatory infection
Thrombosis	Clot formation
Embolism	Solid, liquid, or gas traveling in the circulatory system
Fluid overload	More fluid than the circulatory system is able to handle
Rapid medication overdose	
Hypersensitivity	Allergic response
Precipitation	Formation of deposits that separate from a solution
Incompatibility with other medications or solutions	
Transmission of human immunodeficiency virus	
Transmission of hepatitis	

Review Questions and Activities

1. Define venipuncture and intravenous infusion therapy.
2. List three indications for intravenous infusion therapy.

3. Make a two-column list of the advantages and disadvantages of venipuncture and intravenous therapy as discussed in this chapter.

Chapter 2

Fluid and Electrolyte Fundamentals Related to Intravenous Infusion Therapy

LEARNING OBJECTIVES

Upon completion of this chapter, the reader should be able to:

✳ Define homeostasis.

✳ Differentiate among the structural and functional differences of the intracellular and extracellular fluid compartments.

✳ Explain the function of the cell and cell membrane in fluid and electrolyte balance.

✳ Relate how carbohydrates, lipids, and proteins contribute to cellular physiology.

✳ Describe the different mechanisms for cellular membrane transport.

✳ Illustrate the series of events that maintains the cellular membrane potential.

✳ Compare the three buffer systems in the body and their role in regulating acid-base balance.

✳ Interpret the physiology of the two acid-base imbalances in the body: respiratory and metabolic.

✳ Outline the functions of the electrolytes described in this chapter.

✳ Evaluate how imbalances in electrolyte concentrations in the body affect homeostasis.

Whenever the CMA is providing care to a patient, it is his duty to intervene in such a way so as to safely promote or restore her comfort and well-being. He is responsible for supporting her bio-psycho-social integrity through independent nursing actions, by carrying out dependent actions based on medical directives, and through interdependent actions.

When the patient's condition warrants intravenous medication and infusion therapy, the CMA is responsible for knowing why such interventions are necessary and how they will affect the patient. He is expected to understand the pathophysiology of her fluid and electrolyte and acid-base status and relate it to her need for intravenous intervention.

Under no circumstances should the CMA ever perform any procedure or administer any product unless he knows what it is, why it is ordered, and how it will affect the patient. Once treatment is initiated, he is responsible for continual assessment and evaluation of the patient's progress, the status of her laboratory and diagnostic results, and her response to treatment. Should there be any questions or concerns, the CMA must define the problem(s), consult his resources appropriately, and determine how to rectify the situation. He is responsible for documenting all care and patient responses and reporting and recording any untoward occurrences. The CMA is accountable to the patient and must provide for her comfort and safety at all times.

This chapter provides a review and overview of the basic principles of fluid and electrolyte balance and imbalance that serve as the basis for understanding and safely managing infusion therapy. The content contained herein integrates and builds on the knowledge learned in biology, anatomy, physiology, chemistry, and physics.

The CMA who initiates, maintains, and monitors intravenous infusions must comprehend the concepts and principles of fluids and electrolytes as well as their relationship to the physiology of health, illness, and disease processes. Such knowledge is a prerequisite for the provision of safe patient care. Because imbalances can occur suddenly, the CMA must be alert to such changes and intervene appropriately, in a timely manner. Communication with the patient, astute observation of her condition, knowledge of her history and disease, along with frequent review of laboratory values, diagnostic tests, medication, and parenteral fluid orders, are all critical assessment factors.

FLUIDS AND HOMEOSTASIS

The nineteenth-century French physiologist Claude Bernard originated the concept that the *milieu intérieur,* or **internal environment,** of the body, which remains relatively constant despite external environmental changes, is formed by the fluids that surround and bathe all body cells. These fluids, which make up the extracellular fluid, communicate with the body's organs, tissues, and structures to make exchanges with the body's external surroundings, thus contributing to a state of balance and stability.

The human body normally undergoes a continuous series of self-regulating adjustments to maintain a balance between its internal environment and the external forces that affect it. The physiologic term for this dynamic process that contributes to a state of internal constancy is **homeostasis.** Homeostasis, along with **adaptation,** the process whereby the body adjusts to the ever-changing environment, serves to keep the human body functioning well despite changes in its surroundings. When any component of the internal environment deviates from its normal state, homeostasis is jeopardized and illness ensues.

The term *homeostasis,* when first introduced by the physiologist W. B. Cannon in 1926, referred to a relatively stable state of internal equilibrium as well as the coordination of all bodily processes that contribute to such balance. Since then, the definition of homeostasis has evolved to include the constancy and coordination of the human being as a dynamically integrated organism, encompassing the biologic, physiologic, psychologic, sociocultural, and religious aspects of the person.

Water

Water is the primary chemical component within the human organism and accounts for 50%–70% of adult body weight. It varies with differences in sex, weight, fat content, and age. Individuals with a greater proportion of lean tissue mass have a higher percentage of body water than those whose bodies carry more fat. Neutral fat, most common in body tissues, contains very little water. Table 2-1 compares the approximate body water content among various age groups. Water serves as the vehicle for the delivery of chemicals and nutrients to body cells and tissues and for the excretion of waste products. It also is the medium in which biochemical reactions take place. In addition, water contributes to body temperature regulation, cushions organs and joints, and provides body contour and form through hydration of tissue structures. Homeostasis is preserved through the intake and output of water. Under normal circumstances water volume is regulated by fluids released during metabolic processes and by the intake of food and fluids. Water is the main substance the body is able to perceive a need for, being signaled through the mechanism of thirst.

Water balance is regulated through neurosecretions of the hypothalamus (where antidiuretic hormone [ADH], or vasopressin, is formed in the peraventricular and supraoptic

Table 2-1 | Approximate Body Water Content as Percentage of Body Weight

BODY WATER			
Age	Total	ECF	ICF
Children			
Newborn	79%	45%	34%
2–30 d	74%	40%	34%
1–12 m	63%	30%	33%
1–2 yr	59%	24%	35%
2–8 yr	62%	25%	37%
Men			
9–16 yr	59%	26%	33%
17–35 yr	60%	28%	32%
36–69 yr	55%	25%	30%
70+ yr	51%	25%	26%
Women			
9–15 yr	56%	25%	31%
16–35 yr	50%	25%	25%
36–59 yr	48%	23%	25%
60+ yr	43%	21%	22%

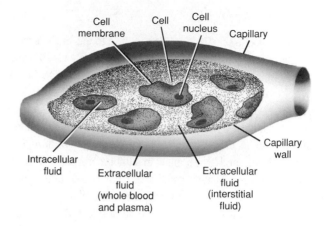

Figure 2-1 | Intracellular and extracellular fluids

Table 2-2 | Distribution of Body Water

PERCENTAGE OF TOTAL BODY WEIGHT		
	Adult Male	Adult Female
Total body water	60.0%	50.0%
Intracellular fluid	45.0%	35.0%
Extracellular fluid	15.0%	15.0%
Interstitial fluid	11.0%	10.0%
Intravascular fluid	4.5%	4.3%

nuclei) and via the actions of aldosterone (the mineralo-corticoid secreted from the adrenal cortex). ADH acts directly on the collecting ducts and tubules of the kidneys to bring about water reabsorption. Aldosterone maintains water balance by regulating sodium metabolism in the kidneys. When there is decreased renal blood flow, aldosterone causes sodium retention, which, in turn, causes water retention.

Water Distribution

All fluids in the body are made up primarily of water, within which various materials are dissolved. The total volume of water in the body is distributed among two large compartments, the intracellular and the extracellular. The cell membrane, which is selectively permeable, separates these two areas. The extracellular compartment is further divided into subcompartments (Figure 2-1). Fluid composition within the two major compartments is unique in chemical formulation.

Although the two compartments are structurally different and carry out separate functions, they are in a constant state of interaction with each other. The amount of fluid as well as the manner in which it is distributed and used in these compartments is vital to homeostasis (Table 2-2). An understanding of the similarities and differences between these two areas and knowing how various illnesses and disease entities can bring about imbalances are of utmost importance for the CMA.

Intracellular Fluid

Intracellular fluid (ICF) is fluid contained within the cells of the body. It comprises approximately two-thirds of the total body fluid. Since the entire amount of fluid in the body comprises about 60% of total body weight, the ICF contributes to about 40% of that weight. The fluid within each cell is made up of materials individual to that cell. The concentration of these intracellular materials—potassium, magnesium, and phosphate ions—is much the same in the trillions of cells throughout the body. Because of this similarity, the intracellular fluid is classified as one large cellular component known as the intracellular fluid compartment.

Extracellular Fluid

The **extracellular fluid (ECF)** is fluid found in the spaces outside of the cells and comprises approximately one-third of the total body fluid, about 20% of total body weight. The ECF is rich in oxygen and carbon dioxide for nutrient and waste exchange, glucose for energy supply and demand, and amino acids and fatty acids for growth, repair, and health maintenance. It also contains large quantities of the electrolytes sodium, calcium, chloride, and bicarbonate. In addition, the ECF transports cholesterol, urea, lactate, creatinine, sulfates, and other products. The ECF is in constant movement within the systemic circulation, coming in contact with tissue fluids throughout the body. The ECF, as mentioned earlier, is referred to as the body's internal environment because it contributes to the homeostatic balance necessary to sustain a healthy human organism.

The two main functions of the ECF are (1) to maintain cell membrane permeability and membrane potential for appropriate membrane function, and (2) to serve as the vehicle for the movement of life-sustaining substances to and from various areas of the body.

The ECF compartment is divided into three subcomponents: the intravascular, the interstitial, and the transcellular compartments.

The Intravascular Compartment

The **intravascular fluid (IVF)** contained within the blood vessels of the body is also called *plasma*. Plasma is the liquid portion of blood and lymph and contains serum (the water portion of the blood left after coagulation), protein, and chemical products. The IVF serves as a vehicle for the transport and exchange of nutrients.

The Interstitial Compartment

Interstitial fluid (ISF) is the solution that exists in the small spaces and gaps between body structures, cells, and tissues. Lymph is formed in tissue spaces throughout the body and is the ISF that circulates within the lymphatic vessels; it varies in composition in different areas of the body. Lymph contains proteins, salts, organic substances (glucose, fats, urea, and creatinine), and water and is filtered in lymph nodes during its circulation throughout the lymphatic vessels. Toxins and foreign matter, such as bacteria, are filtered by the lymphatic system.

The Transcellular Compartment

Transcellular fluid (TSF) is formed as a by-product during the process of cellular activity. It consists of specialized fluids, which make up the smallest amount of ECF, and includes mucus, ocular fluids, sweat, secretions of the genitourinary tract, cerebrospinal fluid, and pleural, pericardial, and peritoneal secretions.

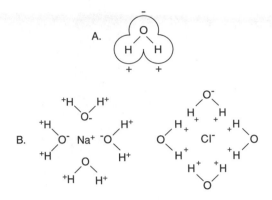

Figure 2-2 | A. Water is a polar molecule; B. Dissolution of ions in water

THE COMPOSITION OF BODY FLUIDS

Water is the main constituent of all body fluids. Within these fluids are numerous minerals and organic compounds. Water is a **polar molecule:** One part of its structure is negative and the other is positive, thus making it neutral as a whole (Figure 2-2). In the body, water acts as a **solvent,** able to hold substances and act to dissolve them. **Solutes** are the substances dissolved in the water (the solvent). The combination of the solute and the solvent forms a **solution.** Because water is polar, substances such as strong acids, bases, ions, and hydroxyl (-OH) groups gravitate around the water molecule, attach to it, and dissolve.

Two major categories of solutes exist in body fluids: electrolytes and nonelectrolytes. It is important to comprehend their differences in order to understand their interaction, their method of movement, and their utilization by the body.

Electrolytes

Electrolytes make up about 95% of the body's solute molecules and are chemicals that carry an electrical charge. Electrically charged molecules are called **ions.** When dispersed in fluid, electrolytes dissociate into constituent ions and convert the solution into a product capable of conducting electricity. Acids, bases, and salts that dissociate when dissolved in water are called *electrolytes.* Ions with a negative charge are called **anions.** Ions with a positive charge are called **cations.** The two are polar, meaning that they are attracted to each other, the anions gravitating toward the positive poles (cations) and vice versa. For chemical-combining activity to occur, there does not have to be the same number of anions and cations, but there must exist a balance in the number of positive and negative ions (charges). Because they separate into charged particles, electrolytes are expressed in milliequivalents per liter (mEq/L), or the number of electrical charges per liter of fluid. A **milliequivalent,** a measurement of the concentration of electrolytes in a volume of solution, refers to the ability of ions to combine chemically, which is dependent on the **valence** (electrical charge) of the ions. Electrolytes are sometimes measured in milligrams per deciliter (mg/dl).

Electrolytes are crucial to the body for the distribution and movement of water and for the maintenance of acid-base balance. They provide the chemicals needed to carry out cellular reactions and to regulate mechanisms at the cell membrane that allow transmission of electrochemical impulses in muscle and nerve fibers. It is very important to remember that any disruption of electrolyte balance can result in a pathophysiologic state.

In the intracellular compartment there are large amounts of potassium, magnesium, and phosphate, but small amounts of sodium, chloride, sulfate, and bicarbonate. By contrast, in the extracellular compartment, there are large concentrations of sodium, chlorides, and bicarbonate ions (Table 2-3). The difference between the two compartments is responsible for permeability of the cell membrane and for electrical potentials occurring across the cell membrane, which allow nerve fibers to conduct impulses and muscle fibers to contract. Since the electri-

cal content between these two areas is different, the concentration is maintained by a mechanism known as the **sodium-potassium pump** (described later in the chapter). This pump, necessary for all cells, is present in cell membranes to draw sodium out of the cell and pull potassium in. It exists to maintain the balanced concentration of ions and is vital to cellular respiration and metabolism.

The calcium in the extracellular fluid is especially vital to homeostasis in regulating the degree of cell membrane permeability. The concentration of calcium is inversely proportionate to the permeability of the membrane; if the calcium level is high, permeability decreases, if the calcium level is low, permeability increases.

In caring for patients, the CMA must have a solid, working understanding of electrolytes and fluid balance and the factors affecting their gains or losses. He needs to monitor these levels and be alert to the signs and symptoms of changes. It is important not only to recognize problems and abnormalities that indicate an imbalance, but also to intervene quickly to correct the situation. When delivering infusion therapy, recognition and intervention become even more critical.

Nonelectrolytes

Nonelectrolytes present in body fluids are solutes that do not carry electrical charges, nor do they separate into particles when dispersed in fluid. Solutes incapable of dissociation include glucose, urea, creatinine, and bilirubin.

Glucose is a large, lipid-insoluble molecule that slowly crosses the cell membrane and affects water movement. It is normally present in both whole blood and plasma and cannot enter the cell unless it attaches to a carrier outside of the cell membrane that will render it lipid soluble.

Urea, a metabolic end-product of protein metabolism, is a small molecule that freely crosses the cell membrane. Urea quantities equalize between the intracellular and extracellular compartments. It has little effect on water movement.

Creatinine, a by-product of muscle catabolism, is derived from the breakdown of muscle creatine phosphate. Bilirubin, an end-product of red blood cell destruction and hemoglobin decomposition, circulates throughout the blood and interstitial fluid.

THE MOVEMENT OF BODY FLUIDS

Water, the principal component of all body fluids, is the medium in which most chemical reactions occur. Body fluids exist in a dynamic state with materials constantly moving into

Table 2-3 | Chemical Compositions of the Extracellular and Intracellular Fluid Compartments

	EXTRA-CELLULAR FLUID	INTRA-CELLULAR FLUID
Sodium (Na$^+$)	142 mEq/L	10 mEq/L
Potassium (K$^+$)	5 mEq/L	141 mEq/L
Calcium (Ca^{++})	5 mEq/L	0–1 mEq/L
Magnesium (Mg^{++})	3 mEq/L	60 mEq/L
Chloride (Cl$^-$)	103 mEq/L	4 mEq/L
Bicarbonate (HCO$_2^-$)	28 mEq/L	10 mEq/L
Phosphate (PO$_4$)	4 mEq/L	75 mEq/L
Sulfate (SO$_4$)	1 mEq/L	2 mEq/L
Protein	17 mEq/L	60 mEq/L
Glucose	90 mg/dl	0–20 mg/dl
Partial pressure of oxygen (PO$_2$)	35 mm Hg	20 mm Hg
Partial pressure of carbon dioxide (PCO$_2$)	46 mm Hg	50 mm Hg
pH	7.4	7.0

and out of cells. When the body is healthy, the movement of water is balanced among the fluid compartments. It is important to understand the mechanisms of fluid movement in the body in order to fully grasp the concepts of fluid and electrolyte balance and replacement during infusion therapy.

The Cell and the Cell Membrane

The cell is the structural and functional unit of all living organisms. It is composed of protoplasm, a complex mixture of organic and inorganic substances, and is surrounded by the cell membrane, a chemically active regulatory matrix.

Nucleus, Nucleolus, Protoplasm, Enzymes, and the Cell Membrane

The **nucleus** is the integral body in the protoplasm of the cell crucial for cell growth, metabolism, reproduction, and the transmission of cellular traits. The **nucleolus** is a spherical body of dense fibers and granules where ribonucleoprotein is formed. Ribonucleoproteins are composed of protein and ribonucleic acid, a substance that controls protein synthesis. **Protoplasm** refers to the substance of the cell and is made of five basic elements: water, electrolytes, carbohydrates, lipids, and proteins. **Protoplasm** (99%) is composed chiefly of carbon, hydrogen, oxygen, and nitrogen. The remaining 1% is sodium, potassium, chlorine, phosphorus, calcium, magnesium, and sulfur, along with traces of copper, iodine, iron, and fluorine. The fluid medium of the protoplasm is water, in which some substances are dissolved in solution and others are suspended as small particles. The water allows the dissolved substances and the suspended particles to be transported from one part of the cell to another.

The protoplasm also contains **enzymes,** organic activators known as **catalysts.** Enzymes are highly specialized molecules that coordinate and control cellular chemical reactions and serve as activators for the timing or speed of cellular reactions. They initiate and carry out change in other substances, yet their individual composition is not altered; they can produce unlimited quantities of the end-products of reactions. They are **reaction-specific,** meaning they act only on certain substances or groups of closely related materials. Enzymes operate at individually optimum temperature ranges and specific degrees of acidity or alkalinity. They can be inactivated or inhibited by temperature extremes, states of dehydration, or by the presence of heavy metals or salts. They sometimes need the presence of other substances to activate their reactions. Specific substances that combine with enzymes and work only with certain enzymes are called **coenzymes.** Nonspecific substances that assist with enzymatic reactions are called **activators.**

In the body, as the extracellular fluid circulates among cells and permeates capillary walls, the cells are nourished with the materials they need to function. The cells, however, are unable to use these substances until they are transported through the cell membrane into the cell. The cell membrane (or plasma membrane) consists primarily of lipids (70% phospholipids, 25% cholesterol, and 5% glycolipids) and proteins, as well as minute water-filled pores.

Carbohydrates

Carbohydrates are organic compounds made up of carbon, hydrogen, and oxygen and are classified according to the amount of sugar in their chemical makeup. The **monosaccharides** are simple sugars whose structure cannot be further broken down by hydrolysis and include glucose, fructose, and galactose. **Disaccharides** are double sugars formed from two monosaccharides and include sucrose (table sugar), lactose (milk sugar), and maltose (malt sugar). **Polysaccharides** are large molecules made up of numerous glucose molecules and include starch (the stored form of glucose in plants), glycogen (the starch stored in the muscles and liver of vertebrates), and cellulose (the structural skeleton for plant cells such as wood and cotton).

Glucose, a monosaccharide and the most important carbohydrate in the body, is the main source of energy for cells and is transported in the blood. The concentration of glucose in the blood (approximately 0.1%) is maintained at a fairly constant range of 80 mg/dl to 120 mg/dl. Once in the cell, it combines with oxygen (**oxidation**) to produce energy. Glucose not used by the cell is converted to **glycogen** by the liver and stored in all body tissues, but mainly in muscles and the liver. The stored glycogen is available for metabolism when needed. During periods of starvation, glycogen is formed from fat (**glyconeogenesis**) and acts as a protein sparer to prevent the use of protein for energy needs.

In the tissues, glucose may be used to form fat or may be oxidized to carbon dioxide and water. Free glucose cannot be used by the tissues until it undergoes a complex series of reactions. It must be penetrated with phosphorus (**phosphorylation**) by adenosine triphosphate (ATP) through the enzymatic action of hexokinase (which produces glucose-6-phosphate). Oxidation of glucose to carbon dioxide and water occurs after further enzymatic and hormonal action and the formation of intermediate components (lactic acid and pyruvic acid).

Fructose is the sweetest of the monosaccharides and is found in fruits, honey, sugar cane, and corn syrup. It is converted to glycogen and used by the body in the same manner as glucose.

Galactose is also a simple sugar. During metabolic processes, galactose and glucose are formed during the catabolism (breakdown) of lactose.

Lipids

Lipids are molecules that contain the elements carbon, hydrogen, and oxygen in the form of phospholipids, steroids, and fats. They are responsible for the structural integrity of the cell membrane and are categorized as **surfactants** (surface-active agents). Lipids have a dual nature because they are polar and charged (**hydrophilic**—attracted to water) on the phosphoric-acid portion of the molecule and nonpolar and uncharged (**hydrophobic**—repelled by water) on the fatty-acid portion. This makeup permits them to alter the interaction of molecules, therefore decreasing the surface tension of water. Because the cell membrane is surrounded by an aqueous environment on each side, the hydrophobic ends of the molecules group together in the middle of the membrane (Figure 2-3). The hydrophilic ends of the molecules exist on the cell membrane exposed to water on both surfaces of the membrane, producing a double layer of phospholipids within the cell membrane. The hydrophobic center of the membrane prevents water and water-soluble molecules from passing through. This structural makeup contributes to one of the most important functions of the membrane—making it nonpermeable to most water-soluble molecules. Some of these molecules do pass through the cell membrane, however, because of the selective transport properties of the proteins. Even though membrane structure is maintained by the lipids, its functions are controlled by the proteins.

Proteins

Proteins, found in the cells of all living organisms, are organic compounds composed of carbon, hydrogen, oxygen, and nitrogen molecules, and usually phosphorus and sulfur as well. They are composed of molecular units called **amino acids.** These compounds serve as the building blocks of protein and are also the end-products of protein digestion. Of the amino acids required for human growth and repair, some are supplied by ingested food (essential amino acids) and others are produced by the body (nonessential amino acids). Proteins that contain all of the essential amino acids are called **complete proteins** and include meat, eggs, milk, and cheese. Those that do not contain all the essential amino acids, such as vegetables and grains, are called **incomplete proteins.**

Amino acids do not undergo any changes as they pass through the intestines, portal circulation, the liver, and into the general circulation. In the body, tissues are amino-acid specific; they absorb amino acids from the circulation according to which protein they need to manufacture. Any proteins that are not metabolized by the tissues are converted into urea **(deaminization).**

Proteins provide several important functions within the cell membrane. In addition to transporting molecules across the membrane, they provide for its structural support and control and act as enzymes to serve as pumps for the enzymatic regulation of chemical reactions on the cell surface. They function as receptors for hormones approaching the membrane surface, and work as antigens, which identify and recognize blood and tissue type.

Proteins also serve as transporters for amino acids and simple sugars and provide pores or channels for the passage of electrolytes. These protein pores in the cell membrane, which carry a positive charge, are lined with positively charged calcium ions. Because of this makeup, positively charged ions, such as sodium and potassium, have difficulty

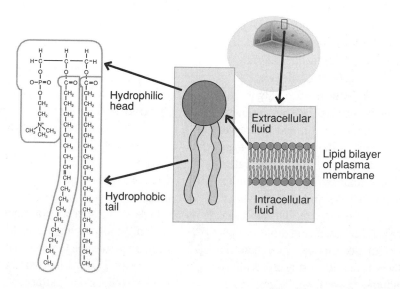

Figure 2-3 | Cell membrane phospholipids

passing through the pores. Whenever they attempt passage, the two positive charges repel each other. Negatively charged ions pass through the membrane pores easily.

Mechanisms of Fluid Movement

Passage of substances across membranes is accomplished in one of two ways, depending on the substances being taken in or moved out. Passive transport, in which there is no expenditure of cellular energy, occurs spontaneously through any semipermeable layer. Biologic energy is not required for this process. Active transport requires a source of biologic activity and cellular metabolic energy for movement of particles across the cell membrane.

Passive Transport

Passive transport (or **noncarrier-mediated transport**) is the movement of solutes through membranes without the expenditure of energy. It includes passive diffusion, osmosis, facilitated diffusion, and filtration.

Passive Diffusion

Passive (simple) diffusion is the process in which ions, water, and lipid-soluble molecules move randomly in all directions from an area of high concentration to a lower solute concentration through the pores in the membrane or through the matrix of the membrane (Figure 2-4). The rate at which diffusion occurs depends on the variations in electrical potentials across membranes. For simple diffusion to occur, the particles must dissolve or be small enough to pass through the membrane. When in solution, particles move about randomly in any direction. If the molecules become more populous in one area of the solution than in another area, a concentration difference, or **concentration gradient**, results, and the particles will move to evenly redistribute themselves until they reach a state of equilibrium. This movement abolishes the concentration difference and is called **net diffusion.**

Net diffusion depends on membrane permeability, the differences in the concentrations on each side of the membrane, the differences in electric potentials, and differences in pressure across membranes. It is this passive movement from an area of higher concentration to lower concentration along a concentration gradient that results in simple diffusion. The random motion of molecules and ions in all directions occurs because of kinetic energy. As the movement continues, heat is produced and released, and diffusion continues. In diffusion, any substance that can move into the cell can move out. It is the net quantity of substances diffusing through the cell membrane, rather than the gross quantity, that is important to cellular function.

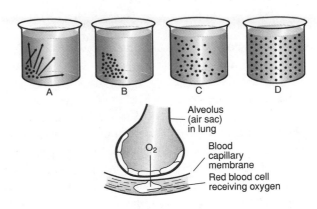

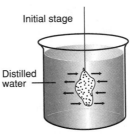 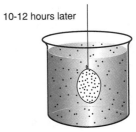

(A) A small lump of sugar is placed into a beaker of water; its molecules dissolve and begin to diffuse outward. (B and C) The sugar molecules continue to diffuse through the water from an area of greater concentration to an area of lesser concentration. (D) Over a long period of time, the sugar molecules are evenly distributed throughout the water, reaching a state of equilibrium.

Example of diffusion in the human body: Oxygen diffuses from an alveolus in a lung where it is in greater concentration, across the blood capillary membrane, into a red blood cell where it is in lesser concentration.

Figure 2-4 | Passive (simple) diffusion

(A) Initially, the sausage casing contains a solution of gelatin, salt, and sucrose. The casing is permeable to water and salt molecules only. Since the concentration of water molecules is greater outside the casing, water molecules will diffuse into the casing. The opposite situation exists for the salt.

(B) The sausage casing swells due to the net movement of water molecules inward. However, the volume of distilled water in the beaker remains constant.

Figure 2-5 | Osmosis: A sausage casing as an example of a selective permeable membrane

Osmosis

Osmosis is the passage of water through a semipermeable membrane from an area with a lower concentration of solutes to an area with a higher concentration of solutes (Figure 2-5). For a membrane to be semipermeable, it has to be more permeable to water than to solutes.

Osmosis governs the movement of body fluids between the intracellular and extracellular fluid compartments, thus affecting the volumes within each. The semipermeable membrane selectively controls the passage of solutes and serves to separate the major fluid compartments.

Through the process of osmosis, water flows through the semipermeable membrane to the side with the higher concentration of particles that cannot diffuse to the side with the lower concentration. It is the difference in the concentration of nondiffusable particles that controls water flow. Once the concentrations of solutes are equal on each side of the membrane, the flow of water stops and the solutions are **isosmotic** to each other, comparable in molecular concentration. Any change in the volume of solutes or water content in either compartment brings about an osmotic water shift.

Whereas diffusion is the passive flow of particles from an area of higher concentration to one of lower concentration, osmosis is the movement of water across a semipermeable membrane from an area of lower concentration to one of higher concentration. Both mechanisms involve movement across a concentration gradient, but diffusion moves solutes and osmosis moves water (solvent). Osmosis cannot occur unless the membrane is more permeable to water than to solutes; water movement is enhanced because of the greater concentration of solutes.

Hydrostatic pressure refers to the physical force of water as it pushes against vessel walls or cellular membranes (Figure 2-6). **Hydraulic pressure** is the force of gravitational pressure that acts on hydrostatic pressure

combined with the pumping pressure of the heart. **Osmotic pressure** is the amount of hydrostatic pressure needed to draw a solvent across a membrane and develops as a result of a high concentration of particles colliding with one another. As the number of solutes increases, there is less space for them to move, so they come in contact with one another more frequently. This results in increased osmotic pressure, which causes the movement of fluid (Figure 2-7). Total osmotic pressure in the extracellular fluid results from the movement of small molecules, ions, and proteins contained in it. The small molecules easily cross back and forth across membranes and have little effect on movement of water or osmotic pressure. The osmotic pressure created by the movement of dissolved ions is termed **crystalloid osmotic pressure.** The osmotic pressure that develops at a membrane because of proteins is the **colloid osmotic pressure** or **oncotic pressure.**

The osmotic activity of a solution is described according to its osmolarity, its osmolality, or both. **Osmolarity (tonicity)** refers to the concentration of solute particles contained in a unit volume of solvent and is usually expressed as milliosmols per liter or mOsm/L. The osmolarity of a solution varies with changes in temperature because liquids expand with increasing temperature (Figure 2-8).

In contrast, **osmolality** (also called *tonicity*) describes the total number of solute particles in a unit weight of solvent and is usually expressed as milliosmols per kilogram or mOsm/kg. The osmol unit is used because osmotic pressure is determined by the number of particles, rather

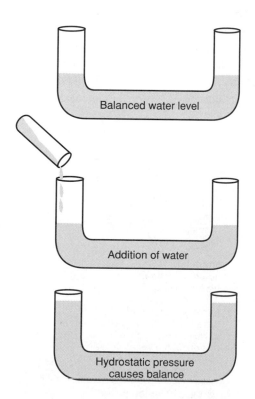

Figure 2-6 | Hydrostatic pressure

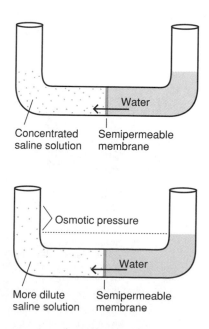

Figure 2-7 | Osmotic pressure

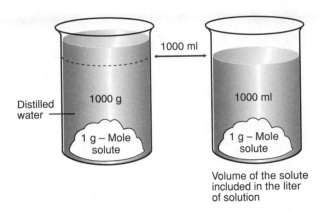

Figure 2-8 | Osmolality and osmolarity

than the mass, of a solute. As a general rule, the osmol is too big a unit for describing osmotic activity in bodily solutes, so the milliosmol is used ($\frac{1}{1000}$ osmol). Both osmolarity and osmolality are used to characterize tonicity, but clinically, osmolality is the more commonly used system of fluid measurement because normal body solutions are very dilute. Temperature does not affect osmolality.

An osmol equals the molecular weight in grams of the number of particles in one mole of a nonionizing material, such as sodium, calcium, urea, or glucose. One mole of such a substance, when added to water, results in a solution with one osmol or particle. Ionizing substances (capable of dissociating in solution and conducting electricity), when placed in water, result in the formation of a solution with more than one osmol. If a mole of potassium chloride is placed in water, there is a separation of ions resulting in a solution with two osmols, one of potassium and one of chloride.

Under normal circumstances, body fluids are dilute solutions. Because of this characteristic, there is very little difference

between the osmolarity and osmolality of body fluids. However, the fluid in the intravascular compartment is slightly greater than in other spaces because it contains plasma proteins.

A solution with an osmolality (or osmolarity) higher than another solution is considered **hypertonic (hyperosmolar).** A cell placed in a hypertonic solution would shrink, or crenate, because water would be osmotically drawn from it. In contrast, a solution that has an osmolality lower than another solution is called a **hypotonic (hyposmolar) solution.** Pure water is hypotonic compared with body fluids, so if a cell is placed in it, the water is osmotically drawn across the membrane causing the cell to swell. A solution that is **isotonic (isosmolar)** has the same osmotic pressure as the comparison solution. The osmolality of plasma (approximately 290–300 mOsm/L) is generally used as the standard for comparison. The tonicity of plasma or extracellular fluid is clinically and physiologically significant with regard to the osmotic shift of water between the fluid compartments (Figure 2-9).

During illness, it becomes a challenge to maintain the proper balance of fluids and electrolytes between the intracellular and extracellular compartments. When dealing with fluid replacement therapy, the CMA must understand the interrelationships that exist between these two compartments and the osmotic factors that contribute to fluid shifts.

Facilitated Diffusion

The cellular membrane allows free movement for the diffusion of lipid-soluble, nonpolar (uncharged) molecules, such as oxygen, the steroid hormones, and fatty acids. In addition, small molecules that have polar bonds but do not carry electrical charges, such as carbon dioxide, urea, and ethanol, are also able to pass with ease back and forth across the cell membrane. Water diffuses through because its molecules are small and uncharged. Charged inorganic ions can only pass

Hypertonic solution

Hypotonic solution

Isotonic solution

Hypertonic solution (seawater)
A red blood cell will shrink and wrinkle up because water molecules are moving out of the cell.

Hypotonic solution (freshwater)
A red blood cell will swell and burst because water molecules are moving into the cell.

Isotonic solution (human blood serum)
A red blood cell remains unchanged because the movement of water molecules into and out of the cell is the same.

Figure 2-9 | Movement of water molecules in hypertonic, hypotonic, and isotonic solutions

through the membrane via **ion channels,** submicroscopic passageways present in the membrane matrix.

Lipid solubility determines whether a substance is able to pass through the cell membrane. Large polar (charged) lipid-insoluble materials cross the cell membrane only with the help of solute-specific carriers called **transport proteins** present within the cell membrane. The process by which material combines with carriers to cross the cell membrane is called **facilitated diffusion** or **carrier-mediated diffusion** (Figure 2-10). It is through this mechanism that amino acids and sugars, especially glucose, are transported into the cell. Once inside the cell, sugar molecules or amino acids break away from the carrier, and the carrier returns to the outside surface of the membrane to pick up more products for diffusion into the cell. The speed with which this process takes place depends on the amount of carrier present, the difference in the concentration of molecules on each side of the cell

membrane, and the speed of the chemical reactions. In the case of glucose, the rate of transport by the carrier is increased because of the hormone insulin.

Facilitated diffusion is somewhat similar to active transport. In diffusion, the movement of molecules is from an area of higher concentration to one of a lower concentration, and in active transport the molecules move from an area of lower concentration through the membrane to an area of higher concentration with the help of biologic, metabolic energy.

Filtration

Filtration is the movement of fluid and diffusible particles through a membrane from an area of greater hydrostatic pressure to one of lesser hydrostatic pressure. While diffusion moves in either direction across a membrane, filtration moves in one direction, owing to the mechanisms of hydrostatic, osmotic, and interstitial fluid pressures that expedite net fluid transport across the membrane. Filtration is similar to pouring a solution through a sieve. The size of the openings in the sieve determines the size of particle to be filtered (Figure 2-11).

In the body, arterial blood is transported via the arteries to the arterioles and then to the arterial capillary beds. From there the fluid enters the interstitial fluid where the cellular exchange of nutrients and wastes occurs. Once this exchange has taken place, the fluid returns to the venous circulation via the venous capillary beds, venules, and veins (Figure 2-12). Fluid movement from the arterial capillary beds into the interstitial compartment occurs through filtration. The mean capillary pressure is 17 mm Hg.

Proteins are abundant in the circulating plasma and serve to maintain osmotic pressure at the capillary membrane by not permitting the movement of fluid from the

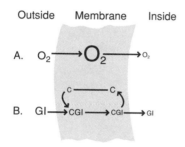

Outside   Membrane   Inside

A. $O_2 \longrightarrow O_2 \longrightarrow O_2$

B. $GI \longrightarrow CGI \longrightarrow CGI \longrightarrow GI$

Figure 2-10 | Facilitated diffusion: A. Free diffusion of oxygen through the lipid matrix of the cell membrane; B. Facilitated (carrier-mediated) diffusion of glucose through the membrane lipid matrix

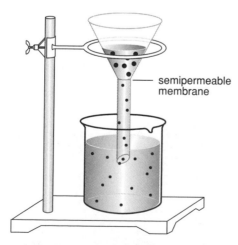

semipermeable membrane

A. Filtration: Small molecules are filtered through the semipermeable membrane, while the large molecules remain in the funnel.

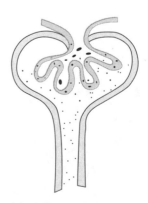

B. Example of filtration in the human body: Glomerulus of kidney; large particles like red blood cells and proteins remain in the blood, and small molecules like urea and water are excreted as a metabolic excretory product—urine.

Figure 2-11 | Filtration

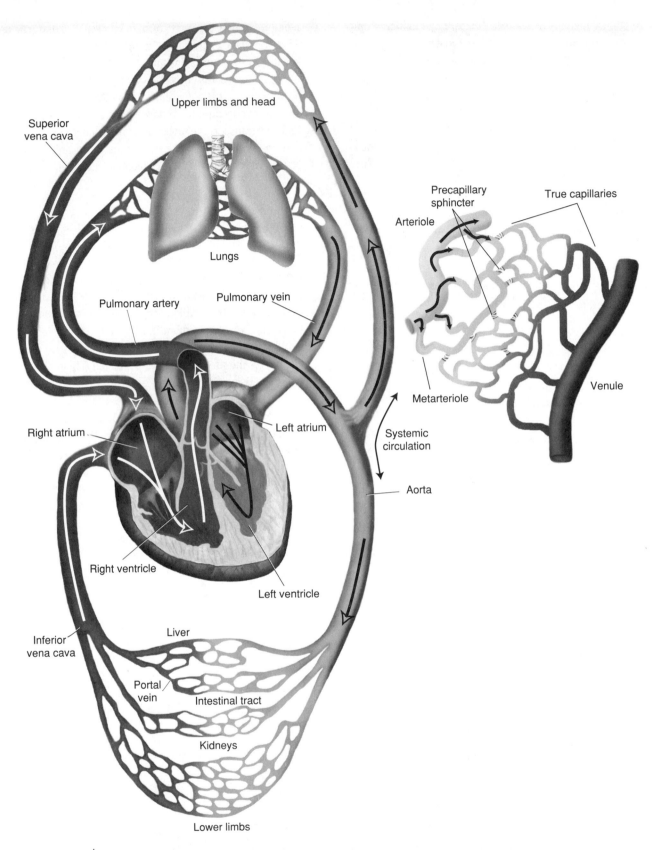

Figure 2-12 | Systemic circulation

plasma into the interstitial fluid compartment. This osmotic pressure, brought about by the dissolved proteins (colloids), is called *oncotic pressure* or *colloid osmotic pressure*, which is 28 mm Hg in the plasma. In general, the size of capillary pores is too small to allow for the passage of plasma proteins into the interstitial fluid spaces. There are, however, some larger pores that allow very small amounts of plasma proteins to filter into the ISF compartment. This amounts to about 0.3%, making the colloid osmotic pressure of the ISF about 5 mm Hg. The hydrostatic pressure in the ISF is about −6.3 mm Hg (or 6.3 mm Hg below atmospheric pressure).

The process of water and electrolyte filtration occurring through the capillary membranes is enhanced by the mechanical forces of blood pressure and gravity, so the capillary pressure at the arterial ends is ±15 mm Hg greater than at the venous ends, making the mean capillary pressure about ±17 mm Hg. As a result of this pressure difference, some fluid filters out of the arterial capillaries, flows through the interstitial spaces, and is reabsorbed into the venous capillary network.

Starling's law of capillaries (Figure 2-13) maintains that, under normal circumstances, fluid filtered out of the arterial end of the capillary bed and reabsorbed at the venous end is exactly the same, creating a state of near equilibrium. It is not exactly the same, however, because of the difference in hydrostatic pressure between the arterial and venous capillary beds. The forces that move fluid out of the arterial end of the network amount to a total of 28.3 mm Hg (mean capillary pressure of 17 mm Hg + negative interstitial pressure of 6.3 mm Hg + ISF colloid pressure 5 mm Hg). The forces that move fluid back into circulation at the venous capillary bed total 28 mm Hg (colloid osmotic or oncotic pressure). The small amount of excess filtration remaining in the interstitial compartment, referred to as **net filtration** (0.3 mm Hg), is returned to the circulation by way of the lymphatic system (Table 2-4).

Of major importance is that the lymphatics carry this excess fluid, proteins, and large particulate matter that cannot be reabsorbed by the venous capillary bed out of the ISF compartment. This minute excess or net filtration

(that only amounts to about 0.3 mm Hg) accounts for 1.7 ml/min of fluid. If the lymphatics were not continually removing this small amount of fluid, there would be a buildup of 2,448 ml in the interstitial compartment over a 24-hour period, which would result in death.

Active Transport

Active transport is the process whereby molecules are moved against a concentration gradient, pressure gradient, or electrochemical gradient by utilizing cellular energy sources. As with facilitated diffusion, transport is through membranes by carriers. Active transport differs from diffusion, however, because substances are capable of crossing membranes even when there is a higher concentration on the side of the membrane the substance is transferring to, and because energy is needed to surpass the concentration gradient.

There exists some scientific debate regarding the details and intricacies of energy supply for the active transport system. What is known and agreed upon by the scientific community, however, is that ATP provides the energy for transport, that there is a chemical joining of the substance to be transported with a protein carrier, and that the process can be accomplished only with the assistance of enzymatic activity. Active transport carriers are sometimes referred to as *pumps*.

Table 2-4 | Starling's Law of capillaries

SUMMATION OF FORCES	MILLIMETERS OF MERCURY (MM HG)
Forces Moving Fluid Out of the Capillary	
Mean arterial capillary pressure	17.0 mm Hg
Negative interstitial fluid pressure	+ 6.3 mm Hg
Interstitial fluid colloid osmotic pressure	+ 5.0 mm Hg
Total outward pressure	= 28.3 mm Hg
Forces Moving Fluid into the Capillary	
Plasma colloid osmotic pressure	28.0 mm Hg
Total inward pressure	= 28.0 mm Hg
	28.3 mm Hg
	− 28.0 mm Hg
Net outward pressure	= 0.3 mm Hg
(per minute filtration)	= 1.7 ml/min

1.7 ml × 60 min = 102 ml/hr × 24 hr = 2,448 ml/d
(Daily net filtration returned to circulation by the lymphatics)

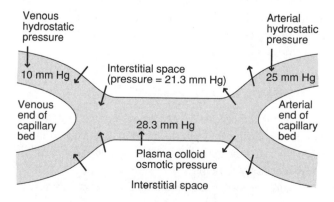

Figure 2-13 | Starling's Law of capillaries

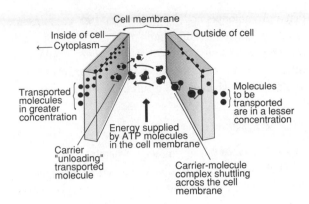

Figure 2-14 | Active transport

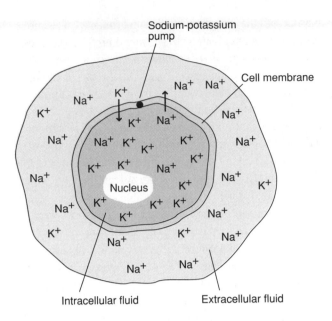

Figure 2-15 | Sodium-potassium pump

ATP

Every cell in the body contains enzymes for splitting proteins, fats, and carbohydrates into amino acids, fatty acids, and glucose, respectively. These chemicals are metabolized with oxygen to form carbon dioxide and water. In the process of accomplishing this metabolic conversion, large amounts of energy are produced. The energy is used to convert **adenosine diphosphate (ADP)** to **adenosine triphosphate (ATP),** which then provides the energy needed for cellular chemical reactions to take place. ATP is present in all body cells but is especially abundant in muscle cells (Figure 2-14).

Active transport occurs when ATP hydrolysis energizes a protein carrier. As with facilitated diffusion, a carrier attaches to a substance crossing the cell membrane and the two diffuse into the cell. ATP is released on the inside of the cell membrane to trigger an enzyme-catalyzed reaction that causes the substance and carrier to lose their affinity for each other and to dissociate. The carrier diffuses out of the cell, and the substance that was split from the carrier, because of its membrane insolubility, remains.

Sodium-Potassium Pump

The sodium-potassium pump is an active transport system. It serves as a transport carrier to pick up and transport a substance across a membrane, detach from it, and then return to the outside to transport additional material. In addition, the sodium-potassium pump exchanges ions or molecules with other ions or molecules (Figure 2-15). It is present in all cells of the body, but is especially active in muscle and nerve cells and the cells of the kidney tubules.

The sodium-potassium pump is a mechanism that results in most of the body's potassium remaining in the intracellular fluid and most of the sodium remaining in the extracellular fluid. This pump is vital to physiologic functioning for the transmission of electrical impulses, to the secretory func-

tioning of glands, and to prevent all cells from swelling and bursting.

Sodium concentration is high in the ECF and low in the ICF. Potassium is low in the ECF and high in the ICF. Because of the pores that exist in the cell membrane, there is some diffusion of sodium and potassium. If this diffusion were allowed to continue, the concentration of sodium would equalize over time, and the cells would swell and rupture. The sodium-potassium pump is a carrier that transports sodium out of the cell and pumps potassium back into the cell. The concentrations of sodium and potassium do not change as a result of diffusion because of the sodium-potassium pump. The energy needed for this pump to work comes from the enzyme ATPase, which is present in the carrier itself, and acts to break down ATP.

The sodium-potassium pump is more effective in transporting sodium than potassium and usually carries three sodium ions for every two potassium ions. This contributes to a **potential difference** (charge separator) providing voltage across the membrane. The sodium-potassium pump contributes to the membrane by pumping more sodium out than potassium in. This promotes a constant membrane potential.

Transport by Vesicle Formation

In order for the cell to live and grow, it must maintain a source of nourishment from the surrounding fluids. It must also be able to excrete wastes and destroy and expel harmful and unnecessary substances.

In addition to the passive and active transport systems, a mechanism is required to move larger molecules that cannot pass through the cell membrane by these methods. These substances include certain fluids and larger extracellular molecules, such as proteins and polysaccharides.

Endocytosis

Endocytosis is a process whereby the cell ingests substances that are too large to be taken in through passive or active transport systems. Whenever these materials present themselves to the surface of the cell membrane, attributes of the surface tension change so that the membrane is able to fold inward and surround these materials. These invaginated areas then break away from the cell membrane and form individual vessels that travel into the cellular cytoplasm. Pinocytosis and phagocytosis are types of endocytosis, both requiring metabolic energy.

Pinocytosis

Pinocytosis is the endocytic process in which invagination of the cell membrane by the larger molecules occurs, and channels are made that encapsulate to form **vacuoles,** clear fluid or air-filled spaces in the protoplasm. Vacuoles break away from the cell membrane and combine with **lysosomes,** intracellular digestive systems containing hydrolytic enzymes that break down proteins and some carbohydrates for cellular use. Pinocytosis occurs in reaction to strong electrolyte solutions, proteins, and other macromolecules. Without this process, proteins would have no other means of penetrating the cell membrane (Figure 2-16).

Phagocytosis

Phagocytosis is the process whereby the cell selectively ingests large particles of material. The process is analogous to pinocytosis, but this system involves the taking in of bacteria, other cells, or particles of tissue degeneration. If the system were not selectively specific, phagocytes would ingest normal body structures as well.

As with pinocytosis, lysosomes act on phagocytic vesicles. Hydrolases are used to digest proteins, glycogen, nucleic acids, and other substances so the vesicles are able to function as digestive bodies. Any matter that is not broken down and digested by lysosomal activity is transported out of the cell by the process of exocytosis.

Exocytosis

In some situations, intracellular molecules are too large to be transported out of the cell by active or passive transport. When this is the case, the molecules join with the cell membrane and exit the cell in the process of **exocytosis,** which is similar to pinocytosis, but a reverse form of it (Figure 2-17).

Movement of Electrical Potentials

It is extremely important for the CMA to fully understand the physiology and movement of electrical potentials across the cell membrane because so many medications administered to patients, especially via the IV route, affect the electrical activity of muscles and nerves. For example, the heart, a mass of cardiac muscle, is innervated and regulated by a nerve conduction system. The CMA employed in critical care specialty areas is often responsible for giving drugs according to changes in electrocardiograms (EKGs).

The capability of nerve and muscle to make and transmit membrane potential changes is called **excitability** or **irritability.** Neurons are able to transmit hundreds of impulses per second.

The inside of the cell carries a negative charge, while the outside is positively charged, resulting in the potential difference (voltage) called the **membrane potential.** These electrical charges, separated by the cell membrane, have the capability to work if they come together. This

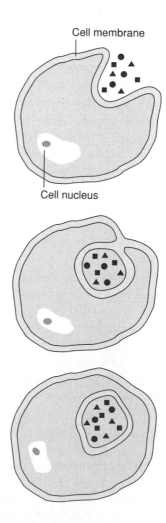

Figure 2-16 | Pinocytosis

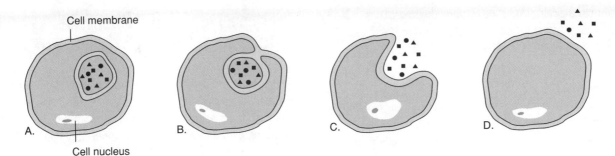

Cell membrane

Cell nucleus

Figure 2-17 | Exocytosis

condition exists in all body cells. The difference in charge is the result of several factors: the negatively charged molecules inside the cell, the permeability properties of the cell membrane, and the action of the sodium-potassium pump that moves sodium and potassium against their concentration gradients.

Within the cell, proteins and organic substances carry negative charges. They do not leave the cell and are known as *fixed anions*. They do, however, attract small organic ions of sodium, potassium, and calcium, which are able to diffuse through from the extracellular fluid.

The cell membrane is more permeable to potassium than to other cations, so potassium is more concentrated in the intracellular compartment. The reason for this is the presence of polypeptide ion channels, known as **sodium-potassium gates,** which open and close under certain conditions. There are two different ionic channels for potassium: one that has no gates and thus is always open, and another that has gates that close when the cell is at rest. Sodium channels have gates that are closed when the cell is at rest. The cell at rest is more permeable to potassium than sodium. Sodium and potassium gates are voltage regulated, opening or closing according to membrane potentials.

The inside of the cell is more negatively charged than the outside and creates a difference in electrical charges called the **resting membrane potential,** present when there is no cellular stimulation (Figure 2-18). The voltage difference is the result of the extracellular concentration of sodium ions and the intracellular concentration of potassium ions maintained by the sodium-potassium pump, which moves sodium out and potassium in. This resting membrane, one hundred times more permeable to potassium than to sodium, allows for some potassium diffusion into the ECF from its higher concentration in the ICF, thus leaving more negatively charged anions in the ICF to maintain the resting membrane potential. This resting membrane potential (−65 to −85 mV) occurs when there are more anions inside the cell and no impulses produced.

Stimulation by mechanical, chemical, or electrical means creates a change in the resting membrane potential of nerve

and muscle cells, resulting in a nerve impulse or **action potential.** This is an electrical occurrence in which the polarity of the membrane potential is reversed rapidly and then restored. Any time a resting cell membrane is stimulated, it becomes more permeable to sodium, allowing sodium to move into the cell, thus decreasing the membrane potential from a negative value to zero. This reversal of membrane polarity during the production of action potentials is called **depolarization.** Depolarization occurs because large amounts of sodium are leaking into the cell, which the membrane cannot keep out. The intracellular side of the membrane becomes less negative than the outside. In order for the membrane potential to change and rapid polarity reversal to occur, a **threshold potential** of 15 mV–20 mV must be reached. Once reached, the cell continues to depolarize, even without additional stimulation. As sodium diffuses into the cell, the membrane potential falls to zero and then rapidly depolarizes, becoming positive (+40 mV). If a stimulus is weaker than the threshold potential, a nerve impulse (action potential) will not occur. This is known as the *all-or-none law* because an impulse is either propagated or not. There is no such entity as a partial impulse.

The cell membrane is not able to react to any other stimulation during most of an action potential because of changes occurring in membrane permeability. This time interval is known as the **absolute refractory period.** The **relative refractory period** occurs when potassium permeability increases toward the end of an action potential and only an extremely strong stimulus can generate another action potential. One action potential cannot begin until the one before it is finished. Each action potential serves as the stimulus for another to occur, so there is a constant and continuous wavelike spread of action potentials across a membrane.

With depolarization, the sodium gates close, the potassium gates open, and potassium ions rapidly leave the cell and return the membrane interior to the normal negative state. This results in **repolarization,** the reestablishment of the resting membrane potential. It occurs in less than a

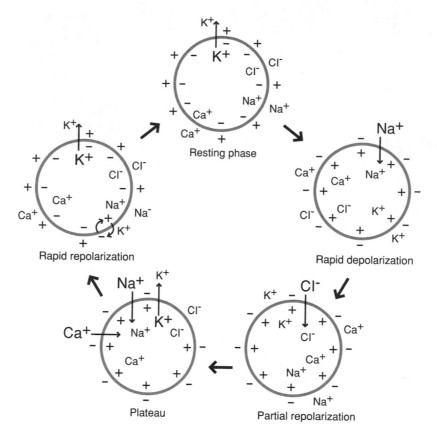

Figure 2-18 | Cell membrane voltage

millisecond (ms). The balance of sodium and potassium is not stabilized until the sodium-potassium pump, through active transport, removes excess sodium from the cell.

BODY SYSTEMS: FLUID AND ELECTROLYTE REGULATION

To fully comprehend body water content, its constituents, and its movement between compartments, it is necessary to review how balances are maintained and regulated. Fluid and electrolyte balance is maintained through the intake of food and fluids, known as **exogenous** sources, and the output of excess water and waste products. **Endogenous** production of water is that produced within the body through chemical oxidation processes. Endogenous sources of water are small compared with exogenous sources.

Regulation of body water occurs as the result of various organs and tissues working together to maintain a state of equilibrium. When the body is in a state of health, fluid intake and loss is about the same over a 72-hour period. Fluid intake and urine output are about equal, while water

formed through the oxidation of food and fluid equals that lost through perspiration, respiration, and gastrointestinal excretion.

It is necessary for the CMA to understand the normal mechanisms of intake, output, and regulation in order to facilitate the identification of abnormalities and to intervene appropriately. When homeostasis is compromised and imbalances occur, the CMA is responsible for managing an important exogenous source of fluid replacement: intravenous infusions.

The Renal System

When addressing water balance in the body, the kidneys play a major role in controlling output, regulating fluid and electrolyte balance, and adjusting acid-base balance. Urine, formed by means of reabsorption and filtration, is composed of 95% water and 5% organic and inorganic material removed from the blood. In the glomeruli, where plasma filtration occurs, the rate of filtration is determined by systemic arterial pressure and plasma oncotic (colloid) pressure, as well as the hydrostatic pressure in the Bowman's capsule. Under normal conditions, the glomerular membrane prevents passage of large molecules, such as proteins and blood cells.

The renal tubules reabsorb 99% of the glomerular filtrate and return it to the extracellular fluid. The 1% that remains is excreted in the form of urine as a mixture of water, solutes, and wastes.

The Cardiovascular System

In order for the kidneys to reabsorb and secrete properly, the heart and blood vessels must be capable of pumping adequately. This driving force enables plasma filtration to occur across the glomerular membrane, resulting in the formation of urine. The cardiovascular system pumps to distribute water and nutrients to all organs and tissues and to remove waste products.

The Lymphatic System

The lymphatic system serves as an adjunct to the cardiovascular system by removing excess interstitial fluid, in the form of lymph, and returning it to the circulatory system. If it were not for the lymphatics, the inward force at the arterial capillary bed into the interstitial fluid compartment, which exceeds the outgoing force at the venous end, would result in fluid overload in the interstitial fluid. This would bring about a state of edema that would prove to be fatal within a matter of hours.

The Nervous System

The nervous system masterminds fluid and electrolyte balance through the regulation of sodium and water. It does this by stimulating the secretions of various endocrine glands.

Baroreceptors, pressure-sensitive nerve endings in the aortic arch, arteries, veins, atria of the heart, and carotid sinuses, respond to changes in volume in the extracellular fluid. Therefore, with overhydration or underhydration, they affect blood flow. They signal receptors in the brain to stimulate the posterior pituitary gland to secrete stored antidiuretic hormone. The hypothalamus triggers the sensation of thirst as a result of the baroreceptor responses to changes in osmolality, prompts fluid intake, and thus increases fluid volume.

The Endocrine System

The endocrine system responds selectively to the regulation and maintenance of fluid and electrolyte balance through hormonal production. Endocrine secretion is controlled by the nervous system, by chemicals in the blood, or through the action of other hormones.

Antidiuretic Hormone (ADH)

Antidiuretic hormone (ADH), also called *vasopressin,* is secreted by the posterior pituitary gland and regulates water retention and excretion. When there is an excess of sodium in the extracellular fluid or reduced blood volume, hypertonicity or diminished circulation signals the release of ADH by the posterior lobe of the pituitary gland. This results in the sensation of thirst while conserving body water through reabsorption (Figure 2-19). ADH is released in response to physical and emotional stressors, excessive physical activity, some anesthetics, morphine, barbiturates, and pain.

In contrast, when the extracellular fluid becomes hypotonic, if there is increased blood volume, or if the body becomes hypothermic, the pituitary is signaled to inhibit the release of ADH. This, in turn, stimulates the excretion of urine. Alcohol acts as a diuretic in this manner. ADH, therefore, regulates extracellular osmolality while aldosterone regulates extracellular volume.

Aldosterone

Aldosterone, a mineralocorticoid secreted by the adrenal glands, plays a major role in regulating distal tubular reabsorption of sodium in the kidneys, thus promoting water reabsorption and increasing blood volume. It regulates potassium concentrations by stimulating potassium secretion into the distal tubules and collecting ducts of the kidneys.

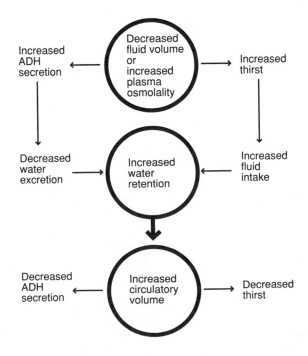

Figure 2-19 | Thirst mechanism and ADH secretion

When the body is exposed to physical and psychic stress, has diminished sodium levels, or when the extracellular volume decreases, aldosterone is secreted to promote the reabsorption of water and sodium by the kidneys. It also promotes sodium retention (and potassium excretion) through its action on the gastrointestinal tract, salivary glands, and sweat glands.

Thyroid Hormone

The thyroid gland stores and secretes thyroid hormone, which influences metabolic rate and blood flow. Increased blood flow results in satisfactory renal perfusion and enhances urinary output. The thyroid also stores and releases calcitonin, which assists in the regulation of calcium levels in the blood and bones.

Parathyroid Hormone (PTH)

The level of calcium and phosphate is regulated by parathyroid hormone (parathormone) secretions. Calcium and phosphate homeostasis is physiologically necessary for bone and tooth formation, acid-base balance, cell membrane permeability, nerve and muscle functioning (especially the myocardium), and for enzyme activation.

Serum calcium homeostasis is achieved through a specialized parathyroid feedback system. When extracellular calcium levels drop, the parathyroid glands are stimulated to secrete parathormone, which acts on the bones to move calcium into the blood. Should the bones be deficient in calcium, the hormone stimulates the kidney tubules and the intestinal tract to reabsorb calcium. If blood levels of phosphate drop, the hormone stimulates its reabsorption in the kidney tubules. If abnormal increases occur, urinary excretion balances the excess of phosphates.

The Respiratory System

The lungs, through the process of internal and external respiration, regulate the exchange of oxygen and carbon dioxide in the body. The lungs also control acid-base balance through the production of carbonic acid. The carbonic acid-sodium bicarbonate system is the body's most important buffer system. In addition, the lungs control fluid balance by removing water from the body through the process of external respiration.

The Gastrointestinal System

The gastrointestinal tract absorbs nutrients and water, and serves as the main reservoir for the intake of fluids. It also removes a small portion of body water in feces. Many illnesses and diseases contribute to large body water loss through the gastrointestinal tract.

The Integumentary System

Body water is lost through the skin in the form of perspiration, or sensible loss. Insensible losses of water occur continuously and cannot be felt or seen, but can amount to a minimum of a pint of fluid per day. Loss of body water through the skin can vary greatly, depending on such variables as internal body temperature, external environmental temperature, physical exertion, illness, or injury.

ACID-BASE BALANCE

In order for homeostasis to be maintained, an equalization must exist between the acidity and alkalinity of body fluids, known as **acid-base balance.** Whether a solution is acid or alkaline depends on its concentration of hydrogen and hydroxyl ions.

An **acid** is any substance that releases hydrogen ions **(hydrogen ion donor)** when placed in a solution. Within the body are **nonvolatile (fixed) acids** derived from the metabolic breakdown **(catabolism)** of proteins and fats. The fixed acids that result from protein catabolism are lactic and sulfuric acids, and acetoacetic acid from fat metabolism. Hydrogen ions that come from fixed acids are excreted by the kidneys. Carbonic acid is a volatile or nonfixed acid that is reciprocal with carbon dioxide and water in the body and dissociates into hydrogen and bicarbonate ions. A **volatile acid** can be vaporized or evaporated and is the means by which carbon dioxide in the ECF is transformed in the lungs to be removed during the expiratory phase of respiration.

A **base**, or alkali, is any substance that releases hydroxyl ions **(hydrogen ion acceptor)** in a solution and is able to accept and combine with hydrogen ions. Bases are derived from the metabolic breakdown of citrate, lactate, and isocitrate to carbon dioxide and water. They are found in most foods but are predominant in fruits and vegetables.

A **salt** is made up of the negative ion of any acid (except hydroxyl) and the positive ion of any base (except hydrogen). It results from the chemical interaction within a solution where the acid and base neutralize each other. **Neutralization** is the process whereby opposing forces balance each other so that neither force dominates.

The chemical unit of measurement used to describe the degree of acidity or alkalinity of a substance is known as the **potential of hydrogen** or **pH.** The degree of pH is gauged on a scale of zero to fourteen, with seven indicating neutrality. The neutrality of a solution means that its concentration of opposing forces balance each other, making it neither acid

Acid ⟶ OH^-

Base ⟶ H^+

Water ⟶ H_2O or HOH

Dissociates into hydrogen and hydroxyl ions

$$H_2O + H_2O = H_3O^+ + OH^-$$

Figure 2-20 | Water as an acid and a base

nor alkaline. Pure water has a pH of 7.0. It can dissociate into hydrogen and hydroxyl ions and act as both an acid and a base (Figure 2-20).

There is an inverse correlation between acid-base properties: As the hydrogen ion concentration increases, the pH decreases (acidity); as the concentration of hydrogen ions decreases, the pH rises (alkalinity). Acids are neutralized with bases and vice versa. As the acidity of a solution increases, with an increase in the number of hydrogen ions, the pH level drops below 7.0, and as alkalinity increases, and hydroxyl ions exceed the concentration of hydrogen ions, the pH rises above 7.0. **Acidosis** is the accumulation of excess acids (hydrogen ions) or a deficiency of base (bicarbonate ions), resulting in a pH less than 7.0. **Alkalosis** is the reduction of acids (hydrogen ions) and an increase of base (bicarbonate ions), resulting in a pH greater than 7.0. The pH of plasma is maintained within the slightly alkaline range of 7.35 to 7.45.

Buffer Systems

Fluids within the intracellular and extracellular spaces must be equalized in terms of acidity and alkalinity. In order for this balance to remain, chemical and physiologic buffers exist. A **buffer** is a substance that maintains the body's acid-base balance by regulating hydrogen ion concentration. It is reaction-specific and only comes into action in response to abnormal changes in acidity or alkalinity. A buffer system is the combination of an acid and a base, and is sometimes referred to as a *buffer pair*.

For normal cellular activity to occur, the hydrogen ion concentration of the body's fluid must be sustained within a very limited range. This concentration is carefully controlled by three major buffer systems that work to maintain acid-base balance: (1) the carbonic acid-bicarbonate system, (2) the phosphate buffer system, and (3) the protein buffer system. They are extremely important in maintaining homeostasis and any deviation from the normal pH range can cause major disturbances in cellular, enzymatic, and neuromuscular activity within the body.

The Carbonic Acid-Bicarbonate Buffer System

The most important buffering system, which exists in the extracellular fluid compartment and serves to maintain acid-base balance, is the carbonic acid-sodium bicarbonate buffer system, which operates in the lungs and kidneys. Under normal circumstances, the body maintains a balanced ratio of one part carbonic acid (1.2 mmol/L) to twenty parts bicarbonate (24 mEq/L) in order to maintain a pH of 7.40 (Figure 2-21).

The carbonic acid supply is regulated by the respiratory system. Carbon dioxide, as it is formed during cellular metabolic processes, is returned to the extracellular fluid where the enzyme carbonic anhydrase acts on the water and carbon dioxide to form volatile carbonic acid. At the alveolar capillary bed, carbon dioxide is exchanged for oxygen during internal respiration. The lungs remove the carbon dioxide from the body by means of external respiration. Whenever the carbon dioxide level rises, the respiratory center of the brain in the medulla is stimulated. It signals the lungs to increase the rate and depth of respirations and rid the body of excess carbon dioxide. When carbon dioxide levels drop too low, the same mechanisms trigger a decrease in the rate and depth of respirations so that the 1:20 carbonic acid-bicarbonate ratio is maintained by holding back carbon dioxide so it can be transformed into carbonic acid.

The kidneys fine-tune the pH by supporting respiratory regulation of acid-base balance. In the renal tubules of the kidneys, nonvolatile acids are removed. During the formation of urine, acid and alkaline phosphates are altered to produce an acid urine. This mechanism conserves sodium, potassium, magnesium, and calcium, all of which maintain the body's fixed base. In the presence of acidosis, the kidneys assist in the regulation of acid-base balance through the excretion of hydrogen ions and the retention of bicarbonate

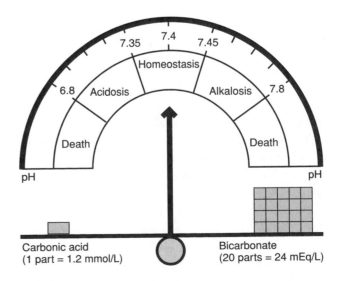

Figure 2-21 | Acid-base scale

ions. They also manufacture bicarbonate from carbon dioxide and water. In alkalotic situations, the kidneys retain hydrogen ions and excrete bicarbonate ions.

The kidneys and lungs function as compensatory systems in balancing acids and bases, maintaining the 1:20 ratio of carbonic acid to bicarbonate. While the respiratory adjustments of acid-base balance occur rapidly, renal mechanisms take longer to restore pH neutrality (up to 72 hr).

The Phosphate Buffer System

Phosphates serve as intracellular and extracellular buffers. The concentration of phosphates is greatest within the cell, making phosphates powerful intracellular buffers. Because of this, the normal hydrogen ion concentrations within the cell can be maintained, which results in acid-base balance.

The Protein Buffer System

The protein buffer system, the largest and strongest buffer system in the body, exists in both the intracellular and extracellular compartments, but is mainly a mechanism of the intracellular fluid. It is able to maintain acid-base balance because the proteins carry numerous negative charges that can buffer positively charged hydrogen ions. Some proteins are unique, however, in that one part of their molecule is able to accept hydrogen ions, while another portion can release hydrogen ions.

Hemoglobin, which carries a negative charge, acts as a strong protein buffer. When carbon dioxide diffuses into a red blood cell, it reacts with part of the hemoglobin molecule to form carbaminohemoglobin, which combines with water to form carbonic acid. The carbonic acid is catalyzed by the enzyme carbonic anhydrase to dissociate into hydrogen and bicarbonate ions. The negatively charged bicarbonate ions diffuse out of the red blood cell into the plasma, allowing negatively charged chloride ions to diffuse into the cell in their place. This phenomenon is known as the *chloride shift*. The hydrogen ions derived from the carbonic acid dissociation are buffered because they combine with the negatively charged hemoglobin.

Acid-Base Imbalances

Whenever there is a change in the hydrogen ion concentration of the blood, acid-base imbalances can occur. The imbalances that relate to alterations in carbonic acid levels are referred to as respiratory disturbances, and those imbalances that are directed toward changes in bicarbonate ratios are considered metabolic disturbances. Any malfunction of the buffer systems results in respiratory acidosis or alkalosis, metabolic acidosis or alkalosis, or a combination.

Respiratory Acidosis (Carbonic Acid Excess)

Respiratory acidosis is the acid-base imbalance with an abnormally elevated hydrogen ion concentration and an excess of carbonic acid. This is the most common of the acid-base imbalances and refers to acidosis caused by a buildup of carbon dioxide in the body. The carbonic acid accumulation is the result of pulmonary hypoventilation. **Hypercapnia,** the increase of carbon dioxide in the blood, with resultant increase in the partial pressure of carbon dioxide (PCO_2) in the plasma, results from the retention of carbon dioxide by the lungs.

In respiratory acidosis, the excess carbon dioxide in the extracellular fluid lowers the carbonic acid-bicarbonate ratio. The kidneys compensate for respiratory alkalosis by increasing the plasma bicarbonate concentration, which helps return the carbonic acid-sodium bicarbonate ratio to normal, thus restoring the pH to normal (Figure 2-22).

Etiology and Contributing Factors

Respiratory acidosis, which may be acute or chronic, is usually the result of altered pulmonary ventilation owing to disease of the respiratory tract. It occurs with asthma, chronic obstructive pulmonary disease (COPD), pneumonia, bronchiectasis, and cardiopulmonary arrest. It is also associated with extreme abdominal pain, disorders that affect the respiratory muscles, pneumothorax, extreme obesity, and inadequate ventilation. In some instances, anesthetics, sedatives (including alcohol), hypnotics, and barbiturates contribute to this problem. Respiratory acidosis may be compensated by the kidneys or uncompensated.

Clinical Manifestations and Defining Characteristics

Clinically, the individual with respiratory acidosis may be weak and sluggish, and experience confusion and disorientation, which are signs of central nervous system depression. There may be a productive cough, dyspnea, and cyanosis, along with a barrel chest in patients with chronic lung disease.

If there is no renal compensation for the respiratory acidosis, the partial pressure of carbon dioxide rises abnormally (>45 mm Hg). The plasma pH is low (<7.35) and the plasma bicarbonate levels are normal. If the kidneys compensate for the respiratory acidosis, the plasma bicarbonate concentration will rise (>28 mEq/L) and the plasma pH will return to normal.

Intravenous Infusion Implications

The goal of treatment is to return the pH and the carbonic acid-bicarbonate ratio to normal, if the underlying cause of the acidosis can be corrected. If there is chronic lung disease, the intention is to enhance ventilation as much as possible.

Parenteral infusion therapy is not a primary treatment modality, although intravenous antibiotics and bronchodilators may be indicated. In this situation an intravenous infusion is usually in place to access the systemic circulation should the need arise. In severe cases, bicarbonate or one of its precursors (gluconate or lactate) may be required.

Respiratory Alkalosis (Carbonic Acid Deficit)

Respiratory alkalosis is an acid-base imbalance when plasma pH is high and the hydrogen ion concentration is abnormally low, with a deficiency of carbonic acid. This condition results in an increased carbonic acid-bicarbonate ratio and is relatively uncommon.

The kidneys are the only compensatory mechanism for respiratory alkalosis, and lowering the bicarbonate concentration restores the normal carbonic acid-bicarbonate ratio, thus returning the pH to normal (Figure 2-22).

Etiology and Contributing Factors

Respiratory alkalosis is caused by hyperventilation and the excessive loss of carbon dioxide. There is a decrease in the partial pressure of plasma carbon dioxide that results in hypocapnia. Both the rate and depth of respirations increase. It can occur as a secondary compensatory mechanism for metabolic acidosis.

The most common etiology is hyperventilation brought on by anxiety and tension. High altitudes induce hyperventilation owing to decreased atmospheric oxygen. Physical disorders and illnesses such as liver cirrhosis, hyperthyroidism, gram-negative sepsis, fever, and peritonitis, and some cardiopulmonary maladies, such as pulmonary edema or pulmonary embolism, are associated with hyperventilation. Central nervous system lesions, in which the

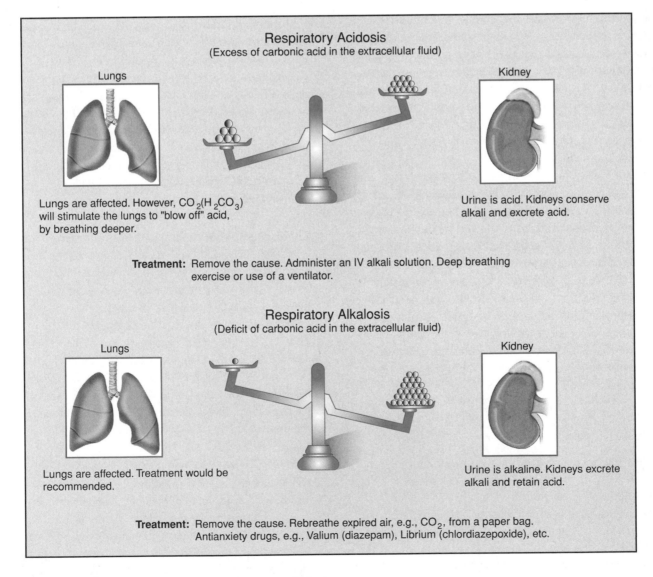

Respiratory Acidosis
(Excess of carbonic acid in the extracellular fluid)

Lungs

Kidney

Lungs are affected. However, $CO_2(H_2CO_3)$ will stimulate the lungs to "blow off" acid, by breathing deeper.

Urine is acid. Kidneys conserve alkali and excrete acid.

Treatment: Remove the cause. Administer an IV alkali solution. Deep breathing exercise or use of a ventilator.

Respiratory Alkalosis
(Deficit of carbonic acid in the extracellular fluid)

Lungs

Kidney

Lungs are affected. Treatment would be recommended.

Urine is alkaline. Kidneys excrete alkali and retain acid.

Treatment: Remove the cause. Rebreathe expired air, e.g., CO_2, from a paper bag. Antianxiety drugs, e.g., Valium (diazepam), Librium (chlordiazepoxide), etc.

Figure 2-22 | Respiratory acidosis and respiratory alkalosis

respiratory center in the brain is affected, induce respiratory alkalosis. These include tumors, trauma, encephalitis, and neurosurgery. Salicylate poisoning in its early stages induces hyperventilation. Asthmatic individuals often hyperventilate in response to air-hunger anxiety.

Clinical Manifestations and Defining Characteristics

Hyperventilation, with deep respirations, rapid respirations, or both, is the chief sign of respiratory alkalosis. Patients often complain of **paresthesias,** sensations of numbness or tingling, especially in the extremities. They often experience light-headedness, sweating, heart palpitations, and muscle cramping. Agitation and mental restlessness occur and may progress to hysteria and a state of temporary unconsciousness. In severe cases there can be tetany, convulsions, and coma, as seen in alcohol withdrawal (delirium tremens).

The levels of plasma pH (>7.45) and urine pH (>7.0) rise, while the partial pressure of carbon dioxide (<35 mm Hg) and the level of plasma bicarbonate fall (<21 mEq/L).

Intravenous Infusion Implications

As with all acid-base imbalances, the goal of treatment is to correct the underlying cause of the respiratory alkalosis and return the carbonic acid-sodium bicarbonate ratio to 1:20. Parenteral therapy is not a primary intervention, although it is used to support the kidneys in their compensatory attempts to retain chloride ions and excrete bicarbonate ions.

Intravenous infusions are used to replace the water lost during hyperventilation and to provide the nonbicarbonate chloride ions needed to replace lost bicarbonate ions. Even though the total concentration of calcium may be normal on laboratory reports, the CMA must be alert to the onset of tetany, which might occur in respiratory alkalosis because of a reduction in ionized calcium. Sodium and potassium ions are lost with increased chloride concentrations and need to be replaced. If calcium levels are replenished too rapidly, tetany may be induced.

Metabolic Acidosis (Base Bicarbonate Deficit)

Metabolic acidosis describes any acidotic condition related to an excess of noncarbonic acid concentrations and is characterized by a deficiency of base bicarbonate. Both the lungs and the kidneys compensate for this situation (Figure 2-23).

Etiology and Contributing Factors

There are several factors that contribute to the development of metabolic acidosis, and any one factor or a combination of factors can precipitate the disturbance. Whenever there is an abnormal increase in acid production, it can lead to a bicarbonate ion deficiency, a decrease in the carbonic acid-sodium bicarbonate ratio, an elevated hydrogen ion concentration, and a lowering of the pH.

Conditions that increase acid production are fever, infection, renal impairment, shock, salicylate poisoning, starvation, and impaired metabolic activity. The keto-acidosis that occurs in uncontrolled diabetes mellitus is a major cause of metabolic acidosis. Impaired cellular metabolism that occurs with fever and infectious processes, anesthesia, and circulatory failure contribute. In liver diseases such as hepatitis and cirrhosis, acidosis occurs as well. Other causes are disturbances in dietary intake associated with starvation, increased fat intake, or reduced carbohydrate intake. Situations when acids remain in the body are diarrhea, from loss of base in the stool, and renal insufficiency, when the kidneys are unable to rid the body of acids.

Clinical Manifestations and Defining Characteristics

Individuals with mild metabolic acidosis can be asymptomatic. As the situation worsens there may be weakness, malaise, nausea, vomiting, and abdominal pain. There is often deep, rapid breathing or shortness of breath with air hunger. If the condition becomes severe, the patient becomes stuporous and may lapse into coma. The pH of the urine (<6.0) and plasma (<7.35) is low, as are plasma bicarbonate concentrations (<21 mEq/L). Depending on compensatory mechanisms, the partial pressure of carbon dioxide (PCO_2) is normal or low.

Intravenous Infusion Implications

The primary concern is to correct the acidosis, identify and remove the underlying causes, and prevent both from recurring. Metabolic acidosis can be produced by the parenteral administration of acidifying salts. If there is excessive delivery of sodium chloride and ammonium chloride, the extracellular fluid may become overloaded with chloride, thus lowering the concentration of bicarbonate.

Fluid volume deficits and electrolyte imbalances that coexist with metabolic acidosis must be adjusted with intravenous fluids and electrolytes and monitored carefully. Special attention to potassium levels is critical. The CMA may be directed to administer sodium bicarbonate or sodium lactate if the acidosis is severe, or if interventions fail to treat the underlying cause.

Metabolic Alkalosis (Bicarbonate Excess)

Metabolic alkalosis describes all cases of alkalosis not caused by a carbonic-acid deficit. It occurs when the level of base bicarbonate is abnormally high or there is a decrease in the

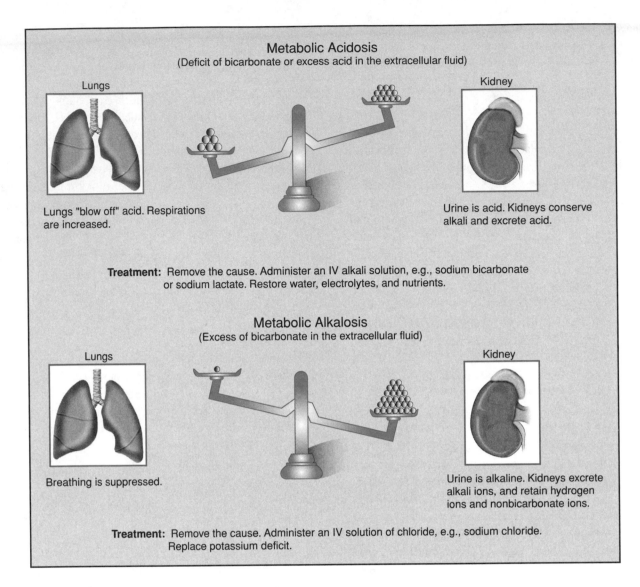

Metabolic Acidosis
(Deficit of bicarbonate or excess acid in the extracellular fluid)

Lungs

Kidney

Lungs "blow off" acid. Respirations are increased.

Urine is acid. Kidneys conserve alkali and excrete acid.

Treatment: Remove the cause. Administer an IV alkali solution, e.g., sodium bicarbonate or sodium lactate. Restore water, electrolytes, and nutrients.

Metabolic Alkalosis
(Excess of bicarbonate in the extracellular fluid)

Lungs

Kidney

Breathing is suppressed.

Urine is alkaline. Kidneys excrete alkali ions, and retain hydrogen ions and nonbicarbonate ions.

Treatment: Remove the cause. Administer an IV solution of chloride, e.g., sodium chloride. Replace potassium deficit.

Figure 2-23 | Metabolic acidosis and metabolic alkalosis

hydrogen ion concentration. With an excess of bicarbonate, there is an elevation in the carbonic acid-bicarbonate ratio.

Metabolic alkalosis is compensated for by the lungs and by the kidneys, but a compensatory respiratory acidosis usually occurs to restore the plasma pH by realigning the carbonic acid-bicarbonate ratio (Figure 2-23).

Etiology and Contributing Factors

Metabolic alkalosis occurs as a result of excessive intake of alkalis, such as sodium bicarbonate (baking soda) or the loss of acid, which results in an increased bicarbonate level. Vomiting and diarrhea can result in a loss of chloride and hydrogen ions, which causes an increase in blood bicarbonate, as well as a potassium deficit. Adrenal malfunction and renal failure can cause metabolic alkalosis, as can potent diuretics, tissue destruction, and hypercalcemia.

Clinical Manifestations and Defining Characteristics

Breathing patterns are depressed both in rate and in depth, a respiratory compensatory mechanism to raise the partial pressure of carbon dioxide and thus restore the carbonic acid-bicarbonate ratio. In contrast to metabolic acidosis, where there is central nervous system depression, there is hyperexcitability with hypertonicity of muscle activity and hyperactive reflexes. In severe metabolic alkalosis, there may be tetany and convulsions because of calcium loss. The plasma bicarbonate concentration is elevated (>28 mEq/L) as is the pH of the plasma (>7.45) and the urine (>7.0). The plasma concentrations of potassium and chloride are low.

Intravenous Infusion Implications

As with acidosis, treatment for metabolic alkalosis involves correcting the underlying cause, if possible. Infusion therapy often includes the administration of electrolytes. Since bicarbonate excess is usually associated with potassium deficit, the hypokalemic condition must be alleviated. The administration of chloride ions, which are retained by the body in place of excess bicarbonate ions, relieves the base bicarbonate excess characteristic of metabolic alkalosis. Fluid and electrolyte therapy is usually a necessary component of treatment. In severe cases, the careful administration of ammonium chloride, an acidifying salt, may be necessary. Whenever electrolyte solutions are administered intravenously, the CMA must be vigilant to thoroughly assess the patient's general condition, intake and output, and related laboratory values, in addition to monitoring and maintaining the infusions.

ELECTROLYTE BALANCES AND IMBALANCES

Fluid and electrolytes must be balanced within a narrow margin for homeostasis to be sustained. Illness and disease processes can easily disrupt this balance, often placing the patient in jeopardy.

For the CMA to provide safe care and effectively manage patient situations, it is necessary to understand the underlying concepts of electrolytes and their role in supporting homeostasis. He must be able to identify the causes of fluid-electrolyte and acid-base imbalances and recognize them in the clinical setting. When imbalances occur, not only is the CMA responsible for recognizing them, he is also responsible for reporting and intervening to correct any irregularities discovered.

While possessing a sound understanding of body fluids and their mechanisms of movement, the CMA also needs to fully comprehend the role of each major electrolyte and how it is regulated. By comprehending how electrolytes function to promote health, the CMA is able to identify how electrolyte imbalance relates to illness and disease, and thus intervene appropriately.

In managing intravenous infusions, the CMA is confronted with several interrelated responsibilities: maintaining fluid regulation so that a balance between loss and replacement exists, monitoring the patient's physical and psychological status, and administrating various products that promote fluid-electrolyte and acid-base equilibrium.

In this chapter, the major electrolyte imbalances and general treatment parameters will be addressed. Interventions with various replacement modalities will be covered later in the text, when specific solutions and guidelines for administration will be covered.

When referring to electrolyte imbalances, it should be remembered that they can be primary or secondary in nature. Primary imbalances exist in and of themselves, whereas secondary imbalances occur as a result of another pathophysiologic phenomenon.

Sodium

Sodium is the major cation (Na^+) of the extracellular fluid compartment and is regulated by ADH and aldosterone. Sodium is one of the primary regulators of fluid balance in the body. Sodium is excreted mainly by the kidneys, which regulate its reabsorption and excretion, depending on sodium intake. Sodium concentration in the plasma is maintained at a constant level and averages 135–145 mEq/L.

Purpose

As discussed earlier, sodium plays a primary role in the transmission of neuromuscular impulses and the maintenance of the cellular membrane potential. It is the principal regulator of osmotic pressure in the extracellular fluid.

Sodium Deficit

Primary sodium deficit results in the redistribution of water between the fluid compartments and changes in extracellular osmolality. **Hyponatremia** is an abnormal decrease in plasma sodium levels. When sodium output exceeds its intake, a deficit results. Any abnormal loss of body water produces a state of **dehydration. Hypertonic dehydration** occurs when there is a greater loss of water than salt, which leads to increased sodium concentration and increased osmolality of the extracellular fluid. When salt loss exceeds water loss, **hypotonic dehydration** occurs; **isotonic dehydration** is the result of a proportional loss of water and sodium.

Etiology and Contributing Factors

Hyponatremia can be caused by inadequate dietary intake of sodium or from excessive loss. Salt is lost from body fluids through several routes: urine, perspiration, vomiting, diarrhea, gastric suction, and potent diuretic therapy. If there is adrenal malfunction, the lack of aldosterone impairs kidney tubule reabsorption of sodium. In renal disease, acute or chronic, sodium loss in the urine is common. The administration of large volumes of intravenous 5% Dextrose in water or excessive drinking of pure (electrolyte-free) water can aggravate hyponatremia. When there is excessive sodium loss, replacement must come, not from pure water, but from fluids with sodium and chlorides because chloride loss accompanies sodium loss.

Clinical Manifestations and Defining Characteristics

The signs and symptoms associated with sodium deficiency, depending on its severity, can range anywhere from mild cramping to cardiovascular collapse. In severe hyponatremia, lethargy and stupor are the result of increased water uptake by the cells in the central nervous system. There may be fatigue, headache, muscle weakness, nausea, vomiting, abdominal cramping, and seizures. Postural hypotension, reduced urine output, and tachycardia are secondary to hypovolemia. The patient may go into a state of shock, manifested by signs of cold, clammy skin, diaphoresis, and cyanosis.

Interventions and Treatment

Prevention of hyponatremia is most important and results from a thorough history along with observation and assessment of the patient's physical findings. The most important prevention mechanism is the oral or parenteral administration of salt to maintain sodium balance.

Once hyponatremia occurs, treatment is guided by serum sodium levels with the goal of restoring the normal sodium concentration of the extracellular fluid, of reestablishing normal osmolality, and correcting fluid shift to the intracellular compartment. If losses occur, they should be replaced with solutions containing sodium and other electrolytes based on the extent of deficit.

Sodium Excess

Hypernatremia is an excess of sodium in the blood, resulting from positive sodium balance, and occurs when sodium intake exceeds loss. Primary hypernatremia is not a common electrolyte imbalance. Under normal circumstances, since sodium and water follow each other, an excess of sodium does not usually occur because water is retained to dilute the sodium.

Etiology and Contributing Factors

The cause of primary hypernatremia relates to excessive ingestion of salt without a corresponding water intake. The intravenous administration of excessive volumes of isotonic or hypertonic saline solutions leads to salt intoxication.

In primary sodium excess, there is salt intoxication with hypernatremia, an increase of fluid osmolality, and redistribution of water between the intracellular and extracellular fluids. Because of the elevated concentration of sodium in the extracellular compartment, water shifts out of the cell in order to promote osmotic balance. While this movement promotes extracellular volume, it does so at the expense of the intracellular fluid.

Clinical Manifestations and Defining Characteristics

The patient with hypernatremia is extremely thirsty with dry mucous membranes. The tongue is dry, red, and edematous, and the body temperature is elevated. As hypernatremia becomes more severe, the patient may become depressed, fatigued, and lapse into coma. Intracranial hemorrhage can occur. The serum sodium concentration (>145 mEq/L) and serum osmolality (>295 mOsm/kg) rise.

Interventions and Treatment

The primary treatment consists of removing the excess sodium from the body by limiting dietary and parenteral sources of intake. In addition, sodium-free fluids are infused to lower the serum sodium concentration and osmolality. In doing this, however, the extracellular compartment may expand. This fluid volume overload can result in pulmonary edema and heart failure. Sometimes dialysis may be the only recourse to lower serum sodium levels.

Potassium

Potassium (K^+) is the major cation of the intracellular compartment; its concentration is 3.5–5.0 mEq/L. Most of the body's potassium is found in voluntary muscle groups, with a substantial amount present in the skin, superficial tissues, and the red blood cells.

Potassium is regulated by the kidney tubules, where potassium ions exchange with sodium ions, and by the secretion of aldosterone, which controls potassium concentrations in the extracellular compartment. Aldosterone enhances renal tubular reabsorption of sodium and promotes the renal excretion of potassium and hydrogen ions. Gastrointestinal secretions of potassium are high, so a large amount is passed out through the feces. Because of the excretion through the renal and gastrointestinal systems, potassium must be replaced daily through dietary intake. If vomiting or diarrhea occurs, large amounts of these electrolytes are lost. Potassium is excreted through perspiration and is rapidly lost whenever there is tissue damage.

Purpose

Potassium maintains intracellular homeostasis and determines the cell's resting membrane potential. It assists various enzyme systems in catalyzing reactions and participates in protein synthesis and carbohydrate metabolism. Potassium is of vital importance in the transmission of electrical impulses in the cardiovascular, respiratory, and gastrointestinal systems.

Potassium Deficit

Hypokalemia is an abnormally low serum concentration of potassium that reflects an extracellular deficiency of the electrolyte. This is a fairly common deficiency, especially in hospitalized individuals. In some instances the levels can drop dangerously low before the imbalance is recognized. It is important to remember that, under normal conditions, losses of 25–50 mEq per day are expected.

Etiology and Contributing Factors

Several factors contribute to hypokalemia. Decreased dietary intake, especially in the older person, is common. During periods of fasting, as much as 40–50 mEq can be lost per day. Impaired potassium conservation occurs when sodium needs to be retained, as in periods of alkalosis or acidosis. The hydrogen ion deficit of alkalosis interferes with potassium conservation because there is a greater secretion of potassium into the distal portion of the renal tubules rather than hydrogen ions. With acidosis, potassium excretion is increased because of the mobilization of potassium from the intracellular compartment to the extracellular compartment.

Diuretic therapy is a very common cause of hypokalemia, especially when there are dietary restrictions of sodium. Vomiting, diarrhea, disease (e.g., inflammatory bowel disorder), and surgical procedures (e.g., ileostomy) of the gastrointestinal tract, where potassium levels are usually high, can deplete potassium stores rapidly. Other situations that precipitate the condition are tissue destruction (e.g., burns or crushing injuries), diabetes insipidus, hyperinsulinism, and malnutrition.

Clinical Manifestations and Defining Characteristics

Many of the signs and symptoms of hypokalemia are nonspecific and can relate to many different illnesses. The clinical picture of potassium deficiency is evidenced by an alteration in cardiovascular, respiratory, gastrointestinal, renal, and neuromuscular activity. Pulses are weak, heart sounds are faint, and the patient is prone to dysrhythmias. Respirations are shallow, and there is mental depression. There may be muscle weakness, depressed or absent reflexes, and paralysis. The patient complains of excessive thirst **(polydipsia),** excessive urination **(polyuria),** and may be anorexic. There is often nausea, vomiting, and diarrhea.

MEDICAL ASSISTING TIP

Adding Potassium to an Infusion Container

Always check agency policy regarding the amount of potassium that can be added to an infusion container. The amount may vary from one workplace to another.

The EKG will exhibit flattened or inverted T waves and S-T segment depression as well as premature ventricular contractions (PVCs). Serum concentration levels of potassium fall below normal (<3.5 mEq/L) and arterial blood gases show an increase in pH and bicarbonate levels.

Interventions and Treatment

Once the diagnosis of hypokalemia is made, oral replacement, parenteral potassium replacement, or both, must be undertaken, depending on the patient's condition. It is also necessary to determine the underlying cause of the deficit so that future losses can be prevented.

Potassium deficit is not usually an isolated imbalance, so the administration of water and other electrolytes may be needed. Before replacement therapy is started, it is necessary to determine renal function, since potassium is mainly excreted by the kidneys. If there is renal impairment, a buildup of potassium in the body can be toxic.

Replacement therapy for severe hypokalemia is undertaken with intravenous supplementations, under very close supervision, to prevent acute potassium intoxication. The dose should never exceed 80 mEq/L of potassium, and 40 mEq/L is preferable. Potassium must never be administered intravenously without diluting it in adequate volumes of fluid. Direct, undiluted administration usually results in cardiac arrest. The rate of administration should not exceed 20 mEq per minute.

MEDICAL ASSISTING ALERT

Potassium Dilution

Potassium must always be adequately diluted prior to intravenous administration to prevent cardiac dysrhythmias or even cardiac arrest. The maximum dose should be 80 mEq/L and must be administered only with caution and meticulous supervision. Never administer IV potassium by direct IV bolus.

During potassium replacement, serum electrolyte levels must be evaluated frequently. The patient must be meticulously observed for manifestations of both deficit and excess.

Potassium Excess

Hyperkalemia is an abnormal excess of potassium in the blood, mainly limited to the extracellular fluid. This condition is not as common as hypokalemia, but must be treated quickly because it is potentially life threatening.

Etiology and Contributing Factors

Hyperkalemia usually results from an increase in potassium intake without a corresponding excretion, but it can also occur because of a redistribution of the electrolyte from intracellular fluid to extracellular fluid. In general, excess dietary intake of potassium is not a cause of hyperkalemia unless there is altered renal function to impede its excretion in the urine.

Excessive oral or intravenous administration of potassium supplements contributes to hyperkalemia, as does the intake of potassium-sparing diuretics. Whenever there is tissue trauma from burns or crushing injuries, potassium leaks out of the cells and into the extracellular compartment, resulting in hyperkalemia. It is also associated with adrenal cortical insufficiency, such as Addison's disease, and a deficiency of aldosterone. Hyperkalemia occurs with diminished urinary output **(oliguria)** or total absence of urinary output (anuria) seen in renal failure.

Clinical Manifestations and Defining Characteristics

Hyperkalemia occurs when the serum potassium level rises (>5.0 mEq/L). The patient presents with muscle weakness, paresthesia, and even paralysis. There is often dizziness **(vertigo)** and painful muscle cramps. Gastrointestinal hyperactivity is usually present with nausea, intestinal colic, and diarrhea. The EKG shows peaked T waves and depressed S-T segments. If hyperkalemia is severe, the P wave flattens and the QRS complex widens.

Interventions and Treatment

The first step in treatment comes with the recognition of precipitating factors of hyperkalemia so that life-threatening situations of severe potassium excess are avoided. The goal of treatment is to remove the extracellular overload of the electrolyte. This can be accomplished through dietary restriction of potassium (in mild cases) or through the administration of oral or parenteral sodium chloride (to individuals who can tolerate the sodium load), which enhances urinary loss of potassium. If renal function is inadequate, potassium-free hydrating solutions can be given.

In hyperkalemic emergencies, the most rapid method of correction comes with the administration of glucose, insulin, and sodium polystyrene sulfonate, which promotes extracellular potassium movement into the cell. If acidosis is the problem, intravenous administration of sodium bicarbonate will move the potassium in the same manner. Diuretics may be given. Cardiac toxicity from elevated potassium levels may be alleviated by administering calcium gluconate or calcium carbonate. If renal insufficiency is present, dialysis may be needed to lower potassium levels.

Calcium

Calcium (Ca^{++}) is the most plentiful electrolyte in the body, with 99% of it stored in the bones and teeth. The 1% in the extracellular fluid is a minute amount, but maintenance of that concentration is of physiologic significance. Normal serum levels range between 4.4 mEq/L and 5.5 mEq/L.

Dietary calcium is absorbed in the small intestine (depending on pH and the presence of vitamin D), with about 80% excreted in the feces and the rest excreted in the urine. A very small amount can be lost through the skin with hyperthyroidism. Under normal conditions, urinary loss of calcium should balance its gastrointestinal absorption. With decreasing acidity, calcium is less readily absorbed in the bowel.

Purpose

Calcium is necessary for the strength and rigidity of bones and for normal coagulation of blood. It is extremely important for neuromuscular activity, especially myocardial stimulation. It has a role in cell membrane behavior by activating or inhibiting enzymatic activity.

Although the amount of calcium in the extracellular fluid is small, it is a vital component. Fifty percent is ionized and diffusible and governs parathormone secretion. The nonionized amount of serum calcium is bound to plasma proteins, mainly albumin.

The ionizing ability of the extracellular calcium is affected by acid-base balance. The increased pH of alkalosis decreases the serum concentration of ionized calcium, whereas the decreased pH of acidosis results in an increase of ionized calcium, at the expense of protein-bound nonionized calcium. A patient in acidosis may have a normal ionized calcium concentration while the total serum concentration will be low. For this reason, the determination of total serum calcium concentration must include serum albumin levels.

Calcium Deficit

Hypocalcemia is an abnormally low concentration of calcium in the blood. It is usually reflected in extracellular deficiency with the main problem a reduction of ionized calcium.

Etiology and Contributing Factors

There are numerous mechanisms that contribute to the development of hypocalcemia and a variety of illnesses and disease processes that cause the condition. One of the most common causes is hypoparathyroidism, where the mechanisms that regulate serum calcium concentrations are disrupted.

Nondietary vitamin D deficiency, due to pancreatitis, small bowel malabsorption, gastrointestinal shunt operations, or other intestinal disorders, is a cause, along with inadequate sun exposure. Because milk and many other food sources are fortified with vitamin D, dietary deficiency is rarely a problem in developed countries of the world. Burns and massive subcutaneous tissue infections induce calcium loss. Hypocalcemia can be induced through the administration of phosphate salts and alkalizing agents used to counteract acidosis, along with other drugs.

Clinical Manifestations and Contributing Factors

The extent of hypocalcemia necessary to elicit symptoms varies greatly among individuals. The EKG shows a normal T wave, but a prolonged Q-T interval because of a lengthened S-T segment. There is commonly the sensation of tingling and numbness of the circumoral area and the fingers. There can be abdominal and muscle cramps as well as spasm of both smooth (involuntary) and striated (voluntary, skeletal) muscles. Spasms of muscles in the face, larynx, bronchi, gastrointestinal tract, and the hands and feet can occur. Tetany is evidenced by a positive **Chvostek's sign** (unilateral facial muscle spasms when the 7th cranial or facial nerve is tapped anterior to the ear) and a positive **Trousseau's sign** (spasmodic contractions of the hands elicited by inflating a blood pressure cuff above systolic pressure for three minutes). There can be hyperactive deep tendon reflexes, depression, mood swings, memory impairment, hallucinations, and seizures.

Individuals with hypoparathyroidism and chronic hypocalcemia tend to have very dry skin, coarse hair with **alopecia** (hair loss), deformed nails, and poorly developed teeth. Cataracts are often a problem. An accompanying hyperphosphatemia may occur, with decreased urinary excretion of both calcium and phosphate.

Interventions and Treatment

In order to reestablish a normal serum concentration of ionized calcium, the underlying cause must be identified and treated. Increased dietary intake of calcium-rich foods is necessary along with oral calcium supplements. In emergency situations, with severe tetany and convulsions, intravenous calcium gluconate is usually administered. When the cause of an individual's hypocalcemia cannot be removed or controlled, continuous calcium salt infusions are given. If there is no response, low magnesium levels may be the problem, something common in patients with malabsorption syndromes, malnutrition, and alcoholism. Vitamin D supplements are administered to facilitate the absorption of calcium from the bowel.

Calcium Excess

Hypercalcemia is an abnormal excess of extracellular calcium. The main alteration is an excess of the ionized portion of calcium; serum levels exceed 5.3 mEq/L.

Etiology and Contributing Factors

Hypercalcemia results from several diseases and conditions. It occurs as a result of primary hyperparathyroidism where there is excessive parathormone secretion. A condition known as hypervitaminosis D occurs when there is increased bone resorption of the nutrient.

Hypercalcemia is a common complication associated with various malignant processes, including breast carcinoma, multiple myeloma, leukemia, and lymphoma, as well as lung and kidney neoplasms.

During periods of immobilization, there is decreased bone formation and bone resorption. Hypercalcemia occurs when the rate of demineralization exceeds the ability of the kidney to excrete the excess calcium.

Clinical Manifestations and Defining Characteristics

In hypercalcemia, there is a decrease in neuromuscular excitability, with reduced muscle tone and fatigue. Nausea, vomiting, anorexia, and weight loss are common. There is often deep bone pain related to pathologic fractures, and flank pain associated with the development of calcium renal stones because the kidneys cannot function appropriately with the increased calcium load.

In addition to increased serum calcium levels, the Q-T interval on the EKG is prolonged. In hyperparathyroidism, there is radiologic evidence of bone demineralization with cavitation.

When acute hypercalcemic crisis occurs, serum calcium levels rise drastically, resulting in a potentially fatal situation. There is intractable nausea, vomiting, polydipsia, polyuria, and dehydration, which lead to electrolyte imbalances. Delirium and coma usually follow.

Interventions and Treatment

If a patient has mild calcium elevation and is free of symptoms, treatment is conservative while its cause is determined. With acute hypercalcemic crisis, emergency measures must be initiated. Treatment of the underlying cause of excess calcium is directed toward lowering its concentration. Hypercalcemia with hypoparathyroidism may require surgical excision of the glands. Ambulation of an immobilized person often corrects hypercalcemia. Administration of sufficient fluids, while restricting calcium intake, is usually effective. Steroid treatment helps to counteract the hypercalcemia associated with malignancies.

Calcium-free fluid infusions are indicated in acute hypercalcemic crisis to hydrate the patient and promote urinary loss of calcium. Use of infusions containing calcium and phosphorus must be avoided. With extremely severe cases, dialysis is indicated to rid the body of excess calcium.

```
┌─────────────────────────────────────────────┐
│  M E D I C A L   A S S I S T I N G   A L E R T │
│                                               │
│  *Hypercalcemic Patients*                     │
│                                               │
│  In patients with hypercalcemia, intravenous  │
│  fluids must not contain calcium or phosphorus.│
└─────────────────────────────────────────────┘
```

Magnesium

Magnesium (Mg^{++}) is exceeded only by potassium in abundance in the intracellular compartment. It is regulated, with calcium, by the parathyroids. Approximately 50% is found in the bones, with the rest present in various organs, especially the heart, liver, and skeletal muscle. Most of the body's magnesium is ionized, while only about 30% is bound to protein. So, like calcium, albumin levels must be considered when assessing magnesium levels in the body.

The kidneys provide the main route for excretion of magnesium. When there is a deficiency, the kidneys conserve magnesium by excreting more potassium. Absorption of magnesium occurs in the small intestine. The body absorbs less than half of the magnesium ingested, unless more is needed, and excretes the excess in the stool. Normal blood magnesium level is 1.5–2.5 mEq/L.

Purpose

One of the main functions of magnesium is enzymatic cellular activation, especially for protein and carbohydrate metabolism. It is needed by nerve tissue, skeletal muscles, and the heart. Magnesium activates the sodium-potassium pump and is needed to maintain calcium levels within the cell.

Magnesium Deficit

Hypomagnesemia is an abnormal decrease in the serum concentration of magnesium. The condition reflects a deficiency in the ionized portion of the cation in the extracellular fluid.

Etiology and Contributing Factors

The causes of hypomagnesemia include decreased dietary intake, impaired absorption, excessive loss, or excessive use of magnesium-free infusions and thiazide diuretics. Vomiting, diarrhea, and intestinal surgeries contribute to magnesium loss as do malabsorption syndromes, parathyroid disease, alcoholism, and malnutrition. Cirrhosis, pancreatitis, vitamin D intoxication, chronic renal diseases, and diabetic acidosis also cause magnesium loss.

Clinical Manifestations and Defining Characteristics

Because magnesium deficits are accompanied by other electrolyte imbalances, the clinical picture of hypomagnesemia may mimic other situations, especially hypocalcemia. Hypomagnesemia leads to corresponding losses of sodium, calcium, and phosphorus. Until levels drop below 1.0 mEq/L, there may be no evidence of a problem.

The main nonspecific signs and symptoms of magnesium deficiency relate to increased neuromuscular irritability. Nonspecific T-wave alterations on the EKG may be present. There is usually confusion, agitation, hyperactive deep tendon reflexes, **nystagmus** (involuntary slow or rapid rhythmical eyeball oscillations that may be rotary [counterclockwise] or vertical [up-down motion]), painful paresthesias, tetany, and seizure disorders.

There may be tachycardia, dysrhythmias, and blood pressure deviations. Nausea, vomiting, anorexia, and abdominal distention occur.

Interventions and Treatment

Administration of oral, intramuscular, and intravenous magnesium salts is the main treatment modality. When seizures or dysrhythmias occur, high doses are given rapidly by the intravenous route.

Magnesium Excess

Hypermagnesemia is an abnormally high serum concentration of magnesium. This is a very rare imbalance.

Etiology and Contributing Factors

Renal failure, in which the kidneys fail to rid the body of excess magnesium (and other compounds), is the major cause of magnesium excess. Hypermagnesemia can also result from diabetic acidosis, hyperparathyroidism, and toxemia of pregnancy.

Clinical Manifestations and Defining Characteristics

There is usually neuromuscular depression that can lead to peripheral muscle paralysis, respiratory depression, hypotension, and cardiac arrest. The EKG shows a prolonged QRS interval with atrioventricular block. There is central nervous system depression that results in drowsiness progressing to coma, and the patient complains of feeling hot and thirsty. Nausea and vomiting are usually present.

Interventions and Treatment

Since most situations of excess magnesium are the result of renal failure, magnesium compounds must be avoided and parenteral magnesium solutions should not be used. Calcium gluconate is used to reverse the depressant effects caused by excess magnesium. Respiratory support may be needed.

Chloride

Chloride is the major extracellular anion (Cl^-), joining with sodium to make saline. Most of it is present in the interstitial fluid, the lymph, and blood, with a very small amount present inside the cell. The normal serum concentration of chloride is 100–110 mEq/L.

Purpose

Chloride serves to maintain the osmotic pressure of the blood. Chloride levels decline in relationship to decreases in sodium, a result of water excess or deficit. Whenever a sodium ion is reabsorbed by the kidneys, a chloride (or bicarbonate) ion is also reabsorbed to preserve acid-base neutrality. The ratio of sodium to chloride is normally 3:2. As discussed earlier, chloride plays a major role in acid-base balance.

Chloride Deficit and Excess

An abnormal decrease in serum chloride is called **hypochloremia.** When chloride levels fall, there is a compensatory rise in bicarbonate levels so that the number of anions and cations in the extracellular fluid balance. Hypochloremia can result from hypokalemic compensation and from diuretic loss of chloride over sodium. During vomiting and diarrhea, chloride is lost with sodium. **Hyperchloremia** is the abnormal elevation of serum chloride concentrations.

Clinical manifestations and treatment of hypochloremia and hyperchloremia are basically those associated with metabolic alkalosis and acidosis. (See Acid-Base Imbalances.)

Phosphorus (Phosphate)

Phosphorus (P^+) exists in the body as organic and inorganic salts with the bulk (85%) of it present in the bones as cellular organic salts. Most of the element exists in the body as phosphate (PO_4^-), making it the major ion of the intracellular compartment. It is well absorbed by the intestine and excreted by the kidneys. The normal serum concentration is 1.7–2.6 mEq/L or 2.5–4.5 mg/dl.

Purpose

Together with calcium, phosphate is regulated by parathormone, and plays an integral part in bone and tooth development. It is necessary for protein, fat, and carbohydrate metabolism and for the production and storage of ATP. Most of the B vitamins must combine with phosphorus in order to work. Phosphorus is needed for nerve and muscle functions and helps maintain the body's acid-base balance.

Phosphorus Deficit

An abnormal decrease in serum phosphorus is called **hypophosphatemia.** Under normal conditions, the kidneys reabsorb about 88% of ingested phosphorus. The intestine absorbs phosphorus more readily than it does calcium, so the kidneys excrete it more readily.

Etiology and Contributing Factors

Hypophosphatemia is usually related to deficient dietary intake or faulty absorption from the bowel because of vomiting, diarrhea, or vitamin D deficiency. Whenever there is a disruption of carbohydrate metabolism, as in diabetic acidosis or fever, phosphorus levels decline. Thiazide diuretics and hypoparathyroidism increase the loss of phosphorus from the kidney. Loss also occurs in the presence of potassium and magnesium deficiencies. Frequent ingestion of antacids, which are not absorbed, contributes to phosphorus depletion.

Clinical Manifestations and Defining Characteristics

The usual symptoms of acute phosphorus deficiency are muscle weakness and skeletal soreness, with progression to confusion and disorientation, convulsions, and coma. If the condition is chronic, there is memory loss, anorexia, and malaise, along with bone pain and joint stiffness.

Interventions and Treatment

As with all imbalances, prevention is the best treatment. Dietary supplementation is recommended for mild deficiency, and oral supplements are recommended for moderate deficiencies. In severe loss or when there is inadequate bowel function, intravenous sodium or potassium phosphate is used.

Phosphorus Excess

Hyperphosphatemia is the abnormal excess of serum phosphorus. The kidneys, when functioning normally, excrete excess phosphorus on a continual basis.

Etiology and Contributing Factors

Renal failure, acute and chronic, is the main cause of phosphorus excess. Hyperphosphatemia occurs with hyperthyroidism, excessive bone growth, or excessive doses of vitamin D. Some forms of cancer chemotherapy destroy cells, resulting in the release of large amounts of phosphorus into the circulation.

Clinical Manifestations and Defining Characteristics

There is little subjective evidence of transient phosphorus excess, and the symptoms that exist vary among patients. If the condition is severe, nausea, vomiting, and anorexia may occur. There may be digital and circumoral numbness, tingling, muscle spasms, and tetany. Tachycardia may be present and the EKG will record shortened S-T and Q-T intervals.

With chronic hyperphosphatemia, the kidneys and other soft tissues of the body are compromised. Calcium phosphate builds up in the kidneys, joints, and skin. The arteries, heart, gastric mucosa, and eyes may be affected.

Interventions and Treatment

Treatment, unless phosphorus excess results from dietary or drug sources, is aimed at remediating or controlling the underlying disorder. For hyperparathyroidism, surgical removal of the glands may be indicated. Dialysis is indicated for individuals with renal failure. In acute situations, intravenous administration of calcium may be necessary.

The usual treatment is dietary restriction of phosphorus and the administration of magnesium, calcium, or aluminum antacids that bind the phosphorus to solids in the intestine, thus removing it in the stools.

Review Questions and Activities

1. Why is it necessary for the CMA to understand fluid and electrolyte acid-base balance?

2. Make a two-column figure listing the components of the intracellular fluid compartment in one column and the components of the extracellular compartment in the other column.

3. What is the function of the cell membrane in maintaining electrolyte balance?

4. What are the differences among the passive transport, active transport, and vesicle transport of substances into and out of the cell?

5. Diagram the series of events that occur in the cell membrane to illustrate the membrane at rest, at depolarization, and at repolarization.

6. What is the difference between respiratory and metabolic acidosis? Between respiratory and metabolic alkalosis?

7. How does each of the three buffer systems of the body maintain acid-base balance?

8. Make a table listing the electrolytes sodium, potassium, calcium, magnesium, chloride, and phosphate. In the appropriate columns, identify two functions of each electrolyte, and two physiologic occurrences that result from (1) a deficiency, and (2) an excess of the electrolyte.

9. Create a physiologic flow sheet that illustrates how fluid and electrolyte acid-base balance contributes to homeostasis.

Chapter 3

Infection Control and Safety Measures Related to Intravenous Infusion Therapy

LEARNING OBJECTIVES

Upon completion of this chapter, the reader should be able to:

* Explain why hand hygiene is the single most important means of preventing the spread of infection.

* Discuss ways to break the chain of infection.

* State the CDC-recommended guidelines regarding postexposure prophylaxis following occupational exposure to HIV.

* Examine the rulings of the Occupational Safety and Health Administration as they pertain to health care personnel.

* Compare and contrast the advantages and disadvantages of the antiseptic agents used most often for intravenous therapy.

* Describe the recommended dressings available for intravenous infusion sites.

* Outline the approved protocols for intravenous tubing care.

* Evaluate the role of the CMA in preventing nosocomial infections as they apply to intravenous infusion therapy.

INFECTION CONTROL

The goal of infection control is to break the chain of infection at any link that will bring about the prevention of disease or its transmission. By following the guidelines of the Centers for Disease Control (CDC) and the enforcement directives of the Occupational Safety and Health Administration (OSHA) and the Association of Practitioners in Infection Control and Epidemiology, Inc. (APIC), and by adhering to professional standards of care and practice, the goal of infection control can be achieved for both the patient and health care personnel.

When infection occurs, it is important to identify it as soon as possible, determine the circumstances that precipitated it, use the most efficient means to eradicate it, and alter conditions in such a way so as to prevent its recurrence (Figure 3-1).

Nosocomial Infections

An infection that develops in a patient during or after and as a result of a stay in a health care setting is called a **nosocomial infection.** It is distinctly different from a **community-acquired infection,** which is acquired or incubating prior to an admission to a health care facility.

Nosocomial infections and medical errors, collectively referred to as preventable "adverse health events," are responsible for 44,000 to 98,000 deaths per year at a cost of $17–$29 billion (Institute of Medicine, 1999). Hospital-acquired infections affect approximately two million persons each year (Gaynes et al., 2001). There are three major influences related to nosocomial infections: overuse of antimicrobial products (which decrease resistance), failure of hospital personnel to follow basic infection control practices (espe-

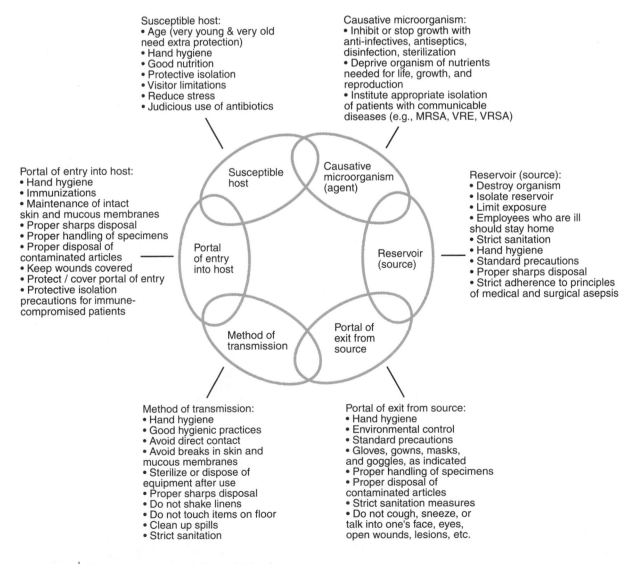

Susceptible host:
• Age (very young & very old need extra protection)
• Hand hygiene
• Good nutrition
• Protective isolation
• Visitor limitations
• Reduce stress
• Judicious use of antibiotics

Causative microorganism:
• Inhibit or stop growth with anti-infectives, antiseptics, disinfection, sterilization
• Deprive organism of nutrients needed for life, growth, and reproduction
• Institute appropriate isolation of patients with communicable diseases (e.g., MRSA, VRE, VRSA)

Portal of entry into host:
• Hand hygiene
• Immunizations
• Maintenance of intact skin and mucous membranes
• Proper sharps disposal
• Proper handling of specimens
• Proper disposal of contaminated articles
• Keep wounds covered
• Protect / cover portal of entry
• Protective isolation precautions for immune-compromised patients

Reservoir (source):
• Destroy organism
• Isolate reservoir
• Limit exposure
• Employees who are ill should stay home
• Strict sanitation
• Hand hygiene
• Standard precautions
• Proper sharps disposal
• Strict adherence to principles of medical and surgical asepsis

Method of transmission:
• Hand hygiene
• Good hygienic practices
• Avoid direct contact
• Avoid breaks in skin and mucous membranes
• Sterilize or dispose of equipment after use
• Proper sharps disposal
• Do not shake linens
• Do not touch items on floor
• Clean up spills
• Strict sanitation

Portal of exit from source:
• Hand hygiene
• Environmental control
• Standard precautions
• Gloves, gowns, masks, and goggles, as indicated
• Proper handling of specimens
• Proper disposal of contaminated articles
• Strict sanitation measures
• Do not cough, sneeze, or talk into one's face, eyes, open wounds, lesions, etc.

Figure 3-1 | Methods to break the chain of infection

cially proper hand hygiene), and an increase in the immuno-compromised patient population (Weinstein, 1998).

An estimated 200,000 nosocomial BSIs occur each year, most of which are related to the use of an intravascular device (CDC, Guideline for Prevention of Intravascular Device-Related Infections, 2001a). Intravascular catheter-related infections are a major cause of morbidity and mortality in the United States. Coagulase-negative staphylococci, *S. aureus*, aerobic gram-negative bacilli, and *Candida albicans* most commonly cause catheter-related BSIs (Mermel et al., 2001). The CDC estimates that one-third of all nosocomial infections are preventable.

Nosocomial infections usually target those who are immunocompromised as a result of advanced age, underlying disease processes, or medical/surgical interventions. Nosocomial infection rates in intensive care units (ICUs) occur at three times the rate of other areas within a hospital, with the sites of infection and the pathogens involved being directly related to ICU treatment (Weinstein, 1998). ICU patients with invasive vascular catheters and monitoring devices have the highest incidence of BSIs.

The predominant organism that is responsible for intravenous catheter infections and the main organism that resides on the skin is *S. aureus*, which enters the bloodstream from the catheter lumen or the outside of the catheter surface (Sadovsky, 2000). *S. aureus* is capable of collecting on clothing, blankets, walls, and medical equipment. It is the number one cause of hospital infections, is blamed for about 13% of the nation's nosocomial infections, and kills over 80,000 people annually (CDC, *CDC Guideline for Prevention of Intravascular Device-Related Infections*, 2002).

Nosocomial infections present a major health care problem, with serious consequences in terms of **morbidity** (the incidence of illness), **mortality** (the incidence of deaths), and the millions of dollars spent each year on diagnosing and treating them. In addition, there are major legal ramifications for health care personnel and their employers whenever nosocomial infections occur. The public has the right to a safe level of care when entering any health care setting and at the very least should be protected from infection occurring as a direct result of care in such an environment.

The most common organisms responsible for nosocomial infections are *Escherichia coli*, *Pseudomonas aeruginosa*, enterococci, and staphylococci. *Staphylococcus epidermidis* accounts for the majority of intravenous cannula-related nosocomial infections (CDC, 1995). Contamination from the patient's own skin or that of the CMA (with eventual cannula colonization) accounted for 28% of all BSIs reported to the National Nosocomial Infection Surveillance System (NNISS). Since the mid-1980s, there has been an increase in the proportion of nosocomial BSIs due to gram-positive, rather than gram-negative, species (CDC, 1995). The major portion of the overall increase in nosocomial BSIs has been due to four

pathogens: coagulase-negative staphylococci (CoNS), *Candida spp.*, enterococci, and *Staphylococcus aureus*. Fungal pathogens account for an increasing proportion of BSIs as well. Between 1980 and 1990, in reports to NNIS, there had been nearly a fivefold increase in the rate of nosocomial fungal BSIs, with *Candida spp.* (particularly *Candida albicans*) accounting for more than 75% of all reported infections (CDC, 1995). It was hypothesized that candidemia arises from the endogenous flora of colonized patients. Recent epidemiologic investigations, however, point to exogenous infection resulting from the "administration of contaminated fluids, use of contaminated equipment, cross-infection, and the colonized hands of health care workers" (CDC, 1995).

In the past, people were admitted to health care facilities—especially hospitals—for conditions that today are treated largely on an outpatient basis or at home. With the changes in technology, Medicare, and the insurance industry, patients admitted to hospitals are "sicker and leave quicker" than ever before. Because of this, patients are susceptible to contracting nosocomial infections through exposure to numerous sources of contamination—other patients, health care personnel, visitors, equipment, machinery, treatment modalities—all harboring potential pathogens. This is especially true if the patients are immunocompromised, very old, or very young. The population at large is living longer with an upward trend in the number of senior citizens. Infants and children who in the past did not survive because of prematurity, low birth weight, and exposure to communicable diseases are now kept alive by advanced technology. The elderly, who often have pre-existing illness, and multiple disease processes, and who are on numerous medications, are much more susceptible to infection than the general adult population, as are the very young. The treatment regimens for such patients often include the intravenous administration of fluids, nutrients, blood products, and life-saving medications. Nosocomial infections that are contracted as a result of intravenous infusion can be prevented or reduced considerably through diligent infection control practices.

Nosocomial infections must be prevented at all cost by carefully observing every patient for any signs or symptoms of infection. For the patient undergoing infusion therapy, any untoward reactions should immediately be evaluated and the necessary measures taken to prevent complications. Health care personnel must utilize standard precautions or body substance isolation (BSI) and follow all required isolation protocols and infection control policies and procedures. Documentation must be accurate and individualized for every patient.

Hand Hygiene

Clean hands, achieved through proper hand hygiene, are the single most important factor in preventing the spread of dangerous germs and antibiotic resistance in health care settings. Good hand hygiene can be achieved through the use of either a waterless, alcohol-based product or appropriate handwashing (Table 3-1) with an antibacterial soap and water with adequate rinsing (CDC, Centers for Disease Control: MMWR—Morbidity and Mortality Weekly Report—Recommendations and Reports. October 25, 2002/Vol. 51/No RR-216. *Guideline for Hand Hygiene in Health-Care Settings: Recommendations of the Healthcare Infection Control*

Practices Advisory Committee and the HICPAC/SHEA/APIC/IDSA Hand Hygiene Task Force. 2002d).

Hand hygiene by washing must be carried out properly by washing with running water, soap (an emulsifier), and vigorous friction for a period of at least 10–15 seconds, covering all hand surfaces, followed by thorough rinsing and drying. For routine patient care, there are no specific guidelines that dictate what type of soap is to be used by health care personnel

---

Table 3-1 | Hand Hygiene Guidelines

Hand hygiene can be accomplished with proper handwashing or with the use of alcohol-based handrubs.

WHEN
Upon arrival…
Before preparing…
Before preparing medications
Before and after…
Before donning gloves
(Gloves are *not* a substitute for handwashing or hand antisepsis with alcohol-based handrubs.)
After removing gloves (as mandated by OSHA)
Before and after personal…
Before and after eating
Before leaving work
After any exposure…
Handwashing is to be carried out

WITH
Running water at a comfortable temperature
Soap (emulsifier). Use the correct kind, depending on the degree of contamination and the level and type of antimicrobial effectiveness required. Plain soap mechanically removes transient bacteria from the skin, but does not kill the bacteria released by the shedding of dead skin cells. Antimicrobial soap mechanically removes, kills, or inhibits bacteria, depending on the levels of product activity. Antiseptic hand rubs kill or inhibit bacteria, depending on the levels of product activity, but do not remove soil.
Friction (vigorous rubbing)
Towels (paper, from dispenser) or warm air dryer for drying

HOW
Wet hands and wrists.
Apply the correct soap or antiseptic.
Apply vigorous friction, and maintain the vigorous rubbing for 10 to 15 seconds (longer if hands are visibly soiled), covering all hand surfaces, including thumbs and between the backs of fingers, with particular attention to fingertips and nails.
Rinse, in a flowing stream of water, from the wrists to finger tips. In the absence of water, use alternative agents (detergent-based towelettes to remove light soil; alcohol-based to reduce microbial flora).
Dry wrists and hands thoroughly with paper towel from wrists to finger tips (while water is still running) or with automated dryers. Activate lever-operated towel dispensers before washing and activate hand dryers with elbow.
Drop towel into waste container (without touching the container).
Obtain a dry paper towel and turn off the faucets (unless automated sinks are available). The dry towel is a more effective barrier to use to touch the contaminated faucet; a used towel is a weak barrier and bacteria may be "wicked" back onto the hand.

for hand hygiene. Employer guidelines should be followed. Prior to invasive procedures, such as the insertion of intravenous devices or before manipulating central venous access lines, many practitioners of infection control recommend handwashing using antiseptic or antimicrobial compounds that contain germicidal properties, such as chlorhexidine gluconate or iodine. A **germicide** is an agent capable of killing germs. The germicides contained in any handwashing agents must be those listed as safe by the Environmental Protection Agency (EPA). Plain soap mechanically removes transient bacteria from the skin but does not kill the bacteria released by the shedding of dead skin cells. The term **antimicrobial** refers to any product that hinders the pathogenic activity of microorganisms on any surface. Antimicrobial soap products mechanically remove, kill, or inhibit bacterial growth. They have varying levels of action and may display bactericidal activity (killing of organisms), bacteriostatic activity (inhibition of organisms), or persistent activity (sustained reduction or inhibition of organisms over time). An **antiseptic** is a product that can safely be applied to the skin or the surface of mucous membranes, thus inhibiting microbial growth or destroying organisms. Antiseptic hand rubs, which have varying levels of activity, may kill or inhibit bacteria but do not remove soil.

Hand hygiene must be performed before and after each patient contact, after contact with patient belongings, after contact with blood and body substances, before setting up equipment, before and after performing patient-related procedures, before eating, and after performing personal hygiene measures (e.g., toilet use). Hand hygiene is a medical aseptic technique that removes infectious organisms. **Asepsis** is the absence of infectious organisms. **Medical asepsis** (clean technique) refers to the absence of pathogenic organisms, whereas **surgical asepsis** (sterile technique) describes the removal of all microorganisms, pathogenic or nonpathogenic.

When in doubt, carry out proper hand hygiene thoroughly and frequently! The wearing of gloves does not preclude the need for hand hygiene. When health care personnel clean their hands frequently and correctly, they lower the populations of transient flora on their hands and inhibit the shedding of resident flora. Inherent in the practice of hand hygiene is educating others (health care personnel, students, patients, family members, and visitors) in the use of infection control protocols. In addition to hand hygiene, good personal hygiene must be maintained and fingernails should be kept clean and short. If nail polish is worn, it should be clear (so as not to obliterate visible dirt under nails) and free of chips so particles do not come off during patient care procedures. Artificial fingernails should not be worn because they increase the growth of gram-negative bacteria and fungus and may also breach the integrity of gloves (Larson, 1996).

Long natural nails and artificial nails harbor significantly more bacteria—both before and after handwashing—than do short natural nails. Both the CDC and APIC recommend that surgical and perioperative personnel wear short, natural nails due to the fact that handwashing is less effective at reducing bacterial colonization on hands with artificial nails. A study of 27 people with artificial nails colonized with gram-negative rods showed that the nails remained colonized with the organism following a five-minute surgical scrub (APIC, 2000). The most noteworthy link between long and artificial nails and a major *Pseudomonas aeruginosa* outbreak was published by the CDC in February 2000. Over a 15-month period, 16 neonate deaths were attributed to infant exposure to two nurses—one with long natural nails and a nurse with long artificial nails—in a newborn nursery. Both nurses harbored the *Pseudomonas* organism under their fingernails (Moolenaar et al., 2000). Another report confirms that three patients who acquired post-laminectomy deep-wound *Candida albicans* were linked to an operating room technician with artificial nails (Parry et al., 2001).

Short is a term used to describe nail length, but what does it mean? As a general guide, a fingernail that extends beyond the fingertip is considered too long. When gloves are routinely worn, tears occur in the glove's fingertips if the nails protrude over the edge of the fingertip, thus compromising barrier protection. In addition, patients can be harmed during routine care when nails are too long. "A sign of healthy fingernails is well-manicured nails—clean, short, with jagged nail tips smoothed away and with surrounding skin intact" (Wen-Tsung et al., 2002).

Some policy manuals recommend that nail polish, if worn, should be clear (so as not to obliterate visible dirt under nails) and free of chips so particles do not come off during patient-care procedures. Although this is considered safe by some, small polish chips may not be obvious to the wearer. Nail polish deteriorates, chips, and breaks away from the nail surface. The time it takes varies, based on the age of the polish, its adherence characteristics, the health of the nail, and the wearer's activity. Polish fragments are foreign bodies that can potentially cause a reaction when deposited in wounds through glove tears. Dermatologists report that reactions to nail hardeners and lacquers cause **onycholysis**, or loosening or detachment of the nail from the nailbed (Berger et al., 2000). "Studies have documented that subungual areas of the hand harbor high concentrations of bacteria, most frequently coagulase-negative staphylococci, gram-negative rods (including Pseudomonas spp.), Corynebacteria, and yeasts. . . . Even after careful handwashing or the use of surgical scrubs, personnel often harbor substantial numbers of potential pathogens in the subungual spaces" (CDC, 2002d, *Guideline for Hand Hygiene in Health-Care Settings*). Even though rings do not interfere with handwashing, they should be avoided in high-risk patient care areas because bacterial counts increase under rings (Jacobson, 1985).

Standard Precautions

In 1987, the CDC published *Recommendations for Prevention of HIV Transmission in Health Care Settings*. This was an update of its 1983 guidelines for handling blood and body fluids, in which precautions were listed for only those patients who were known to have, or were suspected of having, infected bloodborne pathogens. Because of the AIDS epidemic, the 1987 document "emphasizes the need for health care workers to consider *all* patients as potentially infected with HIV and/or other bloodborne pathogens and to adhere rigorously to infection-control precautions for minimizing the risk of exposure to blood and body fluids of all patients." Under Standard Precautions, blood and certain other bodily fluids of all patients are considered potentially infectious for human immunodeficiency virus (HIV), hepatitis viruses, and other bloodborne pathogens.

Standard Precautions pertain to blood and any other body fluids containing visible blood, as well as semen and vaginal secretions. Since the risk of transmission of HIV and hepatitis viruses is not known fully, and research is ongoing in this area, the CDC extends Standard Precautions to cerebrospinal, synovial, pleural, peritoneal, pericardial, and amniotic fluids.

Unless there is visible blood, Standard Precautions do not apply to feces, urine, vomitus, nasal secretions, saliva, spu-

tum, tears, and perspiration. Although the risk of transmitting HIV and hepatitis from these fluids is very low, common sense should be used in handling such materials. Health care personnel must remember that these may be sources of contamination from other organisms. Breast milk, although implicated in the perinatal transmission of HIV and the hepatitis B-specific antigen (HBsAG), is not considered an occupational threat to health care personnel.

Standard Precautions are not considered to be a replacement for routine infection control protocols, but serve as a supplement to them. The need for other disease category-specific isolation procedures, such as respiratory or enteric precautions, still prevails. Good judgment must always be used, along with good hand hygiene and the wearing of gloves (Table 3-2), to prevent contamination of hands.

Occupational Safety and Health Administration Guidelines

Blood and other potentially infectious materials have long been recognized as a potential threat to the health of employees who are exposed to these materials by **percutaneous contact** (penetration of the skin). Injuries from contaminated needles and other sharps have been associated with an increased risk of disease from more than 20 infectious agents. The primary agents of concern in current occupational settings are the human immunodeficiency virus (HIV), hepatitis B virus (HBV), and hepatitis C virus (HCV) (OSHA, 2001).

The CDC has estimated that health care personnel in hospital settings sustain 384,325 percutaneous injuries involving contaminated sharps annually. When nonhospital health care personnel are included, the best estimate of the number of percutaneous injuries involving contaminated sharps is 590,164 per year (CDC, 2001a, Guidelines for Prevention of Intravascular Device-Related Infections). When these injuries involve exposure to infectious agents, the affected workers are at risk of contracting disease. Workers may also suffer from adverse side effects of drugs used for postexposure prophylaxis and from psychological stress due to the threat of infection following an exposure incident.

To reduce the health risk to personnel whose duties involve exposure to blood or other potentially infectious materials, OSHA promulgated the Blood Borne Pathogen (BBP) standard on December 6, 1991. The provisions of the standard were based on the Agency's determination that a combination of engineering and work practice controls, personal protective equipment, training, medical surveillance, hepatitis B vaccination, signs and labels, and other requirements would minimize the risk of disease transmission. Since the inception of this standard, needlesticks and other percutaneous injuries resulting in exposure to blood or other

Table 3-2 | Glove Guidelines (Source: APIC, 1999)

GLOVE GUIDELINES

Type to use:	**Medical grade examination (nonsterile) or surgical (sterile)**
	Natural rubber latex. The natural rubber provides dexterity, durability, flexibility, and tactile sensitivity and is preferred for procedures that are moderate-to-high risk for exposure to blood and other potentially infectious materials and when nonsterile hand protection is indicated. Change every 15–30 minutes, depending on the procedure, the amount of blood/fluid exposure, and contact with sharps.
	Nitrile. The preferred choice for latex-sensitive individuals and those with moderate-to-high risk for exposure to blood and other potential contaminants. Higher chemical resistance than latex to hydrocarbon-based products (lanolin, mineral oil, petrolatum).
	Vinyl synthetic. Appropriate for short-term use involving minimal stress on the glove and low risk of exposure to blood and other potentially infectious materials.
When to wear:	• Handling contaminants • Reasonable likelihood for contact with blood, potentially infectious materials, mucous membranes, and nonintact skin • Touching potentially contaminated items or surfaces • Vascular access procedures
What to do:	• Wear correct size • Keep fingernails short to prevent tears • Wash hands before and after use • Change frequently, depending on length of exposure to blood, potential sources of infection, contaminants, and procedure length • Change between patients • Change between tasks on same patient • Change both gloves (if double-gloving for safety) and wash hands before starting another task • Generously use water-soluble lotions/moisturizers (approved for health care use) to prevent skin abrasions
What not to do:	• Use nonmedical-grade gloves for direct patient care • Use gloves when there is no potential for contact with blood or contaminants (such as taking vital signs or charting) • Use hydrocarbon-based hand products with natural rubber latex gloves (which will cause gloves to break down within minutes of exposure) • Use fragranced hand-care products (which will cause chemical irritation to hands) • Store gloves near heat, sunlight, electrical machines, or areas of temperature extremes

potentially infectious materials continue to be of concern due to the high frequency of their occurrence and the severity of the health effects associated with exposure.

Since publication of the BBP standard, a wide variety of medical devices have been developed to reduce the risk of needlesticks and other sharps injuries. These "safer medical devices" replace sharps with non-needle devices or incorporate safety features designed to reduce the likelihood of injury. In 1998, OSHA solicited information on occupational exposure to bloodborne pathogens due to percutaneous injury. Based in part on the information received, OSHA pursued an approach to minimize the risk of occupational exposure to BBP that involves (1) a revised recordkeeping mechanism requiring that all percutaneous injuries from contaminated needles and other sharps be recorded on OSHA logs, (2) a revised compliance directive for the BBP standard (November 5, 1999), and (3) the placing of an amendment of the BBP standard on its regulatory agenda to more effectively address sharps injuries.

In response to OSHA's findings, the growing concern over bloodborne pathogen exposures from sharps injuries, and technological developments that increase employee protection,

Congress was prompted to take action. On November 6, 2000, the Needlestick Safety and Prevention Act (Pub. L. 106-430) was signed into law by President Clinton. The Act required OSHA to revise the Blood Borne Pathogen standard, with specific language included in the Act, within six months of the enactment.

The revised Blood Borne Pathogen standard took effect on April 18, 2001. The revised definitions do not reflect any new requirements being placed on employers with regard to protecting workers from sharps injuries, but are meant only to clarify the original standard of 1991 and to reflect the development of new, safer medical devices since that time.

The revisions to OSHA's BBP Standard required under the Needlestick Safety and Prevention Act are broadly categorized into the following four areas.

1. Modification of definitions relating to engineering controls.

The revised standard adds *sharps with engineered sharps injury protections* and defines this term as "a non-needle sharp or a needle device used for withdrawing body fluids, accessing a vein or artery, or administering medications or other fluids, with a built-in safety feature or mechanism that effectively reduces the risk of an exposure incident." This term encompasses a broad array of devices that make injury involving a contaminated sharp less likely, and includes, but is not limited to, syringes with a sliding sheath that shields the attached needle after use; needles that retract into a syringe after use; shielded or retracting catheters used to access the bloodstream for intravenous administration of medication or fluids; and intravenous medication delivery systems that administer medication or fluids through a catheter port or connector site using a needle that is housed in a protective covering.

The revised standard also adds the term *needleless system,* which is defined as "a device that does not use needles for: (A) The collection of bodily fluids or withdrawal of body fluids after initial venous or arterial access is established; (B) the administration of medication or fluids; or (C) any other procedure involving the potential for occupational exposure to bloodborne pathogens due to percutaneous injuries from contaminated sharps." Needleless systems provide an alternative to needles for specified procedures, thereby reducing the risk of percutaneous injury involving contaminated sharps. Examples of needleless systems include, but are not limited to, intravenous medication delivery systems that administer medication or fluids through a catheter port or connector site using a blunt cannula or other non-needle connection, and jet injection systems that deliver subcutaneous or intramuscular injections of liquid medication through the skin without use of a needle.

The definition of *engineering controls* has been modified to include "safer medical devices, such as sharps with engineered sharps injury protections and needleless systems." This change clarifies that safer medical devices are considered to be engineering controls under the standard. The term *engineering control* includes all control measures that isolate or remove a hazard from the workplace, encompassing not only sharps with engineered sharps injury protections and needleless systems but also other medical devices designed to reduce the risk of percutaneous exposure to bloodborne pathogens. Examples include blunt suture needles and plastic or mylar-wrapped glass capillary tubes, as well as controls that are not medical devices, such as sharps disposal containers and biosafety cabinets.

2. Revision and updating of the Exposure Control Plans.

The review and update of the plan is now required to "(A) reflect changes in technology that eliminate or reduce exposure to bloodborne pathogens; and (B) document annually consideration and implementation of appropriate commercially available and effective safer medical devices designed to eliminate or minimize occupational exposure." Thus, the additional provisions require that employers, in their written Exposure Control Plans, account for innovations in procedure and technological developments that reduce the risk of exposure incidents. The revised Exposure Control Plan requirements make clear that employers must implement the safer medical devices that are appropriate, commercially available, and effective.

3. Solicitation of employee input.

The revised standard now requires that "An employer, who is required to establish an Exposure Control Plan, shall solicit input from nonmanagerial employees responsible for direct patient care who are potentially exposed to injuries from contaminated sharps in the identification, evaluation, and selection of effective engineering and work practice controls and shall document the solicitation in the Exposure Control Plan." This change represents a new requirement, which is performance-oriented. No specific procedures for obtaining employee input are prescribed. This provides the employer with flexibility to solicit employee input in any manner appropriate to the circumstances of the workplace. The revised standard requires that solicitation of input from employees be documented in the Exposure Control Plan.

4. Recordkeeping.

The recordkeeping requirements of the standard have been amended to add the paragraph that now states: "The employer shall establish and maintain a sharps injury log for the recording of percutaneous injuries from contaminated sharps. The information in the sharps injury log shall be recorded and maintained in such manner as to protect the confidentiality of the injured employee. The sharps injury log shall contain, at a minimum: (A) the type and brand of device involved in the incident, (B) the department or work area where the exposure incident occurred, and (C) an explanation of how the incident occurred." The level of detail presented should be sufficient to allow ready identification of the device, location, and circumstances surrounding an exposure incident (e.g., the procedure being performed, the body part affected, objects or substances involved and how they were involved) so that the intended evaluation of risk and device effectiveness can be accomplished.

If data from the log are made available to other parties, any information that directly identifies an employee (e.g., name, address, social security number, payroll number) or information that could reasonably be used to identify indirectly a specific employee (e.g., exact age, date of initial employment) must be withheld.

Guidelines for Intravenous Care

The CDC estimates that, each year, nearly two million patients in the United States get an infection in hospitals, and about 90,000 of these patients die as a result of their infections. Infections are also a complication of care in other settings, including long-term care facilities, clinics, and dialysis centers (CDC, *Guidelines for the Prevention of Intravascular Catheter-Related Infections,* 2002a).

The patient undergoing infusion therapy is exposed to the risk of infection because the skin barrier is intentionally broken with an IV device, thus allowing for the free flow of organisms into the circulatory system. The incidence of catheter-related bloodstream infection (CRBSI) varies considerably by type of catheter, frequency of catheter manipulation, and patient-related factors, such as underlying disease and acuteness of illness (CDC, *Guidelines for the Prevention of Intravascular Catheter-Related Infections,* 2002a). The CMA is in a critical position to prevent infections from occurring. She does this through good and frequent hand hygiene and aseptic practices while caring for patients and by performing procedures correctly and in a safe manner.

One of the most serious complications of IV therapy involves sepsis, a pathologic state, usually with fever, that is the result of microorganisms in the bloodstream. Microorganisms usually gain access to the blood at the catheter or needle insertion site, but they can also enter via contaminated tubing and fluid. For the patient who is receiving several different medications and fluids intravenously, organisms can enter through injection ports, the fluid, or the filter systems.

Because the CMA has many responsibilities in her day-to-day routine, it is easy to overlook areas of infection control. Unfortunately, and all too often in health care, asepsis is neglected in the interest of saving time. This trend has evolved as a result of the numerous antibiotics available to "chase infections," so prevention of infection has become less important than fixing it after the fact. This negligent mindset needs to be replaced with the philosophy that an ounce of prevention is worth a pound of cure. This is especially important because the excessive use of antibiotics in a patient weakens her response to them over time. Because society has become so litigious, physicians often prescribe antibiotics prophylactically or unnecessarily (such as for colds, which are nonbacterial), to appease the patient or "just to be safe." Physicians should responsibly prescribe antibiotics only where needed and not use powerful broad-spectrum agents if a lesser, precisely indicated agent will suffice (Zuger, 1995).

MEDICAL ASSISTING ALERT

Nosocomial Infection from Resistant Organisms

In principle, it may be possible for a patient who develops a nosocomial infection caused by a resistant organism to recover damages resulting from the organism's resistance if he or she can prove that the resistance was caused by the physician's or hospital's indiscriminate use of antibiotics (Kaunitz, 1996).

As discussed earlier, microbiologists are witnessing the emergence of bacterial strains that are developing resistance to many of the antibiotics available. With each new generation, they are becoming more virulent and more resistant to treatment. Bacteria responsible for hospital-acquired infections have gradually developed resistance to common antibiotics; although MRSA was initially the multidrug-resistant organism of concern, now others have emerged.

MEDICAL ASSISTING ALERT

Preventing Antimicrobial Resistance

The Centers for Disease Control and Prevention (CDC) has launched a campaign aimed at clinicians called "Prevent Antimicrobial Resistance." The campaign focuses on four key strategies for preventing antimicrobial resistance in healthcare settings:

1. Preventing infection
2. Diagnosing and treating infection effectively
3. Using antimicrobials wisely
4. Preventing transmission of drug-resistant pathogens

Within these strategies are 12 action steps derived from evidenced-based guidelines and recommendations developed by the CDC that clinicians can take to prevent antimicrobial resistance in hospitalized adults.

These action steps include:
Action Step 1: Vaccinate
Action Step 2: Get the catheters out
Action Step 3: Target the pathogen
Action Step 4: Access the experts
Action Step 5: Practice antimircobial control
Action Step 6: Use local data
Action Step 7: Treat infection, not contamination
Action Step 8: Treat infection, not colonization
Action Step 9: Know when to say "no" to vanco(mycin)
Action Step 10: Stop antimicrobial treatment when infection is treated or unlikely
Action Step 11: Isolate the pathogen
Action Step 12: Break the chain of contagion

CDC is partnering with professional medical organizations, including the Infectious Diseases Society of America, the American Society for Microbiology, the National Foundation for Infectious Diseases, national medical centers, and other health care institutions to distribute, implement, and evaluate campaign materials. The materials include a slide set, posters, brochures, and a pocket-sized clinician reminder card listing the 12 action steps. The campaign also features a Web site (www.cdc.gov/drugresistance/healthcare).

MEDICAL ASSISTING TIP

Patient Teaching and Antibiotics

The CMA plays a major role in slowing the epidemic of drug-resistant infections by teaching patients about the judicious use of antibiotics. Teaching should include the following.

- Advise patients to comply with physician directives when antibiotics are not prescribed for the common cold or flu—viral infections for which antibiotics are ineffective.
- Caution patients not to push their physicians to prescribe antibiotics "just in case."
- Remind patients that it is important when antibiotics are ordered for bacterial infections to take the prescribed dose at the proper time intervals for the full duration of treatment and to follow guidelines regarding food and fluid intake that may affect the drug's efficacy.
- Explain that taking antibiotics according to prescription guidelines may prevent reinfection and future resistance to lifesaving antimicrobials.

A great deal of research has been done (and continues to be done) regarding the safest and best protocols for infusion therapy. The studies look at the devices used, the antiseptic preparation and site care, dressing changes, patient comfort, time, and cost effectiveness. The CMA who is primarily responsible for initiating, monitoring, maintaining, and discontinuing intravenous treatment makes use of the research by following the guidelines provided by the CDC and protocols mandated by OSHA, and by adhering to employer policies and procedures that apply to the area where she works.

Antiseptic Agents

An antiseptic is an agent that, when applied topically, is capable of killing microorganisms on the skin or inhibiting their growth. An antiseptic works by interrupting the cell's metabolic activity by chemically destroying cellular components, by interfering with the cell's protein structure, or by weakening the cell membrane so that the cell's contents are able to escape, thus destroying the organism. Proper skin cleansing and antisepsis of the cannula-insertion site and surrounding area is considered one of the most important measures for preventing catheter-related infections, and reducing the numbers of resident and transient skin organisms (CDC, 2002a).

MEDICAL ASSISTING ALERT

The Consequences of Carelessness

The CMA must always keep in mind that carelessness and failure to follow proper protocols can cause a patient a great deal of discomfort, extend treatment time, and increase health care costs. The worst-case scenario is when a nosocomial infection results in disability or death. In spite of strict adherence to principles of asepsis and infection control, some patients still contract nosocomial infections.

The antiseptic products most often studied and compared in recent years are alcohol, iodine/iodophors, and chlorhexidine gluconate. These three, employed alone or in combination with other products, are often used for skin antisepsis during intravenous therapy. The CDC recommendations regarding cutaneous antisepsis are as follows:

Disinfect clean skin with an appropriate antiseptic before catheter insertion and during dressing changes. Although a 2% chlorhexidine-based preparation is preferred, tincture of iodine, iodophor, or 70% alcohol can be used . . . Allow the antiseptic to remain on the insertion site and to air dry before catheter insertion. Allow povidone iodine to remain on the skin for at least 2 minutes, or longer if it is not yet dry before insertion. Do not apply organic solvents (e.g., acetone and ether) to the skin before insertion of catheters or during dressing changes (CDC, *Guidelines for the Prevention of Intravascular Catheter-Related Infections*, 2002a).

MEDICAL ASSISTING TIP

Ensuring the Efficacy of Antiseptics

Prior to the application of any antiseptic, the skin must be physically clean because organic matter can inactivate the efficacy of antiseptics.

70% Isopropyl Alcohol

Seventy percent isopropyl alcohol (isopropanol) or ETOH (ethyl alcohol) inhibits bacterial growth and is often used as a topical skin disinfectant. Alcohol is a good fat solvent; it exerts its effect by denaturing protein. It is one of the safest products for the purpose of antisepsis and is cost effective. (Toxic reactions have occurred in children following full body sponging for fever.) It is the antiseptic of choice when patients are allergic to iodine-containing products.

MEDICAL ASSISTING TIP

Proper Application of Alcohol and Iodine

When alcohol and iodine preparations are used together for skin antisepsis prior to IV cannulation, the procedure for applying them is as follows.

1. Vigorously apply the alcohol to the site, using enough alcohol to keep the site wet for one minute. Alcohol is applied first because it does not exert a residual effect.
2. Allow the site to air dry.
3. Apply the iodine to the site.

If applied to the skin with friction and allowed to air dry, isopropanol is able to kill bacteria (**bactericidal**) within two minutes. (The CMA must never blow on the site or fan the area with her hand.) While it is rapid-acting, it does not exert a residual antiseptic effect. Alcohol is effective against most gram-negative and gram-positive organisms, tubercle bacilli, and many fungi and viruses (including HIV), but it is not effective against spores.

MEDICAL ASSISTING ALERT

Be Aware of the Effects of Alcohol

Alcohol causes a burning sensation with discomfort when applied to open wounds or cuts. When used on intact skin, it may cause drying and irritation on some patients. When applied as a skin prep, alcohol causes subcutaneous vasodilation, which enhances the ability to see the veins prior to needle or catheter insertion. Because of this vasodilating effect, alcohol should not be used to discontinue an IV infusion because vasodilation enhances bleeding; a 2×2-inch gauze should be used instead.

Commercially packaged skin wipes saturated with 70% isopropyl alcohol for one-time use are commonly used instead of multiuse containers, which may become contaminated. Also available for cleansing the site (usually on central line insertions) are cotton-tipped alcohol applicator sticks.

Alcohol is often used in combination with iodine as a skin prep prior to IV insertions. When used in tandem, the alcohol should be applied first and allowed to air dry, followed by the iodine preparation. In some institutions, alcohol is used after the iodine preparation has been applied in order to decolor the area and allow for better vein visibility during venipuncture. This is not good practice and should be avoided because the alcohol negates the residual effect of the other products and alcohol does not provide a prolonged cutaneous antiseptic effect. The Infusion Nurses' Society (INS) recommends that "Antimicrobial solutions that should be used for site care include 2% tincture of iodine, 10% povidone-iodine, alcohol, or chlorhexidine, as single agents or in combination" (INS, 2000, Standard 57, S55).

Iodine Preparations

Iodine solutions are frequently used for skin preparation prior to venipuncture. Iodine is a potent antimicrobial, exerting its effects on gram-negative and gram-positive bacteria, viruses, fungi, yeasts, and protozoa. It penetrates the cell wall, causing intracellular oxidation with resultant release of free iodine within the microbial contents to (probably) disrupt protein and nucleic acid structure and synthesis. It is also cost effective, while producing minimal toxicity (although prolonged use of iodine can result in systemic absorption). Incidences of hypothyroidism have occurred in newborn infants treated topically with iodine. Iodine also stains the skin, interfering with the ability to see deep veins.

Tincture of iodine is a simple solution of 2% iodine and sodium iodide in dilute alcohol. It is capable of killing all bacteria present on the skin within 1.5 minutes. It causes less stinging than alcohol when applied to broken skin. Bandaging over tincture of iodine is not recommended, as it may cause skin irritation and discomfort.

MEDICAL ASSISTING TIP

Iodine Allergies

Before using any iodine-containing product on a patient, it is very important for the CMA to find out if the patient is allergic to iodine or has had any unusual reaction (local or systemic) from its use. If the patient does not know if she is allergic to iodine, the CMA should ask her if she is allergic to shellfish (which contain iodine). As with all medications, the CMA must watch for hypersensitivity reactions.

Iodophors, such as povidone-iodine (the most common iodophor), are concentrations of iodine mixed with other substances that act as carriers to produce a substantial release of iodine on the skin, providing longer germicidal activity. Because they are weaker than other iodine compounds, there is reduced toxicity and less irritation and staining of the skin. Because the iodine is released gradually, a contact time of two minutes is necessary to allow for optimum microbial kill. If adequate time is not allowed for iodophor action, the use of tincture of iodine, with its more rapid action, should be considered. The site area may be covered with a dressing because there is less skin irritation. Iodophors burn less than alcohol or other iodine compounds, but they are not as effective as iodine solutions and iodine tinctures. Povidone-iodine is available in several forms: saturated disks, swabs, cotton-tipped applicator sticks, and cotton-tipped plastic ampules.

A shortcoming of iodophors is that their antimicrobial properties are neutralized in the presence of proteinaceous material such as blood and pus.

Chlorhexidine Gluconate

Chlorhexidine gluconate (CHG) is a potent, broad-spectrum cationic biguanide antiseptic available in various strengths. Clinical trials have shown that CHG is bactericidal on contact (through cell wall disruption) and displays persistent antimicrobial activity against a wide range of gram-positive and gram-negative bacteria, having residual antibacterial properties that last for hours after application. Organic material has little effect on CHG. CHG has a minimal effect on tubercle bacilli and is less active against fungi, but is active against many viruses. The major advantage of CHG is its ability to bind to skin protein, leaving a residue with persistent antimicrobial effects for up to six hours after application. In a randomized clinical trial using 70% alcohol, 10% povidone-iodine, and 2% CHG (as cutaneous antiseptics for the prevention of catheter-related infections [CRI] in central venous and arterial catheters), the rate of catheter-related BSIs, when CHG was used, was 84% lower than the rates when the other two regimens were used (Maki, Ringer, & Alvarado, 1991). In July 2000, the U.S. Food and Drug Administration (FDA) approved a 2% tincture of chlorhexidine preparation for skin antisepsis. CHG rarely produces reactions and is not absorbed through the skin. CHG has, however, been reported to cause deafness when instilled into the middle ear through a perforated ear drum. If it enters the eye, it must be flushed out immediately, as prolonged contact can cause serious and permanent eye injury.

Because of its properties, CHG is approved by the FDA as a preoperative skin prep in a 4% strength (for areas other than the face and head), as a skin wound cleanser, for use as a surgical scrub, as a handwashing agent for health care personnel, and for preoperative showering or bathing for the patient.

Numerous studies have compared the efficacy of the three antiseptics discussed in this chapter, along with others that are available and approved by the FDA. The "perfect" agent has not been found—one that would kill all microorganisms on the skin, inhibit regrowth, be nontoxic and nonirritating to the patient, be convenient to use and nonstaining, save time, and be cost effective. In terms of antimicrobial efficacy and infection control, all of the research substantiates three very important facts: (1) hand hygiene continues to be the most important factor in preventing the spread of infection; (2) the proper application of an antiseptic to the intravenous insertion site prior to venipuncture and routinely thereafter with dressing changes is needed; and (3) dressings and tubing should be changed at specified, CDC-approved intervals using aseptic technique.

Antimicrobial Ointments

Studies regarding the application of antimicrobial ointments to the catheter insertion site at the time of placement and during dressing changes have produced conflicting results over the years. "The rates of catheter colonization with *Candida spp.* might be increased with the use of antibiotic ointments that have no fungicidal activity." Current CDC guidelines state: "Do not use topical antibiotic ointment or creams on insertion sites (except when using dialysis catheters) because of their potential to promote fungal infections and antimicrobial resistance." Studies conclude that mupirocin ointment is effective at reducing the risk for CRBSI, but its use has also been associated with mupirocin resistance. In addition, the ointment may adversely affect the integrity of polyurethane catheters: "To avoid compromising the integrity of the catheter, any ointment that is applied to the catheter insertion site should be checked against the catheter and ointment manufacturers' recommendations regarding the compatibility" (CDC, 2002b).

Catheter-related bloodstream infections are more commonly associated with the use of central venous catheters than with small, peripheral catheters. The microbes that colonize the catheter hub and the skin area surrounding the insertion site are the source of most catheter-related infections. Preventive strategies must be aimed at reducing microbial colonization at the insertion site and hub and minimizing the bacterial spread extraluminally (from the skin) or intraluminally (from the hub toward the catheter tip lying in the bloodstream) (Mermel, 2000).

The factors most obviously associated with the increased risk of catheter-related infection include prolonged duration of placement, frequent manipulation, use of thrombogenic catheter materials, an inadequate sterile barrier protecting the catheter insertion site, and inadequate sterile technique during catheter insertion. Some experts suggest, above and beyond what the CDC recommends, that preventive strategies to preclude infection incorporate enhanced skill and care during catheter placement, maximal sterile barriers, the use of antimicrobial catheters, the (preferable) use of the CHG for topical antisepsis, and flushing the catheter with antimicrobial and antiatherogenic agents (Sadovsky,

2000). The development of protocols to ensure that the proper technique is followed and that adequate catheter maintenance is performed should be a priority in all patient care settings.

Alcohol Gels

The spread of microbes in hospitals is making patients who are already ill even worse, with a resultant estimated 20,000 deaths each year (Haney, 2002). One feasible solution appears to be the use of waterless, alcohol-based disinfectants. Hospitals are placing dispensers of alcohol gels either near patient beds or outside patient rooms, where nurses and other health care personnel can apply and rub the solution on while on the move. The disinfectant dries as the skin absorbs it. Research findings, as presented by the American Society for Microbiology in September 2002, suggest that alcohol-based rinses kill more germs, require no sink or water, and are easier to use than soap and water. The alcohol formulas are available as rinses, foams, gels, or lotions. The procedure for use is to place a dime-size spot of the material on one palm, then rub the hands together until it dries—about 15 seconds. The solutions contain moisturizers, so they do not dry the skin.

Recent guidelines from the CDC recommend the use of sinkless, alcohol-based hand degerming gels exclusively, except when workers' hands are visibly soiled—or use of the gels in conjunction with the traditional soap-and-water treatment (CDC, 2002d, Guideline for Hand Hygiene).

In 2000, researchers at the Veterans Administration Medical Center in Washington, DC, measured the effects of switching to alcohol rinses. Dispensers were put in all patient rooms and outpatient facilities. New cases of nosocomial drug-resistant staphylococcal infections decreased 21%, while resistant enterococcus dropped 43%. After four years of use at the University of Geneva Hospital in Switzerland, hospital-acquired infections were cut in half (Haney, 2002).

Dressings and Intravenous Site Maintenance

As previously discussed, preventing infections related to intravascular access depends on the aseptic practices and precautions used prior to and during the insertion of an IV device. Once in place, the entry site of the needle or catheter must be properly secured and maintained. In forthcoming chapters, the techniques for site preparation and maintenance will be covered in detail. From an infection control standpoint, it is important to review accepted dressing change and site maintenance protocols here.

There has been much discussion over IV site dressings in terms of safety and efficacy in preventing infections, durability, patient comfort, practitioner convenience, and cost

effectiveness. The types of protective coverings used as recommended by the CDC are "either sterile gauze or sterile, transparent, semipermeable membrane dressings to cover the catheter site" (CDC, 2002b).

Transparent dressings vary among manufacturers in terms of their physical properties. Although their appearances are similar, there are differences regarding the transmission of oxygen and moisture vapor, as well as their ability to adhere to the skin. These dressings are reliable in securing the cannula, provide a means for continuous visual inspection and palpation of the IV site (thus allowing for quick assessment and identification of redness, swelling, warmth, or dislodgement even before the patient may sense any discomfort), and allow patients to bathe and shower without saturating the dressing. They also require less frequent changes than do gauze and tape dressings, thereby saving personnel time. Many IV practitioners prefer transparent dressings because they can be placed directly over the hub of the needle or catheter, thus stabilizing the IV device. When using these dressings, it is very important not to cover them with tape or other dressing materials that would obliterate the IV insertion site. "Products employed to stabilize the catheter should include sterile tapes, transparent semipermeable membrane (TSM) dressings, sutures, manufactured catheter securement devices, and sterile surgical strips" (INS, Standard 49, S 43, 2000).

When using a gauze dressing, the hub of the needle or catheter must still be stabilized in a sterile manner. As soon as the IV device is in place, tape must be used to prevent dislodgement and movement. Once the IV device is adequately secured, the sterile gauze may be applied. A major advantage of this type of dressing is that the patient who may be uncomfortable about seeing a needle or catheter in her body is spared from looking at it.

With either type of dressing, it is always important to note on the dressing the type and size of the needle or catheter, the date and time of insertion, and the initials of the person who inserted it. This should be placed to the side of the insertion site, so as not to manipulate the IV device or obliterate visualization of the insertion site. This is an excellent communication tool for everyone who assesses the dressing because at a glance all of the important information about the IV device is available.

Studies have shown that the type of dressings used may not be as important as the manner in which they are applied, maintained, and monitored. In the largest controlled trial of dressing regimens (on more than 2000 peripheral catheters) done thus far, the findings of Dr. Maki and associates suggest that the rate of catheter colonization among IV sites dressed with transparent dressings (5.7%) is comparable to that of those dressed with gauze (4.6%) and there are no clinically significant differences in either the incidences of catheter-site colonization or phlebitis between the two groups (CDC, 2002).

A meta-analysis has assessed studies that compared the risk for catheter-related BSIs for groups using transparent dressings versus groups using gauze dressing. The risk for CRBSIs did not differ between the groups. The choice of dressing can be a matter of preference. If blood is oozing from the catheter insertion site, gauze dressing might be preferred. . . . Data suggest that transparent dressing can be safely left on peripheral venous catheters for the duration of catheter insertion . . . (CDC, 2002a).

The monitoring of intravascular devices and dressings should be done on a daily basis (CDC, 2002), and such interventions should be manipulated as little as possible. Patient complaints must always be thoroughly investigated and resolved.

The CDC (2002) recommends that the IV dressing be left in place until the catheter is removed or changed or it becomes damp, loosened, or soiled. IV site dressings need to be changed more frequently in diaphoretic patients.

The dressing must be securely applied so as to prevent dislodgement of the intravascular device. The CMA must be careful not to manipulate the catheter, as this irritates the intima of the vein and increases the risk of phlebitis and infection. She must also take precautions to prevent inadvertent removal of the cannula during dressing changes.

Intravascular Catheters

An intravenous catheter usually remains in place longer than a needle because it is used for prolonged therapy. The patient's risk for developing an infection depends on the manner of site preparation and insertion, the site location, the size of the catheter, the patient's condition, and the length of time the IV device remains in place. Any time the skin is punctured, for any reason, one of the body's natural defenses is to prevent blood loss, so the process of clot formation begins. Fibrin, a protein, develops in the process of blood clotting. Fibrin forms around (fibrin sheath) and on the tip of the catheter, sometimes forming a tail protruding from the tip of the catheter. Microorganisms have an affinity to this fibrin sheath, which generally develops within 48 hours of catheter insertion.

The correlation between infectious morbidity and the IV cannula makeup has been studied extensively. Peripheral cannulas made with Teflon® or polyurethane are associated with fewer infectious complications than those composed of polyvinyl chloride (PVC) or polyethylene. In one major study, polyurethane catheters were associated with nearly a 30% lower risk of phlebitis when compared with those made of Teflon®, yet neither was associated with bloodstream infections (while PVC and polyethylene cannulas were affiliated with BSI rates up to 5%). The CDC recommends cannula selection "based on the intended purpose, duration of use, known complications, and experience at the institution . . .

(using) a Teflon® catheter, polyurethane catheter, or a steel needle" (CDC, 2002).

Certain types of catheters and cuffs that are coated with or impregnated with antimicrobial or antiseptic agents, although more costly, have been shown to decrease the risk for CRBSIs and have the potential to decrease hospital costs associated with treating CRBSIs. Catheters coated with chlorhexidine/silver sulfadiazine only on the external lumen surface have been studied as a means to reduce CRBSI (and) . . . reduced the risk for CRBSI compared with standard noncoated catheters. A second-generation catheter has been developed with chlorhexidine coating on both the internal and external luminal surfaces, with the external surface having three times the amount of chlorhexidine and extended release of the surface-bound antiseptics than that in the first-generation products. Preliminary studies indicate that prolonged antiinfective activity provides improved efficacy in preventing infection (CDC, 2002a).

Ionic platinum/silver metals have broad antimicrobial activity and have been FDA-approved for use on catheters and cuffs in the United States. Further studies need to be done to support their prolonged antimicrobial effect. Ionic silver has also been used in subcutaneous collagen cuffs attached to CVCs. The ionic silver provides antimicrobial activity and the cuff provides a mechanical barrier to the migration of microorganisms along the external surface of the catheter. Further studies are needed on these as well, to determine long-term efficacy.

Changing Regimens for Intravascular Devices and Administration Sets

An important consideration in the prevention of phlebitis and catheter-related infections is the routine replacement of intravascular catheters. Although studies of short peripheral catheters indicate that the incidence of thrombophlebitis and bacterial colonization increases when they are left in place longer than 72 hours, the rates of phlebitis are not substantially different when left in place for 96 hours. "Because phlebitis and catheter colonization have been associated with an increased risk for catheter-related infection, short peripheral catheter sites commonly are rotated at 72- to 96-hour intervals to reduce both the risk for infection and client discomfort associated with phlebitis" (CDC, 2002a). Additional CDC (2002a) guidelines include the following.

1. Prompt removal of any intravascular catheter that is no longer essential
2. No routine replacement of central venous or arterial catheters solely for the purpose of reducing the incidence of infection
3. Leaving peripheral venous catheters in place in children until IV therapy is completed, unless complications occur

4. Replacement of catheters when adherence to aseptic technique cannot be ensured (i.e., when inserted during a medical emergency), as soon as possible, and after no longer than 48 hours
5. Use of clinical judgment to determine when to replace a catheter that could be a source of infection (e.g., do not routinely replace venous catheters in clients whose only indication of infection is fever)
6. No routine replacement of venous catheters in clients who are bacteremic or fungemic if the source of infection is unlikely to be the catheter
7. Replacement of any short-term CVC if purulence is observed at the insertion site, which indicates infection
8. Replacement of all CVCs if the client is hemodynamically unstable and CRBSI is suspected
9. Avoidance of the use of the guidewire technique to replace catheters in clients suspected of having catheter-related infection

The data from several well-controlled studies regarding the optimal interval for changing IV administration sets (not used for blood or blood products, lipids, or TPN) have resulted in the conclusion that it is both safe and cost effective to change them no more frequently than at 72-hour intervals unless catheter-related infection is suspected or documented (CDC, 2002). Tubings used to administer blood, blood products, or lipid emulsions (those combined with amino acids and glucose in a 3-in-1 admixture or infused separately) should be changed within 24 hours of initiating the infusion. When the solution contains only dextrose and amino acids, the administration set does not need to be replaced more frequently than 72 hours. Tubing used to administer propofol infusions is to be replaced every 6 or 12 hours, depending on its use, and according to recommendations from the manufacturer (CDC, 2002). Parenteral nutrition and any infusates that, if contaminated, may support microbial growth may necessitate more frequent tubing changes. In this situation, it is important for the CMA to follow institutional guidelines and INS standards. When blood and blood products are administered, many institutions advise that the tubing should be changed with every unit infused. Fat emulsions usually have special tubing that can only be used with lipids. The tubing is generally changed every 24 hours if the solution is infused continuously. If used intermittently, the tubing is changed at the start of each new unit.

Filters

Filters were once used extensively in the practice of IV therapy (when CMAs performed admixture procedures) to reduce the risk of infection from infusate contamination, for the removal of particulate matter, as well as to reduce the risk of phlebitis in clients receiving high doses of IV medication. Because of the potential undesirable effects of blockage (which increases line manipulation) and reduction of drug dosage, filters are no longer advocated by the CDC (CDC, 2002). It has been suggested that the routine use of in-line filters actually may contribute to infection (because when the bacteria are trapped and die, their toxins can escape the filter and circulate in the bloodstream) and increase cost and personnel time. Pre-use filtration by the pharmacy is safer, more practical, and cost effective.

Policies and procedures regarding the use of filters vary among employment settings. Many institutions use some type of filter for total parenteral nutrition (TPN) and there is a special lipid filter, with larger pores, that is available for use with some fat emulsions. The CMA is expected to know and follow the protocols set forth by her employer. According to the INS, "the indications and protocol for the use of bacterial/particulate-retentive, air-eliminating, and blood and blood component filters should be established in organizational policies and procedures" (INS, Standard 38, S33, 2000). If filters are used, they should be replaced with each new administration set, or sooner if they become occluded or do not allow the infusion to be delivered at the scheduled rate.

Fluids

The 2002 CDC guidelines regarding the "hang time" of parenteral fluids are as follows.

1. Lipid-containing solutions (such as 3-in-1) should be completed within 24 hours of hanging the solution.
2. Lipid emulsions, when administered alone, should be completed within 12 hours of hanging. If the client's fluid volume is a consideration, the infusion can be completed within 24 hours.
3. Blood and blood products are to be completed within 4 hours of hanging.

The CDC has not set forth recommendations regarding the "hang" time limit for other parenteral infusates. Most institutions dictate that the maximum time any infusate may hang at room temperature is not to exceed 24 hours.

If there is any suspicion that any infusion is contaminated, it must be discontinued immediately and saved for laboratory testing. Blood and blood products, which provide an excellent environment for microbial growth, should never stay at room temperature for more than 4 hours. If the CMA anticipates that a unit will take longer than that to infuse, she must notify the blood bank so smaller quantities can be dispensed.

CMA Responsibilities

The CMA who initiates, monitors, and maintains IV infusion therapy is responsible for the patient's safety and comfort while strictly adhering to infection control measures. With

MEDICAL ASSISIING TIP

CDC Definitions

According to the CDC, the following definitions relate to intravenous cannula-related infection.

Colonized catheter: Growth of more than 15 colony-forming units from a proximal or distal catheter segment in the absence of accompanying clinical symptoms

Catheter-related bloodstream infection: Isolation of the same organism ... from a ... culture of a catheter segment and from the blood ... of a patient with accompanying clinical symptoms of BSI and no other apparent source of infection ....

Infusate-related bloodstream infection: Isolation of the same organism from infusate and from separate percutaneous blood cultures, with no other identifiable source of infection

Exit-site infection: Erythema, tenderness, induration, or purulence within 2 cm of the skin at the exit site of the catheter

Pocket infection: Erythema and necrosis of the skin over the reservoir of a totally implantable device or purulent exudate in the subcutaneous pocket containing the reservoir

Tunnel infection: Erythema, tenderness, and induration in the tissues overlying the catheter and more than 2 cm from the exit site

From: *Federal Register,* Vol. 60 (September 27, 1995)

MEDICAL ASSISTING TIP

Hand Hygiene

- Alcohol-based handrubs significantly reduce the number of microorganisms on skin, are fast acting, and cause less skin irritation.
- When using an alcohol-based handrub, apply product to palm of one hand and rub hands together, covering all surfaces of hands and fingers, until hands are dry. Note that the volume needed to reduce the number of bacteria on hands varies by product.
- Handwashing with soap and water remains a sensible strategy for hand hygiene in nonhealth care settings and is recommended by CDC and other experts.
- When health care personnels' hands are visibly soiled, they should wash with soap and water.
- The use of gloves does not eliminate the need for hand hygiene. Likewise, the use of hand hygiene does not eliminate the need for gloves. Gloves reduce hand contamination by 70% to 80%, prevent cross-contamination, and protect clients and health care personnel from infection. Handrubs should be used before and after each client, just as gloves should be changed before and after each client.
- Health care personnel should avoid wearing artificial nails and keep natural nails less than one quarter of an inch long.

(CDC, 2002a)

the large number of patients receiving some type of IV therapy, the CMA must use all the necessary measures to prevent the occurrence of nosocomial infections. The CMA must follow the guidelines set forth by the CDC, the mandates of OSHA, and her employer's directives. She is also wise to incorporate the INS standards of practice in order to maintain the health and safety of her patients, their families, her coworkers, other health care personnel, and herself.

The CMA must be able to recognize the signs and symptoms of infection so that treatment can be initiated to avert the complications of infectious disease. Some infectious processes are easy to identify while others are more difficult to detect. Early recognition depends on the patient's general state of health, her age and nutritional status, her ability to communicate, the organism(s) involved, and the body system(s) affected.

Fever is usually the first sign of infection, but that may not always be the case. Localized infection is usually recognized by inflammation (redness, heat, pain) and swelling.

The inflammatory response is a protective mechanism the body uses in an attempt to protect itself from pathogenic invasion. Later in the text, when the complications of IV therapy are covered, the signs and symptoms of IV-related inflammatory responses and infection will be detailed.

Although concern for the welfare of her patients is important, the CMA must also take the necessary measures to protect herself. She needs to take care of herself through rest, exercise, good hygienic practices, safe social interactions, and a healthy diet. If she is ill, she should not go to work because she will not only jeopardize her own health but endanger the patients in her care. If she has fever or is ill more than two days, she should seek medical attention.

In the workplace, the CMA is expected to follow procedures correctly and in a safe manner so as not to acquire diseases from the patients or transfer them to others. Proper hand hygiene remains the most important thing the CMA can do to prevent picking up an infection or communicating it to others. Appropriate hand hygiene and strict adherence to Standard Precautions are infection control procedures that must be practiced and taught in all settings, including the patient's home. It is essential that the CMA follow the guidelines for wearing gloves and other protective barriers such as gowns, masks, and goggles. A good way to remember when to wear gloves is to follow the advice of many infection control practitioners: If it's wet, wear gloves. As discussed earlier, Standard Precautions are mandated for all health care personnel.

It is important for the CMA to understand how disease is transmitted, but it is equally important that she teach others as well. Patients are often concerned that they might pick up a disease such as AIDS while in the hospital or health care environment. Many misinformed individuals are afraid to donate blood for fear of getting AIDS. It is important for the CMA to reassure patients that HIV can only be transmitted through intimate sexual contact, percutaneous exposure to blood, or through prenatal transmission from mother to infant. Whereas HIV does not survive well outside the body, it can remain viable in blood spills. If the CMA has a cut or open sore that comes in contact with HIV-positive blood, transmission of the virus can occur. The risk of HIV transmission is greater if there is contact with a large volume of blood and if the source patient is in the end stage of AIDS (CDC, 1995). Should occupational HIV exposure occur, prompt treatment is important to decrease the risk of HIV seroconversion. It is essential for the CMA to wear gloves when handling blood and body fluids. Spills and splatters need to be cleaned up immediately. Gloves never take the place of hand hygiene, which is to be done immediately following removal of the gloves.

The hepatitis B and C viruses are far more resilient than HIV when they exit the body. HBV and HCV can survive outside the body on inanimate objects up to 2 weeks. They are serious diseases that can become chronic and progress to cirrhosis, liver cancer, and death. HBV can be prevented with a vaccine, available without cost (due to OSHA regulations) to all health care personnel by their employers. Everyone who works in the health care industry or any other occupation where the possibility of exposure to blood and body fluids is likely should be vaccinated.

Needlesticks continue to be a problem that wearing gloves does not safeguard against. The most frequent cause of bloodborne infections in health care settings—with nurses sustaining the most—are needlesticks. While the use of Standard Precautions can help prevent the spread of bloodborne pathogens, studies show that, even when completely followed, they prevent only about one in three needlestick wounds (APIC, 2000) due to the fact that gloves and other barriers are not impermeable to sharp items.

Needleless systems and protective needle devices are, or should be, in effect in all clinical agencies. As stated earlier, the

MEDICAL ASSISTING TIP

Initiate Prompt Treatment Following Exposure to HIV

The CDC (2001e) recommends that health care practitioners (HCP) occupationally exposed to HIV be treated within one to two hours of exposure. Postexposure prophylaxis (PEP) decreases the risk of HIV seroconversion by almost 70%. Most HIV exposures warrant a two-drug regimen using two nucleoside analogues, ziduvudine (ADV) and lamivudine (3TC), or 3TC and d4T, or d4T and ddI. The addition of a third drug should be considered for exposures that pose an increased risk for transmission. Selection of the PEP regimen should consider the comparative risk represented by the exposure and information about the exposure source, including history of and response to antiretroviral therapy based on clinical response, CD4+ T-cell counts, viral load measurements, and current disease stage. When the source person's virus is known or suspected to be resistant to one or more of the drugs considered for the PEP regimen, the selection of drugs to which the source person's virus is unlikely to be resistant is recommended; expert consultation is advised. If this information is not immediately available, initiation of PEP, if indicated, should not be delayed; changes in the PEP regimen can be made after PEP has been started, as appropriate. Reevaluation of the exposed person should be considered within 72 hours postexposure, especially as additional information about the exposure or source person becomes available.

PEP should be administered over 4 weeks, with follow-up counseling and medical evaluations for at least 6 months following exposure (at 6 weeks, 12 weeks, and 6 months).

For additional information, the following agencies should be contacted:

- CDC
- Hepatitis Hotline
- National AIDS Clearinghouse
- Needlestick! Web site
- PEPline

Needlestick Safety and Prevention Act was passed in the United States in November 2000 in the effort to eliminate needlestick injuries. Protective devices encompass two broad categories: (1) automatically-activated protection (where the device mechanizes at the appropriate point in time), and (2) user-activated protection (where the user must activate the safety device). The CMA must use extreme care in handling and disposing of needles, syringes, and other sharp items. Studies illustrate that as many as one-third of all reported sharps injuries are related to the disposal practices (APIC, 2000).

Even with advanced safety technology and improved protective needle devices, the use of sharps disposal containers remains the vanguard against injuries. Used needles are not to be recapped, broken, bent, or cut. Used syringes, needles, scalpel blades, and all disposable sharps must be properly placed, immediately after use, in puncture-resistant containers for disposal. The blades of safety razors must be handled with care, and then discarded in sharps containers. Razor blades are not to be used between patients. The disposal containers for sharps must be in closest proximity, as is practical, to the area where sharp items are implemented. If a needle is used, and an appropriate disposal container is not nearby (point-of-use disposal), the cap may be "scooped up" with the needle, using one hand, and then carried to the sharps container (Figure 3-2). The cap is not, under any circumstances, to be pushed into place over the needle. "Needles/stylets (sharps) shall be disposed of in nonpermeable tamper-proof containers. Needles/stylets (sharps) shall not be broken, bent, or recapped with two hands" (INS, 2000, Standard 31, S29).

Whenever there is any doubt regarding infection control protocols, the CMA is expected to follow the guidelines set forth by the CDC, OSHA, the employer infection control department, and the agency-approved policy and procedure manuals (Table 3-3). If she is still not sure about something related to her safety or the safety of others, she should contact an infection control practitioner. Under no circumstances should she ever perform any task in a manner that could result in injury or the spread of infection.

Table 3-3 | Infection Control and Safety Measures

Know where policy and procedure manuals are located in your agency and use them. Consult with the infection control practitioner in your agency whenever necessary.

Use the appropriate process to assess the patient's level of consciousness, orientation, and ability to comprehend instructions.

Know and understand all procedures before performing them.

Know and understand the principles of use regarding safety-engineered devices in your agency. You should be trained in their use and have the opportunity to practice using such devices. Do not use any device if you have not received sufficient instruction and the opportunity to perform, at the very least, one demonstration before a person who is knowledgeable regarding the product's use. Once trained, properly use safety devices every time they are indicated.

Explain all procedures to the patient and explain her role in carrying out the procedures. A well-informed patient is more willing to become actively involved and comply.

Use proper hand hygiene before and after all physical patient contacts, patient care procedures, and donning and removing gloves.

Avoid eating and drinking in areas where blood or body fluids may be present.

Protect yourself. Do not touch your eyes, insert/remove contact lenses, or apply makeup in patient care areas.

Know where safety disposal containers for sharp items are located.

Never recap sharps (or use the one-handed technique when not in close proximity to an approved disposal container).

Dispose of sharp items immediately after use.

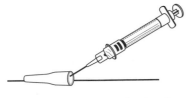

1. Scoop into cap using one hand. Do not touch the cap with the other hand.

2. Slide needle into cap resting on table.

3. Holding the barrel of the syringe in one hand, carry to the sharps container. Do not push the cap onto the syringe.

Figure 3-2 | Scoop technique

CRITICAL THINKING

Don't Start or Promote Unsafe Habits

Glove layering, when the health care person puts on several pairs of gloves and removes one pair to attend to another patient or task without washing his hands, should never be permitted. New gloves are to be worn with each new patient or procedure, and hands must be washed as soon as the gloves are removed and discarded. You, the CMA, play a vital role in preventing bad habits from getting started and in stopping them once they are identified.

MEDICAL ASSISTING TIP

Internet Resources on Infection Control

American Journal of Infection Control: http://www1.mosby.com/Mosby/Periodicals/Medical/AJIC/ict.html

Antibiotic Guide: Treatment Recommendations for Common Infections: http://www.intmed.mcw.edu/drug/InfectionRx.html

Association for Professionals in Infections Control and Epidemiology: http://www.apic.org

BroadStreetSolutions: http://broadstreetsolutions.com

Infection Control Services: http://infectioncenter.com

National Center for Infectious Diseases: http://www.cdc.gov/ncidod/ncid.htm

National Foundation for Infectious Diseases: http://www.nfid.org

Review Questions and Activities

1. List five major responsibilities of the CMA who manages intravenous infusion therapy.
2. Describe the function of the two federal agencies, the CDC and OSHA, and how they operate to protect both the patient and the health care worker.
3. Make a two-column listing that enumerates the variables that affect the disease process from the standpoint of the host and the microorganism.
4. Outline the six links in the chain of infection, and for each link, list three measures that might prevent the transmission of infection.
5. Identify 10 fomites that might be responsible for the inanimate spread of infection.
6. Make a chart of the process of handwashing that you could put by the sinks in your workplace. Be creative so it will be an attention-getter and promote good hand hygiene.
7. Describe what the term *Standard Precautions* means, why it came into existence, and list five substances that are addressed in this category.
8. List and compare the advantages and disadvantages of the three antiseptic agents discussed in this chapter.
9. Using your clinical agency's policy and procedure manual, locate the recommended infection control protocols regarding intravascular catheters, IV site dressings, administration sets, and IV line filters. Compare these guidelines with those of the CDC.
10. Describe the manner in which needles and sharps are to be handled so as to prevent injury to you, your patient, and other health care personnel.
11. What can you do to prevent the spread of infection?

Chapter 4

Risks, Complications, and Adverse Reactions Associated with Intravenous Infusion Therapy

LEARNING OBJECTIVES

Upon completion of this chapter, the reader should be able to:

✳ Differentiate between local and systemic complications associated with intravenous infusion therapy.

✳ Describe the signs and symptoms of the following local complications of infusion therapy:

– Pain and irritation

– Infiltration and extravasation

– Occlusion and loss of patency

– Phlebitis

– Thrombosis and thrombophlebitis

– Hematoma formation

– Venous spasm

– Vessel collapse

– Cellulitis

✳ Explain the interventions for each of the local complications of infusion therapy listed.

✳ List five commonly used vesicant drugs that cause damage with extravasation.

✳ Outline the physiologic processes that occur with cellular and tissue damage.

✳ Interpret the sequence of events that reflects the progression of phlebitis to thrombophlebitis.

✳ Examine how nerve, tendon, ligament, and limb damage can occur as a result of intravenous therapy.

✳ Describe the signs and symptoms of the following systemic complications associated with intravenous infusion therapy:

- Contamination and infection

- Drug and fluid interactions

- Hypersensitivity reactions

- Sepsis

- Emboli (blood clot, air, and catheter)

- Speed shock

✳ Explain the interventions associated with each of the systemic complications listed.

Because intravenous infusion therapy breaks the skin barrier, one of the body's major natural defenses, and further invades and accesses the circulatory system, it carries with it numerous inherent risks and potential complications. To avoid complications associated with such therapy, the CMA should be knowledgeable of every likely complication that might develop. When a problem develops, however, it is important to recognize it as soon as possible so appropriate interventions can be taken.

The CMA must understand the signs and symptoms of each type of complication along with its etiology and defining characteristics. With this information, he can carry out the interventions that are germane to the complication. Complications of IV therapy can be classified as local, systemic, or a combination of the two.

LOCAL PROBLEMS AND COMPLICATIONS

Local complications are adverse reactions that occur at the insertion site of an IV device or close to the IV site. The majority of complications in IV therapy are local problems, and are usually less serious than systemic problems. This does not imply they can be taken lightly. The CMA must always keep in mind that he must intervene appropriately when local complications first arise to prevent progression to systemic complications that can further compromise the patient.

Localized infusion-related complications include pain and irritation at or near the IV site, infiltration and extravasation, cannula dislodgement, catheter or needle occlusion, and phlebitis. Also included are hematoma, venous spasm,

vessel collapse, cellulitis, thrombosis and thrombophlebitis, and nerve, tendon, ligament, or limb damage. Each of these complications will be covered in detail throughout the course of this chapter.

Pain and Irritation

Pain, according to the International Association for the Study of Pain, is "the sensatory and emotional experience associated with actual or potential tissue damage . . . pain includes not only the perception of an uncomfortable stimulus but also the response to that perception" (Thomas, 2001). Pain at the intravenous site is **homotropic:** the sensation of discomfort occurs at the point of injury. The insertion site of the IV device or the inner lining of the vein wall **(intima)** where the infusate comes in contact with it can cause homotropic pain. Pain can be **inflammatory,** which occurs with the increased pressure that accompanies the inflammatory response. **Irritation** is synonymous with tenderness.

Etiology and Defining Characteristics

With infusion therapy, pain can develop as a result of various physical and emotional situations. Pain that radiates proximally (upward) from the IV insertion site is usually a sensation of burning or stinging resulting from the infusion of a fluid or medication with a high or low osmolarity or pH. In addition, severe pain at the IV site can result from mechanical irritation by the IV device, or nerve, tendon, or ligament damage as well as venous spasm (Table 4-1).

Localized pain can be associated with or be a precursor to any of the intravenous complications discussed in this chapter. Because the symptom of pain can be related to numerous complications, the CMA must understand all the problems

Table 4-1 | Pain Associated with Infusion Therapy

SYMPTOM(S)	ETIOLOGY/ CONTRIBUTING FACTORS
Pain at insertion site	• Infiltration/extravasation • Phlebitis/thrombosis • Hematoma • Cellulitis • Type of insertion device • Method of insertion • Location of infusion site • Improperly secured IV device • Length of time device in place
Vein irritation (burning-stinging sensation)	• Type of insertion device • Method of insertion • Fluid pH • Fluid osmolality • Fluid temperature • Irritating medications • Length of time device in place • Infusate contamination • Rate of infusion
Severe pain radiating away from site, loss of sensation, or paralysis	• Damage to nerves, tendons, or ligaments from improper insertion or location of IV device • Pressure buildup from extravasation of fluid or irritating substances into surrounding area

that might occur, know the assessment variables associated with such problems, and be able to intervene appropriately. Under no circumstances should patient complaints of pain be deferred or ignored. Pain is a warning sign that more serious problems might be developing.

When cellular or tissue injury occurs, pain-producing substances (bradykinin, histamine, and serotonin) and other products are produced and released by the body. These chemicals are responsible for the impulses that result in the sensation of pain. Once cell injury occurs, prostaglandins are synthesized and released to exert a local effect that activates pain receptors and augments histamine and bradykinin activity. The neurotransmitters epinephrine, norepinephrine, dopamine, and acetylcholine enhance pain transmission at the local level, but are released centrally.

MEDICAL ASSISTING ALERT

Preventing a Systemic Complication

What starts out as a local infusion-related complication can quickly progress to one that is systemic if assessment, problem identification, and appropriate interventions are not immediately taken to correct the situation.

Assessment and Interventions

Pain is evidenced by a sympathetic response, which brings about an increase in cardiac rate (**tachycardia**) and output, elevated blood pressure, and increased respiratory rate, sometimes with hyperventilation. The patient often experiences the fright–flight–fight (–freeze) response that brings with it pupil dilation, peripheral vasoconstriction, hypermotility, and excessive perspiration of the palms of the hands and the soles of the feet.

Because pain is subjective, it is extremely important for the CMA to assess, intervene, and evaluate each patient on an individual basis. He must never overlook the fact that there are psychological and emotional factors as well as physical components that influence pain. Religious, cultural, and social considerations must be incorporated into assessment and evaluation, and it is important to be alert for both verbal and nonverbal indicators of pain. The inconveniences and interferences as well as the fear and anxiety associated with illness and disease are important considerations for the CMA. The CMA must make every attempt to evaluate the patient's pain through therapeutic communication skills (Table 4-2). In addition to the patient's verbalizations and actions, the CMA can recognize pain and irritation through touch and visual inspection of the IV site. Signs of blanching or redness over the vein and the sensation of warmth over the site validate the patient's complaints.

Once pain is properly assessed, the CMA must determine the most appropriate intervention(s). Depending on his findings, his actions might include discontinuing and restarting the present infusion, changing the position of the extremity, adjusting the flow rate, retaping the site, applying warm or cool compresses, or notifying the physician. He must know which fluids and medications cause pain or irritation during the process of infusion so he can take the necessary measures to prepare the patient and

---

MEDICAL ASSISTING TIP

A Patient's Descriptions of Pain

Pain associated with IV infusion therapy may be described by a patient as follows:
- A burning or stinging sensation at the IV site
- A dull, aching sensation with a feeling of tightness or hardness (induration) at the site
- A shooting pain that radiates upward along the vein wall
- Tenderness above the cannula insertion site
- A cramping or gripping sensation (venospasm)

Table 4-2 | Communication with the Patient: A Guideline for Pain Assessment

1. Tell me about the pain you are having.

2. Where does it hurt?

3. When did it start?

4. Is the pain in one spot, or does it radiate (move) to other places?

5. What kind of pain is it?

   Aching?   Gnawing?

   Burning?   Stabbing or piercing?

   Dull?   Throbbing?

6. Does it hurt constantly, or at intervals?

7. When is the pain most severe?

8. Are there any other symptoms of discomfort?

9. Rate the pain on a scale of 1 to 10, with 0 to 1 indicating no pain and 10 being the worst pain.

10. Tell me anything else about your pain that is important to you.

NOTE: For patients with cognitive dysfunction or verbal or language barriers, a useful visual tool, such as the Wong-Baker Faces Rating Scale, may be used.

reduce the pain as much as possible (Table 4-3). A great deal of discomfort can be avoided by making changes in the amount of diluent used for some medications or by slowing the rate of infusion, if these measures are not contraindicated. The use of distraction, visualization, and other psychoemotional tools should not be forgotten when attempting to reduce the pain associated with IV therapy.

Many times a patient senses pain simply because the IV device is in place. This may occur because of anxiety and misconceptions regarding therapy. Thorough explanations along with reassurances from the CMA are very important in such cases. The patient often becomes more relaxed about having an IV device and infusion if he knows why it is needed, how it works to his benefit, and the estimated length of time it will be in place. It cannot be stressed enough how important the CMA's interactions with the patient are in terms of his progress and response to care.

Infiltration and Extravasation

In the past, the terms *infiltration* and *extravasation* were often used interchangeably. **Infiltration,** a broader term, is the process in which a substance enters or infuses into another substance or a surrounding area. Infiltration may be an intentional or unintentional process. **Extravasation,** a

MEDICAL ASSISTING TIP

The Well-Informed Patient

A patient who is well informed regarding his condition and treatment regimen perceives himself as an active participant in his care, thus making him more relaxed and better able to adapt to the stress of illness and therapy.

more specific term, refers to the actual (unintentional) escape or leakage of material from a vessel into the surrounding tissue. IV infiltration is defined as the escape, or outflow, of nonvesicant infusate from a vessel into the surrounding tissue. IV extravasation is the escape, or outflow, of a vesicant solution from a vessel into the surrounding tissue. A **vesicant** is an agent that is irritating and causes blistering.

Infiltration and extravasation are probably the most frequently encountered problems associated with infusion therapy. Unfortunately, because they are so common, they are sometimes overlooked or not addressed as soon as they should be, yet they can produce debilitating effects.

Etiology and Defining Characteristics

Infiltration and extravasation can arise from several situations (Table 4-4). Dislodgement of the catheter or needle cannula from the intima of the vein wall during venipuncture is a common occurrence. Puncture of the distal vein wall during venipuncture also occurs. Sometimes the infusate leaks into the surrounding tissue from the cannula's insertion site. This is usually related to the cannula being too large for the diameter of the vein (resulting from insertion of an oversized cannula), or the narrowing of the vein lumen from surrounding pressure (as with the edema accompanying the inflammatory response). In addition, the wall of the vein may weaken and rupture from the inappropriate choice of vein or site or from previous venipunctures. Irritating infusates can weaken the vein wall to the point of rupture as can the delivery of fluid under high pressure. Infiltration can occur because of mechanical pressure from the cannula against the vein wall that results in breakage (especially with steel needles). Any time an IV device is overmanipulated, the wall of the vein becomes compromised and infiltration can occur. Poor or improper taping is another problem. If enough tape is not applied or not placed in the right area, the vein can be irritated because the cannula is unstable. Tape applied too tightly to the skin above the cannula tip can act as a tourniquet, disrupt flow, and rupture the vein wall.

Table 4-3 | Pain Related to the Administration of Some of the Commonly Used Medications and Infusates

MEDICATION OR INFUSATE	ASSOCIATED DISCOMFORT
Amino acids (proteins) in 10% dextrose	Venous inflammation
Ampicillins (antibiotics)	Infusion site pain; venous irritation
BCNU (carmustine) (alkylating agent)	Venous pain
Cephalosporins (antibiotics)	Infusion site pain; venous inflammation
Dextrose solutions (10% to 50%)	Venous irritation
Diazepam (depressant; sedative/hypnotic)	Infusion site pain; venous Inflammation
DTIC (dacarbazine) (alkylating agent)	Infusion site pain; venospasm
Erythromycins (antibiotics)	Venous pain; venous inflammation
Foscarnet sodium (antiviral)	Infusion site irritation
Ganciclovir sodium (antiviral)	Infusion site pain; venous inflammation
Imipenem-cilastin (antibacterial)	Infusion site pain; venous inflammation
Iron dextran	Infusion site inflammation
Lymphocyte immune globulin	Infusion site pain
Methocarbamol (skeletal muscle relaxant)	Infusion site pain
Miconazole (antifungal)	Venous inflammation
Mitomycin (antibiotic; antitumor)	Infusion site pain
Penicillins (antibiotics)	Infusion site pain; venous inflammation
Potassium acetate and potassium chloride (electrolytes)	Infusion site pain; venous burning
Ranitidine (histamine receptor antagonist)	Burning and itching at infusion site
Streptozocin (antibiotic; antitumor)	Venous irritation
Tetanus antitoxin (antitoxin)	Infusion site pain
Thiotepa (alkylating agent)	Infusion site pain
Vancomycin hydrochloride (antibiotic)	Infusion site pain
Vinblastine sulfate (alkaloid)	Venous inflammation

MEDICAL ASSISTING TIP

Avoiding Infiltration or Extravasation

Prevention, a result of frequent assessment and good CMA–patient communication, is the best safeguard for avoiding infiltration or extravasation.

Assessment and Interventions

Pain at or near the IV site may or may not be present depending on the chemical nature of the infusate, the amount of infiltration, the patient's pain threshold, or his level of consciousness. This is why frequent assessment is so important. The CMA must always keep in mind, too, that a minute amount of extravasation from a vesicant can be far more dangerous than a large amount of infiltrated isotonic infusate. The INS recommends that the Infiltration Scale (Table 4-5) "should be standardized and used in documenting the infiltration; infiltration should be graded according to the most severe presenting indicator" (INS, Standard 60, S57).

Depending on the amount of leakage, there might be swelling around the IV site (ventral or dorsal) or edema that extends proximal or distal to the IV site. Contingent on the amount of fluid that escapes, the skin may be taut or rigid, with blanching and a sensation of coolness. The more

Table 4-4 | Major Causes of Infiltration or Extravasation

- Puncture of the distal vein wall during venipuncture
- Puncture of any portion of the vein wall by mechanical friction from the catheter/needle cannula
- Dislodgement of the catheter/needle cannula from the intima of the vein
- Poorly secured (taped) IV device (too loose, too tight, or secured incorrectly)
- Poor vein or site selection
- Improper cannula size
- High delivery rate or pressure of the infusate
- Overmanipulation of the IV device, the site, or both
- Irritating infusate that inflames the intima of the vein and causes it to weaken

Table 4-5 | INS Infiltration Scale (INS, 2000)

GRADE	CLINICAL CRITERIA
0	No symptoms
1	Skin blanched Edema <1 inch in any direction Cool to touch With or without pain
2	Skin blanched Edema 1–6 inches in any direction Cool to touch With or without pain
3	Skin blanched, translucent Gross edema >6 inches in any direction Cool to touch Mild–moderate pain Possible numbness
4	Skin blanched, translucent Skin tight, leaking Skin discolored, bruised, swollen Gross edema >6 inches in any direction Deep-pitting tissue edema Circulatory impairment Moderate–severe pain Infiltration of any amount of blood product, irritant, or vesicant

infusate that is exuded, the tighter the skin becomes and the cooler the temperature. The dressing may be damp or wet. If an infiltration is left unchecked, the site may become dark in color owing to tissue injury.

MEDICAL ASSISTING TIP

Recognizing Infiltration

Because a fibrin sheath develops around the tip of the cannula, it may prevent the backflow of blood during aspiration, even though the IV fluid is infusing. Likewise, the presence of a blood return does not necessarily preclude infiltration.

Sometimes, before obvious signs and symptoms of infiltration are evident, the infusion may begin to run at a slower than prescribed rate or cease to flow. The backflow of blood into the tubing may or may not occur when checking for cannula placement in the vein, and therefore is not a reliable indicator of extravasation.

Another way to determine if infusate is leaking is to apply fingertip pressure to the vein just above the cannula tip or to briefly place a tourniquet above the IV site while the fluid is infusing. If the cannula is in place and there is no break in the patency of the vein, the infusate will stop dripping. If the infusion continues to drip when these measures are instituted, there is leakage into the surrounding tissue.

Once infiltration is determined, the infusion must be stopped, the catheter or needle removed, and pressure applied to the insertion site until bleeding is arrested. It may be the responsibility of the CMA to initiate interventions that will reduce or avert tissue damage. Continued observation, assessment, and client education are critical to a positive outcome. Complete and accurate documentation in the medical record is necessary and all reports related to the incident must be completed per agency policy.

If there is only a small escape of fluid, the CMA may apply firm pressure to the site with a 2 × 2-inch gauze for a few minutes. If a large amount of fluid has escaped into the surrounding tissue, some seepage of serous-like fluid may continue from the puncture site. If this is the case, a light dressing should be applied. It is important to assess for circulatory competence by checking for capillary refill and checking pulses proximal and distal to the area of infiltration. The extremity, depending on individual patient circumstances, agency protocols, and medical orders, may be elevated and the patient should be encouraged to actively move it to assist in the absorption and removal of the excess fluid. If infiltration is small, the intermittent application of ice packs may relieve swelling and discomfort. Ice is usually applied at 15- to 30-minute on/off intervals depending on agency policy. For larger infiltrations, the application of continuous warm compresses may be necessary to assist in the

MEDICAL ASSISTING TIP

Signs and Symptoms of Infiltration and Extravasation

- Pain at or near the insertion site
- Swelling proximal to or distal to the IV site
- Puffiness of the dependent part of limb or body
- Taut, rigid skin around IV site
- Blanching and coolness of skin around IV site
- Damp or wet dressing
- Slowed infusion rate
- No backflow of blood into IV tubing when clamp is fully opened and solution container is lowered below IV site
- No backflow of blood into IV tubing when tubing is pinched above cannula hub
- Infusion stops running
- The infusion continues to infuse when pressure is applied to the vein above the tip of the cannula

MEDICAL ASSISTING TIP

How to Treat Infiltration

The use of warm compresses to treat infiltration has become controversial. It has been found that cold compresses may be better for some infiltrated infusates and warm compresses may be more effective for others. It has also been documented that elevation of the infiltrated extremity may be painful for the patient (Masoorli, 1997). To act in the best interest of the patient, following IV infiltration, consult with the physician for orders regarding compresses and elevation.

reabsorption of fluid, but only if agency approved and medically indicated.

If extravasation occurs, the IV must be stopped immediately or discontinued directly following the aspiration of drug left in the cannula and instillation of a prescribed antidote (anti-inflammatory or neutralizing agent) into the cannula, the notification of the physician, and the initiation of the appropriate antidote into the surrounding tissue, following the doctor's orders and institutional protocols. Whenever an antidote is administered by injection, it is important to use a small-gauge intradermal or subcutaneous needle (27–25ga) to minimize further tissue injury. It is also important to frequently

check capillary refill and pulses to assess circulatory status in the extremity. Because procedural policies vary among agencies, it is the responsibility of the CMA to know and understand employer guidelines regarding extravasated drugs, the equipment needed, and the method(s) in which to utilize the counteragent(s) (Table 4-6).

If treatment is not promptly executed for extravasated irritants or vesicants, tissue sloughing or destruction may ensue. In addition, there may be nerve and blood vessel damage to the limb and loss of functional use. Severe pain and burning may be present. In some cases, surgical excision of large portions of the extremity—or even amputation—is the only alternative. The CMA must remember, too, that the antidotes for infiltration sometimes carry serious side effects that also need to be addressed. He must also understand that some of these remedies must be started within a certain time frame or they will not be effective. Table 4-6 lists the antidotes commonly used for extravasation. It is always important to follow agency protocols and medical directives when using them. Once treatment is initiated for extravasation, the CMA must restart the IV as soon as possible proximal to the previously cannulated site or in another location so as not to interrupt the scheduled rate of infusion.

Documentation must be thorough and accurate regarding all pertinent events regarding the signs and symptoms of the infiltration, written and verbal communications, interventions, and the patient response patterns.

Catheter and Needle Displacement

Displacement of the catheter or needle means that the cannula has shifted from its intended placement site in the vein. It also can mean that the cannula is inadvertently removed from the vein.

Etiology and Defining Characteristics

Catheter or needle displacement usually occurs because the cannula was inadequately secured after its insertion into the vein. It also occurs when the tape around the site becomes loose or detaches from the skin. Tape detachment occurs because the wrong type of tape was used, or the site becomes damp or wet from perspiration or contact with external sources of moisture. When infiltration occurs, the cannula can be physically pushed out of its position in the vein from the pressure of the fluid in the tissues surrounding the needle or catheter.

Cannulas that are placed in the radial or metacarpal veins can easily become dislodged or pulled out during routine patient movements such as transfer from a bed to a chair, getting up for ambulation, or during the routine activities of daily living in which the hand and wrist are

Table 4-6 | Extravasation Antidotes for Irritating or Vesicant Drugs

The 15 antidotes listed in the table are to be used alone, or in combination, for extravasation of the following drugs, based on agency/institutional protocols and medical directives.

CLASSIFICATION	MEDICATION	ANTIDOTE(S)
Adrenergic Agents (sympathomimetics) (Generally cause sloughing and tissue necrosis with extravasation)*	Amrinone (Inocor)	1, 5, 11, 13
	Dobutamine HCl (Dobutrex)	1, 5, 11, 13
	Dopamine (Intropin)	1, 5, 11, 13
	Epinephrine (Adrenaline)	1, 5, 11, 13
	Isoproterenol (Isuprel)	1, 5, 11, 13
	Metaraminol bitartrate (Aramine)	1, 5, 11, 13
	Methoxamine HCl (Vasoxyl)	1, 5, 11, 13
	Norepinephrine (Levophed [levarterenol])	1, 5, 11, 13
	Phenylephrine HCl (Neo-Synephrine)	1, 5, 11, 13
Alkalinizing Agents (Generally cause ulceration, sloughing, cellulitis, and tissue necrosis with extravasation)	Sodium bicarbonate	1, 7 and/or 8, 11, + 13
	Tromethamine (Tham-E)	8 + 5 or 8 + 7
Alkylating Agents (Generally cause sloughing and tissue necrosis)	Carmustine (BCNU) [irritant]	1, 6 or 7, 11, 13
	Mechlorethamine (nitrogen mustard; mustargen)[vesicant]	1, 9, 12 (ice), 13
	Streptozocin (Zancosar) [vesicant]	1, 6 or 7, 11
Antihypertensives	Nitroprusside sodium (Nipride)	1, 9
Antineoplastic Agents (DNA/RNA inhibitors or mitotic inhibitors) (Generally cause severe tissue sloughing and necrosis with extravasation)	Dacarbazine (DTIC) [vesicant]	1, 6 or 7, 11, 13
	Etoposide (VePesid) [irritant]	1, 6, 11, 13
	Vinblastine sulfate (Velban) [vesicant]	1, 6 or 7, 13
	Vincristine sulfate (Oncovin)[vesicant]	1, 6 or 7, 11, 13
	Vindesine sulfate (Eldisine) [vesicant]	1, 6 or 7, 11, 13
Antibiotic Antineoplastic Agents (Generally cause stinging, burning, severe cellulitis, and tissue necrosis with extravasation)	Dactinomycin (Actinomycin D) [vesicant]	1, 4, 6 or 7, 12, 13
	Daunorubicin HCl (daunomycin, Cerubidine) [vesicant]	2, 4, 6 or 7, 12, 13, 15
	Doxorubicin HCl (Adriamycin)	2, 4, 6 or 7, 12, 13, 15
	Idarubicin HCl (Idamycin) [vesicant]	1, 3, 4, 6 or 7, 12 (ice), 13, 15
	Mitomycin C (Mutamycin) [vesicant]	2, 6, 13
	Plicamycin (Mithramycin) [vesicant]	1, 6, 11
Chemotherapy (others) [vesicants]	Bisantrene	2, 10
	Dacarbazine (DTIC-Dome)	2, 10
	Mitoxantrone (DHAD)	2, 10
Electrolytes (Vein irritants that generally cause necrosis, sloughing, cellulitis, and tissue necrosis with extravasation)	Calcium salts / Ca carbonate / Ca chloride / Ca gluconate / Ca lactate / Ca glucepate / Potassium salts	1, 7, or 8, 11, 13
Hypertonic (<10%)	Dextrose Solutions	1, 7, 11, 13
Penicillins (Some can cause sterile abscesses, thrombophlebitis, and severe pain with extravasation)	Nafcillin (Nafcil; Unipen) / Ampicillin sodium (Unasyn) / Azlocillin sodium (Azlin)	1, 7

Antidotes (1–15):

1. Stop the infusion immediately. Aspirat any remaining drug in the cannula with a syringe. Administer antidote into the cannula per physician orders, then discontinue the IV.
2. Stop the infusion and aspirate any remaining drug in the cannula with a syringe. Administer sodium bicarbonate (neutralizing agent) or a corticosteroid (anti-inflammatory agent) into the cannula and discontinue the IV.
3. Aspirate as much of the extravasated drug as possible from the tissue.**
4. Flush the extravasated area with normal saline (0.9% NaCl).**
5. As soon as possible, liberally inject 5 to 10 mg of phentolamine mesylate into the extravasated area to prevent dermal necrosis and sloughing.**
6. Inject long-acting dexamethasone or other corticosteroid to produce anti-inflammatory effect.**
7. Inject hyaluronidase throughout the area to dilute the extravasated drug.**
8. Inject 1% procaine to reduce venospasm.*
9. Inject isotonic sodium thiosulfate into the indurated area.**
10. Inject 4% sodium bicarbonate.**
11. Apply warm, moist compresses to enhance blood flow and transport extravasate out of tissues.
12. Apply cold compresses or ice packs (20 min/hr until inflammation dissipates) to reduce inflammation and arrest tissue destruction.
13. Elevate extremity to enhance fluid drainage.
14. Actively move extremity to enhance fluid drainage.
15. Consult reconstructive surgeon. Excision of the involved area may be indicated for necrosis or persistent pain at the site.

*Antidotes for alkylating agents are ineffective if more than 12 hr have passed since the extravasation occurred.

**Always use a small-gauge (27 to 25 ga.) intradermal or subcutaneous needle.

used. It is easy, too, for the IV device or tubing to get caught on clothing, bed linens, and side rails. Catheter dislodgement often happens while the patient is being transferred from his bed to a wheelchair or gurney for transport to other areas.

Assessment and Interventions

Prior to inserting an intravenous cannula, the CMA must make a detailed assessment of the patient's level of consciousness, activity, and movement so as to allow for as much freedom as possible without disturbing the IV device. It is also a good idea, if possible, to place the IV in the patient's nondominant hand if he is ambulatory and carrying out self-care activities.

By using the most appropriate site and the correct type of tape and dressing, the IV device should remain intact. The dressing should allow for frequent inspection of the site so that any change in cannula position can be expediently recognized.

The CMA should also explain to the patient his role in caring for the IV, if he is able to do so. He should be advised to call for assistance when carrying out activities that may compromise his IV and to call the CMA if he notices any change in the IV's placement or experiences any discomfort or change in sensation around the site.

A transparent dressing placed over the insertion site that covers the hub of the cannula is ideal for visually inspecting the insertion site for displacement. The hub and the IV tubing should be secured with tape placed in a chevron formation (Figure 4-1) and all loops of tubing should be secured so they do not catch on anything. Should the tape become loose, the CMA must resecure the cannula and tubing immediately. If a portion of the cannula extrudes from the vein, it should not be pushed back into the vein. Rather, it should be checked for infiltration. If still in the vein and infusing properly, it may be further secured with tape to keep it in place and avoid further movement out of the vein.

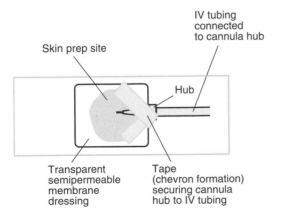

Figure 4-1 | Proper taping of IV site

Occlusion and Loss of Patency

Occlusion occurs when there is some type of blockage that interferes with the passage of infusate into the vein. It can occur at any point within the vein, the cannula, or the tubing. Loss of patency is probably one of the easiest complications to prevent.

Etiology and Defining Characteristics

Loss of patency can occur for reasons ranging from the simple to the more complex. Whatever the cause, measures must be taken as soon as the problem is identified so that the integrity of the infusion can be restored.

An easily identified and remedied problem is tubing that is kinked or bent because the patient has rolled over onto it. If an IV device is inserted near a joint, such as the antecubital space, the line may occlude when the patient flexes his arm. Sometimes the line is clamped off as a result of the patient, his visitors, or untrained personnel manipulating the line. Most often, however, flow is impeded when the IV line is changed from an electronic infusion device to gravity flow, such as during showering or ambulation when the flow rate is not properly maintained. Also, if a line is kept open at too slow a rate, the fluid flow may cease, especially if the patient is hypertensive.

If the infusate runs out and is not immediately replaced, occlusion can occur because of the backflow of venous blood into the cannula and tubing. This is caused by the loss of gravitational flow that is overtaken by venous pressure. If such a situation is left unchecked for even a short period of time, the backed-up blood will clot, thus obstructing the IV cannula as well as the infusion tubing.

The fibrin sheath that forms around and over the tip of a cannula can also disrupt the flow of fluid. Usually this does not cause obstruction unless the cannula is left in place longer than the recommended time. If, during cannulation, the intima of the vein is damaged, platelets may attach to the injured area and obstruct flow.

When too large a cannula is used to access the vein, the tip of the catheter may press against the vein wall, thus disrupting or inhibiting the prescribed rate of infusate flow. For a vein that is kept open with an intermittent infusion plug (saline or heparin lock), but not properly flushed at the prescribed intervals, occlusion can occur.

Assessment and Interventions

The first sign that there is obstruction of the IV line is a slowing or stopping of the infusate. There is often a backup of blood from the cannula into the IV tubing. The IV site usually appears normal.

Since loss of patency can easily be prevented, the CMA can usually maintain the integrity of the IV with thorough assessment of the patient, his position, his IV site, and the flow of infusate through the IV tubing. Patient teaching directed at maintaining the extremity properly positioned and keeping the tubing free of kinks is very important. The patient must not lie on the tubing or manipulate the tubing clamps or the controls on his electronic infusion device.

MEDICAL ASSISTING TIP

Signs and Symptoms of Occlusion and Loss of Patency

- Slowed rate of infusion even if clamp is opened or height of infusate is raised
- Infusion stops infusing
- Infusion site pain (with normal appearance)
- Blood backs up from the cannula into the IV tubing

MEDICAL ASSISTING ALERT

Veins That Are in Close Proximity to a Joint

If possible, the CMA should avoid cannulating veins that are in close proximity to joints. If a steel needle is used and the patient flexes an arm or wrist, the needle can puncture the vein wall and damage surrounding nerves, vessels, and tissues. Although somewhat flexible, an intravenous catheter can become occluded or break off with repeated movement or flexion of a joint. If veins near moveable joints cannot be avoided for use, the CMA must take measures to prevent flexure through patient compliance or the use of arm boards or soft splints.

Patients, visitors, and health care personnel must be advised that only properly trained personnel may handle IV products and equipment. The CMA must maintain the infusion rate at a flow that will keep the line open and prevent backflow of blood into the cannula and tubing. This is especially important for patients with hypertension, when venous pressure may exceed gravitational flow. When the patient is receiving continuous infusions, the CMA must have the next container of infusate ready to hang in advance of the previous one running out.

Intermittent infusion devices (saline or heparin locks) are to be flushed routinely with normal saline or heparin (if ordered) according to protocols. If electronic infusion devices are used, the CMA must monitor them and determine whether the controller or pump mode of flow is to be used. Any time a patient is removed from these machines, the CMA must be careful to manually adjust the IV flow rate. The clamps should never be closed completely (to avoid occlusion), nor should they be left wide open (to avoid fluid overload).

Despite using all measures to prevent the loss of patency, if an obstruction occurs, the CMA must intervene accordingly. If there are no problems with the position of the cannula, the taping, the tubing, or height of the infusate (which should be approximately 36 inches above the IV site), but the flow rate is impeded, the CMA should suspect that the line is occluded and perform the following interventions:

1. Using the fingertips, pinch the IV tubing open and closed or gently milk it, in an attempt to free a cannula tip that is positioned against the vein wall and obstructing flow.
2. If the fluid still doesn't infuse properly, attempt to irrigate the line with normal saline in a 3- or 5-cc syringe (2 cc of normal saline in a 3-cc syringe; 3 to 4 cc in a 5-cc syringe). Should there be any resistance when light pressure is applied to the plunger, stop.

MEDICAL ASSISTING ALERT

The Importance of Gentle Flushing When Irrigating

When attempting to irrigate an IV, if there is any resistance when gentle pressure is exerted on the syringe plunger, STOP. The application of force could dislodge the obstruction and send it traveling in the circulatory system. Remember, the term **irrigate** means to cleanse a canal with *gentle* flushing. It does not mean to force fluid through the canal.

3. Try to aspirate, in an attempt to remove the obstruction. If this fails, stop.
4. Discontinue the IV and restart the infusion in another location.
5. Document all assessment findings, interventions, and patient responses.

```
MEDICAL ASSISTING ALERT
```

Syringe Sizes for Irrigating

Never use smaller than a 2-cc or 3-cc syringe to irrigate or aspirate clots in an IV line. A smaller syringe creates excess pressure that can damage the intima of the vein.

Phlebitis

Phlebitis is the inflammation of a vein. **Inflammation** is part of the body's normal immune response to any type of injury or invasion. Phlebitis, along with infiltration, is a fairly common complication of infusion therapy that can occur as a result of various situations. It can lead to permanent vein damage and other serious complications if left unchecked. Phlebitis can be caused by mechanical, bacterial, or chemical sources, or a combination of them.

Etiology and Defining Characteristics

Phlebitis occurs because of local vasodilation with increased blood flow, augmented vascular permeability, and the movement of white blood cells (especially the neutrophils) from the blood into the area of injury. Plasma moves from the capillaries into the surrounding tissues. This phenomenon results in localized swelling, which in turn results in pain from the pressure of the edema on surrounding nerve endings. As inflammation of the vein progresses, white blood cells (leukocytes) and tissue cells (histocytes) are destroyed by lysosomes emitted from macrophages. This action results in warmth and redness. Pus, the end-product of dead leukocytes, accumulates and can result in **suppurative** phlebitis. As inflammation progresses, the bacterial toxins and proteins released by the invading organisms signal the hypothalamus to elevate body temperature above normal. Prostaglandins are released from phospholipids in the cell membrane, which also contributes to the inflammatory processes of pain and fever.

There are several types of IV therapy-related phlebitis that the CMA must understand.

1. Bacterial phlebitis.

    With the breakage of the skin's protective barrier and a portal of entry into the circulatory system that occurs with venipuncture, pathogenic organisms can gain access and stimulate inflammation, thus producing bacterial phlebitis. Phlebitis can also occur if a cannula is left in the vein longer than the prescribed or recommended time or if contaminated fluid or infusates are used.

2. Chemical phlebitis.

    When the vein becomes inflamed by irritating or vesicant solutions, chemical phlebitis occurs. This is the result of contact with infusates with high or low osmolarities or those with a high or low pH, especially if small veins are used for venous access.

3. Mechanical phlebitis.

    With mechanical phlebitis, the inflammation may develop as a result of the physical trauma from the skin puncture and the movement of the cannula into the vein during insertion. It can arise with any subsequent manipulation and movement of the cannula that alters the integrity of the internal vein wall. Sometimes it is caused by a clot at the tip of the catheter—the consequence of platelet aggregation around the injured vein wall. If a cannula is too large for the vein and prevents the free flow of blood around it, phlebitis can occur. The simple fact that a foreign object (the cannula) is present in the vein is enough to initiate an inflammatory response.

```
MEDICAL ASSISTING TIP
```

Signs and Symptoms of Phlebitis

- Erythema at the site
- Pain or burning at the site and along the length of the vein
- Warmth over the site
- Edema at the site
- Vein hard, red, and cordlike
- Slowed infusion rate
- Temperature elevation one degree or more above baseline

Assessment and Interventions

Prevention is the best intervention for phlebitis and other complications of IV therapy. Measures the CMA must take to prevent phlebitis begin before the IV infusion is even started. It is important to know what infusates will be administered and understand their expected therapeutic outcomes and side effects. Solution containers, tubings, and insertion devices must be checked to be sure there are no breaks in their integrity, and expiration dates must be verified. During preparation, solutions must be checked for clarity, the presence of particulate matter, and discoloration. During set-up of the infusion and priming the tubing, measures must be taken to avoid contamination. Asepsis and good hand hygiene are vital to safe preparation.

The CMA must properly assess the proposed IV site and determine that the vein intended for venous infusion is appropriate for the infusate that will be delivered. He must determine whether an IV catheter or needle should be used. Steel needles pose a greater chance for infiltration compared to catheters, but cause a lower incidence of phlebitis. The INS recommends that stainless steel needles be "limited to short-term or single-dose administration" (INS, 2000, Standard 44, S39). The CMA must select the smallest length and gauge cannula that will allow for the free flow of blood around it yet safely deliver the infusate. Veins in the legs should be avoided because of their propensity for phlebitis.

Prior to starting the infusion, the CMA must prepare the patient psychologically and physically. He needs to explain what will be done and why, and the approximate length of time the infusion will be in place. Patient teaching is so important at this time because the CMA can enlist the patient's help in troubleshooting potential problems, especially during home infusion therapy. It is wise to take the patient's temperature and record it in the chart to have as a preinfusion baseline.

Once the equipment is set up and the CMA is ready to cannulate the vein and start the infusion, he should wash his hands thoroughly, preferably with an antimicrobial emulsion, and don gloves. Following the institution or agency protocols, the CMA must use strict aseptic technique when starting the IV and dressing the site to prevent bacterial seeding. Tape should be applied to keep the IV secure but not so tight as to constrict circulation and interfere with the infusion. Once the infusion is running, there should be minimal manipulation of the cannula and site so as to avoid the mechanical trauma that predisposes to phlebitis.

If an additive is ordered for the infusate, the CMA should use a filter needle to draw it up into a syringe. Once drawn up, the needle is to be replaced with a regular needle (or appropriate needleless device) before injecting it into the IV solution. Using a filter needle followed by the regular needle reduces the chance for contamination of the IV infusate with particulate matter. When medications are given by direct intravenous injection, by bolus into the tubing, or by piggyback, it is important to administer them at the prescribed rate. If given too fast, the vein can become chemically damaged because the venous blood is unable to properly dilute them.

The CMA must be alert to the signs and symptoms of phlebitis. By recognizing them as early as possible, he can act to prevent further complications, especially the development of infection. Usually, the initial sign of phlebitis is **erythema** (redness) at the IV site with the patient complaining of pain or burning in that area. There may be edema. Upon palpation, the site feels warm and the patient experiences discomfort when the skin over the tip of the catheter is touched. The vein may feel **indurated** (hard) with a red streak on the skin that runs the length of the inflamed vein. The indurated vein may look and feel like a reddened cord. There may be temperature elevation and drainage from the IV site.

At the first sign of phlebitis, the IV infusion must be discontinued and the cannula removed. If there is fever and drainage at the site, especially if it is purulent, the physician must be notified. Depending on agency protocols, the infection control nurse or office manager should be notified and the site or cannula, or both, cultured. The appearance of the site and the patient's communications are to be thoroughly documented. When purulent drainage is present, or when "an infusion-related infection is suspected, the catheter, the delivery system, the access site, and/or the infusate shale be cultured using septic technique and observing Standard Precautions. The Semiquantitative culture technique should be used for obtaining a culture" (INS, 2000, Standard 63, S59).

There are various rating systems used to classify phlebitis. Agencies may use the INS-recommended phlebitis scale (Table 4-7), one of several scales developed by various IV product manufacturers, or they may develop their own. It is important to use the selected scale consistently in order to maintain a uniform tool for assessment, reporting, and documentation purposes.

After the IV is discontinued, warm compresses may be applied to the skin over the phlebitis, depending on agency protocols. The IV should be restarted in another place as soon as possible so as not to disrupt the infusion schedule. New tubing and infusate should be used. This is important because the phlebitis may have resulted from bacterial contamination that originated or migrated into the tubing or infusate.

Sometimes there are no signs or symptoms of phlebitis until after an IV or intermittent infusion device has been

Table 4-7 | INS Phlebitis Grading Scale* (for infusion phelibitis and postinfusion phlebitis)

CRITERIA	GRADE 0	GRADE 1	GRADE 2	GRADE 3	GRADE 4
No symptoms	✳				
Erythema at access site with or without pain		✳			
Pain at access site with erythema and/or edema			✳		
Pain at access site with erythema and/or edema				✳	
Streak formation				✳	
Palpable venous cord				✳	
Pain at access site with erythema and/or edema					✳
Streak formation					✳
Palpable venous cord					✳
> 1 inch in length					
Purulent drainage					✳

INS, 2000, standard 59, S56

discontinued. This is known as **postinfusion phlebitis** and it usually occurs within 48 hours of removal. Postinfusion phlebitis may be a delayed reaction or the result of improperly discontinuing an IV. The signs, symptoms, and treatment are the same as for phlebitis.

Thrombosis and Thrombophlebitis

Thrombophlebitis is the inflammation of a vessel due to the development of a **thrombus,** an abnormal blood clot, that obstructs or occludes the vessel. **Thrombosis** is the process whereby the clot develops. **Superficial thrombophlebitis** involves the subcutaneous vessels of the arms and legs that usually are cannulated for IV therapy. If left unchecked or inadequately treated, it may progress to **deep vein thrombosis (DVT),** which involves inflammation of the larger, deeper veins of the extremities, usually the legs. As blood flows past the clot, there is always the possibility that a portion of it will break away and travel throughout the circulatory system until it lodges in a major vessel and obstructs blood flow.

Etiology and Defining Characteristics

Thrombophlebitis is often the sequela of phlebitis (Figure 4-2). Its etiology as related to IV therapy is, therefore, usually the same. When the endothelial lining of a blood vessel becomes traumatized, as with phlebitis, the clotting process is initiated. Once a clot forms, blood flow is inhibited or stopped, a condition known as **venous stasis.** The clot then often continues to grow in the direction of the slow-moving blood.

Thrombophlebitis very often occurs when veins in the legs are used for IV therapy. Unless an emergency situation exists in which no other site is available, the leg veins should not be used in adults.

Assessment and Interventions

Since thrombophlebitis can result in serious complications, even death, prevention should always be the primary therapeutic regimen. The initial sign of thrombophlebitis is usually a slowing of the prescribed infusion rate, although the IV site may look and feel normal. As it persists, there may be pain and burning at the IV site with warmth, redness, cording, and induration of the vein. As inflammation progresses there is usually fever and malaise. As with phlebitis, baseline vital signs should be assessed prior to IV therapy and the patient's level of consciousness must be closely monitored so any untoward changes can be quickly identified.

Whenever hypertonic or highly acidic infusions are prescribed, the CMA must always be alert to the possibility of thrombophlebitis. If an infusion is discontinued and treatment is initiated at the first sign of superficial thrombophlebitis, further complications do not usually ensue and DVT does not develop.

When the lower extremities must be used for IV therapy, there is always the possibility that DVT will occur. If the leg veins must be used, the CMA must take precautions to avoid venous stasis. If possible, the patient should ambulate to promote venous return or perform active and passive range of motion (ROM) exercises in the extremity. Prolonged immobility or positioning the limb in a dependent position when sitting or standing must be avoided and the limb elevated when the patient is in bed.

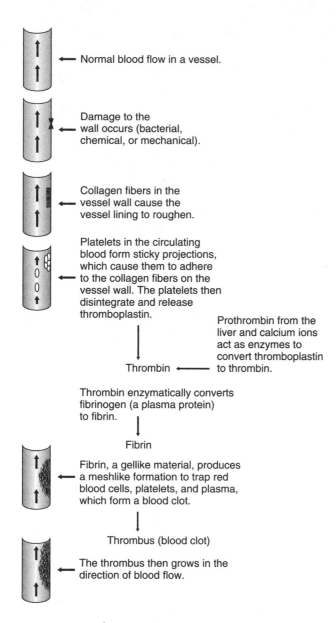

Normal blood flow in a vessel.

Damage to the wall occurs (bacterial, chemical, or mechanical).

Collagen fibers in the vessel wall cause the vessel lining to roughen.

Platelets in the circulating blood form sticky projections, which cause them to adhere to the collagen fibers on the vessel wall. The platelets then disintegrate and release thromboplastin.

Prothrombin from the liver and calcium ions act as enzymes to convert thromboplastin to thrombin.

Thrombin ← to thrombin.

Thrombin enzymatically converts fibrinogen (a plasma protein) to fibrin.

Fibrin

Fibrin, a gellike material, produces a meshlike formation to trap red blood cells, platelets, and plasma, which form a blood clot.

Thrombus (blood clot)

The thrombus then grows in the direction of blood flow.

Figure 4-2 | Progression of phlebitis to thrombophlebitis

MEDICAL ASSISTING ALERT

Avoiding DVT

Due to the possible development of DVT, the leg veins should not be used for IV therapy, unless an emergency situation arises in which other veins are inaccessible. As soon as another site can be accessed, the site must be changed.

Unfortunately, the clinical signs and symptoms of DVT are nonspecific and there may be no warning until acute respiratory distress occurs when a clot breaks away and lodges in the lung. Since a slowing of the IV infusion rate and swelling of the

extremity are the most reliable indicators of thrombophlebitis and further complications, the CMA should frequently assess the site and flow rate. If the area of inflammation is extensive, there will be reduced venous return resulting in mottling, cyanosis, or both. The skin temperature can be increased and superficial veins may be dilated. Although not always a good indicator, if the IV is in the leg, there may be a positive **Homan's sign**—calf pain with dorsiflexion of the foot.

Once identified, thrombophlebitis must be treated expeditiously. The IV must be discontinued and restarted elsewhere. The physician should be consulted as to whether the extremity should be elevated and warm, moist compresses applied. The physician may order antiembolic stockings and/or the use of sequential compression devices (SCDs). The CMA must strictly follow the treatment regime, which usually includes the administration of anticoagulant and antiinflammatory drugs and a balanced routine of active and passive activity and rest. Reporting and documentation must be thorough and accurate.

Hematoma

A **hematoma** is the accumulation of clotted blood in the tissue **interstices** (spaces). It results from the loss of integrity in a vessel wall due to disease or trauma that allows the escape of blood in the surrounding area. The result is **ecchymosis**—a black-and-blue skin discoloration.

Etiology and Defining Characteristics

Whenever a vessel is damaged, platelets migrate to the site to patch it and prevent blood loss. The presence of platelets also signals the activation of the clotting mechanism with the formation of fibrin from circulating fibrinogen.

MEDICAL ASSISTING TIP

Signs and Symptoms of Thrombophlebitis

- Slowed or stopped infusion rate
- Aching or burning sensation at the infusion site
- Elevation in temperature one degree or more above baseline
- Skin warm and red around IV site
- Cording of the infusion vein
- Malaise
- Swelling and edema of the extremity
- Throbbing pain in the limb
- Mottling and cyanosis of the extremity
- Diminished arterial pulses
- Pallor

The usual cause of hematoma formation is faulty venipuncture technique, where the cannula passes through the distal vein wall. It can also occur with infiltration following cannulation of a vein. Sometimes a hematoma develops following successful venipuncture when the flow control clamp for the infusion is opened before the tourniquet is removed. The fluid pressure distal to the tourniquet causes the vessel to rupture.

MEDICAL ASSISTING TIP

Releasing the Tourniquet after Cannulation

Once a vein is successfully cannulated for an infusion, release the tourniquet before opening the flow control clamp on the IV tubing. Failure to do so causes excess pressure to build up distal to the tourniquet and ruptures the vein.

If the lumen of the cannula is too large for the vein to accommodate it, vessel rupture can occur. If the cannula is too long for the vein, it may sever the vessel at a junction where the vein merges with another portion of the vein. For patients with fragile skin and veins, the pressure of the tourniquet, if applied too tightly, can cause a hematoma to form when the vein is punctured. Also, if venipuncture has been unsuccessful and the CMA attempts to start the IV in a nearby area, the application of the tourniquet can cause the first puncture site to break open and bleed.

A hematoma can form when inadequate pressure is applied following a blood sampling stick or the discontinuation of an infusion or heparin lock. Even though bleeding has been arrested, it can start again if the patient lowers the extremity too soon after the cannula has been removed, especially if a pressure dressing has not been applied.

MEDICAL ASSISTING TIP

Signs and Symptoms of Hematoma

- Ecchymosis over and around insertion area
- Pain at the site
- Swelling and hardness at the insertion site
- Inability to advance the cannula all the way into the vein during insertion
- Inability to flush the IV line

Assessment and Interventions

Although hematoma formation cannot always be avoided, the incidence can be reduced with thorough assessment of the patient's skin and vein integrity. The method of cannulation may need to be altered, especially for patients with fragile veins, paper-thin skin, or veins that roll—those that move laterally when manipulated. For patients with veins that tend to roll, rather than insert the cannula directly over the vein, it may be preferable to enter indirectly from the side and gently advance the cannula into the vein. This also decreases the chance of puncturing the opposite vein wall. For patients with very fragile veins, it is sometimes necessary to cannulate the vein bevel down, rather than the usual bevel-up method, as a means to prevent puncture of the opposite vein wall. It is also important to select a cannula that is not too large or too long for the vein. It may be beneficial to use a blood pressure cuff rather than a tourniquet to restrict venous flow during venipuncture. For patients with fragile veins, it is preferable not to use a tourniquet at all.

The tourniquet must never be applied above the site of a recent lab stick, unsuccessful venous cannulation (where the vessel has been nicked), or following the discontinuation of an IV. Once a vein is cannulated for an infusion, the tourniquet must be immediately removed.

A hematoma is fairly easy to identify because the area around the venipuncture site is usually ecchymotic. It may also be tender or painful and edematous. If a large amount of blood has escaped, the area will be raised and hard. If these indicators are not evident, the CMA may suspect hematoma formation when he is unable to advance the cannula into the vein during insertion or meets with resistance when attempting to irrigate.

Once a hematoma is identified, the IV must be discontinued, and a 2 × 2-inch gauze pressure dressing applied. Alcohol should not be used when removing the cannula because it enhances bleeding and may cause stinging at the puncture site. Once bleeding has stopped, the extremity may be elevated and warm moist compresses applied, depending on the severity of the hematoma. The CMA should follow agency protocols and medical directives regarding treatment interventions.

Venous Spasm

Venous spasm is the sudden involuntary movement or contraction of a vessel wall. It occurs as a result of trauma or irritation from chemicals or temperature extremes and is usually painful. A strong, painful spasm is a **cramp.**

Etiology and Defining Characteristics

Venous spasm is usually caused by the administration of an irritating infusate with a high osmolarity or a high or low

MEDICAL ASSISTING ALERT

Infusates That May Cause Venous Spasm

- Cold solutions
- Dextrose solutions with concentrations greater than 12.5%
- Infusates with a high or low pH
- Diazepam (Valium)
- Nafcillin sodium (Nafcil; Unipen)
- Phenytoin (Dilantin)
- Potassium chloride solutions
- Propofol (Diprivan)
- Vancomycin HCl

pH. The delivery of cold or viscous infusates can also precipitate venous spasm. For some patients, the entrance of the IV cannula into the vein can result in spasm, especially if the cannula is too large to allow for adequate hemodilution. Venous spasm often occurs if a solution is infused too rapidly, particularly with a small-gauge cannula. The vasovagal response resulting from pain or anxiety also contributes to venous spasm.

MEDICAL ASSISTING TIP

Signs and Symptoms of Venous Spasm

- Slowed infusion rate
- Stopped infusion rate
- Severe pain from the IV site radiating up the extremity
- Blanching over the IV site
- Redness over and around the IV site

Assessment and Interventions

In most situations, venous spasm is a complication that can be prevented. When it does occur, it is identified by a slowing of the infusion rate due to the wavelike contractions of the vessel wall. The patient complains of a sharp, painful sensation that radiates from the IV site up the extremity. Some patients say it feels like an electric shock going up the arm. The skin over the vein may blanch or it can be red, an indication of phlebitis.

Venous spasm can be prevented by using a large vein and a small-gauge cannula so that blood flow is unrestricted

and allows for dilution of the infusate. Fluids should be administered at room temperature. Refrigerated medications must be taken out of the refrigerator for the minimum time needed to get them to room temperature. A blood warmer can be used to prevent venous spasm during a transfusion. Irritating solutions should be well diluted. The CMA must assess the patient's anxiety level and his pain threshold, then take the necessary measures to help him relax.

Once venous spasm occurs, it can usually be reversed by decreasing the infusion rate. The application of warm compresses to the area surrounding the IV site can be used if the infusate is cold. If not contraindicated, and with a medical order, some irritating infusates can be buffered by adding sodium bicarbonate. A pharmacist should be consulted regarding the amount of buffer to add. When a vein continues to spasm in spite of these measures, the IV must be discontinued and restarted in a larger vein.

Vessel Collapse

When the walls of a vein or artery retract abnormally, **vessel collapse** occurs. This is one of the less commonly encountered complications of IV therapy.

Etiology and Defining Characteristics

Vessel collapse usually occurs as a result of decreased circulation, as seen with excessive blood or fluid loss and shock. The veins in the extremities constrict in an attempt to shunt blood and oxygen to the brain and vital organs. When negative pressure is exerted on a vessel from aspiration of an IV line with a syringe, vessel collapse can occur.

MEDICAL ASSISTING TIP

Signs and Symptoms of Vessel Collapse

- Inability to see a vein
- Inability to feel a vein
- Loss of vessel elasticity
- Vessel feels flat or flaccid
- Reduced or stopped infusion flow

Assessment and Interventions

When attempting to cannulate a vein, the CMA may identify that the vessel is collapsed because he cannot see or palpate the vein. If the vein is palpable, it has little elasticity and feels flaccid and flat. If an infusion is already running and the vessel collapses, the fluid flow will cease. When aspirating to check for patency or to remove a blockage, a vessel may collapse due to the negative pressure exerted on the vessel wall. This usually happens when a small-capacity syringe, 1 cc or smaller, is used.

Whatever the cause of the vessel collapse, the CMA must restart the IV elsewhere, preferably in a larger vein. If the patient is in shock, this may not be possible, and a physician may have to insert a central venous line. The CMA, then, must stay with the patient, provide reassurance, assist with the central venous cannulation, and keep the patient warm. He should lower the patient's head and elevate his legs to promote venous return, and carefully monitor vital signs. Accurate reporting and documentation is critical in such a situation.

Cellulitis

Cellulitis is the diffuse inflammation and infection of cellular and subcutaneous connective tissue. It is bacterial in nature and, although localized, it has poorly defined borders and spreads to surrounding areas by way of watery seepage that extends along tissue spaces. If severe, cellulitis can lead to abscess formation and ulceration of the body's deeper tissues. It often spreads to the lymphatic system.

Etiology and Defining Characteristics

Cellulitis associated with IV therapy occurs in response to the invasion and multiplication of bacteria, usually the *Staphylococcus* and *Streptococcus* strains. The portal of entry is usually the IV puncture site. The organisms may come from the CMA during venipuncture or dressing changes or they may migrate to the IV insertion site from the patient's body. Poor aseptic technique and the failure to follow established infection control protocols are usually to blame for the development of cellulitis.

Assessment and Interventions

With cellulitis there is tenderness, pain, induration, and edema (pitting or nonpitting) when pressure is applied. The site feels warm and the skin has the roughened appearance of orange peel **(peau d'orange).** If the cellulitis has spread to the lymphatics, there may be red streaks on the skin over the vessels. Vesicles may form and there is often purulent exudate. The patient presents with fever, chills, and malaise.

The intervention measures for cellulitis are similar to those for infiltration, extravasation, and phlebitis. The IV must be discontinued and started elsewhere. The CMA may have to assist the physician with the incision and drainage of an abscess. The limb may be elevated to reduce edema. Cool compresses to promote

MEDICAL ASSISTING TIP

Signs and Symptoms of Cellulitis

- **Tenderness**
- **Pain**
- **Warmth**
- **Edema**
- **Induration**
- **Red streaking on skin**
- *Peau d'orange*
- **Vesicles**
- **Abscess formation with pus**
- **Ulceration**
- **Fever**
- **Chills**
- **Malaise**

comfort are often alternated with warm, moist compresses to promote circulation, depending on medical directives and agency protocols. Hand hygiene must be meticulous and gloves are to be worn when tending to the cellulitis. Sterile dressings should be used. The CMA must assess for the signs and symptoms of systemic infection and sepsis. Antibiotics, analgesics, and antipyretics are generally administered.

Documentation must be thorough and accurate. It should reflect the signs and symptoms that led to the cellulitis as well as its progression, the description of the healing process, and the patient's response to treatment.

Nerve, Tendon, Ligament, and Limb Damage

In addition to the tissue damage already covered, there can be nerve, tendon, and ligament damage that can occur as a result of IV therapy. Some complications can progress to the loss of function in an extremity or to amputation of the limb.

Etiology and Defining Characteristics

The major causes of functional and structural damage are the incorrect insertion and placement of the IV cannula or improper securing and stabilization of the cannula and IV line after insertion. Problems usually occur when the selected IV site is in close proximity to a joint and the IV site is not naturally splinted by bone. If the IV must be placed near a joint, problems occur because of failure to artificially splint the joint. Damage can also result from extravasated solution, from the pressure of infiltrated infusate, the pressure and anatomic displacement caused by a hematoma, or the sequelae of cellulitis.

Assessment and Interventions

When starting an IV, the CMA must know the circulatory anatomy so the appropriate vein is properly accessed and damage is not done to the surrounding areas during cannulation. The cannula must never be moved back and forth in the subcutaneous tissue in an attempt to find a vein. Not only can damage be done to nerves, tendons, and ligaments, but an artery can be punctured.

The extremity in which the IV is placed must be frequently assessed and accurately documented. The skin should be warm and dry with normal color. The nurse must be alert to altered circulation, movement, and sensation. The patient should be able to move the extremity distal to the IV insertion site to promote circulation. In the home care setting, the CMA must teach the patient and his family what to look for and report.

SYSTEMIC COMPLICATIONS OF INFUSION THERAPY

Several of the local complications already covered can serve as warning signs for and precursors to the development of systemic problems of infusion therapy. Other systemic problems occur because of contamination, drug and fluid interactions, hypersensitivity reactions, sepsis, and emboli.

Contamination and Infection

Contamination is the introduction of microorganisms or particulate matter into a normally sterile environment. With intravenous therapy, the serious consequences of infection can result from a break in asepsis at any point in the manufacture of IV products or the delivery of infusion therapy.

Etiology and Defining Characteristics

Although the most infrequent cause, contamination can result from breaks in asepsis during the manufacture, packaging, and storage of infusates, medications, and delivery systems. It occurs most frequently, however, during the setup and administration of infusion therapy. During preparation, any break in aseptic technique on the part of the CMA can provide an entry port for microorganisms. The use of three-way stopcocks, which are frequently handled, often serve as the entry site for contaminants.

Assessment and Interventions

Although the CMA cannot be sure that the infusates and delivery systems are sterile, he must use every means to ensure that they are safe. Such measures include visually examining all containers and equipment for the presence of particulate matter, leaks or breaks, and discoloration along with verification of expiration dates. Following agency protocols, the cannula, tubings, and infusates must be changed on schedule. Filters and extension tubings should only be used when necessary and according to policy.

Frequent assessment of the patient and his IV site alert the CMA to any problems that might arise as the result of contamination. The first signs of contamination are the same as those with sepsis. There may be chills, malaise, a fever, and an elevated leukocyte count with no apparent etiology. The IV site will look normal, unless there is phlebitis.

Once it is determined or suspected that contamination has occurred, the IV must be discontinued. The IV should be restarted at another site with new tubing and fresh infusate. The physician and the infection control department should be notified. The cannula, connection sites, tubing, and infusate should be cultured.

Sepsis

Sepsis is the (usually) febrile disease process that results from the presence of microorganisms or their toxic products in the circulatory system. Approximately 700,000 cases of severe sepsis (that associated with acute multiple organ dysfunction syndrome (MODS), hypoperfusion, and shock), occur in the United States annually (Linde-Zwirble et al., 1999). According to the CDC, it is the leading cause of death in noncoronary ICU patients in the United States (Sands et al., 1997) and the 11th leading cause of death overall (CDC, *National Vital Statistics Report,* 2000). On a worldwide scale, this amounts to several million cases annually. Sepsis results in mortality rates that range from 28% to 50% (Natanson et al., 1997; Zeni et al., 1997). The widespread use of broad-spectrum antibiotics, which has increased the rates of both antibiotic resistance and nosocomial infections, will have a direct impact on the rising incidence of sepsis (Opal & Cohen, 1999).

Etiology and Defining Characteristics

The organisms that are usually responsible for sepsis in the nonimmunocompromised adult are the gram-negative (*Escherichia, Klebsiella, Pseudomonas, Enterobacter, Serratia, Proteus,* and *Neisseria* species) and gram-positive (*Staphylococcus* and *Streptococcus* species) organisms, anaerobes, and

the yeast *Candida* (Gorbach, Mensa, & Gatell, 1999). Sepsis is caused by the gram-negative *Escherichia coli, Pseudomonas,* and *Klebsiella* species 65% to 70% of the time (White, 1997).

IV infusion-related sepsis is most often attributed to *Staphylococcus aureus* and *S. epidermidis* bacteria, the *Candida albicans* yeast (Sanford, Gilbert, & Sande, 2002), and the coliform species *Escherichia, Enterobacter,* and *Klebsiella* (CDC, 2001). Vascular system septicemia, introduced by way of IV catheters, foreign bodies, and surgical interventions, is generally caused by the *Enterobacter, Serratia, S. epidermidis, Pseudomonas,* enterococci, and *Candida* pathogens (Myers, 1996).

Assessment and Interventions

Because of the widely disseminated infection that occurs with sepsis, fever develops (as the body's attempt to provide an unfavorable environment for organism growth and reproduction). The fever and toxins from the organisms stimulate cellular metabolism and vasodilation, causing the patient to look flushed, with warm, dry skin. He has general malaise, chills, and headache.

With vasodilation there is decreased peripheral resistance, causing a drop in blood pressure and reduced cardiac output. The heart compensates for loss of vascular volume by increasing its rate in order to shunt blood to the vital organs. Because of this, the extremities are somewhat dehydrated, pale in color, and cool to the touch. The patient complains of thirst. Renal compensation for decreased vascular volume results in oliguria.

When the bacterial toxins increase cellular metabolism, intravascular clotting may be stimulated, leading to the development of microclots throughout the body, a condition called **disseminated intravascular coagulation (DIC).** The clots clog capillaries, impair tissue profusion, and damage vital organs because they are deprived of nutrients. The DIC eventually uses up the available clotting factors in the blood, so hemorrhage into the tissues, especially those of the gastrointestinal tract, occurs.

The body will continue to compensate, but if sepsis is not halted, decompensation occurs. The metabolism of all cells shuts down and the vital organs are damaged. The patient becomes stuporous or comatose. The circulatory system becomes involved and circulatory collapse ensues. Despite adequate fluid resuscitation, severe hypotension occurs (systolic BP <90 mm Hg) and septic shock ensues. Simultaneous and progressive organ failure (CNS, lungs, liver, heart, GI tract, kidneys) or MODS occurs. Once this happens and cardiac output falls below 40% of normal, death soon follows.

Sepsis must be treated aggressively to prevent septic shock and death. Figure 4-3 illustrates the pathophysiology of the progression of sepsis from contamination through septic shock. Interventions are aimed at treating the cause of sepsis with antibiotic therapy and preventing or reversing shock. The patient should be kept flat with his legs elevated (modified Trendelenburg position). Oral fluids are given to relieve thirst and IV infusions must be maintained. Chilling must be prevented, but the patient should not be kept so warm as to cause peripheral vasodilation. Medications are given as necessary to support blood pressure, circulation, and promote comfort. If the patient is disoriented, he must be protected from injury. Accurate monitoring of vital signs is necessary.

Because the patient is weak, care is planned to conserve his strength and allow for frequent rest. Care is directed toward supporting the patient as symptoms develop. The patient must be observed for internal bleeding. If DIC occurs, there may be purpura or frank bleeding from mucous membranes, the IV site, and all body orifices. Pressure and cool compresses may be applied to sites of bleeding and the CMA will be involved in blood product replacement therapy.

Dyspnea and cyanosis require oxygen administration and positioning to assist the patient's breathing. Fever is treated with prescribed antipyretics, cool sponges, and fluid replacement. For muscle and joint pain, analgesics are

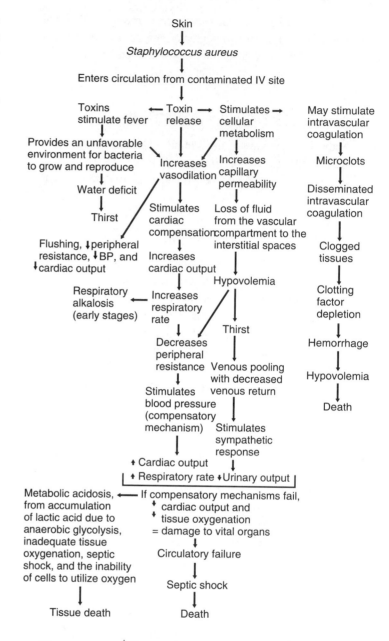

Figure 4-3 | Progression of sepsis

administered and the patient must be positioned to minimize pressure on sore areas. It is important for the CMA to promote self-care within the patient's limitations, encourage therapeutic communication, and support the patient and his family emotionally and psychologically.

Numerous investigational compounds have been studied for the treatment of sepsis (Natanson et al., 1998; Zeni, 1997). Many of these investigational therapies may have been unsuccessful because they modulated only a single pathophysiologic component of sepsis. Current research supports the use of recombinant human-activated protein C (drotrecogin alfa activated), the first drug found to fight sepsis. Those given this drug, a genetically engineered protein and natural blood product that helps prevent clotting and inflammation, have a 19% greater chance of survival. It is estimated that one life out of every sixteen patients with sepsis could be saved (Bernard et al., 2001).

Medication and Fluid Interactions

Many combinations of medication and fluid are delivered during the course of infusion therapy. The concurrent administration of some products can result in unintended or undesirable effects.

Etiology and Defining Characteristics

Incompatibility refers to the qualities of certain fluids and medications that cause unintended effects when they are mixed (drugs with drugs, drugs with fluids, or fluids with fluids). Refer to Table 4-8 for common drug–drug incompatibilities. When two or more agents are mixed, the intended action of either drug or fluid may be neutralized, intensified, or weakened. The mixture may form a **precipitation**—the suspension or crystallization of particles that occurs due to the mixing of incompatible solutions or adding solutes to incompatible solutions. Precipitation results in the occlusion of an intravenous line. **Antagonism** means that the combined effect of two or more agents is less than the sum of each one acting alone, while **synergism** means that the combined effect is greater than the sum of each one acting independently. **Idiosyncrasy** is an unusual or abnormal response to a medication or fluid. The interactions between some medications or fluids can also alter or distort laboratory tests.

Table 4-8 | Significant Drug–Drug Interactions

The following drugs are generally incompatible when combined with any other products.

- Aminoglycosides
- Chlordiazepoxide
- Diazepam
- Digitalis glycosides
- Pentobarbital
- Phenobarbital
- Phenytoin
- Secobarbital
- Sodium bicarbonate
- Theophylline derivatives

An interaction occurring because a medication acts not only on the tissue or system it is targeted for but also on other structures is known as a **side effect.** A common example is the IV administration of meperidine (Demerol) for the alleviation of postoperative pain, which also exerts a depressant effect on the central nervous system, resulting in drowsiness.

Absorption is the process in which a drug or fluid moves from the site of administration (such as the mouth, in the gastrointestinal system) to body fluids (blood, in the circulatory system) to the intended site of action (such as the heart) to elicit a therapeutic effect (e.g., increased cardiac output). With intravenous administration, the medication is directly absorbed into the blood and is immediately distributed to its target tissue. **Biotransformation** is the actual breakdown and metabolism of a drug; **elimination** is its removal from the body. Drug interactions can occur at any point during the processes of absorption, distribution, biotransformation, or elimination.

Assessment and Interventions

The CMA must never under any circumstance administer an intravenous medication or solution unless he knows what it is and its intended effect on the patient. This includes knowing whether it is compatible when mixed with other drugs or fluids. He must also know which drugs cannot be given by direct IV push because they need to be diluted with another fluid of a specified volume prior to intravenous administration (e.g., IV potassium supplements).

With the multitude of drugs and IV infusates on the market today, it is not possible for the CMA to know everything about every product. He is expected, however, to know where to find information about every medication and fluid to be given and refer to the source prior to administration. Consultation with a pharmacist is necessary when any doubts regarding drug and fluid compatibilities exist. He should be familiar with the current *Physicians' Desk Reference* in order to understand the manufacturer's guidelines regarding medication use and admixture preparation. A drug compatibility chart should be available, and it is recommended that the CMA refer to a drug handbook or reference guide to understand the implications associated with intravenous infusions. Whenever an IV medication or fluid is administered for the first time to a patient, the CMA is expected to stay with the patient long enough to determine if the patient will develop any untoward or unexpected reactions.

Hypersensitivity Reaction

A **hypersensitivity** reaction is the profound physiologic response of the body to an antigen. It is one of the most serious consequences of infusion therapy. It transpires when the immune system fails to protect the body against foreign materials. **Allergy** is the acquired abnormal immune response to an **allergen** (any substance that causes an immune response) following **sensitization,** or the first exposure to the allergen. More precisely, an allergen is an antigen that reacts specifically to a **reagin**—a type of immunoglobulin E (IgE). An **antigen** is an agent that is capable of stimulating antibodies. It is a protein that coats the surface of specific tissue cells (e.g., muscle, bone) and identifies them as part of the body, rather than as "strangers" or invaders.

Etiology and Defining Characteristics

Some individuals are more prone to allergic reactions because they carry in their systems large volumes of IgE antibodies, rather than IgG antibodies, which are more common in the general population. These people tend to be drug-sensitive. When an allergen enters the body, an allergen-reagin reaction occurs, which subsequently develops into an allergic reaction because the IgE antibodies bind to cells in the lungs and mucous membranes of the respiratory tract or skin cells.

IgE antibodies are attracted to basophils and mast cells, which can bind with up to a half million IgE molecules. Whenever allergens bind with these molecules, the cell membranes are altered and many of the basophils and masts rupture and release substances that cause blood vessel dilation and damage to tissues by enzymes (**proteases**) that break down proteins. There is increased capillary permeability, which allows fluid to leak into the tissues, and smooth muscle contraction occurs. These reactions are the result of histamine release, toxin secretions (called *slow-reacting substance of anaphylaxis*), heparin, and factors that activate platelets. Enzymes that are attracted to eosinophils and neutrophils are also released.

MEDICAL ASSISTING ALERT

Effects of Anaphylaxis

Anaphylaxis, also called anaphylactic shock, is a severe allergic reaction that results from an allergen moving throughout the circulatory system. The allergen comes in contact with the basophils in the blood and the mast cells that exist near the surface of small blood vessels, which results in a substantial release of histamine. This causes massive peripheral dilation, which deprives the vital organs of blood and oxygen, along with increased capillary permeability and plasma loss from the circulation. Shock and death can ensue within minutes if treatment is not initiated.

Assessment and Interventions

A thorough patient history is very important in eliciting information regarding a patient's allergic status. Proper patient identification and assessment for allergies are crucial in both the acute care and home care settings. Immediately before medications are administered, especially those delivered intravenously, it is a good idea to question the patient again regarding allergies. In addition to prescription medications, the CMA needs to verify allergies to over-the-counter (OTC) medications, foods, topical preparations (especially iodine, if it is used as an IV site prep), and tape. If there is a known history of allergies, patient teaching should include recommending the use of a Medic Alert identification bracelet.

The signs and symptoms of a hypersensitivity reaction can range from mild to severe, can affect several body systems (Table 4-9), and may develop rapidly, gradually, or be delayed hours after the allergen has been delivered. There is often pain and edema around the IV site along with a characteristic **red flare,** due to the local release of histamine and resulting vasodilation. There is red streaking on the skin over venous routes and there may be a rash, with itching. Because of smooth muscle contractions, the patient often presents wheezing and bronchospasm, palpitations, gastric and intestinal cramping, and nausea with vomiting. The patient may have a headache, feel anxious or agitated, or be confused.

MEDICAL ASSISTING TIP

Hypersensitivity in Intravenous Infusions

With intravenous infusions, hypersensitivity to the infusate, its preservatives, or to IV medications can occur. The patient may be allergic to the cannula, skin antiseptic preparation, or tape. Depending on where a specific type of allergen-reagin reaction occurs, the result can be anything from rashes, itching, and hives, to bronchial spasm and anaphylaxis.

Embolism

An **embolus** (plural **emboli**) is an aggregate of undissolved material in the blood that is carried by circulatory flow. It may be solid, liquid, or gaseous. An **endogenous embolus** arises from within the body and usually consists of clotted blood (thrombus), tissue particles, tumor cell mass, or fat globules (that arise from skeletal trauma). An **exogenous embolus** originates outside of the body and is

Table 4-9 | Systemic Signs and Symptoms of a Hypersensitivity Reaction

CARDIOVASCULAR/ CIRCULATORY SYSTEM	GASTROINTESTINAL/ DIGESTIVE SYSTEM	INTEGUMENTARY SYSTEM
• Facial edema	• Dysphagia (difficulty swallowing)	• Flushing
• Generalized edema	• Gastric cramping	• Red flare
• Erythema along veins	• Intestinal cramping	• Rash
• Palpitations	• Nausea	• IV site edema
• Hypotension	• Vomiting	• Pruritus (itching)
• Cardiac arrest		• Urticaria (hives)
NERVOUS SYSTEM	**RESPIRATORY SYSTEM**	**SPECIAL SENSES**
• Agitation	• Nasal congestion	• Pruritus (itching)
• Anxiety	• Rhinorrhea (runny nose)	• Watery eyes
• Confusion	• Cough	• Scratchy throat
• Disorientation	• Sensation of tightness in throat	• Tinnitus (ringing in ears)
• Headache	• Mucous membrane edema	• Buzzing sound in ears
• Paresthesias (loss of sensation or numbness/tingling)	• Wheezing	• Throbbing sensation in ears
• Vertigo	• Bronchospasm	• Tingling/numbness in fingers and/or toes
	• Respiratory obstruction	• Vertigo
	• Respiratory arrest	

MEDICAL ASSISTING ALERT

Proper Actions in a Hypersensitivity Reaction

At the first indication of a hypersensitivity reaction, the CMA must either discontinue the infusion and keep the vein open with normal saline or, if the reaction is mild, slow the IV to a KVO (keep vein open) rate until further orders can be obtained. NEVER REMOVE THE CANNULA! Vital signs are to be taken and the physician notified. The CMA must stay with the patient, reassure him, and keep him warm. Emergency equipment must be readily available. Emergency drugs are administered according to agency policy and physician orders. Documentation must be complete, accurate, and reflect all necessary assessment data, problem identification, and interventions.

introduced into the bloodstream. It consists of particulate matter (such as hair, glass, or other particles), liquids, or gaseous material (such as room air). When an embolus meets with a vessel that is smaller than its diameter, it obstructs the vessel, blocks blood flow, and deprives the area distal to the embolism of blood and oxygen, a condition known as **ischemia.** The result is usually **infarction**—an area of **necrosis** (death of tissue) following the loss of blood supply. An embolus is named according to the vessel or organ it obstructs, usually cerebral, myocardial, pulmonary, or renal. Even the smallest embolus will be caught in a pulmonary vessel. Emboli that arise in veins, because of slower blood flow, are more common than those that arise in arteries.

Etiology and Contributing factors

Risk factors that predispose to embolic formation are impaired mobility and circulation, advanced age, recent surgery, obesity, and thrombophlebitis. In IV therapy, the emboli that most frequently occur result from dislodgement of a thrombus, the accidental admission of air into the circulatory system, or catheter embolism.

Blood Clot

The flow of blood past a thrombosis or any mechanical manipulation of the thrombotic area can cause a portion of the clot to break off and become an embolism, which can then break into multiple emboli. With IV therapy, the cause is usually the result of trauma to the intima of a vein. Bedridden patients are more prone to thromboembolic formation because of immobility (and the resulting venous stasis). About one in ten times an embolus travels through the right atrium and ventricle and lodges in the arterioles of the lung(s), resulting in massive pulmonary embolism (Guyton & Hall, 1997).

Just as a thrombus increases in size on a vein wall, the embolism, if not treated, continues to grow where it lodges in a pulmonary vessel, usually resulting in a fatal outcome. Small emboli may circulate until they become trapped in coronary vessels and cause a myocardial infarction, or lodge in cerebral vessels and effect a cerebral vascular accident, or stroke.

Air Embolism

Vessels can also be obstructed by air that enters the circulation through severed IV lines, tubings that are not primed with infusate, vented infusion containers that are allowed to run dry, or disconnected and loose tubing junctions. Piggyback lines that run dry can predispose to air entry if the primary tubing does not have a back-check valve proximal to the highest injection port. Air embolization occurs more frequently with improper handling of central venous catheters than with peripheral lines.

When air is present in the infusion line, it must be removed so it does not enter the patient's bloodstream. When clearing the line of air by using a syringe connected to an injection port, the plunger must not be removed prior to attachment to the infusion line. If the plunger is removed, air can enter the bloodstream when the flow control clamp is open and the tubing proximal to the cannula hub is not closed off. The plunger should always remain in the syringe barrel to assist with air removal by manually drawing back on the plunger.

Room air is approximately 70% nitrogen and, although blood is able to dissolve nitrogen relatively fast, it cannot do so rapidly enough when there is a large amount. As a result, the blood in the capillary beds and arterioles becomes displaced by the air, so there is ischemia and necrosis distal to the air blockage (Figure 4-4).

Catheter Embolism

When a portion of an IV catheter breaks off, it can become an embolism. This can occur when a through-the-needle catheter (TNC) is inserted and a portion of it is sheared off, usually because the catheter is moved back and forth through the needle. It also happens when an over-the-needle catheter (ONC) is in place and the stylet is advanced back into the catheter.

Other Causes for Embolic Formation

Any particle in the blood can initiate the coagulation process. Other sources of embolism can be hair from the patient's

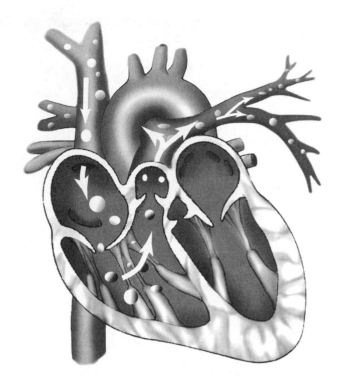

Figure 4-4 | Anatomy of an air embolism

extremity, and cotton, gauze, or linen fibers that enter the blood during venous cannulation. A clot on the tip of a cannula can be propelled into the circulation with improper irrigation technique. Failure to use a filter needle when drawing up IV additives from an ampule or vial can result in the introduction of glass or rubber-stopper fragments. Inadequately diluted solute-solvent admixtures can introduce particles of undissolved medications, which can embolize or attract platelets, which will form an even larger embolism. Bacteria circulating independently do not act as emboli, but if clusters form (when there is contamination to a vein at an IV puncture site), they may deteriorate the vein intima and cause shreds of the vein to break off.

Assessment and Interventions

Emboli, no matter how small, will cause pulmonary embolism. If large enough, death is usually instantaneous. Care is primarily aimed at prevention of thrombosis and emboli.

Blood Clot

If a clot lodges in a small branch of the pulmonary artery, the patient usually is tachypneic, dyspneic, and has fever. He complains of chest pain and has a cough, which sometimes produces hemoptysis. Although a small embolism may not elicit any symptoms, it usually progresses to a larger one because its presence initiates the coagulation process.

MEDICAL ASSISTING TIP

Signs and Symptoms of Pulmonary Embolism

- Dyspnea
- Tachypnea
- Cardiac arrhythmia
- Hypotension
- Diaphoresis
- Anxiety
- Substernal pressure
- Chest pain with inhalation and exhalation
- Localized decreased breath sounds
- Pleural friction rub
- Cough (often with hemoptysis)

CRITICAL THINKING

Discerning the Causes and Diagnosis of Chest Pain

Is your patient who is complaining of chest pain suffering from an infarction or something else? How do you know?

This is a frightening situation and can present a confusing dilemma. The CMA must be able to accurately assess the etiology of chest pain in any patient. This is especially important in the home care setting because of the potential need for emergency transport to a hospital. The CMA should remember that **angina pectoris** is chest pain caused by coronary artery spasm or constriction, not by an obstruction from a clot. The patient usually complains of substernal pressure that radiates to the neck, jaw, and down the right shoulder and arm. There may be dyspnea, diaphoresis, and pallor. It is usually temporary, reversible, and relieved with rest and nitroglycerin. A **myocardial infarction (MI)** results from prolonged ischemia from an infarcted vessel that causes hypoxia and irreversible damage to the myocardium if treatment is not initiated immediately. The symptoms may be similar to those of angina, or there may be no symptomatology (called silent heart attack). A patient having an MI does not experience relief of symptoms from rest and nitroglycerin.

When central organs are obstructed, pain and dysfunction result from infarction and necrosis. Renal vessel obstruction causes flank pain and oliguria. With mesenteric blockage, the patient has abdominal pain and cramping with impaired bowel mobility. Wherever blood flow is impeded, the necrotic tissue that results provides an ideal medium for bacterial growth and reproduction, which further compromises the patient.

Patient care is primarily aimed at the prevention of thrombosis. For patients who are at risk for thrombus development, the CMA may be required to administer low-dose heparin or oral anticoagulants. He may need to plan activity and movement to discourage venous stasis. For IV therapy, leg veins must be avoided and it is important to use a cannula that is not too large for the vein. Blood products must be administered through appropriate filters. When checking for the patency of an IV line, fluid must never be forced into a line if there is any resistance to flow. Proper site preparation and cannulation technique must be used to prevent phlebitis, so that the sequence of events leading to embolization does not occur.

Should thrombosis occur, anticoagulants must be administered as ordered. It is important to give heparin (which rapidly acts to increase blood-clotting time) as scheduled to prevent the development of further thrombi. In some situations, the CMA may be required to administer thrombolytic drugs. Antiembolic stockings, or SCDs, are often used for both the prevention and treatment of thrombosis.

The CMA must promote comfort and gas exchange by elevating the head of the bed, assisting with coughing and deep breathing (unless contraindicated), administering analgesics, and maintaining a restful environment. To promote tissue perfusion, she must assist the patient with ROM

exercises and active foot dorsiflexion. The leg must be inspected regularly but never massaged, to avoid breaking off a portion of the thrombus.

It is necessary to accurately document all signs and symptoms associated with thrombosis and monitor and report laboratory coagulation studies. The patency of the IV infusion must be maintained in case emergency venous access is needed.

Air Embolism

With infusion therapy, the possibility of air embolism is always present. The amount of air needed to cause death is not precisely known, but can occur with as little as 10 cc, depending on the patient's size and condition. Once an air embolism occurs, the situation becomes very serious. Therefore, it is important to prevent the entry of air into the circulatory system.

The CMA can prevent air embolism by removing air from tubings and syringes prior to IV cannulation. It is important to secure all tubing junctions with tape and it is preferable to use Luer-lok connections as well. When accessing or changing lines on central venous infusions, the patient's head should be lowered (below the level of the heart) to raise thoracic venous pressure above atmospheric pressure, or instruct the patient to perform the Valsalva maneuver.

Instructing a Patient in the Valsalva Maneuver

Whenever a central venous line is accessed or changed, it is important to instruct the patient to perform a Valsalva maneuver. Ask him to take in a deep breath and, while holding it, bear down or push as if having a bowel movement.

The signs and symptoms of air embolism are associated with vascular collapse and can be nonspecific. The patient may become extremely anxious and, if able, verbalize that death is approaching. There is dyspnea, hypotension, and tachypnea. The physician, on auscultation, may hear a loud, churning sound over the heart, called a *cog wheel murmur*. It occurs because air and blood are obstructing ventricular output.

Signs and Symptoms of Air Embolism

- Extreme anxiety—fear of impending death
- Light-headedness and confusion
- Nausea
- Substernal pain
- Tachypnea
- Hypotension
- Cog wheel murmur

Treatment for air embolism is supportive, but the CMA must act quickly. If known, the source of air entry must be blocked. If cardiac arrest occurs, CPR must be initiated. Otherwise, the patient must be positioned on his left side with his head lowered below heart level (left lateral Trendelenburg). This traps air in the right atrium of the heart, keeping it from passing into the right ventricle and on to the pulmonary artery and lungs. One hundred percent oxygen is delivered by mask to assist in reducing the embolism by assisting in the dissolution of nitrogen in the blood. If hemodynamic monitoring is being done and a lumen of the central line opens in the right atrium, medical intervention may include aspiration of air from the heart.

If the patient is conscious, he must be reassured and supported. Vital signs must be monitored and the patient observed for impending cardiac arrest. As with any situation, documentation must be thorough and accurate.

Catheter Embolism

With catheter embolism, the patient may complain of sudden, severe pain at the IV site and there will be a reduced or absent blood return upon checking for placement. If the catheter lodges in the pulmonary circulation or a chamber of the heart, there will be hypotension, tachycardia, chest pain, and cyanosis. The patient may lose consciousness. If the catheter does not migrate, the patient may be asymptomatic and the CMA will discover that the catheter is severed when she removes the cannula.

Catheter embolism can be prevented by inserting ONCs or TNCs according to procedure. As a general practice, infusions should never be started near a joint, where bending of the extremity could cause the catheter to break. If there is no other place, the joint must be prevented from flexure by placing it on an arm board.

Once it is ascertained that a catheter has broken, a tourniquet should be applied high on the extremity to limit venous flow and prevent embolism. Arterial circulation must not be impeded, so the CMA must be able to palpate a pulse distal to the tourniquet. The physician and radiologist must be notified and a new infusion must be started immediately. The patient must be kept on bed rest, receive cardiopulmonary support, and be prepared for x-ray or surgery. The catheter may have to be surgically removed or retrieved under angiography. The patient needs to be emotionally supported.

Documentation must include the patient's signs and symptoms, vital signs and level of consciousness, and the amount of catheter that is missing when the cannula is removed. The portion removed should be saved to determine the cause of breakage.

Other Causes of Embolic Formation

When embolism by thrombus, air, or catheter is ruled out, identification and treatment of other sources of embolism is usually symptomatic and supportive. Unless verified by x-ray or discovered during surgery or autopsy, other causes of embolism may not be determined.

Speed Shock

Speed shock is the systemic reaction to the rapid or excessive infusion of medication or infusate into the circulation. The body reacts by flushing, shock, or cardiac arrest.

Etiology and Defining Characteristics

With rapid administration of a fluid or medication, there is inadequate dilution with the circulating blood. The vital organs, therefore, are "shocked" by a toxic dose.

Speed shock can occur when a flow control clamp is inadvertently left completely open, allowing a large volume of fluid to infuse rapidly. It can also occur when an electronic infusion device (EID) is programmed incorrectly. Whenever an IV bolus or piggyback infusion of medication is given rapidly, plasma concentrations can reach unsafe or toxic proportions.

MEDICAL ASSISTING TIP

Signs and Symptoms of Speed Shock

- Flushing of head and neck
- Feeling of apprehension
- Hypertension
- Pounding headache
- Dyspnea
- Chest pain
- Chills
- Loss of consciousness
- Cardiac arrest

Assessment and Interventions

With speed shock, the first sign is usually flushing of the head and neck with the patient complaining of a severe, pounding headache and a feeling of apprehension. (The patient may correlate the sensation, although more powerful, to that occurring when ice cream or a cold beverage is consumed too fast.) There is hypertension, tachycardia with arrhythmia, dyspnea, and loss of consciousness. Cardiac arrest can occur.

If cardiac arrest occurs, CPR must be initiated. The infusion must be slowed or stopped (and the vein kept open with another infusate), and the physician notified. Vital signs, level of consciousness, and neurologic checks must be evaluated and documented.

The best intervention for speed shock is prevention. A medication should never be given without reading and following the manufacturer's guidelines. For highly toxic medications, an EID or a volume-controlled set with microdrop delivery should be used.

Review Questions and Activities

1. List the local complications of infusion therapy and briefly outline how each one can progress to a systemic problem.
2. Name five commonly administered intravenous drugs that have vesicant properties.
3. Look up in your drug guide and your institution's procedure manual the antidotes for the five vesicants listed in the previous question.
4. Outline the sequence of events in the progression of phlebitis to thrombophlebitis and embolism.
5. Explain the variables that contribute to a hypersensitivity reaction.

Chapter 5

Intravenous Infusion Preparations

Upon completion of this chapter, the reader should be able to:

✳ Review the physiologic principles of osmolality as they relate to body fluids.

✳ List the indications for intravenous infusion therapy.

✳ Differentiate between crystalloid, colloid, and hydrating infusions.

✳ List the basic principles for determining the tonicity of an infusion.

✳ Discuss the purpose and use of the commonly used isotonic, hypotonic, and hypertonic infusions.

✳ Identify the interventions and precautions associated with the use of isotonic, hypotonic, and hypertonic infusions.

In addition to having a substantial knowledge of the principles of fluid, electrolyte, and acid-base balance, the CMA must also understand the principles of fluid volume maintenance, replacement, and restoration in order to safely manage infusion therapy and promote a state of homeostasis for the patient. Although the physician prescribes infusions, the CMA must know what they are, confirm if they are appropriate for the patient, and administer them correctly.

Body water, which accounts for 50%–70% of adult body weight, is distributed between the ICF and the ECF compartments. The ECF is further divided into subcompartments, which are in a state of dynamic movement, constantly bathing the cells to maintain homeostasis (Figure 5-1). Electrolytes, which make up about 95% of the body's solute molecules, are crucial to the distribution and movement of water and for the maintenance of acid-base balance. They provide the chemicals needed to carry out cellular reactions and regulate vital cellular control mechanisms.

In the average adult, daily water requirements are approximately 30 ml/kg (13.6 ml/lb) of body weight. The recommended dietary allowances (RDA) in kilocalories (kcal) are estimated at 33 kilocalories per kilogram or 15 kilocalories per pound of ideal body weight, with 46% derived from carbohydrates, 30% from fat, and 24% from protein. In addition, the body must be supplemented with electrolytes, vitamins, minerals, and various trace elements to maintain homeostasis (Dudek, 2001).

MEDICAL ASSISTING TIP

Approximate Intake Requirements

The approximate daily average intake requirements of a moderately active adult who weighs 145 lb (65.9 kg) is as follows:

Water	1974 ml
Calories	2174.5
Carbohydrates (46%)	1000.04 kcal
Fats (30%)	652.20 kcal
Proteins (24%)	521.76 kcal
Sodium	1100–3300 mg
Potassium	1875–5624 mg
Chloride	1700–5100 mg
Calcium	800–1200 mg
Magnesium	325 mg
Phosphorus	800–1200 mg

Plus vitamins, minerals, and trace elements (Dudek, 2001)

Extracellular fluid compartment (ECF)

Cell	
(ICF) Intracellular fluid	ECF is composed of:
	Plasma (in the intravascular compartment)
	ISF (interstitial fluid) (in the space between the cells)
	Lymph (in lymphatic vessels)
	Bone (water bound to intracellular bone)
	Connective tissue (water bound to dense connective tissue)
	Transcellular fluids (formed as a result of cellular activity):
	Mucus
	Digestive juices
	Fluid in the lumen of the gastrointestinal tract
	Serous fluid
	Synovial fluid
	Cerebrospinal fluid (CSF)
	Ocular fluid
	Genitourinary secretions

Figure 5-1 | Total blood volume distribution between the ICF and ECF

OSMOLALITY AND OSMOLARITY

Osmolality is the osmotic pull or pressure exerted by all particles per unit of water (expressed as milliosmoles per kilogram of water), and **osmolarity** is the osmotic pull (pressure) exerted by all particles per unit of solution (expressed as milliosmoles per liter of solution). A unit of osmotic pressure is the osmole (Osm) and the milliosmole (mOsm) is $1/1000$th of an osmole. Osmotic pressure determines osmotic activity (Kee & Paulanka, 2004).

Osmolality is influenced by the quantity of dissolved particles that exert an osmotic pull in the intracellular and extracellular fluids. The primary solutes are serum sodium, urea, and glucose. Under normal circumstances, as the CMA will recall, there is very little difference between the osmolality of body fluids. Plasma (in the intravascular compartment) contains proteins and has a slightly higher osmolality than fluid in other areas. The concentration of plasma, though, is only about 25% of that found in the ICF. Interstitial fluid has little to no protein.

It is the responsibility of the CMA to know whether a prescribed infusate is hypertonic, hypotonic, or isotonic, and to determine which route is appropriate for its administration. Plasma, under normal conditions, has approximately 280–300 mOsm/L and is isotonic (or isosmotic). Anything below this range is considered hypotonic, while anything above

MEDICAL ASSISTING TIP

Differentiating Osmolality and Osmolarity

Both osmolality and osmolarity are used to characterize tonicity. Since body solutions are very dilute, *osmolality* is the term used to clinically characterize tonicity. *Osmolarity* describes the tonicity of infusions that are administered intravenously.

it is hypertonic. The normal isotonic plasma level is used as the standard for comparing the tonicity of intravenous infusions. With parenteral fluid administration, the IV infusion is determined by the average serum osmolality (290 mOsm). The normal osmolality range is +50 mOsm or −50 mOsm of 290 mOsm (Kee & Paulanka, 2004). An infusion with about the same osmolality of serum is categorized as isotonic. If it is +50 mOsm higher, it is hypertonic (340 mOsm or more), and if it is −50 mOsm below 290, it is hypotonic (240 mOsm or less).

MEDICAL ASSISTING TIP

Differentiating Plasma and Serum

Plasma is the liquid portion of the blood without corpuscles and consists of serum (plasma that has lost its fibrinogen, or Factor I, due to the clotting process), protein, and chemicals.

When the body is in a healthy state, there is a normal pattern of water intake and loss (Figure 5-2) and a balanced movement of water molecules back and forth between the fluid compartments. This movement is controlled by colloid osmotic and hydrostatic pressures as well as the sodium-potassium pump and ATP.

MEDICAL ASSISTING TIP

Differentiating Hydrostatic Pressure and Osmotic Pressure

Hydrostatic pressure is regulated by the number of molecules contained in a given volume of fluid. Osmotic pressure is governed by the number of solutes contained in a volume of solution.

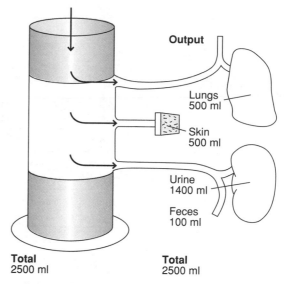

Figure 5-2 | Normal pattern of water intake and loss

During illness and disease, physical and chemical alterations occur that impede the normal regulatory mechanisms that contribute to fluid balance (Table 5-1). When one or more of these controls falters, interventions are aimed at restoring and supporting homeostasis through the implementation of intravenous infusion therapy.

CLASSIFICATIONS OF INFUSATES

The five basic classifications of IV infusions are crystalloids, colloids, hydrating solutions (sources of free water and calories), hypertonic-hyperosmolar preparations, and blood or blood components (Kee & Paulanka, 2004).

Crystalloids

Crystalloids are materials that are capable of **crystallization,** or have the ability to form crystals. Crystalloids are solutes that, when placed in a solvent, homogeneously mix with and dissolve into a solution and cannot be distinguished from the resultant solution. Because of this, crystalloid solutions are considered true solutions and are able to diffuse through membranes. Crystalloid infusions are usually electrolyte solutions that may be isotonic, hypotonic, or hypertonic.

Colloids

Colloids are glutinous substances whose particles, when submerged in a solvent, cannot form a true solution because

Table 5-1 | Regulators of Fluid Balance

REGULATORS	ACTIONS
Thirst	An indicator of fluid need.
Electrolytes Sodium (Na)	Sodium promotes water retention. With a water deficit, more sodium is reabsorbed from the renal tubules.
Protein, albumin	Protein and albumin promote body fluid retention. These nondiffusable substances increase the colloid osmotic (oncotic) pressure.
Hormones Antidiuretic hormone (ADH)	ADH is produced by the hypothalamus and stored in the posterior pituitary gland (neurohypophysis). ADH is secreted when there is an ECF volume deficit. ADH promotes water reabsorption from the distal tubules of the kidneys.
Aldosterone	Aldosterone is secreted from the adrenal cortex. It promotes sodium reabsorption from the renal tubules.
Renin	Decreased renal blood flow increases the release of renin from the juxtaglomerular cells of the kidneys. Renin promotes peripheral vasoconstriction and the release of aldosterone (sodium and water retention).
Lymphatics	Plasma protein that shifts to the tissue spaces cannot be reabsorbed into the blood vessels. Thus, the lymphatic system promotes the return of water and protein from the interstitial spaces to the vascular spaces.
Skin	Skin excretes approximately 500 ml of water daily through normal perspiration.
Lungs	Lungs excrete approximately 500 ml of water daily with normal breathing.
Kidneys	The kidneys excrete 1200 to 1500 ml of body water daily. The amount of water excretion may vary according to fluid intake and fluid loss.

From *Fluids and Electrolytes with Clinical Applications: A Programmed Approach* (7th ed.), by J. L. Kee, B. J. Paulanka, & L. Purnell, 2004, Clifton Park, NY: Delmar Learning.

their molecules, when thoroughly dispersed, do not dissolve, but remain uniformly suspended and distributed throughout the fluid. Because of this, such fluids have a cloudy appearance. The particles of colloidal dispersions are too large to pass through cell membranes.

Intravenous colloid infusions raise colloid osmotic pressure, and thus are often called *plasma* or *volume expanders*. When small amounts of plasma proteins are forced into the interstitium at the arterial end of the circulation, because of the increased pressure, they cannot return at the venous capillary end, so they are removed by way of lymph vessels. The colloid infusions that are commonly used consist of albumin, dextran, plasmanate, and the artificial blood substitute, hetastarch.

Hydrating Solutions

Various infusions are frequently administered to patients to supplement caloric intake, supply nutrients, provide free water for maintenance or rehydration, or promote effective renal output. When used, their chemical makeup or rate of administration is adjusted so the equilibria of body fluids are not disturbed. Glucose solutions are most often used. When glucose and other nutrients are administered in water, they are quickly metabolized, leaving an excess of water. This is why glucose solutions are often called *hydrating solutions*. Any water that is not needed by the body is excreted by the kidneys in the form of dilute urine.

MEDICAL ASSISTING TIP

Frequently Used Hydrating Solutions

Hydrating solutions that are often infused for maintenance, rehydration, and to enhance renal output are as follows.

Dextrose 2½% in 0.45% saline
Dextrose 5% in water
Dextrose 5% in 0.45% saline
Sodium chloride 0.45%
Dextrose 5% in 0.2% saline

DETERMINING TONICITY

Depending on the type of infusate, the addition of glucose and electrolytes determines the tonicity of the infusion. Osmotic pressure, remember, is determined by the measurement of the total number of particles in a volume of solution.

Electrolyte Solutions

One gram mole of a substance that is nonpermeable and non-ionizable equals one osmole. If the substance is capable of ionization, such as sodium chloride, 0.5 g of the mole of the substance equals one osmole. As discussed earlier, because the osmole unit is too big in relation to body fluid osmolality, the milliosmole unit is used. With electrolyte-containing infusates, each milliequivalent of an electrolyte equals one milliosmole. Milliequivalents measure how many chemically active ions are present in a solution.

When a monovalent electrolyte, such as normal saline, is placed in a solvent and ionized, or separated, the amount of electrolyte is equal to the sum of the separated ions. Sodium chloride contains 154 mEq/L of sodium and 154 mEq/L of chloride. The osmolarity, therefore, is about 308 mOsm/L. 0.45% NaCl (half-strength saline) has 77 mEq/L of sodium and 77 mEq/L of chloride, making the osmolarity 154 mEq/L.

Dextrose Solutions

Dextrose solutions, which are frequently used as infusates, are manufactured as percentage concentrations in water or sodium chloride. Remember that percentage solutions express the number of grams of solute per 100 g of solvent. A 5% dextrose in water (D_5W) infusion contains 5 g of dextrose in 100 ml of water. One ml of water equals one gram.

MEDICAL ASSISTING TIP

Percentage Solutions

Percentage solutions express the number of grams of solute per 100 g (100 ml) of solvent.

INFUSATES: CATEGORIES OF TONICITY

When the body is in a state of homeostasis, the serum osmolality is the same as that in other body fluids, approximately 280–300 mOsm/L. IV infusions are isotonic, hypotonic, or hypertonic when compared to serum osmolality.

It is important for the CMA to understand the tonicity of every infusion order so she can determine if it is safe for her patient, discern what type of vein to access for the infusion, and regulate the rate appropriately.

Isotonic Infusates

Isotonic or isosmotic infusates have the same tonicity as body fluids. Because of this, they do not alter osmolality and, once infused, they remain within the intravascular space because osmotic pressure is equal between the intracellular and extra-

cellular compartments. For this reason, they are used to treat hypotension resulting from hypovolemia. Isotonic infusions, because they are compatible with the plasma, can be administered at a more rapid rate than hypo or hypertonic solutions. Figure 5-3 illustrates how red blood cells (RBCs) maintain their size and shape when placed in an isotonic solution of 0.9% NaCl. Isotonic infusions are primarily used to expand the intravascular compartment, as depicted in Figure 5-4. Table 5-2 outlines the various isotonic infusions available, their indications for use, and precautions associated with them.

Hypotonic Infusions

Hypotonic infusions lower serum osmolality by causing fluid to shift out of the blood and into the cells and interstitial spaces. These solutions are used to hydrate the intracellular and interstitial compartments and lower sodium levels. The rate of administration of hypotonic infusions must be carefully controlled to prevent water from hemolyzing RBCs (rupture). Figure 5-5 illustrates how hemolysis occurs when

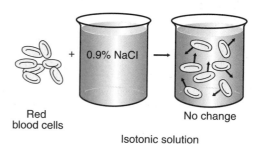

Red blood cells   + 0.9% NaCl   →   No change

Isotonic solution

Figure 5-3 | Red blood cells maintain their size and shape in isotonic 0.9% NaCl.

Physiologic effect of an isotonic infusion

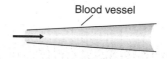

Blood vessel

Figure 5-4 | Isotonic infusion expands the intravascular space because osmotic pressure is equal.

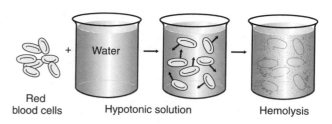

Red blood cells   + Water   →   Hypotonic solution   →   Hemolysis

Figure 5-5 | Red blood cells hemolyze when placed in hypotonic (free) water.

Table 5-2 | Isotonic Infusions: Indications for Use and Precautions

INFUSION	OSMO-LARITY	INDICATIONS AND INCOMPATIBILITIES	PRECAUTIONS, COMMENTS, CONTRAINDICATIONS
5% dextrose in water (D₅W) 50 g dextrose per liter pH 4.5 (3.5–6.5)	252.52 mOsm/L	**Indications** Hydration: replaces water losses in dehydration Provides free water for the excretion of solutes Provides 20 kcal/100 ml (200 kcal/L) Diluent for medications **Incompatibilities** Ampicillin sodium (after 2 hr) Diazepam Erythromycin lactobinate (after 6 hr) Fat emulsions Phenytoin sodium Procainamide Sodium bicarbonate Warfarin sodium Whole blood Vitamin B₁₂	D₅W is isotonic in the container. Once infused, the dextrose is rapidly metabolized and the infusion becomes hypotonic Do not administer to patients with increased intracranial pressure because it is hypotonic in the body and will increase edema D₅W does not contain electrolytes Because of excess ADH secretions, as a stress response to surgery, use cautiously in the early postoperative period to prevent water intoxication Hypokalemia can occur because, during the cellular use of glucose, potassium shifts from the ECF to the ICF Use cautiously in patients with signs of fluid overload and CHF Can cause dehydration from osmotic diuresis if infused too rapidly D₅W may alter insulin or oral hypoglycemic needs in diabetics Contraindicated in diabetic coma Contraindicated in patients allergic to corn and corn products
Normal saline (0.9% NaCl) Na 154 mEq/L Cl 154 mEq/L pH 5 (4.5–7.0)	308 mOsm/L	**Indications** Replaces ECF losses by expanding the intravascular space when chloride loss is greater than sodium loss Corrects hyponatremia Corrects hypovolemia Replaces sodium losses Corrects mild metabolic acidosis Corrects metabolic alkalosis when fluid depletion exists because the chloride ions cause a decrease in bicarbonate ions Only infusate compatible with blood; used to initiate and follow transfusions Diluent for medications Used as an irrigant for intravascular devices Maintains patency of heparin locks **Incompatibilities** Amphotericin B Chlordiazepoxide hydrochloride Diazepam Fat emulsions Levarterenol Mannitol Methylprednisolone sodium succinate Phenytoin sodium	Accurately monitor I & O Can cause intravascular overload Can cause hypokalemia because saline promotes potassium excretion Can cause hypernatremia Can induce hyperchloremic acidosis due to loss of bicarbonate ions Normal saline can cause sodium retention during the intraoperative and early postoperative periods Does not provide free water Does not provide calories Use with caution in patients with decreased renal function Use with caution in patients with altered circulatory function Use with caution in the elderly Contraindicated in the presence of edema with sodium retention Causes excess sodium retention when used with glucocorticoids

continues

Table 5-2 | Isotonic Infusions: Indications for Use and Precautions (*continued*)

INFUSION	OSMO-LARITY	INDICATIONS AND INCOMPATIBILITIES	PRECAUTIONS, COMMENTS, CONTRAINDICATIONS
Dextrose in Saline Solutions		**Indications**	To prevent circulatory overload, use with caution in the following:
0.2% dextrose in 0.9% NaCl	318.1 mOsm/L	Rehydration by replenishment of salt and water	patients with CHF
2 g dextrose per liter (10.1 mOsm/L)		Fluid replacement for burns	patients with pulmonary edema
Na 154 mEq/L		Supply calories	patients with edema with sodium retention
Cl 154 mEq/L		Reduce nitrogen depletion	patients undergoing corticosteroid therapy
pH 4.5 (3.5–6.5)		Used in place of plasma expanders (until they are available) to treat circulatory insufficiency and shock	patients with urinary obstruction
2.5% dextrose in 0.45% NaCl	264.86 mOsm/L	Hypotonic saline with dextrose infusions (2.5 % D in 0.45 NaCl and 5% D in 0.2% NaCl) are used to establish renal function prior to electrolyte administration	Maintain strict I & O Contraindicated in patients in diabetic coma Contraindicated in patients with allergies to corn and corn products
25 g dextrose per liter (126.26 mOsm/L)		D_5 in 0.2% NaCl is used as a maintenance infusion	May falsely elevate BUN laboratory reports
Na 69.3 mEq/L			Once renal function is assured, electrolytes must be supplemented to prevent hypokalemia
Cl 69.3 mEq/L		**Incompatibilities**	
pH 4.0 (3.5–6.5)		Amphotericin B	
5% dextrose in 0.2% NaCl	314.12 mOsm/L	Ampicillin sodium Diazepam	
50 g dextrose per liter (252.52 mOsm/L)		Erythromycin lactobinate Mannitol	
Na 30.8 mEq/L		Phenytoin	
Cl 30.8 mEq/L		Warfarin sodium	
pH 4.0 (3.5–6.5)		Whole blood	
Ringer's solution	310 mOsm/L	**Indications**	Provides no calories (When dextrose is added to Ringer's solution, the dextrose provides calories and spares protein loss)
Na 147 mEq/L		Restores fluid balance	
K 4 mEq/L		Restores electrolyte balance	May exacerbate the following:
Ca 4 mEq/L		Replaces ECF loss resulting from dehydration, gastrointestinal losses, and fistula drainage	sodium retention
Cl 155 mEq/L			CHF
pH 5.5 (5.0–7.5)		Used instead of lactated Ringer's when patients have liver disease and are unable to metabolize lactate	renal insufficiency Maintain strict I & O
		May be used as a blood replacement for a short period of time	Added potassium is needed to correct severe hypokalemia Contraindicated in renal failure
		Incompatibilities	
		Ampicillin sodium Cefamandole Cyphradine Chlordiazepoxide Diazepam Erythromycin lactobinate Methicillin Phenytoin Potassium phosphate Sodium bicarbonate Whole blood	

continues

Table 5-2 | Isotonic Infusions: Indications for Use and Precautions (*continued*)

INFUSION	OSMO-LARITY	INDICATIONS AND INCOMPATIBILITIES	PRECAUTIONS, COMMENTS, CONTRAINDICATIONS

Lactated Ringer's (Hartmann's solution)
 	
Na 130 mEq/L
Cl 109 mEq/L
K 4 mEq/L
Ca 3 mEq/L
Lactate 28 mEq/L
pH 6.5
(6.0–7.5)
	274 mOsm/L	**Indications**
		Restores fluid volume deficit
		Used for rehydration in *most* types of dehydration
		Replaces fluid lost as a result of *bile loss*, *burns*, or *diarrhea*
		Treats mild metabolic acidosis
		Treats diabetic ketoacidosis
		Treats salicylate overdose
		
		Incompatibilities
		Amphotericin B
		Ampicillin sodium
		Cefamandole
		Cephradine
		Chlordiazepoxide
		Diazepam
		Erythromycin lactobinate
		Methicillin
		Methylprednisolone sodium succinate
		Oxytetracycline
		Phenytoin sodium
		Potassium phosphate
		Sodium bicarbonate
		Thiopental
		Warfarin
		Whole blood
			Resembles blood serum electrolyte content
			Provides 9 calories from lactate
			Lactate is metabolized to bicarbonate in the liver
			Does not provide free water for renal excretion
			Can precipitate hypernatremia because the amount of potassium is not sufficient for daily requirements
			Hyperkalemia can develop with use of potassium-sparing diuretics and potassium supplementation
			Contraindicated with severe metabolic acidosis and alkalosis
			Contraindicated in hypoxia
			Contraindicated with hepatic disease where the liver is unable to metabolize lactate
			May exacerbate the following:
			  CHF
			  edema
			  sodium retention

Multiple Electrolyte Solutions
Plasma-Lyte R® (Baxter)
Isolyte E® (McGaw)
 	
Na 140 mEq/L
Cl 103 mEq/L
K 10 mEq/L
Ca 5 mEq/L
Mg 3 mEq/L
Acetate 47 mEq/L
Lactate 8 mEq/L
pH 5.5
(4.0–6.5)
	316 mOsm/L	**Indications**
		Replace water and electrolytes caused by the following:
		  severe diarrhea
		  severe vomiting
		  gastric suctioning
			Monitor electrolytes because, once the deficits have been replaced, hyperkalemia can occur
			Monitor I & O
			Observe for signs of circulatory overload

Plasma-Lyte 148® Na 140 mEq/L Cl 98 mEq/L K 5 mEq/L Ca 0 Mg 3 mEq/L Acetate 27 mEq/L Gluconate 23 mEq/L pH 5.5 (4.0–6.5)	296 mOsm/L		
Plasma-Lyte A®	296 mOsm/L	Plasma-Lyte® has the same constituents as Plasma-Lyte 148,® but has a pH of 7.4 (6.5–8.0) and is used in anesthesia	
Gastric replacement solutions			In addition to the constituents in the electrolyte replacement solutions, gastric replacement fluids have the addition of ammonium ions

continues

Table 5-2 | Isotonic Infusions: Indications for Use and Precautions (*continued*)

INFUSION	OSMO-LARITY	INDICATIONS AND INCOMPATIBILITIES	PRECAUTIONS, COMMENTS, CONTRAINDICATIONS
Alkalinizing Fluids **Sodium lactate ⅙ molar (M/6 sodium lactate)** Na 167 mEq/L Lactate 167 mEq/L pH 6.5 (6.0–7.3)	334 mOsm/L	**Indications** Mild to moderate acidosis, not for the treatment of lactic acidosis Alkalinization of urine **Incompatibilities** Oxytetracycline Sodium bicarbonate	Contraindicated in lactic acidosis Contraindicated with hypernatremia Contraindicated in hypoxic patients Can exacerbate respiratory or metabolic alkalosis Use with caution when administering to patients with conditions that increase lactate use, such as hepatic insufficiency Monitor glucose, electrolytes, and acid-base balance Strict I & O Daily weight Monitor for fluid retention Administer with caution to patients with altered (reduced) tissue perfusion
Sodium bicarbonate ⅙ molar (1.45% sodium bicarbonate) Na 166.70 mEq/L HCO₃ 166.70 mEq/L pH 8.0 (7.0–8.5)	333 mOsm/L	**Indications** Treats systemic acidosis Increases serum bicarbonate and buffers excess hydrogen Alkalinization of urine **Incompatabilities** Numerous; consult pharmacist **Drug Interactions** Numerous; consult pharmacist	Contraindicated in chloride depletion from gastrointestinal losses Contraindicated in hypocalcemia Use with caution in patients with renal insufficiency Use extreme caution in patients with edema due to sodium retention Monitor for signs of alkalosis (overdose) Take precautions to prevent extravasation
Acidifying Fluids **0.9% sodium chloride**	308 mOsm/L	**Indications** Corrects metabolic alkalosis when fluid depletion exists because the chloride ions cause a decrease in bicarbonate ions	See comments under normal saline
Ammonium chloride solution 0.9% NH₄ 168 mEq/L Cl 168 mEq/L	336 mOsm/L	Systemic acidifier indicated for severe metabolic alkalosis resulting from vomiting, gastric suctioning, or chloride depletion from diuretic use Rids body of excess hydrogen ions in metabolic acidosis and supplies chloride Ammonium ion is converted to hydrogen ion and ammonium then excreted as urea in the urine **Incompatibilities** Alkalides and their carbonates Dimenhydrinate Levorphanol tartrate Methadone Potent oxidizing agents Warfarin	Can produce dangerous dysrhythmias Accurate I & O Accurate respiratory assessment Seizure precautions Contraindicated in severe liver disease because the liver is unable to convert ammonium ions to urea; ammonia retention results in hepatic coma Contraindicated in primary respiratory alkalosis due to chance of development of systemic acidosis

continues

Table 5-2 | Isotonic Infusions: Indications for Use and Precautions (*continued*)

INFUSION	OSMO-LARITY	INDICATIONS AND INCOMPATIBILITIES	PRECAUTIONS, COMMENTS, CONTRAINDICATIONS
Mannitol 5% in 0.45 NaCl (Osmitrol,® Resectisol®) pH 5.0 (4.5–7.0)	274 mOsm/L	**Indications** Diuresis Treatment of oliguria Reduction of increased intracranial pressure Reduction of cerebrospinal fluid pressure Reduction of intraocular pressure **Incompatibilities** Blood products Imipenem/cilastic sodium	Strict I & O Hourly vital signs Closely monitor BUN and electrolytes, especially sodium and potassium levels Contraindicated with anuria due to possibility of circulatory overload Can cause renal failure May induce dangerous dysrhythmias May exacerbate intracranial bleeding May cause congestive heart failure in patients with cardiopulmonary compromise May exacerbate electrolyte imbalances Monitor for rebound increase in intracranial, cerebrospinal, and intraocular pressures within 12 to 24 hours after administration
Plasma Volume Expanders **Dextran 70 and 0.9% NaCl** (6% Gentran® 70 and 0.9% NaCl) Na 154 mEq/L Cl 154 mEq/L pH 5.0 (4.0–6.5) **Dextran 40 and 0.9% NaCl** (10% Gentran® and 0.9% NaCl) Na 154 mEq/L Cl 154 mEq/L pH 5.0 (3.5–7.0) **Dextran 40 and D₅W** (10% Gentran® and D₅W) pH 4.0 (3.0–7.0)	308 mOsm/L 308 mOsm/L 255 mOsm/L	**Indications** Restoration of circulatory dynamics Fluid replacement Treatment of perioperative shock Used prophylactically in surgical patients at risk for acute thrombosis and embolization Hemorrhage Trauma Moves water from body tissues to increase urinary output **Incompatibilities** Ascorbic acid Chlortetracycline Phytonadione Promethazine Protein hydrosylate	**Caution:** Never add any medications to dextran infusions. **Contraindicated with:** Cardiac decompensation Coagulation defects Corticosteroid therapy Hypersensitivity to dextran Hypervolemia Pulmonary edema Renal failure Severe bleeding disorders Monitor for any signs of allergic reaction Never administer near site of trauma or infection Monitor I & O hourly Monitor pulse, blood pressure, and central venous pressure (CVP) hourly Monitor specific gravity Monitor for fluid overload Monitor for signs of bleeding Monitor for exacerbation of bleeding Monitor site of infusion for venous thrombosis and phlebitis **Comments:** Solution must be clear—not cloudy Crystallization may occur; before administration, submerge bottle in warm water to dissolve crystals

continues

Table 5-2 | Isotonic Infusions: Indications for Use and Precautions (*continued*)

INFUSION	OSMO-LARITY	INDICATIONS AND INCOMPATIBILITIES	PRECAUTIONS, COMMENTS, CONTRAINDICATIONS
Hetastarch (HES) 6% in 0.9% NaCl Na 154 mEq/L Cl 154 mEq/L pH 5.5	308 mOsm/L	**Indications** Similar to dextran but causes fewer allergic reactions Used in shock due to sepsis, acute hemorrhage, or burns Similar to human albumin in colloidal properties **Incompatibilities** Amikacin Ampicillin Cefamandol Cefazolin Cefonicid Cefoperazone Cefotaxime Cefoxitin Cephalothin Gentamicin Phenytoin Ranitidine Theophylline Tobramycin	Contraindicated with severe bleeding disorders Contraindicated in congestive and renal failure Maintain strict I & O Monitor CVP and PCWP (hemodynamic monitoring) to assess for circulatory overload

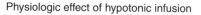

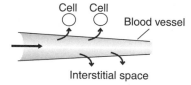

Physiologic effect of hypotonic infusion

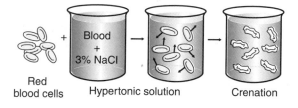

Figure 5-6 | Hypotonic infusion lowers serum osmolality by causing fluid to shift out of the intravascular space and into the cells and interstitial spaces.

Figure 5-7 | Red blood cells crenate when placed in hypertonic 3% NaCl.

RBCs are placed in hypotonic free water, with water passing from the blood vessels into the cells, causing the RBC to burst. Because hypotonic infusions hydrate the intracellular compartment, care must be taken to prevent circulatory depletion. They should not be administered to hypotensive patients, as this can further lower blood pressure. Figure 5-6 shows the physiologic effect of the administration of a hypotonic infusion. Table 5-3 lists the hypotonic infusions available, their indications for use, and the precautions associated with them.

Hypertonic Infusions

Hypertonic infusions raise serum osmolality by causing a pull of fluids from the intracellular and interstitial compartments into the blood vessels. They act to greatly expand the intravascular compartment and are administered when there is a serious saline depletion. Extreme caution must be exercised with hypertonic infusions to prevent circulatory overload. They also are irritating to the intima of veins. Figure 5-7 shows how RBCs crenate (shrink) when

Table 5-3 | Hypotonic Infusions: Indications for Use and Precautions

INFUSION	OSMO-LARITY	INDICATIONS AND INCOMPATIBILITIES	PRECAUTIONS, COMMENTS, CONTRAINDICATIONS
Dextrose in Water Solutions **2.5% dextrose in water** **25 g dextrose per liter** pH 4.5 (3.6–6.5) **5% dextrose in water** (Reminder: D$_5$W is isotonic, but it becomes hypotonic when it is infused because the dextrose is metabolized rapidly.)	126 mOsm/L 252.52 mOsm/L	**Indications** Provides 85 kcal/L Diluent for medications Provides hydration to cells in hyperglycemic situations and in cellular dehydration associated with diuretic administration Review Table 5-2: Isotonic Infusions **Incompatibilities** Refer to isotonic dextrose in water above	Depletes intravascular compartment Monitor for signs of cardiovascular collapse from fluid volume depletion Contraindicated in patients with increased intracranial pressure Contraindicated in patients with decreased serum protein levels Assess for hypokalemia after prolonged use without potassium supplementation Review under isotonic infusions. D$_5$W is isotonic in the container. Once it is infused, the dextrose is rapidly metabolized, and the infusion becomes hypotonic. Review Table 5-2: Isotonic Infusions
Sodium Chloride Solutions **0.45% (half normal)** **saline** pH 5.0 (4.5–7.0)	154 mOsm/L	**Indications** Used when fluid losses exceed electrolyte depletion Preferable to 0.9% NaCl for electrolyte restoration of sodium and chlorides Provides free water for the renal elimination of solutes Lowers serum osmolality by moving body fluid from the blood vessels into the cells and interstitium Used in hyperosmolar diabetes when dextrose is contraindicated, but fluid without excess sodium is indicated **Incompatibilities** Amphotericin B Levarterenol Mannitol	Contraindicated in hypernatremia Use with caution in situations of fluid retention Assess for cellular dehydration
Dextrose in Sodium Chloride Solutions No hypotonic infusions			
Multiple Electrolyte Solutions **Plasma-Lyte 56® or** **Normosol R® injection** Na 40 mEq/L Cl 40 mEq/L K 13 mEq/L Mg 3 mEq/L Acetate 16 mEq/L pH 5.5 (4.0–6.0)	112 mOsm/L	**Indications** Maintenance solution; provides free water and electrolytes Provides water for retention of needed electrolytes and the excretion of excesses **Incompatibilities** Refer to isotonic multiple electrolyte solutions	Monitor I & O Monitor electrolyte levels Use with caution in patients with impaired renal function Observe for signs of hyperkalemia Weigh daily to assess for water retention and intoxication
Sterile water for **injection** pH 5.5 (5.0–7.0)	0 mOsm/L	**Indications** Use as a diluent	Never administer free water alone, as it causes cell rupture

placed in a hypertonic solution. Figure 5-8 illustrates the physiologic effect of a hypertonic infusion. Table 5-4 lists the hypertonic infusates available, their indications, and the precautions associated with their use.

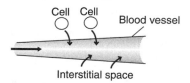

Figure 5-8 | Hypertonic infusion raises serum osmolality by causing a pull of fluids from the intracellular and interstitial compartments into the intravascular compartment.

Table 5-4 | Hypertonic Infusions: Indications for Use and Precautions

INFUSION	OSMO-LARITY	INDICATIONS AND INCOMPATIBILITIES	PRECAUTIONS, COMMENTS, CONTRAINDICATIONS
Dextrose in Water Solutions		**Indications**	Monitor for hyperglycemia and glycosuria
		Nonelectrolyte source of calories (protein-sparing) and water	Monitor for sepsis, with high glucose concentrations
			Accurate I & O
10% dextrose in water	505 mOsm/L	Provides 340 kcal/L	10% solution should be administered in a large arm vein. The
20% dextrose in water	1,010 mOsm/L	Provides 680 kcal/L	site must be assessed frequently for pain, phlebitis, and
30% dextrose in water	1,510 mOsm/L	Provides 1,020 kcal/L	thrombosis
40% dextrose in water	2,020 mOsm/L	Provides 1,360 kcal/L	Solutions over 10% must be delivered via a central line into a
50% dextrose in water	2,520 mOsm/L	Provides 1,700 kcal/L	large vessel for adequate dilution and the prevention of
60% dextrose in water	3,030 mOsm/L	Provides 2,040 kcal/L	peripheral vein sclerosis
70% dextrose in water	3,530 mOsm/L	Provides 2,380 kcal/L	
pH 4.5 for all strengths			
Sodium Chloride Solutions		**Indications**	Hypertonic saline solutions must be given with extreme care and should be administered only in critical care areas
2.225% NaCl	685.30 mOsm/L	Hypertonic NaCl injections are indicated for severe sodium depletion accompanied by	Strict I & O
Na 342.65 mEq/L		abnormal neurologic functioning	Assess for fluid overload
Cl 342.65 mEq/L		Used when sodium losses exceed fluid losses	Monitor renal function
3.0% NaCl	924 mOsm/L	Used in crisis associated with Addison's	Assess for hypernatremia
Na 462 mEq/L		disease	Contraindicated in CHF, fluid retention, impaired renal function, and hypernatremia
Cl 462 mEq/L		Used in diabetic coma	
5.0% NaCl	1,540 mOsm/L	**Incompatibilities**	Do not administer more than 2 mEq/L/hr
Na 770 mEq/L		Amphotericin B	The strength and rate of administration of these infusions depends on the patient's age, weight, and clinical condition
Cl 770 mEq/L		Benzquinamide	
		Chlordiazepoxide	
pH 5.0		Diazepam	
(4.5–7.0) for all strengths		Fat emulsions	
		Levarterenol	
		Mannitol	
		Methylprednisolone sodium succinate	
		Phenytoin sodium	

continues

Table 5-4 | Hypertonic Infusions: Indications for Use and Precautions (*continued*)

INFUSION	OSMO-LARITY	INDICATIONS AND INCOMPATIBILITIES	PRECAUTIONS, COMMENTS, CONTRAINDICATIONS
Dextrose in Sodium Chloride Solutions **5% dextrose in 0.45 NaCl** Dextrose 252.52 mOsm/L Na 69.3 mEq/L Cl 69.3 mEq/L **5% dextrose in 0.9 NaCl** Dextrose 252.52 mOsm/L Na 154 mEq/L Cl 154 mEq/L **10% dextrose in 0.9 NaCl** Dextrose 505.04 mOsm/L Na 154 mEq/L Cl 154 mEq/L pH 4.0 (3.5–6.5) for all strengths	391.12 mOsm/L 560.52 mOsm/L 813.04 mOsm/L	**Indications** Indicated for shock and circulatory insufficiency until plasma volume expander is available Treats severe dehydration Replaces fluid losses from burns With hypertonic dextrose in saline solutions, the concentrations and rate are determined by the patient's weight, circulatory status, and electrolyte-acid-base balance. **Incompatibilities** Amphotericin B Ampicillin sodium Amsacrine Diazepam Erythromycin lactobinate Mannitol Phenytoin Warfarin Whole blood	Strict I & O Daily weight Monitor for fluid overload Monitor for electrolytes with prolonged therapy Use with caution in the elderly Use with caution in patients with renal obstruction and patients with renal disease Contraindicated in conditions associated with fluid retention Use with extreme caution in patients with diabetes Contraindicated in diabetic coma
5% dextrose in Ringer's injection Dextrose 252.52 mOsm/L Na 147.5 mEq/L Cl 156 mEq/L K 4 mEq/L Ca 4.5 mEq/L pH 4.0	564.52 mOsm/L	**Indications** Provides calories from dextrose and spares protein with electrolyte composition similar to that of plasma Replaces ECF losses and replaces electrolytes **Incompatibilities** Refer to isotonic Ringer's solution	Contraindicated in renal failure Use with caution in patients with CHF Monitor electrolytes Use with caution in hypernatremic and hypercalcemic patients
5% dextrose and lactated Ringer's injection Dextrose 252.52 mOsm/L Na 130 mEq/L Cl 109 mEq/L K 4 mEq/L Ca 3 mEq/L Lactate 28 mEq/L pH 5.0	526.52 mOsm/L	**Indications** Treats mild metabolic acidosis Provides 170 kcal from dextrose and 9 kcal from lactate per liter Replaces fluid losses from burns	Dextrose and lactated Ringer's infusions are contraindicated in lactic acidosis Use with caution in metabolic or respiratory alkalosis Use with caution in patients with hepatic insufficiency Monitor for circulatory overload Contraindicated in diabetic ketoacidosis Because of lactate, excess administration could cause metabolic acidosis
10% dextrose and lactated Ringer's injection Dextrose 505.04 mOsm/L remaining constituents same as 5% solution	779.04 mOsm/L	Treats mild metabolic acidosis Provides 340 kcal from dextrose Spares protein Replaces fluid losses from burns **Incompatibilities** Refer to isotonic lactated Ringer's solution	

continues

Table 5-4 | Hypertonic Infusions: Indications for Use and Precautions (*continued*)

INFUSION	OSMO-LARITY	INDICATIONS AND INCOMPATIBILITIES	PRECAUTIONS, COMMENTS, CONTRAINDICATIONS
Electrolyte Solutions		**Indications**	With all electrolyte infusions, monitor electrolytes carefully, monitor for fluid overload; and perform hemodynamic monitoring in patients with renal, and cardiovascular impairment
5% dextrose and Electrolyte # 75 injection Dextrose 252.52 mOsm/L Na 40 mEq/L Cl 48 mEq/L K 35 mEq/L Lactate 20 mEq/L Phosphate (as HPO_4^-) 15 mEq/L pH 5.0	410.52 mEq/L	Fluid replacement Fluid and electrolyte maintenance Treats mild metabolic acidosis	
5% dextrose and Plasma-Lyte 56® Dextrose 252.52 mOsm/L Na 40 mEq/L Cl 40 mEq/L K 13 mEq/L Mg 3 mEq/L Acetate 16 mEq/L pH 5.5	364.52 mOsm/L	Fluid replacement Fluid and electrolyte maintenance	
5% dextrose and Plasma-Lyte M® Dextrose 252.52 mEq/L Na 40 mEq/L Cl 40 mEq/L K 16 mEq/L Ca 5 mEq/L Mg 3 mEq/L Acetate 12 mEq/L Lactate 12 mEq/L pH 5.0	380.52 mOsm/L	Fluid replacement Fluid and electrolyte maintenance Treats very mild metabolic acidosis	
5% dextrose and Plasma-Lyte 148® Dextrose 252.52 mOsm/L Na 140 mEq/L Cl 98 mEq/L K 5 mEq/L Mg 3 mEq/L Acetate 27 mEq/L Gluconate 23 mEq/L pH 5.0	548.52 mOsm/L	Fluid replacement solution Electrolyte replacement	With all electrolyte infusions, monitor electrolyte levels, maintain strict I & O, assess for hypernatremia, and monitor for fluid overload
5% dextrose and Plasma-Lyte R® Dextrose 252.52 mEq/L Na 140 mEq/L Cl 103 mEq/L K 10 mEq/L Ca 5 mEq/L Mg 3 mEq/L Acetate 47 mEq/L Lactate 8 mEq/L pH 5.0	568.52 mOsm/L	Fluid replacement solution Electrolyte replacement	Because of the addition of lactate, contraindicated in patients with liver impairment

continues

Table 5-4 | Hypertonic Infusions: Indications for Use and Precautions (*continued*)

INFUSION	OSMO-LARITY	INDICATIONS AND INCOMPATIBILITIES	PRECAUTIONS, COMMENTS, CONTRAINDICATIONS
Invert Sugar as Fructose and Dextrose Solutions **5% Travert® and Electrolyte # 2 injection** Dextrose 252.52 mOsm/L Na 56 mEq/L Cl 56 mEq/L K 25 mEq/L Mg 6 mEq/L Lactate 25 mEq/L Phosphate (as HPO$_4^-$) 12.5 mEq/L pH 4.5 **10% Travert® and Electrolyte # 2 injection** Dextrose 505.04 mOsm/L Electrolytes are same as 5% solution	433.02 mOsm/L 685.54 mOsm/L	**Indications** Provide calories in the form of carbohydrates More rapidly metabolized and can be administered more rapidly than dextrose Use for diabetic patients because insulin is not required for the metabolism of these carbohydrate forms Supply electrolytes at the maintenance level Provide fluid replacement and maintenance **Incompatibilities** Aminophylline Amobarbital Ampicillin sodium Blood products Diazepam Penicillin G Phenytoin Warfarin Thiopental sodium	These infusions are equimolar mixtures of fructose and dextrose Contraindicated for patients with fructose intolerance Strict I & O Use with caution in patients with conditions associated with fluid overload Do not use small peripheral veins for administration Do not exceed 1g/kg/hr Monitor for lactic acidosis Contraindicated in patients with gout because hyperuricemia may occur as an adverse reaction to the invert sugar Assess for fluid overload The 10% solution delivers more calories in less fluid (up to 3 L/day is safe and provides 340 kcal/L)
Mannitol 10% mannitol solution 15% mannitol solution 20% mannitol solution	 549 mOsm/L 823 mOsm/L 1,098 mOsm/L	**Indications** Osmotic diuretic Reduces intraocular, intracranial, and intraspinal pressures by raising plasma osmolality and causing fluids in these areas to diffuse back into the plasma and intravascular space Used to measure glomerular filtration rate Promotes excretion of toxic substances Promotes diuresis during oliguric phase of acute renal failure **Incompatibilities** Refer to isotonic mannitol infusions	Contraindicated in anuria Contraindicated in patients who are severely dehydrated Use with extreme caution in patients with congestive heart failure or pulmonary edema Use filter with 15% and 20% solution Strict I & O with output measurements every 30 to 60 minutes Hemodynamic monitoring Monitor electrolytes and BUN Weigh daily, or more frequently
Amino Acid (Protein) Solutions Aminess® Aminosyn® Branch-Amin® FreAmine® HepAmine® Nephramine® Novamine® ProcalAmine® RenAmine® Travasol® TrophAmine®	Range from 400 mOsm/L to 1,600 mOsm/L	**Indications** These are nutritional agents indicated for use when oral routes of nutrition are not possible or are inadequate due to disease, surgery, severe infections, chemotherapy, or severe anorexia Refer to Chapter 13 for complete information on the use of these products **Incompatibilities** Do not add anything without consultation with a pharmacist	Numerous precautions and guidelines are associated with use of these products These hypertonic preparations range in amino acid content from 3.5% to 10%, with or without electrolytes; they also are available in preparations with 5% to 50% dextrose

continues

Table 5-4 | Hypertonic Infusions: Indications for Use and Precautions (*continued*)

INFUSION	OSMO-LARITY	INDICATIONS AND INCOMPATIBILITIES	PRECAUTIONS, COMMENTS, CONTRAINDICATIONS
Alcohol in Dextrose and Water Infusions		**Indications**	Contraindicated in
5% alcohol and 5% dextrose in water	1,010.08 mOsm/L	Caloric provisions are: dextrose 3.4 kcal/g, alcohol 5.6 kcal/ml	alcoholism diabetic coma epilepsy
Alcohol 252.52 mOsm/L		Fluid replacement	urinary tract infections
Dextrose 252.52 mOsm/L		**Incompatibilities**	Use with caution in diabetes mellitus
pH 4.5		Check with pharmacist before mixing anything with these infusions	Monitor for intoxication
10% alcohol and 5% dextrose in water	757.56 mOsm/L		Monitor for hyperglycemia
Alcohol 505.04 mOsm/L			Monitor for glycosuria
Dextrose 252.52 mOsm/L			Strict I & O
			Drug Interactions
			There are many drug interactions because of the alcohol in these infusions. Many medications are potentiated or have a reduced effect when given concurrently with alcohol infusions. Note the medications the patient is taking and determine untoward interactions.
Alkalinizing Agents		**Indications**	Contraindicated with
Sodium bicarbonate 5% 595 mEq/L (0.595/mL)	595 mOsm/L	Alkalinizing agent for temporary treatment of severe metabolic acidosis	acidosis (respiratory) alkalosis (metabolic and respiratory) edema
Sodium bicarbonate 7.5% 892.50 mEq/L (0.893/mL)	893 mOsm/L	Increases plasma bicarbonate and buffers excess hydrogen ion concentration	hypertension hypocalcemia hypochloremia
Sodium bicarbonate 8.4% 999.60 mEq/L (0.999/mL)	1,000 mOsm/l	Dosage corresponds to degree of acidosis according to pH (<7.25), PO$_2$, PCO$_2$, and electrolytes	impaired renal function
pH 7.75 (7.0–8.5)		Treats hyperkalemia	Use with extreme caution in patients with sodium retention
		Used as a buffer to raise the pH of intravenous infusates	Use with caution in patients on corticosteroids
		Treatment for barbiturate and salicylate intoxication	Excessive or rapid administration can result in intracranial hemorrhage
		Incompatibilities	Extravasation can result in severe tissue damage
		Numerous; consult pharmacist	Flush IV line before and after injection

Review Questions and Activities

1. List two infusions for each category (crystalloid, colloid, and hydrating solutions) and calculate the caloric content and osmolarity of each.
2. List five indications for IV therapy.
3. List why the following might be ordered:
   a. Dextrose
   b. Dextran
   c. Sodium bicarbonate
   d. normal saline
4. Describe what happens when hypotonic solutions are not properly used.
5. Describe what happens when hypertonic solutions are not properly used.

Chapter 6

Patient Preparation and Site Selection for Peripheral Intravenous Infusion Therapy

LEARNING OBJECTIVES

Upon completion of this chapter, the reader should be able to:

* List the major advantages and disadvantages of intravenous or intravascular infusion therapy.

* Discuss the importance of psychological preparation for the patient who is about to undergo infusion therapy and for the CMA who administers it.

* Review the components of physical preparation for the patient about to undergo infusion therapy in terms of safety, comfort, and position.

* List and describe each of the sites that may be accessed by the CMA and used for peripheral intravenous infusion therapy.

* Assess the factors that determine the choice and selection of sites for peripheral venipuncture and infusion therapy.

There are distinct advantages and disadvantages to deliberate before instituting peripheral infusion therapy. Although the advantages usually outweigh the disadvantages, the decision must be based on the patient's situation and the pharmacokinetics and bioavailability of the products that need to be administered. **Pharmacokinetics** is the study of drug action and metabolism in the body, including the processes of absorption, distribution, duration of action, and methods of excretion. **Bioavailability** refers to the rate and concentration of drug entry into the circulatory system and its pharmacologic response at the site of action. Both of these factors must always be considered when deciding to administer fluids or medications to a patient. Table 6-1 compares and contrasts the advantages and disadvantages of peripheral IV therapy.

PATIENT PREPARATION

The administration of peripheral IV therapy has become commonplace in most health care settings. In the interest of cost containment, governmental and insurance regulations are becoming more and more stringent, leaving the acute care setting available to only the sickest patients, or those in need of special procedures who cannot be accommodated safely on an outpatient basis or in the home. Ninety percent or more of the patients in some hospital units may be receiving some form of IV therapy via peripheral or central venous access lines. For those undergoing outpatient surgical procedures, peripheral infusions run throughout most of their stay. Due to the limitations dictated by Medicare and Diagnosis Related Groups (DRGs), the insurance industry, and the shift to managed care, as well as personal preferences, many patients are receiving intravenous therapies at home. There has been a dramatic conversion to IV home care for antibiotic and chemotherapy administration, hydration, pain control, hyperalimentation, as well as advanced HIV disease-related therapies, and the administration of growth hormone and immune globulins. In addition, dobutamine (for patients with severe congestive heart failure who are not candidates for heart transplantation) and tocolytic therapy (to prevent the premature onset of contractions in women who have not sustained full-term pregnancies) are being administered in the home.

Psychological Preparation

A person who is psychologically prepared for an event is better equipped to cope with the circumstances of that situation.

Table 6-1 | Advantages and Disadvantages of Peripheral IV Infusion Therapy

ADVANTAGES	DISADVANTAGES
1. It provides a route for immediate availability to the systemic circulation without regard to gastrointestinal functioning or subcutaneous or intramuscular conditions.	1. There is a greater possibility of a serious allergic reaction occurring because of rapid delivery to the systemic circulation. Once administered, an IV drug cannot be retrieved.
2. Drug absorption is more predictable.	2. There is always the possibility of fluid overload.
3. Blood levels of the drug can be maintained for even distribution and titrated according to the patient's needs.	3. Should an error occur in dosage or administration, the potential for dangerous outcomes is amplified.
4. It provides a reliable route for emergency conditions.	4. There is always the possibility of infection and sepsis whenever the skin barrier is breached through percutaneous puncture.
5. It is ideal for drugs that cannot be given orally due to poor absorption and failure to reach the general circulation for systemic distribution.	5. There is pain associated with cannula insertion as well as psychological discomfort associated with the knowledge that an indwelling device is in place.
6. It provides a route for drugs that cannot be given by other routes (such as heparin, which cannot be given orally or intramuscularly).	6. There may be impaired mobility, depending on placement of the IV.
7. It is often the only available route for the unconscious or uncooperative patient.	7. The potential for nerve or vessel damage exists with improper venipuncture technique and incorrect cannula placement.
8. It is ideal for patients who are nauseated, vomiting, or have any gastrointestinal disruptions.	8. There may be pain associated with the administration of irritating drugs.
9. There is less discomfort because, once initiated, the site may be accessed for 72 hours or more.	9. Tissue damage can occur with extravasation of vesicants.
	10. There is always the potential for phlebitis, thrombophlebitis, or embolization.

This holds true for any new experience in life, but is even more important for the person who is ill, in an unfamiliar environment, and in need of services and procedures to which she is unaccustomed. The patient undergoing infusion therapy is usually very sick and has multiple lifestyle changes and personal crises to deal with. Any event, no matter how insignificant it may seem to someone else, can produce added stress for the patient.

When a patient is in need of IV therapy, it is imperative that she is mentally and emotionally prepared. For most people, the thought of being stuck with a needle is not pleasant. Even though the need for treatment is inevitable, the circumstances surrounding the situation can be manipulated so that the experience is less traumatic.

MEDICAL ASSISTING TIP

IV CMA Responsibility

Because IV therapy is so frequently employed, the CMA may look at it as a very ordinary, almost mundane, activity. This attitude can be very dangerous in terms of both patient safety and CMA liability. From the patient's perspective, the need to undergo IV therapy can be an anxiety-producing, traumatic event—something definitely not perceived as a routine, everyday experience. For this reason, the CMA must take all the appropriate measures to prepare the patient psychologically and physically so that she can adapt as favorably as possible to the experience. While the CMA who administers IV therapy must be highly skilled in the technical details of infusion therapy, she must also possess the knowledge and sensitivity to deal with the psychosocial issues as well, especially in the home care setting.

The CMA must always remember that psychological preparation not only helps the patient adapt, but also facilitates the initiation of IV therapy for the CMA. If venipuncture and the introduction of the cannula into the vein is to proceed smoothly, the patient must be relaxed. If she is not at ease, she experiences a sympathetic response, also called the *fright, flight, fight, freeze reaction*. When this occurs, the veins may spasm or constrict. The blood is then shunted from the peripheral circulation to the vital organs, thus making venous access very difficult, if not impossible. Extreme anxiety can cause **syncope** (fainting), the result of a vasovagal response.

Time, explanations, and honesty are the CMA's best allies when it comes to the patient's psychological preparation.

CRITICAL THINKING

The Environment of a Traumatic Situation

Can you recall a traumatic situation you have experienced? What was it? What events, no matter how small or seemingly insignificant, comforted you? Which made the situation worse? How can you apply your experience to a patient situation?

When the CMA takes the time to explain the forthcoming procedure, and allows time for the patient to ask questions, caring and trust are imparted, and obstacles to communication are breached. The CMA must be honest regarding the procedure in terms of the expected time the IV will be needed, why it is needed, and the amount of discomfort, immobility, and inconvenience that will be associated with it. If a CMA tells a patient that needlesticks or injections will not hurt, but feel just like a "little" mosquito bite, he is not being honest. A mosquito bite is not evident until after the venom has been injected and the area starts to itch; the sting itself is painless. Needlesticks, for the most part, do impart various degrees of discomfort. The patient needs to know that the pain is temporary and should diminish once the cannula is in place.

MEDICAL ASSISTING TIP

Pain Reduction

It is imperative that the CMA be honest regarding the type and severity of discomfort associated with any procedure. If pain is anticipated, the patient should be told. He should be instructed regarding any measures that might make it less distressing for him, then be reassured that the CMA will do everything possible to expedite the procedure and make it as painless for him as she can. The CMA should intervene to make any painful procedure less uncomfortable by employing appropriate (and substantiated) physical, pharmacological, and psychological measures.

It is always a good idea to explain the positive aspects of any procedure in terms of how the patient will benefit from the therapy. Sometimes, just the thought that what is being done is expected to promote health and comfort relieves much of the pain and stress associated with illness and treatment. The CMA's demeanor is also significant, making it very important that he appear confident and knowledgeable in order to elicit the patient's cooperation and decrease anxiety.

Physical Preparation

In addition to psychological preparation, if the patient is to adapt to treatment, she must be physically prepared. Physical comfort, along with the confidence that she is in a safe environment and under the care of competent individuals, constitutes expectations that are the right of every patient. In readying a patient for venipuncture and infusion therapy, there are several prerequisites that must be addressed, primarily those of safety, comfort, and correct positioning.

Safety

The assessments and interventions that promote and contribute to the patient's safety prior to the initiation of peripheral infusion therapy include, but are not limited to, the following:

1. Verification of the physician's order
2. Correct patient identification
3. Validation that the ordered infusion is appropriate for the patient
4. Confirmation that the patient is not allergic to anything that is to be administered
5. Confirmation that all supplies and equipment for venipuncture are sterile and handled aseptically, and that they have not exceeded their expiration dates
6. Documentation of significant laboratory and diagnostic reports
7. Strict asepsis in the preparation of all products to be used for venipuncture and IV infusion
8. The provision of a safe environment for the patient during infusion therapy in terms of bed rails, restraints, movement, and ambulation
9. Assessment and selection of the peripheral vessel that is appropriate for the type of infusion(s) ordered
10. Teaching measures that will instruct the patient about what she needs to report in terms of activity, discomfort, or signs and symptoms associated with any untoward reaction

Comfort

The administration of any peripheral infusion imposes some degree of restriction for the patient in terms of mobility and sustaining activities of daily living (ADLs). Although the ambulatory patient may get up and move around during IV therapy, measures must be employed to prevent dislodgement of the cannula or disconnection of any portions of the setup. Should the closed, sterile system be breached, the potential for contamination and the introduction of infection escalates.

MEDICAL ASSISTING TIP

Veins to Avoid

It is important to remember that veins in the limb located on the side of the body where a radical mastectomy with lymph node stripping and dissection has been performed are to be avoided due to altered circulation and impaired venous return. Likewise, an edematous extremity or extremity that has sustained third-degree burns should also be bypassed. If the IV is being inserted to provide access during surgery, the access site should present minimal interference with the surgical procedure or positioning during the intraoperative and postoperative periods.

Prior to the initiation of IV therapy, there are several assessments and interventions that need to be employed in the interest of the patient's physical comfort. These include, but are not limited to the following:

1. Determining whether the patient is right handed or left handed (The CMA should make all efforts to access an appropriate vein in the patient's nondominant hand, so the patient can carry out ADLs without compromising the IV. The CMA should also avoid using veins in areas of flexion or in the antecubital fossa unless such areas are immobilized in a safe manner.)
2. Allowing the patient to carry out ADLs (bathing or showering, oral care, hair care, toileting) prior to the initiation of therapy, if time permits
3. Securing IV tubing that is of a length appropriate for minimally restricted movement by the patient during the infusion
4. Providing loose-fitting bed clothes that will not restrict movement or fluid flow, and will allow for easy removal when they need to be changed without interfering with the IV
5. Providing privacy

MEDICAL ASSISTING ALERT

Hemodialysis Considerations

Never access, for peripheral intravenous therapy, an arteriovenous fistula, graft, or shunt that has been surgically placed for hemodialysis (Figure 6-1). In fact, the arm in which one of these devices is present should not be used for IV therapy, blood pressure monitoring, or any procedure that might restrict blood flow to the dialysis access site.

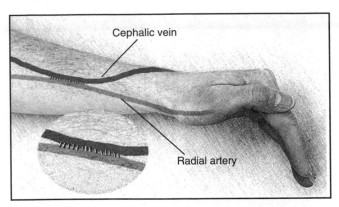

A. An arteriovenous fistula is the direct communication between an artery and a vein, in which a surgical incision is made into each vessel, after which the two are sutured together.

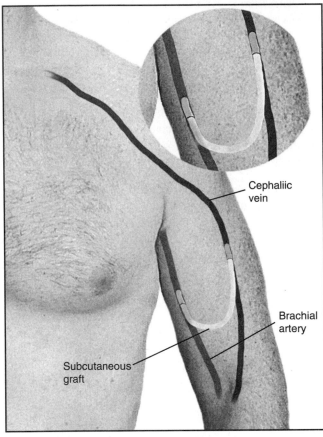

B. An arteriovenous graft is where a natural graft (autograft or bovine graft) is tunneled under the skin and connected to the distal end of an artery and the proximal end of a vein.

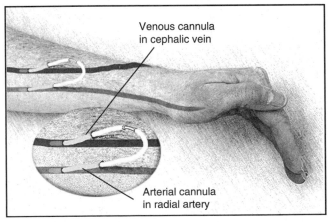

C. A shunt is an artificially constructed passage to divert blood flow from an artery to a vein, in which one transparent silicon cannula is threaded into an artery and another into a vein. The two are tunneled to the surface of the limb and connected to form a loop by joining them together with a silicon connector.

Figure 6-1 | Surgical arteriovenous communications: (A) arteriovenous fistula; (B) arteriovenous graft; (C) arteriovenous shunt

Position

Prior to the initiation of IV therapy, the patient should be positioned in a manner that allows for optimum conditions for venous access. Although cannulation can be performed when the patient is in a flat, supine position, it is preferable that she be placed in the **Fowler's position:** semi-sitting, with the torso and head elevated between 40 and 60 degrees (Figure 6-2). The knees may be flexed and supported by pillows **(semi-Fowler's position).** The arms should be positioned so that they are at the patient's side, with the intended site of venipuncture at a level lower than the heart, to promote venous filling.

Measures need to be taken to make the patient as comfortable as possible during infusion therapy. She should understand that she can move the extremity with the IV, rather than keep it totally immobile, so circulation is maintained. An arm board may be unnecessary if the CMA appropriately selects and cannulates the vein, allowing for natural anatomic splinting by the bones. Should immobilization of the extremity be required, the CMA must follow agency policy and procedural guidelines regarding the use of arm boards, restraints, or any stabilization devices. "Protocol for the use of restraints shall be consistent with state and federal regulations . . . shall be in accordance with the order of a physician or a prescriber authorized by the state Nurse Practice Act" (INS, 2000, Standard 37, S33). When an arm board is applied, the CMA must protect circulatory status and flow, and be able to monitor the infusion site. "An arm board should be used to facilitate infusion delivery when the catheter is placed in or around an area of extremity flexion" (INS, 2000, Standard 36, S32). The CMA must always keep in mind the potential for nerve and muscle damage that can accompany the use of restraining devices. It is important to remove any device at frequent intervals in order to adequately assess circulatory status. "The arm board should be removed and the patient's extremity circulatory status should be assessed at established intervals" (INS, 2000, Standard 36, S33). Pillows can be provided to support the extremity and to position the patient comfortably. Depending on her condition, the patient may be able to ambulate and shower, as long as the cannula and IV equipment are secured and the insertion site is protected from moisture and contamination.

INTRAVASCULAR SITE SELECTION

There are many factors that must be considered, from patient, medical assisting, and medical perspectives, when selecting an appropriate intravascular site. The site selected should provide the most appropriate access to the vessel for the intended therapy and accommodate administration of the prescribed infusion while minimizing any associated risks or complications. **Intravascular** access refers to entrance into arteries, veins, or capillaries. Veins, because they are so profuse and can usually be accessed easily, are most commonly used, and are predominantly focused on in this text, with this chapter addressing commonly used peripheral venous sites.

When the CMA is responsible for initiating infusion therapy, he must take into consideration the patient's age, health status, diagnosis, condition of the site to be accessed, and the purpose, duration, and possible side effects of therapy. The CMA is expected to have a sound understanding of the anatomy and physiology of the vascular system and the access sites that may be used whether he initiates the therapy or manages and monitors the infusion started by someone else.

Peripheral Intravenous Routes

When selecting an appropriate vein for infusion therapy, the CMA must take into consideration, based on the patient's circumstances, the purpose of therapy, the proposed duration that the IV will be needed, and the condition and location of usable veins.

Prior to setting up or bringing any IV equipment to the patient's bedside, the CMA should spend some time with the patient, explaining all components of the proposed therapy and providing some time for the patient to ask questions. At this time the CMA can visually inspect the patient's skin and veins and palpate proposed access sites to locate the most appropriate vessel in which to initiate therapy. He might want to apply a tourniquet, shine a flashlight over the arm, or utilize a device such as the Venoscope II Transilluminator

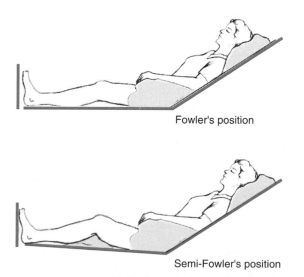

Fowler's position

Semi-Fowler's position

Figure 6-2 | Fowler's and semi-Fowler's positions

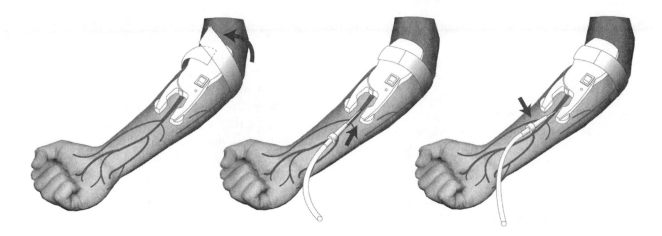

Figure 6-3 | The Venoscope II Transilluminator® (Courtesy of Venoscope, LLC, Lafayette, LA)

(Figure 6-3) to detect the most suitable veins for use. When it is decided which vein will be employed using one of these measures, the CMA might want to mark the intended vein with a surgical marking pen. During this time, he can also predict the ease or difficulty of venous access and determine the measures he might need to take to facilitate successful venipuncture. Before starting the IV, the patient's permission must be obtained.

There are several issues that must be addressed and considered prior to commencing infusion therapy. These include things that the CMA should accomplish and those that he must avoid, that is, the dos and don'ts of IV site selection and therapy initiation (Table 6-2).

Upper Extremity Access Sites

Venous cannulation, for infusion therapy, should begin at the distal-most area of the upper extremity and proceed proximally, with subsequent cannulation being made proximal to the previously cannulated site. Table 6-3 profiles which veins should be used and their indications for use. As always, when electing to cannulate a particular vein for any infusion, the CMA must assess the patient and his condition, the indication(s) for therapy, the product(s) to be infused, and the projected time the therapy will be employed. "Site selection for vascular access shall include assessment of the patient's condition, infusion device history, and type and duration of therapy" (INS, 2000, Standard 43, S37).

Veins of the Hands

The digital veins of the hands are the small vessels in the dorsal and lateral sections of the digits, or fingers. They are small and communicate to form the metacarpal veins, those that lie on the dorsum of the hand over the metacarpal

bones, and are tributaries of the dorsal venous arch. Figure 6-4 illustrates the venous circulation of the hand.

Veins of the Arms

The cephalic vein emanates from the metacarpal vein at the radial portion of the lower forearm and proceeds upward, above the radial-humeral joint, on the radial margin of the upper arm, at which point it becomes the upper cephalic vein. The accessory cephalic vein branches off from the cephalic vein and continues to run along the radial surface of the forearm, whereas the median cephalic vein branches toward the inner aspect of the forearm.

The basilic vein radiates upward from the metacarpal veins on the ulnar aspect of the forearm, past the elbow to the upper arm, with the median basilic branching on the palmar side of the forearm. In the upper arm, the basilic and cephalic veins merge with the axillary vein, which leads into the subclavian vein. Figures 6-5 and 6-6 illustrate the venous circulation of the arms and upper body.

The antecubital veins (also called *median veins* because they extend centrally from the palmar region of the forearm) are three vessels that lead into the **cubital fossa**—the triangular region that lies anterior to and below the elbow. The median cephalic branches from the cephalic vein on the radial aspect of the arm, the median basilic emanates from the basilic vein on the ulnar side, and the median cubital branches from the basilic vein in front of the elbow. Table 6-3 compares and contrasts the indications and uses for peripheral access sites of the hands and arms.

Veins of the Upper Body

The veins of the upper body consist of larger vessels that channel blood to the heart. The subclavian veins originate from the axillary veins where the cephalic and basilic veins

Table 6-2 | The Dos and Don'ts of IV Site Selection

DO	RATIONALE
Use the distal veins of the upper extremities first, with subsequent venipunctures proximal to the previous sites.	The venous network above previously used sites will not be punctured. By alternating limbs, the previously used vein can heal.
Palpate the veins prior to venipuncture.	From palpation, the CMA can determine the condition of the patient's veins, differentiate them from arteries, and locate deeper, larger veins, which are stronger and more suitable for IV therapy.
Use veins appropriate for the prescribed infusate. Larger veins should be used for irritating or hypertonic preparations.	Hypertonic or irritating infusates cause discomfort when infused into small veins where there is reduced hemodilution and the intima of the vein can be damaged.
Use veins that will most likely sustain the infusion for 48 to 72 hours.	With prolonged infusion therapy, all measures must be taken to preserve peripheral veins.
Use the smallest cannula that will deliver the prescribed infusate.	The cannula size should allow for adequate blood flow and hemodilution while delivering the infusate at the appropriate rate and causing minimal discomfort.

DON'T	RATIONALE
Do not use the veins of the lower extremities in adults and children who are walking. If an emergency exists and they must be used, change the site as soon as the patient is stabilized.	The circulation in these veins is more sluggish than in the upper body, thereby increasing the risk of phlebitis, thrombosis, and embolism.
Do not use veins that are irritated or sclerosed from previous use.	Use of such veins produces undue discomfort for the patient and increases trauma and the possibility of phlebitis and infection.
Avoid areas of flexion, unless the joint is immobilized.	The catheter may kink and restrict the flow of fluid, or it may break. If a steel needle is used, it may puncture the vessel wall, infiltrate, or cause damage to surrounding tissues and nerves. Using these areas limits the patient's movement and independence.
Avoid veins in the antecubital fossa.	It is difficult to adequately immobilize this area and movement of the cannula can result in infiltration and mechanical phlebitis. Damage to the antecubital veins restricts use of distal veins in the extremity that feed into these vessels.
Do not use a tourniquet on fragile veins.	The pressure of the tourniquet may cause rupture of the venous wall during venipuncture, resulting in hematoma and damage to the vein.
Do not use the veins in an extremity: • On the side of the body where a radical mastectomy has been performed with lymph node dissection/stripping • That is impaired as a result of a CVA • That is partially amputated, or has undergone reconstructive or orthopedic surgery • That has sustained third degree burns	Circulation in these areas is impaired, with altered venous and lymphatic flow, which can cause or exacerbate edema.
Do not use an arteriovenous fistula, shunt, or graft for peripheral infusion therapy.	These routes, which are surgically constructed, must be preserved for hemodialysis access.

Table 6-3 | Upper Extremity Venous Access Sites: Indications for Use

VEINS	Digital	Metacarpal	Cephalic	Accessory Cephalic	Median Cephalic (Antecubital)	Basilic	Median Basilic (Antecubital)	Median Cubital (Antecubital)	Median Antebrachial
USAGE CHARACTERISTICS									
Ideal for short-term use	✓	✓							
Use with small-gauge cannula	✓	✓							
Use with nonirritating fluids	✓	✓							
Naturally splinted by bone		✓	✓	✓		✓			
Requires artificial splinting	✓				✓		✓	✓	✓
Accommodates large-gauge cannula			✓	✓	✓	✓	✓	✓	
Accommodates longer cannula			✓	✓		✓			
Close proximity to artery					✓			✓	
Thin-walled vein	✓	✓							
ADVANTAGES									
Best choice for early IV use		✓							
Easy access		✓	✓	✓	✓	✓	✓	✓	
Good visibility		✓	✓		✓	✓	✓		
Does not impair mobility			✓	✓		✓			
Allows for good hemodilution			✓	✓	✓	✓	✓	✓	✓
Ideal for phlebotomy					✓		✓	✓	
Ideal for blood transfusion				✓	✓	✓			
DISADVANTAGES									
Impairs mobility	✓	✓			✓		✓	✓	✓
Discomfort on insertion	✓	✓				✓	✓		✓
Infiltrates easily	✓						✓	✓	✓
Tends to roll with venipuncture			✓			✓			✓
Difficult to splint	✓				✓			✓	✓
Vessels, tissues, nerves are easily damaged					✓		✓	✓	✓
Difficult to visualize with edema or obesity	✓		✓	✓	✓				
Inflames easily		✓							

merge in the upper chest and shoulder regions. The internal and external jugular veins drain blood from the head and neck regions into the superior vena cava, the large vessel that empties into the right atrium of the heart.

Lower Extremity Access Sites

"Veins of the lower extremities should not be used routinely in the adult population due to risk of embolism and throm-bophlebitis" (INS, 200, Standard 43, S37). Although not recommended for use in adults or walking children because of circulatory compromise and the potential for thromboembolic disorders, the lower extremity vessels (Figure 6-7) sometimes have to be accessed in emergency situations. If used, there needs to be a written medical order as well as agency policy to uphold this procedure. There must be full documentation to support the reason for lower extremity cannulation and the site must be changed as soon as the

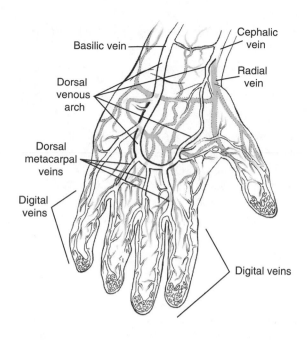

Figure 6-4 | Superficial and deep veins of the hand

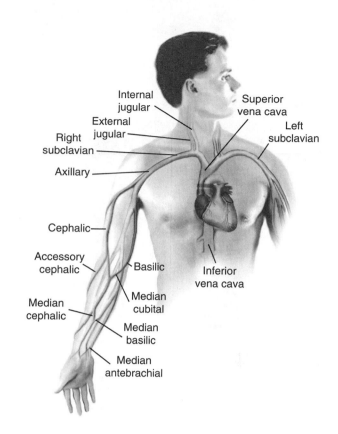

Figure 6-5 | Superficial and deep veins of the arm and upper torso

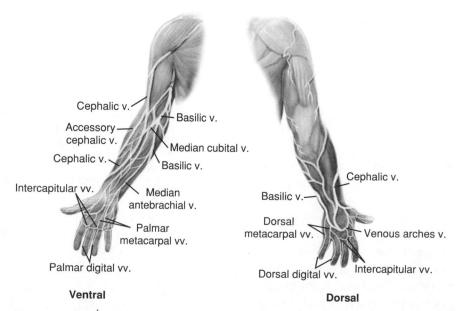

Ventral

Dorsal

Figure 6-6 | Superficial and deep veins of the arm

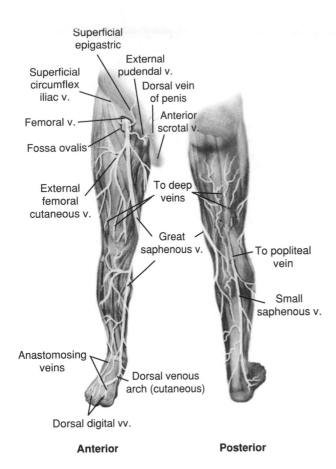

Anterior   **Posterior**

Figure 6-7 | Superficial veins of the lower limbs

patient's condition warrants it. If it is absolutely necessary to use the leg veins, the best choices are usually those on the dorsum of the foot, over the metatarsal bones, or the saphenous vein, where it surfaces in the ankle area.

CRITICAL THINKING

How Do You Handle a Patient Who Refuses a Procedure?

Your patient, whose physician has ordered an intravenous infusion, refuses to allow you to start it. He is pale, trembling, and the palms of his hands are cool and clammy. What would you say? What would you do? What are his rights? What is your responsibility?

To begin with, always bear in mind that a patient has the right to refuse treatment, but before notifying the physician of this, you have several options

Listen. Give him a chance to verbalize his feelings and fears.

Be nonjudgmental. Maintain eye contact and interest in what he has to say.

Reassure. Assure him that nothing will be done without his consent. Clearly state that he certainly has the right to refuse treatment and that you will abide by his wishes.

Investigate. Try and find out why he does not want the treatment—again, in a nonjudgmental manner. He may have had an unfavorable experience in the past and need clarification and explanations.

Explain. When a patient is apprehensive, he may need reinforcement as to why treatment is needed and how it can help him.

Report. If he still refuses, notify the physician.

Document. Record all assessment data, verbal and nonverbal, to substantiate the refusal.

Review Questions and Activities

1. List five factors the CMA must consider when choosing an IV site.
2. In light of the physiology and mechanics of circulatory and lymphatic flow, explain why an IV infusion should not be initiated in the extremity on the side of the body where a radical mastectomy has been performed.
3. Draw a two-column chart to compare arteries, arterioles, capillaries, venules, and veins, in terms of their size, structure, anatomic location, elasticity, and blood flow.
4. Based on the following information, what measures would you take to prepare this patient physically and psychologically for her prescribed treatment regimen? What, specifically, would you say and do regarding the IV you must start?

Miss Lucci is a 22-year-old college student admitted to your unit for a possible ruptured ovarian cyst. Her physician has ordered several diagnostic tests and has given stat orders for her to be NPO with continuous IVs infusing at 125 cc/hr. As you begin to perform your admission assessment and explain what the doctor has prescribed, Miss Lucci begins to tremble and cry, saying, "I am so afraid. The thought of being stuck with needles terrifies me. I feel like I am going to faint."

Chapter 7

Equipment and Supplies Employed in the Preparation and Administration of Intravenous Infusion Therapy

LEARNING OBJECTIVES

Upon completion of this chapter, the reader should be able to:

✳ Analyze and identify the CMA's role and responsibility regarding the use of equipment and supplies used for infusion therapy.

✳ Identify the types of infusate containers available and indications for their use.

✳ Describe the features of the various primary and secondary infusate administration sets and the accessory devices that can be used with them.

✳ Explain how needleless systems and needlestick protection devices operate.

✳ Distinguish between the commonly used peripheral venous access devices.

✳ List the materials used to prepare and maintain the integrity of the percutaneous infusion site.

✳ Differentiate between the types of manual, gravity control, and electronic infusion devices used to regulate intravenous infusions.

The practice of intravenous infusion therapy has rapidly advanced to one of the most sophisticated specialty areas. The knowledge, skill, and expertise required to perform procedures in this highly technical realm involve the use of some traditional, but mostly innovative, state-of-the-art equipment. Such items pass through many hands and fall under the guidelines and requirements set forth by federal, state, and local authorities, as well as private, legal, and financial sectors. These groups, via their dictates, are committed to a universal cause—the well-being and safety of all health care consumers and providers.

The equipment and supplies available for use in the delivery of infusion therapy are constantly being evaluated and updated. Manufacturers strive to provide equipment that is on the cutting edge in terms of patient safety and comfort, nursing productivity, cost-effectiveness, and environmental preservation.

It is the responsibility of the CMA to develop and maintain expertise in the use and maintenance of any equipment utilized in the delivery of IV therapy. He is obligated to understand how various products function and know where to turn for information and problem solving. The CMA is often involved in clinical trials of products as well as the decision-making processes regarding what supplies will be adopted for use in his place of employment.

INFUSATE CONTAINERS

The containers used for the delivery of intravenous infusions, for the most part, are made of flexible plastic materials. Because of the chemical makeup of some infusates, however, glass containers are also used. When using any of these containers, the CMA must always do several things prior to setting up and administering the infusate to ensure patient safety. He must read the label to ascertain that the infusate is the correct one ordered for his patient and check the expiration date. He must evaluate the container, making sure that all seals are intact and that there are no breaks in its integrity. The fluid should be checked for clarity and the absence of particulate matter. Manufacturer and additive labels are affixed to containers in an inverted position so they can easily be read when the container is hanging upside down on an IV pole.

Glass Containers

Glass containers are vacuum systems that require a vent to replace infused fluid with air. The vacuum must be released in order for the solution to flow. The venting can be accomplished with use of vented administration set tubing or through an internal system in which the bottle contains a tube that allows air to enter and collect in the space above the fluid level. In the vented administration set, the bottle is sealed with a solid rubber stopper with one hole, covered by a latex rubber disc that maintains the vacuum. Once the disc is removed and the administration set attached, filtered air enters the container through an airway that is built into the administration set spike. With the internal system, the rubber closure for the bottle has two openings, one with a filtered strawlike tube that extends into the bottle and one for the administration set (both sealed with a latex rubber disc that preserves the vacuum inside the bottle). Once the latex disc is removed and the container is spiked, air enters into the solution container through the filtered tube. In both systems, the vacuum-preserving latex disc is secured with an aluminum, peel-off band. Fluid graduation marks are molded into the glass. At the bottom of the bottle is an aluminum band and bail for hanging on an IV pole when the bottle is inverted (Figure 7-1).

A.

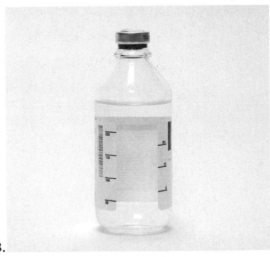

B.

Figure 7-1 | Glass IV bottles (B. Courtesy of Baxter Healthcare Corporation)

Once a glass solution bottle is opened by a pharmacist for the introduction of an admixture, it is sealed with a tamper-proof closure to prevent alteration of the infusate after it leaves the pharmacy. This device cannot be removed without being torn. If it is not fully intact, the infusate must not be used.

Plastic Containers

Plastic containers that house intravenous infusates are constructed of semirigid or flexible materials. Even though they can be punctured or broken, they have a greater safety factor and are more functional than glass bottles, especially in emergency and community health settings.

Individual plastic containers are made of the same materials, rather than a combination of glass, plastic, rubber, and metal (found in glass systems). Semirigid containers are generally made of biologically inert, nontoxic PVC (polyvinyl chloride) or polyolefin. To provide flexibility in the manufacture of pliable, collapsible bags, the phthalate plasticizer DEHP (Di [2-ethylhexyl] phthalate) has been added to the PVC for many years. Some companies have elected not to use PVC/DEHP due to concerns regarding the safety of exposure to this chemical. The FDA issued a public health notification regarding the use of the DEHP plasticizer and its ability to leach out of plastic medical devices into the solutions that come in contact with the plastic. The amount of DEHP that will leach out depends on the temperature, the lipid content of the liquid, and the duration of contact with the plastic. Exposure to DEHP has produced a range of

adverse effects in laboratory animals. Of greatest concern, based on existing studies, are the effects the chemical may have on the male reproductive system and the production of normal sperm (FDA Center for Devices and Radiological Health, 2002b). Most infusion companies are no longer making IV bags with PVC/DEHP, even though the International Agency for Research on Cancer (IARC) has reclassified DEHP as "not classifiable as to carcinogenicity to humans" (IARC, 2000). Instead, manufacturers are using polyolefin, a biologically inert, clear, flexible, non-DEHP nontoxic plastic that is ecologically favorable because it is biodegradable and will incinerate into carbon dioxide and water. Infusion containers made with polyolefin are as drug-compatible as those made of glass.

Flexible Plastic Containers

The soft plastic containers, which are most common and widely used, are totally closed systems that do not require venting because they are not vacuum sealed (Figure 7-2). They are free of air and impervious to moisture. Because they can withstand extremes of temperature, these bags are used for additives that must be stored under refrigeration or require freezing prior to administration. These bags are available in a wider variety of sizes than other containers, ranging from 50 to 2000 ml. The major problems associated with the use of

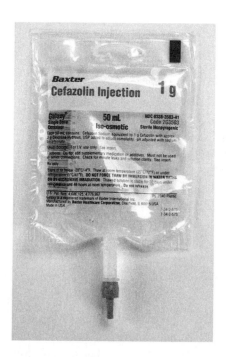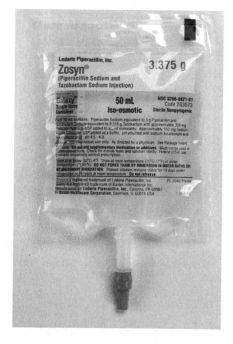

Figure 7-2 | Flexible IV Containers (Courtesy of Baxter Healthcare Corporation)

plastic IV bags is that they can be easily punctured during spiking and small breaches in the integrity of the plastic may go unnoticed, thus allowing for the entry of organisms into the system.

Unless admixtures have been added in the pharmacy, flexible plastic IV bags are contained in an opaque, outer plastic wrap that must be torn off to expose the IV container. Extending from the top of all flexible IV bags is a flat continuation of the plastic that has a hole for hanging on an IV pole. Depending on the manufacturer, there may be one or two extensions protruding from the bottom of the bag. If there are two, one is the administration set port, encased in a protective, easily removable plastic pigtail that maintains the port's sterility prior to spiking, and the other is an injection port for adding medication. Inside the administration port (about 0.5 in) is a polyvinyl diaphragm that prevents loss of infusate prior to spiking, even if the pigtail is removed. When this diaphragm is punctured with the administration set spike, infusate flows into the administration set. Once pierced, the diaphragm is not resealable. The other extension from the IV bag is covered by a latex rubber medication port that allows for introduction of additives via a syringe and needle or needleless connection plug. When there is only one extension from the bag for the administration set, the medication port, which is a resealable latex disk, is found on the lower portion of the IV bag.

Information regarding the product, expiration date, and fluid graduation marks are imprinted into the plastic by the manufacturer. Never write directly on a flexible plastic bag with a ballpoint pen or any type of indelible marker. The pen may puncture the bag and the indelible marker ink may absorb into the plastic and contaminate the infusate. If additional information is to be added, it must be affixed with a label.

As with glass containers, tamperproof additive caps are available for use with flexible plastic IV bags (Figure 7-3). The cap fits over the medication port and indicates that a pharmacist has added medication to the infusate and that the admixture has not been tampered with since leaving the pharmacy.

Flexible plastic IV bags are used for reduced-volume (50 or 100 ml) piggyback containers of 5% dextrose in water and 0.9% sodium chloride (Figure 7-4). Medications are added to these bags for intermittent administration. For commonly used drugs, especially antibiotics, the plastic minibags are

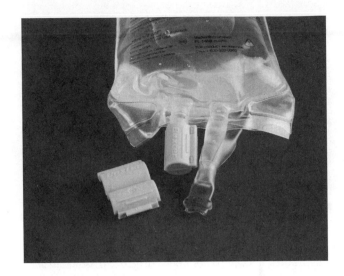

Figure 7-3 | Additive cap for VIAFLEX plastic container used to provide evidence that medication has been added to VIAFLEX containers (Courtesy of Baxter Healthcare Corporation)

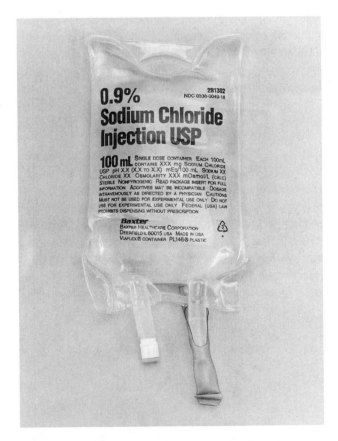

Figure 7-4 | MiniBag® Reduced-Volume Piggyback Container (Courtesy of Baxter Healthcare Corporation)

MEDICAL ASSISTING ALERT

Writing on IV Bags

Never write directly on a flexible plastic IV bag with a ballpoint pen or any type of indelible marker.

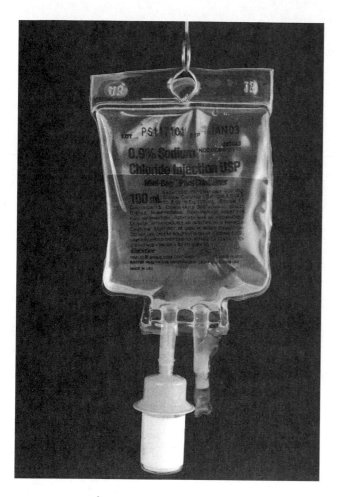

Figure 7-5 | MiniBag Plus® (Courtesy of Baxter Healthcare Corporation)

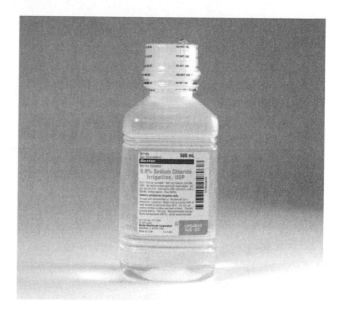

Figure 7-6 | Rigid Plastic Container (Courtesy of Baxter Healthcare Corporation)

while others, like glass bottles, have a vent mechanism that allows air to enter the system and replace the fluid. These containers combine the characteristics of glass bottles (form, easy-to-read calibration marks, and prevention of chemical leaching) with those of flexible bags (shatter-proof, ease of storage and transport, and reduced chance of puncture).

filled with ready-to-use medications at the time of manufacture. It is the responsibility of the CMA to know which of these need to be refrigerated or kept at room temperature prior to administration. Some minibags, such as the MiniBag Plus® system by Baxter (Figure 7-5), are manufactured with the capability of attaching a vial of medication. By manipulating the minibag and the medication vial, the medication and diluent can be mixed immediately prior to administration, thus eliminating the need for refrigeration.

Semirigid Plastic Containers

Semirigid containers (Figure 7-6) are made of polyolefin and do not contain plasticizers, thus preventing chemical leaching and the extraction of DEHP into the solution they enclose. They are ideal for use, too, when the additive is of a chemical nature that predisposes it to bind to the interior of pliable plastic bags, thus altering the proper drug delivery dosage. Some types are non-air-dependent systems and do not require venting because they collapse as they empty,

INFUSATE ADMINISTRATION SETS

The IV administration set is the tubing that delivers fluid or medication from the infusate container to the patient (Figure 7-7). Administration sets range in style from basic, general-purpose ones to complex, multifeature, multifunction sets. The traits they all have in common are a spike insert (usually with a finger guard for ease of insertion) at one end that fits into the administration set port of the infusate container, followed by a drip chamber, where solution flows prior to its entry into the tubing. The tubing on all sets has a screw, roller, and slide clamp (screw and roller clamps usually also have slide clamps lower down the tubing) that provides a means for the CMA to regulate flow using one hand (Figure 7-8). (While screw and roller clamps are used to regulate the drops of the infusate flow, the slide clamp functions only as an on-off clasp.) The tubing terminates in a sterile-capped adapter to which a cannula hub can be attached. The adapter may be straight, where it fits directly into the cannula hub (with a direct push, without twisting), or manually twists and screws on to the hub of

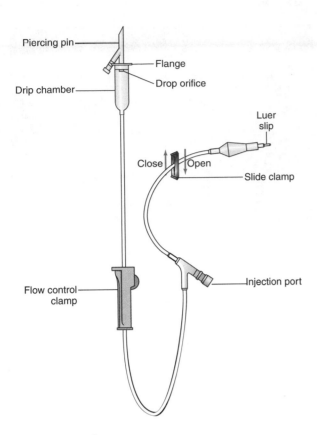

Figure 7-7 | Basic Administration Set

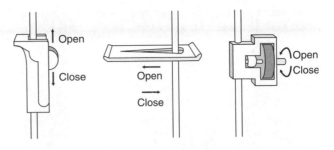

Figure 7-8 | Administration Set Tubing Clamps

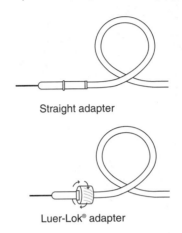

Figure 7-9 | Straight and Luer-Lok® Cannula Hub Adapters

the cannula, which provides a firm attachment that cannot be pulled out (Luer-Lok®) (Figure 7-9).

Administration sets are available as vented systems, which are used for vacuum infusate containers that do not have their own built-in mechanisms for air displacement (glass and some semirigid bottles), or nonvented systems, for use with flexible plastic bags and other nonvacuum receptacles. They are also available for exclusive use with electronic infusion devices (EIDs), and vary according to the manufacturer.

Administration sets, based on their manufacturer-specific proportions, primarily determine the rate at which fluid can be delivered to the patient. In order for the CMA to accurately manage the delivery of infusate to a patient, he must know how much fluid the administration set he is using transports. This is determined by the drop factor.

Drop Factor

The **drop factor** is the number of drops needed to deliver 1 ml of fluid and is based on the size of the hollow, internal diameter (bore) of the administration tubing. The drop factor is clearly stated on the administration set package. Sets are made to deliver either macrodrops or microdrops. Macrodrip sets deliver 10 to 20 drops/ml, while microdrip tubings dispense 60 drops/

ml (minidrip) (Figures 7-10 and 7-11). The CMA may calculate the rate of IV flow in drops per minute. In addition to these standard tubings, there are also specialized extra large (macrobore) and extra small (microbore) tubings that are used in specialized settings and circumstances. The former are used in emergency surgical and trauma situations when large volumes of blood or fluid must be infused rapidly. The latter are designed for the delivery of small amounts of precisely controlled fluid or medication in situations where volume restriction is critical, such as for neonatal care and for epidural infusions.

MEDICAL ASSISTING TIP

Four Essentials of IV Infusions

In order to correctly deliver and manage an intravenous infusion, the CMA must know four things:

1. The prescribed volume to be infused
2. The prescribed time for the infusion
3. The drop factor
4. The mathematical formula needed to calculate the rate

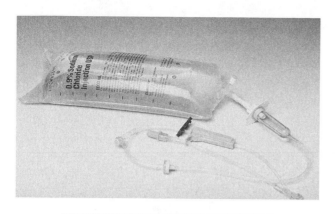

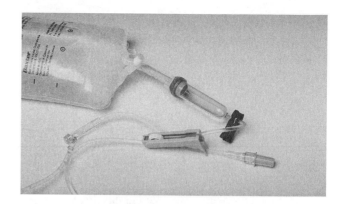

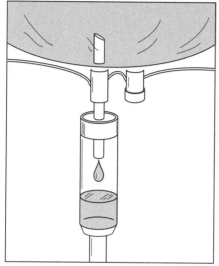

Figure 7-10 | Macrodrip Tubing

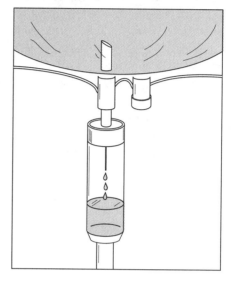

Figure 7-11 | Microdrip Tubing

Primary Administration Sets

Primary administration sets (also referred to as *basic* or *standard sets*) are those that are spiked into one (single line) or two (Y-type sets) main infusate containers and carry fluid via one tube directly to the patient. At the distal end, where they attach to the cannula, they may terminate in straight, flashtube, or Luer-Lok® male adapters. Primary tubing sets are available in macrodrop or microdrop sizes and come in varying lengths to accommodate patient needs (Figure 7-12). They are available with or without check valves to prevent retrograde flow, and may contain one or several injection ports. It is from the primary sets that secondary administration tubings are added as well as other attachments, such as extension tubings, flow control devices, filters, and various adapters.

Single Line Primary Administration Sets

Single line primary sets have one spike that extends proximally from the drip chamber that is inserted into one main bag of infusate. The tubing distal to the drip chamber ter-

minates in the male-adapter end that connects to the hub of the vascular access device in the patient.

Y-Type Primary Administration Sets

Y-type administration sets have two equal-length tubes (each having its own roller clamp and, sometimes, its own drip chamber) that extend above one drip chamber and are able to access two primary infusates simultaneously or alternately. The fluids reach the patient via one common tubing that extends distally from the common drip chamber, making it necessary for the two infusates to be compatible with each other. Such tubings are frequently used in emergency, surgical, and critical care situations and often have macrobore tubing, designed to deliver large quantities of infusate over a faster period than could be accomplished with standard macrodrop administration sets. Blood administration tubings are Y-type sets, but differ somewhat in design from standard primary Y-type sets.

It is crucial for the CMA to understand the physical principles associated with venting and the use of Y-type sets in order

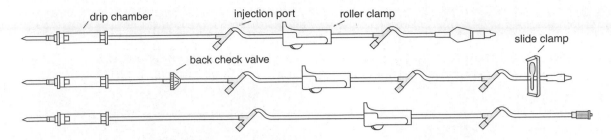

Figure 7-12 | Primary Administration Set

to prevent the possibility of air entering the circulatory system, resulting in air embolism. Y-type sets are not vented and, therefore, must be used only with collapsible infusion containers. Because flexible plastic containers collapse, there is no air in the system. If Y-type sets are used with vented containers and one bottle infuses before the other, the empty receptacle functions as a vent (due to atmospheric pressure in the bottle and tubing exiting it, that exceeds that in the tubing distal to the control clamp). Air then enters the tubing and is siphoned into the circulation, causing a potentially fatal air embolism.

MEDICAL ASSISTING ALERT

Preventing an Air Embolism

Y-type administration sets should be used only with nonvacuum, flexible, collapsible, infusion containers where there is no air in the system and venting is unnecessary. If vented containers are used in a Y set, air can be drawn into the circulatory system and result in an air embolism if the vented container empties before the infusate in the other container is finished infusing.

Check Valves

A **check valve** (also termed *back-check* or *one-way valve*) functions to prevent retrograde solution flow (Figure 7-13). Check valves are in-line components of many primary administration sets. They are most commonly used when secondary IV lines are in place for intermittent infusion to inhibit the back flow of secondary infusate into the primary infusate. They also serve to constrain the backflow of blood from the cannula into the IV tubing.

The mechanism of action of the check valve is as follows.

1. The primary infusate is infusing at the prescribed rate by gravity (and is not clamped off prior to the initiation of the piggyback infusion).

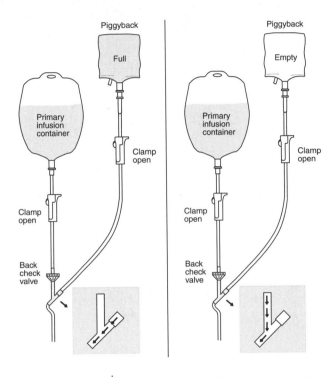

Figure 7-13 | Check Valve and Its Mechanics of Function

2. The secondary infusate, of a lesser volume, is piggybacked into the primary line.
3. The level of the secondary infusate container is elevated above the level of the primary container.
4. The clamp on the tubing of the secondary container is opened, activating the back-check valve due to the pressure exerted by the piggyback solution. (Elevation and gravity increase pressure in the smaller secondary container, even though the primary container is larger.)
5. When the secondary infusate container empties and its fluid descends into its tubing, the decreased pressure in this line (and the greater pressure in the primary line) causes the back-check valve to release, thus activating flow in the primary line, which resumes at its previously set rate.

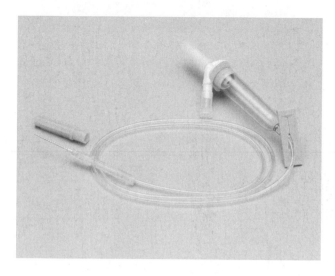

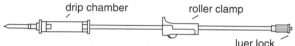

Figure 7-14 | Secondary Administration Set

Secondary Administration Sets

Secondary administration sets are often referred to as *piggyback* or *add-a-line sets* and are used to deliver continuous or intermittent doses of fluid or medication (Figure 7-14). These sets are ideal—and widely used—because patients do not have to undergo additional venipunctures and the primary IV does not have to be interrupted for administration of these therapies. They are usually connected with a needle or needleless adapter into an injection port immediately distal to the back-check valve of the primary tubing. Some primary administration sets are available with a closed-system connection to the secondary line so that the system does not have to be breached, thus avoiding the possibility of microbial introduction into the setup.

Volume-Control Administration Sets

Volume-control administration sets are limited-volume, cylindrical solution compartments that extend from the primary infusate container and have their own tubing that joins with the patient's IV cannula (Figure 7-15). They are designed to accurately calibrate and dispense restricted quantities of fluid or medication. While these are used widely in pediatric infusion therapy, they are also used to administer small quantities of critical medications and to limit IV intake in adult patients who are severely restricted in their fluid intake. Though sometimes used for intermittent medication delivery, even though they

alter the infusion schedule of the primary infusate, they have largely been replaced by secondary administration sets for this purpose.

Blood and Blood Product Administration Sets

Blood administration sets are generally Y-type tubing devices, for use with primary infusates of 0.9% sodium chloride and blood and blood products (Figure 7-16), although straight-line sets are used when blood or blood constituents are the only components to be infused. They must be used in conjunction with cannulas that are large enough for red blood cells to pass through. These sets are blood-product specific and contain in-line filters with a pore size of 170 (minimum) to 260 µm that are designed to screen out clots and other debris that accumulate during the processing, transport, and storage of blood products. The use of blood administration sets should not exceed a 4-hour time period, as bacterial contamination can develop and the filters become less effective. Specialty sets are available for the administration of platelets, cryoprecipitate, and direct IV push of small aggregates of blood component.

Blood administration sets are designed for infusion by gravity or for use with electromechanical infusion devices that have been tested and approved for blood component delivery. They are manufactured for use with special blood administration equipment, such as special filters, specifically designed external pressure infusion cuffs (that do not exceed 300 torr and are used only with large-bore cannulas), and for connection with in-line blood warming devices that do not exceed 38°C (Figure 7-17).

Lipid Administration Sets

Lipids, or fat emulsions, are supplied in glass containers and require special, vented tubing that is supplied by the pharmacy with the release of each bottle of fat emulsion. Lipid-containing infusates have been known to leach phthalates from the bags and tubings of PVC with DEHP. As a result of this concern, fat emulsions are supplied in glass containers, accompanied by nonphthalate infusion sets.

Accessory Devices for Use with IV Administration Sets

There are numerous accessory products for use with primary IV lines. Ancillary add-on devices should only be used when an integral tubing system, containing all the components needed to deliver an infusion, is not available. Whenever an infusion line is breached in order to add nonessential

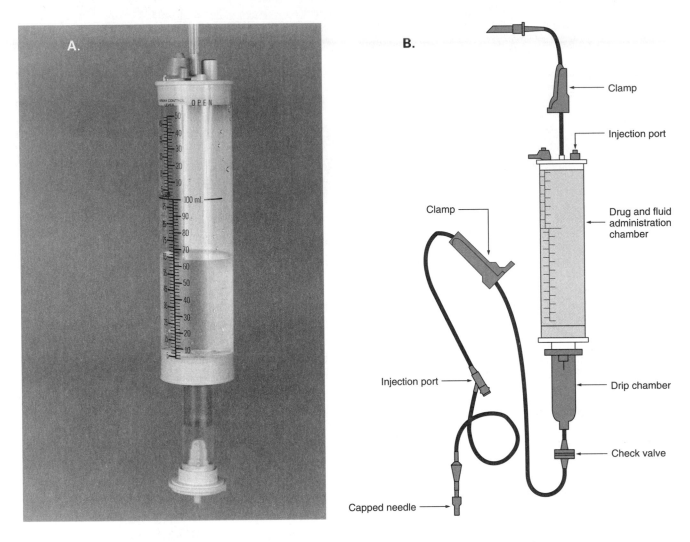

Figure 7-15 | Volume-Control Administration Set (A. Courtesy of Baxter Healthcare Corporation)

components, the potential for inadvertent contamination occurs.

Filters

An **IV filter** is a porous medium through which impurities and particulate matter in an infusate pass, for the purpose of separating and trapping them, thus preventing them from entering the patient's circulation during infusion therapy. Filters are available as integral components of IV administration sets (Figure 7-18) or can be added on (Figure 7-19). As a general rule, the CDC (2001a) does not recommend the use of filters for nonblood infusates. When any filter is used, it is important that the CMA follow the manufacturer's guidelines, so as not to damage the membrane.

Extension Sets

An **extension set** is a segment of IV tubing that is added to a primary administration line for the purpose of adding length (Figure 7-20). Extension tubings come in a variety of sizes to meet individual clinical needs, so the CMA should use only the length necessary to provide the needed elongation. If too short, the purpose is not accomplished; if too long, there is the possibility of kinking, catching on equipment, or falling on the floor and being stepped on. For purposes of

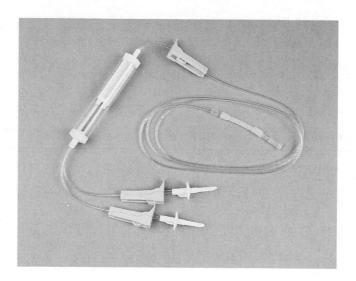

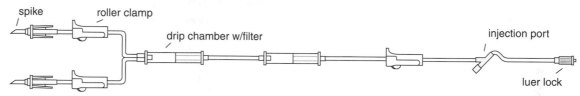

Y-type, drip chamber with (170μ) blood filter, pump chamber, three roller clamps, injection site 6" above distal end, two-piece male Luer-Lok® adapter.

Figure 7-16 | Y-type Blood Administration Set

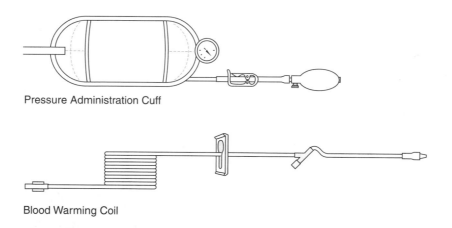

Pressure Administration Cuff

Blood Warming Coil

Figure 7-17 | Blood Administration Accessory Equipment

safety and infection control, extension tubings should always have Luer-Lok® adapters on both ends to avoid an inadvertent disconnection. Unless absolutely necessary, the CDC does not recommend the routine use of extra tubing (CDC, 2001).

Adapters and Connectors

Connectors attached to IV administration sets are special tubings or adapters that add versatility to the infusion line. They should

be used only when they are absolutely necessary and their features are not available in integral systems (CDC, 2001). The CMA must remember that every time a closed system is breached, the potential for contamination and infection increases.

When using any type of adapter or connector, the CMA must know its priming volume. The **priming volume** is the amount of infusate needed to replace the air in the IV adapter or connecting device. Failure to add the appropriate quantity of fluid could result in an air embolism.

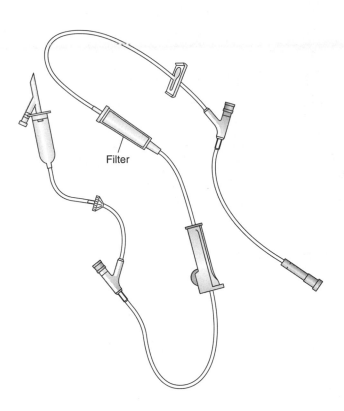

Figure 7-18 | In-line Filter

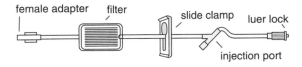

Figure 7-19 | While not normallly recommended, this is an example of a type of add-on filter that could be used.

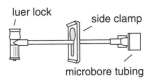

Figure 7-20 | Extension Tubings

Stopcocks

A **stopcock** is a device that controls the directional flow of infusate through manual manipulation of a direction-regulating valve (Figure 7-21). IV infusion stopcocks operate as three- or four-way mechanisms. A three-way stopcock connects two lines of fluid to a patient and provides a mechanism for either one to run to the patient (like a faucet where either the hot or the cold water can run [alone] into a

container). In a four-way stopcock, the valve can be manipulated so that one or both lines can run to the patient alone or in combination (like a faucet where hot water can run, cold water can run, or both can run together).

Ports and Connectors

Ports and connectors are adapters that can be added to infusion lines, serving as add-on viaducts that couple with the cannula hub or other IV lines. These are available as T ports, J loops, U connectors, or Y connectors (Figure 7-22). There are also add-ons, referred to as *PRN adapters* or *injection caps* (Figure 7-23), that affix only to the cannula hub (when there is no further use for continuous fluid administration) for intermittent use, or to keep the cannula line to the vein open. Ports are designed with integral injection sites for needleless access. A needleless system is the preferred method to access an injection/access port. Port systems are manufactured with one connection or as multiflow structures (containing one, two, or three injection ports).

The T port attaches to the cannula at the rigid portion of the device (where the top of the T has an injection port on one side and the cannula connector on the other), which extends to a 4- to 6-in. segment of tubing (the "leg" of the T), containing a slide clamp, that Luer-Loks® to the IV administration tubing. T ports are suitable for patients who are ambulatory and can be disconnected from their IV line for short periods of time for showering, ambulating, or other activities.

Serving essentially the same purpose as T ports, J loops and U connectors are rigid in form, making them more cumbersome to handle, thus predisposing to inadvertent cannula movement during use. They do not have slide clamps, so the introduction of air or the retrograde flow of blood during connection or disconnection from the cannula hub is a possibility. Some do not have injection ports.

The Y connector is a device that provides an access route for two IV fluids to infuse at the same time. The upper "arms" of the Y connect to the infusates, while the "leg" of Y attaches to the cannula hub.

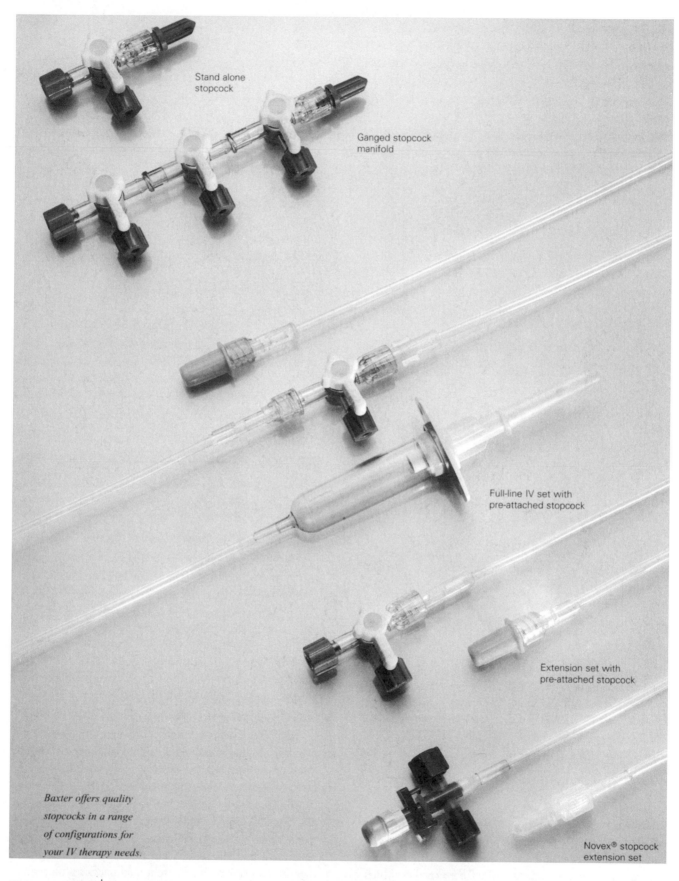

Stand alone
stopcock

Ganged stopcock
manifold

Full-line IV set with
pre-attached stopcock

Extension set with
pre-attached stopcock

*Baxter offers quality
stopcocks in a range
of configurations for
your IV therapy needs.*

Novex® stopcock
extension set

Figure 7-21 | Stopcocks (Courtesy of Baxter Healthcare Systems)

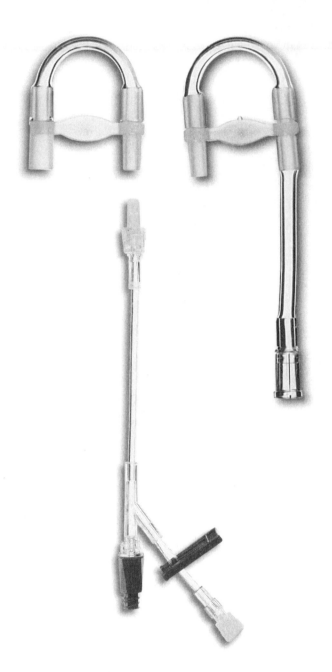

Figure 7-22 | Ports and Connectors (Courtesy of BD Medical Systems)

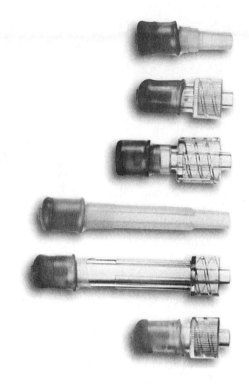

Figure 7-23 | PRN Adapters (Courtesy of BD Medical Systems)

MEDICAL ASSISTING TIP

Knowing Your Equipment

The CMA must be familiar with all types of ports and connectors available in his place of employment and choose the one most congruous with the patient's situation. There are advantages and disadvantages associated with all of the devices on the market and the CMA must keep in mind the potential outcomes associated with their use.

NEEDLELESS SYSTEMS AND NEEDLESTICK SAFETY SYSTEMS

According to the CDC, 384,000 percutaneous injuries (needlesticks and other sharps injuries) occur annually among health care workers in U.S. hospitals. Among these injuries, 236,000 resulted from hollow-bore needles, which have the greatest potential to transmit bloodborne pathogens (General Accounting Office, 2000). Numerous studies have documented the efficacy of needleless IV-access devices in reducing the risk of IV-related injuries.

Needleless systems are state-of-the art technology in the practice of intravenous therapy. Other than the initial stick to insert the cannula into the patient's vein, there is no need for further use of needles during treatment.

Needleless systems eliminate up to 80% of needles and are used to connect IV devices, administer infusates and medications, and sample blood. Some, such as Burron Medical's SAFSITE™ System, are made in such a way that they are compatible with different manufacturers' IV administration sets and extension tubings, syringes, catheters, and medication vials. Others, such as Baxter's Interlink™ access system (Figure 7-24) offer complete needleless programs designed for use with their own equipment.

Although not needleless, other products have been developed to prevent needlestick injuries, such as self-sheathing needles and needle-locking devices, used in IV therapy as well as other parenteral routes. Figure 7-25 illustrates how the Critikon PROTECTIV™ IV catheter safety system works.

VENOUS ACCESS DEVICES

There are numerous venous access devices on the market that are available for one-time use, short-term use, or extended use, which are left in place and remain functional for months, even years. Most of these are inserted by nurses (some requiring nurses to have special training or certification), while others are inserted by physicians

Securing the locking cannula

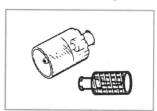

1. The InterLink™ Threaded Lock Cannula is a streamlined locking device for securing I.V. catheter connections.

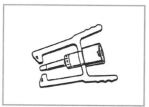

1. The InterLink™ Lever Lock Cannula is an easy-to-use device for securing I.V. connections.

Y-Site access

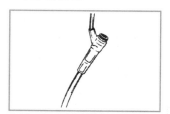

1. The InterLink™ Set allows access to the I.V. line without a needle.

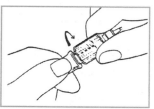

2. Insert InterLink™ Threaded Lock Cannula into InterLink™ injection site.

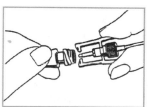

2. Grasp levers and insert the InterLink™ Lever Lock Cannula into InterLink™ injection site.

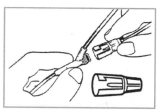

2. The InterLink™ Y-Lock inserts and twists into the InterLink™ Y-Site for a safe and secure connection.

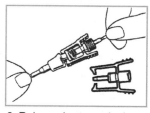

3. Rotate InterLink™ Threaded Lock Cannula clockwise until securely engaged.

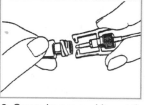

3. Release levers to lock cannula into place.

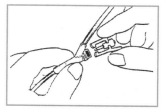

3. The InterLink™ Lever Lock Cannula is an easy-to-use device for securing I.V. connections.

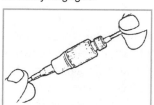

4. The Threaded Lock Cannula provides a closed system that minimizes touch contamination.

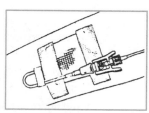

4. The Lever Lock Cannula rests comfortably against patient's skin.

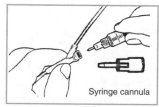

Syringe cannula

4. An InterLink™ Cannula attached to a syringe is ideal for injecting bolus dose medications into the InterLink™ Y-Site.

Figure 7-24 | Interlink™ Needleless System (Courtesy of BD Medical Systems)

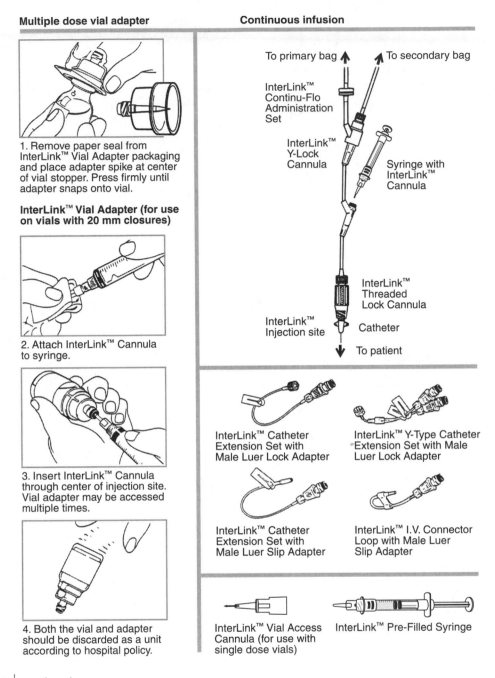

Multiple dose vial adapter

1. Remove paper seal from InterLink™ Vial Adapter packaging and place adapter spike at center of vial stopper. Press firmly until adapter snaps onto vial.

InterLink™ Vial Adapter (for use on vials with 20 mm closures)

2. Attach InterLink™ Cannula to syringe.

3. Insert InterLink™ Cannula through center of injection site. Vial adapter may be accessed multiple times.

4. Both the vial and adapter should be discarded as a unit according to hospital policy.

Continuous infusion

To primary bag

To secondary bag

InterLink™ Continu-Flo Administration Set

InterLink™ Y-Lock Cannula

Syringe with InterLink™ Cannula

InterLink™ Threaded Lock Cannula

InterLink™ Injection site

Catheter

To patient

InterLink™ Catheter Extension Set with Male Luer Lock Adapter

InterLink™ Y-Type Catheter Extension Set with Male Luer Lock Adapter

InterLink™ Catheter Extension Set with Male Luer Slip Adapter

InterLink™ I.V. Connector Loop with Male Luer Slip Adapter

InterLink™ Vial Access Cannula (for use with single dose vials)

InterLink™ Pre-Filled Syringe

Figure 7-24 | continued

(usually anesthesiologists or surgeons) or nurse anesthetists. Once inserted, however, the responsibility for patient monitoring, management, and maintenance may become the primary responsibility of the CMA in collaboration with the physician and other health care workers.

Peripheral Venous Access Devices

Peripheral venous access devices range in variety from straight steel and winged needles to catheters made of

Teflon,® polyurethane, PVC, polyethylene, silicone, or other materials. They vary in length and gauge to meet the needs of a wide variety of patients, ranging from the premature neonate (with tiny, difficult-to-access veins) to the elderly (with delicate, fragile, easily broken veins).

Straight Steel Needles

Straight steel needles come in a variety of gauges (27 ga to 14 ga) and lengths (¼ in. to 3 in.). The hub can attach to the

PROTECTIV™ I.V. CATHETER SAFETY SYSTEM.

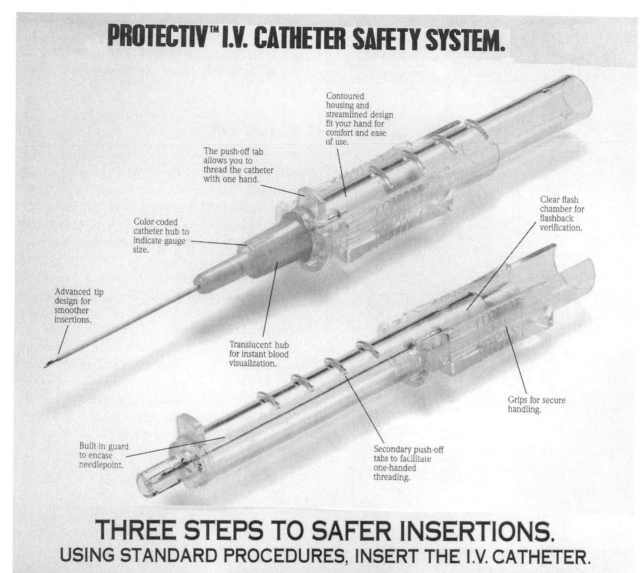

Contoured housing and streamlined design fit your hand for comfort and ease of use.

The push-off tab allows you to thread the catheter with one hand.

Clear flash chamber for flashback verification.

Color-coded catheter hub to indicate gauge size.

Advanced tip design for smoother insertions.

Translucent hub for instant blood visualization.

Grips for secure handling.

Built-in guard to encase needlepoint.

Secondary push-off tabs to facilitate one-handed threading.

THREE STEPS TO SAFER INSERTIONS.
USING STANDARD PROCEDURES, INSERT THE I.V. CATHETER.

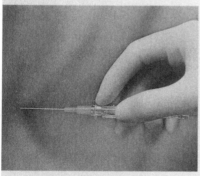

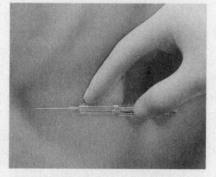

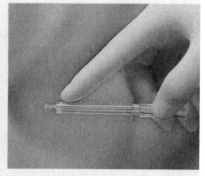

1. Position the forefinger behind the push-off tab to begin threading the catheter.

2. Slide the catheter off the introducer needle while gliding the protective guard over the needle. Listen for the "click" that tells you the needle is safely locked into place.

3. The needle is now encased and locked inside the guard. Simply remove it from the catheter hub and dispose.

Figure 7-25 | PROTECTIV™ IV Catheter Safety System (Courtesy of Ethicon Endosurgery, a Johnson & Johnson Company)

MEDICAL ASSISTING ALERT

What to Do Following Blood Exposure

- Wash any needlestick punctures and cuts with soap and water.
- Flush splashes to the nose, mouth, or skin with water; irrigate the eyes with clean water, 0.9% sodium chloride solution, or sterile ophthalmic irrigants.
- Report the exposure to the department responsible for managing exposures.
- Start postexposure treatment, if recommended, as soon as possible.

tip of a syringe or to infusate tubing with either a straight connector or Luer-Lok™ adapter (Figure 7-26). For IV use, needles should have a sharp, well-tapered bevel for ease of insertion and less patient discomfort.

Steel needles were commonly used for all vein cannulations prior to the introduction of IV catheters. They are rarely

used today except for the direct delivery of IV medication, due to the fact that they tend to dislodge and infiltrate more frequently than catheters. "The use of stainless steel needles should be limited to short-term or single-dose administration" (INS, 2000, Standard 44, S39).

Winged Needles

Winged needles have one wing or two (referred to as *butterflies*) that connect with the needle on one side and a segment of infusion tubing, ending in a hub and protective cap, on the other (Figure 7-27). The wings are the portion of the device that are held in an upright position between the thumb and forefinger during needle insertion to facilitate movement into the vein. Once the needle is in the vein, the wings are placed in a flat position and taped to the skin to secure the device. Prior to insertion, the tubing, which varies in length from 3½ in. to 12 in., should be primed with normal saline to prevent the entry of air into the circulation.

If secured properly, winged needles stay in the vein quite well and provide a good means of venous access for short-term infusions of 24 hours or less. Nonetheless, they are not frequently used for adult infusion therapy other than to deliver one-time IV medications or to draw blood. They continue to be used in pediatric services to access surface veins in the head (referred to as *scalp-vein needles*).

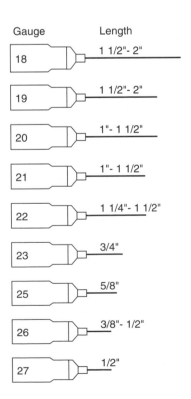

Figure 7-26 | Straight Steel Needles

MINICATH™

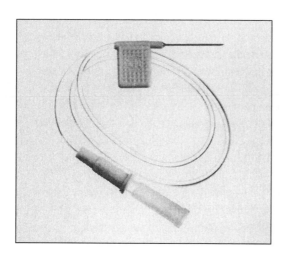

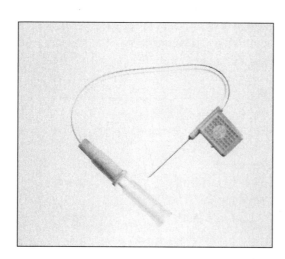

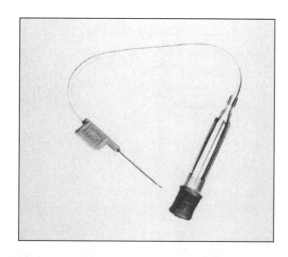

E-Z SET™

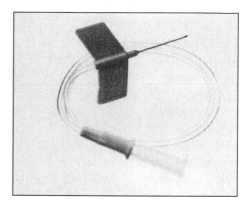

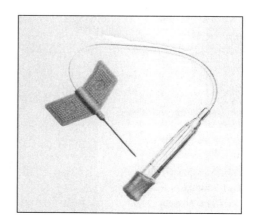

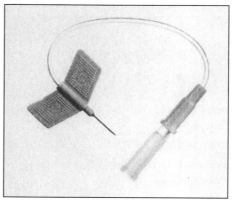

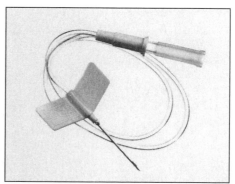

Figure 7-27 | Winged Infusion Sets (Courtesy of BD Medical Systems)

Peripheral Venous Access Catheters

A peripheral venous access catheter, the most commonly used IV device, is used to enter the superficial and deep veins of an extremity, the neck, or the head (Figure 7-28). It is a two-part flexible cannula in tandem with a rigid needle or stylet that is used as a guide to puncture and insert the catheter into the vein. The stylet connects with a clear chamber that allows for visualization of blood return, indicating successful venipuncture, and facilitates removal of the needle. The hub of the cannula is plastic and color-coded to indicate length and gauge. It can range in length from ¼ in. to 12 in. (midline or midarm cannulas) and can be thin- or thick-walled. Every catheter should be radiopaque so that it can be detected radiologically should it break off and embolize. There are numerous varieties and sizes of periph-

eral catheters available, all manufactured with safety, ease of insertion, convenience, and cost-effectiveness in mind.

The over-the-needle peripheral catheter (ONC) is a flexible cannula that encases a steel needle or stylet device and is the most commonly used peripheral IV device. Once the vein is accessed, the catheter is threaded into the vessel, and the stylet is withdrawn. Venous access can be discerned by a retrograde flow of blood from the vein into the flash chamber, a plastic compartment in back of the cannula hub, or with immediate visualization of blood in the catheter via a notched needle, such as INSYTE-N® (Figure 7-29).

The through-the-needle catheter (TNC) is the opposite of the ONC, as the flexible cannula is encircled by the steel needle. As originally designed (and infrequently used today), the needle is withdrawn once venous access is achieved and secured in a protective shield outside the body on the skin. The TNC, mainly seen in peripherally inserted central venous access devices, has a steel or plastic encasement that can be removed after the catheter is advanced into the vein. The steel needle has a slit along the length of its shaft that can be split apart and removed, whereas the plastic type can be peeled off. Due to the risk of puncture or shearing, through-the-needle catheters are not used for routine peripheral venous access.

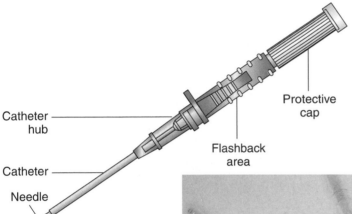

Catheter hub

Flashback area

Protective cap

Catheter

Needle

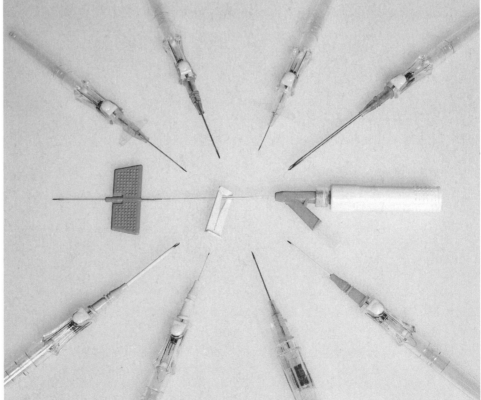

Figure 7-28 | Over-the-needle Catheter

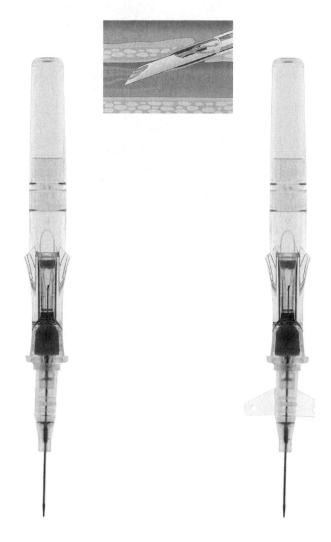

Figure 7-29 | INSYTE-N® IV Catheter with notched needle (which confirms venipuncture at the point of insertion) (Courtesy of BD Medical Systems)

Catheters are made of various biocompatible materials designed for ease of insertion, while preventing vein irritation and reducing the propensity for infection. Teflon® has been used extensively in the past, but newer, state-of-the-art materials are being developed on a regular basis.

Central Venous Access Catheters

Central access catheters encompass a wide variety of devices that may be peripherally inserted or surgically implanted. The use of these products is often design-specific.

VEIN ILLUMINATION DEVICES

The use of illumination devices has facilitated the practice of intravenous access and infusion therapy for patients who are

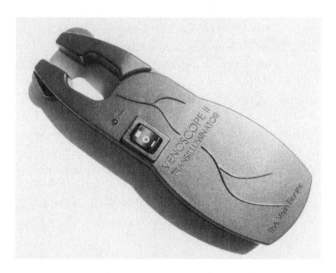

Figure 7-30 | Venoscope II Transilluminator (Courtesy of Venoscope, LLC)

in need of IVs but have veins that can neither be seen nor palpated. The Venoscope II® Transilluminator works by directing a high-intensity cool light down into the subcutaneous tissue and creating a uniform area of orange-like reflection from the fatty tissue (Figure 7-30). The light is flush with the skin; by moving it around the extremity, a dark line can be seen between the two arms of the Venoscope II, which is the vein. The vein's deoxygenated blood absorbs the light, whereas the fatty tissue reflects the light.

After the vein is recognized, the CMA depresses both arms of the light on either side of the dark line to determine if the vein is soft and patent or hard and sclerotic. If the line disappears and then reappears when pressure is released, it is a vein that is capable of transmitting fluids and medications. If the dark line does not disappear and reappear (blanch), it is not a vein and an attempt at cannulation should not be undertaken.

INFUSION SITE PREPARATION AND MAINTENANCE MATERIALS

Prior to the insertion of a venous access device, the appropriate dressing materials must be obtained and the skin must be properly cleansed. Once in place, the IV device must be suitably secured to allow for regular site assessment, the prevention of cannula movement or dislodgment, and to maintain asepsis and prevent catheter-related infection (CRI). This is accomplished with the use of several items, procured individually or in kits. Selection of such articles is based on individual patient situations and conditions, following the recommendations set forth by the CDC, INS standards, and agency protocols.

Skin Preparations

Prior to the insertion of a vascular access device, the client's skin must be prepared, using an antimicrobial barrier. One of the most important measures for preventing CRIs, in addition to strict attention to proper hand hygiene, is antisepsis of the insertion site. In the United States, povidone iodine has been the most commonly used antiseptic for cleansing catheter insertion sites. However, preparation of central venous and arterial sites with a 2% aqueous chlorhexidine gluconate has been shown to lower infection rates as compared to site preparation with 10% povidone-iodine or 70% alcohol. The rate of catheter-related bloodstream infections when CHG was used was 84% lower than

the rates when the two other antiseptic regimens were used (CDC, 2002a). Commercially available products containing 2% CHG were not available in the United States until July 2000, when the U.S. Food and Drug Administration (FDA) approved a 2% aqueous chlorhexidine preparation for skin antisepsis.

The CDC, in the Guidelines For Prevention of Intravascular Device-Related Infections, 2002, suggests that the skin, prior to catheter insertion and during dressing changes, be cleansed with an appropriate antiseptic. A 2% chlorhexidine-based preparation is preferred, but an iodophor, tincture of iodine, or 70% alcohol may also be used (CDC, 2002a). The antiseptic must remain on the insertion site and be allowed to air dry before catheter insertion. Povidone iodine is to remain on the skin for at least two minutes, or longer if it is not yet dry before insertion. The use of organic solvents (e.g., acetone and ether) on the skin before insertion of catheters or during dressing changes is not recommended. When CHG or povidone iodine are used in conjunction with alcohol, the alcohol must always be used first. The alcohol must not be used to wipe off the iodophor because the iodophor exerts a prolonged antimicrobial effect. Skin preparations are available in the form of swabsticks, prep pads, or plastic (cotton-tipped) squeezable vials for one-time use (Figure 7-31).

It is not recommended that antimicrobial ointments be applied to the catheter site at the time of catheter insertion or during routine dressing changes. The use of polyantibiotic ointments that are not fungicidal may significantly increase the rate of colonization of the catheter by *Candida* species (CDC, 2002a).

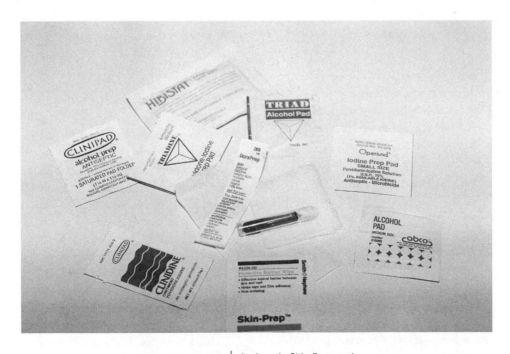

Figure 7-31 | Antiseptic Skin Preparations

Dressings

The dressing used to cover the skin surrounding a percutaneous device should be either a sterile gauze or a sterile, transparent, semipermeable dressing (CDC, 2002a). Tunneled CVC sites that are well healed might not require dressings. Transparent, semipermeable polyurethane dressings are popular among practitioners because they reliably secure the vascular access device, allow for continuous visual inspection of the catheter site, let patients bathe and shower without saturating the dressing, and require less frequent changes than do standard gauze and tape dressings; the use of these dressings saves personnel time. Data suggest that transparent dressings can be safely left on peripheral venous catheters for the duration of catheter insertion without increasing the risk for thrombophlebitis (CDC, 2002a). The choice of dressing can be a matter of preference. If blood is oozing from the catheter insertion site, a gauze dressing might be preferred.

If the patient is diaphoretic, or if the site is bleeding or oozing, a gauze dressing is preferable to a transparent, semipermeable dressing. A catheter-site dressing is to be replaced if it becomes damp, loosened, or visibly soiled. The dressing is to be changed at least weekly for the adult and adolescent patient depending on the circumstances of the individual patient. Topical antibiotic ointments or creams are not recommended for use on insertion sites (except when using dialysis catheters) because of their potential to promote fungal infections and antimicrobial resistance (CDC, 2002a).

There are several types of transparent membrane dressings (TMDs) available that vary in size and thickness and are designed for one- or two-handed application. They are also referred to as *transparent semipermeable membranes* (TSMs). The newer gauze dressings combine the dressing and tape in one component, such as 3M™ Medipore and pad adhesive wound dressing and Smith and Nephew's Primapore.™ ConMed™'s Veni-Gard® features a transparent membrane, a waterproof foam perimeter, and pre-cut accessory tape strips all in one (Figure 7-32).

A hydrophilic chlorhexidine-impregnated sponge (Biopatch™) is used by some agencies. It is placed over the site of short-term arterial and central venous catheters and

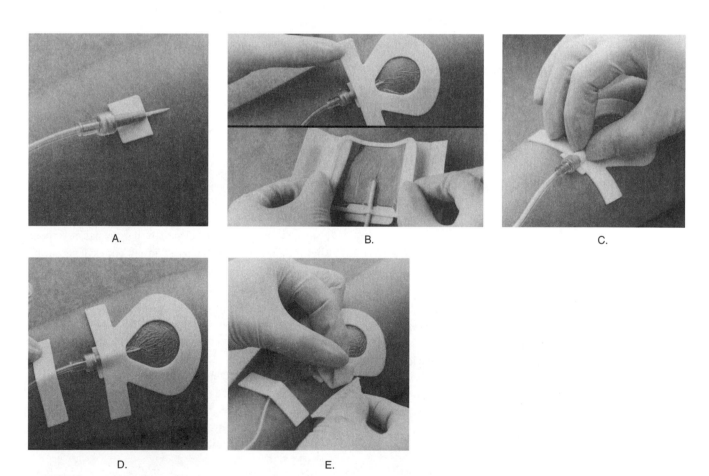

A.　　　　　　　　　　B.　　　　　　　　　　C.

D.　　　　　　　　　　E.

Figure 7-32 | Veni-Gard® Transparent Membrane Dressing with Waterproof Foam Perimeter and Pre-cut Accessory Strips. Guidelines for use: A. Place foam pad. B. Apply dressing. C. Pinch to occlude. D. Secure with accessories. E. Remove with alcohol. (Courtesy of ConMed™ Corporation)

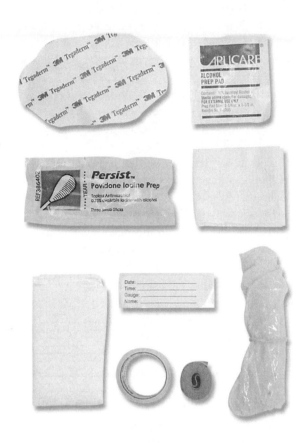

Figure 7-33 | IV Start Kit (Courtesy of BD Medical Systems)

has been shown to reduce the risk for catheter colonization and CRBSI (CDC, 2002a). Thus far, adverse systemic effects have not resulted from use of this device. When used, however, it should be according to institutional policy, after the skin has been prepped with an appropriate (agency-approved) antimicrobial barrier.

Kits

There are various prepackaged kits used to start IVs. They are supplied with or without peripheral venous access devices and contain all of the routinely used equipment needed to start an IV (Figure 7-33), including the tourniquet, antiseptic skin prep, gauze, tape, and a dressing.

In general, if available in an agency, the prepackaged starter kits are used only when IV therapy is initiated. If the vein is not accessed on the first attempt or when site dressings need to be reinforced or redressed, just the supplies needed are procured.

INFUSION REGULATION SYSTEMS

Traditionally, IVs infuse by gravity flow, measured in drops per minute (gtt/min), which the CMA adjusts manually with the roller or screw clamp on the administration set. Now there are numerous mechanical and electronic devices available that assist the CMA in maintaining the infusion rate.

Mechanical Gravity Control Devices

Mechanical gravity control devices such as the Baxter Control-A-Flo® infusion regulator (Figure 7-34) are flow-regulating mechanisms that attach to the primary infusion administration sets and are manually set to deliver specified volumes of fluid per hour. They are available as dials, with clocklike faces, or as barrel-shaped devices with cylindrical controls. There are flow markings, which are approximate, that must be verified by counting the drops per minute, based on the administration set drop factor.

There are several of these devices on the market, all with varying degrees of accuracy. There can be discrepancies of up to ±25% due to the patient's condition, positioning, activity level, and venous pressure. Restriction of fluid flow can occur because of kinking or obstruction of the IV tubing. These generally should be used only for short periods, such as for transport of patients between services, and must be checked frequently for infusion accuracy. The 3M™ IV Flow Regulator has a patented, pressure-sensitive membrane that compensates for fluctuations in pressure, providing a constant volumetric output to maintain the set flow rate within ±10%. It self-adjusts to compensate for patient movement and venous pressure changes, so it may be safely used with lipids and antibiotics, as well as for hydration.

Electronic Infusion Control Devices

Electronic infusion devices (EIDs) are regulating mechanisms that are powered by electricity, battery packs, or both. They have evolved over the past 25 years into safe, accurate, state-of-the art infusion-regulating machines that deliver fluids and medications accurately (±5%) and are capable of being programmed to infuse several infusates at different rates and volumes simultaneously. They have sensors that detect air in the line, changes in pressure, and signal when infusions have terminated. The CMA is alerted to problems through systems of light-emitting diode (LED) or liquid crystal display (LCD) read-outs, alarms that sound, and lights that flash. Most newer models have built-in mechanisms to prevent unintended free flow of infusate to the patient, should the administration set be removed from the machine (Figure 7-35).

It would be almost impossible for the CMA to be familiar with all of the EIDs on the market today. It is important that he learn how to use correctly the product line his agency has adopted and be able to program it safely, use its features to the fullest capacity, and know how to troubleshoot problems. An EID, no matter how sophisticated, is not a substitute for regular patient observation and evaluation.

EIDs operate through various mechanisms; the two most common are peristalsis-driven and cassette operated. In the peristaltic system, fluid is propelled through the infusion line when intermittent wavelike movement (from rotary-driven cams or fingerlike projections) exerts pressure on a portion of the administration tubing that is housed in the EID. The cassette system has a mechanism in the machine that accepts set-selective disposable administration tubing that controls the volume of infusate being delivered to the patient.

Electronic infusion devices are driven by one of two methods: the controller mode or the pump mode. Some machines are designed to function as both, such as those in the IMED® line, which offers more versatility.

Controllers

An EID with a controller mode functions as an electronic "eye" that "watches" the drops flow, according to the preset rate through a drop sensor system. It generates gravitational flow. There is no force exerted by the EID, so the flow rate is influenced by the height at which the IV container is hung. When hung 36 in. above the IV site, there should be sufficient pressure for the infusate to infuse by gravitation into a peripheral vascular line. Should any resistance to flow develop, the alarm on the machine will sound.

Pumps

An EID that functions in the pump mode provides a driving force to overcome resistance to pressure in order to propel the infusate. It generates positive pressure flow. If the fluid does not flow by gravity, the pump produces the needed pressure for the infusion. There is greater delivery accuracy with a pump. A pump has preset pressure restrictions, so it cannot overcome forces that exceed its maximum preset pressure. Pressure is gauged in pounds per square inch (psi), with up to 15 psi considered a safe maximum. Pressure greater than this in the infusion line signals the alarm to sound on the pump. Pump devices that generate positive pressure flow include peristaltic, syringe, and pulsatile pumps.

"The safety features . . . should be of prime consideration . . . (and) include, but are not limited to, audible alarms, battery life and operation indicators, anti-free-flow protection, adjustable occlusion pressure levels, accuracy of delivery indicator, drug dosage calculation, in-line pressure monitoring, and antitamper mechanisms" (INS, 2000, Standard 39-II, S35). As sophisticated as an EID may be, it is never to be used as a substitute for patient care and

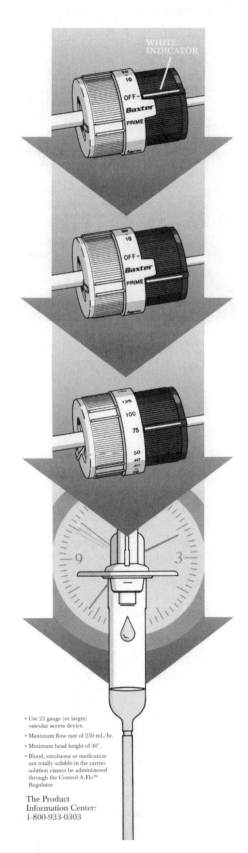

• Use 22 gauge (or larger) vascular access device.
• Maximum flow rate of 250 mL/hr.
• Minimum head height of 30".
• Blood, emulsions or medication not totally soluble in the carrier solution cannot be administered through the Control-A-Flo™ Regulator.

The Product Information Center: 1-800-933-0303

Figure 7-34 | Control-A-Flo® (Courtesy of Baxter Healthcare Corporation)

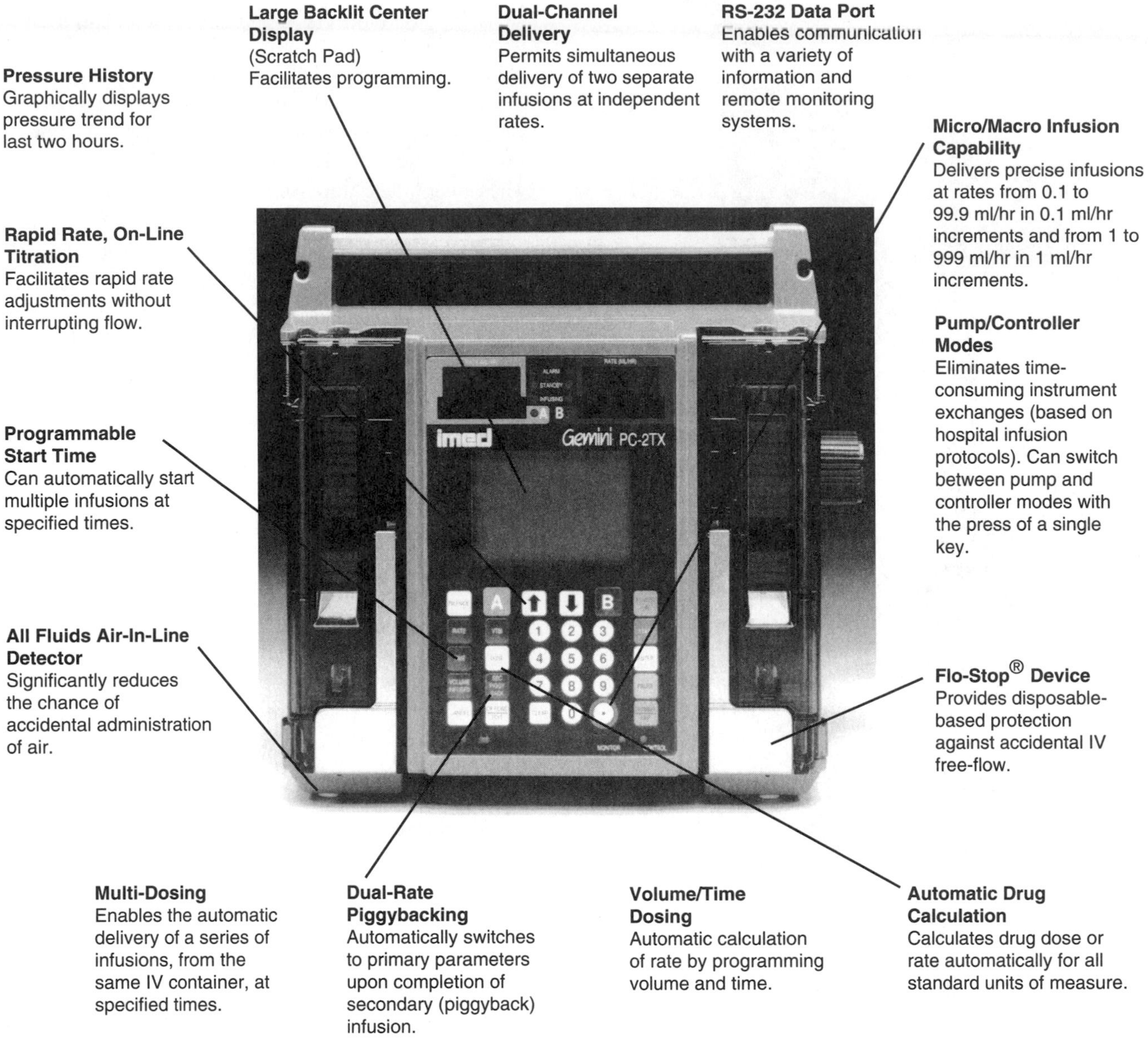

Pressure History
Graphically displays
pressure trend for
last two hours.

**Large Backlit Center
Display**
(Scratch Pad)
Facilitates programming.

**Dual-Channel
Delivery**
Permits simultaneous
delivery of two separate
infusions at independent
rates.

RS-232 Data Port
Enables communication
with a variety of
information and
remote monitoring
systems.

**Rapid Rate, On-Line
Titration**
Facilitates rapid rate
adjustments without
interrupting flow.

**Micro/Macro Infusion
Capability**
Delivers precise infusions
at rates from 0.1 to
99.9 ml/hr in 0.1 ml/hr
increments and from 1 to
999 ml/hr in 1 ml/hr
increments.

**Programmable
Start Time**
Can automatically start
multiple infusions at
specified times.

**Pump/Controller
Modes**
Eliminates time-
consuming instrument
exchanges (based on
hospital infusion
protocols). Can switch
between pump and
controller modes with
the press of a single
key.

**All Fluids Air-In-Line
Detector**
Significantly reduces
the chance of
accidental administration
of air.

Flo-Stop® Device
Provides disposable-
based protection
against accidental IV
free-flow.

Multi-Dosing
Enables the automatic
delivery of a series of
infusions, from the
same IV container, at
specified times.

**Dual-Rate
Piggybacking**
Automatically switches
to primary parameters
upon completion of
secondary (piggyback)
infusion.

**Volume/Time
Dosing**
Automatic calculation
of rate by programming
volume and time.

**Automatic Drug
Calculation**
Calculates drug dose or
rate automatically for all
standard units of measure.

Figure 7-35 | The Gemini PC-2tx™ Volumetric Pump/Controller (Courtesy of Alaris Medical Systems)

supervision. The CMA always maintains responsibility and accountability for monitoring the patient, the prescribed infusion, and the proper flow rate. The CMA may be expected to be able to properly manage the brand of EID used by the employing agency. When using an EID, the manufacturer's guidelines should be adhered to and precautions regarding electrical safety must be followed (INS 2000, Standard 39-II, S35).

Syringe Pumps

The syringe pump is a syringe barrel with a capacity of up to 60 ml and a plunger that operates electronically. A lead, screw motor-driven system pushes the plunger to deliver fluid or medication at a rate of 0.01 to 99.9 ml/hr (Figure 7-36), depending on the model. It is a precisely accurate delivery system that can be used to administer very small volumes. Some models have program modes capable of admin-

istration in mcg/kg/min, mcg/min, and ml/hr. The syringe, which is usually filled in the pharmacy, can be safely stored at room temperature or under refrigeration prior to use.

Most syringe pumps are designed to deliver continuous and bolus doses. They are frequently used in neonatal care, critical care, and anesthesia services, but are also used for patient-controlled analgesia.

Patient-Controlled Analgesia Systems

Patient-controlled analgesia (PCA) is a drug administration system that enables the patient to self-administer and regulate the delivery of medication for pain control on an as-needed (prn) basis. The candidate for this device must be mentally lucid in order to use the device correctly. The advantage of such a system is that the patient can administer a bolus of analgesic with the simple press of a button

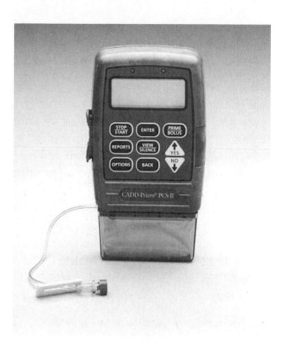

Figure 7-36 | CADD-Micro™ Ambulatory Infusion Pump (Courtesy of Deltec, Inc.)

before the pain becomes too severe, thus maintaining a relatively pain-free state. When this method is used, much less medication is usually required by the patient.

PCAs are available in a variety of models, with variations in size, weight, portability, and volume delivery, depending on patient needs. Some can deliver continuous as well as bolus, intermittent, and taper-down dosages. The ones used in hospitals and other health care facilities are usually larger, heavier, and require suspension on an IV pole or table, while those designed for ambulatory patients are smaller, lightweight, and less bulky (Figure 7-37).

PCA can be used to deliver medication via IV, epidural, or subcutaneous routes. It must be programmed, according to medical orders, to regulate drug dosage, time intervals between boluses, and lock-out intervals (the period of time following drug delivery when the machine will not release any additional medication). The CMA should have knowledge of analgesic pharmacokinetics and equianalgesic dosing, contraindications, side effects, appropriate administration modalities, and anticipated outcome, and should document this information in the patient's medical record (INS, 2000, Standard 72, S 68). The CMA should be educated and competent in the preparation and use of the PCA device, including programming the device to deliver prescribed therapy, administration and maintenance procedures, and use of lock-out devices (INS, 2000, Standard 72, S 65).

Ambulatory and Disposable Infusion Systems

Ambulatory infusion systems are designed for patients who need parenteral medication or nutritional support, yet are

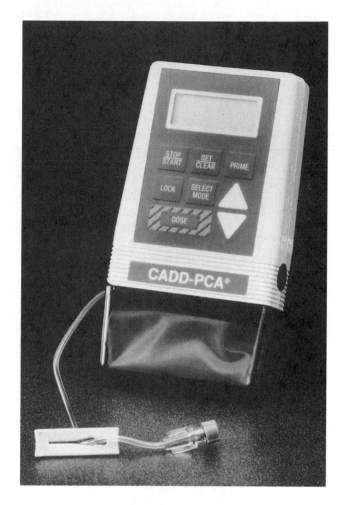

Figure 7-37 | CADD-PCA® (Courtesy of Deltec, Inc.)

able to be at home and maintain varying levels and degrees of activity. Some PCAs, as discussed previously, fall into this category, along with a large variety of others. These systems are usually lightweight, portable (with carrying cases, belt attachments, or back packs), and are powered by alkaline batteries or rechargeable NiCd batteries, but also have AC power adapters. The manufacturers of most ambulatory systems have 24-hour clinical communication centers that link the patient with the infusion service. They all furnish patient education information that is easy to follow, in written and audiovisual formats.

Disposable Infusion Devices

Disposable infusion devices are the newest innovations to facilitate home infusion therapy. They are closed-system mechanisms that have preattached administration tubings and air elimination filters. They are self-priming and are programmed to deliver specified volumes of infusate (50 to 250 ml) at predetermined rates. Disposable infusion structures are either elastomeric or positive-pressure systems. Although costly, patients prefer them over traditional

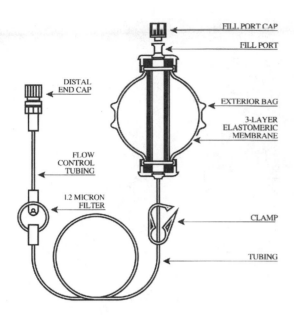

Figure 7-38 | Eclipse™ Elastometric Infusion System (Courtesy of I-FLOW Corporation)

ambulatory infusion devices because they are simple to learn, uncomplicated to use, and are completely disposable.

The framework of an elastomeric system consists of a protective outer shell, the elastomeric infusion membrane (preattached to the administration set), a 1.2 μ filter, and a volume control regulator. The driving force is the elastomeric membrane (like a balloon), which generates pressure as it collapses which, in turn, provides the thrust that delivers the infusate. The flow control device, along with the pressure in the elastomeric membrane, determines the infusion rate. The Eclipse™ (Figure 7-38) from BLOCK Medical is just one example of an elastomeric infusion structure. Other commonly used systems are the Homepump™ (BLOCK), Baxter's Intermate® (Figure 7-39), McGaw's Readymed™, and MedFlo® (Secure Medical).

A positive-pressure system, such as the SideKick® (I-Flow Corporation), has a disposable infusion system cartridge (the DISC) encased in a reusable positive-pressure infuser. The encasement has a top and bottom half, both of which are joined when screwed together. There is a spring coil in the top half of the infuser, and the DISC is loaded into the bottom half. When the two halves are screwed together, the spring exerts

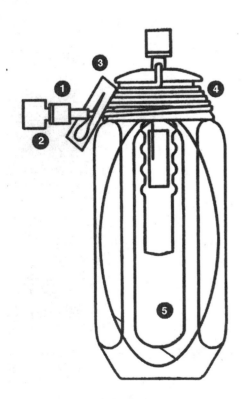

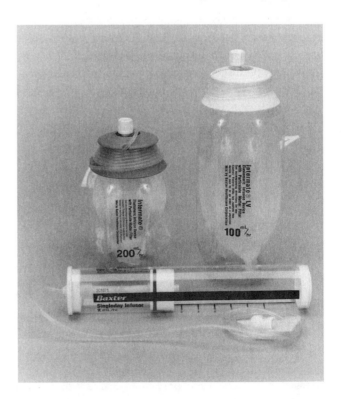

Figure 7-39 | Intermate® and Infusion Elastomeric Systems. 1. Luer-Lok connector attaches the Intermate system tubing directly to IV line. 2. Winged Luer-Lok cap protects the Luer-Lok connector. 3. Slide clamp stops fluid medication when pushed to the closed position. Medication flows when clamp is in the open position. 4. Tubing carries the fluid medication. 5. Balloon holds the fluid medication. When filled, the balloon moves medication down the delivery tubing. (Courtesy of Baxter Healthcare Corporation)

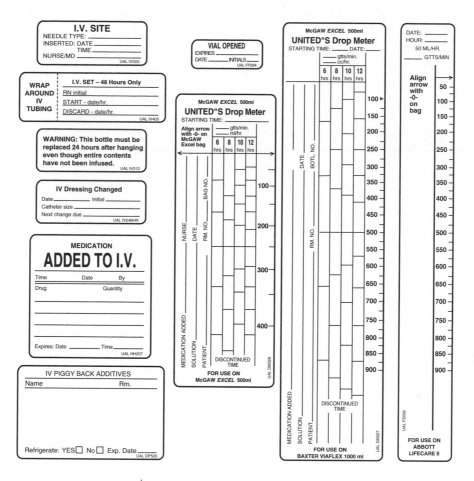

Figure 7-40 | IV Labels (Courtesy of United Ad Label Company, Inc.)

pressure on the DISC, and the infusate flows through the administration tubing (Figure 7-39).

LABELS

Labels are a quality assurance tool that alert all members of the health care team to the status of intravenous infusions (Figure 7-40). Legible labeling provides pertinent and easily identified information regarding the cannula, dressing, infusate, medication, and administration set. Labels must be affixed to infusate containers, administration set (primary and secondary) tubings, and dressing sites. They may also be placed on the patient's bed and chart. The main purpose of labels in IV therapy is to denote start, stop, and discontinuation times.

HANGING DEVICES FOR IV EQUIPMENT

There are many hanging devices available to hold IV containers and infusion devices (Figure 7-41). They vary according to the setting in which they are used. They consist of a pole with hanging loops or projections that are usually mounted on wheels, but may also be stationary or attached to the patient's bed or chair. Some are heavy and constructed to hold several infusate containers, machines, monitors, and other devices, while others are lightweight and portable and designed for ease of movement and ambulation.

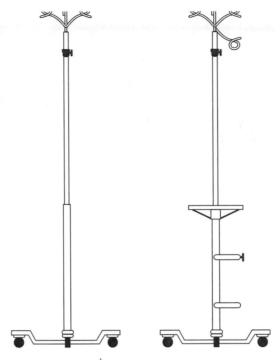

Figure 7-41 │ IV Poles

Review Questions and Activities

1. If you see that someone has written on a plastic IV infusate container with an indelible marker, what should you do? How would you go about ensuring that such a practice be stopped?

2. Explain and diagram the difference between straight adapters and Luer-Lok® adapters.

3. Explain the concept of priming volume for IV administration sets and cannulae.

4. Why have needleless systems developed? How do they relate to OSHA guidelines regarding needlestick injuries?

5. List the three most common bloodborne pathogens that can be transmitted through needlestick injuries.

6. Differentiate between a straight steel needle and a winged (butterfly) infusion set.

7. Differentiate between an over-the-needle (ONC) and a through-the-needle (TNC) IV catheter.

8. Describe the differences of mechanical gravity control devices, electronic infusion controllers and pumps, and syringe pumps.

Chapter 8

The Delivery, Care, Maintenance, and Discontinuation of Intravenous Infusion Therapy

LEARNING OBJECTIVES

Upon completion of this chapter, the reader should be able to:

※ Review the components of the medical order for IV infusion therapy.

※ State the correct use of a tourniquet for peripheral venous access in terms of indications, application, and duration.

※ Compare the general procedures and sequencing used to enhance venous identification and access with those procedures needed for patients with compromised circulatory conditions.

※ Evaluate the CMA's role in identifying allergies to tape, iodine, and latex products.

※ Assemble the items required to initiate a primary peripheral IV infusion.

※ Analyze the components of labeling, reporting, and documentation, and their importance, in the practice of peripheral infusion therapy.

MEDICAL ASSISTING TIP

Principles of Safe Practice

It is important to remember that, while procedures and protocols may vary from state to state or agency to agency, the underlying principles regarding safe practice in the delivery of IV therapy do not change.

MEDICAL ASSISTING TIP

Physician's Orders

The physician's order for any infusion must include all of the following, written on the patient's medical record.

1. Date and time of day
2. Infusate name
3. Route of administration
4. Dosage of infusate
5. Volume to be infused
6. Rate of infusion
7. Duration of infusion
8. Physician's signature

Medical Order

Infusion therapy is a collaborative function that integrates medicine, medical assisting, and pharmacology. It cannot be initiated without the order of a physician or legally authorized prescriber. The order must be appropriate for the patient and properly written in the medical record. "Verbal orders should be signed by the physician within an appropriate time frame in accordance with state and federal regulations and organizational policies and procedures" (INS, 2000, Standard 10, S18) (Figure 8-1). The essentials of any prescription include the patient's name and location; the date (and preferably the time); the name of the medication or infusate, including the dose, quantity, frequency, route, and necessary directions or precautions regarding administration; and the physician's signature. Generic or brand names may be used.

Legibility, which depends on the handwriting of the physician and the experience of the CMA and pharmacists reading

medical orders, must also be considered. Whenever there is any doubt regarding legibility or the intention of the physician, it must be questioned. Never make assumptions! An order for initiation of therapy should be written and signed by the prescriber and must be "clear, concise, legible, and complete before the CMA may initiate therapy" (INS, 2000, Standard 10, S18). If the order is not clear, the CMA must contact the prescriber for clarification.

Although abbreviations are not recommended because of possible misinterpretations that may result in errors, they are

Date	Time ordered	Physician's orders	✔	Time noted	Nurses signature
3/10/00	0900	① Start I.V. c̄ #18g ONC: 1000cc D5W c̄ 20 mEq KCl @ 125cc/hr. Follow c̄ D5W @ 100cc/hr.			
		② Cimetidine 300mg I.V. STAT, then 300mg IVPB q 8h			
		③ Piperacillin Sodium 3Gm IVPB q 6h			
		④ T&C for 2u packed cells. B. Raab, M.D.			

Dansig, John M-44
2-23445-4   D.O.B.: 01-04-56
Rm 322-A
Dr. Bernice Raab

Allergies: NKA

Figure 8-1 | Infusion orders

widely used. It is very important that the physician, CMA, and pharmacist comprehend, and are in accord with, the commonly used abbreviations in the setting in which they practice. Doubts must always be clarified.

There are many different brands of drugs available within the same category. They may be identical to each other in terms of their chemical makeup or pharmacologic properties. This is often the case with antibiotic classifications, such as the ampicillins and the cephalosporins. In order to minimize duplication, most institutions have instituted the formulary system, a program in which only one drug (a generic equivalent) from a particular category is selected for use, rather than stocking every one on the market. The CMA should be aware of the formulary system so as not to be confused when the medical order is written for a brand name drug, but the pharmacy dispenses a generic equivalent.

Formulary drugs are decided upon by pharmacy and therapeutics (P & T) committees within institutions (made up of pharmacists, nurses, physicians from various services, infection control personnel, and others) with selection criteria usually including safety, therapeutic effect, and cost. These panels authorize the pharmacy to stock and dispense the generic equivalents of the various brands of drugs ordered by physicians.

Hand Hygiene

It cannot be stressed often enough that proper hand hygiene is the single most important means of preventing the spread of infection. The CMA must clean her hands by washing or use of an alcohol-based rub or gel before gathering and setting up equipment and before using it on a patient. Hand hygiene must be carried out immediately after contact with a patient or his belongings and before touching other patients or items. Hands are to be sanitized before donning gloves and immediately upon removal. Since touch contamination is a common source for the transmission of pathogens, proper hand hygiene reduces the risk of cross-contamination. Hands are to be cleansed by washing or with the use of alcohol-based rubs or gels (CDC, 2002d).

Patient Preparation and Vein Evaluation

Once the CMA has verified an IV order, but before preparing the necessary equipment and transporting it to the patient's room, it is important to take a few minutes to apprise the patient of the situation. This prepares him psychologically, allows for questions and explanations, and gives the CMA an opportunity to evaluate venous accessibility. This not only gives the CMA a better idea of what she will be dealing with, but also provides the opportunity to reassure the patient and establish rapport.

MEDICAL ASSISTING TIP

Preparing the Patient Psychologically

When the CMA takes the time to psychologically prepare a patient for infusion therapy by providing explanations, allowing for questions and answers, and accepting expressions of feelings, venous access is facilitated and the patient better adapts to the procedures associated with the therapy. When the patient is ill-prepared and frightened, peripheral venous constriction occurs and venipuncture becomes difficult or impossible to accomplish.

CRITICAL THINKING

Using Guided Imagery to Facilitate Venipuncture

Can you recall a situation when you were uncomfortable, felt queasy, or were frightened? Of course. We all have. When confronted with a situation in which your patient is extremely frightened and agitated by the thought of being stuck with a needle and having an IV started, creativity may be your best ally.

Guided imagery, in which you ask the patient to imagine a place that makes him feel relaxed and comfortable, is a way to alleviate your patient's anxiety and fears. Some people refer to this as a "happy place."

When first learning to use guided imagery, it is helpful to ask yourself what would make you feel comfortable when you encounter a difficult situation. Sometimes what works for you would help your patient cope more effectively.

During this short period that precedes the initiation of infusion therapy, when the CMA has the opportunity to assess and evaluate the patient's veins, she should have a tourniquet available in order to examine one or several areas for the best possible venipuncture site. If the CMA foresees that finding a suitable vein may be difficult, there are measures that can be taken to enhance venous access. Even if a nurse is inserting the IV, a CMA may be asked to assess the vein and prepare the patient.

Tourniquet Application

A **tourniquet** is an encircling device consisting of a segment of rubber tubing or a strip of Velcro® strapping that temporarily arrests blood flow to or from a distal vessel. A blood pressure cuff is sometimes used as a tourniquet by inflating it to a reading midway between the patient's systolic and diastolic pressures or just below his diastolic pressure. Unless disposable tourniquets are available, reusable ones should be disinfected between use or covered with a throwaway plastic sheath during use to avoid cross-contamination between patients. Remember: Tourniquets may be a source of latex exposure.

The most important thing to remember when utilizing a tourniquet is to apply it so that only venous, and not arterial, blood flow is suppressed. To ensure this, the CMA must always be able to palpate or auscultate a pulse distal to the tourniquet.

MEDICAL ASSISTING ALERT

Avoiding Tourniquet Paralysis

When applying a tourniquet, never apply it so tightly that it obstructs arterial flow, nor leave it in place longer than four to six minutes. Tourniquet paralysis from injury to a nerve can occur if the tourniquet is applied too tightly or left for too long a period. To confirm that only venous flow is suppressed, the CMA must always be able to palpate or auscultate a pulse distal to the tourniquet.

Methods to Enhance Venous Access

If after assessing the patient's veins the CMA finds an appropriate site for venipuncture, she then prepares the necessary equipment for infusion therapy. Should she find that venous access may be difficult, there are steps that should be taken to facilitate cannulation and insertion.

The following procedures, used alone or in conjunction with the others, are commonly employed, in the ensuing order, to expedite venous access. Be sure to explain to the patient what will be done before each procedure is initiated.

1. *Gravity.* Place the extremity intended for venipuncture below the level of the patient's heart for several minutes. If the veins do not distend, do this with a tourniquet in place.
2. *Fist clenching.* Ask the patient to open and close his fist or squeeze and release his hand around a rolled wash cloth or the lowered bed rail. If the veins do not distend, do this with a tourniquet in place.
3. *Friction.* Gently stroke the skin over the veins intended for venipuncture. Doing this with an alcohol pledget

creates heat, which enhances venous distention. If the veins do not engorge, do this with a tourniquet in place.
4. *Percussion.* Gently tap the area of skin over a vein using the thumb and index (or third) finger, or pat the area using light to moderate force (to engorge the vein with blood). If veins do not engorge, do these maneuvers with a tourniquet in place.
5. *Compresses.* With the extremity placed below the level of the patient's heart, apply warm compresses for 10 to 15 minutes prior to venipuncture. Immediately before the intended IV site is to be prepped with an antiseptic, fresh, warm compresses may be applied for a few additional minutes, with a tourniquet in place, to further enhance vein distention.
6. *Multiple tourniquets.* This process increases tissue oncotic pressure and forces blood into collateral veins to distend them. It is employed when the usual veins accessed for IV therapy are not viable and collateral vessels must be used. The process is as follows.
   (a) Apply one tourniquet to the upper arm (about 2 to 3 inches above the antecubital fossa) for two minutes while applying pressure with downward stroking movements from the tourniquet to the hand. Check for arterial pulses distal to this tourniquet.
   (b) After two minutes, apply a second tourniquet to the forearm about 2 to 3 inches below the antecubital fossa and continue with the downward stroking movements. At this point, collateral veins usually become visible.
   (c) If collateral veins do not appear after two minutes, place a third tourniquet above the wrist and release the tourniquet on the upper arm. Continue to stroke the hands to locate collaterals in the hands and fingers.
   (d) Remove all tourniquets before six minutes have passed.
   (e) Should a venous access site still not present itself, the physician should be notified.
7. *Transillumination.* Darken the room so that the lighting is dim and hold the VENOSCOPE® II Transilluminater so that the arms are flush against the patient's skin. Gradually slide the device along the extremity until a dark shadowy line appears between the fiberoptic arms, indicating that a vein is present. Apply downward pressure over the two arms to check for blanching.

Veins in the lower extremity should not be used. If they must be accessed, there should be a medical order. They are used only for a short period of time until other upper body sites can be found or placement of a central line can be instituted. When lower extremity veins are used, there must be frequent circulatory assessments and range-of-motion exercises (active, passive, or both) must be instituted to maintain adequate venous return.

MEDICAL ASSISTING TIP

Checking for Blanching

Remember: For a vein to be viable, it must be able to be blanched. To check for blanching, apply downward pressure over or on each side of a vein. If the vein disappears with the pressure, then reappears when the pressure is removed, the vein is viable. A sclerotic vein will not blanch.

Hair Removal

If necessary, prior to initiating IV therapy, hair may need to be removed. This should be done only if there is enough hair to impede vein visualization, site disinfection, cannula insertion, or dressing adherence. Hair is to be removed by gently clipping it close to the skin, without scratching the skin. Shaving, because of the potential for microabrasion and the introduction of contaminants, should not be used, nor should depilatories be applied because of the possibility for skin irritation or allergic reactions (INS, 2000, Standard 45, S40). An electric shaver may be used, depending on institutional policy, if it belongs to the patient or if the shaving heads can be changed or disinfected between patient use. An electric shaver should not be used if breaches in skin integrity result from its use.

Special Considerations Regarding Venous Access

In addition to the previously discussed problems, other circumstances and conditions may impede venous access. In these situations, there are special techniques the CMA may need to utilize to facilitate cannulation.

Patients Receiving Anticoagulation Therapy

Patients receiving anticoagulants are prone to bleeding that can range from local ecchymoses to major hemorrhagic complications. A primary consideration for such patients is to monitor them closely and avoid any procedures that might enhance bleeding during IV therapy.

Precautions are especially necessary when IV therapy is being initiated. If possible, tourniquets should be avoided to prevent subcutaneous bleeding and bruising. If they must be used, they should be applied as loosely as possible. Venous distention may be accomplished using gentle constriction with towels, cotton batting, or even the hands of another person encircling the extremity and applying gentle pressure during cannulation.

During the application of the antimicrobial preparation, care must be taken to avoid excess pressure. The smallest cannula that will accommodate the vein and deliver the ordered infusate should be selected to prevent unnecessary traction against the skin during cannulation. Dressings must be removed gently, using alcohol or an adhesive solvent, to avoid any tearing movement that might result in superficial bruising. If cannulation is not successful after the vein has been entered, measures must be taken to diminish bleeding into the surrounding tissues and reduce bruising.

Patients with Altered Skin and Vessels

Special precautions must be taken if patients have irritated, burned, or diseased skin. Alternate measures, in accord with institutional policies, may need to be taken during skin antisepsis to prevent further irritation and discomfort. Since photoexposure may cause discomfort, special indirect lighting is usually employed when locating a vein and during cannulation. Venous distention may be achieved using measures similar to those required for patients receiving anticoagulants.

For patients with fragile, delicate veins, the use of tourniquets is discouraged. These fine vessels may break ("blow") when they distend with tourniquet application or when accessed during venipuncture. Such veins are usually seen in frail, elderly patients and patients receiving corticosteroid therapy.

Some patients develop sclerosed veins from frequent IV therapy, collagen-related disease processes, or illicit intravenous drug use. These veins are hard and often cordlike, nonelastic, and do not blanch when pressure is applied over or around them. Sclerotic veins cannot be accessed, so transillumination may be needed to locate deeper veins. The multiple tourniquet technique to find collateral vessels may also be used.

CRITICAL THINKING

Respecting a Patient's Privacy While Maintaining IV Care Priorities

Sometimes the CMA is faced with a situation in which there are no viable peripheral veins for infusion therapy because the patient has a history of illicit IV drug use. The physician may need to put an IV line in a central vein in the neck area. In such a circumstance, when the patient's family members come to visit, they may ask you why the IV is in such an unusual place. A parent might say to you, "When I needed one, the CMA put it in a vein in my forearm. Why does my son need it in his neck?" How would you handle this situation? What are your patient's rights regarding confidentiality in this case?

Patients with Peripheral Edema

Venous access in patients with peripheral edema is very difficult and not without risk. Because of increased oncotic pressure in the tissues that surround the vessels, venous access is complicated. If cannulation is successful, the vessel may collapse from the oncotic pressure created by the edema. When venous access is achieved and maintained, another potential problem, infiltration (because of the edema) is hard to identify. Should infiltration occur, **compartment syndrome,** in which the function and viability of nerves and vessels are threatened when they are confined and constricted by fluid pressure, can result.

Because veins cannot be visualized, the CMA must locate veins based on anatomical landmarks. Venous access is best accomplished by applying digital pressure with the heel of the hand (for 15 to 20 seconds over the proposed vein) to displace tissue pressure. When the pressure is removed, the edema is temporarily gone (displaced) and the vein can be seen. Cannulation must follow quickly or the edema will shift back and obliterate the vein again. For the purpose of asepsis, and since the CMA must work quickly, it is a good idea to have prepped the intended venipuncture area first and apply digital pressure with a sterile glove prior to cannulation. Some CMAs apply the pressure using a 70% alcohol pledget.

Obese Patients

Obese patients may have easy-to-visualize surface veins or deeply imbedded vessels, depending on how the adipose tissue displaces them. If they migrate toward the surface of the extremity, cannulation is accomplished as it would be for an average-sized person. For deep vessels, anatomical landmarks must be used in conjunction with a longer cannula that can gain access to them. Multiple tourniquets and vein illumination may also be necessary.

Allergies

It cannot be stressed often enough that the CMA must take advantage of every possible situation to determine whether or not a patient has allergies. These include medications, foods, animal and insect matter, latex, and environmental substances. The patient and family should be questioned during the initial assessment and the history, and also throughout the course of care. Questions regarding allergies should always be asked prior to giving medications, especially those administered parenterally. The CMA must know where emergency drugs used to counteract allergic reactions are located. Once it is determined that a patient has allergies, such information must be placed in the medical record and clearly labeled on his identification bracelet, chart, bed, MAR, and on all communication media with the pharmacy, x-ray, and laboratory departments, and all other services used by the patient.

Iodine Allergy

With infusion therapy, it is important to determine whether a patient is allergic to iodine and its derivatives, since such products are often used in skin antisepsis. If a patient does not know whether or not he is allergic to iodine, he should be questioned regarding allergies to fish, especially shellfish. If there is any doubt, iodine preparations should not be used. If a patient has a known allergy to iodine, the prepping solution of choice is 70% isopropyl alcohol. The alcohol is to be applied with friction for a minimum of 30 seconds or until the final applicator is visually clean. CHG, if institutionally-approved, may also be used.

Tape Allergy

Another consideration regarding allergies concerns tape. Many people who have not had problems with tape or dressings in the past develop sensitivities to it over time. It is important to assess for any problems with tape that may develop during the course of care and be alert to redness, rashes, or patient complaints of itching when tape is used. The problem with tape may be associated with the adhesive used on it or the fact that it is made of latex.

Latex Allergy

Latex refers to the natural rubber product manufactured from a milky fluid that is primarily obtained from the rubber tree (*Hevea brasiliensis*). Latex has become a major health concern with patients and health care personnel having developed, or become aware of, an allergy to latex. Increasing numbers of people in the workplace have been affected due to the extensive use of the product as a component of many medical and consumer devices. Some synthetic rubber materials may be referred to as "latex" even though they do not contain the protein that produces latex allergy.

MEDICAL ASSISTING ALERT

Powdered Gloves and Hand Creams

The starch powder used to coat and lubricate some latex gloves becomes coated with latex protein and is inhaled during glove application and removal. It is better to use powder-free gloves. Oil-based hand creams and lotions should not be used with gloves because they cause latex deterioration, which increases exposure to latex proteins (Petsonk, 1997).

MEDICAL ASSISTING TIP

Latex Reactions

Patients at risk for latex-related reactions include the following.

1. **Women (who account for 75% of all reported cases)**
2. **Asthmatics**
3. **Persons with histories of allergies**
4. **Persons with occupational latex exposure, such as health care workers, artists, painters, and rubber industry workers**
5. **Persons with allergies to fruits and vegetables, especially avocados, bananas, chestnuts, kiwis, and other tropical fruits (due to reciprocal reaction of these foods and latex allergens)**
6. **Persons who undergo intermittent catheterization**
7. **Persons with long histories of genitourinary or intraabdominal surgeries**

It is estimated that 10–17% of health care workers have already become sensitized to latex, and over 2% have occupational-induced asthma as a result of latex exposure. The Food and Drug Administration (FDA) has received more than 1,000 reports of adverse health effects from exposure to latex, including 15 deaths due to such exposure (OSHA, 2002). Documented reactions to latex include mild contact dermatitis, rhinitis, conjunctivitis, urticaria, bronchospasm, and severe systemic anaphylaxis.

The FDA and OSHA advise health care professionals to identify latex-sensitive patients and be prepared to treat them. Many common household items contain latex or its by-products. Home-bound patients who perform self-catheterization or undergo intermittent catheterization are at risk for latex-related allergic reactions. Allergic individuals must avoid latex products and use appropriate substitutes

MEDICAL ASSISTING ALERT

Reporting Latex Reactions

The FDA asks that incidents of adverse reactions to latex or other materials used in medical devices be reported to the FDA Problem Reporting Program (through the U.S. Pharmacopeia) at 1-800-638-6725.

that meet federal safety guidelines. Synthetic rubbers, polyethylene, silicone, or vinyl can be used effectively as alternatives to natural rubber latex. Latex materials labeled "hypoallergenic" are not necessarily latex-free and may not prevent adverse reactions because they may contain the latex proteins and chemicals responsible for sensitization.

The FDA recommendations to health professionals include the following.

1. Questioning for latex sensitivity during the taking of general histories on all patients
2. Using devices made with alternative materials, such as plastic
3. Being alert to the fact that an allergic reaction may occur whenever latex-containing devices are used, especially when the latex comes in contact with mucous membranes
4. Alerting patients with suspected allergic reactions to latex to possible latex sensitivity and advising them to consider immunologic evaluation
5. Advising patients to tell health professionals and emergency personnel about their latex sensitivity and consider advising them to wear a medical identification bracelet

MEDICAL ASSISTING ALERT

Latex Exposure

Latex-allergic individuals must not be exposed to people or items that might have aerosolized latex on them. Never go near a latex-allergic person while wearing clothes, such as OR scrubs, that have powder on them. Always wash hands thoroughly immediately after removing latex gloves. Exposure to aerosolized latex persists for 12 to 16 hours after latex gloves are removed (Jezierski, 1997).

INITIATION OF INFUSION THERAPY

After all of the preparatory steps have been taken, the CMA is ready to gather and set up the appropriate equipment and start the infusion. She must check the order, identify that it is for the right patient, and verify infusate compatibility. The infusate container should be compared directly with the physician's order to be sure it is correct, and pharmacy admixtures must be verified. If the IV order is for blood or blood products, anticoagulants, or chemotherapy, institutional protocols usually require verification checks by two licensed nurses. It is very important for the CMA to know what is required by the agency that employs her.

Equipment Preparation and Setup

The equipment needed for the infusion should be set up away from the patient's room in an environment that minimizes the chance for contamination. If possible, a separate room or area that has good lighting is preferable. Noise and traffic should be kept to a minimum so there is no unnecessary distraction for the CMA and the least amount of air movement. All nonsterile supplies such as any outer packaging, IV poles, or electronic infusion devices must be clean.

Primary Infusion Setup

Prior to starting an intravenous infusion, the correct infusate needs to be set up with a primary administration set. If piggyback medications or secondary infusions are ordered or anticipated, procure a set that has a check valve and injection ports. The interior of the tubing, both ends, as well as the IV fluid, need to be kept sterile to avoid contamination. Gravity flow tubing, or tubing that is not pump specific, is available in macrodrip (usually 15 drops per ml) and microdrip (usually 60 drops per ml).

Many tubings are specifically used for certain types of IV pumps. Although the principles for setting up the infusion remain the same, directions should be checked for any specific tubing, as manufacturers may have slight variations for setting up their particular brand of tubing.

To set up a primary infusion, the CMA must strictly adhere to established step-by-step protocols. Check your facility's protocol before starting IVs.

Administration Guidelines for Peripheral Infusion Therapy

With all of the proper equipment ready and the correct infusion prepared, the CMA can proceed to the patient. As discussed earlier, the ideal situation is one in which the CMA has had the opportunity to establish rapport, give thorough ex-

planations regarding the prescribed therapy, assess the patient and his venous status, and allow for questions and answers. Even if time is of the essence, shortcuts cannot be taken when it comes to safety, comfort, and communication. Patient identity must be verified, and asepsis must be a major concern. Allergies and fluid or medication compatibilities need to be double-checked. The room should be equipped to accommodate both the patient and the CMA, and it should have good lighting and a comfortable temperature. If time and the patient's condition permits, he should be given the opportunity to use the bathroom prior to starting the IV. If possible, site selection should be in the patient's nondominant hand or arm so he can carry out routine activities of daily living during infusion therapy. If the extremity to be used for the IV is not clean, it should be washed with soap and water, rinsed, and dried prior to precannulation antisepsis. The bed should be elevated so the CMA can comfortably assess the patient, prepare the IV site, and initiate the infusion. For the patient's safety and convenience, the bed should be returned to its low position after the infusion is started.

Starting an Infusion

The ensuing guidelines and protocols should be closely followed for the safe administration of any infusion.

1. Ask the patient to state his full name, if he is able to do so. Verify identity with the chart and the identification bracelet.
2. Introduce yourself to the patient.
3. Provide privacy.
4. Explain the proposed procedures in terms the patient can understand. Remember, the patient has the right to know what is being done and the right to refuse treatment.
5. Elevate the bed to a level conducive to starting the IV to prevent straining the CMA's back.
6. Place the patient in a semi-Fowler's or Fowler's position.
7. Protect the patient's clothing and bedding with an underpad or towel.
8. Carry out proper hand hygiene.
9. Set up all of the necessary supplies on the bedside stand or overbed table in the order they will be used, and tear or cut tape strips into the needed lengths. A few strips of paper tape should be available in addition to the start-kit tape. Because paper tape is easy to handle while wearing gloves and is easily removable, it is good to use it to stabilize the IV tubing, once it has been connected to the cannula, while the IV site dressing is being applied. Without this, it is easy for the weight of the tubing to pull the cannula out of the vein before the site dressing and regular tape are applied.

CRITICAL THINKING

Maintaining Priorities

You are preparing to set up an IV infusion that is ordered stat. The only IV pole on your office was just used by another patient and is contaminated with splatters of blood. What would you do in this situation?

10. Gloves are worn to protect the CMA from exposure to blood and do not need to be sterile. For the convenience of the CMA, it is suggested that, before donning them, all of the supplies needed to perform venipuncture and dressing of the IV site be arranged, the vein selected, and the site prepped. The gloves can be applied while the final antiseptic is drying.

11. Select a vein based on the type of infusion therapy and the anticipated duration.

12. Apply a tourniquet 2 to 3 inches below the antecubital fossa for venous access in the lower arm or hand. For veins that are not readily visible, as with the obese person, position the tourniquet 2 to 3 inches above the intended venipuncture site. Depending on the CMA's experience and the time needed for cannulation, the tourniquet may be left on during site preparation or removed. If it is anticipated that more than 4 to 6 minutes will be needed from the time of tourniquet placement to venous cannulation, the tourniquet should be applied, the vein located, the tourniquet removed, the site prepped, and the tourniquet reapplied before cannulation.

Preparing the Site

Correct infusion site preparation is necessary to prevent injury and the introduction of microorganisms that can predispose an individual to infection. Skin preparation can be done using 70% isopropyl alcohol and 2% aqueous chlorhexiden gluconate, povidone-iodine, or 70% tincture of iodine. Institutional policy should be followed.

Preparing the Local Anesthesia

The use of local anesthetics for peripheral cannulation is dictated by institutional policy. The most common products used are lidocaine, normal saline, and EMLA® cream.

Lidocaine

The routine use of lidocaine is generally not recommended. Most CMAs agree that the risks of allergic reaction, inadvertent injection into a vessel, the need for an additional needle stick, and vein obliteration (due to tunica media relaxation) outweigh the benefits of reduced anxiety and increased comfort. They believe that one stick for cannulation done expeditiously is safer and causes the patient the least amount of distress. However, when used, 0.05 to 0.2 ml of 1% lidocaine (Xylocaine) without epinephrine is injected with a 27- to 25-ga., ¼- to ½-inch needle into the tissue below or to the side of the intended cannulation site. When a superficial wheal forms, it is massaged with an alcohol pledget to speed absorption and prevent obliteration of the vein. The anesthetic effect usually occurs within ten seconds. Always follow institutional policy regarding this practice.

Normal Saline

Normal saline (NS), or 0.9% bacteriostatic sodium chloride, produces essentially the same anesthetic effect as lidocaine. The ethyl alcohol used as the preservative causes the numbing sensation. The NS does not cause smooth muscle relaxation of the vein wall, nor does it sting (as lidocaine does). A larger volume of NS can be injected, making the anesthetic more powerful. To make the procedure virtually painless, the needle (27- to 25-ga., ¼- to ½-inch) should be introduced bevel down. Before inserting the needle, apply pressure with the needle bevel down for a few seconds, then pass the needle under the skin. Inject the NS over the vein, then on each side of the vein. Most CMAs who routinely use local anesthesia injections prior to cannulation prefer normal saline to lidocaine since it does not have the potential to cause an untoward effect.

EMLA® Cream

EMLA® cream is a eutectic mixture of 2.5% lidocaine and 2.5% prilocaine as an oil in water emulsion. It is applied to intact skin under an occlusive dressing. It provides dermal analgesia by releasing lidocaine and prilocaine from the cream into the epidermal and dermal layers of the skin in the vicinity of dermal pain receptors and nerve endings. EMLA® works well when time is not a major consideration. The onset, depth, and duration of dermal analgesia depends on the duration of application. For IV therapy, it should be in place for at least one hour prior to venipuncture and cannula placement. It is used frequently for peripherally inserted central lines and in pediatric settings. Because it causes relaxation of the tunica media, the vein may be obliterated and difficult to access.

Astrazeneca, Inc. recommends the following steps for the application of EMLA® cream.

1. Remove the backing from an EMLA® patch (Figure 8-2A).

2. Peel the paper liner from the paper framed dressing.

3. Apply the EMLA® patch, being careful not to spread out the cream. Smooth down the dressing edges carefully and be sure the dressing is secure to avoid leakage (Figure 8-2B). (This is especially important when the patient is a child.)

4. Remove the paper frame. The time of application can be marked directly on the occlusive dressing. (Figure 8-2C) EMLA® cream must be applied at least one hour before the start of a routine procedure and two hours before the start of a painful procedure.

5. Remove the occlusive dressing, wipe off the EMLA® cream, clean the entire area with an antiseptic solution, and prepare the patient for the procedure. The skin anesthesia will be effective for at least one hour after removal of the occlusive dressing.

(Reproduced with permission of AstraZeneca, Wilmington, DE)

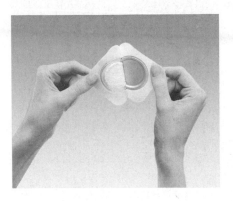 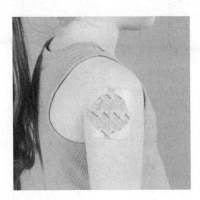 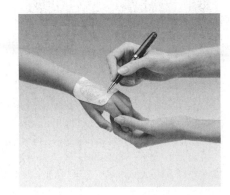

Figure 8-2 | (A) Peel the backing from the EMLA® patch. (B) Apply the patch to the skin. (C) Label the dressing around the patch. *Courtesy of AstraZeneca, LP, Wayne, PA*

Iontophoresis

The skin can be desensitized using iontophoresis of lidocaine (Numby Stuff by Iomed), an alternative to EMLA®, when time is of the essence. Whereas EMLA® takes about an hour to exert the effect of numbness, iontophoresis takes about ten minutes. It is a fast, noninvasive system that utilizes a mild electrical current to deliver local anesthetic to the skin without causing tissue distortion (such as the wheal that occurs with injection). The system consists of a set of electrode pads. One pad, which contains Iontocaine (2% lidocaine and epinephrine 1:100,000 topical solution), is placed over the intended venipuncture site. The other electrode is placed on the skin about 4 to 6 inches (10–15 cm) away from the drug-delivery site. A handheld device controls a steady, low electrical flow of current that initiates the delivery of ion salts into the skin layers to provide local anesthesia to a depth of up to 10 mm.

Vein Cannulation

Prior to cannulation, take the distal end of the IV administration tubing that is hanging over the IV pole and position it in close proximity to the IV insertion site. Gently loosen the cap, but do not remove it. Sterility must be maintained until it is connected to the cannula hub.

Over-the-Needle Catheter (ONC) Insertion

The most commonly used angiocatheter to start an infusion is the over-the-needle catheter (ONC). An ONC is a flexible catheter, encased with a metal stylet, that is used to pierce the skin and vein, and that attaches to the infusion tubing (once the stylet has been removed). The ONC has essentially replaced straight, steel needles that were, at one time, the main delivery device for fluids into the vein.

An ONC can be inserted using a one-handed or two-handed technique (Figure 8-3). It can be threaded into the vein or "floated" in. The CMA's experience and the manufacturer's guidelines determine what method should be used.

Figure 8-4 illustrates cannulation with a Y-type catheter. In this type of system, the stylet is removed from an accessory port rather than through the insertion route. With this method, the administration set tubing can be connected prior to cannulation, providing a bloodless IV start.

If cannulation is unsuccessful, the entire procedure must be repeated at another site. It is not recommended that cannulation be attempted by the same CMA more than two times (INS, 2000, Standard 48 S43), as this may put undue stress on the patient and the CMA, both tending to lose con-

---

MEDICAL ASSISTING TIP

Cannulating ONCs

The two methods used to cannulate ONCs follow.

1. **One-handed technique.** Using one hand (while the other anchors the vein), the skin is entered, the vein cannulated, and (with the index finger or thumb) the cannula is advanced off the needle/stylet and into the vein, and the needle is discarded or retracted into its protective shield.

2. **Two-handed method.** The cannula is inserted into the vein, using one hand, while the other anchors the vein. Once a backflash of blood occurs, one hand (that anchored) is used to stabilize the cannula hub while the other removes the needle/stylet.

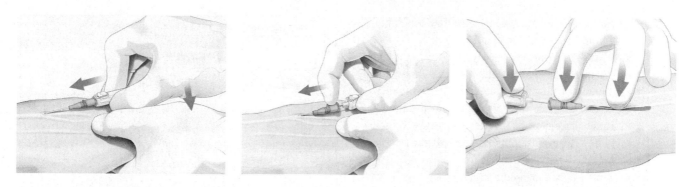

Figure 8-3 | Over-the-needle catheters can be inserted using a one-handed technique in which the catheter is inserted into the vein (A) and the index finger is used to slide the catheter into the vein while the needle is being retracted (B) or by using a two-handed technique in which one hand anchors the vein and holds the catheter while the other retracts the needle (C). *Courtesy of BD Medical Systems, Franklin Lakes, NJ*

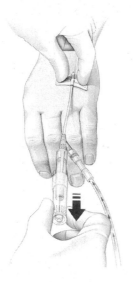

Figure 8-4 | Y-style catheter allows bloodless insertion of an IV because the infusate can begin flowing before removing the stylet. *Courtesy of BD Medical Systems, Franklin Lakes, NJ*

fidence. If possible, another person should attempt to perform the procedure. The CMA should not allow herself to become distressed over this or let it diminish her self-confidence. As proficient as she may be at venipuncture and cannulation, there are times when the procedure does not progress as planned. It is better to be forthright about this (in her own regard and for the patient's sake) and let someone else attempt cannulation.

Straight Needle

Straight needles are seldom used anymore for infusion therapy, but are still used for blood sampling and blood do-

> ## MEDICAL ASSISTING ALERT
>
> ### *Flashback*
>
> Flashback may occur when the needle (only), and not the catheter tip, has entered the vein. Do not use flashback as a signal to withdraw the needle.

nation. When they are used to deliver infusates, it is best to use veins that are naturally splinted by bone to hinder movement of the needle within the vein. Steel needles must never be used to deliver fluids or medications that may cause tissue necrosis should extravasation occur. The correct method follows.

1. Select the smallest needle that will accommodate the vein yet deliver the ordered infusate. The needle can be inserted using one of two methods, depending on the CMA's preference and the condition of the patient's vein.
   (a) Connect the needle to the end of the administration set tubing, remove the needle cap while maintaining its sterility, and slowly open the tubing clamp to purge the needle of any air. Reclamp the tubing and recap the needle.
   (b) Prepare the site and don gloves.
   (c) Enter the vein, bevel up, and advance the needle into the vein. Once in the vein, there may be a small back-flash of blood into the IV tubing, depending on venous pressure, to verify placement. If this does not occur, slowly open the tubing clamp and slowly run the infusate, watching the site and

palpating around it. A cool sensation and skin-tightening would indicate infiltration. If the site looks and feels normal, loosely tape the IV tubing with paper tape to the patient's arm. Lower the IV container below the IV site with the clamp fully open. A retrograde flow of blood into the tubing indicates placement in the vein. Hang the IV and regulate it. The site should be dressed and secured in the same manner as an ONC.

2. The other method used to insert a steel needle is to connect it to a syringe containing 3 cc to 5 cc of normal saline.
   (a) Prime the needle and enter the vein, bevel up. To verify placement, pull back on the syringe plunger to visualize a backflow of blood.
   (b) Secure the needle, remove the syringe, connect the cannula hub to the administration set, and regulate the infusion. Secure and dress the site.

IV therapy can be administered through a winged infusion set, also known as a *butterfly needle*. This is a short metal needle that lies within the vein during infusion therapy. The needle extends from soft plastic wings and is connected to a short, permanently attached, extension tubing. The wings provide a means to stabilize the cannula when secured with tape. The wings are flexible and can be bent upward to act as a handle when inserting the needle. Since this is a metal needle, there is an increased chance of the needle becoming dislodged during therapy. Winged metal needles are usually used to provide IV therapy to infants or for very short-term drug or fluid administration, such as a one-time order. It is generally a CMA judgment, based on accurate assessment, as to which type of device is most appropriate for a particular client. The most common site for insertion of a

---

MEDICAL ASSISTING TIP

To prevent blood leakage while removing the needle and connecting the administration set tubing, apply digital pressure to the vein just above the catheter tip, using the fourth or fifth finger of the nondominant hand, while holding the cannula hub securely with the thumb and index finger.

For patients with thin, fragile veins, this practice is not recommended, as the pressure—especially if it is inadvertently applied over the tip of the catheter—could bruise the vein wall. In this situation, work quickly to connect the cannula hub with the administration set tubing. This is why it is important to shield the area under the extremity with a protective cover.

MEDICAL ASSISTING ALERT

Maximum Cannula Use

Never stick a patient more than one time with the same cannula. If venipuncture is unsuccessful, the cannula must be properly disposed of and a new one inserted.

MEDICAL ASSISTING ALERT

Avoiding a Catheter Embolus

Do not, under any circumstances, reinsert the needle into the catheter at any time. The needle could sever the catheter, resulting in a catheter embolus.

MEDICAL ASSISTING TIP

Advancing the Catheter

It is suggested that the catheter not be advanced completely up to the hub, but that approximately ⅛ in. of catheter remain visible outside of the body. In the rare, unforeseen event that the catheter and hub should separate, the catheter could be retrieved with forceps.

---

winged needle is the dorsal surface of the hand and the smaller veins in the forearm.

Securing the IV Site with Dressings and Tape

As discussed earlier, the IV site can be dressed with a transparent membrane dressing or a gauze-and-tape covering, depending on the patient's clinical situation and institutional policy. The most important factor, regardless of the type of dressing used, is that the site must be able to be assessed frequently in order to troubleshoot problems. The dressing should be secured around the catheter hub to protect the IV site and to prevent the dressing from coming off. Additional tape is only to be used to secure the administration set tubing. In an oriented, noncombative adult, the IV site dressing and two to three additional strips of tape are generally all that are required to maintain an IV. Additional adhesion is superfluous in that it adds unnecessary bulk, is a potential skin irritant, and provides a medium for contamination. To avoid circulatory impairment, tape must never encircle an extremity.

Two major considerations must be kept in mind when using any IV site dressing.

1. The dressing should mold to the catheter insertion site and surrounding area so that there are no gaps or openings where contaminants can enter.

2. The dressing must be placed so that it covers only the IV site and extends up to the top margin of the cannula hub. No tape or dressing should cover the connection between the IV device and the administration set tubing. When this connection site is secured with the dressing, there is manipulation of the cannula and IV site should the administration set need to be changed, have extensions or connectors added to it, or if the infusion is disconnected and converted to an intermittent administration system.

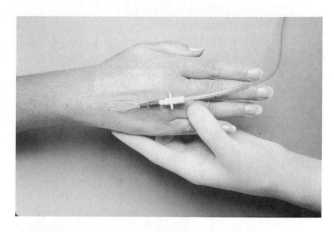

Figure 8-5 | Transparent semipermeable membrane dressing

MEDICAL ASSISTING ALERT

Applying Tape to an IV Site

When applying tape to an IV site or when taping an immobilizing device in place, never encircle the entire extremity with tape. This could cause circulatory impairment, especially if edema sets in or if infiltration occurs.

MEDICAL ASSISTING TIP

Tape or Dressing Removal

To prevent a skin tear when removing tape or a transparent dressing, remember the following rule: "Don't remove the tape from the skin; remove the skin from the tape."

Transparent Dressings

The transparent semipermeable dressing (TSD) (Figure 8-5) or transparent membrane dressing (TMD) is often preferred because the IV insertion site can be easily assessed. Manufacturer instructions must be followed when using TSDs. Instructions for the application of a TSD follow.

1. Apply to dry skin.
2. Remove backing papers according to directions.
3. Gently lift the catheter, and carefully mold the transparent film around the sides of the catheter hub to form a seal.
4. Remove any additional backings or paper frames around dressing, as directed.
5. Apply additional tapes, as needed, to secure IV tubing, but do not obliterate the IV insertion site.
6. Do not apply tape over a transparent dressing.

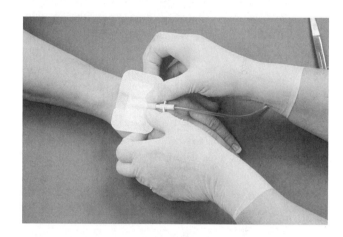

Figure 8-6 | All-in-one gauze-tape dressing

To remove a transparent dressing, gently move the skin away from the dressing using either the stretch technique or the alcohol technique. With the stretch technique, the dressing is stretched parallel to the patient's skin in small increments until the dressing has been removed. With the alcohol (or adhesive remover) technique, the dressing is lifted around the edges and the solvent is used to break down the adhesive seal and remove the dressing.

Gauze and Tape Dressings

If an all-in-one gauze-tape dressing (Figure 8-6) is used, follow the manufacturer's directions for application and removal. If a ready-made dressing is not available, the IV site must be covered with a sterile (preferably nonadherent) gauze that covers the prepped area. It should be taped so that there are no openings for contaminants to enter. When gauze-tape dressings are used, established institutional protocols must be followed regarding scheduled removal for changing and to assess the IV site.

Catheter Stabilization and Taping

"Cannulas shall be stabilized in a manner that does not interfere with assessment and monitoring of the infusion site or impede delivery of the prescribed therapy" (INS, 2000, Standard 49, S43). In the past, it was recommended that the needle or catheter be stabilized by taping over or around its hub in a chevron, H, or U formation before applying the dressing. Since it is now encouraged that nothing that is not sterile come in contact with the IV site once it is prepped and cannulated other than the sterile dressing, this practice is not recommended. Some agencies recommend predressing taping regimens for certain patient populations, such as pediatrics and geriatrics. Unless institutional policy dictates otherwise, there should be nothing placed between the catheter and the dressing.

In general, if an IV site requires additional protection, as for a pediatric or combative patient, the better alternative is to use a self-adherent wrap over the basic IV dressing, one that does not require adhesive, pins, or clips (Figure 8-7). The wrap stays in place to protect the IV, can be removed easily for site assessment, and can be reapplied. The use of roller bandages is not advised because they may impede circulatory flow and do not allow for visual inspection of the cannula site. "Site protection material shall allow visual inspection of the site and shall be placed so as not to impede circulation or impede infusion through the access device" (INS, 2000, Standard 49, S43).

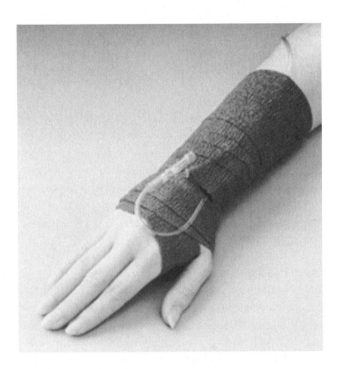

Figure 8-7 | 3M™ Coban™ Self-Adherent Wrap to secure and protect an IV over the basic site dressing. *Courtesy of 3M Health Care, St. Paul. MN*

Completing the Procedure

Lower the bed and document the procedure.

Documentation

Once the infusion is initiated, the CMA must document the following information in the CMA's notes (Figure 8-8) of the medical record.

1. Date and time started
2. Insertion site and its appearance
3. Size and type of cannulation device
4. Name of the infusate and the rate
5. Type of dressing applied
6. Number and locations of attempted cannulations and the condition of the sites (and any remedial procedures needed)
7. Patient's response to the procedure

Armboards

Unless absolutely necessary (and then only when an IV device is in an area of flexion), it is better not to restrict the patient's extremity on an armboard (INS, 2000, Standard 36, S32). If an IV device is positional in a vein, a rolled washcloth or gauze roll can often be used to support and better position it and reestablish infusate flow.

If an armboard is indispensable for the maintenance of an IV, extreme care must be taken to ensure that the area it is applied to has optimum circulation and remains functional. Measures are to be instituted to prevent restriction, discomfort, or injury while allowing for infusion site monitoring. The armboard must be removed at established intervals in order to assess circulation and movement. Federal and state mandates must be followed regarding the use of armboards and restraints and the issue must be addressed, in writing, in agency policy. If extremity restraints are ordered, care must be taken to position them away from the IV site and cannula.

PERIPHERAL INFUSION THERAPY: MAINTENANCE AND MONITORING

Once IV therapy has been initiated, it is vitally important to observe and assess the patient, monitor the IV site, and maintain the equipment. Strict adherence to safety protocols and the detection of problems, should they arise, are the most important mechanisms in preventing the complications associated with infusion therapy.

Observation and Assessment

The patient undergoing any type of infusion therapy should be monitored every hour at a minimum. If the individual's condi-

CMA's Notes

DATE	TIME	ASSESSMENT DATA	CMAs INTERVENTIONS	EVALUATION
6-2-99	0840	Pt. c/o "burning and stinging" when ONC inserted. 6 mm raised, circular ecchymotic area around insertion site after ONC removal.	Venipuncture attempted in Rt. dorsal metacarpal vein over 3rd finger with 20 g 1" Jelco ONC. 2" × 2" pressure dressing applied following removal.	Pt. said it is "sore, but feels OK."
	0855		20 g 1¼" Jelco ONC inserted above Lt. dorsal venous arch into cephalic vein. 1000 cc D$_5$W @ 125 cc/hr per IMED (controlled mode). Op Site TSM to site.	Pt. says site and arm "feels fine."

Figure 8-8 | Documentation in the CMA's notes

CMA's Notes

DATE	TIME	ASSESSMENT DATA	CMAs INTERVENTIONS	EVALUATION
8-7-98	0430	Pt. states, "I have such terrible pain in my whole arm that it woke me up. It feels like it is on fire where the needle is." Cannula insertion site (Lt. dorsal metacarpal area) is reddened, warm to the touch, and tender. Lower arm and hand are edematous. T: 101.2, P: 94, R: 26, BP: 136/90.	IV d.c. 'd, Lt. hand and forearm wrapped in moist, warm compresses and elevated on 2 pillows. Dr. Gand called (per Exchange Operator #22) regarding fever.	Pt. says Lt. arm "feels better, but the hand still hurts."
	0455		Acetaminophen gr × "p.o." IV restarted in Rt. cephalic vein (above the wrist) with 20 g 1" Insyte ONC at 100 cc/hr per IVAC pump. Tegaderm TSM to site.	Pt. says he feels better and wants to go back to sleep.
	0550	Pt. asleep. T: 99.1, P: 82, R: 18, BP: 128/90.		

Figure 8-9 | Documentation in the CMA's notes regarding a change in the patient's status and reporting

MEDICAL ASSISTING TIP

Patient-Family Teaching for Home-Bound Patients

For home-bound patients, where frequent assessment is not feasible, the patient and family should be instructed regarding IV therapy. It is important that they understand what to look for and what situations require reporting.

tion warrants it, more frequent checks may be necessary. He must be observed as well as questioned regarding his status. Any change in his color, skin turgor, level of consciousness, or vital signs must be investigated, documented, and reported (Figure 8-9). Observation includes not only the patient but any IV equipment used. There must be thorough and accurate verbal and written communication among all personnel caring for him.

Monitoring is especially important during the period following the initiation of infusion therapy and the introduction of new medications. It is very important that the CMA stay with the patient for a short period whenever anything new is delivered. Even though a patient may not have experienced problems with something in the past, especially if taken orally, that cannot be taken for granted. Time is of the essence when problems arise with parenteral fluids or drugs, and measures must be instituted swiftly to counteract any untoward events. Monitoring is an integral part of quality improvement and risk management and it ensures patient safety. Although in your facility nurses may be required to do formal assessments, you should report to the nurses any problems that you notice.

Documentation and Reporting

It has been stressed repeatedly that the CMA must document and report all pertinent information regarding the patient's status. The saying, "not documented, not done" has become a legal standard. The patient's chart (the medical record) is where all pertinent communications regarding a patient's care and status must be documented, in addition to other forms required by the institution. Remember: Documentation includes labeling.

Documentation entails recording infusion-related information in the following areas.

1. MAR
2. CMA's notes
3. Infusion flow sheets
4. Intake and output records
5. General or equipment flow sheets
6. Laboratory, radiology, and other ancillary department requisitions
7. Labels
   (a) ALLERGIC: place on and in the patient's chart, room, and bed, and all communication channels with other personnel and departments, regarding allergies and drug reactions, and attach the appropriate identification bracelet to the patient
   (b) IV site, next to the dressing, with the date and time of the cannulation; the type of device, including length and gauge; and the CMA's initials
   (c) Administration set tubing (date and time of initiation or change)
   (d) Infusate containers (date and time of start, flow level strips, medications added)

Documentation and reporting go hand-in-hand. One without the other is insufficient.

Reporting includes verbal communication to the physician supported by written notes to other personnel, to pharmacy, to the family, and to ancillary departments regarding any pertinent occurrences and changes regarding the patient's status. Even though information is written in the patient's chart, failure to report it to the appropriate individuals means communication is incomplete and may be invalidated in a court of law.

Infusion Site Maintenance

The proper maintenance of the IV site is essential to preventing complications. Since the site provides accessibility to the circulatory system, measures must be taken to avoid microbial contamination and chemical or mechanical trauma. The policies and procedures of the institution regarding the frequency of site monitoring and maintenance should be followed. In addition, monitoring must be dictated by the patient's condition and age, the type of infusion device, the kind of therapy he is receiving, and the setting in which care is delivered.

The most recent CDC Guidelines regarding IV site care (CDC, 2001c) recommend the following.

1. The IV insertion site is to be visually inspected and manually palpated, through the intact dressing, on a daily basis. If the dressing prevents palpation and visualization because it is large or bulky, it must be removed for assessment and a new one reapplied.
2. Hands are to be washed, using an antiseptic-containing product, before palpating, inserting, changing, or dressing any intravascular device.
3. Wear (sterile or nonsterile) vinyl or latex gloves during insertion of intravascular catheters and during dressing changes (per OSHA Standards).
4. Dressings are to be left in place until the catheter is removed or changed, or the dressing becomes damp, loosened, or soiled. Dressings need to be changed more frequently for patients who are diaphoretic.

MEDICAL ASSISTING TIP

Accurate Charting

Accurate charting is always your best legal defense should litigation occur. Always chart the following.

1. The date and time of insertion.
2. The vein cannulated. Be specific. Know your peripheral venous anatomy. If necessary, document why you chose a particular vein. Document the condition of the vein in terms of its softness, hardness, and resiliency.
3. The device used. Include the brand name and style, the gauge, and length.
4. The infusate administered.
5. The method of infusion: gravity, electronic infusion device (controller or pump mode and the name brand and model number).
6. The patient's reaction to the procedure, and any comments he makes.

Equipment Protocols

The equipment used for infusion therapy must be used correctly, regularly monitored, and properly maintained for the safety of the patient and the personnel using it. The CDC guidelines regarding IV equipment (CDC, 2002a) include the following.

1. Select the catheter, insertion technique, and insertion site with the lowest risk for complications (infectious and noninfectious) for the anticipated type and duration of IV therapy.

2. Allow the antiseptic (2% aqueous chlorhexidine gluconate [CHG], 10% povidone-iodine, 2% tincture of iodine, or 70% alcohol) to remain on the insertion site and to air dry before catheter insertion. Allow the povidone-iodine to remain on the skin for at least two minutes, or longer if it is not yet dry, before insertion. Do not apply organic solvents (e.g., acetone and ether) to the skin before insertion of catheters or during dressing changes.

3. Once an intravascular device is inserted, the date and time of insertion must be recorded in an obvious location near the insertion site (e.g., on [and to the side of] the dressing or on the bed).

4. In adults, replace short, peripheral venous catheters at least every 72–96 hours to reduce the risk for phlebitis. If sites for venous access are limited and no evidence of phlebitis or infection is present, peripheral venous catheters can be left in place for longer periods, although the patient and the insertion sites should be closely monitored. Do not routinely replace midline catheters to reduce the risk for infection. In pediatric patients, leave peripheral venous catheters in place until IV therapy is completed, unless a complication (e.g., phlebitis and infiltration) occurs.

5. When adherence to aseptic technique cannot be ensured (i.e., when catheters are inserted during a medical emergency), replace all catheters as soon as possible and after no longer than 48 hours.

6. Use clinical judgment to determine when to replace a catheter that could be a source of infection. Replace any short-term CVC if purulence is observed at the insertion site, which indicates infection.

7. Promptly remove any intravascular catheter that is no longer essential.

8. Replace administration sets, including secondary sets and add-on devices, no more frequently than at 72-hour intervals, unless catheter-related infection is suspected or documented. Replace tubing used to administer blood, blood products, or lipid emulsions (those combined with amino acids and glucose in a 3-in-1 admixture or infused separately) within 24 hours of initiating the infusion. If the solution contains only dextrose and amino acids, the administration set does not need to be replaced more frequently than every 72 hours. Replace tubing used to administer propofol infusions every 6 or 12 hours, depending on its use, per the manufacturer's recommendation.

9. Complete the infusion of lipid-containing solutions (e.g., 3-in-1 solutions) within 24 hours of hanging the solution. Complete the infusion of lipid emulsions alone within 12 hours of hanging the emulsion. If volume considerations require more time, the infusion should be completed within 24 hours. Complete infusions of blood or other blood products within 4 hours of hanging the blood. No recommendation can be made for the hang time of other parenteral fluids, but most agencies do not recommend leaving any infusate hanging for more than 24 hours.

10. Change the needleless components at least as frequently as the administration set. Change caps no more frequently than every 72 hours or according to manufacturers' recommendations. Ensure that all components of the system are compatible to minimize leaks and breaks in the system. Minimize contamination risk by wiping the access port with an appropriate antiseptic and accessing the port only with sterile devices.

11. Do not use filters routinely for infection-control purposes.

IV Medication Administration During Infusion Therapy

When IV medications are ordered while an infusion is running, there are several administration options. They may be added to the primary infusate container, given via a secondary administration set, added through an injection port in the primary administration tubing, or given by direct injection into another vein that is not concurrently receiving any infusates. If the first three options are used, it is critical that the CMA check for chemical, physical, and therapeutic compatibility between the medications and the delivery systems.

Adding Medications to the Infusion Container

In general, admixtures are dispensed directly into infusate containers in the pharmacy by pharmacists who use strict asepsis. Admixing is done under laminar air flow hoods, where air is constantly filtered of contaminants. **Laminar air flow** refers to air that moves along separate but parallel flow paths into filters where contaminants are removed. It was common practice in the not-too-distant past for nurses to prepare their own admixtures for primary infusions. The

CDC now recommends that all parenteral admixtures be aseptically prepared in the pharmacy under laminar-flow hoods (CDC, 2002a).

In some circumstances the CMA may have to add newly ordered medications to an already hanging infusion. Prior to doing this, several areas need to be addressed.

1. *Compatibility.* The CMA must verify that the drug can be mixed with the existing infusate.
2. *Concentration.* Depending on the amount of infusate remaining in the primary container, would the addition of the medication render a safe dilution? (An example here would involve adding potassium chloride to a primary container. Unless there is enough infusate to dilute the drug, the concentration of KCl might be too great, which could result in a cardiac dysrhythmia.)
3. *Stability.* How long will the drug be stable once it is added to the infusion?

If, after all precautions are taken and the CMA does add medication to a primary container, she must prepare the admixture using strict asepsis. If taken from a glass ampule, a depth-filter needle must be used to draw up the medication to remove any glass fragments that may have fallen into the solution when the ampule was broken. It must be replaced with a standard needle or appropriate needleless device before expelling the drug from the syringe into the IV container.

The administration set tubing must be clamped and the infusion container must be removed from the IV pole prior to injecting the drug. The injection port must be swabbed with 70% alcohol, the medication injected, and then the bag or bottle must be gently rocked back and forth to thoroughly mix the added drug with the fluid. It can then be rehung, the clamp opened, and the rate adjusted. The container must be labeled to indicate what drug and dose was added, the date and time, the amount of infusate in the container when the admixture was prepared, the name of the person who prepared and added it, and the expiration time.

Secondary Medication Administration Piggybacked into the Primary Infusion Line

The secondary infusion is initiated after the primary infusion is in progress. It is the most common method to administer IV medications concurrently with the primary infusion. It is coupled to the primary infusion line at the first injection port below the check valve.

The piggyback is able to function concurrently with a primary infusion only when it is suspended higher than the primary line (which must have a back-check valve). By opening the clamp on the secondary line, the primary infusion temporarily stops flowing. When the piggyback

infusion is complete and the infusate in its tubing falls below the level of the primary line drip chamber, the back-check valve opens and the primary infusion resumes.

MEDICAL ASSISTING TIP

Adding Medication to an Existing Infusion Container

When adding a medication to an existing infusion container, *never* inject it into the bag or bottle while it is hanging and infusing. This would deliver the drug to the base of the container, where it would infuse as a bolus dose to the patient. There are documented cases where this practice has resulted in serious complications and death.

Adding Medications Through the Infusion Line

Some IV medications that would normally be delivered directly into the vein by bolus injection can be administered through an injection port in the primary administration set if the patient already has an IV running.

When administering any IV push medication, it is very important to check for compatibility between the infusing product and the drug. Failure to do so could cause a precipitate to form, which could obstruct the infusion line or, if it entered the patient, could damage the vein or embolize. It is also critical that any required interventions that accompany the drug's administration be verified. These often include vital signs (which may be required before, during, and after administration), patient teaching regarding sensations he may experience during or following administration, the amount of time needed to safely inject the drug, side effects associated with too-rapid infusion, and patient safety precautions.

MEDICAL ASSISTING TIP

Bolus Injection

The term *bolus injection* actually refers to the slow injection of a drug directly into a vein. Contrary to what some CMAs believe, it does not mean to administer the drug via an existing infusion line.

DISCONTINUATION OF PERIPHERAL INFUSIONS WHILE RETAINING VENOUS PATENCY

Once a primary infusion is no longer needed, the bag or bottle and administration set tubings can be removed, and an intermittent infusion plug can be attached to the hub of the cannula. This is usually done in order to keep the IV line available in case it is needed later or to keep it for administering intermittent medications.

After verifying the order, the CMA obtains an intermittent infusion plug, also called a *male adapter plug* (formerly called a *heparin lock*) and a 2 cc syringe of 0.9% NaCl. The appropriate needleless connectors are used for access to the intermittent infusion plug. The infusion is turned off, gloves are applied, and the administration set tubing is disconnected from the cannula. The sterile cap on the intermittent plug is removed and the adapter is attached to the cannula hub. The rubber stopper is swabbed with 70% alcohol and 2 cc of normal saline is injected to flush the cannula.

In the past, the saline flush was followed by 1 ml of heparin (10 units per ml). The CDC (CDC, 2001) recommends that heparin be used only when intermittent infusion devices are used for blood sampling. Normal (0.9%) saline is just as effective as heparin in maintaining catheter patency and reducing phlebitis among peripheral catheters. In addition, recent in vitro studies have suggested that the growth of coagulase-negative staphylococci (CoNS) on catheters may be intensified in the presence of heparin. CoNS growth is inhibited by edetic acid (EDTA), making it the subject of clinical trials and testing to judge its efficacy for use in catheter flushing. Until further clinical trials substantiate otherwise, heparin is no longer routinely recommended for intermittent flushing.

When an intermittent line is inserted but no IV medications are ordered, the usual maintenance routine is to assess the site, check for cannula patency, and instill 2 cc of 0.9% saline every 8 to 12 hours. To check for patency, the syringe is attached to the intermittent plug and the plunger is pulled back to elicit a blood return. There may or may not be a return because a fibrin shield forms at the tip of most cannulas (a homeostatic defense mechanism that occurs when the skin barrier is broken) that prevents retrograde blood flow, yet allows infusates to pass into the system. If there is no blood return, the CMA should gently inject the saline while palpating the infusion site and observing. If the cannula is out of the vein, the saline will infiltrate the surrounding tissue, raising it, and giving it a cool feeling. Otherwise, the saline will enter the cannula and vein to maintain patency.

When any medication is administered into an intermittent infusion device, the protocol to be followed is the S-A-S method.

1. Carry out proper hand hygiene.
2. Assess the site.
3. Don gloves.
4. Disinfect the cannula port.
5. Verify cannula and venous patency. If resistance is met, do not exert pressure on the syringe plunger to restore patency.
6. Slowly instill 2 ml of normal saline (0.9% NaCl) to clear the lock—**S**.
7. Administer the prescribed medication—**A**.
8. Flush with normal saline to clear the lock—**S**.
9. Maintain positive pressure during and after flushes to prevent reflux of blood. (See *Medical Assisting Tip*.)
10. Remove gloves and carry out proper hand hygiene.
11. Document according to agency policy.

If multiple IV medications are ordered at one time, the normal saline is to be instilled between the administration of each one. The normal saline must always be given after any medications are injected to clear the cannula of the drug and maintain patency. Positive pressure must be maintained within the cannula lumen during and following a flush to prevent reflux of blood into the lumen.

In the event that heparin is ordered, the traditional S-A-S-H sequence protocol would be used.

1. Carry out proper hand hygiene.
2. Assess the site.
3. Don gloves.
4. Disinfect the cannula port.
5. Verify cannula and venous patency. If resistance is met, do not exert pressure on the syringe plunger to restore patency.
6. Slowly instill 2 ml of normal saline (0.9% NaCl) to clear the lock—**S**.
7. Administer the prescribed medication—**A**.
8. Flush with normal saline to clear the lock—**S**.
9. Connect the heparin-filled syringe (usually 1 ml of 10 units/ml) to the cannula port and flush—**H**.
10. Maintain positive pressure during and after flushes to prevent reflux of blood. (See *Medical Assisting Tip*.)
11. Remove gloves and carry out proper hand hygiene.
12. Document according to agency policy.

Do not use the S-A-S-H method for peripheral IV lines unless it is backed by institutional policy or specifically ordered by the physician.

Turbulent flushing may assist in minimizing fibrin collection and clot formation on peripheral catheters, just as it does with central lines This type of flushing is accomplished by exerting a driving motion on the syringe plunger with a

MEDICAL ASSISTING ALERT

Maintaining Positive Pressure in Cannula Lumen

It is imperative that positive pressure be maintained within the lumen of the catheter during and following the administration of a flush solution to prevent reflux of blood into the cannula lumen. A positive displacement device helps to eliminate fluid backflow by generating a positive pulse of fluid directed toward the catheter tip as the male Luer-Lok adapter is removed from the device. When flushing a positive displacement device, remove the syringe *before* clamping.

MEDICAL ASSISTING TIP

Positive Pressure Technique

- When using a blunt cannula or needle, withdraw the blunt cannula or needle as the last 0.5 ml is flushed inward.
- When using a Luer activated device:
  - As the last 0.5 ml is flushed inward, clamp the extension tubing.
  or
  - Maintain pressure on the plunger and clamp the extension set at either end.

pulsatile, push-pause technique. This introduces turbulence into the cannula of the IV device, which creates a swirling (true flushing motion). The result is a vigorous movement that can remove blood cells, fibrin, or protein buildup on the walls of the cannula.

DISCONTINUATION OF PERIPHERAL INFUSION LINES

An IV is discontinued when ordered by the physician, when the infusion line is no longer needed, or if it must be terminated because of complications.

MEDICATION ADMINISTRATION BY DIRECT INTRAVENOUS BOLUS DELIVERY

When the patient does not have an infusion line in place but requires intravenous medications, the medication must be injected directly into the vein. Either a straight needle or a winged tip administration set connected to a syringe can be used.

Straight Needle and Syringe

For medications that can be injected over a short time period (usually less than 60 seconds), a straight needle attached to a syringe is generally used.

Winged Administration Set and Syringe

A winged administration set is generally used when the medication to be administered takes more than a minute to inject (such as IV phenytoin, where the rate is not to exceed 50 mg/min). Using this method, the CMA can comfortably position herself next to the patient without straining her back. If any interventions need to be taken during administration of the medication (such as blood pressure or pulse monitoring), the syringe can be set down next to the patient's extremity or taped to it without the needle becoming dislodged from the vein.

MEDICAL ASSISTING ALERT

Time Parameters

The term *IV bolus* or *IV push* does not indicate an appropriate injection rate. If the prescriber does not order time parameters, it is the CMA's responsibility to consult with the phyisican as well as a reliable drug reference source, or confer with a pharmacist to obtain a protocol for the length of time needed to administer the ordered dose. Certain drugs, such as digoxin, when administered too rapidly can cause severe bradycardia or death from cardiac arrest.

Review Questions and Activities

1. Describe the various roles of the CMA in infusion therapy.
2. List the necessary components of a physician's order.
3. Describe patient preparation for IV therapy.
4. List methods to enhance venous access.
5. List the steps involved in starting IV therapy.
6. Describe how to secure an IV site.
7. Describe how to document the discontinuation of IV therapy.

Aitken, D. R., & Minton, J. P. (1984). The pinch-off sign: A warning of impending problems with permanent subclavian catheters. *American Journal of Surgery, 148,* 633–636.

Allen, K. (2000). How to remove a Huber needle without sticking yourself. *Nursing, 30*(10), 55–56.

Alvarado-Ramy, F., Alter, M.J., Bower, W., Henderson, D.K., Sohn, A.H., & Sinkowitz-Cochran, R.L. (2001). Management of occupational exposures to hepatitis C virus: Current practice and controversies. *Infection Control and Hospital Epidemiology, 22*(1), 53–55.

American Association of Blood Banks. (1990). *Technical manual* (10th ed.). Arlington, VA: Author.

American Heart Association. (2001). *Textbook of pediatric advanced life support.* Dallas, Texas: Author.

American Heart Association. (2002). *PALS Provider Manual.* Dallas, Texas: Author

American Nurses Association. (1980). *Nursing: A social policy statement.* Kansas City, MO: Author.

American Nurses Association. (1991). *Standards of clinical nursing practice.* Washington, DC: American Nurses Publishing.

American Nurses Association. (1995). *Nursing's social policy statement.* Washington, DC: American Nurses Publishing.

American Nurses Association. (2001). *Scope and standards of gerontological nursing practice* (2nd ed.). Washington, DC: American Nurses Publishing.

Association for Professionals in Infection Control and Epidemiology (2000). *APIC infection control and applied epidemiology: Principles and practices.* St. Louis, MO: Mosby.

Axton, S. E., & Hall, B. (1994). An innovative method of administering IV medications in children. *Pediatric Nursing, 20*(4), 341–344.

Banks, M. A. (1994). Home infusion of intravenous immunoglobulin. *Journal of Intravenous Nursing, 6,* 299–310.

Barber, Phil. (2002, September 27). Dirty Work: From hurried handwashing to faux fingernails, a disturbing rise in hospital-acquired infections prompts facilities to crack down. *Nurse Week: South Central Edition, 7*(19).

Beam, T. R., Goodman, E. I., Maki, D. G., Farr, B. M., & Mayhall, C. G. (1990). Preventing central venous catheter-related complications, a roundtable discussion. *Infections in Surgery, 10,* 1–13.

Behrman, R. E., Kliegman, R., & Jenson, H. B. (Eds.). (2001). *Nelson Textbook of Pediatrics* (16th ed.). Philadelphia: W. B. Saunders.

Bennett, J., & Brachman, P. S. (Eds.). (1998). *Hospital infections* (4th ed.). Philadelphia: Lippincott Williams & Wilkins.

Berger, T. G., James, W. D., & Odom, R. B. (2000). *Andrew's Diseases of the Skin* (9th ed.). Philadelphia: W. B. Saunders.

Bernard, G. R., Vincent, J.-L., Laterre, P.-F., LaRosa, S. P., Dhainaut, J.-F., Lopez-Rodriguez, A., et al., for The Recombinant Human Activated Protein C Worldwide Evaluation in Severe Sepsis (PROWESS) Study Group (2001, March 8). Efficacy and safety of recombinant human activated protein C for severe sepsis. *The New England Journal of Medicine.*

Brunner, L. S. (2001). *Lippincott manual of nursing practice* (7th ed.). Philadelphia: Lippincott Williams & Wilkins.

Burggraf, Virginia (2001). What the future holds for gerontology. *Nursing, 31*(1), 52.

California Department of Health Sciences. (2002, January 24). *SHARPS Injury Control Program.* Retrieved April 7, 2003, from http://www.dhs.ca.gov/ohb/sharps/default.htm

Carlson, R. D. (1992, January). Antiseptic-releasing catheter reduces infections: An interview with Dennis Maki, M.D. *Oncology Times, 14,* 1.

Carpenito, L. J. (2002). *Handbook of nursing diagnosis* (9th ed.). Philadelphia: Lippincott Williams & Wilkins.

Carrico, R.M. (2001). What to do if you're exposed to a bloodborne pathogen. *Home Healthcare Nurse, 19*(6), 362–368.

Carrieri, V. K., Lindsey, A. M., & West, E. M. (2003, March). *Pathophysiological phenomena in nursing: Human responses to illness* (3rd ed.). Philadelphia: W. B. Saunders.

Centers for Disease Control and Prevention (CDC). (1988). Update: Universal precautions for prevention and transmission of human immunodeficiency virus, hepatitis B virus, and other blood-borne pathogens in health care settings. *Morbidity and Mortality Weekly Report, 37*(24), 377–388.

Centers for Disease Control and Prevention (CDC). (1995a). A case-control study of HIV seroconversion in health care workers after percutaneous exposure to HIV-infected blood—France, United Kingdom, and United States, January 1988–August 1994. *Morbidity and Mortality Weekly Report, 44,* 929–933.

Centers for Disease Control and Prevention (CDC). (1995b). *HIV/AIDS Surveillance Report, 1,* 15.

Centers for Disease Control and Prevention (CDC). (1995c). Intravascular device-related infections prevention: Guideline availability notice. *Fed. Reg., Part II, 60*(187), 49978–50006.

Centers for Disease Control and Prevention (CDC). (1995d, September 22). Recommendations for preventing the spread of vancomycin resistance: Recommendations of the Hospital Infection Control Practices Advisory Committee (HICPAC). *Morbidity and Mortality Weekly Report, 44*(RR-12), 1–13. Retrieved April 7, 2003, from http://www.cdc.gov/mmwr/PDF/RR/RR4412.pdf

Centers for Disease Control and Prevention (CDC). (1996, June 7). Update: Provisional public health service recommendations for chemoprophylaxis after occupational exposure to HIV. *Morbidity and Mortality Weekly Report, 45*(22), 468–472. Retrieved April 7, 2003 from http://www.cdc.gov/mmwr/PDF/wk/mm4522.pdf

Centers for Disease Control and Prevention (CDC). (1997, December 26). Immunization of health-care workers: Recommendations of the Advisory Committee on Immunization Practices (ACIP) and the Hospital Infection Control Practices Advisory Committee (HICPAC). *Morbidity and Mortality Weekly Report, 46*(RR-18), 1–42. Retrieved April 7, 2003, from http://www.cdc.gov/epo/mmwr/preview/mmwrhtml/00050577.htm

Centers for Disease Control and Prevention (CDC). (1998a, May 15). *Appendix: First-Line Drugs for HIV Postexposure Prophylaxis (PEP).* Retrieved April 7, 2003 from http://www.cdc.gov/epo/mmwr/preview/mmwrhtml/00052801.htm

Centers for Disease Control and Prevention (CDC). (1998b). *Guideline for infection control in health care personnel, 1998.* Retrieved April 7, 2003 from http://www.cdc.gov/ncidod/hip/GUIDE/InfectControl98.pdf

Centers for Disease Control and Prevention (CDC). (1998c, May 15). *Public Health Service Guidelines for the Management of Health-Care Worker Exposures to HIV and Recommendations for Postexposure Prophylaxis.* Retrieved April 7, 2003 from http://www.cdc.gov/epo/mmwr/preview/mmwrhtml/00052722.htm

Centers for Disease Control and Prevention (CDC). (1998d, October 16). *Recommendations for Prevention and Control of Hepatitis C Virus (HCV) Infection and HCV-Related Chronic Disease.* Retrieved April 7, 2003 from http://www.cdc.gov/epo/mmwr/preview/mmwrhtml/00055154.htm

Centers for Disease Control and Prevention (CDC). (1998e). *Recommendations for prevention of infections in health care personnel.* Atlanta, GA: Centers for Disease Control and Prevention, The Hospital Infection Control Advisory Committee.

Centers for Disease Control and Prevention (CDC). (2001a). *Guideline for the Prevention of Intravascular Device-Related Infections.* Atlanta, GA: Author.

Centers for Disease Control and Prevention (CDC). (2001b). Recommendations for preventing transmission of infections among chronic hemodialysis patients. *Morbidity and Mortality Weekly Report 50*(RR-5), 1–43.

Centers for Disease Control and Prevention (CDC). (2001c, October 12). Deaths: Leading causes for 1999. *National Vital Stat Rep 49*(11):1–87. (DHHS Publication No.(PHS)2002 –1120 PRS 01-0594 (10/2001)). Retrieved April 7, 2003, from http://www.cdc.gov/nchs/data/nvsr/nvsr49/nvsr49_11.pdf

Centers for Disease Control and Prevention (CDC). (2001d). Updated U.S. public health service guidelines for the management of occupational exposures to HBV, HCV, and HIV and recommendations for postexposure prophylaxis. *Morbidity and Mortality Weekly Report 50*(RR-11):1–52. Retrieved April 7, 2003, from http://www.cdc.gov/mmwr/PDF/rr/rr5011.pdf

Centers for Disease Control and Prevention (CDC). (2002a, August 9). Guidelines for the prevention of intravascular catheter-related infections. *Morbidity and Mortality Weekly Report 51*(RR-10), 1–26.

Centers for Disease Control and Prevention (CDC). (2002b). Guidelines for the use of antiretroviral agents in HIV-infected adults and adolescents. *Morbidity and Mortality Weekly Report 51*(RR-7), 1–55.

Centers for Disease Control and Prevention (CDC). (2002c, October 25). Guidelines for hand hygiene in health-care settings: Recommendations of the Healthcare Infections Control Practices Advisory Committee and the HICPAC/SHEA/APIC/IDSA Hand Hygiene Task Force. *Morbidity and Mortality Weekly Report 51*(RR-16).

Centers for Disease Control and Prevention (CDC). (2003a). CDC prevention guidelines database. Retrieved April 7, 2003, from http://aepo-xdv-www.epo.cdc.gov/wonder/PrevGuid/PrevGuid.shtml

Centers for Disease Control and Prevention (CDC). (2003b). *Morbidity and Mortality Weekly Report (MMWR) home page*. Retrieved April 7, 2003, from http://www2.cdc.gov/mmwr/mmwr.html

Chaisson, R. E., Keruly, J. C., & Moore, R. D. (1995). Race, sex, drug use, and progression of human immunodeficiency virus disease. *New England Journal of Medicine, 333*(12), 751–756.

Chamberland, M. E. & Bell, D. M. (1992). HIV transmission from health care worker to patient. What is the risk? (Editorial). *Annals of Internal Medicine, 116,* 871–873.

Chamberland, M. E., Epstein, J., Dodd, R. Y., Persing, D., Will, R. G., DeMaria, A., Jr., et al. (1998). Blood safety. *Emerging Infectious Diseases, 4*(3).

Chiarello, L., Cardo, D.M., Panlilio, A.L., Alter, M.J., & Gerberding, J. (2001). Risks and prevention of blood-borne virus transmission from infected healthcare providers. *Seminars in Infection Control, 1*(1): 61–72.

Clinical. (2000). Giving up before surgery? *Nursing, 30*(7): 64.

Combating Infection (2001). Handwashing: First defense against infection. *Nursing, 31*(9): 20.

Combating Infection (2001). Handwashing: First defense against infection. *Nursing, 31*(10): 30.

Corbbett, J. V. (2000). *Laboratory tests & diagnostic procedures with nursing diagnoses* (5th ed.). Upper Saddle River, NJ: Prentice Hall.

Craven, R. F., & Hirnie, C. J. (2002). *Fundamentals of nursing: Human health & function* (4th ed.). Philadelphia: Lippincott Williams & Wilkins.

Crismon, C. (1992). Errors in subclavian administration of P.O. meds continue. *R.N. Update, 23*(3), 4.

Cunha, B. A. (2002). *Antibiotic Essentials.* Royal Oak, Michigan: Physicians' Press.

Curley, M. A. Q. & Moloney-Harmon, P. A. (2001). *Critical care nursing of infants and children* (2nd ed.). Philadelphia: Elsevier Health Sciences.

Daniels, J. M., & Smith, L. M. (1998). *Clinical calculations: A unified approach* (4th ed.). Albany, NY: Delmar Learning.

Decreases Seen in Leading Causes of Death. (2001, June 26). United Press International, on NewsMax.com.

DeCrosta, T. (1986a). Every patient is a target. Part I: The problem. *Nursing Life, 5,* 18–22.

DeCrosta, T. (1986b). Every patient is a target. Part II: Fighting the problem. *Nursing Life, 6,* 45–47.

DR Intravenous Therapy Consulting, Inc. (2003, February 15). *DR Intravenous Therapy Consulting home page*. Retrieved April 7, 2003, from www.drivt.com

Drinker, C. K., Drinker, K. R., & Lund, C. C. (1992). The circulation in the mammalian bone marrow. *American Journal of Physiology, 62*(1), 1–92.

Dudek, S. G. (2001). *Nutrition essentials for nursing practice* (4th ed.). Philadelphia: Lippincott Williams & Wilkins.

Ebersole, P., & Hess, P. (1998). *Toward healthy aging: Human needs and nursing response* (5th ed.). St. Louis, MO: Mosby.

Edlich, R. F., & Watkins, F. H. (1997). Glove powder—Facts and fiction. In *Surgical services management*. Denver, CO: Association of Operating Room Nurses.

Ehrlich, A. (2000). *Medical terminology for health professions* (4th ed.). Albany, NY: Delmar Learning.

Erbelding, E. J. (1999, May). Resistance testing: A primer for clinicians. *The Hopkins HIV Report, 11*(3), 1, 8, 9.

Ernst, J. (2001). Guide to needlestick prevention devices: Is your phlebotomy technique putting you at risk? *Home Healthcare Nurse, 19*(6): 345–347.

Estes, M. E. Z. (2002). Health assessment and physical examination (2nd ed.). Clifton Park, NY: Delmar Thomson Learning.

Evans, C. A., Kenny, P. J., & Rizzuto, C. (1993). Caring for the confused geriatric surgical patient. *Geriatric Nursing, 14*(5), 237–241.

Farber, T. M. (1991, September 29 – October 2). *ARROWgard™ antiseptic surface—Toxicology review.* Paper presented at the 31st Interscience Conference on Antimicrobial Agents & Chemotherapeutic Agents.

Fitzpatrick, L. (2002). When to administer modified blood products. *Nursing, 32*(5): 36–42.

Fong, E., & Scott, A. (2004). *Body structures and functions* (10th ed.). Clifton Park, NY: Delmar Learning.

Fraser, D. (1993). Patient assessment: Infection in the elderly. *Journal of Gerontological Nursing,19*(7), 5–11.

Friedman, G., Silva, E., & Vincent J.-L. (1998) Has the mortality of septic shock changed with time? *Crit Care Med., 26,* 2078–2086.

Friedman, M. M. (2001). The impact of the Needlestick Safety and Prevention Act on home care and hospice organizations. *Home Healthcare Nurse, 19*(6): 356–360.

Friend, T. (1997, January 22). Hospital's drug errors cost lives, drain resources. *USA Today,* p. D1.

Gahart, B. L. & Nazareno, A. R. (2003) *Intravenous Medications* (19th ed.). St. Louis, MO: Mosby.

Gaynes, R., Richards, C., Edwards, J., Emori, T. G., Horan, T., Alonso-Echanove, J., et al. (2001). Feeding back surveillance data to prevent hospital-acquired infections. *Emerging Infectious Diseases, 7*(2).

Gelb, L. (1991). *Food and Drug Administration medical alert*. Rockville, MD: U.S. Department of Health and Human Services.

Genentech. (2002). *Genentech products—disease education—central venous access devices*. Retrieved October 2, 2002 from www.gene.com/gene/products/education/cardiovascular/cvads.jsp

Gianino, S., Seltzer, R., & Eisenberg, P. (1996). The ABCs of TPN. *RN, 59*(2), 42–47.

Goodwin, D. (1992). Critical pathways in home health care. *Nursing Administration Quarterly, 22*(2), 35–40.

Gorbach, S. L., Mensa, J., & Gatell, J. M. (1999). *Pocket book of antimicrobial therapy & prevention*. Baltimore: Williams & Wilkins.

Guyton, A. C., & Hall, J. C. (1997). *Human physiology and mechanisms of disease* (6th ed.). Philadelphia: W. B. Saunders.

Guyton, A. C., & Hall, J.C. (2000). *Textbook of medical physiology* (10th ed.). Philadelphia: W. B. Saunders.

Hadaway, L. C. (2000a). IV rounds: Flushing to reduce central catheter occlusions. *Nursing, 30*(10), 74.

Hadaway, L. C. (2000b). IV rounds: Managing vascular access device occlusions, part 1. *Nursing, 30*(7), 29.

Hadaway, L. C. (2000c). IV rounds: Managing vascular access device occlusions, part 2. *Nursing, 30*(8), 14.

Hadaway, L. C. (2002). What you can do to decrease catheter-related infections. *Nursing, 32*(9), 46–48.

Haiduven, D. J., DeMaio, T. M., & Stevens, D. A. (1992). A five-year study of needlestick injuries: Significant reduction associated with communication, education, and convenient placement of sharps containers. *Infection Control and Hospital Epidemiology, 13*(5), 265–271.

Halderman, Francie. (2000). Selecting a vascular access device. *Nursing, 30*(11), 59–61.

Hall, J. K. (2002). *Law and Ethics for Clinicians*. Philadelphia: Jackhal.

Haney, Daniel Q. (2002, September 29). Alcohol gels speed hospital scrubbing. *Associated Press,* as reported in *The El Paso Times,* p. 7A.

Hawkins, D. A., Asboe, D., Barlow, K., Evans, B. (2001). Seroconversion to HIV-1 following a needlestick injury despite combination post-exposure prophylaxis. *Journal of Infection, 43*(1), 12–15.

Hazinski, M. F. (1992). *Nursing care of the critically ill child* (2nd ed.). St. Louis, MO: Mosby.

Henderson, D. K. (2001). HIV postexposure prophylaxis in the 21st century. *Emerging Infectious Diseases, 7*(2), 254–258.

Herbst, S. F. (1993). Accumulation of blood products and drug precipitates in VADs: A set-up for trouble. *Journal of Vascular Access Network, 3*(3), 9–13.

Hibberd, P. L. (1995). Patients, needles, and health care workers. *Journal of Intravenous Nursing, 18*(2), 65–76.

Hogstel, M. O. (2001). *Gerontology: Nursing Care of the Older Adult*. Clifton Park, NY: Delmar Learning.

Hospital Nursing Newsline. (2001). T-PA clears clogged catheters too. *Nursing, 31*(5), 32–38.

Hrouda, B. S. (2002). Warming up to IV infusion. *Nursing, 32*(3), 54–55.

Hunt, M. L. (1995). *Baxter training manual for intravenous admixture personnel* (5th ed.). Chicago: Precept Press.

Infusion Nurses Society. (2000). Infusion nursing standards of practice. *Journal of Intravenous Nursing* (Supplement). Note: This journal is now the *Journal of Infusion Nursing*.

INSERT Intravenous Access Network. (2003). *INSERT Intravenous Access Network home page*. Retrieved April 7, 2003, from www.ivteam.com

Institute of Medicine. (1999). *To err is human*. Washington: National Academy Press.

International Agency for Research on Cancer (IARC). (2000, February 28). *DEHP confirmed as non-carcinogenic: International Agency for Research on Cancer (IARC) reclassifies DEHP as non-carcinogenic to humans* [Press Release]. Brussels, Belgium: European Council for Plasticisers and Intermediates (ECPI). Retrieved April 7, 2003, from http://www.ecpi.org/pressrelease/current/index.asp

International Health Care Worker Safety Center, University of Virginia. (2001, April 18). *Safety devices*. Retrieved April 7, 2003, from http://www.people.virginia.edu/~epinet/products.html

Intravenous Nurses Society. (1998). Revised intravenous standards of practice. *Journal of Intravenous Nursing* (Supplement).

Intravenous therapy: The right stuff. (1994). Infection-control/Update 94. *Nursing, 24*(10), 54.

Iyer, P. W. (1991). Thirteen charting rules to keep you legally safe. *Nursing, 21*(6), 40–45.

Jackson, D. (1995). Latex allergy and anaphylaxis—What to do? *Journal of Intravenous Nursing, 18*(1), 33–52.

Jacobson, G. (1985). Handwashing, ring-wearing, and number of organisms. *Nursing Research, 34,* 186–187.

Jagger, J., and Perry, J. (2001a). Risky phlebotomy with a syringe. *Nursing, 31*(2), 73.

Jagger, J., and Perry, J. (2001b). Exposure prevention, point by point. *Nursing, 31*(6), 12–15.

Jagger, J., and Perry, J. (2001c). Beware of glass capillary tubes. *Nursing, 31*(11), 92.

Jagger, J., and Perry, J. (2002). Exposure safety: Realistic expectations for safety devices. *Nursing, 32*(3), 72.

Jagger, J., Hunt, E. H., Brand-Elnaggar, J., & Pearson, R. D. (1988). Rates of needlestick injury caused by various devices in a university hospital. *New England Journal of Medicine, 319*(5), 284–288.

James, L., & Hadaway, L. C. (1993). A retrospective look at tip location and complications of peripherally inserted central catheter lines. *Journal of Intravenous Nursing, 16*(2), 104–109.

Jezierski, M. (1997). Creating a latex-safe environment: Riddle Memorial Hospital's response to protect patients and employees. *Journal of Emergency Nursing, 23,* 191–198.

Johnson, M. (1998). *Working on a miracle.* New York: Bantam Doubleday Dell.

Joint Commission on Accreditation of Healthcare Organizations. (2002). *Comprehensive accreditation manual for hospitals: The official handbook.* Chicago: Author.

Kallenborn, J. C., Price, T. G., Carrico, R., & Davidson, A. B. (2001). Emergency department management of occupational exposures: Cost analysis of rapid HIV test. *Infection Control and Hospital Epidemiology, 22*(5), 289-293.

Kaunitz, K. K. (1996). Legal issues. In *APIC infection control and applied epidemiology: Principles and practice.* St. Louis, MO: Mosby.

Kee, J. L., & Paulanka, B. J. (2004). *Fluids and electrolytes with clinical applications: A programmed approach* (7th ed.). Clifton Park, NY: Delmar Learning.

Kelly, L. Y., & Joel, L. A. (1999). *Dimensions of professional nursing* (8th ed.). New York: McGraw-Hill.

Kenny, P. (1996). Managing HIV infection: How to bolster your patient's fragile health. *Nursing, 26*(8), 26–35.

Kite, P. (1999, October 30). Rapid Diagnosis of Central-Venous-Catheter-Related Bloodstream Infection without Catheter Removal. *Lancet.*

Kozier, B., Erb, G., & Olivieri, R. (1999). *Fundamentals of nursing: Concepts, process, and practice* (6th ed.). Redwood City, CA: Prentice Hall.

Larsen, E. A. (1988). APIC guidelines for infection control practice: Guideline for use of topical antimicrobial agents. *American Journal of Infection Control, 16*(6), 253–266.

Larson, E. L. (1996). Handwashing and skin preparation for invasive procedures. In *APIC infection control and applied epidemiology: Principles and practice.* St. Louis, MO: Mosby.

Lauer, G.M., & Walker, B.D. (2001). Hepatitis C virus infection. *New England Journal of Medcine, 345*(1), 41–52.

Lawson, M. (1991). Partial occlusion of indwelling central venous catheters. *Journal of Intravenous Nursing, 14*(3), 157–159.

Leddy, S., & Pepper, J. M. (1998). *Conceptual bases of professional nursing* (4th ed.). Philadelphia: Lippincott Williams & Wilkins.

LeMone, P. and Burke, K. M. (2000). *Medical-surgical nursing: Critical thinking in client care.* Upper Saddle River, NJ: Prentice Hall Health.

Lenox, A. C. (1990). IV therapy: Reducing the risk of infection. *Nursing, 20*(3), 60–61.

Levi, M, & ten Cate H. Disseminated intravascular coagulation. *New England Journal of Medcine, 341*(8), 586-592.

Linde-Zwirble W. T., Angus D. C., & Carcillo J. Age-specific incidence and outcome of sepsis in the US [abstract]. Critical Care Medicine, *27,* 3.

Lindley, C. M., & Deloatch, K. H. (1993). *Infusion technology manual: A self-instructional approach.* Bethesda, MD: American Society of Hospital Pharmacists.

Litjen, T., Hawk, III, J. C., Sterling, M. L. (2001, April 9). Preventing needlestick injuries in health care settings. *Archives of Internal Medicine, 161.*

Loftis, P. A., & Glover, T. L. (1993). *Decision-making in gerontologic nursing.* St. Louis, MO: Mosby.

Maki, D. G. (1989). Infection control and hospital epidemiology. *Infection Control and Hospital Epidemiology, 10*(6), 243–247.

Maki, D. G., & Ringer, M. (1987a). Evaluation of four dressing regimens for peripheral venous catheters, including gauze, a transparent dressing, and an iodophor-impregnated transparent dressing. *Journal of the American Medical Association, 258,* 2396–2403.

Maki, D. G., Botticelli, J. T., LeRoy, M. L., & Thielke, T. S. (1987b). Prospective study of replacing administration sets for intravenous therapy at 48-hour versus 72-hour intervals: 72 hours is safe and cost-effective. *Journal of the American Medical Association, 258*(13), 1777–1781.

Maki, D. G., Cobb, L., Garman, J. K., Shapiro, J. M., Ringer, M., & Helgerson, R. B. (1988). An attachable silver-impregnated cuff for prevention of infection with central venous catheters: A prospective randomized multicenter trial. *American Journal of Medicine, 85,* 307–314.

Maki, D. G., Ringer, M., & Alvarado, C. J. (1991). Prospective randomized trial of povidone-iodone, alcohol, and chlorhexidine for prevention of infection associated with central venous and arterial catheters. *Lancet, 338,* 339–343.

Maki, D. G., Wheeler, S. J., Stoltz, S. M., & Mermel, L. A. (1991, September 30 – October 2). Clinical trial of a novel antiseptic central venous catheter. In *Program and Abstracts of the 31st Interscience Conference in Antimicrobial Agents and Chemotherapy* (Abstract # 461, p. 176).

Malloy, J. (1991). Administering intraperitoneal chemotherapy: A new approach. *Nursing, 21,* 59–61.

Management of central venous catheter occlusions: The emerging role of alteplase. (1999, October). Littleton, CO: Postgraduate Institute for Medicine, sponsored by Genentech, Inc.

Masoorli, S. (1995). Know the pitfalls of IV therapy. *Nursing Service Risk Advisor, 95,* 2.

Masoorli, S. (1996). Home IV therapy comes of age. *RN,* *59*(10), 22–26.

Masoorli, S. (1997). Consult stat: Never assume anything when a patient's IV infiltrates. *Nursing, 60*(7), 65.

Masoorli, S. (1999). Iatrogenic injuries: Air embolism. *RN, 62*(11), 32–35.

Masoorli, S., & Angeles, T. (2002). Getting a line on central vascular access devices. *Nursing, 32*(4), 36–45.

Mawyer, D, & Perry, J. (2001). One nurse's fight. *RN, 64*(4), 59–60.

Mayhall, G. C. (Ed.). (1999). *Hospital epidemiology and infection control* (2nd ed.). Philadelphia: Lippincott Williams & Wilkins.

Mazur, S. (1997). *A different method of vein stimulation.* Presented at a PICC seminar sponsored by BARD Access Systems. (Available from BARD Access Systems, 5425 West Amelia Earhart Drive, Salt Lake City, UT 84116)

McCance, K. L. & Huether, S. E. (2001). *Pathophysiology: The biologic basis for disease in adults and children* (4th ed.). St. Louis, MO: Mosby.

McCloskey, J. C., & Bulechek, G. M. (Eds.). (2000). *Nursing interventions classification (NIC)* (3rd ed.). St. Louis, MO: Mosby.

McConnell, E. A. (1986). What the experts say: Air embolism in patients with central venous catheters. *Nursing Life, 2,* 47–49.

McCormick, R. D., Meisch, M. G., Ircink, F. G., & Maki, D. G. (1991). Epidemiology of hospital sharps injuries: A 14-year prospective study in the pre-AIDS and AIDS eras. *American Journal of Medicine, 91*(Supplement 3B).

McGovern, K. (1992). Ten golden rules for administering drugs safely. *Nursing, 22*(3), 49–56.

Mears, C. (1992). PICC and MLC lines: Options worth exploring. *Nursing, 22*(10), 52–55.

Medical Educational Services, Inc., & Kellett, P. B. (1996). *How to make your medical facility latex-safe.* Knoxville, TN: Medical Educational Services, Inc.

Merchant, R. C., Keshavarz, R. (2001). Human immunodeficiency virus postexposure prophylaxis for adolescents and children. *Pediatrics, 108*(2), E38.

Mermel, L. A. (2000, March 7). Prevention of intravascular catheter-related infectioins. *Annals of Internal Medicine, 132,* 391–402.

Mermel, L. A., Farr, B. M., Sherertz, R. J., Raad, I. I., O'Grady, N., Harris, J. S., & Craven, D. E. (2001, April). Guidelines for the management of intravascular catheter-related infections. *Infection Control and Hospital Epidemiology (Special Report), 22*(4).

Messner, R. L., & Pinkerman, M. L. (1992). Preventing peripheral IV infection. *Nursing, 22*(6), 34–41.

Metheny, N. M. (2000). *Fluid and electrolyte balance: Nursing considerations* (4th ed.). Philadelphia: Lippincott-Raven.

Millam, D. A. (1988). Managing complications of IV therapy. *Nursing, 18*(3), 34–42.

Millam, D. A. (1992). Starting IVs: How to develop your expertise. *Nursing, 22,* 33–48.

Millam, D. A., & Boutotte, J. (1993). Infection control update. *Nursing, 23*(10), 61–68.

Mirrop, M. (1992). *Intravenous catheterization: A guide to proper insertion techniques.* Tampa, FL: Critikon.

Moolenaar, R. L., Crutcher, J. M., San Joaquin, V. H., & Sewell, L. V. (2000). A prolonged outbreak of Pseudomonas aeruginosa in a neonatal intensive care unit: Did staff fingernails play a role in disease transmission? *Infection Control and Hospital Epidemiology, 21,* 80–85.

Moore, Kathleen. (1999). Consult Stat: AACN guidelines contain latest on PA catheter care. *RN, 62*(12), 71.

Moulton, P. J., Wray-Langevine, J., & Boyer, C. G. (1997). Implementing clinical pathways: One agency's experience. *Home Healthcare Nurse, 15*(5), 343–354.

Moureau, Nancy. (2001). Preventing complications with vascular access devices. *Nursing, 31*(7). 52–55.

Natanson, C., Esposito, C. J., Banks, S. M. (1998). The sirens' songs of confirmatory sepsis trials: Selection bias and sampling error. *Critical Care Medicine, 26,* 1927–1931.

National Alliance for Infusion Therapy. (1992). Home infusion fact sheet. *Journal of Nursing Administration, 22,* 8.

National Association for Home Care. (1999). *Basic statistics about home care.* Washington, DC: Author.

National Center for Chronic Disease Prevention and Health Promotion. (2002). *Healthy aging 2000.* Atlanta: Centers for Disease Control and Prevention.

National Center on Health Statistics. (2002). *Older Americans 2000: Key indicators of well-being.* Bethesda, MD: U. S. Department of Health and Human Services, National Institutes of Health.

National Institute for Occupational Safety and Health (NIOSH). (1997, June). *Preventing Allergic Reactions to Natural Rubber Latex in the Workplace* [DHHS (NIOSH) Publication No. 97-135]. Retrieved April 7, 2003, from http://www.cdc.gov/niosh/latexalt.html

National Institute for Occupational Safety and Health (NIOSH). (1998, January). *Selecting, Evaluating, and Using Sharps Disposal Containers* [DHHS (NIOSH) Publication No. 97-111]. Retrieved April 7, 2003, from http://www.cdc.gov/niosh/sharps1.html

Needlestick Safety and Prevention Act, Pub. L. No. 106-430 (2000). Retrieved April 7, 2003, from http://thomas.loc.gov/bss/d106/d106laws.html

Nightingale, F. (1992). *Notes on nursing: What it is and what it is not.* New York: Lippincott Williams & Wilkins.

North American Nursing Diagnosis Association (2001). *NANDA nursing diagnoses: Definitions and classification 1995–1996.* Philadelphia: Author.

A nurse with a mission: Lynda Arnold. (1996). *Advances in Exposure Prevention, 2*(2), 1, 10–11.

Nurses Service Organization. (1992). Q & As. *Nurses Service Organization Risk Advisor*. (Available from Nurses Service Organization, 159 E. County Line Road, Hatboro, PA 19040)

Occupational Safety & Health Administration (OSHA). (2001, November 27). *Enforcement procedures for the occupational exposure to blood borne pathogens, standard number: 1910.1030* [OSHA Instruction CPL 2-2.69]. Washington, D.C.: Author.

Occupational Safety & Health Administration (OSHA). (2002, August 26). *Safety and Health Topics: Latex Allergy*. Washington, D.C.: Author.

Occupational Safety and Health Administration (OSHA). (1999, February 22). *Glass capillary tubes: Joint safety advisory about potential risks.* Retrieved April 7, 2003, from http://www.osha.gov/pls/oshaweb/owadisp.show_document?p_table=INTERPRETATIONS&p_id=22695

Occupational Safety and Health Administration (OSHA). (2003, March 19). *Safety and health topics: Needlestick prevention*. Retrieved April 7, 2003, from http://www.osha-slc.gov/SLTC/needlestick/index.html

Opal, S. M. & Cohen, J. (1999). Clinical gram-positive sepsis: Does it fundamentally differ from gram-negative bacterial sepsis? *Critical Care Medicine, 27,* 1608–1616.

Otto, S. E. (1995). Advanced concepts in chemotherapy drug delivery. *Journal of Intravenous Nursing, 18*(4) 170–176.

Palmer, S., Giddens, J., & Palmer, D. (1996). *Infection control*. El Paso, TX: Skidmore-Roth Publishing, Inc.

Parry, M. F., Grant, B., Yukna, M., Adler-Klein, D., McLeod, G. X., Taddonio, R., Rosenstein, C. (2001). Candida Osteomyelitis and Diskitis after Spinal Surgery: An outbreak that Implicates Artificial Nail Use. *Clinical Infectious Diseases, 32*(3), 352–357.

Peck, K. R., & Altieri, M. (1988). Intraosseous infusions: An old technique with modern applications. *Pediatric Nursing, 14*(4), 296–298.

Pennsylvania Medical Society Center for Professional Drug Education. (2002, February 10). *Drug Alert! Streptase is not indicated for restoration of patency of intravenous catheters*. Retrieved April 7, 2003, from http://www.counterdetails.org/alert.html

Perry, J. (2001a). Attention All Nurses! *American Journal of Nursing, 101*(9), 24AA–24CC.

Perry, J. (2001b). The Bloodborne Pathogens Standard, 2001. *Nursing, 31*(6), 16.

Perry, J. (2001c). The Bloodborne Pathogens Standard, 2001: What's changed? *Nursing Management, 32*(6), 25–26.

Perry, J., Parker, G., & Jagger, J. (2001). Percutaneous injuries in home healthcare settings. *Home Healthcare Nurse, 19*(6), 342–344.

Perry, J. (2001d). The Bloodborne Pathogens Standard, 2001: What's changed. *Dimensions of Critical Care Nursing, 20*(5), 44–45.

Perry, J. (2001e). When home is where the risk is. *Home Healthcare Nurse, 19*(6), 338–341.

Petsonk, E. L. (1997). Nurses should take action to avoid occupational latex allergy. *Journal of Emergency Nursing, 23*(2), 91.

Phifer, T. J., Bridges, M., & Conrad, S. A. (1991). The residual central venous catheter track—An occult source of lethal air embolism: Case report. *Journal of Intravenous Nursing, 31,* 1558–1560.

Phipps, W. J., Long, B. C., Woods, N. W., & Cassmeyer, V. L. (2003). *Medical-surgical nursing: Concepts and clinical practice* (7th ed.). St. Louis, MO: Mosby.

Pickar, G. D. (1999). *Dosage calculations* (6th ed.). Albany, NY: Delmar.

Potts, N. (2002). Pediatric nursing: Caring for children and their families. Clifton Park, NY: Delmar Thomson Learning.

Pozzar, G. D. (2002). *Legal aspects of health care administration* (8th ed.). Gaithersburg, MD: Aspen.

Pugliese, G., Germanson, T. P., Bartley, J., Luca, J., Lamerato, L., & Cox, J. (2001). Evaluating sharps safety devices: Meeting OSHA's intent. *Infection Control & Hospital Epidemiology, 22*(7), 456–458.

Pugliese, G., & Salahuddin, M. (Eds.). (1999) Sharps injury prevention program: A step-by-sep guide. Chicago: American Hospital Association..

Rangel-Frausto, M. S., Pittet, D., & Costigan, M. (1995). The natural history of the systemic inflammatory response syndrome (SIRS): A prospective study. *Journal of the American Medical Association, 273,* 117–123.

Rathbun, J. (1996). A plague upon our houses. *Columns, The University of Washington Alumni Magazine, 16*(2), 14–17.

Reddy, Sumana. (1998, January 1). Latex allergy. *American Family Physician*.

Reiss, B. S., & Evans, M. E. (2002). *Pharmacological aspects of nursing care* (6th ed.). Albany, NY: Delmar.

Reiss, P. (1996). Battling the superbugs. *RN, 59*(3), 36–40.

Rhinehart, Emily. (2002). Infection control in home care. *Emerging Infectious Diseases, 7*(2).

Rice, J., & Skelley, E. G. (2001). *Medications and mathematics for the nurse* (9th ed.). Albany, NY: Delmar.

RN News Watch Clinical Highlights. (1999). Autologous blood donation isn't crucial anymore. *RN, 62*(4), 18–19.

Robertson, K. J. (1995). The role of the IV specialist in health care reform. *Journal of Intravenous Nursing, 18*(3), 130–144.

Sadovsky, R. (2000, August 15). Preventing Intravascular Catheter-Related Infections. *American Family Physician*.

Sandford, J. P., Gilbert, D. N., & Sande, M. A. (2002). *Guide to antimicrobial therapy* (32nd ed.). Dallas, TX: Antimicrobial Therapy, Inc.

Sands, K. E, Bates, D. W., & Lanken, P. N. (1997). Epidemiology of sepsis syndrome in 8 academic medical centers. *Journal of the American Medical Association, 278,* 234–240.

Sansivero, G. E. (1995). Why a PICC? What you need to know. *Nursing, 18*(3), 34–42.

Sapolsky, R. M. (1992). Stress and neuroendocrine changes during aging. *Generations, 16*(4), 35–38.

Scher, R. K. & Daniel, C.R. (1990). *Nails: therapy, diagnosis, surgery* (pp. 220–222). Philadelphia: W. B. Saunders.

Scott, B. D. (1996). *Techniques of regional anesthesia.* Norwalk, CT: Appleton & Lange/Mediglobe.

Spratto, G. R., & Woods, A. L. (2003). *PDR nurse's drug handbook.* Clifton Park, NY: Delmar Learning.

Springhouse Corporation. (2001a). *Clinical laboratory tests: Values & implications* (3rd ed.). Springhouse, PA: Author.

Springhouse Corporation. (2001b). *Professional guide to diseases* (7th ed.). Springhouse, PA: Author.

Springhouse Corporation. (2002). *Illustrated manual of nursing practice.* Springhouse, PA: Author.

St. Marie, B. (1994). *Management of cancer pain with epidural morphine independent study module.* St. Paul, MN: Sims Deltec, Inc. and Wyeth-Ayerst Laboratories.

Stedman's medical dictionary (27th ed.). (2000). Baltimore: Williams & Wilkins.

Stone, S. (1999). *Clinical gerontological nursing* (2nd ed.). Philadelphia: W. B. Saunders.

Swearingen, P. (2002). *Medical-surgical nursing diagnosis & interventions* (5th ed.). St. Louis, MO: Mosby.

Taber's Cyclopedic Medical Dictionary (19th ed.). (2001). Philadelphia: F.A. Davis Company.

Tappen, R. M., & Beckerman, A. (1993). A vulnerable population: Multiproblem older adults in acute care. *Journal of Gerontological Nursing, 19*(11), 38–42.

Thielen, J. B. (1996). Air emboli: A potentially lethal complication of central venous lines. *Focus on Critical Care, 17*(5), 374–383.

Thielen, J. B., & Nyquist, J. (1992). Subclavian catheter removal. *Journal of Intravenous Nursing, 14,* 114–118.

Townsend, Carolynn E. & Roth, R. (2002). *Nutrition & diet therapy* (8th ed). Clifton Park, NY: Delmar Learning.

Training for Development of Innovative Control Technologies (TDICT) Project. (n.d.) *Safety feature evaluation forms.* Retrieved April 7, 2003, from http://www.tdict.org/criteria.html

Ulrich, S. P., Canale, S. W., & Wendell, S. A. (2001). *Nursing care planning guides: A nursing diagnosis approach* (5th ed.). Philadelphia: W. B. Saunders.

U.S. Bureau of the Census. (2000, January 13). *Current population reports: Projections of the total resident population by 5 year age groups, race, and hispanic origin with special age categories: middle series, 1999 to 2000.* Washington, D.C.: Author.

U.S. Bureau of the Census (2002). *A profile of older americans: 2001.* Washington, D.C.: U.S. Administration on Aging.

U.S. Department of Health and Human Services (DHHS). (1990). *Transfusion therapy guidelines for nurses* [NIH Pub. No. 90-2668]. Bethesda, MD: National Institutes of Health.

U.S. Department of Health and Human Services (DHHS). (1991). *Transfusion alert: Use of autologous blood* [NIH Pub. No. 91-3038]. Bethesda, MD: National Institutes of Health.

U.S. Department of Health and Human Services (DHHS). (2001, January 18). *New needlestick rule: Occupational exposure to bloodborne pathogens; needlestick and other sharps injuries; final rule* [Federal Register# 66:5317-5325]. Atlanta, GA: Centers for Disease Control and Prevention.

U.S. Department of Veterans Affairs (VA). (2002, February 8). *Safety sharp device contracts.* Retrieved April 7, 2003, from http://www.va.gov/vasafety/page.cfm?pg=542

U.S. Food and Drug Administration (FDA). (1999a, January 25). *Important drug warning: Safety information regarding the use of Abbokinase (Urokinase).* Rockville, MD: Public Health Service.

U.S. Food and Drug Administration (FDA). (1999b, March 25). *Statement on latex allergies by Elizabeth D. Jacobson, Ph.D., Acting Director, Center for Devices and Radiological Health before the House Committee on Education and the Workforce, Subcommittee on Oversight and Investigations.* Rockville, MD: U.S. Department of Health and Human Services.

U.S. Food and Drug Administration (FDA). (2002a, February). *Keeping blood transfusions safe: FDA's Multi-layered protections for donated blood* [Publication No. FS 02-1]. Rockville, MD: U.S. Department of Health and Human Services.

U.S. Food and Drug Administration (FDA). (2002b, July 12). *Public Health Notification: PVC Devices Containing the Plasticizer DEHP.* Rockville, MD: U.S. Department of Health and Human Services.

U.S. Food and Drug Administration (FDA). (2003) *Safety alerts, public health advisories and notices from CDRH.* Retrieved April 7, 2003, from http://www.fda.gov/cdrh/safety.html

U.S. General Accounting Office. (2000, November 17). *Occupational safety: Selected cost and benefit implications of needlestick prevention devices for hospitals* [DCGAO-01-60R,: pp. 1–18]. Washington, DC: Author.

Veal, D. F., Altman, C. E., McKinnon, B. T., & Fillingim, O. (1995). Evaluation of flow rates for six disposable infusion devices. *American Journal of Health-System Pharmacists, 52,* 500–504.

Vervloet, M.G., Thijs, L. G., & Hack, C. E. (1998). Derangements of coagulation and fibrinolysis in critically ill patients with sepsis and septic shock. *Seminars in Thrombotic Hemostasis, 24,* 33–44.

Viall, C. D. (1990). Your complete guide to central venous catheters. *Nursing, 2,* 34–41.

Weinstein, Robert A. (1998, July-Sept,). Nosocomial Infection Update. *Emerging Infectious Diseases, 4*(3).

Wen-Tsung, L., Chih-Chien, A., & Mong-Ling C. (2002) A nursery outbreak of Staphylococcus aureus pyoderma originating from a nurse with paronychia. *Infection Control and Hospital Epidemiology, 23,* 153–155.

Wenzel, R. P., Rinsky, M. R., Ulevitch, R. J., et al. (1996). Current understanding of sepsis. *Clinical Infectious Diseases, 22,* 407–413.

Whaley, L. F., & Wong, D. L. (2001). *Nursing care of infants and children* (6th ed.). St. Louis, MO: Mosby.

Wheeler, A. P. & Bernard, G. R. (1999). Treating patients with severe sepsis. *New England Journal of Medicine, 340,* 207–214.

White, K. M. (1997). Understanding the hemodynamics of sepsis. In *Critical care choices 1997.* Bethlehem, PA: Springhouse Corp.

Whitehouse, M. J. (1992a). Nursing assessment of the elderly patient. *Journal of Intravenous Nursing, 15* (Supplement), S14–S17.

Whitehouse, M. J. (1992b). The physiology of aging. *Journal of Intravenous Nursing, 15* (Supplement), S7–S13.

Wilkes, G. M., Burke, M. B., & Ingwersen, K. (2002). *Oncology nursing drug handbook.* Boston: Jones and Bartlett Publishers, Inc..

Wilkinson, J. M. (2002). *Nursing diagnosis handbook with NIC interventions and NOC outcomes* (7th Ed.). Upper Saddle River, NJ: Prentice Hall.

Yamamoto, A. J., Solomon, J. A., Soulen, M. C., Tang, J., Parkinson, K., & Lin, R. (2002). Sutureless securement device reduces implications of peripherally inserted central venous catheters. *Journal of Vascular and Interventional Radiology, 13,* 77–81.

Zeni, F., Freeman, B., & Natanson, C. Anti-inflammatory therapies to treat sepsis and septic shock: A reassessment. *Critical Care Medicine, 25,* 1095–1100.

Zuger, A. (1995). When microbes can't be stopped. *Healthnews, 1*(4), 4.

Appendix A Review Test A

The AAMA will highlight which test you should take.

Final Review Questions

Select the best answer.

1. Which of the following is an advantage of IV therapy?
   a. possibility of fluid overload
   b. rapid distribution of electrolytes
   c. incompatibility of medications
   d. increased possibility of sepsis
   e. increased chance of embolism

2. The major component of the human body is
   a. blood
   b. amino acids
   c. oxygen
   d. water
   e. nitrogen

3. Which of the following is the abbreviation for potassium?
   a. Po
   b. Pt
   c. Cl
   d. Ps
   e. K

4. The monosaccharide found in honey is
   a. sucrose
   b. fructose
   c. lactose
   d. galactose
   e. glucose

5. Water moving through a sieve when spaghetti is drained is an example of which of the following?
   a. osmosis
   b. passive diffusion
   c. passive transport
   d. net diffusion
   e. filtration

6. Which term refers to the physical force of water as it pushes against vessel walls or cellular membrane?
   a. osmosis pressure
   b. hydrostatic pressure
   c. hydraulic pressure
   d. blood pressure
   e. pulse pressure

7. Which term refers to the concentration of solute particles contained in a unit volume of fluid?
   a. electricity
   b. osmolarity
   c. polarity
   d. hydraulic pressure
   e. hydrostatic pressure

8. What is the process whereby the cell ingests substances that are too large to be taken in through passive or active transport systems?
   a. endocytosis
   b. pinocytosis
   c. phagocytosis
   d. exocytosis

9. The system that excretes antidiuretic hormone is
   a. renal
   b. cardiovascular
   c. nervous
   d. endocrine
   e. lymphatic

10. The pH of plasma should be
    a. 7.00–7.10
    b. 7.15–7.25
    c. 7.25–7.35
    d. 7.35–7.45
    e. 7.45–7.55

11. Potassium should have a concentration of what amount in the body?
    a. 3.0–.3.5 mEq/L
    b. 3.5–5.0 mEq/L
    c. 5.0–7.5 mEq/L
    d. 10–15 mEq/L
    e. 15–45 mEq/L

12. What is the major extracellular anion?
    a. magnesium
    b. potassium
    c. sodium
    d. calcium
    e. chloride

13. Which of the following is NOT involved in tooth development?
    a. phosphorus
    b. parathormone
    c. calcium
    d. sodium

14. Which of the following words means the "evidence of illness"?
    a. nosocomial
    b. morbidity
    c. mortality
    d. epidemiology

15. Enforcing infection control directives is the responsibility of the
    a. CDC
    b. FDA
    c. OSHA
    d. INS
    e. APIC

16. Which of the following is NOT a pain-producing substance?
    a. bradykinin
    b. histamine
    c. serotonin
    d. macrophage

17. Which of the following is seen ONLY in infiltrates which are rated "4" on the INS infiltrate scale?
    a. skin blanched
    b. cool to touch
    c. moderate to severe pain
    d. edema 1-6 inches in any direction
    e. numbness

18. Pus accumulating at an IV site usually indicates
    a. infiltration
    b. displacement
    c. occlusion
    d. phlebitis
    e. extravasation

19. Which of the following is NOT a sign of phlebitis?
    a. erythema
    b. induration
    c. increased temperature
    d. drainage
    e. coolness to touch

20. Which of the following is a sign of vessel collapse?
    a. blanching over the IV site
    b. vessel feels flat
    c. severe pain
    d. decreased infusion rate
    e. redness over site

21. Which of the following usually accounts for 1400 mL of fluid output per day?
    a. lungs
    b. skin
    c. urine
    d. feces

22. Which of the following is a hypertonic hydrating solution?
    a. dextrose 2.5%
    b. sodium chloride 0.9%
    c. dextran
    d. sodium bicarbonate 1.45%
    e. 5% dextrose in Ringer's injection

23. Which of the following is hypotonic hydrating solution?
    a. dextrose 2.5%
    b. sodium chloride 0.9%
    c. lactated Ringer's
    d. sodium bicarbonate 1.45%
    e. 5% dextrose in Ringer's injection

24. Which of the following is a volume expander?
    a. dextran
    b. sodium bicarbonate
    c. lactated Ringer's
    d. dextrose
    e. saline

25. Which of the following is NOT a sign of a hypersensitivity reaction?
    a. agitation
    b. tinnitus
    c. palpitations
    d. pallor
    e. pruritus

26. Which of the following is an advantage of IV therapy?
    a. fluid overload
    b. pain
    c. phlebitis
    d. absorption
    e. impaired mobility

27. Which artery is in the hand?
    a. metacarpal
    b. radial
    c. cephalic
    d. basilica
    e. subclavian

28. Which of the following is made of silicon?
    a. bovine graft
    b. autograft
    c. shunt
    d. arteriovenous fistula

29. Which position should the patient assume for dialysis?
    a. supine
    b. lithotomy
    c. Trendelenburg's
    d. Sims's
    e. Fowler's

30. Which of the following is a correct statement about selecting veins for IV therapy?
    a. Veins of the lower extremity are best.
    b. Use the side of the mastectomy because those veins are not accessed as much and are better.
    c. After the patient has a CVA, it is best to use the numb side because it decreases pain.
    d. Change the vein site every 72 hours.
    e. Using the veins in the hand decreases pain and increases mobility.

31. Which of the following is NOT necessary for the CMA to have to calculate an infusion rate?
    a. prescription of volume to be infused
    b. prescription of time to be infused
    c. the drop factor of the IV set

d. the name of the manufacturer of the drug
    e. the mathematical formula for calculating rate

32. If you need to infuse 85-105 mL/minute, you should use which of the following gauge needles?
    a. 16 g
    b. 24 g
    c. 22 g
    d. 20 g
    e. 18 g

33. Which of the following is a device that controls the directional flow of the infusate through manual manipulation?
    a. stopcock
    b. filter
    c. extension tubing
    d. adapter
    e. clamp

34. Which of the following is NOT necessary for a physician order?
    a. cost of prescription
    b. route of administration
    c. time of infusion
    d. amount of infusate
    e. physician signature on order

35. Which of the following will NOT promote venous access?
    a. ice
    b. fist clenching
    c. friction
    d. percussion
    e. warm compresses

36. Which of the following is the percentage of healthcare workers who are allergic to latex?
    a. 1–5 %
    b. 10–17 %
    c. 25–30 %
    d. 50–75%
    e. 75–90%

37. Which of the following is not a risk factor for allergy to latex?
    a. use of nitrile gloves
    b. female gender
    c. bladder self-catheterization
    d. history of asthma
    e. allergy to bananas

38. Where is the best location for venous access to the lower arm?

    a. 1 inch above the antecubital fossa

    b. 1 inch below the antecubital fossa

    c. 2 inches below the antecubital fossa

    d. 6 inches below the antecubital fossa

    e. on the wrist

39. Which is the best skin preparation for a porta-catheter implantation in the chest?

    a. 70% isopropyl alcohol

    b. 2% aqueous choride hexiden gluconate

    c. povidone-iodine

    d. 70% tincture of iodine

40. Which is the correct percentage for normal saline?

    a. 0.9

    b. 9

    c. 0.5

    d. 5

    e. 100

41. If a registered nurse inserts an IV catheter, who documents this in the patient record?

    a. the physician

    b. the CMA

    c. the registered nurse

    d. the administrative assistant

42. How often should an IV site be changed?

    a. every 8 hours

    b. every 12 hours

    c. every 24 hours

    d. every 72 hours

    e. once per week

43. To remember the order of intermittent IV flushing, use which of the following memory tools?

    a. SAS

    b. SASH

    c. SA

    d. SAH

    e. ASH

44. Which of the following locations NEVER use CMAs for IV therapy?

    a. dialysis clinics

    b. emergent care facilities

    c. home health

    d. emergency departments

45. The vein is irritated and the patient is complaining of a burning sensation. Which of the following is not a cause of this pain?

    a. fluid temperature

    b. infiltration

    c. phlebitis

    d. cellulitis

    e. improper securing of tape

46. Which of the following is NOT a cause of an infiltration?

    a. cannula size is incorrect

    b. the infusate is irritating

    c. the catheter is dislodged

    d. infection has begun

    e. the rate of delivery was set too high

47. Which of the following is seen only in INS grade 4 phlebitis?

    a. pus

    b. palpable venous cord

    c. streak formation

    d. pain

    e. edema

48. Which of the following is NOT a sign/symptom of thrombophlebitis?

    a. malaise

    b. edema

    c. cold skin

    d. pallor

    e. slowed infusion rate

49. Which of the following is the single most important practice to break the chain of infection?

    a. documentation

    b. change the IV site frequently

    c. using the correct size cannula

    d. handwashing

    e. impermeable dressing over site

50. If a CMA wants to know whether she is allowed to insert IVs in her facility, she should check with which of the following?

    a. AAMA

    b. AMA

    c. INS

    d. State Board of Nursing

    e. her own facility

Review Test A Answer Sheet

Name _____ Date _____

Directions:

1. Fill in only one circle using pencil representing your answer for each question.
2. Keeping your marks inside the circle, blacken the circle completely.
3. Completely erase any answer you wish to change, and make no stray marks.

Correct: Ⓐ ● Ⓒ Ⓓ Ⓔ   Wrong: ⊗ Ⓑ Ⓞ Ⓒ̸ Ⓔ̸

1 Ⓐ Ⓑ Ⓒ Ⓓ Ⓔ   26 Ⓐ Ⓑ Ⓒ Ⓓ Ⓔ
2 Ⓐ Ⓑ Ⓒ Ⓓ Ⓔ   27 Ⓐ Ⓑ Ⓒ Ⓓ Ⓔ
3 Ⓐ Ⓑ Ⓒ Ⓓ Ⓔ   28 Ⓐ Ⓑ Ⓒ Ⓓ Ⓔ
4 Ⓐ Ⓑ Ⓒ Ⓓ Ⓔ   29 Ⓐ Ⓑ Ⓒ Ⓓ Ⓔ
5 Ⓐ Ⓑ Ⓒ Ⓓ Ⓔ   30 Ⓐ Ⓑ Ⓒ Ⓓ Ⓔ
6 Ⓐ Ⓑ Ⓒ Ⓓ Ⓔ   31 Ⓐ Ⓑ Ⓒ Ⓓ Ⓔ
7 Ⓐ Ⓑ Ⓒ Ⓓ Ⓔ   32 Ⓐ Ⓑ Ⓒ Ⓓ Ⓔ
8 Ⓐ Ⓑ Ⓒ Ⓓ Ⓔ   33 Ⓐ Ⓑ Ⓒ Ⓓ Ⓔ
9 Ⓐ Ⓑ Ⓒ Ⓓ Ⓔ   34 Ⓐ Ⓑ Ⓒ Ⓓ Ⓔ
10 Ⓐ Ⓑ Ⓒ Ⓓ Ⓔ   35 Ⓐ Ⓑ Ⓒ Ⓓ Ⓔ
11 Ⓐ Ⓓ Ⓒ Ⓓ Ⓔ   36 Ⓐ Ⓑ Ⓒ Ⓓ Ⓔ
12 Ⓐ Ⓑ Ⓒ Ⓓ Ⓔ   37 Ⓐ Ⓑ Ⓒ Ⓓ Ⓔ
13 Ⓐ Ⓑ Ⓒ Ⓓ Ⓔ   38 Ⓐ Ⓑ Ⓒ Ⓓ Ⓔ
14 Ⓐ Ⓑ Ⓒ Ⓓ Ⓔ   39 Ⓐ Ⓑ Ⓒ Ⓓ Ⓔ
15 Ⓐ Ⓑ Ⓒ Ⓓ Ⓔ   40 Ⓐ Ⓑ Ⓒ Ⓓ Ⓔ
16 Ⓐ Ⓑ Ⓒ Ⓓ Ⓔ   41 Ⓐ Ⓑ Ⓒ Ⓓ Ⓔ
17 Ⓐ Ⓑ Ⓒ Ⓓ Ⓔ   42 Ⓐ Ⓑ Ⓒ Ⓓ Ⓔ
18 Ⓐ Ⓑ Ⓒ Ⓓ Ⓔ   43 Ⓐ Ⓑ Ⓒ Ⓓ Ⓔ
19 Ⓐ Ⓑ Ⓒ Ⓓ Ⓔ   44 Ⓐ Ⓑ Ⓒ Ⓓ Ⓔ
20 Ⓐ Ⓑ Ⓒ Ⓓ Ⓔ   45 Ⓐ Ⓑ Ⓒ Ⓓ Ⓔ
21 Ⓐ Ⓑ Ⓒ Ⓓ Ⓔ   46 Ⓐ Ⓑ Ⓒ Ⓓ Ⓔ
22 Ⓐ Ⓑ Ⓒ Ⓓ Ⓔ   47 Ⓐ Ⓑ Ⓒ Ⓓ Ⓔ
23 Ⓐ Ⓑ Ⓒ Ⓓ Ⓔ   48 Ⓐ Ⓑ Ⓒ Ⓓ Ⓔ
24 Ⓐ Ⓑ Ⓒ Ⓓ Ⓔ   49 Ⓐ Ⓑ Ⓒ Ⓓ Ⓔ
25 Ⓐ Ⓑ Ⓒ Ⓓ Ⓔ   50 Ⓐ Ⓑ Ⓒ Ⓓ Ⓔ

For AAMA credit, return this answer sheet to AAMA, 20 North Wacker Drive, Suite 1575, Chicago, IL 60606.

Review Test B

True/False. Write *true* if the statement is true and *false* if it is incorrect.

_____ 1. Women have a greater percentage of water in their bodies than men.

_____ 2. The newborn has a greater percentage of water than the adult in his body.

_____ 3. Extracellular fluid is found in the spaces outside the cells.

_____ 4. Solvents are substances dissolved in water.

_____ 5. Cations have a negative charge.

_____ 6. During periods of starvation, glycogen is formed from fat.

_____ 7. The molecular unit of protein is the amino acid.

_____ 8. Lipids contain carbon, hydrogen, and oxygen.

_____ 9. Filtration is the passage of water through a semipermeable membrane from an area with a lower concentration of solutes to an area with a higher concentration of solutes.

_____ 10. For a membrane to be semipermeable, it has to be more permeable to water than to solutes.

_____ 11. A solution with an osmolarity higher than another solution is hypotonic.

_____ 12. ATP stands for adenosine diphosphate.

_____ 13. The refractory period occurs when the cell membrane is not able to react to other stimulation.

_____ 14. Acids tend to have lower pH than alkaline solutions.

_____ 15. The treatment for respiratory alkalosis is antianxiety drugs.

_____ 16. The treatment for metabolic acidosis is IV chloride therapy.

_____ 17. Hypokalemia is low calcium in the blood.

_____ 18. Calcium is the most plentiful electrolyte in the body.

_____ 19. An infection that develops in a patient during a stay in a health care setting is called a nosocomial infection.

_____ 20. The most effective way to break the chain of infection is handwashing.

_____ 21. Vancomycin can cause infusion site pain.

_____ 22. Elevating the extremity after an infiltration may decrease pain.

_____ 23. It is usually best to put the IV into the patient's nondominant hand rather than the dominant hand.

_____ 24. Cannulas placed in the metacarpal veins are the most secure.

_____ 25. Slowed rate of infusion could indicate occlusion of the vein.

_____ 26. Osmolarity is the osmotic pull or pressure exerted by all particles per unit of water.

_____ 27. Skin usually excretes approximately 1200 mL of water daily.

_____ 28. Crystalloids are gelatinous substances whose particles, when submerged in a solvent, cannot form a true solution.

_____ 29. Cells in hypertonic solution shrink.

_____ 30. An antagonist is a usual response to a medication.

_____ 31. IV therapy is advantageous with the unconscious patient.

_____ 32. The cephalic vein is located in the head.

_____ 33. The lymph system usually equalizes fluid volume.

_____ 34. IVs can be placed on a nurse's order.

_____ 35. A shunt is an artificially constructed passage to divert blood flow from an artery to a vein.

_____ 36. Glass containers are no longer used.

_____ 37. The drop factor is the number of drops needed to deliver 1 mL of fluid.

_____ 38. Filters prevent retrograde solution flow.

_____ 39. Blood should be administered only through IV sets specifically designed for blood administration.

_____ 40. Lipids are always supplied in plastic containers.

_____ 41. More needlesticks occur with IV catheters than syringes.

_____ 42. A 19 gauge needle has a larger lumen than a 27 gauge needle.

_____ 43. Using alcohol on an insertion site decreases the risk of infection more than using 2% aqueous cholorhexidine gluconate.

_____ 44. Transillumination should be done in the dark.

_____ 45. Hair may be shaved before IV insertion.

_____ 46. Many patients who are allergic to shellfish are also allergic to iodine.

_____ 47. The macrodrip rate is 15 drops/mL.

_____ 48. Psychological preparation is part of the preparation of the patient receiving IV therapy.

_____ 49. If 10 minutes have elapsed since you placed the tourniquet on the site but you have not been able to draw blood, remove the tourniquet.

_____ 50. A CMA should always check with the facility for IV therapy protocols, as they vary from one facility to the next.

Review Test B Answer Sheet

Name _____ Date _____

Directions:

1. Fill in only one circle using pencil representing your answer for each question.
2. Keeping your marks inside the circle, blacken the circle completely.
3. Completely erase any answer you wish to change, and make no stray marks.

Correct: Ⓐ ● Ⓒ Ⓓ Ⓔ   Wrong: ⊗ Ⓑ Ⓞ ⊘ ⊘

1	Ⓣ Ⓕ		26	Ⓣ Ⓕ	
2	Ⓣ Ⓕ		27	Ⓣ Ⓕ	
3	Ⓣ Ⓕ		28	Ⓣ Ⓕ	
4	Ⓣ Ⓕ		29	Ⓣ Ⓕ	
5	Ⓣ Ⓕ		30	Ⓣ Ⓕ	
6	Ⓣ Ⓕ		31	Ⓣ Ⓕ	
7	Ⓣ Ⓕ		32	Ⓣ Ⓕ	
8	Ⓣ Ⓕ		33	Ⓣ Ⓕ	
9	Ⓣ Ⓕ		34	Ⓣ Ⓕ	
10	Ⓣ Ⓕ		35	Ⓣ Ⓕ	
11	Ⓣ Ⓕ		36	Ⓣ Ⓕ	
12	Ⓣ Ⓕ		37	Ⓣ Ⓕ	
13	Ⓣ Ⓕ		38	Ⓣ Ⓕ	
14	Ⓣ Ⓕ		39	Ⓣ Ⓕ	
15	Ⓣ Ⓕ		40	Ⓣ Ⓕ	
16	Ⓣ Ⓕ		41	Ⓣ Ⓕ	
17	Ⓣ Ⓕ		42	Ⓣ Ⓕ	
18	Ⓣ Ⓕ		43	Ⓣ Ⓕ	
19	Ⓣ Ⓕ		44	Ⓣ Ⓕ	
20	Ⓣ Ⓕ		45	Ⓣ Ⓕ	
21	Ⓣ Ⓕ		46	Ⓣ Ⓕ	
22	Ⓣ Ⓕ		47	Ⓣ Ⓕ	
23	Ⓣ Ⓕ		48	Ⓣ Ⓕ	
24	Ⓣ Ⓕ		49	Ⓣ Ⓕ	
25	Ⓣ Ⓕ		50	Ⓣ Ⓕ	

For AAMA credit, return this answer sheet to AAMA, 20 North Wacker Drive, Suite 1575, Chicago, IL 60606.